THE FLUID PANTHEON

GODS OF MEDIEVAL JAPAN

GODS *of* MEDIEVAL JAPAN

VOLUME 1
THE FLUID PANTHEON

BERNARD FAURE

UNIVERSITY OF HAWAI'I PRESS
HONOLULU

21 20 19 18 17 16   6 5 4 3 2 1

Library of Congress Cataloging-in-Publication Data

Faure, Bernard, author.
  Gods of medieval Japan / Bernard Faure.
    pages cm
  Includes bibliographical references and index.
  ISBN 978-0-8248-3933-8 volume 1 (cloth : alk. paper)
  1. Buddhist gods—Japan. 2. Buddhism—Japan—History—1185–1600.
3. Japan—Religion—1185–1600. I. Title.
  BQ4660.J3F38 2015
  294.3'42110952—dc23
                                        2014046113

Publication of this book has been assisted by grants from the following:

Hiroshi Nitta Publication Fund of the Donald Keene Center of Japanese Culture, Columbia University

Nobuko Seriguchi and George Akita in memory of Mark M. Akita and Florence T. Akita

The School of Pacific and Asian Studies, University of Hawai'i, Mānoa

The Suntory Foundation

Designed by Mardee Melton

CONTENTS

ACKNOWLEDGMENTS

I dedicate this book to the memory of five departed "kings of knowledge," my mentors Rolf Stein and Bernard Frank, and my friends Anna Seidel, Louis Frédéric, and Michel Strickmann. It would also not have been possible without the support of all the lesser deities and kindred spirits—academic and non-academic—as numerous as the sands of the Ganges, or at least too numerous to cite. Special mention should be made, however, of Allan Grapard and Robert Duquenne; and of Iyanaga Nobumi, whose work and comments, in his books, personal conversations, and online discussions, have been a constant source of inspiration; of Dominic Steavu, Sujung Kim, and Luke Thompson, who have helped me with revising the manuscript; of Patricia Crosby at the University of Hawai'i Press, whose trust and support have reinvigorated me; and of Stuart Kiang, the Press's copy editor, who has had the unrewarding task of making my tedious prose readable. I am greatly indebted to them all. I would also like to thank the Department of East Asian Languages and Cultures and the Donald Keene Center at Columbia University for their generous financial support of this undertaking. May the merits of the book, however small, be redistributed evenly among them; as to its many flaws, may the compassionate, bodhisattva-like reader forgive them. Finally, I also ask forgiveness from the spirits of the trees that have been cut for the many drafts and printouts of this book.

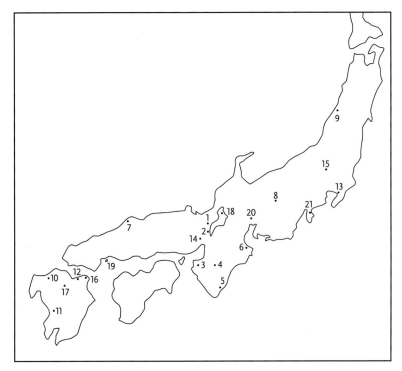

MAIN CULTIC SITES DISCUSSED IN THIS BOOK

1. Hieizan
2. Onjōji
3. Kōyasan
4. Yoshino
5. Kumano
6. Ise
7. Izumo
8. Suwa
9. Haguro
10. Dazaifu
11. Yatsushiro
12. Usa Hachiman
13. Chiba
14. Nose
15. Nikkō
16. Kunisaki
17. Hikosan
18. Chikubushima
19. Itsukushima (Miyajima)
20. Shinpukuji
21. Shōmyōji

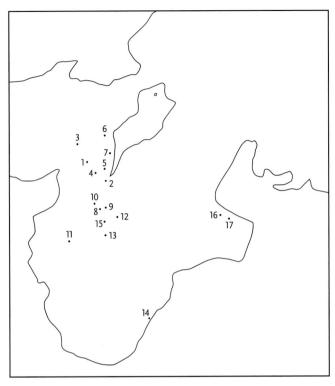

MAIN CULTIC SITES IN THE KYOTO AND THE KINKI AREA

1. Tōji
2. Daigoji
3. Ninnaji
4. Inari
5. Gion
6. Enryakuji (Hieizan)
7. Onjōji
8. Kōfukuji/Kasuga
9. Tōdaiji
10. Saidaiji
11. Kongōbuji (Kōyasan)
12. Murōji (Murōsan)
13. Yoshino
14. Kumano
15. Hasedera
16. Ise
17. Asamagatake

THE ESOTERIC PANTHEON

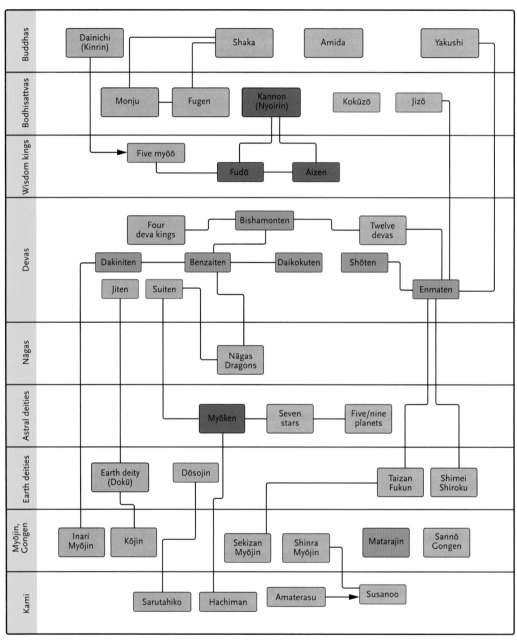

Deities discussed in *The Fluid Pantheon* appear in red; those discussed in *Protectors and Predators*, in blue.

PROLOGUE

Gods: with broad strokes we give them definition
though testy fate wrecks our work again and again.
But they are the immortals. Let us listen
and hear them out, who will hear us in the end.

R. M. RILKE, THE SONNETS TO ORPHEUS

Every god that humanity has ever known is still
  a god today . . .
All the gods, and you see them all if you look, alive
  and moving today,
and alive and moving tomorrow, many tomorrows,
  as yesterdays.

D. H. LAWRENCE, "ALL SORTS OF GODS"

THE RISE OF ESOTERIC BUDDHISM

This book is about the role of the gods in Japanese esoteric Buddhism and their influence on medieval Japanese religion. The Japanese have used a bewildering variety of names to designate the powers that are perceived to influence human life in all kinds of ways, a variety that is ironed out by translation into Western languages. For lack of a better word, I use the term *gods* in the broadest possible sense to designate these multifarious powers touching human life, including not only Japanese *kami* but also buddhas, bodhisattvas, wisdom kings (*myōō*), "bright" deities (*myōjin*), devas, and so on, all the way down to spirits and demons. The terms *god* and *demon*, which are sharply contrasted in the West, seem much less so in the Japanese context. Indeed, as the iconography shows, demons often form part of a powerful god's retinue, with the latter's identity remaining fluid as it spans the spectrum from the divine to the demonic. One of the main tasks of this book is to show that, in spite of the strict hierarchy imposed by Buddhism, gods at various levels of the pantheon share more features and have more affinities than one would expect. While I tend to reserve the word "god" for entities that look more individualized at first glance, and use "deities" more generally to designate powers that seem less well defined, the point is moot, and the difference elusive. Often, one single name will refer to both aspects (individualized and collective) of the same divine/demonic power. A case in point is that of Kōjin 荒神, a name that can designate a relatively individualized god or a category of spirit-like entities (*kōjin*).

The name "esoteric Buddhism" (Mikkyō 密教) designates primarily the two Buddhist schools of Shingon and Tendai, or more precisely Tōmitsu 東密—the esotericism of Tōji 東寺, the monastery founded by Kūkai 空海 (774–835) at the beginning of the ninth century—and Taimitsu 台密—Tendai esotericism, centered on two monasteries, Enryakuji 延暦寺 on Mount Hiei, northeast of the capital, Heian-kyō, and Onjōji 園城寺, better known as Miidera 三井寺, in present-day Ōtsu City. Tendai, a Japanese development of the Chinese Tiantai school (itself named after Mount Tiantai, the school's geographical base), was founded by Saichō 最澄 (767–822), a contemporary of Kūkai.[1] Although its main scriptural authority is the *Lotus Sūtra*, it soon took on an esoteric coloration under the influence of Shingon, in particular with Saichō's disciples Ennin 円仁 (793–864), Enchin 円珍 (814–891), and Annen 安然 (841–889?).

Buddhist scholars have traditionally defined Shingon as "pure esotericism" (*junmitsu*) and contrasted it with "mixed esotericism" (*zōmitsu*).[2] Even those who reject the notion of pure esotericism still cling to that of a "mature" esotericism.[3] More generally, the term Mikkyō itself reflects an attempt to purify the tradition and rid it of the magical and sexual elements that characterized Indian Tantrism. However—and perhaps we should say fortunately—this attempt was a failure. Indeed, never is esoteric Buddhism more "mixed" (or confused) than when it claims to be "pure." Its rituals, as they were performed in China and in Japan, were never as systematic and free of magic as a retrospective view, following centuries of formalization, would have it. Their cohesion, if there is any, is not that of *explicit theology* but a deeper one, which we may call *implicit theology*.[4] In reality, already with Kūkai, esoteric Buddhism had been enriched by various elements—some of which were borrowed from what would later become known as the "Way of Yin and Yang" (Onmyōdō 陰陽道), as well as from Buddhist astrology (Sukuyōdō 宿曜道, Way of Lunar Lodgings and Luminaries) and local cults.[5]

While I follow the general practice of referring to an esoteric Buddhism, meaning Mikkyō, I sometimes use the expression Tantric Buddhism when I want to emphasize the continuity between Mikkyō and its precursors: not only Indian, Tibetan, and Japanese forms of esoteric Buddhism, but also non-Buddhist forms of Indic Tantra, in particular Shaivism. I agree with Iyanaga Nobumi when he argues that "Japanese religion may be, in some aspects, considered as a special local development of Śaiva religiosity."⁶ This is especially true for the god Śiva himself, who, under the names Maheśvara (Daijizaiten 大自在天) and Īśāna (Ishana-ten 伊舎那天), as well as under the guise of other figures, remained very present in Japanese esotericism and was even identified with the *kami* Izanagi and Amaterasu.⁷ While Chinese cultural influence on medieval Japan has been duly acknowledged, Indian influence remains largely unrecognized. Yet this belated recognition must be qualified, for an overemphasis on influences would downplay the agency displayed at every turn by medieval Japanese Buddhists.

Ryūichi Abé has argued that Kūkai's originality lies less in the foundation of a new school (Shingon) than in inaugurating a new type of discourse. While this discourse admittedly had Indian and Chinese predecessors, it was entirely new in Japan.⁸ Nevertheless, the discursive field of esoteric Buddhism remained alive and well after Kūkai through the creative efforts not only of Shingon priests like Ningai 仁海 (951–1046) and Kakuban 覚鑁 (1095–1143), but also of Tendai priests like Ennin, Enchin, Annen, and many others. For all that, we should not overestimate the role played by "eminent" clerics, since many of the cultural, ritual, and mythological innovations that define the period were probably contributed anonymously.

Although Kūkai established Tōji in the capital and Kongōbuji 金剛峰寺 on Mount Kōya, the headquarters of the Shingon school, perhaps as important was the founding of Ninnaji 仁和寺 (in 868) on the northwestern outskirts of the capital, and of Daigoji 醍醐寺 to the southeast of the capital. With the rise of these new centers, Shingon esotericism (Tōmitsu) separated into two main currents, the Hirosawa-ryū 広沢流 and the Ono-ryū 小野流.⁹ Taking their cue from Hayami Tasuku, scholars have often tried to explain the rise of Mikkyō at the end of the Heian period by reference to social upheavals and the competition of various schools (allied with various political factions) for power.¹⁰ The Ono branch of Shingon, for instance, benefited greatly from the political changes of the Insei period (1086–1192). This sociopolitical explanation, while basically correct, still remains insufficient to apprehend the role of the gods in Japanese religion.

Whereas much of Western scholarship to date has focused on Shingon, it is impossible to understand the medieval religious landscape without examining the contribution of Tendai esotericism. The balance that Saichō had maintained between the esoteric and exoteric teachings was abandoned by his disciples Ennin, Enchin, and Annen in favor of esotericism: Enryakuji, the monastery founded by Saichō on Mount Hiei, became a stronghold of Taimitsu. The rivalry between the disciples of Ennin and Enchin led to a schism, resulting in Enchin's founding of Onjōji at the eastern foot of Mount Hiei. The bitter feud between the two branches, known as the Mountain Gate (Sanmon 山門, i.e., Enryakuji) and the Monastery Gate (Jimon 寺門, i.e., Onjōji), continued for centuries, causing at times terrible damage.[11] On the other hand, sectarian rivalries stimulated reflections about doctrine, mythology, and ritual, leading to the constitution of vast syntheses. A case in point is that of the priest Kōgei 皇慶 (var. Kōgyō, 977–1049), who attempted to systematize Taimitsu rituals by fusing them with Tōmitsu rituals. Based on records of his oral teachings, new currents flourished, leading to the formation, during the Insei period, of the "thirteen currents" of Taimitsu. These currents entailed the development of not only new rituals, but also new myths, in particular the mythological development known as Sannō shintō 山王神道.

ANOTHER MIDDLE AGES

Following the work of the Japanese historians Kuroda Toshio (1926–1993) and Amino Yoshihiko (1928–2004), a radical reinterpretation of medieval Japanese Buddhism has taken place, giving precedence to sociopolitical and cultural contexts over traditional doctrinal approaches. This view of the religious significance of the period has led to what has been called a "new medievalism." Taking their cue from these two scholars, recent studies of Japanese Buddhism have attempted to explain religious history in terms of socioeconomic transformations—for instance, the displacement of the Ritsuryō system by the growth of private estates, or manors (shōen 荘園), from the ninth century onward.[12] Another important factor was the vicissitudes of the imperial house in the face of the growing power of the warrior class. This unstable political situation prompted the elaboration of an ideology centered on the imperial regalia and on Buddhist themes such as the Buddha's relics and the wish-fulfilling jewel (J. nyoi hōju 如意宝珠, Skt. cintāmaṇi).

Kuroda defined the medieval period as the time when kenmitsu 顕密 Buddhism (combining exoteric and esoteric teachings) and the kenmon taisei (system of ruling elites) were dominant on the ideological and sociopolitical planes, respectively. This period extended approximately from the mid-Heian to the end of the Muromachi period.[13] The combination of exoteric and esoteric Buddhism flourishing then was a kind of "militant syncretism" that implied the superiority of esotericism. Furthermore, it was loosely articulated: in spite of its ideological penetration through all spheres of Japanese society, the kenmitsu system never became a pensée unique. As we shall see, the esoteric proliferation of symbols even seemed to breed its own antibodies.

Kuroda's untimely death prevented him from revising his model, and later scholars, while building on his insights, have criticized or supplemented that model on a number of points.[14] These criticisms do not diminish the value of the notion of kenmitsu Buddhism.[15] Whatever its problems, Kuroda's approach helped shift the focus of historical research toward more fruitful areas. After him, we can no longer define the evolution of medieval Buddhism solely in terms of the emergence of individual schools like Zen, Jōdo, Shinshū, and Nichiren. At the level of beliefs and practices, for instance, we see a realignment of native and nonnative beliefs within the magnetic fields of Tantric ideology, Indian astrology, Chinese cosmology, and Japanese mythology. Within the sociopolitical system described by Kuroda, various groups competed for power, in part by producing their own symbolism and mythology. These groups included not only the nobility and the large monasteries but also groups of outcasts (*senmin* 賤民), such as actors and blind minstrels, and a kind of cross-fertilization took place. In other words, the *kenmitsu* ideology changed at its point of contact with local culture, and vice versa. Within that broad historical framework, two peaks of symbolic creativity can be identified, occurring during the rule by retired emperors at the end of the eleventh century and the failed attempt at imperial restoration by Emperor Go-Daigo in the Kenmu era, opening the so-called Nanbokuchō period (1336–1392). The cult of the wish-fulfilling jewel, for example, emerged during the former, while one of its aspects, the Joint Ritual of the Three Worthies (Sanzon gōgyō-hō 三尊合行法), to which we will return, developed during the latter.

Amino Yoshihiko emphasized the heteromorphic (*igyō* 異形) nature of medieval kingship at the time of Emperor Go-Daigo and the prevalent interest in new deities, labeled "strange gods" (*ijin* 異神) by Yamamoto Hiroko.[16] The two phenomena seem to have developed in parallel, although the latter slightly predates the former. Given the importance bestowed on hybrid (half-human, half-animal) deities such as Shōten 聖天, Dakiniten 荼吉尼天, and Benzaiten 弁才天 in court rituals, one could indeed speak of a "heteromorphic" legitimacy. The modern fascination with the strange, however, lends itself all too easily to exoticism and runs the risk of feeding a romantic infatuation with the Japanese Middle Ages and its imperial mystique while remaining oblivious to the negative ideological effects of that period's politico-religious dualism.[17] A close examination of beliefs and practices, revealing the indebtedness of medieval Japan to other Asian cultures (India, China, and Korea), is perhaps the best way to deconstruct the Japanocentric tendency of this "new" medievalism. Moreover, in the case of medieval Japan, where central power lacked clear definition or was at least diluted by the presence of several "centers"—those of the reigning emperor, the retired sovereign, and the shōgunate (bakufu)—it may be that traditional center vs. periphery models simply do not work as well, so that an emphasis on margins has less deconstructive power.

One explanation, often invoked, is that competition between the Shingon and Tendai schools to legitimize imperial power and to respond to the needs of the aristocracy in times of crisis lay behind this symbolic effervescence.[18] This theory explains a good deal but limits itself to political considerations—in this case, the interinstitutional competition for patronage. Yet the changing political situation alone does not explain the exegetical, ritual, and mythological creativity of Mikkyō. Although recent scholarship has paid more attention to specific rituals, there is as yet little emphasis on the symbolic realm or on the constraints of symbolic discourse that may in part have determined the evolution of Japanese Buddhism. I am not denying the importance of infrastructure or political events. But it is important to recognize that while symbols are produced by collectivities and individuals, once born they take on a life of their own. I have chosen to focus here on esoteric myths and rituals, and especially on their constant change and resilience. In order to bring their logic and dynamics to light, I have had to consider them in the *longue durée*. The disadvantage of such an approach is, of course, that I have not always provided a sociohistorical context as thick as specialists of this or that particular period might desire. But while there are many studies that attempt to reveal the local and national contexts in all their complexity, studies of Japanese myth and ritual are sometimes still unaware of the extent to which the symbolic logic of those myths and rituals is indebted to India, China, and Korea. One cannot, for instance, understand a "typically" Japanese god like Gozu Tennō 牛頭天王 without taking into account Indian, Chinese, and Korean epidemic deities, as well as the Indian motifs of the taming of Māra and of Rudra/Śiva.[19] Gods can be de-contextualized and re-contextualized, but they always preserve traces of their former contexts, and these traces, when re-actualized, may affect their new status in surprising ways.

RESCUING THE GODS FROM OBLIVION

While this book is indebted to what some have called the new medievalism, it departs from the latter's historical or sociological approach by focusing on the symbolic realm, and particularly on the medieval Japanese pantheon. The Japanese Middle Ages were the site of a prodigious thought experiment, which until recently went almost unnoticed. Its aim was to represent the world in Buddhist mythological terms—through a thorough rewriting of local traditions. This led to the development of what is nowadays called "medieval myth" (*chūsei shinwa*) to distinguish it from classical Shintō mythology.[20]

Yet the gods have long been neglected by Buddhist scholars, for reasons that are not altogether clear. Among possible explanations for that strange blind spot or amnesia, one may cite the fact that they were too quickly relegated to the background as secondary figures in a supposedly atheistic Buddhism. In the specific case of Japan, they were also reduced to abstract and solemn entities by an official ideology that became Shintō, whose nationalist drift led to an eclipse in postwar scholarly studies on the history, nature, and functions of such gods. Recent studies have shown the extent to which the appearance and development of medieval Shintō was influenced by esoteric Buddhism.[21] In particular, research on the phenomenon called medieval Nihongi (*chūsei Nihongi* 中世日本紀) has revealed the part played by Mikkyō in the impressive mythological efflorescence that marked the medieval period, not only in the religious domain but also in the political, artistic, and literary spheres.[22] Medieval theology, by attempting to intertwine good and evil, ended up giving a foothold to demonic forces. This development can be seen in compilations like the *Collection of Leaves Gathered in Mountain Streams* (*Keiran shūyōshū* 渓嵐拾葉集*). On the social plane, this phase corresponds to the period of heteromorphic phenomena, with a concomitant recognition of impure sacredness, represented by the outcasts (*hinin* 非人). From this standpoint and others, the seventeenth century marked a turning point: the eclipse of esoteric Buddhism freed (for better *and* for worse) the gods from their ambivalence, thereby opening up new polarities—between good and evil *numina,* gods and demons—in a movement that paved the way for the separation of Shintō and Buddhism during the Meiji period.

The current disinterest of Western historians of religion in Japanese gods may also betray a lingering Durkheimian influence. Since Émile Durkheim famously claimed that gods were not a central element in the definition of religion, historians of religion have tended to pay less attention to pantheons and their citizens.[23] This disinterest may also reflect the still widely held understanding of Buddhism as rationalist,[24] a teaching founded by a "historical" Buddha who did not believe in any gods. Buddhist scholars were too quick to take this statement at face value and shift their focus to allegedly more noble topics. In doing so, they may have thrown out not only the baby Buddha with the bathwater, but also a number of other divine infants and elephants.

The field of Japanese religions was more affected by this disinterest than the neighboring fields of Indian religions and Chinese religions.[25] For obvious reasons, in Japanese religious studies interest in divine images has been limited primarily to art historians. But even in Japanese art history, we find only a few monographs on specific gods. Actually, what is striking is not so much the absence of studies on the gods, but rather the fact that even in these works, the nature of the gods is often broached with a kind of easy functionalist offhandedness. Yet it is unlikely that this kind of flippancy ever existed in the minds of religious people in Japan, and scholars who claim to respect other people's beliefs should begin by taking those people's gods seriously. According to the functionalist thesis, gods are ciphers—shorthand for social realities. Even if such were the case, my contention is that the gods also have their own level of reality and their own dynamics. We therefore need to "think with" Japanese religion, not simply to describe it with some condescension as an interesting set of now irrelevant beliefs.[26]

The renewal of ritual studies has sometimes paradoxically overshadowed the role of the gods. In the classic study of magic by Henri Hubert and Marcel Mauss, magic rituals work quasi-automatically, and divine or demonic entities have little agency.[27] Of course, Hubert and Mauss's conception was indebted to Vedic ritual, in which gods like Agni and Soma are indeed little more than ritual operators whose existence is dependent on and justified by the ritual.[28]

In many cases, it is the ritual that initially gives consistence to a god, but in those cases it is also true that the god tends to gradually emerge from anonymity and acquire a distinct individuality, or even a full-fledged mythological "personality." Behind the ritual often lurks a psychological element—whether respect or fear—that transforms a vague, demonic presence into a very real enemy, or a somewhat abstract entity into an intimate protector. Yet the *intensity* of a god is never entirely psychological in nature, nor is it only a structural effect: it is essentially the expression of a felt presence—I hesitate to speak of a transcendence—which overflows all structures and irrupts into human reality. *Mana* (as Mauss would have called it), or whatever name we give to this presence or intensity, is not, as Lévi-Strauss argued, merely a kind of zero degree of meaning or a semiological surplus of meaning, the equivalent of *italics* in written English.[29]

Yet rituals, like mythological narratives, often mislead us by attributing a stable individual identity to a god, in a way that is reminiscent of Luis Buñuel's film *The Obscure Object of Desire.* The male protagonist in this film fails to realize that the object of his sexual desire is constantly changing, in spite of its apparent stability. In fact, the role of the woman he desires is played by two actresses, whose appearances are strikingly different. The spectators themselves are to a certain extent victims of the same illusion, akin to what neurologists call "change blindness." (Indeed, a majority of viewers of this film never took notice of the alternation.) Likewise, the gods are elusive figures, whose faces change in accordance with the fluctuations of human fears and desires, even though the deluded mind perceives their nature as stable. While their perceived transcendence is often expressed through metamorphosis, human vision tends to freeze their constant morphing into snapshots, immutable forms, and because of this the metamorphic shimmer is eventually reduced to static identities and contradictory appearances. Eventually a system of images gets elaborated. But these images are only the traces of a vanished intensity, the figments of a forgotten dream—like the embers of what may have been (and perhaps could become again, under certain conditions) a raging fire.

With gods, as with Italo Calvino's cities, "it is as with dreams: everything imaginable can be dreamed, but even the most unexpected dream is a rebus that conceals a desire or, its reverse, a fear. Cities, like dreams, are made of desires and fears, even if the thread of their discourse is secret, their rules are absurd, their perspectives deceitful, and everything conceals something else."[30]

Gods and demons (demonic gods, divine demons) not only provide us with a prism through which we may understand a given society: they also have greater truths to tell us. As the Egyptologist Erik Hornung points out, whatever the nature of the gods may be, whatever the system of concepts or network of associations in which we situate them, all attempts to explain them are actually aimed at expressing the information they convey into a different, less ambiguous language. We feel that they transmit a valuable message about the world and mankind, but we have not yet found a language whose expressive richness rivals theirs. They constantly refer us back to ourselves, revealing the limitations of our conceptual system. If we desire to understand the world, we may always need the gods, as Rainer Maria Rilke and D. H. Lawrence knew well. The disappearance of a god is not only an impoverishment of human reality (imagination being a fundamental part of that reality), it also represents the loss of an opportunity for self-knowledge.[31]

Without denying the explanatory value of the dominant sociological, functionalist interpretation of the gods, I want to relativize it: gods are not soluble in the acids of human sciences; they are not merely social or psychological projections, vectors of social logic, or transparent symbols; they also have a certain degree of *agency.* At one end of the spectrum they are figures of a reality that transcends the symbolic realm, while at the other end they point to the presymbolic, the unnameable, the demonic. In both cases, they represent that *je ne sais quoi* that overflows, infiltrates, and fissures the symbolic realm while also constituting its source or "fundamental ground."

Admittedly, a god's name often is hardly more than a "floating signifier," an impossible algebraic sign whose value constantly changes, but which at all times represents a bundle of social groups and interests. One might object, arguing that there is a danger in defining the gods as "actors." And yet they do acquire a life of their own in people's imagination, and we cannot entirely deny them a kind of paradoxical agency. While they do express social forms, they may also express something else, a more fundamental reality (even if it remains forever elusive or unnameable). Under the influence of Mikkyō, that reality was no longer perceived as an alien and primitive power: it had become interiorized and every individual had to reckon with it.

At this juncture, it may prove useful to introduce the notion of *actor-network* as developed and promoted by Bruno Latour, Michel Callon, and John Law. An actor-network, according to Latour, is "what is made to act by a large star-shaped web of mediators flowing in and out of it.

It is made to exist by its many ties: attachments are first, actors are second."[32] Rather than focusing on individual actors, actor-network theory instead examines the network made up by relationships between actors, looking specifically at how (but not why) a network developed, how the network survives, and how it dissolves or transforms. In this context actors (or "actants" in actor-network theory parlance) are formed largely through their relationships within the network. In addition, actor-network theory does focus first and foremost on the agency of the actor in the usual sense, i.e., as intentional human agency. According to Latour, "instead of opposing the individual level to the mass, or agency to structure, we simply follow how a given element becomes strategic through the number of connections it commands, and how it loses its importance when losing its connections."[33] Elsewhere Latour explains that the "actor" of actor-network "is not the source of an action but the moving target of a vast array of entities swarming toward it."[34] By viewing the Japanese gods as actors in this sense, and by remembering that they are ever-changing nodes within a network constantly in flux, we can more accurately perceive the Japanese gods as the unstable aggregates that they are rather than as static projections of human minds, society, culture, or what have you. Furthermore, actor-network theory allows us to see that the relationship between gods and humans was bidirectional: gods were not only a product, but in taking on a life of their own, they too became active, productive elements within a larger network.

SOURCES

The historian of Japanese religions is confronted with a wealth of sources, still largely untapped, such as the Taishō edition of the Buddhist canon—particularly its iconographic section, known as *Zuzō* 図像—and the recent edition of the Shintō canon known as the *Shintō taikei* 神道大系 (which in spite of its name contains many texts of Mikkyō, Shugendō 修験道, and Onmyōdō inspiration). For the gods of the medieval period in particular, we have a proliferation of sources: collections of foundation stories (*engi*) like the *Origin Stories of Temples and Shrines* (*Jisha engi* 寺社縁起) and the *Collection on the Way of the Gods* (*Shintō shū* 神道集, a late fourteenth-century collection of legends compiled on Mount Hiei); ritual and iconographic compendia like the *Compendium of Iconographic Drawings* (*Zuzōshō* 図像抄) by Yōgen 永厳 (1075–1151) or Ejū 恵什 (1060–1145) and the *Miscellaneous Records on Special Worthies* (*Besson zakki* 別尊雑記) by the Hirosawa branch priest Shinkaku 心覚 (1116–1180); broad mythico-ritual syntheses like the *Asabashō* (1279) by Shōchō 承澄 (1205–1282), the *Compilation of Kakuzen* (*Kakuzenshō* 覚禅鈔, ca. 1198) by Kakuzen (1143–ca. 1213), the *Record of the Forest of Practice* (*Gyōrinshō* 行林抄) by Jōnen 静然 (fl. 1154), and the *Collection of*

Leaves Gathered in Mountain Streams (*Keiran shūyōshū* 渓嵐拾葉集, ca. 1311–1347) by the Enryakuji priest Kōshū 光宗 (1276–1350); and newly rediscovered libraries like those of Shōmyōji 称名寺 (Kanazawa bunko 金沢文庫) in Yokohama and Shinpukuji 真福寺 (Ōsu bunko 大須文庫) in Nagoya. Paradoxically, what characterizes these documents is their quality as "open works."[35] There is properly speaking no original text, only a multitude of oral traditions that complement or contradict each other, and to which new "private" glosses were constantly added. The transmission of such documents was therefore not, as often claimed, a quasi-mechanical process of preservation of atemporal truths, but an ongoing and laborious process "implying a multitude of sources, authors, versions, and interpretations."[36]

Another important iconographic source has been the *Powder Book of Buddhist Drawings from Rokkakudō Nōman-in* (*Rokkakudō Nōman-in butsuga funpon* 六角堂能満院仏画粉本), a copy book of line drawings by the priest Daigan 大願 (1798–ca. 1864) and his workshop. These sketches, which are today in the possession of Kyōto City University of Arts, have been published as a two-volume set entitled *Collection of Buddhist Images* (*Bukkyō zuzō shūsei* 仏教図像聚成), from which I have drawn extensively.[37]

One of the historian's primary tasks is the dating of written sources. In the field of religious practices and beliefs, however, documents are not always the best proof of the importance of a given myth or ritual. Indeed, the history of ideas or of mentalities is not always as fixated on the point of emergence of a phenomenon in written documents. Sometimes a ritual or an icon might reflect an earlier state of things than a text.[38] Variants of a myth or ritual may have the same legitimacy as the "founding myth," if there is ever such a thing. Given the fact that the chronological sequence is not always as clear as historians would want, I use documents and evidence from various periods in order to retrieve a plausible interpretation.

The dual structure of the synthesis of exoteric and esoteric teachings that Kuroda Toshio labeled *kenmitsu* Buddhism created (or gave room to) Janus-faced deities, in the sense that a specific god will present a different face in exoteric and esoteric sources. Furthermore, that face will be differently reflected in the prisms of various literary genres. Yet the prism metaphor should not lead us to believe that there is always an original image or an original textual source. In many cases, we may be dealing with mere virtual origins or family resemblances, a fact hidden by a name that is taken to designate an individual god, when it initially designated a collective entity or a mythological category.

In medieval Mikkyō, traditional doctrinal study gradually gave way to an extreme ritualism, symbolic manipulations mixed with language games that underscore and reveal the mystical nature of language. Next to the scriptural tradition, an oral tradition (*kuden* 口伝), or rather a multitude of secret oral traditions, developed, reinterpreting local customs and legends in language drawn from Buddhist scholasticism. In Tendai, this proliferation of oral traditions accompanied the multiplication of esoteric branches in the twelfth century, after the initial division of the school into two currents, the Eshin-ryū 恵心流 and the Danna-ryū 旦那流.

The so-called oral traditions, expressing experiences, interpretations, and essential points of doctrine and practice, were paradoxically written down in a multitude of short texts known as "cut papers" (*kirigami* 切紙). They came to constitute a large collection of glosses related to certain points of doctrine or meditative practice, as well as to temples and icons, ritual and liturgy, and myths and legends related to the buddhas, the gods, and the patriarchs. These *kirigami* were eventually collected in texts called "documents" (*kiroku* 記録).[39] The documents were compiled under the supervision of a category of specialists, "archivists" or "chroniclers" (*kike* 記家), whose tradition goes back to an Enryakuji priest named Kenshin 顕真(1130–1192). These archivists were not simply content to record past events, they were also masters of creative writing. As such, they were the main actors behind the vast synthesis of Buddhist teachings and local cults that characterizes medieval Tendai. Kōshū, the archivist-author of the *Keiran shūyōshū*,[40] is representative of a current called Kurodani-ryū 黒谷流, after the name of the valley on Mount Hiei where many of the archivists resided. His work is perhaps the best source for understanding the formidable medieval attempt to reinterpret classical Japanese mythology and ritual in Buddhist terms. It is among archivists like him that the so-called Sannō shintō came into existence, paving the way to other forms of Shintō that would eventually escape from their Buddhism framework—among them Ryōbu shintō 両部神道, Ise 伊勢 or Watarai shintō 度会神道, and Miwa shintō 三輪神道.

On the Shingon side, we find monks particularly active in the tradition of Daigoji. It is in this tradition that the myths and rituals around the wish-fulfilling jewel developed the most spectacularly, with priests such as Ningai (951–1046) and Shōken 勝賢 (1138–1196). In Kanto, the priests of Shōmyōji—and in particular the monastery's second abbot, Kenna 劒阿 (1261–1338)—compiled an extensive collection of documents that is still available to us through the Kanazawa Library. (More recently, the Ōsu Library in Nagoya has also revealed a wealth of interesting documents.) These monks were interested in a variety of new gods and brought to the ritual forefront deities such as Benzaiten, Daikokuten 大黒天, Ugajin 宇賀神, Dakiniten, and Kangiten 歓喜天—deities that often were intimately related to the cults of the Buddha's relics and the wish-fulfilling jewel.

Some deities developed as a response of one social group to another: for instance, Myōken Bosatsu 妙見菩薩 was worshiped in Shingon as well as in the Sanmon (Hieizan) branch of Tendai, whereas his alias, Sonjōō 尊星王, was worshiped mainly in the Jimon (Onjōji) branch. Similarly, Dakiniten was worshiped in Shingon whereas Benzaiten was more popular in Tendai. Historians looking into these matters have usually been more interested in the priests who promoted these gods than in the gods themselves. In other words, they have favored human agency over divine agency. Yet agency (human or divine) should neither be ignored nor overemphasized. Historical actors are part of networks, and they are themselves networks.

PROJECT HISTORY

This project was initially conceived as a sequel to my earlier books on the marginalized elements of the Chan/Zen tradition and on Buddhist sexuality and gender. It soon became clear, however, that sexuality itself was only part of a broader symbolic field, structured by desire, death, suffering, evil, and fear. The gods—particularly in Zen and in traditional Buddhism—belong among the figures of exclusion. For many people, Buddhism remains preeminently a religion without gods, and perhaps the proliferation of discourse around the gods was just another way to keep them at bay. But the question remains: how does one account for a proliferation that is so massive that it has practically gone unnoticed until now?[41] Why did so few historians see that nebula spread over the medieval horizon?

As Lévi-Strauss puts it: "[As] the nebula gradually spreads, its nucleus condenses and becomes more organized. Loose threads join up with one another, gaps are closed, connections are established, and something resembling order is to be seen emerging from chaos."[42] Or perhaps I should say, in the case of Buddhism, that something that resembles *another order* transpires behind the manifest order of the orthodox mythology and cosmology. Going one step further, I would argue that something that resembles *another chaos,* or rather a *chaosmos,* to borrow James Joyce's portmanteau word, transpires behind the latent order painstakingly established by Buddhist ideologues and structuralist scholars.[43]

With its emphasis on mythological and ritual components, my approach cuts across sectarian lines and bridges the gap, or undermines the distinction, between elite and popular culture, abstract and concrete religion, central power and peripheral cults. Without going into a historiographical critique of the textbook approach to Japanese religion (and its Meiji representation of Buddhism and Shintō), it reveals that medieval Japanese religion was constituted of a conglomeration of networks. This emphasis on networks should help us stay clear of the Scylla and Charybdis of sectarian scholarship and abstain from jumping out of the frying pan of Shingon theology into the *goma* fire of Tendai rituals.

Beyond the study of concrete cases, I want to reflect on Japanese polytheism and its pantheon (or rather "polytheon"). The recurrent tendency to promote hitherto minor deities to the exalted status of "separate worthies" (*besson* 別尊)—or even, in some cases, to ultimate deity—participates in the same reductionism that shrinks diversity to unity, the concrete to the abstract, the unknown to the known, the wild to the domesticated, and the dangerous to the beneficial. Yet it hits the same stumbling block: the mystery, the hidden aspect (which, paradoxically, can also express the abstract), the infinite potentiality of the divine, and the demonic.

In this book, I attempt to show how ideas and practices proliferated and disseminated outside the framework of esoteric Buddhism, and how some fragments of the medieval discourse survived even in the Edo period. Such a proliferation may give the impression that Buddhist thought somewhere crossed the fine line between creativity and hubris. This proliferation (and perhaps hubris) is similarly reflected in the texture of this hybrid book, which also proceeds from a sense of wonder and puzzlement: wonder at the wondrous creations of the human imagination, at the endless creativity that constitutes a culture; but also puzzlement, due to the fact that, despite all the forgeries and the self-serving arguments, all the power games, and all the reductionist explanations—Marxist, psychological, structuralist, and whatnot—the mystery remains intact.

THE ESSENTIALIST FALLACY

This book rejects the methodological individualism and anthropomorphism that characterize most mythological studies, as seen for instance in descriptions of the birth, growth, and career of specific gods.[44] The gods are multilevel, kaleidoscopic phenomena (some would say *noumena* and *numina*): they exist both at the level of individual belief and at that of collective representations. At the level of society, they represent larger forces, institutions, or groups, which are often in conflict: temples, shrines, lineages, palaces, courtiers, warriors, itinerant priests and artists, Yin-Yang masters, and so on.

The main pitfall in a discussion of Japanese deities is personalism. Authors in need of a narrative tend to isolate characters, without attempting to discern the structures that determine them.[45] While gods can and should be described as *agents,* they are not *persons:* they are rather nodes in constantly changing networks, and their agency too is a network. And even to speak of a network structure may be too optimistic when, to borrow an image from Latour, actors "swarm in all directions like a bee's nest disturbed by a wayward child."[46]

The persistence of a naive personalization engenders all kinds of false problems. After structuralism, this should go without saying. But Japanese scholarship does not seem to have come to terms with structuralism yet, and the essentialist fallacy dominates the study of Japanese religion, not to mention that of Buddhism, a teaching that recurrently denounced the "essentialist" heresy.

A rationalizing narrative tissue constitutes the manifest discourse of mythology and hagiography. Yet there is also another, mostly nondiscursive level, which allows the drift from one figure to another through the intermediary of such and such a mythical or ritual motif. For instance, we find the same rite practiced for Fudō 不動 and Kōjin despite narrational differences. This kind of drift might turn into a nightmare for the monographically inclined narrator. Mythology develops in the tension between these two discourses or levels.

For the sake of the narrative, it may be necessary at times to speak of a specific god as if it were an "individual," and I will occasionally slip back into that language. Nevertheless, we should keep in mind that the name of a god remains shorthand for a given symbolic configuration at a particular moment, and that the nominal continuity may hide a functional discontinuity. It is often pointed out that behind the gods there are always humans who manipulate them. But the gods are not mere puppets, and they escape the humans who naively believe that they manipulate them. Or rather, it may be that both puppet and puppeteer are manipulated, and manipulate one another. Admittedly, behind a god's mask there is a man, but a mask may also hide another mask. The man who wears a mask is already a hybrid being, possessed or traversed by a higher force.

It is a naive functionalist approach that sees the gods merely as symbols for human groups and individuals. Gods are not mere signs, or if they are they have their own semantics and dynamics. Events that take place at the symbolic level do not simply reflect human relationships. Even if the gods only had the life we lend them, this in itself would not be insignificant: imagination has strange powers, and its figments become very real under a certain light—say, the light of stars. Esoteric Buddhist ritual is often described as an attempt to manipulate symbols, and it is indeed that. Yet it also reflects the understanding that reality (divine or demonic powers) cannot simply (or always) be manipulated, that it is resilient, a reminder that all symbolic systems leave a remainder.

A god is always the god of a given place, of a specific collectivity, and the plurality of places and collectivities already entails that of the god.[47] Its image also reflects itself into various prisms: textual (literary genres), ritual, doctrinal, or hagiographic—to name just a few. Yet the inherent multiplicity of medieval Japanese gods is not merely the expression of their diverse social and geographical origins. Such social and geographical determinism is obvious and almost trivial. To use John Law's terminology, a god is a "fractional object"—that is, an object that is "more than one and less than many."[48] Gods are also plural because they owe their being to a network of relations. There may not be two Nyoirin Kannon 如意輪観音, Aizen Myōō 愛染明王, or Benzaiten exactly alike: sometimes an individual name designates a combination of several deities, at other times a specific aspect of a multifaceted deity. Their fractal nature also reflects an essential, ontological multiplicity that cannot and should not be reduced to historical accidents. Gods are nodal points in a changing network of relationships. These knots of meaning do not always have the same value or significance. Their relation calls to mind the neuronal model. Like synapses, certain paths are traced, certain links reinforced, while others soon vanish. This model is what I call *synaptic Buddhism.* But to see the gods as nodes is still to remain indebted to a substantialist epistemology. If some of them may indeed be described in such terms, others—and they are legion—may not. Taking my cue from Étienne Souriau and Tim Ingold, I would rather describe them as modes of existence, relations, lines. For instance, in the relation between one deity and another, the actual god may be the equals sign, the relationship itself, the space-in-between. How do we envision that? We can no longer, in that case, speak of a combinatory pattern, because the combination, being essentially or etymologically binary, implies preexisting entities instead of a primordial relationship. But the same is true for all *relations*—and a new word is needed, which would, as Souriau puts it, "evoke a universe of existence where the only beings are . . . dynamisms or transitions, and where the synaptic (by opposition to the ontic) rules."[49]

METHODOLOGICAL CAVEATS

In the end, it is probably impossible to do justice to these elusive gods, whose intense, vibrant, scintillating, kaleidoscopic nature was infinitely more complex, fluid, and elusive than rigid taxonomies would let us believe. Classification (from *classis* 'army') is in itself a form of power or power grabbing.[50] Nevertheless, as a starting point (and point from which to depart), I have provided a chart showing the categories of the esoteric Buddhist pantheon. Medieval religion presents us with a form of religious or metaphysical thinking, a fascinating "logic" that sometimes goes wild and verges on a doctrinal or mythological delirium. Yet it fulfills an essential function—that of making people feel more secure by putting them into an intimate relationship with the cosmos, by giving meaning to their life (and to their death). To reject all this wholesale would be almost as illusory as to claim to reject dreams: one continues nonetheless to dream, even though impoverished, nightmarish dreams.

This book is, albeit in an oblique way, a reflection about rationality and its limits. Retrospectively, scholarly attempts to establish relations between myths strike me as analogous to the process that led to the constitution of medieval mythology. Inasmuch as scholarship is also a way to confront (or assuage) fears, to trap all those demons in the web of discourse by talking casually, *objectively,* about them and their origins, this book participates in the same taxonomic attempt to reduce the unknown to the known, which I have observed in the case of medieval Japan, and is bound for the same ultimate failure.

Perhaps, as Bruno Latour paradoxically argued, "we have never been modern": in part because, for all our much vaunted rationalism, we continue to create gods and to be manipulated by them, or at least by the powers that we objectify under that name (and a few others). In spite of (and largely owing to) our demythologizing discourse, the reality of our habitual practice has not much evolved. Thus, even if the nature of our gods has changed, we still have something to learn from them and from the way our ancestors (and those of other peoples) dealt with them. Latour's statement extends to the case of the allegedly modern Japanese who, in spite of an aggressive Meiji "Restoration"—which, to use Allan Grapard's label, was rather a "cultural revolution"—have never been able to become fully modern and to erase the cultural memory of earlier centuries when Shintō and Buddhism were not separated like symmetrical mantelpiece ornaments.

Both historicism and structuralism have their methodological pitfalls. On the one hand, an approach that is too anchored in local history tends to mask continuities, not to mention the deep structures that determine that history by providing it with a preconceived ideological framework. On the other hand, any attempt to anchor oneself in the deep structures and the continuities of the *longue durée,* by glossing over the irruption of historical accident, participates in the same domestication of the strange and the atypical. Because it focuses primarily on representations, this book takes at times a loosely structural approach. The textual point of emergence (or disappearance) of those representations may not be as important as historians usually think: to understand them, we must move beyond the narrow framework of a given historical time.

Even though I have grounded my discourse in historical context, my approach is not a historical one in the strict sense. I introduce the historical context whenever possible, but without lingering on it, because local instantiations tend to obscure the broader symbolic logic at work. In matters divine, the historical approach only goes so far and it needs to be supplemented by a variety of structural and poststructural approaches. Confronted with the emergence of a cult, the historian is often content with looking for its origins, which in practice often means looking for the first emergence of the name of a god in a written document. In the worst case scenario, this quasi-obsession with textual origins constrains the historian "to arbitrarily fix a first content to the 'personality' of a god before it begins to get richer—and why not poorer?—in the random course of history and its accidents."[51] The documentary corpus is not homogenous; it is structured (and warped) by the various literary genres that make it up, and the earliest texts do not necessarily represent the most primitive state of the question. As Wittgenstein pointed out, a historical explanation, an explanation as hypothesis of a development, is only *one* kind of summary of the data—of their synopsis.[52]

When the cult of a deity takes off, it acquires a dynamics of its own. Its sum becomes greater than that of its elements, and it cannot be simply reduced to them without a loss. The chariot is no longer the mere sum of its parts, as in the Indian Buddhist monk Nāgasena's famous parable for the emptiness of the self; or, to use Georges Dumézil's slightly different metaphor: "a chair is not only the sum of the pieces of wood, twigs of straw, iron nails that have been used to fabricate it—and it hardly matters in order to understand it to know the age of the wooden pieces of its rungs or its back, because it is the functional arrangement of the parts, it is the whole that explains the elements."[53]

Since I am weaving metaphors, I could also say that I have tried to tease out certain motifs of the rich mythological brocade by hiding the chronological weft thread.[54] The weaving (or textual) metaphor imposes itself, if only because the gods that called my attention are often referred to as "the warp and woof of heaven and earth," that is, the source of all life. Many of them were also, as it were, products of the loom, in the sense that they were promoted by immigrant groups of Korean descent like the Hata (whose name means "loom"), which were instrumental in importing continental technologies like weaving.[55]

Because of the structural nature of the gods, the starting point of this project may seem relatively arbitrary. Perhaps, as Lévi-Strauss points out, the book "would have developed along similar lines if it had had a different starting point."[56] I chose to start from the hierarchical order provided by the official *kenmitsu* pantheon for the sake of convenience, but I soon depart from this official model to emphasize another, more elusive reality. Accordingly, there is only the *appearance* of a narrative, that is, of a chronological development or logical progression: the discussion proceeds "not along a linear axis but in a spiral."[57]

One more caveat: in a book like this, a certain degree of repetition is unavoidable—it echoes the unceasing, tireless repetitions of the textual corpus, and of myth and ritual themselves. Through repetition is the braid of Japanese mythology woven. The reader may get the impression that in the mythological and ritual realms everything goes. This impression would be false, however: even if the diversity of the figures considered is great and perplexing, it represents only a small sample—always the same, and not random—of the totality of the pantheon. In spite of the importance that serendipity plays in it, our *randonnée* across Japanese myth and ritual is not mere *randomness* (as the etymology implies), and the encounters we make along the road will turn out to be significant.[58]

Scholarship means simplification, even when it seems to delight in complexities. While simplification is necessary, it is never neutral: it participates in the same ideo-*logical* nature as classification, mytho-*logy*, and pantheon building. It chooses abstract order at the expense of concrete multiplicity. It is a form of *logos,* or frontal knowledge, which lets slip through its meshes the diagonal, evanescent, transversal "logic" (if this word still applies) of what the ancient Greeks called *mètis* (cunning intelligence). There is of course no escaping the constraints of scholarly discourse when one writes such a book. But this discourse is always performative (and ultimately political): it chooses, for instance, the abstract and logical over the concrete and multiple. Even within that discursive constraint, however, one can be more or less inclined toward the concrete or the abstract. While I did attempt to sort out the large array of documents, doctrines, ideas, and images of medieval esoteric Buddhism, I did so with some reluctance, because I am acutely aware of what is being lost in the process.

Finally, I will probably be reproached for yielding to the encyclopaedic temptation, at risk of slowing the flow of the argument and adding a few more corridors to the labyrinth. I plead guilty. Indeed, the discussion meanders and sometimes seems to get lost in the alluvions of data. I have chosen to do so, however, in order to provide a remedy in part to the uncanny lack of information in Western languages regarding Japanese gods. By trying to kill two birds (presenting facts and discussing ideas) with one stone, I may have failed on both accounts, ending up catching neither the horsefly nor the wasp (*abu hachi torazu*).

SYNOPSIS

Chapter 1, "Twists and Turns," raises a number of methodological issues related to the structuralist approaches of Georges Dumézil and Claude Lévi-Strauss as they may apply to the Japanese pantheon. I argue that while the structuralist method can be useful up to a point, its insights are also the reverse of its blindness; it must therefore be used in combination with other theoretical (or poststructural) approaches, such as those inspired by Deleuze and Guattari's discussion of the rhizome and the actor-network theory of Bruno Latour and John Law.[59]

Chapter 2, "Under the Gaze of the Stars," deals with the Buddhist deity of the pole star, Myōken. Because of its position in the nocturnal sky, the pole star has traditionally been a paradigmatic symbol of the center (cosmological, but also sociopolitical). In spite of his rather obscure Daoist origins, Myōken was deemed a bodhisattva and converged with other, more orthodox esoteric Buddhist symbols of the center like Dainichi (Skt. Mahāvairocana) and Monju (Mañjuśrī). More than the central aspects of Myōken, however, what interests me are his less obvious features, which link him to deities such as the Healing Buddha Yakushi, Aizen Myōō, the water deity Suiten, and the snake god Ugajin, particularly his functions as controller of human destiny, placenta deity, and companion spirit. Giving priority, in a book on Buddhist gods, to a so-called bodhisattva of clearly non-Buddhist origins is meant to underscore the fact that, in spite of his importance, Myōken has been conspicuously absent from modern studies on Japanese religion.

Chapter 3, "The Elusive Center," deals with another symbol of the pivotal center, the wisdom king (Skt. *vidyārāja*) Fudō, "The Unmovable." While discussing his centrality, I also emphasize his elusive nature. The genealogical approach adopted in the first part of the chapter contrasts two aspects of the "official" Fudō, as a servant and as a master (or tamer) of demons. I trace his development from a lowly to an exalted position in the explicit esoteric pantheon, and discuss his main functions (protection of the state and protection of individuals, particularly ascetics). I then sketch out the development of the Fudō cult in Japan before turning to doctrinal developments in which Fudō appears as symbol of the deluded or enlightened mind. In the second part of the chapter, I turn to the implicit theology of Fudō, emphasizing his chthonian nature, the importance of his acolytes (who are also his emanations), his embryological functions, and his affinities with another chthonian god, Kōjin.

Chapter 4, "Lust but Not Least," examines another awe-inspiring wisdom king, Aizen. As in the preceding chapters, the first part deals with the official Aizen as representative of the explicit theology of Mikkyō. Beginning with the political context of the Aizen ritual in medieval Japan, I examine the well-known apotropaic and sexual symbolism of the god. I then turn to his iconography, which reveals fascinating details like his empty third hand, holding the vital essence of human beings. In the second part, I turn to the implicit theology of Aizen as disclosed from a dense network of associations (with deities, for instance, like King Yama, the judge of hell). I also emphasize one of his less well-known aspects, an embryological function, symbolized by his five-finger-high icon, whose size points to that of the fetus in the womb.

Chapter 5, "Fearful Symmetry," takes a closer look at the coupling of Aizen and Fudō, first as a dyad, then as a single two-headed figure. While the dyad lends itself to apotropaic and sexual readings, my contention is that the embryological code was just as important. After tracing that pair's evolution, I examine their conjunction with the wish-fulfilling jewel (and its emanation, the bodhisattva Nyoirin Kannon) in the so-called Joint Ritual of the Three Worthies. This mutilayered ritual, based on Kūkai's apocryphal *Testament*, had apotropaic and soteriological functions. I then turn to another triad, formed by the combination of Aizen and Fudō with the sun goddess Amaterasu, or rather with a special, horse-riding form of the Ise Shrine deity. Finally, I look at another secret rite based on the Aizen-Fudō dyad, the Peasant Aizen ritual, in which the wisdom king is represented in the form of a snake. I conclude by questioning both the dualistic models that form a leitmotif of explicit Mikkyō ideology and the nonduality supposedly provided by ternary models such as the Three Worthies.

Chapter 6, "The Hidden Jewel," examines the cult of the wish-fulfilling jewel (Skt. *cintāmaṇi*) as it developed in relation to the cult of the Buddha's relics. In the Shingon tradition, both cults are traced to Kūkai, and with the growth of Kūkai's legend and the influence of his apocryphal *Testament* from the tenth century onward, the relics and the jewel, which had been functionally similar until then, merged into the object of a single cult. After describing the forms of worship and use of seed-syllables in relic rituals, I examine the symbolism of the relics/jewel in the Daigoji tradition and the emergence of two jewels: a visible one, kept at Tōji, and an invisible one, allegedly buried on Mount Murō (Murōzan 室生山). Along the way, I discuss the creation of artificial jewels by Kūkai and his heirs Hanjun 範俊 and Shōken 勝憲. I then turn to the jewel cult on Mount Murō and examine the various components of that tradition: namely, the role played by Kūkai's disciple Kenne, the legends surrounding Mount Murō and its "dragon hole," the dragon cult and rain rituals, and the apotheosis of Kūkai as the mythical Kōbō Daishi, emanation of the wish-fulfilling jewel. In the concluding section, I question the established theory according to which the jewel cult represents a specific Japanese development brought about by Kūkai and his successors, taking my cue from recent work pointing to influences from the continent. Finally, I return to the question of ternary thinking and suggest that actual practices, in contrast to the symbolism and ideology of the center, created a symbolic proliferation that subverted the ternary schema.

Chapter 7, "Living Jewels," begins by looking at a group of deities who have a jewel as their main attribute or source, including the bodhisattvas Monju and Kokūzō (Skt. Ākāśagarbha), Uhō Dōji (a Buddhist version of Amaterasu), Hachiman, and Ugajin. Then it focuses on one paradigmatic jewel deity, Nyoirin Kannon, and traces the origin of her cult in China and her emergence from a group of six emanations of Kannon. I discuss Nyoirin's various functions—particularly her role as the Seven-star Nyoirin in star rituals and divination rituals—and describe her network, including her associations with Seiryō Gongen (the protector of Daigoji), Kichijōten, and Benzaiten, and her cult at Inari, Ise, and Ishiyamadera 石山寺. I also discuss the legend of the nun Nyoi 如意, one of her manifestations, in connection with the Urashima 浦島 legend, the island of the immortals, and the dragon palace. In the final section, I highlight certain poorly understood aspects of Buddhist material culture by examining a number of portable reliquary shrines centered on Nyoirin.

The apparent coherence of the book, suggested by the synoptic vision presented above, forms a stark contrast to the serendipity of the research that preceded it. Writing a book is often a messy business, like a laboratory experiment. In the end, a book is often evaluated not so much on its findings, but on the way in which the mess has been cleaned up. The laboratory must look perfectly clean and reassuring—no objects misplaced, no loose ends. All trash has to be removed (even if some remains in the trash bin and the storage room—here, the endnotes). And yet the gods studied are, almost by definition, loose ends and figures of the remainder.

At the last stages of revising the manuscript, taking to heart the kind advice of its reviewers, I frantically tried to add sections and subsections, and transitions, all of which are supposed to insure the continuity of a text "through the effects of reference, insistance, and repetition."[60] From that retrospective viewpoint, the synopsis may give the reader a false sense of linearity and logic—two qualities that were sorely missing along the way.

While the structure of the book loosely follows the numerological categories (unity/center, dyad, triad) of esoteric Buddhism, it also attempts to deconstruct them by showing that these ideological structures were constantly subverted and undermined by internal or external elements. This deconstruction will become even more visible when I examine the case of the devas (in particular, the so-called Three Devas) in the companion volume, *Protectors and Predators.*

TWISTS AND TURNS
Pantheons, Structures, Beyond and In Between

For the snark was a Boojum, you see.
LEWIS CARROLL

*The true units are not men; the true actors do not have a
human face. Everything takes place between beings that
cannot be imagined. Man is therefore perhaps not the
unit, the element to choose in order to get to the root of
human things.*

PAUL VALÉRY, *TEL QUEL II*

After dealing with issues proper to the field of Japanese
religions, and defining my approach with regard to that field, I now want
to discuss the theoretical problems raised more generally by the subject(s)
of this book, namely, Japanese gods, and by what could be perceived as
the inherent structuralism of medieval combinatory systems. I will then
question that combinatory logic and its ideological effects. Let me state
at the outset that I find the notion of anything "combinatory" already too
systematic, and that we should keep in mind Samuel Taylor Coleridge's
contrast between mechanical association, or permutation, and the imagination that "dissolves, diffuses, dissipates in order to recreate."[1]

A CALDERIAN PANTHEON

The rise of Mikkyō from the ninth century onward was marked by the
emergence of a new pantheon, that is, an ordered totality of the divine
world. One important aspect of the Tantric pantheon in East Asia is the crucial role played by the "bright kings" or "wisdom kings" (Skt. *vidyārāja*,
J. *myōō* 明王). Jean Przyluski argues that "the class of the *vidyārāja*,
originally formed of metaphysical abstractions, constituted a weak point
in Buddhist doctrine, from which Brahmanical mythology was able to

expel the first occupiers by pouring in it the *trop-plein* of its creations."[2] In Japan, the esoteric Buddhist pantheon was further enriched by an outpouring of ritual and iconographic production, and by the proliferation of discourse(s)—theological, ideological, epic—that marked the Japanese Middle Ages. It unfolded between two poles: that of the high gods, the transcendent buddhas, perceived as distant gods; and that of lower, potentially dangerous entities, who were kept at bay by ritual. Between the two, we find a host of deities which, while more sympathetic to human interests, are essentially ambivalent. (See The Esoteric Pantheon chart on p. xii.)

While its taxonomic aspects are usually emphasized, a pantheon is equally an instrument of production, a generative and transformative matrix.[3] In the same way as the *interpretatio graeca* allowed ancient Greeks to translate near-eastern deities into their pantheon, the *interpretatio buddhica* provided a device for mythological proliferation: although it seemed to reduce foreign gods to local gods, in fact it allowed the introduction of those foreign deities into the local picture and therefore added new valences to local gods. Far from simply registering a preexisting, objective reality, any classification is performative, and to classify gods in a pantheon is to classify desires. Taxonomy is never neutral, it is always a site of tension and contention.[4] When the process loses its dynamics and fluidity, the classification turns into an ideological prison.

The addition of a new deity to the pantheon, or the elevation of a preexisting deity, is among other things a way of asserting sectarian difference. Furthermore, a god is always inscribed in several contexts, which define its meaning and function: narrative contexts (oral or written, mythological or literary), ritual, and social contexts. While the god may be clearly individualized in the narrative field, it may be partly interchangeable with other gods in the ritual field, owing to various functional equivalences.[5] Mythological narratives tend to emphasize the individuality of the gods, but the situation is quite different in the ritual field, where equivalence reigns supreme and "identities" tend to dissolve. As Jean-Pierre Vernant points out, "myths and literary creations emphasize, in their pictures of the gods, the unitary aspect. . . . In the cult, however, it is on the contrary the plurality of aspects of the same god that is emphasized."[6] Ritual brings together deities that seem otherwise distinct, as if they were functionally interchangeable, thereby suggesting that they could easily merge into a unique functional deity.[7] Consequently, ritual yields a more complicated picture of the gods than mythological narrative.[8] Thus, it is easier to classify deities on the basis of narratives than on the basis of ritual, but it may also prove counterproductive. To identify a deity within a pantheon, one must therefore take the various contexts into account. To neglect them is to run the risk of retrieving a static and lifeless pantheon whose classifications have little relevance in practice.[9] The name of a god may represent a negative power that needs to be coerced or placated through the cult.[10] The same appellation, however, can also designate quite different cultic realities. The gods of one social group are often the demons of another.[11] Often, the distinction between gods and demons is just a matter of perspective or of time, reflecting different phases in a process that transforms a demon into a god (and sometimes the opposite).

Philippe Descola emphasizes another *sine qua non* condition for any meaningful taxonomy, namely, discernment of the integrating schemes that allow humans to make sense of the world in which they live. Starting from what he sees as a fundamental, cross-cultural distinction between interiority and physicality, he defines four types of ontology: animist, naturalist, totemist, and analogical. Gods (or myths), depending on which type of ontology they belong to, should not be treated in the same way.[12] The place of myth (and therefore that of the gods) varies in each of these models. A myth does not have the same meaning in animist and analogical cultures, for instance. Admittedly, there are no pure cases, and any particular culture reflects a predominance of one or another of these ontologies.[13] Descola is applying a basic insight of structuralism, namely, the notion that a myth (or god) cannot be treated in isolation but only as part of a larger framework. Yet structuralists themselves tend to forget that insight when they compare myths from societies character- ized by different ontologies, or when they emphasize myth at the expense of ritual. The problem of the "distant vision" advocated by structuralism has to do with its objectivist claim, which in the end is merely the impo- sition of one particular ontology (viz., naturalist) onto another (animist in the case of Amerindian societies and/or analogical in that of Asian societies). In reaction to the reductionist character of such an approach, Descola and Eduardo Viveiros de Castro advocate what they call "perspectivism."[14]

EXPLICIT AND IMPLICIT PANTHEONS

Like the esoteric mandala, the Tantric pantheon is a spatiotemporal struc- ture, a cosmic grid. This grid initially served to limit the profusion of images and sort out the wheat (the buddhas and protecting deities) from the chaff (the demons). It obeyed what Michel Foucault called the prin- ciple of *rarefaction* of discourse. Yet in reality things turned out quite differently. The grid of the pantheon turned into a kind of mycelium, from which gods sprouted like mushrooms.

We need therefore to distinguish between the official or *explicit* pantheon and the latent or *implicit* pantheon. In contrast to the hierarchy of the official pantheon, the gods of the implicit pantheon are caught in various types of transversal relations that determine a "secret, invisible economy, located at the heart of the visible, official economy."[15] Along the same lines, we may contrast the implicit mythology of medieval Japan with its explicit mythology.

Lévi-Strauss (1981) already distinguished between implicit and explicit mythology in his "Finale" to *The Naked Man*.[16] But by implicit mythology he merely meant an impoverished version of the standard myths contained in ritual. Although he never defined what he meant by explicit mythology, it is clearly the only mythology that has value in his eyes, and it has semantic properties that the implicit mythology of rituals does not have. While I use the same terminology, my understanding of the two terms is radically different from his. I want to argue precisely the opposite, while insisting on the inseparability of both types of mythology (and theology).

NAMING THE GODS

What's in a god? From both a structuralist perspective and the Buddhist standpoint of codependent origination (*pratitya-samupāda*), the answer is at the same time simple and infinitely complex: *all the others,* the entire pantheon. Yet the constantly transforming network of a god's identities with other gods does not cancel this god's specificity nor lead to a vague pantheism. Furthermore, not all Asian gods accepted incorporation into the Buddhist pantheon; quite a few in fact asserted their difference. Such deities tend to fall through the cracks of orthodox Buddhist discourse and also are more resistant to a structuralist approach.

While most gods owe their prestige to their place in the pantheon, some of them seem to subvert the classificatory order, ranging over an increasingly broad spectrum of fields and modes of action. Ultimately, they can become subpantheons in themselves. A case in point is that of Avalokiteśvara (Kannon 観音), whose 33,000 manifestations are finally (yet provisionally) subsumed under the rubrics of the Thirty-three or even Six Kannon.

By adapting to various contexts, a high or classical god or goddess fuses with local deities, who are, by the same token, elevated to a higher divine status.[17] A god is obviously many things to many people: an object of perception (in epiphanies, dreams, visions); an explanatory cause for extraordinary events; a recipient of thoughts, prayers, rituals. In a way, a floating—albeit not empty—signifier.

The essentialist or "personalist" approach to the gods fails to recognize that a deity exists only against the background of a social imaginary, that is, within a conceptual field. Indeed, neither a name nor a form suffices to characterize with certitude a god. The same god can receive different interpretations and present a nocturnal, potentially malevolent, quasi-demonic aspect as well as a diurnal, benign, benevolent aspect. This ambivalence, which is central to esoteric Buddhism, resonated with

Japanese notions of the "rough spirit" (*aramitama* 荒魂) and "benign spirit" (*nigimitama* 和魂) of the *kami.*

Scholars face the same difficulty as devotees—namely, how to recognize a divine being with certainty. The problem is expressed by Philippe Borgeaud as follows: "Having once recognized the epiphanic nature of such or such experience, how does one succeed, in the framework of a pantheon, in designating with a proper name, irreducible but necessarily circumstantial, the presence that asserts itself in the proliferation of possibles?" As it appears in cultic practice, a god constitutes "a nodal, conjunctural, problematic point."[18] This is particularly true in the case of those gods which are described as "provisional manifestations" (*gongen* 権現) or "divided bodies" (*bunshin* 分身) of a higher deity.

A name serves an important function as a federating principle, but it masks the constant processes that traverse it. Inside the name of a god, all kinds of symbolic groupings and proliferations take place, of the same type as those occurring outside between two or more deities. Thus, the difference between two forms of a god might be just as great as that between that god and other deities, just as, for Spinoza, the difference between a racehorse and a draft horse is surely greater than that between a draft horse and an ox. For Charles Malamoud, "[the] differences and oppositions between the individual gods who make up the pantheon are secondary to the speculative discussions of a given divine power's many faces and levels of reality."[19] Things become more complex in the case of a dyad (not to mention triads and other groupings), which can be obtained by the division of a single deity (endowed with opposite and symmetrical features) or by the association of two deities with opposite features.

The name of a god is shorthand for what Wittgenstein calls the "craving for generality," that is, "the tendency to look for something in common to all the entities which we commonly subsume under a general term," when the only thing they actually share are "family likenesses."[20] The mirage of a god's individuality, caused by its scintillating name, became increasingly clear to me in each of my unsuccessful attempts to fit "individual" gods into individual chapters of this book, attempts that regularly ended in having to *dis-locate* and spread a god over several chapters while lumping it with others in my discussion of some particular function.

While the nominal approach is inherently defective, neither religion nor scholarship can do without names. When the same deity appears under different names and changes all the time, is it still really the same? Furthermore, different gods can share the same function while a single god fulfills various functions. Gods like Myōken, Benzaiten, and Matarajin are what Bruno Latour calls "hybrids": they are more like networks than like individuals. Their name is not just a proper name: rather, like a word defined by other words in the dictionary, they can be defined by all their relationships with other deities; but, as even Ferdinand de Saussure—the founder of structural linguistics—knew, that may not be enough.[21]

Again, the names of deities like Inari Daimyōjin, Matarajin, or Benzaiten call to mind what Humpty Dumpty calls a portmanteau word, i.e., a word into which two (or more) meanings are packed up.[22] Thus, we should perhaps use neologisms of that kind to describe their complex nature. The "Buddho-Daoist" deity Myōken, for instance, could be described as an "adulescent" (both *adult* and *adolescent*) god. After all, the medieval Japanese themselves (who explained "Inari" as *ine-nari* 稲成 'becoming rice-seedling') were never shy of such wordplays.

Gods (and demons) are figures of infigurability, and their names are those of the Innommable. If they were purely functional, the relative uniformity of their functions would not explain their profusion and their idiosyncrasies: why, for instance, would the god of obstacles Vināyaka have an elephant head if he were just another gatekeeping deity?

THE MEDIEVAL LOGIC OF EQUIVALENCE

Theological discussions often constitute a smokescreen. Yet in some cases they reveal real structures. We can therefore follow them up to a certain point, beyond which they seem to deconstruct themselves. We must also pass beyond (or behind) them in order to reveal the implicit theology of cultic practices, the soft underbelly of Mikkyō.

Divine protectors are often described as variants of each other. But what does it mean to describe different gods as one and the same? The logic of equivalence that links a certain buddha and a certain god derives from their functional similarity—for instance, the fact that they both bring worldly benefits (*genze riyaku* 現世利益). It may also result from a perceived circulation of power, produced essentially by ritual, between them.

Japanese gods tend to proliferate: sometimes the emergence of new deities is a case of one god dividing into several; at other times, it is a case of several deities merging into one. The proliferation of gods also reflects a proliferation of discourse stimulated by hermeneutic techniques: the multiplication of symbolic associations—a kind of free association, although not quite free; a loose symbolism, but not quite loose either; a fuzzy logic, but with concrete aims and results. It is akin to what Pierre Bourdieu called the "logic of practice"—a practical logic that "owes its efficacy to the fact that, through the choice of the fundamental schemes that it applies and through its exploitation of the polysemy of the symbols that it uses, it adjusts in each case to the particular logic of each area of practice."[23] While this logic accounts for the "irresistible analogy" that drives the medieval esoteric pantheon, it also explains "the uncertainties and even incoherence that are encountered as soon as one tries to compare methodically all the particular applications of the systems of schemes."[24]

The combinatory system of medieval Mikkyō is based on a quasi-algebraic principle of "transitive" identification: if an entity a is identified with an entity b, and the latter with an entity c, then a is identical with c.[25] The question remains as to what this kind of identity actually means on the doctrinal, philosophical, ritual, and soteriological planes. Should we see them as mere casual, quasi-automatic combinations? Is $a=b$ an identity between two equal powers on the same plane, or is one more fundamental than the other, in the end capturing or subsuming it?[26] At times, symbolic equivalence amounts to a tautological identity (a equals b); at others, it points to a process (a becomes b).[27] The copula may also introduce a dissymmetry, an inequation that suggests added significance (like the *italics* in a written sentence), or a dissemination that both complements and undermines identity.[28] As Charles Malamoud points out in the Vedic context: "Contrary to appearances, the staggering mechanism of identification and correspondences (between gods, between the different protagonists of the sacrifice, humans, gods, inanimate objects, victims; between the elements of the world, of the ritual, and of the human body) that the *Brāhmaṇas* tirelessly expound functions only because these superimpositions are transitory, mobile, explicitly formulated ad hoc, and because they put into relation notions that are articulated and not confused."[29]

Thus, the apparent simplicity of the equivalence between one god and another should not delude us: it conceals a multitude of possible operations, from an ontological identity to mere affinities, including temporary metamorphosis, functional resemblance, inclusion of the individual into the species, and the relation between manifestation and essence. It could just as well be a substitution or a displacement, veiling and revealing at the same time the nature of a god, and the assertion of one group's power over another.

In this mythological algebra, the equivalence between two gods, like the synonyms in a poem, signifies two different systems or registers, which it allows one to articulate. In the case of a poem, this is, according to Michael Riffaterre, the proof that the *system* has replaced the *referent*.[30] In the case of the Buddhist pantheon, however, things are slightly different.

These identities repeat themselves as in a strange loop, without there ever being a central control system. They mutually reinforce each other, but they also find their anchoring and their limits in the outside reality. The dizzying development of their structural "logic" calls to mind a soap opera in which all possible relationships between protagonists are in turn explored: the good guys of today's show become the bad guys of tomorrow's show, and vice versa—vice reverting to virtue, virtue to vice. In the end, these reinforcing patterns lead to the emergence of *primi inter pares*. The next step would be to see all these emerging deities as facets of a single primordial, universal deity. This pattern, however, is held in check by the constant dissemination of symbols that allows Japanese religion to remain resolutely polytheistic.

The relations between various deities are permitted or triggered by various features: iconographic, symbolic, philosophical, numerological, etc. Everything can become relevant—all is grist to the mill of symbolic thinking. The resources of analogical thought are truly mind-boggling. It is of course impossible, and beyond a certain point useless, to follow all these associations in their intricate detail: I have therefore privileged certain tracks that seemed more relevant to my purpose. Symbolic associations between two or more deities can be triggered by practically anything, including elements such as:

a) A name or semanteme: for example, Uga/Uka/Uke, which connects Uga Benzaiten 宇賀弁才天 with classical deities like Uka no mitama 倉稲魂, Ukemochi 保食神, and Toyouke 豊受.

b) A symbol like the wish-fulfilling jewel (*cintāmaṇi*), which connects Benzaiten with other cintāmani-holding deities such as Nyoirin Kannon, Dakiniten, Aizen, and Daikokuten.

c) A specific theme or root metaphor, like *secrecy*, symbolized by the cave or the womb. This particular theme allows the articulation or identification of various motifs like the Chan patriarch Bodhidharma meditating in a cave on Mount Song in China, the sun goddess Amaterasu hiding in the Heavenly Rock Cave, or the bodhisattva Maitreya waiting in Tuṣita heaven for his final rebirth—and the interpretation of these motifs in terms of Buddhist embryology, as images of the embryo in the womb.

d) A taxonomic marker: a color (for instance, red, which can symbolize fire, the southern direction, purification, blood, fever, epidemics, etc., and the deities associated with those elements); or a direction: for instance, the north, connecting directional or cyclical deities like Bishamonten 毘沙門天, Myōken (god of the pole star), emblematic animals like the Rat and the Tortoise (Xuanwu 玄武, the Dark Warrior of Chinese cosmology), etc.

e) Numerological homologies: for instance, the homology between the seven stars of the Northern Dipper, the seven buddhas Yakushi, and the seven Sannō shrines on Mount Hiei. The ternary structure of Sannō symbolism likewise connects it with many analogous triads, as well as with a host of ternary concepts of Tendai esotericism. In some cases, this numerological structure is revealed by a technique that can be traced back to Chinese glyphomancy, namely, the decomposition of Chinese characters forming a name into meaningful elements.[31]

Through one or several of these hermeneutic (semantic, formal, structural, synechdochal, metaphoric) devices, whose arbitrariness is no longer perceived, various deities can be linked, identified, and eventually perceived as different manifestations of a single deity. Even when none of these principles is at work, two or more deities may be identified on the basis of a visionary or intuitive experience.

Kōshū's *Keiran shūyōshū* 渓嵐拾葉集 is probably one of the best examples of the combinatory thought of medieval esotericism, associating as it does Tendai doctrinal rubrics (for instance, the Three Truths) with the *kami* of classical Japanese mythology, as well as with traditional Buddhist cosmology (with its hierarchy of buddhas, bodhisattvas, and divine or semi-divine, demonic and semi-demonic entities), Chinese cosmology, Indian and Chinese astrology, and all kinds of oral tales and traditions. This analogical thinking is in turn supplemented (and subverted) by concrete cases.[32]

The play of analogies and identities allows the emergence of new lateral, rhizome-like relations between the gods. It causes the symbolic network to extend gradually in all directions, and meaning to circulate in creative ways along its channels. Each deity (or symbolic node) gets enriched, albeit temporarily, by the value of its connections. Far from constituting a tautological structure, a closed system, the network of identities produces a drift, a series of modulations, declinations, productive displacements that shortcut hierarchies, introducing an apparent confusion in the neat paradigmatic and syntagmatic order. Because of its swerve, the loop of identities actually creates differences and increases the network's complexity. Thus, every relationship—between signifier and signified, sign and referent, but also between signifier and signifier (in the case of homophony), sign and sign (in the case of homo*graphy*)—produces new meanings, even if it does not always makes sense to us.[33] The relations between words reveal (and produce) relations between things and between beings. Paradoxically, to the extent that the identity is never simple or total, it leaves or introduces a difference that actually facilitates the god's dissemination. Consequently, in the identity between a god and another, the copula does not express their merging or confusion, but rather their articulation. An alternative and tentative view would be to consider the copula itself as the fundamental ground, the source of the two terms it apparently links, which become its traces.

THE STRUCTURALIST MODEL

Bipartition and the "Already Structural"

With its meta-characters linking scenes and discursive loops, esoteric Buddhist mythology calls to mind a Monty Python film—although perhaps not quite as funny. The mythological palimpsest known as *chūsei Nihongi* 中世日本紀 consists in repetition, transformation, and retranscription, all aspects of the work of cultural memory. In medieval Japan, techniques of myth production were not simply based on oral traditions that transgressed the limits of the standard written version; they also relied on the work of writing. Esoteric texts, for instance, dwell at length on their own symbolism and techniques such as *allegoresis*.[34]

Like fish in water, historical actors never perceive consciously and in its totality their symbolic environment. Our inquiry must therefore strive to go beyond the conscious level. In order to explain the continuity or recurrence of certain religious or mythological themes and patterns, we must, with all due precaution, take into account the collective and individual *imaginaire* or mental universe inhabited by these actors.[35] Historians of religions who take their cues from Lévi-Strauss cannot resist the temptation to formalize these bundles of identities. They would be mistaken, however, to conclude that the structures thus retrieved were actually seen and understood by the actors themselves—even if, in the case of medieval Japan, some clerics like Kōshū, the author of the *Keiran shūyōshū,* and even outsiders like the Nō playwright Konparu Zenchiku 金春禅竹 (1405–?) clearly had an intuitive or intellectual grasp of the system. While scholars should be wary of replicating the biases of Buddhist clerics, they should also take the latter's insights seriously. Oftentimes, Buddhist priests were able to discern, beyond the superficial claims of their orthodoxy, a deeper structural logic that, depending on the case, reinforces or subverts the dominant Buddhist ideology. As Rolf Stein remarks in a passage that deserves to be quoted at length:

> The priests or the worshipers reflected upon the available texts and the visual representations. Certainly they could misunderstand and reinterpret a particular form that had become incomprehensible. But they could also sense, or clearly discover, the connections between diverse characters of the pantheon after an analysis analogous to the one we are able to remake. In following the meanderings of these connections, they could take up again characteristics or characters that had fallen out of use. They could also innovate by originating substitutions, superimpositions, identifications, amalgams, or reassemblances. Having done this, they could hardly keep in mind the historical identity of the characters or their provenance. What interested them were types; what they retained for their combinations were sometimes names or formal characteristics, motifs, or themes, connections or functions in isolation, sometimes several of these elements at once. They proceeded by analogy or by taking their categories of classification into account. But although the various elements that were combined may have had different origins or belonged to various contexts, the choice the worshipers made implies that they recognized a connection between forms and contents.[36]

This example illustrates the resilience of symbolic structures, in spite of any explicit doctrinal transmission. The Buddhist monks who resurrected such structures had some understanding of the symbolic system underlying them. This system was *already structural*, and they were structuralists *avant la lettre*. In this respect, they knew better than some modern scholars who persist in studying Buddhist gods individually without taking into account the binary structure or the larger symbolic system that explains their emergence, and their recurrence in variegated cultural contexts.[37]

The same binary codes (inversion, symmetry, opposition) that are at the very heart of the myth's elaboration according to Lévi-Strauss also characterize esoteric Buddhist mythology. Stein has shown that in the Asian context, the dual structure is characteristic, for instance, of the gate (and gatekeeper) motif. The formal features of gatekeeping deities serve above all to underscore bipartition and bipolarity (as opposition and complementarity).[38] Bipartition can be obtained by splitting a single character (with opposite and symmetrical figures)—like Vajrapāṇi becoming the two "benevolent" kings (Niō 仁王) who protect the Buddhist monastery gates—or by associating two characters with opposite features (slender and potbellied, male and female). It is particularly clear in the coupling of the Indian deities Gaṇeśa and Skanda. Stein has shown how these two gods, who had initially been paired in the myth of Śiva, evolved independently in Indian mythology before being "reunited" in a different form in Chinese Buddhism, where they became the gatekeepers of monasteries, the young warrior Weituo 韋駄 (J. Idaten 韋駄天) and the potbellied Mile 弥勒 (J. Miroku), better known as the "laughing Buddha." This Chinese innovation remains in fact faithful to its Indian prototype in form, content (purity vs. gluttony, abstinence vs. abundance), and function (gatekeeping and protection of secrecy).[39] Contrary to most cases, in which the latent mythology subverts the binary coding of the texts, here it is the latent mythology that is dualistic, against the texts. The same is true in Japan—for instance, with the dyad formed by Fudō and Aizen, but also in the case of single deities like Gaṇeśa (Vināyaka, J. Shōten 聖天) and Vaiśravaṇa (Bishamonten). Bipartition can also be expressed by the splitting of an image into two, which can be represented either face to face (the dual Kangiten) or back to back (the dual Bishamon). We also find some rare cases of dual-bodied Kṣitigharba (Jizō 地蔵) and Ākaśagharba (Kokūzō).[40] According to Stein, the logic of bipartition associated with the gatekeepers explains their back-to-back representations in the sense that these deities are protecting the northern and southern directions. Whereas these dual deities seem eminently "structural," others appear less so. Devas like Aizen and Benzaiten, for example, could almost be called "antistructural," owing to their essential multiplicity, their constant metamorphoses, and their prolific nature and proliferation. Dyadic figures are undeniably important for understanding the emergence, meaning, and functions of medieval deities. Yet these motifs and traditional patterns may in some cases turn out to be red herrings or overdetermined MacGuffins. The binary structure is often the imposition of an ideology that we must deconstruct rather than simply accept. The first step is to describe it, which does not mean to endorse it.

Structuralisms

The functional aspect of gods is obviously important. A given deity can be the spokesperson or protector of one or several groups (professional or otherwise). Indeed, its rise often goes together with that of its clientele. Yet the best approach to understanding medieval Japanese gods may be a loosely structural one. The term *structuralism* usually refers to the theory laid out by Lévi-Strauss in his study of American myths. However, in what may be another case of bipartition that transforms Lévi-Strauss and Dumézil into gatekeepers, it has also been used to characterize Georges Dumézil's approach to the study of Indo-European myths—in spite of Dumézil's protestations.[41]

Unfortunately, neither has written much about Buddhism. While Dumézil has given us tantalizing glimpses of the way in which his structural method could be applied to Buddhism, Lévi-Strauss, in his early work *Tristes Tropiques,* only gives a very idealized description of Buddhism (which he starkly contrasts with Islam), regretting that it did not exert more influence on Western culture. This hasty and hardly "scientific" judgment should be contextualized and seen as what it is—the subjective impressions of a traveler after a short stay in Pakistan.[42]

Confronted with traditional, "nonhistorical" societies, Lévi-Strauss could without too much inconvenience describe myths as ahistorical. For him, a myth, "far from constituting a single entity . . . is a bundle of differential elements."[43] It is "comparable to a word encountered in a document, but not appearing in the dictionary, or even to a proper noun, i.e., a term deprived of context. But to understand the meaning of a term is always to change it in all its contexts."[44] In conversation, he once described the mythological field as rose curves rising out of one another:

> The myth taken as the center radiates variants around it, which form the pattern of rose curves that progressively enlarge and become more complicated. And no matter which variant at the edge you choose for a new center, the same thing happens, producing new rose curves that partly overlap with the first and extend beyond them. And so forth, not indefinitely, but until these incurved constructions bring you back to the starting point. The result is that a once indistinct and confused field reveals a network of lines of force and is seen as being powerfully organized.[45]

The approaches of Lévi-Strauss and Dumézil are in many respects complementary. Neither pays much attention to the historical context. Each has justified his approach, and their reasons are not without merits. Lévi-Strauss is concerned essentially with mythological structures, whereas Dumézil tries to recover or reconstruct the Indo-European ideology—as it found its expression through myths, but also rituals, epic narratives, and so on. While their respective object differs, both aim at retrieving structures of thought. Between the two, it is Dumézil who pays the most attention to the gods. To him, the Indo-European pantheon is at times so well articulated that it may be labeled "already structural." Accordingly, one must place a god in the "polytheic" field that defines it by establishing a list of all its functions, and distinguish its field of action from its specific mode of action. For Lévi-Strauss, a god's agency tends to dissolve between the paradigmatic and syntagmatic axes of the myth.

Even though Dumézil limited himself to the Indo-European sphere, his method remains valid for other cultural spheres.[46] His distinction between a few major deities and a whole host of minor deities attached to concrete aspects of practical life reflects a broad division of the Indo-European universe and society. In the case of medieval Japan, however, that dichotomy is subverted by the fact that the same gods shift constantly from one pole to the other, from elemental nature to culture. To give just one example, Benzaiten is at times a goddess of letters and music, and at other times an elemental deity linked with water and earth. Here the historical context is particularly important.

Unlike Dumézil, who always remained wary of extending his findings about Indo-European societies to Japan, Lévi-Strauss found in Japanese mythology a privileged terrain for his structuralist theory, and in the process he has written fascinating—albeit at times problematic—pages about it.[47]

Strictures and Structures

The theories of Dumézil and Lévi-Strauss have given rise to many critiques.[48] Some of the critiques are fair, others less so, but none of them is devastating in my opinion: they are more like useful correctives—in the sense that they relativize the structuralist method—than definitive rebuttals. This is not the place to rehearse them at length, and I will just emphasize a few points that seem relevant to my purpose.

Dumézil and the God's Mode of Action

Dumézil was interested in the ideological structures of Indo-European societies, not in their mythical structures per se. Yet his methodology provides us with a more complex perception of the gods. One of his main contributions has been to allow us to go beyond the notion of an individualized god. This he did by defining a god through the totality of the positions it occupies. Rather than focusing on explicit statements about a god, one now examines the forms of association or contrast between this god and others.

By breaking away from traditional naturalistic interpretations, Dumézil has helped the study of comparative mythology make a great step forward. Yet his insights have often been downplayed by classicists, and it would be an understatement to say that they have had little impact on the study of Asian religions. Even today, most Japanese scholars still define the *kami* Amaterasu in naturalist terms as a solar symbol.[49] Only recently have some of them begun to examine Amaterasu's alleged identity with the buddha Dainichi and her relations with Buddhist deities like Kannon, Maō 魔王 (Skt. Māra), Aizen, Enmaten 閻魔天, Dakiniten, and Benzaiten. This new approach has already yielded important results.[50]

Yet by contrasting the very variable field of action of a god and his more restricted mode of action, Dumézil seems to take one step back to emphasize the latter, and to freeze the divine character into a static definition. Indeed, he attributes to a given god characteristics that tend to become the "primitive element" in this god's definition. By the same token, other characteristics are perceived as "later additions." Dumézil's emphasis on a specific mode of action, when applied to the Indian context, fails to take into account what, since Friedrich Max Müller, has occasionally been described as the "henotheistic" tendency of Indian religion, namely, the fact that each god or goddess becomes "the god or goddess of everything when cathected in devotion or worship."[51]

Dumézil has been criticized on that ground by the classicist Marcel Detienne. Himself a former structuralist, Detienne rejects the idea that a god can be defined by a differential orientation within a unitary activity.[52] If that were the case, the pantheon would indeed become too static a system, one in which each deity occupies a fixed position in relation to its neighbors, a well-delimited square, defined by a specific character, particular means and modes of action, and singular relationships with the cosmos and with mankind. The god's name would refer to an identity conceived once and for all as the articulated and coherent ensemble of a character, a mode of action, and a precise series of affinities with the world, human society, and the collectivity of other gods.[53]

The Gods in the Details

Detienne emphasizes the problem caused by a definition of a god that rests only on its mode of action. He claims to avoid that pitfall by focusing on concrete elements such as objects, gestures, and situations. He emphasizes the importance of details that allow him to bring to light, to uncover, certain latent but essential meanings, revealing not so much the true nature or function of the god, but rather its specific mode of action. Truly, the god is in the details.[54] In the myth, a detail can shed light on certain aspects—and not the slightest either—of a divine power. It may be, as Detienne argues, that "the surest, if not the most direct way to analyse whole complexes of relations between deities and to avoid being led astray by the immediate forms of gods so prone, ever since the days of their original devotees, to become individuals, is to approach them via concrete details and segments of situation: through objects, gestures, and situations."[55]

In a pregnant symbolic universe, where everything is (or can become) significant, fraught with a latent meaning, the most unexpected details may trigger the analogical process. The most obvious function is not necessarily the most important, let alone the original one.[56] Rather than the *field* of action, then, one should, according to Detienne, privilege the *mode* of action. In the Greek context, Detienne contrasts deities that are clearly distinguished by their name and a few prominent features, as well as by their place in classifications and symbolic systems, with elusive, almost undifferentiated deities, whose name masks or blurs their personality more than it reveals it. The latter escape confusion and anonymity only through repeated oracles, operating almost exclusively through speech.[57] The above distinction is constantly called into question, inasmuch as the deities of the first category become more complex, less transparent, and acquire features of the second, whereas a few deities of the latter category become orthodox and simplified. Detienne's model is not sufficiently dialectical or dynamic to explain this two-way process.

This analysis applies well to the medieval Japanese/Buddhist pantheon. In a first phase, one can show how various deities are connected by an object or symbol (for instance, the wish-fulfilling jewel). Sometimes this connection is explicit, sometimes not. In a second phase, one may attempt to show that this association includes a distinction as to the mode of action—as shown by Detienne in the case of the relations of Athena and Poseidon with the horse.

In the visual arts, an uncanny detail can "dis-locate" a painting and its viewer's perception, revealing a hitherto unseen meaning. Well-known examples of deceptive or ambiguous images include Wittgenstein's rabbit-duck illusion and Salvador Dali's "Slave Market with the Disappearing Bust of Voltaire." Although the alternative view or meaning is not necessarily deeper, the totality cannot be synthesized into a single image, as in the case of binocular vision.[58] Often the artist has purposely set the detail out as a trigger, but it can also be invented (in the archeological sense of "discovery") by the viewer. In the same way, the "details" that I have selected in my discussion of medieval gods may reflect my desire to find certain links between them and to reveal a coherence that runs deeper than that of the official pantheon. While having no claim to truth, this interpretation will hopefully reveal itself as productive. Here a caveat is in order: the obvious detail is not necessarily the most telling one, it could also be a lure.[59] We must check its relevance by placing it into an interpretive field or network. At the same time, we must refrain from thinking that what is revealed in this manner is the main or original function of the deity. While the detail may call into doubt the manifest "personality" of the god, it does not establish another, more real personality. It simply transforms the god into a complex node in a network whose relevance had perhaps until now gone unnoticed. Even better, it suggests that the god, as an actor, is itself a network of the kind described in actor-network theory. The tree does not hide the forest, it reveals it, because the tree itself is a forest, and the god a pantheon. Or rather, there is neither tree (unity) nor forest (totality), but an irreducible multiplicity. The name of a god does not designate a gathering or subsuming (of the multiple into unity), but a metamorphic deployment, a permanent onto/morpho-genesis—"In an uproar and chaos of Peninsulas, Exultant, from their moorings in triumph torn."[60]

Lévi-Strauss and His Critics

Although structuralism provides intelligibility, it is not without its problems. Lévi-Strauss was well aware that the insights yielded by his "vision from afar" presuppose a certain blindness to the contextual, psychological, and phenomenological dimensions of the myths. Yet, as he argues in his introduction to the work of Marcel Mauss, too much reliance on "local knowledge" and native categories might prevent the observer from seeing clearly the deep structures that informed the informant's viewpoint.[61] Without going as far as asserting, as he does, that myths think themselves through humans (and most notably through him), I believe that they have a certain autonomy and are not simply means to solve the logical contradictions experienced by humans in the world.[62]

At first glance, Lévi-Strauss provides us with a useful road map when he writes: "When faced with a problem, myth thinks of it as homologous to problems raised in other domains: cosmological, physical, moral, juridical, social, etc. And it aims to account for all these at once."[63] For him, myths and rituals are merely "different transformations of identical elements": "What a myth says in a language that seems to pertain to one realm spreads to all areas in which a problem of the same formal type may arise."[64] Therefore, mythical thought, when confronted with a problem, puts it in parallel with others. It uses several codes simultaneously. It is always a question of finding in another domain a formal equivalent of the meaning we are looking for. "Meaning is nothing but this use of correspondences."[65] While this may be true in some cases, just the opposite may be true in others. Even in our world of GPSs and fMRIs, however, the paths of the gods (in the "outer" reality or in our brains) may still remain undecipherable. The dream of a total and tautological structure might be just that—a dream. It does not take into account the phenomenon of *emergence,* namely, the fact that certain structures that develop at one level may have no correspondence with those on another level. And this leaves open the question whether some aspects of religious experience may not remain invisible to our intellectual (or neurological) radar, escaping the binary structures of our logical net.

When he developed Marcel Mauss's notion of symbolic exchange, Lévi-Strauss abandoned the Durkheimian theory of the sacred and replaced it with that of the "symbolic"—a notion from which all mystical tendencies had been expurgated. Still he was at pains to explain the "symbolic efficacy" of ritual through a quasi-algebraic manipulation of symbols.[66] The sacred nature of the gods cannot be understood without restoring to some extent the powers of the *imaginaire.*

As Lévi-Strauss notes, different levels of analysis yield different structures. If the historical method is above all humanistic, in the sense that it aims at reducing all historical events to human actions, it also runs the risk of leading to a methodological individualism by reducing historical evolutions to individual decisions and conflicts of interest. The history of mentalities shows that human actions do not always find their source in voluntary acts, but in a social and psychological unconscious. In this sense, humans are not the only, nor even the main, actors—perhaps not even, as Paul Valéry puts it, the meaningful units—of the human comedy or tragedy.

According to Lévi-Strauss's intellectualist and instrumentalist conception, the main function of myths is to attenuate a "logical scandal."[67] The structuralist hypothesis always runs the danger of overextension—a term referring initially to the fact that children learning the rules of language often apply them *logically,* but *incorrectly,* as in the case of irregular verb conjugations and irregular plurals in English.

Sometimes, however, it is the myth itself that creates the scandal instead of attenuating it, let alone solving it. One is tempted to apply to Lévi-Strauss's work Clifford Geertz's tongue-in-cheek remark about Evans-Pritchard's work on the Nuer, namely, that it is an "anthropological geometry book."[68] At the very least, when one speaks of a "grammar" of forms or symbols, one tends to overlook their poetic and emotional power.[69]

In a similar fashion, given the profusion of algebra-like identities among medieval Japanese gods, I run the risk of writing a historical-anthropological algebra book about Japanese religion and turning Buddhist monks into "grammarians of the absolute."[70] Lévi-Strauss himself, admittedly on rare occasions, criticizes this abstract tendency. In his *Conversations* with Didier Eribon, for instance, he emphasizes that structures are not reducible to a system and cannot be conceived separately from the notion of transformation. He rejects abstraction in favor of a "science of the concrete," regretting for instance that the French Revolution "has given people the idea that society is to be ruled by abstract thought, when instead it is formed of habits and customs; by crushing these in the mortar of reason, one pulverizes ways of life founded on a long tradition, reducing individuals to the state of interchangeable and anonymous atoms."[71]

There is a general tendency to deny complexity by separating the antagonists and rejecting on the outside what seems strange and troubling. Taxonomies are dichotomic: they clearly distinguish between dragons and snakes, dogs and wolves. But the realm of the gods could be defined by the French expression *entre chien et loup* 'in between dog and wolf', meaning that ambiguous moment between day and night when all contours and borders become uncertain. It is a time of metamorphoses, when it becomes hard to distinguish between friends and enemies, gods and demons, the beauty and the beast, historians and structuralists.[72] In medieval Japan, dragons and snakes, tortoises and serpents, become intertwined or fuse, as we will see in the cases of Myōken and Benzaiten.

Myth as Ritual

We need not rehearse here the rather pointless debate as to which, of myth and ritual, predates, preempts, or determines the other. A few comments on Lévi-Strauss's interpretation of ritual will suffice. While claiming that myth and ritual are "different transformations of identical elements," Lévi-Strauss sees them as categories stemming from movements of thought that operate in opposite directions: whereas the myth divides reality, ritual attempts to fill the lived experience.[73] In the end, he unabashedly gives myth precedence over ritual, and tackles the latter only—almost as an afterthought—in the "Finale" of his masterwork.[74] Even then, he is mainly interested in binary codes and fails to take into account the performative nature of ritual. Accordingly, what he finds in ritual is merely impoverished, "implicit" mythology, which he contrasts with "explicit" mythology.[75]

Contrary to the Amerindian cases discussed by Lévi-Strauss, Japanese gods exist and thrive mainly through ritual. It is ritual that literally brings them down to earth, in the life of the worshiper, or more precisely in the purified arena prepared for them. It is again through ritual that anonymous and generic entities become individualized as specific "gods" that respond to a proper name. Some will object that this is wishful thinking, and that in the end perhaps the gods will never know that we have given them names, because they are figments of our imagination. Yet imagination has ontological power, and it is ritual, not myth, that brings the gods to life, making them present, to the point of inducing at times possession in their worshipers. Gods and demons crowd at the gate of the ritual arena, they constitute a real danger: real *because* imaginary. Because the practitioners try to identify themselves with ambivalent, possessive, and potentially dangerous deities, self-protection is required at the threshold of most esoteric rituals. There is of course a significant difference between

Tantric visualization and identification with deities perceived as emanations of the cosmic buddha (*gonsha*), on the one hand, and possession by powers that are perceived as alien and often malevolent, on the other. Yet even "high" deities like Benzaiten and Daikokuten are ambivalent in that respect. The priest may have difficulty distinguishing between the wisdom kings (*myōō*) with which he tries to identify himself as manifestations of the Buddha (and of his true self), and the demons by which he might be possessed (or dispossessed), and which are the figure of the inner or external Other. Indeed, with certain deities like Kōjin, a troubling situation arises: the demonic itself is experienced as being the fundamental reality, and there a confusion or transit between self and other—which is also a passage at the limit of madness—is liable to occur.

Medieval gods are caught in a complex and heterogenous web formed by myths, rituals, images, and many other things. Scholars have begun studying ritual in its concrete occurrences, but there is as yet no real *rito*-logy (as there is a *mytho*-logy).[76] Above all, there is no articulation between iconography and the ritual sphere to explain the way in which the "nature" of a god evolves according to encounters between images and symbols.

From my standpoint, the symbolic freeways of official theology have no more value—but also no less—than the byways of implicit theology as found in ritual practice and mythology. If I emphasize the latter, it is because they have been abandoned for too long, overgrown with brambles, and need to be cleared and traveled again. Deleuze and Guattari tackle the question of mythological structures from a slightly different angle. To them, while structuralism claims to deal with transformations, it pays actually little or no attention to "becomings." Indeed, "it is designed precisely to deny or at least denigrate their existence: a correspondence of relations does not add up to a becoming."[77] In other words, "to become is not to progress or regress along a series."[78] For example, Amaterasu's "becoming animal" (snake or fox) is not the same thing as an "animal rebirth," seen as one of the six types of rebirth in the Buddhist soteriological schema.

Unlike the genealogic or arborescent model, the rhizome model proposed by Deleuze and Guattari allows us to see how a single deity disseminates into several others or several deities merge into one. The neat classificatory hierarchy of the pantheon is subverted by transversal or rhizome-like communalities between heterogeneous groups of gods, demons, and buddhas. Instead of the vertical emanations and filiations of the theoretical *honji suijaku* ("original substance and manifest traces") model, we find transversal relations, *par la bande* (in both senses of the word *bande*—margin and group). According to Deleuze and Guattari, the mythologist is only interested in individuals, whereas gods (and demons) are bands that merge into one another. Medieval deities, particularly those of the *kōjin* 荒神 or "wild gods" variety, were nomadic powers—a fact well understood by some of the social groups (itinerant minstrels and outcasts, for example) that worshiped them. The wild gods, on the other hand, slip through the institutional cracks, they relentlessly outflank the system, grid, or pantheon—albeit with varying degrees of success. For the same reason, they elude a straightforward structuralist analysis, which by default has the habit of letting go of the essential, the fluxes, the concrete, and of reducing everything to positions or points, forgetting intensities and becomings. As Eduardo Viveiros de Castro points out, such multiplicity is "non-taxonomic" in that it resists typological categories such as similarity, opposition, analogy, and identity, as well as any kind of hierarchy.[79] By contrast, the traditional buddhas and *kami* represent the institutionalized, enshrined, domesticated divine. How could the linear discourse of orthodoxy follow the ever-changing network in its meanders and ramifications?

Modern scholars too often consider the native's beliefs with condescendence.[80] They usually deny any real existence to the gods by reducing them to signs and symbols and taking away from them that awe-inspiring intensity and essential mobility that constitute their very nature. Trapped in the meshes of a reductionist analysis, the gods fade away—even when they seem at the center of the discourse. Is there a way to speak about them that would re-call them to life, re-animate them, lend them the credit of existence, or at least the benefit of the doubt—if not blind faith or due respect? Ideally, we should, as Jeanne Favret-Saada argues in the case of witchcraft, accept (at least temporarily) the prospect of being "caught" in the starry web of discourse on myth and ritual.[81] Being a participant-observant is of course never easy. The question of empathy is rendered all the more difficult in the case of historians of religion dealing with a distant past. And yet, as they immerse themselves in the world of medieval mythologues, a strange "fusion of horizons" takes place: they begin to understand the inner logic—if not the truth-value—of a discourse that from the outside sounds like a mythomaniac's nonsense. Objectivist scholars will object that precisely when the empathetic interpreters come to believe they are making sense of that sacred delirium, they have fallen prey to it. Yet why study medieval gods if one is not able to listen and fall prey (at least temporarily) to their sirens' song? Indeed, why would we study other people's beliefs at all—if not because we hope to become able to adhere to them, albeit vicariously? Even when they look most rational, when they seem to "make sense," historians of religions and anthropologists often speak from a sense of loss and nostalgia, from a deep-seated desire to reenchant their world.

The ambivalence of the gods is not simply a static structural opposition of features, but rather an essential indecidability, a fluidity, mutability, hesitation, the postponing of any definitive interpretation. Structures

do not explain everything. Sometimes, for instance, an enduring structure hides a change or loss of meaning. Thus, between the Muromachi
and the Edo periods, very little changed in the theological structures of
esoteric Buddhism—and yet everything changed. The edifice remains
in place, but it no longer has the same meaning, as if a new light had,
between morning and evening, totally modified its appearance. Furthermore, as John Law points out, "structure is not free-standing, like
a scaffolding on a building site, but a site of struggle, a relational effect
that recursively generates and reproduces itself."[82] Keeping this in mind,
it should be clear that the "structures" encountered in this work are not
always those of structuralism, they are more akin to the networks of
actor-network theory. They constitute a reading among others, contextual, moving, constantly reorganizing. They do not by any means offer
a "key" to some permanent Japanese/Buddhist mythology. As Law puts
it, the actor-network approach "not only effaces the analytical divisions
between agency and structure . . . , but it also asks us to treat different
materials—people, machines, 'ideas' and all the rest—as interactional
effects rather than primitive causes."[83]

Lévi-Strauss argued that myths have a kaleidoscopic nature that can
be reduced to the variation of a few elements.[84] The metaphor of Indra's
net or of the spiderweb is eminently applicable to mythology.[85] It is difficult to avoid repetitions, because each deity is a bundle of relationships, multifaceted, functionally reflected in many others. Even if one
uncovers basic structures, however, they do not account for the esthetic
pleasure (and at times the vertigo) produced by their apparently infinite
variations.

Analogical thought—whether that of the priest or the scholar—lets
intensities and multiplicities slip through its meshes. The unknown powers that we call "gods," "demons," or "deities" transcend, exceed, and
subvert all structures, even when they appear to be caught in them. As
Maurice Blanchot, speaking of Dionysos, points out, the fragmentation
of the god "is not the rash renunciation of unity, nor a unity that remains
one by becoming plural. Fragmentation is the god itself, that which has
no relation whatsoever with a center and cannot be referred to an origin:
what thought, as a consequence—the thought of the same and of the one,
the thought of theology and that of all the modes of human (or dialectic)
knowledge—could never entertain without falsifying it."[86] Thus, the god's
essential multiplicity can never be reduced to an essence or contained in
a taxonomy, in spite of its being apparently caught in analogical relations
of identity and opposition.

Perhaps we are condemned to oscillate between two incompatible
models. The former is a kind of metaphysics of presence (and absence)
which argues that the reality of the sacred, while initially really experienced as epiphany, is soon lost or diluted in a network of relationships.

The latter model claims that the sacred was never present in the first place, that mythological and ritual networks proliferate around an originary loss, and that all attempts at creating a semblance of presence are vain. Likewise, there is no choosing between the "vision from afar" and "local knowledge." Yet as modern Westerners, removed both temporally and geographically from our object of inquiry, we tend to privilege the former.

Between a close-up vision that risks blinding itself to its object by staring at it, and a "vision from afar" that tends to fuse this object into a mass of materials and to privilege the background over the object itself, there is room for an intermediary position, which will multiply focalizations, shifting from the wide angle to the narrow angle, in a back-and-forth movement between close and distant vision, forefront and background, individual consciousness and collective *imaginaire*. In that passage, that constant to-and-fro motion, the gods may be dwelling. By showing how certain literati have had a tendency to sediment a multitude of features into a single object or to hang various functions onto a portmanteau name, scholars risk yielding to the monographic temptation and to do in turn "constructive mythology." On the other hand, if they are able to avoid that pitfall, their study will be a deconstruction or "de-sedimentation."

SITTING UNDER THE BANYAN TREE

To find our way in the labyrinth of medieval Japanese religion, we need to overcome our instrumentalist and objectivist proclivities. The corridors of that labyrinth are like the half-deserted streets in Eliot's "Love Song of J. Alfred Prufrock"—"streets that follow like a tedious argument/ Of insidious intent/ To lead you to an overwhelming question."[87] All we can do is open a space of indeterminacy and suggest the possibility of an originary experience in which forms and functions fuse into one another, and the divine is perceived as constantly infiltrating, traversing, or overflowing individual consciousness.

To use a fashionable (albeit problematic) scientific metaphor, the fluidity of symbolic associations calls to mind that of neurons and dendrites. By enabling the transition of ideas and images, individuals play as if it were the role of neurotransmitters. What matters here is not so much the content as the network or rather the rhizome that is constantly formed and transformed by these ephemeral yet strangely resilient roots. I feel therefore tempted to speak of "synaptic" Buddhism in spite of the obvious difficulties with such a "modern" and pseudoscientific definition.

Latour's definition of the network emphasizes the role of *mediators,* a term that he contrast with "intermediaries."[88] The latter are transparent, conveying information without altering it, whereas the former are opaque, resistant, irreducible, transforming the information that circulates through them. While mediators have an agency of their own, it does not mean that they are the ultimate causes whose effects are perceived by humans. The same is true of human agency, which cannot be reduced to an individual origin (say, free will) but already implies a complex network of mediations. "So who is pulling the strings? Well, the puppets do in addition to their puppeteers."[89] One thing at least is clear. Even with more complex and fluid notions like those of the network and rhizome—or mycelium— we cannot hope to reach the truth of the gods, but merely to tease out what Deleuze and Guattari call a "plane of consistency" (*plan de consistance*) among others, a constellation of deities that forms a kind of oblique, latent, and temporary pantheon.[90]

BACK TO PHENOMENOLOGY?

True causalities have little or nothing to do with superficial (ideological) structures. We must keep the latter only because of what they tell us of autochthonous visions, which often constitute a form of false consciousness, a way of covering up actual practices. Yet this consciousness cannot simply be rejected as false, as it is also part of reality.[91] We should resist the tendency to focus on "structures"—whether superficial or deep— because the structural meshes tend to let pass through the existential reality, among other things, of fear and magical possession.

Admittedly, there is no way to reach the direct experience of an individual—particularly when that individual has long been dead. Not only is the religious experience of others always mediated by language, more fundamentally it may forever be out of the reach of scholars who cannot construct their object without a priori rejecting the epiphanies that are taken as a "given" by religious people. And yet, despite this network of symbolic equations and the constant exchange of attributes, there is also a certain semantics according to which deities, like words, preserve a part of their history, deposited like sediments in their name and form, and reach a certain degree of individualization that may justify, in some cases, the type of methodological individualism I criticized earlier. One can indeed argue that, inasmuch as they exist as individuals in the minds of people, gods do have a certain (psychological) reality and real effects on their lives.

At the psychological or phenomenological level, that is, from the standpoint of the believer, gods are perceived as real agents. Structural analysis tends to leave out not only the psychological or existential experience, but also the genetic development, the tension and contention between different images of the same deity or the same function played by different deities, the symbolic sedimentation, superscription, or reverberation. To understand the beliefs they discuss, historians of religions sometimes have to yield to the temptation of reckoning with the god's real presence, and experience firsthand its intimacy, its seduction or fearsomeness.[92] Gods are tremendously real, in the sense that they cause tremor and trauma. Japanese gods are often, like Rainer Maria Rilke's angels, terrifying.[93] Entering in contact with them is always fraught with danger and requires ritual protection.

By overemphasizing form—for instance, the formal links or details of the god's appearance—structuralists tend to forget or deny its (perceived) phenomenological presence. And yet, it is through form that presence is supposed to manifest itself—albeit in a domesticated form (even if it looks fierce). The iconographic detail can also be a way to coax fear, to bring the demons out of the darkness in which they hide, to produce them into the light (and also, metaphorically, to guide them from ignorance to awakening).

To "return" to the phenomenological dimension of religious phenomena is by no means to fall back into a kind of epistemological naiveté; quite to the contrary, it is to question our Western epistemological assumptions. It means, among other things, to take seriously the reality of magical powers. The point was made long ago by the Italian anthropologist Ernesto De Martino (1908–1965) in his book *The Magic World* (*Il mondo magico,* 1948). But De Martino remained a voice in the wilderness, quickly disavowed by his political friends and by his mentor, Benedetto Croce (1866–1952), and soon drowned by the clamors of structuralism. Perhaps it is time to listen to this voice again, and the recent work of sociologists like Bruno Latour and anthropologists like Jeanne Favret-Saada, Philippe Descola, Tim Ingold, and Eduardo Viveiros de Castro, albeit quite different in their approaches, seems to point toward the same direction.[94]

Functionalist anthropologists, structuralists, and historians of religion like Mircea Eliade have conveniently forgotten that what is at stake in these rituals and stories is a very real drama, and not just ideas and beliefs.[95] Another important point that is often overlooked is that the psychological—and even physical—reality of premodern people was not the same as ours, and that modern epistemology, in spite of its meteoric success, has no definitive purchase on truth. East Asia, in particular, was a zone of contact and intermingling between what Descola has described as shamanistic and analogical epistemologies (the latter being represented by Chinese correlative thinking and esoteric Buddhism). De Martino also emphasized (twenty years before Foucault) the historicity of our epistemologies, and the reality of magical and supranormal (or paranormal) powers. Likewise, Viveiros de Castro emphasizes a "perspectivism" that helps us to question the presuppositions of our objectivist, naturalist approach. Even then, however, we are condemned to do so on naturalism's terms, and our account of what *we* call *religious phenomena* in another culture can hardly be a fair and balanced one.[96]

Of course, it would be suicidal for a scholar today (just as it was in De Martino's time) to assert the reality of the magical realms that, for instance, medieval Buddhists were describing, and to believe, as did our Romantic precursors, in the possibility of an authentic access to the minds of past and alien people.

All we can do, I believe, is to reflect upon the fact that, as cognitive science and postmodernism have told us, our description of reality is just that, a *description,* and that many other descriptions have been and remain possible. Before rejecting these accounts of the invisible world as superstitions or showing our tolerance (and condescension) by accepting them as "beliefs" (as opposed to our secure knowledge), we should realize that these beliefs and superstitions are made so by our refusal to see them for what they are: modes of existence and subjectivity in worlds that were (and still are) significantly different from the one that our civilization has granted and warranted us. This is not, however, to fall into some cultural relativism in which everything is the same, an intellectual night in which all cats are grey, but to remain aware of the possibility that, as Marcel Mauss once said, there are "many moons, pale, dead or obscure, in the firmament of reason"—but also many yet-to-come sunrises.

CODETTA

Starting (and departing) from the naive vision of methodological (mythological) individualism, we met various methods associated (sometimes unduly) with structuralism and poststructuralism: the structural analysis of Dumézil (revisited by Detienne), the structuralism of Lévi-Strauss (revisited by Viveiros de Castro and Descola), Derridean deconstruction, the nomadic thought of Deleuze and Guattari, and the actor-network theory of Latour and Law.

By focusing on the ideology (the system behind the multiplicity), Dumézil attends only to what Deleuze and Guattari call "territorialization," and he posits as an achieved idealized system—the trifunctional ideology of the Indo-Europeans—something that may only have been actualized in varying degrees depending on the cultural setting. True, Dumézil is well aware of the limits of this model, and he scrupulously avoids bending the facts. In the end, however, he is only interested in the "order" of things, not in their apparently chaotic transformations. Lévi-Strauss's *esprit de système,* on the other hand, leads him to downplay the elements that do not fit his interpretation. A purely structuralist approach, while it provides a pleasant feeling of intelligibility by reducing everything to logical relations, proves too costly inasmuch as it loses sight of the meaning of the practices it studies, discarding their phenomenological (and perhaps ontological) reality and largely ignoring their historical evolution. While a practical purpose can be served by focusing on a specific figure, doing so blurs the constant merging and emerging of symbols, their polysemy and dissemination. Yet the semantic approach remains useful, insofar as it offers a certain organizing principle.

Like their Buddhist predecessors, modern Buddhist scholars have pigeonholed the gods by giving them fixed ranks in the pantheon. Yet the gods stubbornly resist localization and other kinds of reduction—not only on the phenomenological plane, where their epiphanies often overflow their allotted slots, but also on the structural plane, where the chain of their equivalences leads to a profusion, a proliferation, a kind of mythologico-ritual spam that eventually enriches the system's complexity. As Henri Atlan points out, Deleuze and Guattari's notions of "territorialization" and "deterritorialization" correspond to the principles of complexity through noise, a sequence of disorganizations recuperated as reorganization.[97]

I started from the traditional notion of structure and proceeded to turn it against itself (or at least to relativize it) by defining another "formation"—which is not exactly a structure in the strict sense, or at least remains an open structure, with irreducible pockets of nonstructure. To the structural transparence of categories such as buddhas, wisdom kings, and other Buddhist hypostases (*gongen*), I oppose the opacity of the demonic deities known as the "real ones" (*jissha* 実者). But under the influence of the latter, the former in turn tend to become opaque.

Medieval Japanese gods are truly *meta-morphic* in the sense that they constantly *morph* from one form into another. Behind that perpetual morphing, however, does something remain constant that would deserve to be called the true "fundamental ground" (*honji* 本地), though it might not be an individual entity or even a functional kernel? We need to maintain a middle way between fetishizing names and abandoning them as federating and taxonomic principles.

Gods may be part of a semiotic system, but they are not mere signs. They represent not just beliefs but the vanishing trace of a presence, perhaps a floating feeling of uncanniness, fear, or joy caused by a close encounter with an elusive higher power. Discourse about gods reveals not merely the content of beliefs but a certain existential or phenomenological tonality, which is always at risk of slipping through the meshes of symbolic discourse.

While the Buddhist abhorrence of pandemonium led to the constitution of an official pantheon, symbols—like iron filings in a magnetic field—tend to reorganize themselves along unexpected lines of force. Consequently, the Buddhist "ordering of things" was gradually subverted by a deeper kind of reordering at the level of the imaginary rather than the doctrinal level. One should therefore always distinguish between the latent and manifest content of myths—as Freud did for dreams. The symbolic associations of esoteric Buddhism pave the way to all kinds of associations and permutations, thereby allowing some of this latent symbolism to emerge in written texts.[98]

In spite of appearances, I offer no teleological model in which structuralism would eventually be superseded by poststructuralism and actor-network theory. Poststructuralism has too often been misunderstood as simply declaring structuralism false and outdated, but such a frontal critique is precisely what deconstruction is against, albeit in an oblique fashion. Structuralism remains unmatched in its explanation of the *already structural* that constitutes an essential part of Buddhist doctrine, ritual, and mythology. In its search for a fixed syntax of relations that would reflect mental processes and actions, it is not so much defeated as "supplemented" (in the Derridean sense) by poststructuralism and its exploration of limits and incompleteness. While the structuralist approach proves necessary and well adapted to understand the *explicit* mythology of medieval esoteric Buddhism, the poststructural and actor-network theories prove more efficient at teasing out its *implicit* mythology. But these theories should not be turned into yet another orthodoxy. Thus, the rhizome or network is not an *anti*-structure, as it was made to appear at a time when structuralism was the dominant paradigm that needed to be overturned; it is rather the extension of a fluid concept of the structure, one that is arguably *already present* in Lévi-Strauss's work.[99] Philosophers like Deleuze and Guattari, sociologists like Latour and Law, anthropologists like Viveiros de Castro and Ingold all admit the need to attend to both the structure and the rhizome/network, symmetry and transversality, identity and difference, sedentary and nomadic thought. At any rate, it has become too easy to be hypercritical and nomadic.

As Viveiros de Castro points out, nomadic thought has its own dangers and its own sedentarism, and sedentary thought (which is often more nomadic than one imagines) must also be given its share. Lévi-Strauss himself may not be as Lévi-Straussian as one thinks: in many ways he prefigures Deleuze and Guattari.

At any rate, I prefer to stick to a pluralist or eclectic approach, in which both methodologies have their uses. Structuralism accounts for the cultivated spaces, poststructuralism for the grass that grows in the interstices.[100] In the end, perhaps the difference between structure and network is merely one of personal preference, like the gap between the viewpoints of Gulliver's "Big-Endians" and "Small-Endians."[101] Better stick to a twofold principle or yield to alternating temptations.

Structuralism attempted to provide a remedy to the "personalist" and "narrative" fallacies that presented the gods as characters in a story. Nevertheless, by reducing everything to bundles and oppositions, it missed a crucial element, the constantly evolving flux of divine energies. It is admittedly difficult, perhaps impossible, to follow the metamorphoses of the gods in the relatively linear discourse of a book. Books require a narrative, while reality offers no plots. There lies a vexing paradox for an author who tries to discern the lines of dissemination of religious discourse while resisting dissemination in his own attempt to keep his narrative (at least minimally) organized. Even a book that emphasizes deterritorialization cannot but be an example of reterritorialization. But I am confident that it will be deterritorialized again—if not reduced to shreds—by its eager and well-meaning critics, those essential mediators. So be it.

2

UNDER THE GAZE OF THE STARS
Myōken and the Northern Dipper

In the world of Buddhist mythology, as in Blaise Pascal's famous sphere, the center is everywhere and the circumference nowhere. If the center, contrary to appearances, is simply a point like any other, we can enter the mythic world of Japanese religion from any given point—say, its would-be center or northern pole (or both). I begin therefore with Myōken 妙見, a deity who has often been regarded as marginal despite the fact that he, as god of the pole star, became a symbol of the center. This "bodhisattva" of obscure origins is a paradigmatic representative of the gods that we will encounter in this book and its companion volumes. Why choose him over other symbols as an entry point? The choice is not as arbitrary or paradoxical as it may seem. It marks, from the outset, the importance of astral realities in a Buddhism that, in theory at least, downplayed cosmology. Myōken is, in a way, the *punctum saliens*—the leaping point and living heart, "the dynamic center of a universe whose center extends outwards indefinitely into outer space," irradiating its force without limits.[1] In this, of course, he is not alone, indeed he hardly differs from other—more orthodox—esoteric figures like Ichiji Kinrin 一字金輪 (Skt. Ekākṣara-uṣṇīṣacakra), the Single-letter Golden Wheel Buddha. But there is another reason to focus (in an out-of-focus way) on him, namely, the fact that he was all but erased by Meiji reformers and iconoclasts. In this sense, his case is exemplary: he is the cornerstone rejected by the builders. Or one of the cornerstones. Like Dakiniten 荼吉尼天, Gozu Tennō 牛頭天王, and so many other deities that were at the very center of medieval Japanese religion, he was rejected by Meiji ideologues, because he was too "Buddhist" (sad irony), and replaced by two authentically "Shintō" and allegedly native deities, Hachiman 八幡 and Ame no Minakanushi 天御中主. A rapid toponymic survey, however, reveals his extreme importance in situ and may lead us to conclude that, like Inari Daimyōjin, he was one of the great deities of premodern Japan.[2]

FEAR AMONG THE STARS

Looking at the starry heavens, Pascal also famously exclaimed: "The eternal silence of these infinite spaces frightens me." The medieval Japanese were frightened by the night skies too, but not for the same reasons. Despite the theoretical infinity introduced by Mahāyāna cosmology, the world in which they lived was still a closed, finite one. Their fear of the skies was not caused by silence or absence, but rather by the very real and ominous presences of the stars. Indeed, stars and planets were usually perceived as demonic entities that needed to be propitiated. This understanding of astral bodies is particularly obvious in the case of the grouping formed by the pole star and the seven stars of the Northern Dipper (our Ursa Major).

While Japanese star worship is largely indebted to Chinese cosmology, the cosmotheistic nature of esoteric Buddhism provided an easy bridge for cultural translation between Indian and Chinese cosmologies, on the one hand, and between Indian astrology and local Japanese folk beliefs about the stars, on the other. The *Asabashō* by the Tendai priest Shōchō (1205–1282), for instance, notes that Myōken, as the deified pole star, was particularly important in non-Buddhist writings produced and used by Yin-Yang masters (*onmyōji* 陰陽師) and exegetes of the *Book of Changes* (*Yi jing* 易経).[3] Like esoteric star rituals and earth-quelling rituals, Myōken rituals served as a bridge between esoteric Buddhism and the Way of Yin and Yang (Onmyōdō), but they simultaneously constituted an arena of contention.[4]

In this chapter I discuss Myōken's character as a paradigmatic symbol of the cosmic center, focusing in particular on the ways in which this symbolism drew upon conceptions of kingship, Daoist notions, and esoteric Buddhist models. After giving an overview of the development of his cult in Japan, I focus on certain local appropriations of Myōken, and an investigation of the god's varied iconography reveals some connections and implications that are not always explicit in doctrinal texts. Finally, a discussion of Myōken's intimate relationships with certain deities leads me to emphasize the embryological symbolism that underlies his role as a god of destiny. Throughout the chapter I hope to draw the reader's attention to a handful of themes common to most if not all of Myōken's ritual and theological manifestations. Starting from his primary importance as a deity of the center and his concomitant role as regulator of the universe that revolves around him, I highlight his ambiguous and elusive nature: the apparent lack of consistency with regard to his associations with other astral bodies and deities periodically made him a focal point of contestation. Another persistent theme is Myōken's cross-fertilization with other deities and the manner in which he collects characteristics from and imparts attributes to deities of the Daoist, Yin and Yang, esoteric

Buddhist, and imperial traditions of China and Japan. Also significant is his association with water and with metal, which paved the way to his development as an agricultural and martial deity.

SYMBOLS OF THE CENTER

Ichiji Kinrin

I begin with the process whereby the notion of a structure organized around a central focal point gave rise to symbolic competition between rival systems. In the mandala-like grid of esoteric Buddhism, the center was anchored by an abstract and idealized buddha, Ichiji Kinrin 一字金輪 (Fig. 2.1). Ichiji Kinrin is arguably the most important buddha of Japanese esoteric Buddhism. Yet this astral version of the cosmic buddha Vairocana (J. Dainichi 大日, Great Sun) developed particularly in medieval Tendai, in the so-called Blazing Light Ritual (Shijōkō-hō 熾盛光法—hence Kinrin's other name, Shijōkōbutsu 熾盛光仏, or Blazing Light Buddha) (Fig. 2.3). Quoting an oral tradition, the *Kakuzenshō* explains that "blazing light" designates the light that comes out from the pores of Kinrin's body. This light is said to subdue all the astral deities like the sun, the moon, the stars, and the lunar mansions.[5] It is so dazzling that even Avalokiteśvara and Vajrapāṇi faint when looking at it. Only when Kinrin utters the incantation called Butsugen butsumo 仏眼仏母 (Buddha's eye, Mother of the buddhas) can beings again look at him, and this is why he is usually paired with Butsugen, the emanation of that incantation or *dhāraṇī*.

The name Kinrin (Golden Wheel) actually designates two different figures, Shaka Kinrin and Dainichi Kinrin.[6] Dainichi Kinrin is said to dwell in the sun, and he is represented sitting on a

FIGURE 2.1. Ichiji Kinrin mandala. 12th century. Hanging scroll, color on silk. Nara National Museum.

FIGURE 2.2. Kinrin mandala. MOA Museum of Art, Atami City (Shizuoka prefecture). *Zuzō shūsei* 9: 5.

seven-headed lion. Because of the predominance of the solar (and diurnal) symbolism in the case of Dainichi (and Dainichi's association with Shingon), it is Shaka Kinrin who is usually the main deity or *honzon* of the Blazing Light Ritual in Tendai. He is represented in the Northern Dipper mandala as a buddha holding the wheel (one of the seven jewels of the *cakravartin* king). He sits atop Mount Sumeru, the axis mundi of Buddhist cosmology, the summit of which is none other than the pole star. He is therefore symbolically equated with the latter. The term *ichiji* (single letter) refers to the seed-letter *bhrūṃ* (awkwardly transcribed into Japanese as *boron*), out of which this buddha emanates during the esoteric visualization process.

There is also a close relationship between astral cults and the bodhisattva Mañjuśrī (J. Monju 文殊), another cosmic figure often encountered in esoteric Buddhist texts. This embodiment of Buddhist wisdom is also the lord of heaven, and he is represented at the center of the *Diagram of*

FIGURE 2.3. Shijōkōbutsu mandala. Edo period. Sheet, ink on paper. University Art Museum, Kyoto City University of Arts. *BZS* 1035.

the Hora (*Kara zu* 火羅図) (Fig. 2.4). He is said to be the source of all stars. His mouth, in particular, emits a five-colored light that transforms into the five stars or planets while the light rays emanating from his eyes become the sun and the moon, and those emanating from the pores of his skin become the countless stars (see Fig. 2.5). Thus, all stars are said to be transformations of Monju. More specifically, according to one source: "The Northern Dipper is a different name for the bodhisattva Mañjusri."[7] In other words, as we will see, Monju is identical with Myōken.

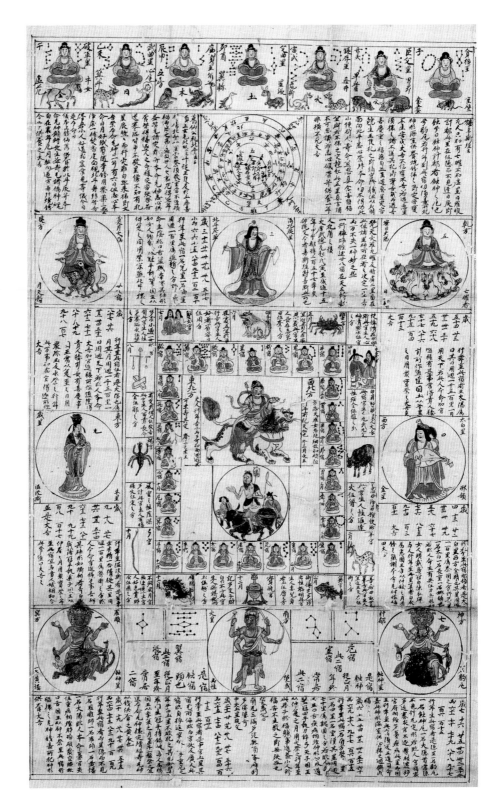

FIGURE 2.4. *Karazu.* 1166. Hand scroll, ink and color on paper. Tōji, Kyoto.

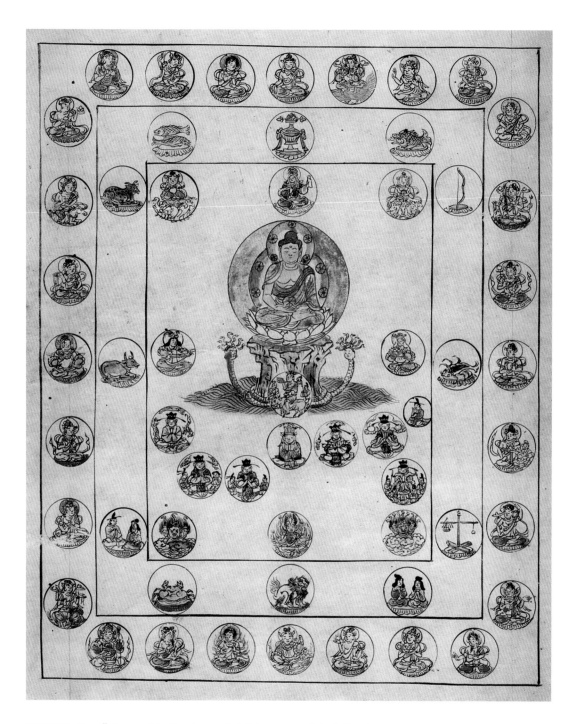

FIGURE 2.5. Star-offering mandala. Kamakura period. Color on paper. Entsūji. *Zuzōshō,*
Tenbu 2, Hokuto-hō.

SILENT NIGHT, SALIENT STAR

In its dream of cosmic control, esoteric Buddhist astrology attempted to include all astral deities and celestial bodies in its mandalas. The aim was to create a centered, internally coherent, and self-enclosed system. As certain astral deities became the foci of specific cults, however, they loosened the shackles of the mandalic system. Myōken is an atypical bodhisattva on the fringes (and at the center) of Mikkyō orthodoxy. While his central position renders him functionally similar and in some respects interchangeable with the cosmic buddha Ichiji Kinrin, his influence reaches beyond Kinrin's radiance to those dark regions beyond the boundaries of the mandala. He is not only the *honzon* of a specific Myōken mandala, he also looks very much like a "real one" (*jissha* 実者, var. 実社), a term designating deities with strong demonic characteristics. Like them, Myōken required from his followers a personal allegiance of a quasi-feudal nature. In this way the process whereby Myōken came to hold the central position of a particular system is the same process that challenged the prescribed structure and orthodoxy of the mandalic grid.

FIGURE 2.6. Myōken mandala. MOA Museum of Art, Atami City (Shizuoka prefecture).

FIGURE 2.7. Myōken mandala. Ink on paper. Collection of Sylvan Barnett and William Burto.

Aspects of Myōken

As a deified form of the pole star, Myōken governs all the movements of the astral bodies. In this traditional capacity he is said to protect the country, expel all malign influences, and increase the wealth and happiness of the people. He is described as the greatest of all the stars of the Jambudvīpa or human realm, the greatest immortal (*sennin* 仙人), and the greatest bodhisattva. The recitation of his mantra is believed to insure that the realm is protected by all the stars and bodhisattvas, and that all baleful influences are eliminated.[8]

Myōken is essentially a Daoist deity in Buddhist garb. Despite the alleged Sanskrit origin of his name (*sudṛṣṭi,* meaning "wonderful sight") and his bodhisattva status, he is conspicuously absent from early Buddhist literature. While his name first appears in apocryphal (i.e., Chinese) scriptures, his origins can be traced back to early Chinese beliefs regarding the pole star and the Northern Dipper.[9] These beliefs weave together several political and religious strands—in particular, a royal ideology in which these stars served as symbols of sovereignty, and a current of Daoist inspiration centered on divinatory talismans.

Royal Symbolism

While the prestige of the pole star is due to its apparent immobility at the center of the boreal hemisphere, that of the Northern Dipper is based on the constellation's regular revolution around the pole, whereby it regulates the hours of the night and the seasons (and, by extension, the destiny of all beings).[10] Owing to these salient characteristics—centrality and a regulating function—these astral bodies came to be associated and even identified with the emperor, who likewise was conceived of as both occupying the central position of the empire and regulating the entire realm between heaven and earth. The locus classicus is Confucius' statement: "He who rules by means of his virtue is like the northern pole star, which keeps its place [as] all the stars turn toward it."[11] That complementarity rendered both the pole star *and* the Northern Dipper symbolically indispensable to the royal institution, since only in unison did these two celestial bodies signify the complete and balanced nature of the emperor. The royal symbolism extended to the comparison of the Northern Dipper with the imperial chariot—its revolution around the pole star being replicated in the emperor's circulation around the Hall of Light (Ch. *mingtang* 明堂) as a symbolic *tour d'horizon* of his empire, the pole star being identified with the primordial, nondual Great Monad (Taiyi 太一).

Daoist Origins

The cult of Myōken grew in large part out of the Daoist worship of the Northern Dipper as found in the imperial rituals of China, Korea, and Japan.[12] As early as the Heian period, the Japanese court was making a ritual lamp offering to the pole star during the third and ninth months, that is, at the time of the equinoxes. As a symbol of the pole star and/or the Northern Dipper, Myōken came to be identified with the Daoist deity Xuanwu 玄武 (J. Genbu 'Dark Warrior'), one of the four theriomorphic spirits associated with the cardinal directions—the one governing the northern quadrant.[13] Xuanwu is usually represented by a snake and a

FIGURE 2.8. Zhenwu and acolytes. Wood, pigment, gilt. Hildburgh Collection. American Museum of Natural History.

tortoise intertwined. The name Xuanwu was changed to Zhenwu 眞武 in 1012, during the Northern Song period, in order to avoid a taboo related to the reigning emperor's name. Zhenwu was no longer represented as a hybrid (tortoise-snake) animal, however, but as a man with unkempt hair, flanked by two acolytes, one of which holds a banner. Following the Song, and particularly during the Ming Dynasty, the growing popularity of Zhenwu's sacred site at Mount Wudang led to his ascension to the pinnacle of the Daoist pantheon.[14] It is, therefore, only after the thirteenth century that the anthropomorphic image of Zhenwu penetrated into Japan.

Under the name of Chintaku Reifujin 鎮宅霊符神 (God of the Numinous Talismans for Stabilizing the House), a title that originally referred to Xuanwu, Myōken became in the Edo period the center of a thriving divinatory tradition stemming from a cult brought by Korean immigrants to Yatsushiro Shrine 八代神社 (Yatsushiro City, Kumamoto prefecture) (Figs. 2.9–2.11). The *honzon* of this cult was a representation of Chintaku Reifujin surrounded by seventy-two talismanic diagrams representing constellations. These talismans, as their names indicate, were used in rituals performed to insure domestic safety; their names appear already in

FIGURE 2.10. Chintaku Reifujin. Edo period. Sheet, ink on paper. University Art Museum, Kyoto City University of Arts. *BZS* 4116.

FIGURE 2.11. (*Opposite*) Chintaku Reifujin with eight trigrams, the Northern Dipper, and seventy-two talismans. Early 18th century. Hanging scroll, colors and gold on silk. Art Institute of Chicago.

FIGURE 2.9. Chintaku Reifujin. Muromachi period. Color on silk. Ichigami Shrine (Shiga prefecture).

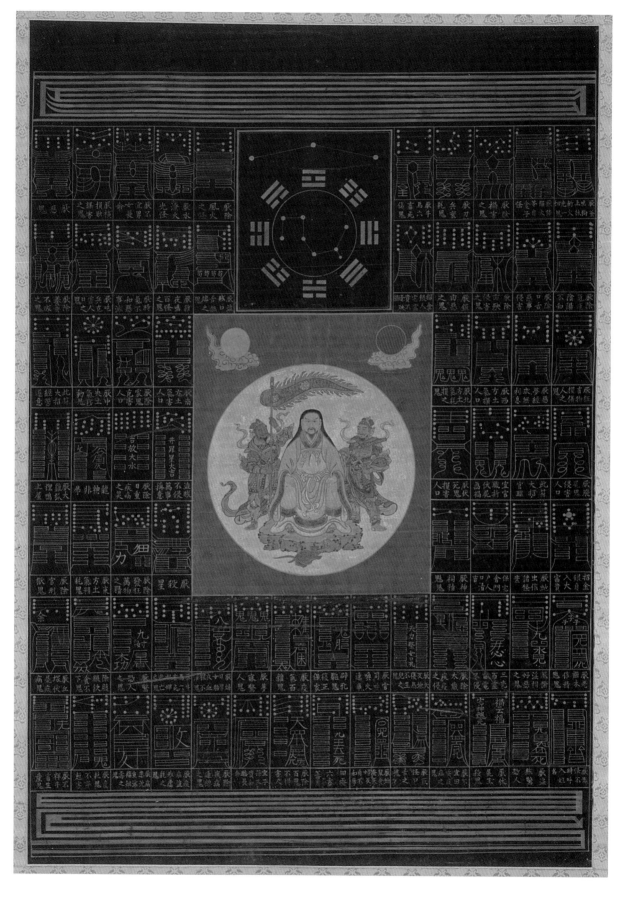

FIGURE 2.12. Hokushin. 14th century. Panel, color on silk. Tōji, Kyoto.

Ge Hong's 葛洪 *Baopuzi* 抱朴子 (4th century).[15] One of the best examples of this iconography is a painting in the Art Institute of Chicago (Fig. 2.11). The Chintaku Reifujin cult is one of the many cults that passed from Onmyōdō to esoteric Buddhism.

MYŌKEN IN ESOTERIC BUDDHISM

The identification of Myōken with the pole star, the Northern Dipper, or both was reinforced and further developed in East Asian esoteric Buddhism (Fig. 2.12). The locus classicus for the esoteric Myōken is the *Dhāraṇī Sūtra [Spoken by] the Seven Buddhas and Eight Bodhisattvas* (*Qifo ba pusa suoshuo tuoluoni shen zhou jing* 七仏八菩薩所説陀羅尼神呪経), in which he declares that he is the bodhisattva of the Northern Chronogram (Hokushin 北辰, a term that can literally mean "Northern Dragon") and that he has vowed to protect all countries. He claims to be "the first among all stars, the true immortal among all immortals, and the commander of all bodhisattvas."[16] The identity between Myōken and Hokushin is reiterated in many sources.

Myōken and the Seven Stars

This passage and others like it suggest that Myōken (Hokushin), as deity of the pole star, is distinct from and rules over the seven stars of the Northern Dipper. In the *Usuzōshi kuketsu* 薄草子口決 by the Shingon priest Raiyu 賴瑜 (1226–1304), we read: "Myōken is the leader of all the stars. The [seven stars of the] Northern Dipper are his retinue."[17] In some cases, however, he becomes identical with them. The *Kakuzenshō,* for example, states: "The seven stars of the Northern Dipper *are* Myōken Bosatsu."[18]

Most sources trace this identity to the aforementioned passage of the *Dhāraṇī Sūtra.* Quoting this same passage in another work, *Dialogue on the Secret Commentary* (*Hishō mondō* 祕鈔問答), Raiyu asks: "If so, is Myōken identical with the Northern Chronogram? Is he or is he not identical with Sonjōō and the pole star?" He goes on to conclude: "The Sonjōō of the Jimon (Onjōji) is the same as the Myōken of Tōmitsu (Shingon), and Myōken is also identical with the Northern Chronogram. Myōken is the king of all stars; the seven stars of the Northern Dipper form his retinue."[19]

Strangely enough, Myōken is more specifically identified with a minor component of the Northern Dipper constellation, the so-called "auxiliary star" (Ch. Fuxing; J. Hosei 補星 or Tenposei 天輔星).[20] This star was known in Indian astronomy as Arundhatī and in Western astronomy as Alcor (i.e., 80 Ursae Majoris). It is depicted in the iconography as a small male deity standing next to the seven goddesses (i.e., the seven stars).[21] While in India the ability to see the faint light of Arundhatī was a test of a person's acuity of vision, being able to make out its dim glow in China was thought to bring the viewer benefits such as longevity. According to the *Secret Instructions of the Seven Principles,* those who manage to glimpse the two minor stars of the Northern Dipper, the eighth (Fuxing) and the ninth (Bixing), are rewarded with a prolongation of three hundred and six hundred years of life, respectively.[22] In medieval Japan, however, the inability to see this star became the omen of an impending death.[23] That Myōken would be associated with this barely visible star rather than with one of the brighter astral members of the constellation is perplexing.

This association further highlights Myōken's elusive identity. Esoteric Buddhist priests debated as to whether Myōken is *the* deity of the pole star or merely *one* of the stars forming the Northern Dipper.[24] In the *Hishō mondō,* Myōken, under the name Hokushin, is said to be the axial star of the Northern Dipper.[25] This could mean that Hokushin is the central star of the Northern Dipper (namely, Rokuson 禄存) or the auxiliary star (Hosei). Alternatively, it could mean that Hokushin is the star around which the Northern Dipper revolves, i.e., the pole star. These two possibilities are depicted in two diagrams contained in the *Onjōji denki* 園城寺伝記.[26] In the first one, Hokushin, identified with Rokuson at the center of gravity of the constellation, is said to be immovable (*fudō* 不動), like the emperor surrounded by his ministers. In the second one, Sonjōō (Myōken) is placed below the seven stars, which are said to be his "lid" (*gai* 蓋) and to revolve around him.[27]

By the Kamakura period, the cult of the Northern Chronogram focused solely on the pole star, thereby drawing a clear distinction between it and the Northern Dipper. Judging from texts such as the *Jakushōdō kokkyōshū* 寂照堂谷響集 by Unshō 運敞 (1614–1693), the identity established in Shingon between Myōken and the Northern Chronogram (Hokushin) prevailed until the Edo period.[28] Yet it was also widely held that Myōken (*qua* Hokushin) or Sonjōō was none other than the seven stars of the Northern Dipper, in spite of all affirmations to the contrary.[29] In these various ways

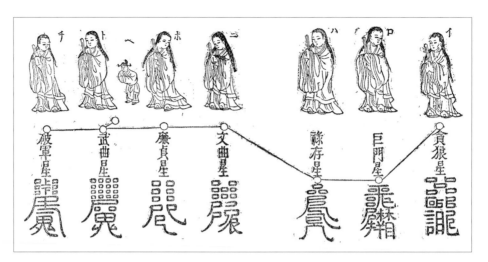

FIGURE 2.13. The seven stars and talismans. *Foshuo beitou qixing yanming jing,* T. 21, 1307.

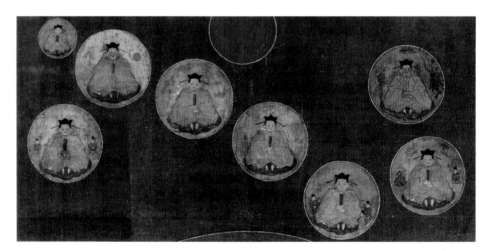

FIGURE 2.14. The seven stars. Detail of Seven-star Nyoirin. 14th–15th century. Hanging scroll, color on silk. Nezu Museum, Tokyo.

esoteric Buddhism reified the links between Myōken and the Northern Dipper. In the end, the debate about Myōken's relationship to specific astral bodies not only hints at the ambiguous nature of this deity but also suggests that his symbolic nature was of greater importance than astronomical realities.

The Seven Stars

The seven stars of the Northern Dipper (a portion of Ursa Major, our Great Bear) (Figs. 2.13–2.17). were known in India since the Vedic period and were even assimilated with the seven sages (ṛṣis). They became especially important in East Asia, however, as they were identified with the power that rules over human destinies, Siming (J. Shimei or Shimyō 司命). They owed their "stardom" to their perennial nature as circumpolar stars, always visible in the northern sky and forming a kind of cosmic clock with the pole star at its center. In China, the cult of the seven stars developed in Daoism before being integrated into esoteric Buddhism.[30] These seven stars were known as Tanlang (J. Tonrō 貪狼 'Greedy Wolf'), Jumen (J. Komon 巨門 'Great Gate'), Lucun (J. Rokuson 禄存 'Persistent Happiness'), Wengu (J. Mongoku 文曲 'Civil Song'), Lianzhen (J. Renjō 廉貞 'Pure Virtue'), Wugu (J. Mugoku 武曲 'Military Song'), and Pojun (J. Hagun 破軍 'Army Destroyer').[31] This cult became particularly important in Korea, as shown by the many sumptuous representations preserved in monasteries such as Donghwasa near Taegu City.[32] In Japan, it preexisted Buddhism, but it came to flourish during the Heian period with the rise of Mikkyō.

In the anonymous *Beidou qixing yanming jing* 北斗七星延命経 (*T.* 21, 1307), for instance, the seven stars are represented in anthropomorphic fashion. There are three types of representations: as *yakṣas,* as bodhisattvas, and as officials. Although they are usually perceived as benevolent figures, their representation as *yakṣas* suggests their latent demonic nature. Apart from such anthropomorphic representations, the seven stars are usually represented in stylized diagrammatic form, as small circles

FIGURE 2.15. The seven stars. Detail of *Karazu.* 1166. Hand scroll, ink and color on paper. Tōji, Kyoto.

FIGURE 2.16. The nine planetary deities. Detail of *Karazu*. 1166. Hand scroll, ink and color on paper. Tōji, Kyoto.

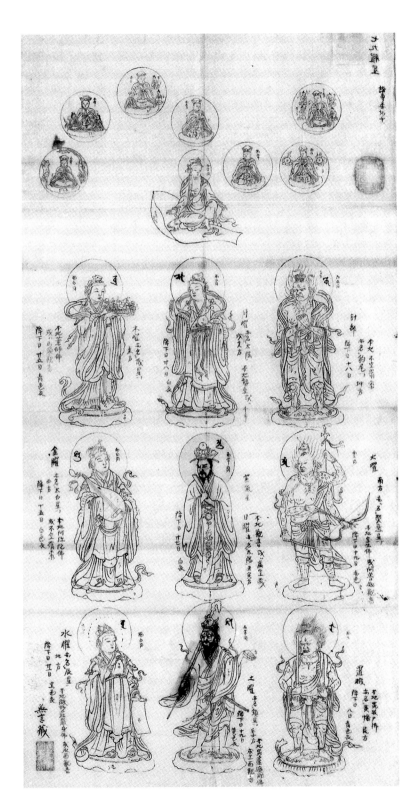

FIGURE 2.17. The seven stars, nine planetary deities, and Northern Dipper. Edo period. Sheet, ink on paper. University Art Museum, Kyoto City University of Arts. *BZS* 2276.

connected by lines (Fig. 2.13). That diagram became a powerful talisman, which contributed to the development of the Northern Dipper cult. It was, for instance, "the powerful charm incised on the vibrant blades of treasure swords."[33] A splendid example is a sword preserved in the Shōsoin in Nara, which shows the Northern Dipper, among other constellations, combined with cloud patterns.

Myōken and the Number Seven

Numerological symbolism has been one of the ways Myōken's network developed, in tandem with the cult of the seven stars. While the number seven is essentially related to the Northern Dipper, it becomes the *chiffre* (shibboleth) of Myōken's secrets. Its symbolism is overdetermined. It also points to the seven "planets" (the five planets, the sun, and the moon) and, under the influence of Western hemerology (mediated by Persia), to the seven days of the week (which are an important if unnoticed contribution of esoteric Buddhism to Japanese culture).

Another group of seven days is that of funerary rituals: the liminal period between death and rebirth, and subsequently the sequence of trials in the other world, came to be defined as one of seven times seven days, and this symbolism played, for instance, a significant role in the Ritual of the Healing Buddha, to which we will return. In this otherworldly context, the number seven also links the seven stars (and Myōken) with the seven mothers (Shichimo) of Enmaten's retinue—a feature shared with the Seven-star Nyoirin (Shichishō Nyoirin 七星如意輪), an astral form of the bodhisattva Kannon 観音. The pattern of the seven stars was also projected over the landscape of China, Korea, and Japan. Examples of such projections include the seven shrines of Hie and their replicas (for instance, the seven shrines of Sonkō-in 尊光院, a temple in Chiba City that was dedicated to Myōken).[34] All these quasi-algebraic equivalences constitute a secondary feature, which sometimes assumes precedence over others.

In the *Chintaku reifu engi shūsetsu,* Myōken declares in an oracle that he has seven bodies or manifestations (shichitai Myōken 七体妙見): Shaka 釈迦, Amida 阿弥陀, Kannon, Jizō 地蔵, Kongōzōō 金剛蔵王, Kokūzō 虚空蔵, and Daiitoku Myōō 大威徳明王. Notice, here, that he is perceived as a source (*honji*) of the buddhas, bodhisattvas, and wisdom kings—and not the other way around, as one would expect from the traditional *honji suijaku* 本地垂迹 model, which held that bodhisattvas and other deities are emanations of buddhas.

As god of the pole star, Myōken is essentially a symbol of oneness— another name for the Great Monad (Taiyi). However, the multiplicity is already inscribed in the bipolar pair he forms with the seven stars. Yet, in the tandem formed by Myōken and the seven stars, the latter slowly move to the foreground.[35] The medieval evolution of Myōken seems to consist in a gradual shift from the monad to the heptad. Thus, toward the end of the medieval period (and in illustrated texts of the early Edo period), Myōken is a deity that is both one and sevenfold. The aura of the seven stars around his head has become an integral part of his image.

A parallel evolution can be seen in the image of the buddha Yakushi 薬師 (Skt. Bhaiṣajyaguru), a cosmic figure that too often is reduced to his medical aspect, whereas his apotropaic function is at least as important. In the *Myōkenji emaki* preserved at Chiba, Yakushi (or rather the seven Yakushi) becomes Myōken's *honji*. However, just as one of the seven Yakushi is the Yakushi *par excellence* (the prototype), among the seven Myōken, we are told, the one that corresponds to that original Yakushi is the Chiba Myōken, and because he also corresponds to one of the seven stars, Hagun (Army Destroyer), this Myōken is *par excellence* the god of battles and the protector of the Chiba clan warriors.

DEVELOPMENT OF THE MYŌKEN CULT

Early Stages

The introduction of the Myōken cult to Japan is traced to the arrival of a Korean prince named Imseong (J. Rinshō 琳聖). According to legend, this prince was the third son of a Paekche king. In 611 (var. 595), during the reign of Empress Suiko (r. 593–628), he came to Japan and settled on Mount Shiragi in Yatsushiro (Higo province, Kyūshū).[36] Not surprisingly, Myōken became popular among clans of Korean descent.[37] He was in particular the tutelary deity of the Ōuchi 大内 lineage in Yamaguchi (Suō province), which claimed descent from Imseong. According to the origin story of that lineage, Imseong landed in Suō province, not Yatsushiro. Another account states that the Myōken cult was brought from Yatsushiro to Suō by members of the Ōuchi lineage. At any rate, the Ōuchi lineage was instrumental in developing the Myōken cult in both places.

One version of the legend of the Korean prince Rinshō Taishi, told in relation to Ōuchi Yoshitaka and the origins of the Ōuchi clan, relates that during the third year of the reign of Empress Suiko (595), on the eighteenth day of the ninth month (the date that was to become Myōken's festival day), a large star fell on Green Willow Bay (Aoyanagi no Ura) in the domain of Jutō 鷲頭 (Eagle's Head) in Tonō district (present-day Yamaguchi prefecture). The star remained suspended on the branch of a pine tree and shone as brightly as the full moon for seven days and nights. An oracle was finally delivered, in which the deity declared: "I am the bodhisattva of the Northern Chronogram, Myōken. In three years, on the second day of the third month, Prince Rinshō will come from the Paekche kingdom to this province. Tell Prince Shōtoku to make him stay here." When the oracle was reported to the capital, Empress Suiko Tennō rejoiced. Three years later, in 598, Rinshō Taishi did land on Tatara Beach in Suō and started spreading the cult of Myōken.[38]

When Emperor Kanmu moved the capital from Nara to Heian-kyō in 794, Myōken was enshrined in Buddhist temples called Reiganji 霊巌寺, located at the four sides of the city for the purpose of protecting it. The most widely known of these was located on the northern hill, Kitayama 北山. It was a large temple, extending over the hill of Funayama 船山 (Takagamine 鷹峯). In 804, Sakanoue no Tamuramarō 田村麻呂, the general in charge of the pacification of the barbarians (seii taishōgun 征夷大将軍), is said to have offered a copy of the Buddhist canon to this temple.

We know from tales found in the *Nihon ryōiki* 日本霊異記 that Myōken was already the object of popular devotion by the early Heian period.[39] In one story, he manifests himself as a deer in order to return stolen silk robes; in another, he appears again as a deer and helps locate a monk who had stolen money donated for the performance of a lamp-offering ritual dedicated to Myōken; in a third story, he rescues a fisherman from drowning. In addition to these types of aid, Myōken was invoked in cases of eye disease.[40] Here, however, we get a hint of Myōken's ambivalence: Myōken could cure diseases, but he could also provoke them. In the diary of Fujiwara no Yukinari 藤原 行成 (972–1027), the eye disease of Ichijō Tennō 一条天皇 (r. 986–1011) is attributed to a curse from Myōken.[41]

During the Heian period, the official ritual was performed every year at the imperial palace on the third day of the third and the ninth months. During this celebration, called *gotō-e* 御灯会 (Assembly of the August Lamps), lamps were offered to the Northern Chronogram (Hokushin) while the emperor, following the Chinese practice, addressed a petition (*saimon* 祭文) to the god.[42] Myōken's cult was not the preserve of the aristocracy, however. The popular cult of Myōken entailed great festivities, including male and female dances. Such celebrations came to be perceived as a threat to public order and were therefore prohibited (for instance, by imperial decrees dated 796 and 811).[43]

Another aspect of Myōken's popularity is revealed by the stone carvings in the so-called holy man's cave (Shōnin-kutsu 上人窟) in the Valley of Hell (Jigokudani 地獄谷, said to be the place where the corpses of executed people were abandoned) behind Kasuga Shrine in Nara. Myōken appears, surrounded by stars, on the right wall of the cave, the central wall being occupied by a triad (Miroku, flanked by Yakushi and Jūichimen Kannon 十一面観音, who happen to be Myōken's two main *honji*), and the left wall by Amida and Senju Kannon 千手観音 (unfortunately damaged).[44]

Myōken and Masakado

In his martial form, Myōken, together with the seven stars of the Northern Dipper, had become popular among warrior groups in Kantō such as the Chiba clan by the end of the Heian period.[45] According to legend, Taira no Masakado had seven doubles (*kagemusha* 影武者), who were none other than the seven stars. He is said to have been protected at first by Myōken and by the god Hachiman (the latter giving him the title of Emperor). The *Shōmonki* 将門記 and other sources, however, attribute the failure of his rebellion against the court in 940 to the fact that his hubris caused him to lose Myōken's support.[46] Masakado's vengeful spirit (*onryō* 怨霊) was deified and was enshrined at the Kanda Myōjin 神田明神 Shrine (in what would become Edo, then Tokyo). His ambiguity as a rebel and a precursor of the warrior class led to his cult's merging with that of Myōken and the pestilence deity Gozu Tennō in a form of worship specific to the Chiba clan.[47]

The Emergence of Local Traditions

Sonjōō at Miidera

Among the various local forms of the Myōken cult, one of the most important was that of Miidera (Onjōji), where he was worshiped under the name of Sonjōō 尊星王 (Figs. 2.18–2.21).[48] At Miidera, the head monastery of the Jimon branch of Tendai, Sonjōō ascended to new cosmic heights, rising to the rank of a demiurge.[49] At some point Miidera priests began to assert that Myōken was not simply the pole-star deity, but a condensation of the entire cosmos. As the priest Chōen 澄圓 (1218–ca. 1290) puts it in his *White Jewel Notes* (*Byakuhō shō* 白宝鈔, 1279): "In heaven, Sonjōō combines all the deities of the planets and constellations; on earth, he is the five phases. All four directional deities and the deities of the sexagenary cycle are no different from Sonjōō. If they are visualized during

FIGURE 2.18. Miidera mandala. Edo period. Hanging scroll, color on silk. Onjōji, Ōtsu City (Shiga prefecture).

FIGURE 2.19. Myōken (Sonjōō) on dragon, surrounded by animals. Color on paper. *Shoson zuzōshū*. Kanazawa bunko.

the ritual, they all become Sonjōō."[50] We are dealing, then, with a higher god that manifests itself as Sonjōō in heaven and as Myōken on earth. Jimon clerics argued that although priests of other schools (Shingon and Sanmon) knew the Myōken ritual, they ignored the secret ritual of Sonjōō, which Enchin had supposedly studied in China and transmitted to Japan.[51] They claimed that only they understood the higher, heavenly form of that deity, which had manifested itself at the site of the sacred spring of Miidera (i.e., the "spring of perfumed water") near the rear of the Buddha Hall. The water gushing forth from this spring was therefore known as the "water of Sonjō" (Sonjō-sui 尊星水).[52] The *Kakuzenshō* quotes a tradition according to which the goddess or "female deva" (*nyoten* 女天) Sonjōō symbolizes the emperor, with seven stars behind him representing his consorts.[53] The same source links this tradition with the practice, initiated by the Miidera priest Kakushū 覚宗 (d. 1167) and later restored by Ryūun 龍雲, of hanging two images or mandalas of Myōken back to back in order to symbolize the sexual union between husband and wife.[54] This representation was also said to symbolize the complementary relationship between the ruler (Sonjōō) and his ministers (the seven stars). Hence, we are told, the depiction of the seven stars behind Sonjōō or on the rim of his mandala.

FIGURE 2.20. Myōken (Sonjōō) on dragon with constellations and animals. 12th century. Ink on paper. *Besson zakki* 48, fig. 263.

FIGURE 2.21. Myōken (Sonjōō) with sun, moon, and animals. Edo period. Color on wood. Onjōji, Ōtsu City (Shiga prefecture).

The secrecy of the Sonjōō ritual did not prevent Miidera's rivals from having a fairly good notion of its content and criticizing it. The *Asabashō,* for instance, claims that the ritual was a fabrication rooted in Onmyōdō. As proof, it cites the ritual's use of the Pace of Xiang (Zō-ho 象歩, probably a variant of the Pace of Yu, Ūho 禹歩), an allegedly Daoist feature.[55] Another central element of the ritual, the offering of twelve cups to Sonjōō, was rejected as a borrowing from the Kichijōten ritual.[56] The author of the *Asabashō* concludes that this secret ritual cannot be traced back to Enchin and reflects a local tradition. The Onjōji tradition linked Sonjōō with the tutelary deity of Miidera. This tradition greatly influenced the development of the cult in Kantō, and most notably among the Chiba clan (to which we will return). Let us now turn to the local developments outside Mikkyō, among warrior families.

The Ōuchi Clan

The main cultic center of Myōken (as Chintaku Reifujin) was the Chintakureifu Shrine of Miyagi-chō in Yatsushiro City (Kumamoto prefecture, Kyūshū).[57] This shrine became famous in the seventeenth century owing to the printing of Chintaku Reifujin talismans. Yatsushiro is still today the site of a large Myōken festival in which two giant (male and female)

FIGURE 2.22. Rinshō
Taishi. Color on paper.
Rurikōji, Yamaguchi City.
Photo Bernard Faure.

snake-tortoises (*kida* 亀蛇) are carried through the streets of the city.[58]

According to another tradition, Prince Rinshō (Fig. 2.22), after landing on a beach called Tatara-hama 多々羅浜, first took the name Tatara.[59] He built himself a dwelling at Aoyanagi no ura (Green Willow Bay), where a star, identified as Myōken, had recently fallen. Then, after moving to Ōuchi Village, he took the name Ōuchi. Thus, he is considered to be the ancestor of the Ōuchi clan, a powerful clan based in the castle town of Yamaguchi (Suō province), and one that played a major role in trade with the continent from the twelfth to the sixteenth century.

In this tradition, Myōken is a fallen star that shines miraculously on a pine tree for seven days and nights. The same topos reappears in the origin story of Seichōji 清澄寺, near Myōkenzan. An anonymous "Dharma master" who practiced on that mountain discovered, near the Dragon Pond, an oak tree (*kashiwa* 柏) that emitted a mysterious light. Then an old man appeared to him, claiming to be Myōken Bosatsu, and told him to carve a statue of Kokūzō with the wood of that tree. The Dharma master eventually carved two statues, one of Kokūzō, the other of Myōken, and built what would become Seichōji to enshrine them. The name of that temple (Pure and Limpid) refers to the miraculous spring that gushed forth at that time.

The man who organized the cultural memory of the Ōuchi clan is Ōuchi no Masatsune 大内正恒. Masatsune received from Uda Tennō 宇多天皇 (r. 887–897) the patronym Ōuchi (a prestigious name, since it evoked the imperial palace, Daidairi 大内裏), as well as the three regions of Suō province, as a reward for performing an exorcism centered on Myōken (Hokushin). Masatsune reorganized Myōken's cult in terms of esoteric Buddhism. He portrayed himself as a seventh-generation descendant (the number is no coincidence) of the Tatara family stemming from Rinshō Taishi, and described the latter as a manifestation (or reincarnation, *goshin* 後身) of the astral deity Kokūzō. By the same token, he became himself a manifestation of the seven-bodied Myōken (and Dainichi), while the intermediary generations were turned into manifestations of Kannon, Monju, Fugen 普賢,

Yakushi, and Shaka. Henceforward, in the Ōuchi clan that stemmed from him, everything was counted by seven or multiples of seven. After the death of Uda Tennō, Masatsune returned to his domain, and restored the Myōken shrines (Kamimiya, Nakamiya) on Mount Jutō.

It was only much later, in the seventeenth generation, that Ōuchi Hiroyo 大内弘世 (1325–1380) built a Lower Shrine (Shimomiya 下宮) at the foot of that mountain, known today as the site of Jutōji 鷲頭寺, in the town of Kudamatsu.[60] His son Yoshihiro, having vanquished the Yamana clan, became deputy shōgun (kanryō 管領) and attributed his victory to the Myōken of Matsushita. He presented Jutōji with a monumental Niō Gate and a five-degree pagoda (like the famous pagoda of Rurikōji 瑠璃光寺, a Sōtō temple in Yamaguchi whose origins are also traced back to Rinshō Taishi). Another interesting detail in that story, which links Myōken with the wish-fulfilling jewel (cintāmaṇi), is that the Dharma master, after receiving a vision of Myōken, buried three jewels in three places, which he called Nyoi-san, Hōju-san, and Mani-san. In 1354, Ōuchi Hirotomo 大内弘巴 restored the Myōken-sha of Kōryūji 興隆寺 in Yamaguchi (Bōshū province).

In the second half of the sixteenth century, the Ōuchi clan was eclipsed by the Mōri 毛利 clan, after being defeated in 1561 at the battle of Itsukushima (the only battle ever fought on that sacred island, a major cultic center of the goddess Benzaiten 弁才天). This was the last phase in a decline initiated by Ōuchi Yoshitaka 大内 (1507–1551). Yoshitaka was a devotee of Myōken, but his hubris seems to have led him astray. Boasting of his royal Korean pedigree, he asked the Korean king to give him some of the lands that had formerly belonged to the kingdom of Paekche.

Just as Taira no Kiyomori, after receiving a prediction of his ascension to power from the Itsukushima deity, had lost that protection because of his hubris, Ōuchi Yoshitaka seems to have lost Myōken's protection. After the destruction of the Ōuchi clan, Myōken's cult was restored by the Mōri clan.

The Chiba Clan

Another stronghold of Myōken worship is Chiba and the sourrounding Bōsō region (Figs. 2.23–2.25). This cult may have been brought to Kantō by Korean immigrants early on. During the Nara period, under the reigns of Tenji Tennō 天智天皇 (r. 661–671) and Jitō Tennō 持統天皇 (r. 686–697), the court on several occasions sent fairly large numbers of immigrants from Silla, Paekche, and Koguryo to the eastern provinces.

It was with the rise of the Chiba clan after the tenth century, however, that Myōken moved to the forefront. The relationship between Myōken and the Chiba clan goes back to the ancestor of that clan, Taira no Yoshifumi 平良文 (d. 952). Yoshifumi, who had allied himself with his nephew Taira no Masakado against his elder brother Kunika 平国香 in 931, is said to have been saved by Myōken during the battle of the

Sometani River (in Ueno province).[61] As the story goes, Masakado and Yoshifumi were about to lose the battle when Myōken, the deity of the neighboring Sokusaiji 息災寺, appeared in the form of a divine youth (*dōji* 童子) and rescued them. When Yoshifumi went to Sokusaiji to express his gratitude, he wondered which particular image, among the seven statues of Myōken enshrined there, had saved him. A voice from the sky told him that it would be the statue whose feet were covered with mud—and he found that one of them had indeed muddy feet. This particular Myōken, identified with one of the seven stars (Hagun, the Army Destroyer), was henceforward worshiped as protector of the Chiba clan, and his image was eventually moved to Sonkō-in 尊光院 (a subtemple of Kongōjuji 金剛授寺) on the Mount of the Northern Dipper (Hokuto-zan 北斗山)—site of the present-day Chiba Shrine in Chiba City.

Myōken's protection had initially extended to Yoshifumi's nephew, the rebel Masakado. The latter's final defeat and his death, a few years later, are interpreted in the Chiba tradition as a reversal of Myōken's favor, indicating that Myōken chose to protect Yoshifumi and his descendants. The original Chiba domain was the Chiba no shō (present-day Chiba City) in the Bōsō 房総 peninsula. The Chiba clan rose to prominence with the victory of Minamoto no Yoritomo over the Heike. Although the clan had issued from the Taira clan, it chose to support Yoritomo and received large domains throughout Japan as a reward. Myōken's cult spread through those domains as a result.

FIGURE 2.23. (*Left*) Chiba Myōken. Kamakura period. Color on wood. Tōsho-chō kōminkan (Chiba prefecture).

FIGURE 2.24. (*Right*) Chintaku Reifujin (Myōken). Edo period. Sheet, ink on paper. University Art Museum, Kyoto City University of Arts. *BZS* 2273.

FIGURE 2.25. Chiba
Myōken. Detail of *Myōkenji
daiengi emaki*. Hand scroll.
Kangiji (Chiba prefecture).

The clan soon divided into two groups, the Kazusa 上総 Chiba and
the Shimōsa 下総 Chiba. The patron deity of both groups was the warrior
deity Hachiman. However, after the defeat of the Kazusa branch at the
battle of Hōji 宝治 in 1247, the Shimōsa branch chose Myōken as its
protector. This Myōken was no longer a water deity, that is, an agricultural deity, or even a state-protecting deity, as he had been for the Heian
court; rather, he was a god of bow and arrows (*kyūzen-shin* 弓箭神), a
god of battles (*ikusa no kami* 戦神). In fact, he shared many affinities with
Hachiman and was in some cases identified with him.[62]

In 1590, toward the end of the long civil war that ravaged Japan, the
Chiba clan chose the wrong side and was destroyed by Toyotomi Hide-
yoshi 豊臣秀吉. Even after their fall, however, Myōken's cult remained
popular in the Bōsō region, as attested by some fifty Myōken shrines and
the many images of the god that remain today in Chiba prefecture.

During the Edo period, several illustrated scrolls centered on Myōken
appeared, among them the *Chiba Myōken daiengi emaki* 千葉妙見大縁
起絵巻 and the *Myōkenji daiengi* 妙見寺大縁起 (Fig. 2.25).[63] Among
the temples that promoted this cult by producing origin stories (*engi*)
and scrolls (*emaki*), one was particularly active: Sonkō-in, a subtemple

FIGURE 2.26. Nose Myōken. Edo period. Sheet, ink on paper. University Art Museum, Kyoto City University of Arts. *BZS* 2275.

of Kongōjuji founded in the year 1000 by Kakusan 覚算, a son of Taira no Tadatsune 平忠常 (975–1031). The latter is well known for his three-year rebellion against the court, which devastated the Bōsō region.

Belief in Myōken as a protector of horses may also explain in part his popularity among members of the Chiba clan, who raised horses on the Shimōsa plateau, as well as of the other great clans of Kantō. These clans contributed to the diffusion of his cult by building chapels dedicated to him.[64] During the medieval period, it was a common annual practice to set ten horses free and designate their meadows as "pasture for Myōken's divine horses" (Myōken jinme no maki 妙見神馬の牧); feudal lords would commonly set two horses free in the same manner. It was forbidden to catch these wild horses, whose number increased over time to reach several thousand.[65]

The Nose Clan

After the conversion of the Chiba clan to the Nichiren sect, the cult of Myōken was also adopted by that sect and Myōken halls flourished throughout Japan. Perhaps the most famous of them is the Myōken-dō 妙見堂 (also known as Nose Myōken 能勢妙見) in Nose, on the northwestern outskirts of Osaka (Fig. 2.26). This cultic center came to be known as the Mount Minobu 身延山 of western Japan—a reference to the mountain in Kantō to which Nichiren withdrew—and it remains the main cultic center of the Nichiren sect in western Japan.[66]

Nose was the domain of the Tada 多田 family, a branch of the Seiwa Genji 清和源. According to the temple tradition, the family traces its origins back to the warrior Minamoto no Raikō (var. Yorimitsu 源頼光), the man who is said to have cut off the head of the demon Shuten Dōji 酒呑童子.[67] The ancestor of that branch, Mitsunaka 満仲 (918–987), was a devotee of Myōken. His grandson Yorikuni 頼国 allegedly brought Myōken's image to the domain and founded the Nose Shrine, ca. 1028–1037. At the beginning of the seventeenth century, Nose Yoritsugu 能勢頼次 converted to Nichiren Buddhism and invited the Nichiren priest Nikken 日乾 (1560–1635), from Mount Minobu 身延山, to come to Nose. Nikken founded Shinnyoji 真如寺, the temple that has jurisdiction over Nose Myōken Hall (the present-day Kaiun-dō 開運堂).

According to a late source, the *Chintaku reifu engi shūsetsu* 鎮宅霊符縁起集説, it was Nikken who equated Myōken with Chintaku Reifujin (i.e., Zhenwu). Cultic practices centered on Chintaku Reifujin had initially been developed by Yin-Yang masters (*onmyōji*). Despite the fact that the cult's main deity was seen as distinct from Myōken, the Buddhist appropriation of Chintaku Reifujin rituals eventually brought about the perception that Myōken and Chintaku Reifujin were identical.[68]

In 1630, the Nichiren priest Nittō Shōnin had a vision of Iwato Myōken Daibosatsu 岩戸妙見大菩薩 in a dream and initiated the god's worship under the name of Hokushin Sonjōō Genbu-shin 北辰尊星王玄武神 (a title that combines the name of Myōken in the Miidera tradition with that of the Daoist Dark Warrior). With the help of the Ichijō family, he founded Enjōji, where he rebuilt the Myōken Hall of Reiganji and turned it into a thriving cultic center, the Iwato Myōken-gū 妙見宮 (popularly known as Takagamine no Myōken-san 鷹峯の妙見様).[69]

The Edo Period

With Nose Myōken we have already moved into the Edo period. Judging from the *Chintaku reifu engi shūsetsu* (printed in 1707), the cult of Myōken experienced a revival of sorts during the Edo period.[70] As one legend has it, in 1265, on the eve of the Mongol invasion, as Nichiren was praying at the Kobayakawa 小早川 house (which later became the headquarters of the sect, the present-day Jusenji 鷲山寺 in Chiba prefecture), the star Venus shone brightly and Myōken appeared to him, riding on an eagle. This image of Myōken, the Washi Myōken Daibosatsu 鷲妙見大菩薩, was transferred in 1771 to Chōkokuji 長国寺 in Asakusa (Tokyo), causing the temple to become the site of a popular market, the Otori ichi 鷲市 (Eagle Market).

During the Edo period, religious specialists called *hakase* 博士, *shomonji* 声聞師 (唱門師), and *sanjo* 散所 played a significant role in the dissemination of Myōken's cult among the population. Myōken was also important in Shugendō thought and practice. Gaynor Sekimori has documented the importance of the Myōken (Sonjōō) ritual—and of star rituals in general—in Nikkō Shugendō. Indeed, a star ritual centered on Sonjōō is still performed today by a *shugen* group at Nikkō. Sekimori explains that in Myōken's rituals "the *shugenja* overcomes baleful stars and invites the influence of good stars by becoming one with Myōken."[71]

An interesting testimony to Myōken's popularity among the people of Edo is that of the painter Hokusai (1760–1849), who was born in Katsushika, a district of Edo known for its Yanagishima Shrine, dedicated to Myōken. Hokusai was a devotee of Myōken and in 1811 even took as one of his pseudonyms Taito 戴斗 "Worshiper of the Dipper".[72]

After the disastrous "cultural revolution" of the early Meiji period (1868–1873), many shrines dedicated to Myōken, particularly in the Bōsō peninsula, shifted allegiance to the *kami* Ame no Minakanushi 天御中主, the primordial *kami* dwelling at the center of heaven. This abstract deity is functionally similar to Myōken, a fact that eased the transfer of many of Myōken's functions—e.g., protection of seaways, safe childbirth, longevity, and fortune—to him. After Meiji the two deities were occasionally conflated or worshiped at the same shrine.[73] While the primordial *kami* is a rather abstract deity, rarely represented, Myōken's iconography, to which we now turn, is strikingly diverse.

ICONOGRAPHY

Myōken's iconography represents a significant departure from the standard symbolism of pole-star deities. In his classic study of esoteric star worship, Morita Ryūsen distinguishes no fewer than forty-two forms of this protean deity.[74] Confronted with this staggering diversity, one cannot help wondering how one passes from one form to another. How were such different forms perceived as expressing one and the same reality, while forms very close to each other express different realities?

While Myōken's iconography reflects the orthodox conceptions of this deity in its various guises—as the pole star, as the Great Monad (Taiyi) of the Chinese imperial cult, as the divinatory god of Daoism (i.e., Zhenwu, Chintaku Reifujin), and as the astral god of esoteric Buddhism—because it simultaneously diverges from this orthodoxy, it serves as a point of transition between the text-sanctioned deity and the *honzon* of secret rituals and popular practice.[75] Because textual sources tell us little about these representations, we must read these images and their symbolism critically, taking into account relevant ritual contexts and Myōken's relationship with other deities. Here I focus on those aspects of Myōken's iconography that reveal his heterodox side, using them as a gateway into the life of the Myōken hidden from the world of texts. After presenting the general features of Myōken's iconography, I outline the characteristics of the esoteric Myōken, then discuss portrayals of Myōken as a divine youth, and finally address a handful of unique features of Myōken's iconography.

In Mikkyō, Myōken is usually represented with two or four arms, standing on a cloud or on a dragon above a cloud. In the two-armed representation he resembles a bodhisattva: seated on a five-colored cloud, he forms the teaching mudrā with one hand while in the other he holds a lotus flower surmounted by a diagram of the seven stars of the Northern Dipper.[76] In the Myōken mandala, Myōken appears in the center as a bodhisattva holding a lotus on which rests a diagram of the Northern Dipper (see, for example, Fig. 2.27). Positioned around him are the seven stars in the form of anthropomorphic deities together with the twelve cyclical signs in the form of animal-headed deities.[77] This representation of Myōken, which appears in the *Besson zakki* 別尊雑記, is dated to the end of the Heian period (twelfth century) (Fig. 2.28).[78]

While the image of Myōken as Chintaku Reifujin was known in medieval Japan, it is another image that came to the forefront in esoteric Buddhism. In the *Myōken Bosatsu zō* 妙見菩薩像, Myōken is shown standing or dancing on the back of a dragon; he holds a bow and bulb-arrows in his upper hands, a brush and a register in his lower hands.

Another characteristic representation, shows Myōken (Sonjōō) within a circle formed by sun and moon disks, each held by an animal (see Fig. 2.19).[79] This image is typical of the Miidera tradition. The Miidera monastery possesses a painting in which a four-armed Myōken holds the sun and moon disks in his upper hands, a staff (*shakujō* 錫杖) and trident in his two lower hands. Three red sun disks and three white moon disks, paired with various animals and in some cases

FIGURE 2.27. Myōken as bodhisattva. 12th century. Color on paper. *Zuzōshō.* Kanazawa bunko.

FIGURE 2.28. Myōken as bodhisattva. 12th century. Ink on paper. *Besson zakki* 48, fig. 258.

FIGURE 2.29. Daishōgun. 12th century. Wood. Nara National Museum.

with talismans, are positioned on the outer rim of the circle. Following the traditional Chinese motif, the sun disks contain a three-legged crow, the moon disks a hare pounding the elixir of immortality. A deer head appears on the head of Sonjōō, as well as above the upper sun and moon disks. The two other sun disks are paired with a tiger and an elephant, the two moon disks with a leopard and a white fox.[80] A wooden statue representing the same motif can still be seen in the main hall of Miidera (see Fig. 2.21). A line drawing shows Myōken at the center of a kind of mandala in which the diagrams of the constellations have been added to the sun and moon disks and their associated animals. In various drawings the disks appear only on the right side of the image, in the direction toward which Myōken and his dragon are turned (see Fig. 2.20).

The Miidera exemplar (see above) shows a four-armed bodhisattva standing on a green dragon with a foot raised behind the opposite knee. Although this form is similar to one of the three standard iconographic descriptions of Myōken, it differs in that the deity's second pair of hands holds a *shakujō* and trident instead of a brush and paper. As for the animals on the outer rim, a deer head appears on the head of Sonjōō and above the upper sun and moon. A similar drawing in the *Besson zakki* instead shows four crocodile-like animals. The Miidera painting, in addition, has a tiger and a panther (or leopard). Both the painting and drawing include an elephant and a white fox.

Later Representations

Another widespread motif is the representation of Myōken on the back of a tortoise, or rather a tortoise intertwined with a snake.[81] In spite of their resemblance, these two images might have different origins—one Daoist (Xuanwu), the other Buddhist (the deva Suiten 水天 and *nāga* symbolism). In the Chinese motif of the four heraldic animals, the northern quadrant is symbolized (and ruled) by Xuanwu (the Dark Warrior), a theriomorphic deity portrayed, already by the third century BCE, as an intertwined tortoise and snake. During the Northern Song, the deity's theriomorphic form gave way to an anthropomorphic form called Zhenwu.[82] In this guise the deity appears as a long-haired man wearing a black robe and holding a sword, known as Chintaku Reifujin. As noted earlier, this motif coexisted in Japan with that of the esoteric Buddhist

Myōken and experienced a rise in popularity in the late medieval and Edo periods.

Early Kamakura-period esoteric Buddhist texts do not mention this form of Myōken, which suggests that the fusion between Zhenwu and Myōken had not yet taken place. The earliest known example is a hanging plaque (*kakebotoke* 賭け仏) from Chiba dated to 1299, in which Myōken, standing on a tortoise, is clearly identified as Zhenwu. A representation of Myōken as Chintaku Reifujin is found in a Miidera painting in which the god is surrounded by the diagrams and corresponding talismans of the seven stars of the Northern Dipper and the seventy-two stars.[83] A similar representation is found in the collection of the Art Institute of Chicago (see Fig. 2.8).

Another typical representation of Myōken as Zhenwu (Reifujin) is found at Tōji.[84] It is distinctly Chinese in style. Myōken leans on a club or sword and his hair falls loosely on his shoulders. In front of him are a snake and a tortoise intertwined. His two attendants hold a banner.[85] In fact, as Nikaidō Yoshihiro points out, the cult of Zhenwu was originally distinct from that of Myōken, and the two cults, in spite of some fusion or confusion, seem to have developed in parallel (as suggested by the existence of two shrines, side by side, in Yatsushiro). Initially, the Jingūji on Mount Shiragi 白木 had three shrines: Upper, Median, and Lower.[86]

From the iconographic standpoint, we can thus distinguish between several distinct Myōken types as influenced by other figures: the eso-teric Myōken (Sonjōō), riding a dragon; Myōken as Xuanwu or Zhenwu (a long-haired deity riding or accompanied by a tortoise intertwined with a snake); Myōken as a water deity, riding a tortoise, like Suiten; and Myōken as a warrior (like Daishōgun 大将軍) or youth. The Chiba Myōken, a youth with long hair, is also a warrior deity, and he represents a combination of Zhenwu and Daishōgun.[87]

THE GOD IN THE DETAILS

The characteristic appearance of the Chiba Myōken, quite different from that which is shown in standard iconographic sources, is that of a deity riding a tortoise-snake and holding the sword of Zhenwu. In this repre-sentation, Myōken's left hand forms a characteristic gesture (the index and medium raised, the thumb curved, joining the annular and auricular fingers). It is a gesture of exorcism and command, known as the sword mudrā, which can also be observed in representations of the directional god Daishōgun.[88] Certain sources affirm the identity between Myōken and Daishōgun, and at the Daishōgun Hachi Shrine (大将軍八神社) in Kyoto, a wooden statue of Daishōgun, identified as Myōken, is flanked by seven similar images of Daishōgun which are equated with the seven stars of the Northern Dipper.

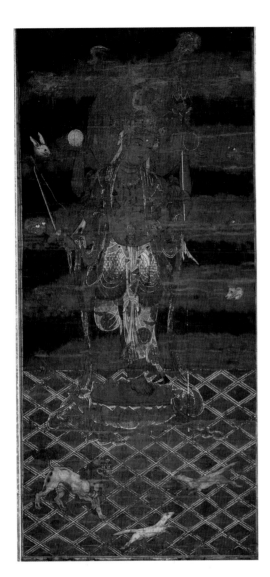

FIGURE 2.30. The Six-letter Worthy (Rokuji-son). 13th century. Color on silk. Hōju-in, Kōyasan.

The Pace of Yu

A Daoist element is evident in the iconography of Sonjōō, particularly in the representation of the god standing on one leg. This posture has been interpreted as referring to the Pace of Yu (Yu bu 禹步, J. Ūho), a Daoist rite in which the officiant traces a celestial pattern on the earth with his steps.[89] While the earliest record we have of the Northern Dipper's form being used as the pattern for this ritual is found in the Shangqing 上清 (Supreme Purity) scriptures, allegedly revealed between 364 and 370, aspects of this practice can be traced back to Han times.[90] The Pace of Yu influenced the ritual of "stamping the ground" (J. *henbai* 反閇), and eventually, during the Northern Song, the two fused together. In Japan, stamping was used in the Onmyōdō and Shugendō traditions as a means of creating sacred boundaries, of arousing earthly powers, and expelling evil influences.[91] Attesting to this connection, the *Asabashō* tells us that the Myōken ritual did not originate in Shingon but was borrowed from Onmyōdō.[92]

This particular iconographic representation of Myōken is strikingly similar to visual portrayals of Rokuji Myōō 六字明王, the central deity of an exorcistic ritual based on the *Six-letter Sūtra* (*Rokujikyō* 六字経).[93] Although Myōken and Rokuji Myōō seem clearly distinct on a ritual plane, their iconographic forms are not easily distinguished: both wear a diadem with an animal, have four or six arms, hold the sun and moon disks in their two hands, and stand on one leg with the other leg folded.[94] This similarity might be due to the fact that Hanjun 範俊 (1038–1112), the patriarch of the Kajūji 観修寺 line of the Ono 小野 school, based his iconographic depiction of Rokuji Myōō on that of Sonjōō. A specific feature in the case of Rokuji Myōō is the animal heads (and talismans) distributed around him—representing, in clockwise fashion from the bottom, the twelve cyclical signs, with one, two, or three foxes (sometimes chased by a lion) below (or in front of) him. The same is true of the Rokuji Myōō painting preserved at Hōju-in (Fig. 2.30). The figure in Fig. 2.31 has no animals around, but there is a monkey head on his headgear. All the exemplars of Rokuji Myōō have bodhisattva-like faces, with one exception (Fig. 2.32), which looks demonic.

FIGURE 2.31. Rokuji Myōō. Edo period. Sheet, ink on paper. University Art Museum, Kyoto City University of Arts. *BZS* 2184.

FIGURE 2.32. Rokuji Myōō. Edo period. Sheet, ink on paper. University Art Museum, Kyoto City University of Arts. *BZS* 2185.

FIGURE 2.33. Rokuji Myōō, with animals. Edo period. Sheet, ink on paper. University Art Museum, Kyoto City University of Arts. *BZS* 1050 (2).

The Deer Head

Another intriguing and perhaps significant detail found in certain representations of Myōken is the animal head atop his headgear (see Figs. 2.7 and 2.34). The *Asabashō* identifies it as a dragon head, perhaps alluding to Myōken's role as a provider of rain. Yet in most representations it is clearly a deer head. No explanation is given in the texts. The first idea that comes to mind is that this image is connected with Kasuga Shrine. As is well known, the deer is the emissary of the Kasuga deity.[95] Yet in spite of the obvious importance of astral cults in the medieval Kōfukuji-Kasuga complex, I have not been able to find any mention of Myōken in Kasuga documents, and I am reduced to indirect symbolic links.

As a symbol of immortality, the deer is the mount or messenger of Fukurokuju 福禄寿, one of the seven gods of fortune of Daoist origin, whose very name evokes the three stars of fortune (*fuku* 福), emoluments (*roku* 禄), and longevity (*ju* 寿). The deer head in Myōken's mandala is

FIGURE 2.34. Myōken with deer head and acolytes. Detail of Myōken mandala. Collection of Sylvan Barnett and William Burto.

also reminiscent of a popular figure of the Kagura tradition named Arahira 荒平, a demonic mountain deity shown with antlers protruding from his head, whose eyes are said to reflect the sun and moon, and his voice to resound like thunder.[96] Indeed, one of Myōken's characteristics is said to be the scent of musk, a fragrant glandular secretion found in a certain type of stag.[97]

In another so-called Myōken mandala, the *honzon*, instead of Myōken, is the planetary deity Saturn—in the form of an old man with an ox head over his head—riding an ox or buffalo. The god holds a staff (*shakujō*) in his left hand, and is flanked by two acolytes and surrounded by the twelve signs of the Western zodiac and the eight other planetary deities.[98]

Providing a possible clue to the significance of the animal symbolism operating in the iconography, the *Besson zakki* contrasts the rituals of the ox king 牛王 and the deer king 鹿王.[99] The ox king ritual, being the better known of the two, is sometimes identified with the rituals of Enmaten (Skt. Yama) and Daiitoku Myōō大威徳明王 (Yamāntaka 'Yama's Terminator'), both of whom are often pictured riding a water buffalo. Here, however, the ox king is defined as the wish-fulfilling jewel of space, whose essence is the great earth of the Dharmadhātu, and he is therefore implicitly equated with the Womb realm; whereas the deer king, whose essence is the perfect freedom of space, symbolizes the Vajra or Diamond realm. Although in these cases the ox and the deer are used as symbolic markers of the ultimate unity of a seemingly dualistic reality, the deer king may also have had a specific relation to Myōken.[100]

Another clue is perhaps given by the *Jingi hishō* 神祇祕抄 in a passage on Kashima Daimyōjin. A gloss explains that the deer represents the

utmost of stupidity among animals and thus symbolizes extreme ignorance—the *aramisaki* 荒御前 (messenger) of the deity of Dharma nature
(*hosshōjin* 法性神) before the opening of the Iron Tower in southern India
(the symbol of ultimate reality in Mikkyō).[101]

The Brush and the Register

As noted above, Myōken (Sonjōō) often holds a brush and a sheet of
paper, on which he records the deeds of beings (Figs. 2.35 and 2.36).
According to various sources, "because the pupils of the eyes of this worthy are pure, he sees things clearly and records good and evil."[102] In this
form, he is the director of destiny, a role usually associated with Enmaten
and his acolytes.

One of Myōken's feminine attributes, the mirror, is said to reflect
both good and evil. While this motif is at first glance related to Enmaten's
mirror, there is an important difference: the latter reveals the good and
evil deeds of the deceased and portrays them as fundamentally irrecon-
cilable, whereas Myōken's mirror is used to highlight the entwinement of

FIGURE 2.35. Myōken with brush and scroll. 12th century.
Ink on paper. *Besson zakki* 48, fig. 260.

FIGURE 2.36. Myōken with brush and scroll. 12th century.
Color on paper. *Zuzōshō*. Kanazawa bunko.

good and evil and their nondual nature. The text illustrates this nonduality through a number of dyads—the two sisters Kichijōten 吉祥天 (Śrī-devī) and Kokuanten 黒闇天 (Devī of Darkness), also known as Kokuniten 黒耳天 (Skt. Kālakarnikā or "Black-eared Devī," i.e., Yama's sister); the beautiful and the ugly; the auspicious and the inauspicious—which are said to always appear together, the former symbolizing ultimate reality (Skt. *dharmatā,* J. *hosshō* 法性), the latter fundamental ignorance (*avidyā,* J. *mumyō* 無明).[103]

Snakes and Dragons

In his role as god of destiny, Myōken (or one of his attendants) is often represented as wrathful in appearance: his hair stands on end, and seven snakes emerge above (or from) it.[104] The snakes' number suggests that they symbolize the seven stars of the Northern Dipper, although the precise relationship between stars and snakes is unclear. In one source, they are described as dragons. This motif of snakes links Myōken with the planetary deities Rāhu (J. Rago 羅喉) and Ketu (J. Keito 計都), an association to which we will return.[105]

FIGURE 2.37. Myōken on dragon. Edo period. Sheet, ink on paper. University Art Museum, Kyoto City University of Arts. *BZS* 2274.

FIGURE 2.38. Myōjō tenshi (Venus). *Zuzō shūsei* 9: 15.

Myōken's Mount

The *Asabashō* mentions that in the Gotō-in 後唐院, a pavilion of Miidera built by Enchin, there is a double-faced mirror that stands erect upon the back of a tortoise. Images are engraved on both faces: the front displays a four-armed Myōken riding a dragon (similar to Figs. 2.37 and 2.38), the back a two-armed Myōken sitting on a lotus. That mirror was deposited by Uji-dono 宇治殿 (i.e., Fujiwara no Yorimichi 藤原頼通, 992–1074) in the treasure house of the Byōdō-in sometime after 1052. The *Asabashō* suggests that this object may be the origin of the two images of Myōken that gained currency among the people, namely, Myōken riding a dragon and Myōken riding a tortoise (similar to Fig. 2.39).[106] The motif of the dragon links Myōken not only with Rāhu but also with the planetary deity

FIGURE 2.39. Myōken on tortoise. 12th century. Ink on paper. *Besson zakki* 48, fig. 261.

FIGURE 2.40. Myōken on tortoise and horses. Ink on paper. Private collection.

Venus and the goddess Benzaiten, while that of the intertwined tortoise links him with water deities like Suiten and the *nāgas*. Marui Keiji distinguishes the latter motif from that of the intertwined snake and tortoise, which clearly derives from the Chinese representation of Xuanwu (the Dark Warrior), and traces it back to Tendai influence.[107]

The tortoise-alone motif is also reminiscent of the figure of Urashima no ko 浦島子 (better known as Urashima Tarō 浦島太郎) and his descent to the palace of the sea king—a symbolic equivalent of Penglai (J. Hōrai 蓬莱, the island of the immortals).[108] Both Penglai and Myōken's heavenly palace are heterotopias, places where time stands (almost) still. We recall that Myōken, as emblem of the center, is both the ruler of time and change and a symbol of eternity.

The Two Acolytes

In this type of representation, Myōken is usually flanked by two acolytes who, according to the *Besson zakki,* are none other than Shimei (Ch. Siming 司命) and Shiroku (Ch. Silu 司祿), the controllers of human destiny.[109] One of them looks like a demon (*yakṣa*), the other like a goddess or bodhisattva (see Figs. 2.41 and 2.42).[110] The former usually presents an inkstone to Myōken; the latter often looks like Myōken and, like him,

FIGURE 2.41. Myōken (Sonjōō) with two acolytes. 12th century. Color on paper. *Zuzōshō.* Kanazawa bunko.

holds a brush and a sheet of paper. Siming and Silu appear in the *Essential Rules of the Seven Stars of the Northern Dipper for Subduing Demons* (*Beidou qixing houmo biyao yigui* 北斗七星護摩秘要儀軌), according to which, on the *gangshen* (J. *kōshin* 庚申) day, they ascend to heaven and report to the heavenly emperor on the good and evil deeds of humans.[111] These two deities are in fact two sides or emanations of a single, older god named Siming 司命. Since Myōken's assistants can be seen as his emanations, Myōken himself becomes functionally similar to Siming. According to the *Scripture on Emoluments and Destiny* (*Luming shu* 禄命書): "There is in the world a god who controls destiny (*siming-shen* 司命神); every year on the *gangshen* 庚辛 [day], he reports the sins of humans to the heavenly emperor." The text concludes that the Buddha, in order to help beings during the final age of the Law, has expounded the ritual of the seven stars.[112] The *Asabashō* points out that while the seven stars are also in charge of recording good and evil deeds, they can, if the appropriate rituals are performed, transfer the names of individuals from the record of death to that of life.[113] Siming and Silu also became the attendants of the underworld judges Enmaten (King Yama) and Taizan Fukun 泰山府君, and are functionally similar to the companion spirits (*kushōjin* 倶生神) who report the good and evil deeds of people to Enmaten.

FIGURE 2.42. Myōken (Sonjōō) with one acolyte. Color on paper. *Shoson zuzōshū*. Kanazawa bunko.

FIGURE 2.46. Rāhu, Ketu, and Saturn. *Kakuzenshō, DNBZ* 49: 46.

FIGURE 2.47. Rāhu on dragon. Detail of *Karazu*. 1166. Hand scroll, ink and color on paper. Tōji, Kyoto.

WATER DEITIES

Mercury

At the root of Myōken's connection to water are his associations with Taiyi and the planetary deity Mercury (Ch. Shuixing 水星 or Shuiyao 水曜, var. Chenxing 辰星). The Great Monad (Taiyi), one of Myōken's prototypes, had already been linked with water by Han times.[138] In Japan, this water symbolism resurfaced at Ise, in particular at the Outer Shrine, where the food goddess Toyouke 豊受 was identified with Taiyi.[139] Myōken's relation to the north and its concomitant element, water, also justified his association with Xuanwu and its theriomorphic emblem, a tortoise and a snake intertwined. Myōken is also often associated with springs: the eponymous spring of Miidera, for instance, is said to have gushed forth after Myōken came down to earth.[140]

Myōken's relationship with the planet Mercury was rooted in the Chinese belief that the northern direction is ruled by the water element.[141] Mercury is equated with the "essence of water" and is said to have given birth to Xuanwu. As noted above, he is usually represented holding a brush and a register and riding a tortoise, just like Myōken.[142] In India, Mercury was identified with the Vedic god Varuṇa, who, under the name Suiten (Water Deva), became one of the twelve directional devas of esoteric Buddhist cosmology.[143]

Suiten and the *Nāgas*

In the *Kakuzenshō,* Suiten is represented frontally as a bodhisattva with seven snakes coming out of his hair, standing on a giant tortoise (Figs. 2.48 and 2.49); as a deva or bodhisattva sitting on a tortoise, with five snakes in his hair, holding a sword and a snake noose (*ryūsaku* 龍索, Skt. *nāgapaśa*) (Figs. 2.50 and 2.51); or as a regular bodhisattva seated on a downward-facing lotus leaf and holding a threefold jewel in front of his chest.

Suiten also provides a link between Myōken and the *nāgas* or dragons, due to the fact that in some cases his mount is not a tortoise, but a dragon.[144]

RULERS OF DESTINY

Enmaten

The close relationship between the seven stars and King Yama (J. Enra-ō or Enmaten) is due to their shared function controlling human longevity. Here Yama is not simply the judge of the dead, but the deva who, when properly worshiped, can alter the registers of life and death, a privilege he shares with Myōken.

Myōken, owing to his eminent position at the apex of the sky, is the god that sees everything. The panoptic metaphor suggests not only his

FIGURE 2.52. Taishakuten. Color on paper. *Shoson zuzōshū*. Kanazawa bunko.

cosmic centrality, but also his position at the heart of human existence.[145] In his capacity as supreme ruler of human destinies, Myōken's role is strikingly similar to that of King Enma and his attendants. In the *Henkushō* 遍口鈔 by Seigen 成賢 (1162–1231), Enma is also said to be the "father of all stars."[146] In the *Ritual Procedure Regarding the Mansions and Luminaries* (*Xiuyao yigui* 宿曜義軌), a text attributed to Yixing, 673–727), astral deities and underworld deities are invoked in tandem.[147] The same is true in the *Betsugyō* 別行 by Kanjo 寛助 (1052–1125).[148]

Enmaten and his retinue (Taizan Fukun, Godō Daijin 五道大神, Shimei 司命, and Shiroku 司禄) are sometimes included in star mandalas.[149] A case in point is a mandala preserved at Hōshaku-in 宝積院, in which the *honzon* Ichiji Kinrin (Shijōkōbutsu) is surrounded by the seven planets, the twelve zodiacal constellations, the twenty-eight lunar mansions, with the seven stars of the Northern Dipper and two figures (one standing on a tortoise, probably Myōken) above, Enmaten and his acolytes below.

The *Kakuzenshō* explains that the incantations and mantras of the Northern Dipper and King Enma are recited together because these two powers are in essence the same. In the star offering the priest therefore recites Enma's mantra, whereas in the Enma offering he recites the incantation of the Northern Dipper.

Taishakuten

In his panoptic function, Myōken is also close to Taishakuten 帝釈天 (Skt. Indra, Ch. Dishi, K. Jeseok) (Figs. 2.52–2.54). In the Vedic tradition, Indra is a warrior god who leads the devas in the eternal cosmic struggle against the asuras. In Buddhism, he has a more pacific role: he is the lord of the Trāyastriṃśa heaven, or heaven of the thirty-three gods, at the apex of the realm of desire and the top of the cosmic mountain, Mount Sumeru. As one of the twelve directional devas, he rules over the eastern direction.

While the Vedic Indra lost much of his prestige in early Buddhism, he again became an important deity in East Asia, particularly in Korean

FIGURE 2.53. Taishakuten. Color on paper. *Shoson zuzōshū*. Kanazawa bunko.

Buddhism, where iconographic representations of Jeseok 帝釈 vie with those of the seven stars and Skanda (Ch. Weituo, K. Witaech'eon 위태천, J. Idaten 韋駄天) in Buddhist monasteries.[150] In Japan, too, apart from being one of the twelve directional devas, he became the object of a flourishing cult during the Edo period.[151]

The main function of the Buddhist Taishakuten is to determine the life span of beings according to their deeds. Like Yama, he is therefore a judge that determines karmic retribution. To that end, he sends the four deva kings on inspection tours through the human realm (Jambudvīpa), or he himself descends to this world to record the deeds of beings.[152] According to the *Sanbōe kotoba* 三宝絵詞 (984) by Minamoto no Tamenori 源為憲, Taishakuten roams through the Jambudvīpa in the first, fifth, and ninth months, and during these periods people must be particularly attentive to their actions.[153]

FIGURE 2.55. Marishiten. Edo period. Color on silk. Ichigami Shrine.

Sometimes the deity rides seven boars, or a cart drawn by seven boars, a clear allusion to the seven stars (and therefore a link to Myōken). In some cases, Marishiten is multiheaded, one of his/her heads being that of a boar.

Like Aizen Myōō, Marishiten is said to dwell in the solar wheel. Like Myōken, he or she protects travelers. What brings this deity closer to Myōken (and Yama), however, is its function as ruler of human destinies. Marishiten is said to write the names of beings in the registers of life and death. The Nō playwright Zenchiku 禅竹, in his *Meishuku shū* 明宿集, lists Marishiten (together with deities such as Benzaiten, Fudō, and Aizen) as one of the manifestations of the Shukujin 宿神 (the deity that rules over *shuku* 宿—in both senses of stars/constellation and human destiny). This theme is one of the leitmotifs of the deities that we will encounter in this book, and it will be further developed in *Protectors and Predators*.

EMBRYOLOGICAL SYMBOLISM

While the symbolism resulting from Myōken's central position and his concomitant cosmological function is obvious, less apparent but just as important for his definition as a god of destiny are his embryological functions—that is, functions relating to prenatal but also to postmortem protection (inasmuch as death is perceived as a prelude to rebirth). In the figure of Myōken the embryological and the panoptic elements merge. For now I shall simply mention a few features that point to Myōken's function as a placenta deity (*enagami* 胞衣神). The *Shiragisan Myōken daibosatsu engi* 白木山妙見大菩薩縁起, for instance, provides a detailed description of Myōken as a deity that protects the fetus inside the womb and continues to protect the individual after his or her birth, throughout life, and beyond death. Myōken is also identified with a specific form of Kōjin known as Placenta Kōjin (Ena Kōjin 胞衣荒神).[173]

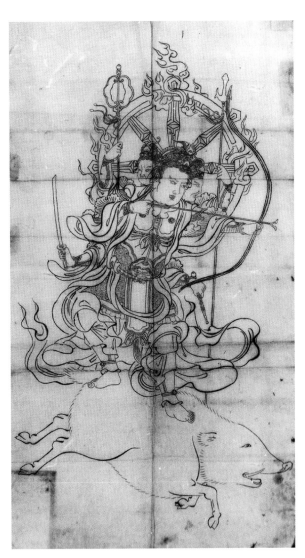

FIGURE 2.56. Marishiten. Edo period. Sheet, ink on paper. University Art Museum, Kyoto City University of Arts. *BZS* 2232.

The first thing to notice is the embryological coding of the red and white symbols—for example, the sun and moon disks that figure so prominently in the iconography of Myōken and similar deities. In esoteric Buddhism these two colors are associated with female blood and male semen, respectively, whose fusion, following sexual union, forms the embryo. The pregnancy of this womb symbolism is reflected in certain images of Myōken as Amaterasu. A case in point is the so-called Iwato Myōken 岩戸妙見 (Myōken of the Rock Cave), the *honzon* of the Myōken Hall of the Nichiren temple Enjōji 円成寺 (also known as Iwato Myōken-gū 岩戸妙見宮), on the northern outskirts of Kyoto.[174] In medieval Japan, Amaterasu's withdrawing to the Heavenly Rock Cave was often interpreted as a symbol of gestation, and her coming out of the cave as a symbol of childbirth.

FIGURE 2.57. Marishiten as bodhisattva. Edo period. Sheet, ink on paper. University Art Museum, Kyoto City University of Arts. *BZS* 2230.

Interestingly, among the protecting deities of Sonkō-in, in the *Myōken engi emaki* of Chiba, we find next to Benzaiten, Inari (Dakiniten), Seiryō Gongen 清滝権現, and Hachiman, a rather obscure deity called Shakujin Daimyōjin 石神大明神.[175] This deity, popularly known as *shaguji,* is often represented by phallic stones, and it is said to symbolize the fetus.[176] It has been well studied by Yanagita Kunio in his classic work *Questions and Answers on the Shakujin (Shakujin mondō* 石神 問答).[177] It is another form of the placenta deity, about which I will have more to say later.

CODETTA

Let us recapitulate. If, in his roles as ruler of heaven and judge of human destinies, Myōken corresponds to what one could call with Dumézil a god of the first function (sovereignty), it seems that, as a warrior deity, he marks a resurgence of the second function (war) in medieval Japanese religion. Yet, as a water deity and an agricultural deity assuring the earth's fertility, as well as a placenta deity that protects human fecundity, he is also, and perhaps above all, a god of the third function (prosperity). In the last analysis, he is a multifunctional deity who overflows the trifunctional framework. In this respect, he resembles Benzaiten and her Indian prototype, Sarasvatī, whose multifunctionality was already recognized by Dumézil himself. However, whereas Dumézil saw in Sarasvatī a trifunctional goddess standing vis-à-vis three male gods who are limited to a single function, Myōken is, with a few exceptions, a male deity (although his image as a youth is somewhat androgynous).

As god of the pole star, Myōken inherited from his Chinese predecessor Taiyi the function of regulator of the cosmos who protects countries and governs individual destinies.[178] Like the dragons or *nāgas* with whom he is associated, he also dispenses rain and rich harvests. He grants longevity, health, and fortune; he is invoked against all kinds of calamities;

in particular, he protects sea travelers. While his heterodox nature as an astral deity initially placed him at a lower rank or on the margins of the Buddhist pantheon, his commanding cosmic position allowed him to move to a central symbolic position and to escape the karmic transmigration that binds devas and humans alike, so that he eventually became the supreme judge of human destinies.

At the apex of the cosmos, Myōken and the seven stars form a paradigm of centrality in heaven that is replicated on earth by the emperor and his ministers. Indeed, all deities associated with the seven stars tend to be perceived as panoptic deities who control human destiny.[179] As we have seen, the list of these functionally similar deities—Buddhist and non-Buddhist—is already long; in a Dumézilian spirit, we could also add to it Indo-European deities such as Chronos and Mithra, masters of time who are also represented at the center of a "star mandala" of sorts, surrounded by the twelve zodiacal signs and other astral symbols.

FIGURE 2.58. Marishiten. Talisman. Sengakuji, Tokyo. Private collection.

Yet the ambiguity of Myōken's identity—he was variously identified with the pole star, the Northern Dipper, and certain stars of Ursa Major—suggests that this deity resists any single location or structural function, be it that of the center or otherwise. Because of his affinities with the dark hole or umbilicus of esoteric cosmology, he is in some sense invisible and therefore cannot be located vis-à-vis other structural constituents. He is what we might call a *poststructural* god. By setting into motion the system whose center he seems to occupy, Myōken becomes its vanishing point. His unruly nature is revealed in his juvenile, wrathful, Medusa-like manifestation—with serpents rising above his head—as well as in his relationships with the dark underworld and the watery realm. His martial manifestation further underscores the nature of this demonic god that rules over human destiny.

Myōken's iconography offers a paradigmatic case of the passage between an explicit, textual symbol and its implicit counterpart. Each element of his semantic constellation can in turn become paradigmatic and open a new chain of equivalences: the symbolism of the north, for example, links him to the water element, and consequently to its emblem, the tortoise-snake (Xuanwu, the Dark Warrior), Suiten, and the *nāgas;* but also to Bishamonten, the ruler of the northern quarter. The symbolism of the center links him to the earth element and to deities like Fudō, Kōjin, Daishōgun, Mahākāla, Kichijōten, Benzaiten, Bishamonten (again); the dragon symbolism to Rāhu, Nyoirin Kannon, and Benzaiten (again). The numerological symbolism—seven, but also eight (that is, seven plus one)—links him to various heptads (the seven stars and seven Yakushi) and octads (Nyoirin and the seven stars, Vināyaka and the seven Mothers). Finally, his panoptic vision and his grasp of the registers of life and death identify him with figures like Taishakuten (Skt. Indra), Enmaten (Skt. Yama), and Taizan Fukun. Thus, Myōken is not only a faint star in the northern sky (whether Polaris or Alcor), he is also the piercing gaze that reaches us and judges us from the unfathomable depths of the sky. Like the divine eye that followed Cain everywhere, the steady stare of that stern star is the very symbol of a transcendent moral conscience.[180]

THE ELUSIVE CENTER
Fudō

"The centre cannot hold."

W. B. YEATS, "The Second Coming"

"This so-called ontological monism has finally to be paid by an inflational proliferation of epistemological dualisms."

EDUARDO VIVEIROS DE CASTRO, *Cannibal Metaphysics*

Another symbol of the unmovable center, at first glance quite different from Myōken, is the wisdom king Fudō Myōō 不動明王 (Skt. Acala, Acalanātha), whose image is inscribed everywhere in the Japanese landscape. While the word "center" in the chapter title points to a cosmological position held by Fudō, and an important function fulfilled, the second word—"elusive"—is the attribute that most accurately describes the deity we now consider. Of Indian provenance, Fudō was initially brought to Japan by esoteric monks in the early Heian period but soon achieved prominence as an integral member of state rituals and, later, privately commissioned rites performed for the aristocracy. Because of his elusive nature and manifold guises, I address in this chapter various forms of Fudō without necessarily positing an "essential" Fudō.

That being said, there is one theme ubiquitous in, and of fundamental importance to, Fudō's centrality to Japanese religious thought and practice: the relationship between conceptions of Fudō as a servant and as a tamer or master. Iconographically the former is portrayed as hideous, wrathful, and servile, while the latter exudes compassion (albeit often wrathfully so) and appears humble, almost humanlike at times. At the heart of the relationship between the two, and of the development of the Fudō cult, was a structural shift whereby Fudō moved from a position of inferiority to one of superiority, from being a mere acolyte to being a mighty demon tamer. The Fudō whom we moderns have been bequeathed in Japan, however, is essentially a composite figure containing elements of both the old and the new Fudōs. The tension between these two aspects of Fudō, as well as their complementary relationship, is a recurrent theme in the study of this deity.

We begin with Fudō's role as a wisdom king and his Indian origins, following the evolution of Fudō as he traveled eastward. As we shall see, it was in India that the distinction and subsequent tension between Fudō (Acala) as acolyte and Fudō as master first emerged. Next we turn to an examination of this deity according to his functions. I have chosen four for close scrutiny: first, Fudō's apotropaic function, followed by his roles in spirit possession, individual protection, and prolongation of life. In sketching the development of the Fudō cult in Japan, I make important distinctions between the three arenas in which the cult evolved: state rituals, private rituals, and the practice of individual ascetics. Following this historical overview, I address two lines of doctrinal interpretation, one focusing on Fudō as a symbol of the center and the other seeing him as representing either enlightenment or ignorance. These two lines express a preoccupation with cosmology, on the one hand, and a concern with Fudō's role in Buddhist soteriology, on the other. Less explicit but indispensable to a comprehensive understanding of Fudō are a number of symbolic tendencies, including Fudō's role as a chthonian power, youthful acolytes and Fudō's relationships to them, the dualistic symbolism found in Fudō's couplings with other deities, his embryological functions, and his association with another elusive yet omnipresent deity named Kōjin.

To minimize confusion in what is an inevitably confusing network of relationships, I use the name Acala (Fudō's Sanskrit name) when discussing this deity's development outside Japan and Fudō when addressing his career in Japan or character at a general level. While Acala and Fudō are in a sense synonymous, they also represent different points on a continuum, which manifest themselves as drastically different characters at times. With this in mind, let us turn to Fudō's elusive origins.

THE WISDOM KINGS

In India, Acala is usually perceived as one of the five wisdom kings (Skt. *vidyārāja,* J. *myōō*) (Figs. 3.1–3.3). The term *vidyārāja* denotes a type of deity originally conceived of as an emanation of *vidyā,* a term that usually means knowledge or wisdom but in the compound *vidyārāja* refers to an incantation.[1] In other words, a *vidyārāja* is the personification of a powerful mantra or *dhāraṇī.*

The Japanese cult of the five wisdom kings—also known as the Five Great Worthies (*godaison* 五大尊)—developed during the Heian period. In the esoteric Buddhist scheme of things, the five wisdom kings are the forms taken by the primordial buddha Dainichi (Mahāvairocana) to tame beings that resist conversion. The raging fire that surrounds them is interpreted symbolically as the fire that purifies the practitioner from all defilements and transmutes passions into awakening, the so-called fire *samādhi* (J. *kashōzanmai* 火生三昧).

Fudō is the *primus inter pares* in the sense that he stands (or sits) at the center of the group, having come to subsume the other four wisdom kings—who thus can be seen as either his retinue or his emanations. According to orthodox esoteric Buddhism, the wisdom kings are in principle motivated (if not moved) by compassion; yet their wrathful appearance betrays the violent nature of the demons or *yakṣa*s from which they developed. This fierceness is reflected in iconographic details such as protruding fangs and the snakes coiled around their torsos and limbs.

The tendency toward individualization exhibited by these five deities derives naturally from the fact that each of the four directional *myōō* was taken as chief deity for one of the four main types of esoteric ritual. According to the esoteric master Amoghavajra (Ch. Bukong 不空, 705–774), Trailokyavijaya (J. Gōzanze 降三世—east) was invoked in rites of increase (*pauṣṭika*, J. *zōyaku* 増益), Kuṇḍalin (J. Gundari 軍荼利—south) in rites of subjugation (*abhicāraka*, J. *chōbuku* 調伏), Yamāntaka (J. Daiitoku 大威徳—west) in rites of attraction (*vaśīkarana*, J. *keiai* 敬愛), and Vajrayakṣa (J. Kongōyasha 金剛夜叉—north) in rites for the elimination of calamities (śantika, J. *sokusai* 息災).[2] As for Fudō, he is a synthetic figure and as such can fulfill the role of chief deity in a number of different rituals, although he is most commonly invoked in subjugation rituals (Fig. 3.4–3.7).

FIGURE 3.1. The five wisdom kings. Edo period. Sheet, ink on paper. University Art Museum, Kyoto City University of Arts. *BZS* 2172.

INDIAN PROTOTYPES

In Japan, Fudō became a thoroughly naturalized citizen, exhibiting many characteristics that can only be traced to Japanese religious thought and praxis, but to understand this multifaceted fellow in his entirety, one must scrutinize his Indian origins. Of particular importance is an examination not only of direct textual references and iconography, but also of his Indian prototypes.

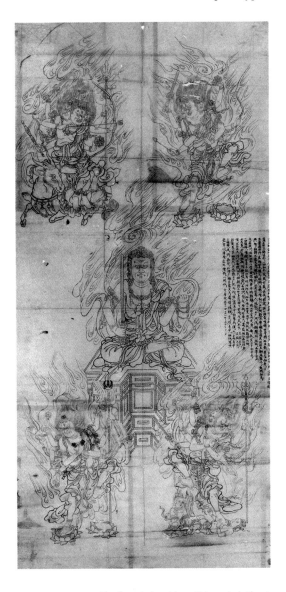

FIGURE 3.2. The five wisdom kings. Edo period. Sheet, ink on paper. University Art Museum, Kyoto City University of Arts. *BZS* 2169.

FIGURE 3.3. Daiitoku Myōō. Edo period. Sheet, ink on paper. University Art Museum, Kyoto City University of Arts. *BZS* 2160.

FIGURE 3.4. Standing Fudō. Talisman. Personal collection.

FIGURE 3.5. Standing Fudō. Wood. Kyoto National Museum.

FIGURE 3.6. Seated Fudō with acolytes. Edo period. Sheet, ink on paper. University Art Museum, Kyoto City University of Arts. *BZS* 2138.

FIGURE 3.7. Fudō and acolytes. Kitano market, Kyoto. Photo Bernard Faure.

In Indian esoteric Buddhism, Acala (i.e., Fudō) is usually represented in a dynamic lunging posture (called, precisely, ācalāsana): his right leg thrust forward while his left knee touches the ground. This posture suggests his close relationship with the earth. It is quite different from Fudō's motionless posture whether he is standing or sitting, which is specific to Japan. Acala first appears in the *Bukong guansuo shenbian zhen'yan jing* 不空羂索神変真言経 (Skt. *Amoghapāśakalparāja-sūtra,* translated by Bodhiruci ca. 707–709), in which he is described as a messenger or servant of the Buddha Vairocana: "The first from the west in the northern quadrant is the acolyte Acala 不動使者. In his left hand he grasps a noose and in his right hand he holds a sword. He is seated in the half-lotus position."[3] But the locus classicus is a passage in the *Mahāvairocana Sūtra* in which Acala appears as one of the deities of the Womb mandala:

> Below the lord of mantras, in the southwestern direction, is Acala, servant of the Tathāgata. He holds the sword of wisdom and the noose (*pāśa*). His hair hangs on his left shoulder. One eye lightly squinting, he gazes intently. Blazing flames radiate from his awe-inspiring body. He dwells on a large rock. On his forehead are wrinkles like waves on the water. He is a young boy with a plump body.[4]

In the commentary on that scripture by the Chinese monk Yixing 一行 (673–727), we read that Acala appeared in the world following Mahāvairocana's vow to save all beings, and that his primary function is to eliminate obstacles to awakening.

Vajrapāṇi

Concerning possible prototypes or precursors, one could theoretically locate Acala's origins in a generic Śiva, but only in the sense that all Tantric deities can in one way or another be traced back to Śiva.[5] Other potential prototype candidates include Trailokyavijaya (another wisdom king whose name is an epithet of Śiva) and the Vedic fire god Agni.[6] Nevertheless, the most likely candidate is Vajrapāṇi (the Vajra Holder) (Figs. 3.8 and 3.9).[7] Étienne Lamotte's remark on Vajrapāṇi could easily be applied to Acala: a protean spirit who was, in spite of a humble origin, "raised to the summit of metaphysical reality and acceded to the rank of supreme being."[8] Yet I do not follow Lamotte when he claims that Vajrapāṇi's success is due "less to a natural and logical evolution of Buddhist conceptions than to a kind of compromise between decadent Buddhism and triumphant Hinduism."[9] I would argue that Vajrapāṇi's success, like that of Fudō and similar figures in the Japanese context, reflects the logic of esoteric Buddhism, a religious trend that can no longer be dismissed as "decadent."

FIGURE 3.8. Shūkongōshin (Vajrapāṇi). 13th century. Color on wood. Kongōbuji.

FIGURE 3.9. Shitsu-kongōshin (Vajrapāṇi). Edo period. Sheet, ink on paper. University Art Museum, Kyoto City University of Arts. *BZS* 2193.

Vajrapāṇi was originally a *yakṣa,* the leader of a privileged class of deities (the *vajrapāṇis*) who escaped the authority of the deva king Vaiśravaṇa and were directly under the authority of Indra (a.k.a. Śakra, the "Powerful One"). Vajrapāṇi is therefore intimately related to Indra, and he served at times as a substitute for that god. He is also the leader of the *guhyaka* and the guardian of the mysteries.[10] Then, as Lamotte notes, "under a separate form, he climbed up again all the degrees that his prototype had climbed down."[11]

As a companion and servant of the Buddha, Vajrapāṇi is represented as a kind of bully who, while remaining invisible, threatens to (and sometimes does) explode the head of those who do not listen to the Master.[12] His role as a protector is exemplified in the episodes in which he subjugates the dragon Apalāla and intercepts the boulder that the jealous Devadatta had thrown at the Buddha.[13]

Vajrapāṇi shares with Ānanda the privileged status of assistant of the Buddha. As intimate companion, he knows all the secrets (*guhya*) of the Master and will therefore become the master of esoteric teachings. Ānanda is his exoteric human counterpart.[14] In Mahāyāna literature, Vajrapāṇi became a kind of double of Ānanda.[15] This "unavoidable acolyte," as Alfred Foucher calls him, is said to follow the Buddha "like his shadow," a topos characteristic of the so-called gods of obstacles that we will find on our way again and again. In the *Golden Light Sūtra*'s discussion of deities who protect this scripture, Vajrapāṇi is still listed as a *yakṣa.* According to one tradition, a buddha is always flanked and protected by five hundred *vajrapāṇis* on either side.[16] Vajrapāṇi is also said to protect bodhisattvas: as soon as a bodhisattva enters the eighth stage or *bhūmi* (*acala-bhūmi,* a name that evokes that of Acala), Vajrapāṇi follows him like his shadow.[17]

With the rise of esoteric Buddhism, however, the nature of Vajrapāṇi changed drastically. His esoteric transformation is reflected in the view that the *vajra* he holds is not a mere weapon but a symbol of his adamantine nature—the diamond-like essence immanent in all beings. This change, which proved to be the key to Vajrapāṇi's long-term success, was further facilitated by the symbolic polysemy of the word *vajra,* meaning both thunderbolt (weapon) and diamond.[18] In the *Mañjuśrīmūlakalpa,* Vajrapāṇi, redefined as Vajrasattva, becomes the leader of the Vajra clan (*kula*) and is positioned next to the buddha Śākyamuni, leader of the Buddha clan, and the bodhisattva Avalokiteśvara, leader of the Lotus clan. In the *Mahāvairocana Sūtra,* Vajrapāṇi, in his capacity as "master of mysteries," engages in dialogue with the buddha Mahāvairocana.[19]

UPWARD BOUND

Acala's rise in the esoteric pantheon from a mere acolyte of the bodhisattva (Avalokiteśvara?) to a demon-subduing deity is spectacular: beginning as a humble errand boy he eventually became Mahāvairocana's "wheel-commanding body" (J. *kyōryōrinshin* 教令輪身). As in the case of Vajrapāṇi, Acala's ascent from the lowly position of servant to that of master was a process in which the periphery swapped positions with the center, the shadow morphed into reality, and the supplement became the essence. Bob Linrothe's remarks on Trailokyavijaya (J. Gōzanze) (see Figs. 3.10 and 3.11) could be applied verbatim to Acala's circumstances: "This is an amazing promotion, from the quasi-coerced, vow-bound assistant of a bodhisattva . . . to a being who fuses the wisdom of all the cosmic buddhas in order to subdue the most powerful god in the universe."[20]

Although Fudō's youthful appearance may suggest a kind of arrested development, the Fudō cult in Japan is definitely not characterized by stasis, but on the contrary by a strong dynamism. The social metaphor of the servant who becomes the ultimate lord—a lowly figure who ascends to the apex of the divine world—was certainly not lost on a socially volatile

FIGURE 3.10. Taming of Daijizaiten (Maheśvara) by Gōzanze (Trailokyavijaya). Detail of *Dato shuji mandara* portable shrine. 1387. Lacquered wood with polychromy. Nara National Museum.

FIGURE 3.11. Taming of Daijizaiten (Maheśvara) by Gōzanze (Trailokyavijaya). 12th century. Ink on paper. *Besson zakki* 33, fig. 168.

FIGURE 3.12. Taming of Daijizaiten (Maheśvara) by Fudō (Acala). 12th century. Ink on paper. *Besson zakki* 32, fig. 165.

medieval society that was witnessing the triumph of inferiors over their superiors (*gekokujō* 下克上). Actually, Fudō did not wait to arrive on Japanese soil to begin this structural shift: while Acala was just a servant (or even a quasi-slave) in the *Mahāvairocana Sūtra,* in Yixing's commentary on this text he has already become the worthy who tames all demons.

In medieval Japan, Fudō and Gōzanze 降三世 were occasionally thought to be identical. The *Kakuzenshō* juxtaposes two theories, one arguing for the identity of Fudō and Gōzanze, the other emphasizing their disparity.[21] Acala already appears in the Tang translations of the *Mahāvairocana Sūtra* by Śubhakarasiṃha and Vajrabodhi, but he does not yet have the eminent status of Trailokyavijaya in the lineage of the *Jingangding jing* (Skt. *Vajraśekhara-sūtra, T.* 18, 865) and the Vajradhātu mandala.[22]

In his *Commentary on the Mahāvairocana Sūtra,* Yixing compares Acala and Trailokyavijaya and presents them as equals. While in the received tradition it is Trailokyavijaya—as a manifestation of Vajrapāṇi—who tames the reluctant Maheśvara (J. Daijizaiten 大自在天), Yixing replaces Trailokyavijaya with Acala (Fig. 3.12).[23] It seems, then, that Yixing was the one responsible for Acala's prestigious promotion to lord of all the devas.[24] In line with this trend, the *Kakuzenshō* contains an illustration of Fudō trampling Daijizaiten.[25] Significantly, it is only in this scene that Fudō is depicted in a dynamic posture, like the Indian Acala. All other Japanese representations show him in either a standing or sitting position, motionless in either posture.[26]

Thus, the image of Fudō as a servant, still found in the *Bukong guansuo shenbian zhen'yan jing,* was gradually overshadowed, only to resurface in a latent form in the doctrine and iconography of medieval esoteric Buddhism, to which we now turn.

RITUAL AND ICONOGRAPHY

In the standard image of Fudō in Japan, the deity holds a sword in his right hand and a noose in his left. Japanese art historians usually distinguish between two iconographic types of Fudō: the so-called Jingoji 神護寺 type and the Nineteen Aspects (*jūkyūsō* 十九相) type; the latter was codified by the Tendai priest Annen 安然 (841–902) and by the Ishiyamadera 石山寺 priest Shunnyū 淳祐(890–953).[27] These two clerics also emphasized the difference between the standing Fudō and the sitting Fudō. From the ritual standpoint, however, a more significant distinction is that between the two-armed (Fig. 3.15) and the four-armed Fudō (Figs. 3.13–3.14). The latter was the *honzon* of subjugation rituals and earth-placating rituals (*anchin-hō* 安鎮法).[28]

The *anchin* ritual is first mentioned in the *Nihonshoki* 日本書紀 in 651, under the reign of Kōtoku Tennō 孝徳天皇 (r. 645–654). It was a rather grand affair, since 2,100 monks and nuns are said to have recited the *Sūtra for Land Pacification* (*Antaku dosoku kyō* 安宅土側経).[29] Such rituals became increasingly important with the development of esoteric Buddhism in the Heian period, and in particular with Tendai esotericism (Taimitsu). They were based on texts such as *Acala's Method for Pacification* (*Budong anzhen fa* 不動安鎮法) [30] or *Acala's Mantra for Pacifying the House* (*Budong zhentuo zhen'yan* 不動鎮宅真言).[31] The *Asabashō* describes one such ritual performed in 972 on behalf of the chancellor (*dajōdaijin* 太政大臣) Fujiwara no Koretada 藤原伊尹 (924–972). On this occasion, dolls made of peach wood were buried, as well as a mandala with Fudō Myōō at its center, surrounded by various devas, the seven planets, the twenty-eight lunar mansions, and dragons.[32] A similar ritual, placing Fudō at the center of the eight directions, is attributed

FIGURE 3.13. Fudō's earth-quelling mandala. Edo period. Sheet, ink on paper. University Art Museum, Kyoto City University of Arts. *BZS* 1065.

FIGURE 3.14. Four-faced Fudō. 13th century. Ink on paper. Kyoto National Museum.

to Amoghavajra.[33] The Fudō in question is the four-armed Fudō, not the two-armed one.[34] According to the *Shijūjō ketsu* 四十帖決 by Chōen 長宴 (1016–1081), "The four-armed Fudō is the lord of the various categories [of gods], whereas the two-armed [Fudō] is the emissary of the Tathāgata."[35] In the Fudō *anchin* ritual attributed to Vajrabodhi, a two-armed Fudō stands at the center, surrounded by eight four-armed Fudō and eight deities, all his emanations, whose role is to guard the eight directions. This two-armed Fudō is said to be the "essence" (*honji*) of the earth deity, Kenrō Jiten 堅牢地天 (or Kenrō Jijin 堅牢地神). This representation probably reflects a later stage when Fudō was already endowed with great prestige.[36]

FIGURE 3.15. *Ninnyōkyō* mandala. Muromachi period. Color on silk. Tōji, Kyoto.

A large-scale Fudō *anchin* ritual was performed before the construction of the imperial palace (*dairi* 内裏) at the heart of the capital and therefore of Japan. It aimed at transforming the whole country into a sacred area (*kekkai* 結界), free of all calamities. To this end, various types of offerings were ritually buried at the center and in the eight directions, while formulas of demonic subjugation were recited. The accompanying dance was a kind of stamping (*henbai* 反閇), whose function was to awaken the positive energies of the earth while driving negative energies into the ground.

Fudō is usually represented within a mandorla of flames. In certain paintings, his entire body (including his sword) is ablaze.[37] His eponymic "unmovability" is implied by his erect, rigid posture. Nevertheless, like his prototype Acala, he is sometimes represented in a dynamic posture. A case in point is a line drawing that depicts him in the midst of flames, lunging toward the left (Fig. 3.16). His feet rest on two lotus pads, he raises a sword with his right arm, and he fiercely glares at a demon whom he holds in supine position on his left arm.[38]

FIGURE 3.16. The demon-pursuing Fudō and two attendants. Edo period. Sheet, ink on paper. University Art Museum, Kyoto City University of Arts. *BZS* 2149.

The monumental representations of official or semi-official worship (*jōroku* 丈六, measuring about 5 m high for a standing image, half that for a sitting image) became increasingly common in the late Heian period (for instance, the Fudō of Hosshōji's 法性寺 Godai-dō 五大堂 was 4 m high) and contrasted starkly with the miniature representations employed in personal devotion. One should not think, however, that there is a direct relationship between Fudō's religious importance and the size of his icons. As we will see, the three-inch Fudō (*sansun* Fudō 三寸不動) is perhaps as significant as the monumental Fudō icons.

FUDŌ'S TRANSFORMATIONS

As previously mentioned, central to the transformation of Acala/Fudō was a change from the position of servant to that of master. As a servant, Fudō is depicted with an unsightly, wrathful appearance, and he exhibits an excessive slavishness; as master, he is characterized by humility, compassion, a humanlike appearance (particularly evident in the iconography), and the ability to subjugate. Here I would like to briefly outline this evolution and its bipartite elaboration into two diametrically opposed, yet complementary and oft-combined, conceptions of Fudō.

The Indian pairing of Trailokyavijaya and Acala, or at least the collection of shared characteristics responsible for their periodic identification, prefigures the Japanese pairing of Aizen 愛染 (Skt. Rāgarāja) and Fudō. In both cases, we start with a rather lowly figure—a *yakṣa*—who eventually ascends to the highest position in the esoteric Buddhist pantheon. If Maheśvara (Śiva) refuses to submit to Trailokyavijaya, it is because he confuses him with the lowly demon he once was. Similarly, Acala's lowliness remains evident in his ugly, lowly appearance, which stands in stark contrast to such exalted figures as the buddhas and bodhisattvas. One cannot blame Maheśvara for his mistake.

In Yixing's *Commentary on the Mahāvairocana Sūtra*, Acala's ugliness is already interpreted (or rather explained away) in allegorical fashion. He is no longer merely Acala the servant, because he is endowed with Mahāvairocana's awesome powers of subjugation. His slavishness has become an expression of humility, a Buddhist virtue, while his wrathful appearance is interpreted as an expression of his "ruthless" compassion. At the same time, says Yixing, Acala's representation as a plump youth renders him the most "human" of the wisdom kings, which perhaps explains why he took precedence over his companions (see Fig. 3.17).

Acala and Trailokyavijaya both serve as symbols of *bodhicitta* (J. *bodaishin* 菩提心), the first thought or seed of

FIGURE 3.17. Youthful Fudō. Detail of *Taizōkai zuzō*. 1194. Ink on paper. Nara National Museum.

his servant before asking him to tame Śiva-Maheśvara.) Unfortunately for Sawa's thesis, the theory of Acala's identity with Śiva is no longer widely accepted, since it relies entirely on a single piece of evidence, namely, the observation that the two deities share the same epithet ("Immovable").

Beginning with the *Budong shishe tuoluoni bimi fa* 不動使者陀羅尼秘密法 (translated by Vajrabodhi; *T.* 21, 1202), the many texts centered on Acala are either contemporary with or slightly posterior to the *Mahāvairocana Sūtra.* These texts can be roughly divided into two distinct traditions: those that present Acala as a servant of the Buddha and those that portray Acala as a powerful tamer of demons. As one might expect, this distinction is not always clear cut and it is not easy to determine the intertextual influence of these chronologically proximate texts, including the role played by the *Mahāvairocana Sūtra* therein.[44]

Moving beyond the bipartite Acala, the classic Fudō known to the Japanese from the Heian period on is in fact the product of an amalgamation of the servant and wrathful wisdom king. Rather than being Indian in provenance, this image emerged and developed in China and Japan, although it was only in Japan that it became prominent as the stereotyped object of a thriving cult.[45] Although the servant Fudō was thoroughly integrated into a Japanese Buddhist philosophical framework, this sort of assimilation was not an inevitable outcome. A deity known in Japan as Shō Mudō 聖無動, for example, exhibits traces of various formidable Indian deities decidedly non-Buddhist in character.

As the once-lowly servant ascended to the exalted rank of protector of the Womb mandala, Fudō's look became increasingly wrathful yet supposedly compassionate. In his capacity as the wheel-commanding body of Dainichi, he took up his position at the center of the mandala and became the leader of the four directional wisdom kings.[46] In this way the wrathful aspect came to dominate images of the solo Fudō. A further development took place when doctrinally inspired details were added to images of Fudō used as the *honzon* in certain rituals. For instance, an undertone of compassion lies just beneath the anger in these images, evoking the qualities of the Buddha's servant. Thus, Fudō's ugliness developed into an expression of anger while his youthfulness served as an indicator of his overflowing energy. The tension (or complementary relationship) between the doctrinal polarities found in Fudō is given greatest iconographic expression in those of Fudō's facial features that lend themselves to a dualistic interpretive model, e.g., his fangs, lips, eyes. This is an archetypical example of doctrinally inspired iconography (as opposed to visionary images).

Sawa sees the two-step transformation of Acala's image as the highest expression of esoteric thought: first, the servant is transformed into a tamer, and second, he becomes an avatar of Mahāvairocana, a role that combines the two aspects represented by the former images, namely, anger and compassion. But where is the compassion in Fudō's figure, apart from pious interpretations? And how does Acala's slavish nature turn into compassion? Sawa does not consider this question, yet his notion of two distinct strands in Fudō's evolution is basically correct. What remains important for our purposes is the distinction between two traditions: the "teratological" Fudō and the "human," more orthodox Fudō.

FUNCTIONS

Let us now take a different approach and examine Fudō according to his functions. Some of these functions, such as that of servant or tamer, have already been mentioned. Here I would like to highlight four additional functions that can be distinguished despite a degree of overlap: an apotropaic function, possession, individual protection, and prolongation of life.

The Apotropaic Function

Fudō's power of subjugation and ability to ward off evil influences can be traced back to Acala's taming of Māra and Maheśvara. In the role of tamer he is identified with the earth deity. For example, in one of the versions of the legend of the Buddha, the earth deity appears twice to help the Buddha defeat Māra, first as a witness to the Buddha's virtue and subsequently as Acala the subduer.[47]

The apotropaic function is particularly evident in ritual texts in which Acala/Fudō appears as protector of the state. One such text, entitled *Secret Ritual for the Protection of the State* (*Chingo kokka hihō* 鎮護国家秘法), is said to have been transmitted secretly by the Indian Tantric master Vajrabodhi.[48] It describes the origins of Acala, the state-protection mission entrusted to him by Vairocana, his mandala, and the forty-eight types of benefit resulting from the performance of his ritual.[49] In this text, the Buddha Vairocana orders Acala to protect beings from the calamities of the final age by assuming leadership of the four great wrathful *vajras,* the devas of the eight directions, the seven planets, the twenty-eight mansions, and the thirty-six animals.

In his *Commentary on the Mahāvairocana Sūtra,* Yixing describes a subjugation rite in which the priest draws a picture of the obstructing demon inside a triangular altar. Having visualized Acala and become one with him, the priest mentally pictures himself trampling the head of the demon, who quickly departs to avoid being killed.[50] Certain ritual texts use the image of Acala's foot as a talisman. Yixing also quotes Mahāvairocana's explanation to Vajrapāṇi of a method used to clear obstructions. The method described entails visualizing Acala using his left foot (his "*samādhi* foot") to crush the obstructing demon's head.[51] Fudō's apotropaic function is further confirmed by his position at the center of the oblation (J. *goma* 護摩, Skt. *homa*) ritual, which is essentially an apotropaic rite.[52]

Possession

An important element of apotropaic rituals is possession (*āveśa*), which can be induced or involuntary. Fudō played a crucial role in both cases, but he was particularly important in esoteric rituals in which a priest induces possession in children.[53] In other words, while Fudō protected people against possession, he was himself a deity known to possess children. His association with possession is well illustrated by an event in the life of the Tendai priest Sōō 相応 (831–918). On one occasion when the daughter of Fujiwara no Yoshisuke 藤原良相 (813–867) was seriously ill, Sōō was asked to pray for her recovery. After Yoshisuke's prayers were answered and the possessing demon was expelled, the grateful father presented Sōō with a Chinese sword on which were engraved and set in gold the following words: "The spell of Fudō Myōō, the mantra with which the buddhas compassionately protect us."[54]

Successful exorcism requires that the possessing spirit be sent back to the source whence it came. This is made clear in one particular exorcistic ritual called King Fudō's Sending Back of the Live Spirits (Fudō-ō *ikiryōgaeshi* 不動王生霊返).[55] The rite requires the ritualist's invocation of protector spirits (known in esoteric Buddhism as *gohō* 護法). These "protectors" are violent deities, and Acala himself, like Vajrapāṇi, may originally have been one of them. Indeed, Fudō and his acolytes are on occasion described as "spell deities" (*susogami*), magic helpers that help a practitioner conjure up spells and cure demonic illnesses.[56] A famous case of possession involving Fudō is that of the Miidera priest Chikō 智光 (d. 970), recorded in the *Soga monogatari* 曽我物語. Chikō had fallen gravely ill and the etiology had been traced to a malevolent spirit. The famous Yin-Yang master (*onmyōji*) Abe no Seimei 安倍晴明 was asked to perform an exorcism, and Chikō's disciple Shōkū 性空 (910–1007) offered himself as substitute. Seimei invoked his spirit helpers, the *shikigami* 式神 (an Onmyōdō counterpart of the *gohō*), but to no avail. Shōkū was on the verge of death when Fudō miraculously intervened and saved both master and disciple.[57]

Individual Protection

Apart from his apotropaic function, Fudō operated as an individual protector (*gohō*) at the service of practitioners. During the performance of esoteric rituals, Fudō was invoked to protect both the ritual arena and the priest.[58] But his protection extended beyond the time and space of the ritual, and he was believed to protect his devotees life after life. At times he did so directly, and at other times he acted through his acolytes (especially Kongara 矜羯羅 and Seitaka 制多迦).[59] In this way, he became the main tutelary deity of Buddhist ascetics and *shugen* 修験 practitioners, who aimed at achieving ritual merging or unity with him. Eminent Buddhist priests, like Kūkai and Kakuban 覚鑁 (1095–1143) in Shingon, and

Enchin and Sōō in Tendai, worshiped him as their personal protector.[60] The large number of monks, particularly well-respected ones, engaging in such personal devotional practices directed toward specified deities resulted in the growth of popular devotion during the medieval period.[61]

In this way, Fudō was not simply Dainichi's servant in the way that Vajrapāṇi was the servant of the Buddha; he was also the servant of the practitioners, eating the food scraps that they offered him.[62] According to the *Budong liyin gui* 不動立印軌 (translated by Amoghavajra, *T.* 21, 1199), "The Worthy Fudō manifests corporeally in order to serve the practitioner, as if [the latter] were the Buddha." Fudō's lowly nature is further revealed by the list of nineteen contemplations wherein one is instructed to contemplate Fudō as one who devours the practitioner's leftovers. In this context "leftovers" is interpreted allegorically as the remainders of karmic hindrances resulting from the practitioner's passions.[63] This detail, which accords with Acala's identification with the wisdom king Ucchuṣma (J. Ususama 烏瑟沙摩 or 烏芻沙摩), is important because it places Fudō firmly in the category of deities that deal with leftovers and impurity, a category studied in depth by Rolf Stein.[64]

In the same vein, Fudō serves as a guide and a protector. He also helps ascetics to purify themselves. He does this by burning all obstacles with the fire of his wisdom, slashing hindrances with his sword, and tying up demons with his noose.[65] Fudō became the paradigmatic protector of ascetics and was associated in particular with those *shugenja* who practiced waterfall askesis. A case in point is the story of the ascetic Mongaku 文覚 (1139–1203), who fell into *samādhi* and subsequently fell quite literally into the rapids of the Nachi waterfall. He was rescued from drowning by Fudō's acolytes Kongara and Seitaka.[66] Also worth mentioning is the case of Gaken 我見, an ascetic who, with Fudō's aid, had a vision of the dragon of the calderal lake atop Mount Aso 阿蘇山 in Kyushu. On his way down the mountain, Gaken met a young woman with whom he desired to have sex. When he kissed the woman (who was actually a female dragon), she cut off his tongue. In shock, Gaken invoked Fudō, and a divine youth appeared to restore his tongue.[67]

Another important feature of Fudō's function as personal guardian is his manifestation as the "body-substituting" Fudō (*mikawari* Fudō 身替り不動). In this capacity he saves his devotees through a somatic transformation whereby their bodies temporarily morph into his. The following example appears in *Tales from Times Now Past* (*Konjaku monogatari shū* 今昔物語集). During the anti-Buddhist campaign of the Huichang era (841–846) in China, the Japanese Tendai priest Ennin (792–862) invoked the name of Fudō just as he was about to be arrested. Soldiers searched the hall in which he had been but he was nowhere to be found. All they found inside was a statue of Fudō, which of course was in fact Ennin himself, magically transformed by the power of Fudō. Fudō also appeared to help

Ennin during the latter's return trip to Japan.[68] Similar stories are found in appreciable number about Buddhist priests in the medieval period.

Another aspect of this particular function that one encounters in numerous legends is Fudō's shouldering of others' suffering, a phenomenon we might call "surrogate suffering." In such cases Fudō calls to mind the bodhisattvas Jizō and Kannon, both of whom are known to take on the burdens of sentient beings in need.[69]

Prolongation of Life

The protective function of Fudō led naturally to a belief in his ability to prolong one's life. Relevant to this capacity was Fudō's relationship with *ḍākiṇīs,* female demons who feed on human flesh and blood. In the *Mahāvairocana Sūtra* these ghoulish creatures are tamed by Mahākāla. In certain variants, it is Acala who plays the role of tamer. In Nobumi Iyanaga's essay on the subjugation of Maheśvara, we read: "Acala is the leader of the jackals (in other words, of the *ḍākiṇīs*). That is why he can subjugate them."[70] It is also for that reason that Fudō was believed to prolong the life of his devotees (usually for one or several six-month periods). The implication was that should a person be attacked by soul stealers, a *goma* ritual centered on the four-armed Fudō was the only means of escaping a rapid, terminal decline.[71] These life-prolonging rituals, known in Japanese as Fudō *enmei-hō* 不動延命法, could be repeated indefinitely to prolong the practitioner's life. Thus, they played a role similar to that of rituals centered on Dakiniten and Aizen.[72]

According to the Tendai priest Keien 慶円 (var. Kyōen, 1140–1223), Fudō's life-prolonging rituals were a specialty of Miidera, but because of their similarity to Dakiniten rituals, they were labeled as heterodox by Enryakuji.[73] The Fudō and Dakiniten rituals, then, present essentially two alternative methods to prolong human life. But whereas the Dakiniten ritual simply prevented premature death—that is, the shortening of one's life span—the Fudō ritual, which could be indefinitely repeated, was said to actually extend it.

We catch another glimpse of the relationship between Fudō and Dakiniten in Seigen's (1162–1231) *Usuzōshi,* in which a disciple asks his master why Fudō is still needed since Mahākāla (J. Daikokuten) is already taming the *ḍākiṇīs.* The master offers two contradictory answers: first, Acala and Mahākāla are both avatars of Vairocana; second, while the *ḍākiṇīs* can only delay a premature death by six months, Fudō can actually prolong it indefinitely by six-month increments.[74] A person whose life is threatened by soul stealers can placate the *ḍākiṇīs* either by worshiping them directly or by seeking aid from more powerful deities such as Mahākāla (Daikokuten) and Acala (Fudō). As we have seen, these formidable deities were able to tame *ḍākiṇīs,* or at least hinder their ghoulish action.

Fudō was also thought to protect against sudden death caused by epidemics. A case in point is the Fudō ritual performed by the Kajūji priest Kanjin 寛信 (1084–1153) during the reign of retired emperor Toba in the midst of an epidemic that was devastating the capital. The ritual involved twenty attendant monks and was performed for a one-week period inside the imperial palace, eventually bringing an end to the epidemic.[75] Fudō and his acolytes were also invoked at the time of death in order to avoid demonic obstacles and obtain a better rebirth.[76] In one fascinating tale the *onmyōji* Abe no Seimei falls into a stupor and is brought in front of King Yama to be judged. He is saved *in extremis* by Fudō, who here plays a role usually attributed to the bodhisattva Jizō. King Yama then bestows upon him the "seal of rebirth in paradise" (*ōjō gokuraku-in* 往生極楽印).[77] Fudō could also be called upon to revive a person who had fallen into a coma. A famous example is that of Lady Murasaki in the *Tale of Genji* (*Genji monogatari* 源氏物語), who is brought back to life for five more years as a result of the performance of a Fudō ritual.[78]

FUDŌ'S CULT IN JAPAN

Images of Fudō and the five wisdom kings were first brought to Japan by Kūkai and his successors. During the Heian period the Fudō cult developed as part of the growing popularity of rituals for the protection of the state.[79] While initially Fudō was simply a *primus inter pares* among the five wisdom kings, he gradually became the object of an independent cult. Nevertheless, the cult of the five wisdom kings remained popular, and one should avoid positing a linear evolution in which the individual deity's prominence grew at the expense of the wisdom king quintet from which he emerged.

Fudō was the *honzon* of earth-placating rituals (*anchin-hō* 安鎮法). His chthonian powers are related—as cause or effect—to his central position in the epistemological model of the five phases (in which the earth element is associated with the center). The most common expression of this pentadic model is the group of the five wisdom kings, but it is also evident in the five-colored Fudō: the Fudō at the center is yellow, the color of the earth element. Fudō gradually subsumed the other four *myōō*, who then came to be perceived as emanating from him. In this development his spatial functions related to the center are evident, but in this capacity he had not yet become a protector of individuals.

The Yellow Fudō (Ki Fudō 黄不動) of Onjōji (Miidera) is an idiosyncratic Japanese image that was not inherited from the continental tradition, and it served as a transition between Fudō as one member of the group of five wisdom kings and the individualized image of Fudō.[80] This Yellow Fudō is known as one of the "three Fudō," the other two being the Blue Fudō of Shōren-in 青蓮院, in Kyoto, and the Red Fudō of Myōō-in

明王院, on Mount Kōya.[81] Muscular (like Vajrapāṇi) and with fangs protruding, Yellow Fudō was a "hidden buddha" that only esoteric masters (*ajari* 阿闍梨) could see and then only during initiation rites (*denpō kanjō* 伝法灌頂).

The Tendai priest Enchin (814–891) is said to have had a vision of the Yellow Fudō in 838 as he was practicing austerities in the mountains. Fudō appeared to him as a golden man and told Enchin that he would "attach himself to him like his shadow" and protect him. Although the earliest iconographic representation of Yellow Fudō is said to be based on Enchin's vision, art historians date it from after Enchin's death.[82] In several hagiographical sources, Enchin himself is said to be a manifestation of Fudō. The *Tales of Times Now Past* gives an account of Enchin's voyage to China in which Fudō manifests himself to the Tendai monk in dire straits. The boat carrying Enchin had drifted to the Ryūkyū Islands for lack of wind. Fudō then appeared and a strong wind arose, pushing the boat toward the mainland. Later, Fudō appeared again to Enchin as the latter was lying sick in bed in China.[83]

As Karen Mack points out, legends around Enchin developed around the Insei period at a time when Onjōji (Jimon 寺門), in its attempt to become independent from Enryakuji (Sanmon 山門), was trying to obtain imperial authorization for an ordination platform. The legend that Fudō transmitted information about the initiation rites to Enchin would have been extremely relevant in that context.[84]

Sōō and Fudō

With the various legends and accounts that I have presented one begins to see that Enchin was instrumental in the emergence of an individualized Fudō cult. Other monks participated in this process, though. One of them was Sōō 相応 (831–918), the founder of Mudōji 無動寺, an important cultic center of Fudō on Mount Hiei.[85] Sōō inherited the Fudō ritual from Ennin and performed it on several important occasions. According to his biography, Sōō was conceived when his mother dreamed that she swallowed a sword. The sword is of course one of the implements carried by Fudō, and this legend can therefore be seen as a pious attempt to establish Sōō's affinity with this Buddhist deity. Furthermore, the link posited relates to Sōō's actual conception and prenatal existence, thereby emphasizing the profundity and duration of the relationship. Sōō's connection to Fudō is of obvious importance, seeing that Fudō is the main object of devotion in *kaihōgyō* 回峰行 practice (the ill-named Hiei "Marathon"), of which Sōō is the purported founder.[86] Sōō is well known as a *shugen* practitioner. One legend tells of his vision of Fudō while practicing under a waterfall on the Kazura River northeast of Kyoto.[87] He jumped into the water and dragged Fudō to the bank, only to realize that he was holding the trunk of a *katsura* tree (a name homonymous with that of the river).

He later carved an image of Fudō from this trunk. On another occasion, Fudō carried Sōō to Tuṣita heaven, but Sōō was unable to enter because he could not recite the *Lotus Sūtra* by heart.[88] According to the *Kazuragawa engi* 葛川縁起, Sōō met an old man near the aforementioned waterfall who told him that he had been the landlord of that area since the beginning of the present age, at which time the three worlds (of desire, form, and formlessness) had not yet separated. He introduced himself as the god Shikobuchi 思古淵 (var. 志古淵) Daimyōjin and also claimed to be an avatar of Fudō.[89] Sōō subsequently founded the Myōō-in 明王院 near that waterfall and enshrined Fudō as its main deity. Sōō was also instrumental in the development of a cult centered on Hira Myōjin 比良明神, in the same area, near the shore of Lake Biwa.

Such apparitions of Fudō were of great importance to the process by which Fudō came to be associated with particular locations within the Tendai tradition. This can be usefully juxtaposed with Fudō's appearances in the ritual arena, in which Fudō is not tied to a particular place and is consequently able to appear anywhere. The waterfall episode, then, indicates an important aspect of the localization of Fudō.

Sōō is also renowned for exorcizing a malevolent spirit that had taken possession of the Somedono 染殿 empress.[90] Furthermore, in 903 Sōō conducted a seven-day Fudō ritual for the recovery of the Vinaya master Genshō 玄昭 (844–915).[91] In the Somedono episode, Shinzei 真済 (also known as Ki no Sōjō 柿本僧正, the monachal rector of the Ki clan), is described as a "heavenly fox" (*tenko* 天狐), a term that could refer to the *tengu,* but also to the spirit-animal associated with Dakiniten, a Japanese transformation of the Indian *ḍākinī.*[92] This image further brings to mind Izuna Gongen 飯網権現, a *shugen* deity that looks like a *tengu,* stands on a fox, and clutches Fudō's symbols, the sword and the noose.[93]

Pacification Rituals

The simultaneous outbreak in 940 of the rebellions of Fujiwara no Sumitomo 藤原純友 in western Japan and Taira no Masakado 平将門 in eastern Japan constituted another turning point in the development of the Fudō cult.[94] In order to quell these rebellions, the court asked esoteric priests to perform rituals of subjugation. The Tendai priests Son'i 尊意 (866–940) and Enshō 延昌 (880–964) performed Fudō rituals at Enryakuji and Hosshōji, respectively. In addition, the "Wave-cleaving Fudō" (Namikiri Fudō 浪切り不動) of Mount Kōya was taken to Owari province, while the Shingon priest Kanjō 寛朝 (916–998) transferred the Fudō statue of Jingoji to Shinshōji 新勝寺 on Mount Narita 成田山 (where it has remained the *honzon* down to the present day).[95] In 923, Son'i had performed a seven-day Fudō ritual to coincide with the birth of the royal consort (*chūgū* 中宮); he had subsequently become the child's protector monk (*gojisō* 護持僧). He also became the *gojisō* of Emperor

Daigo 醍醐 (r. 897–930) after lightning struck the imperial palace in 930, an incident attributed to the vengeful spirit of Sugawara no Michizane 菅原道真. His protection proved insufficient, however, since Emperor Daigo died one year later, a death allegedly caused by the same spirit. In 939, Son'i performed a Fudō ritual at Enryakuji to placate Michizane's spirit, who was thought to be behind the recent rebellion of Masakado. It was said that during this ritual Masakado appeared in the *goma* hearth with his bow and arrows. However, as noted earlier, Son'i died soon after the demise of Masakado, and his death was attributed by some to revenge on the part of Masakado's spirit. Another example of a Fudō-centered ritual performed for the purpose of pacification was that conducted by Chūkai 忠快 (1162–1227), founder of the Ogawa-ryū 小川流 (a branch of Taimitsu). Chūkai performed this particular Fudō ritual in order to quell the rebellion of Wada no Yoshinori 和田義盛 (1147–1213).

Near the end of the Heian period, many private Fudō rituals began to develop alongside the state-centered rites. These rituals were commissioned by individual aristocrats or aristocratic families rather than by the *ritsuryō* 律令 state.[96] The rise of Fudō and other wisdom kings coincided with the growing fear of malevolent spirits intent on taking revenge on their former enemies (*goryō* 御霊), in particular on members of the ruling Fujiwara clan. Fujiwara females, being the weakest members of the clan, were particularly prone to possession by alien forces, and in such cases rituals of subjugation were deemed necessary. Fujiwara no Michinaga 藤原道長 (966–1027?), who had married his three daughters Shōshi 彰子 (988–1078), Kenshi 妍子 (994–1027), and Ishi 威子 (999–1036), to emperors Ichijō 一条 (r. 986–1011), Sanjō 三条 (r. 1011–1016), and Go-Ichijō 後一条 (r. 1016–1036), respectively, called on Fudō and other wisdom kings to insure safe delivery of the imperial heirs. The *Tales of Flowering Fortunes* (*Eiga monogatari* 栄華物語) and other sources give a vivid description of Shōshi's delivery in 1008.[97] The five wisdom kings were also invoked, together with the buddha Yakushi, during the delivery of Taira no Kiyomori's 平清盛 second daughter, Tokuko 徳子 (1155–1213), the future empress dowager Kenrei (Kenreimon'in 建礼門院), in 1178.[98] In the *Tale of the Heike* we are told that during Kenreimon'in's delivery of the future and short-lived emperor Antoku 安徳天皇 (1178–1185), a number of vengeful spirits took advantage of her condition and possessed her. They turned out to be the spirits of former enemies of the Taira clan—e.g., Emperor Sutoku 崇徳 (r. 1123–1142), Fujiwara no Yorinaga 藤原頼長 (1120–1156), Fujiwara bi Narichika 藤原成親 (1138–1177) and his brother, the novice Saikō 西光 (Fujiwara no Moromitsu 藤原師光, d. 1177), and Kikaigashima 鬼界が島 exiles such as the Shingon priest Shunkan 俊寛, 1143–1179).[99] In this case the attendant monks called upon Fudō to help transfer the possessing spirits to mediums.[100] The efficacy of Fudō in cases of childbirth expresses both his (at times black magical) power of subjugation and his power to bestow worldly benefits.

Thanks to the influence of priests like Mongaku and Chūkai, the cult of Fudō developed among warriors during the Kamakura period. In the political struggle between court and bakufu, Fudō was invoked by both sides. For instance, rituals of subjugation aimed at the bakufu were performed by retired emperor Go-Toba during the Jōkyū 承久 Disturbance (1221). One century later, Emperor Go-Daigo 後醍醐, taking as his *honzon* the Red Fudō (Aka Fudō 赤不動, so named because it had allegedly been colored by Enchin's blood), had the priests Enkan 円観 (1281–1356) and Monkan 文観 (1278–1357) perform similar rituals under the pretense of performing childbirth rituals for the imperial consort.[101] The bakufu was informed of this and arrested the two priests. Monkan was sent into exile while Enkan was eventually released. According to the *Taiheiki* 太平記, his release was the result of an ominous dream by Hōjō Takatoki 北条高時 (1303–1333) in which the monkeys of the Sannō deity appeared to protect Enkan, who sat silently in meditation, casting a shadow shaped like Fudō.[102] The *Taiheiki* and similar sources emphasize the efficacy of Fudō's subjugation rituals. But here Fudō's function of individual protection (of Enchin) is transferred to general rituals of subjugation, in this case a ritual of state protection. This latter example is not so different from black magic.

The Diffusion of the Cult

The popularity of Fudō in medieval Japan is indicated by the numerous miracle tales involving him, as well as by the many rock carvings of Fudō. The carved images are either in anthropomorphic form (as a wrathful youth) or in symbolic form (e.g., as a lone sword or as a sword with a dragon coiled around it, called the Kurikara 倶梨伽羅 form) (see Fig. 3.20).[103] Fudō closely followed the bodhisattvas Kannon and Jizō in popularity, and the cultic process that pushed him into the limelight radically changed his nature. Without going into the details of his cult, I would like to note the main elements that may have contributed to its diffusion beyond the monastery walls, first among the nobility, then the warriors, and ultimately the populace at large. In the process Fudō also became the main deity of Shugendō.[104]

One of the most famous representations of Fudō is the Wave-cleaving Fudō on Mount Kōya, a statue allegedly carved by Kūkai while in China. During Kūkai's return trip to Japan, his boat was caught in a storm. He was saved when Fudō appeared and parted the waves with his sword, causing the storm to abate. As already mentioned, this statue was allegedly transferred from Mount Kōya to Owari to serve as the *honzon* of subjugation rituals during the rebellions of Fujiwara no Sumitomo in western Japan and Taira no Masakado in eastern Japan. It was

無動経), a short text recited by *shugenja,* we read: "Because he is in substance identical to space, [Fudō] has no dwelling place. He simply dwells in the mind of beings."[136] After reciting the *sūtra,* the *shugenja* recites the names of Fudō's thirty-six acolytes in order to dispel calamities.

According to a collection of oral traditions concerning the secret rituals practiced in Mount Hiko *shugen,* Fudō allows the practitioner to progress from the initial stage (*bodhicitta,* J. *hosshin* 発心 or *bodaishin* 菩提心) to full buddhahood, he protects and watches over his spiritual growth, and prevents him from regressing or falling into evil paths. He is therefore worshiped as the main deity of the ten realms of rebirth, and his appearance is said to symbolize the ten realms, following a detailed symbolism.[137] At the end of his ascetic practice, the *shugenja* receives Fudō's secret seal (mudrā), and when he forms that mudrā, he identifies himself with Fudō. As symbol of the ten realms, Fudō represents the whole universe, the realms of both delusion and awakening.[138]

En no Gyōja 役行者 is said to be an avatar of Fudō, while his two demonic servants, Zendōki 善童鬼 and Myōdōki 妙童鬼 (or Zenki 前 鬼 and Gōki 後鬼), are identified with Kongara and Seitaka.[139] The two demonic acolytes of En no Gyōja are further identified with the two great mandalas of Shingon, while En no Gyōja sitting between them represents the nonduality of the Womb and Vajra realms. More specifically, the blue demon, corresponding to the Dainichi of the Womb mandala, is said to be the messenger of the good, while the red demon, corresponding to the Dainichi of the Vajra Realm mandala, is said to be the messenger of evil. As such, they correspond to the "companion spirits" (*kushōjin* 俱生神) born at the same time as the individual. In this way, En no Gyōja, representing the nonduality of good and evil as well as Fudō's dharma body (*hosshin* 法身, Skt. *dharmakāya*), overlaps with the individual.[140] Indeed, we know that the practitioner must imagine himself to be identical with Fudō. The triad formed by Fudō and his two acolytes was thus interpreted as symbolizing the practitioner and his two companion spirits.

LATENT SYMBOLISM

Iconographic details trigger imagination and doctrinal innovation. Yet they can function at times as a red herring, distracting us from more essential cultural meanings (for which even an "iconological" interpretation à la Panofsky may not be sufficient). Yet in the case of esoteric Buddhism one cannot simply dismiss the traditional details as irrelevant, since they play an essential role (in principle) in a perfect visualization—the morphing from seed-letter (*bijā*) into conventional (*samaya*) form, and into the living form of the deity, resulting in the creation of a "true" eidetic image without which the ritual would remain dead letter. We must emphasize again the role of visualization as the symbolic matrix that produces the

FIGURE 3.23. (*Left*) Fudō cliff carving. Late Heian/ early Kamakura period. Kumano magaibutsu, Kunisaki peninsula, Kyūshū. Photo Bernard Faure.

FIGURE 3.24. (*Right*) Detail of Fudō cliff carving. Late Heian/early Kamakura period. Kumano magaibutsu, Kunisaki peninsula, Kyūshū. Photo Bernard Faure.

esoteric pantheon, and as a meditative practice that allows the practitioner to mentally manipulate or manufacture (yes, mental images have hands) and thereby control reality. The details, in this case, serve as handles for such handling.[141]

In the case of Fudō, while the symbolism of the center and of the enlightenment and ignorance of the mind is often expressed in texts and images in explicit terms, much of this deity's significance remains unstated, yet everywhere evident. In this section I discuss several strains of implied symbolism operating beneath Fudō's superficial appearance. These are his function as a chthonian deity, his relationships with his acolytes (through which Fudō's previous status as servant is expressed), his position as one member of various dyads, and his role in matters gestational and embryological.

Fudō as Chthonian Power

Fudō is first and foremost a chthonian deity. The identification of Fudō with the earth in the five-phase schema assured this deity a position at the heart of earth-quelling rituals. This facet of Fudō explains his frequent association with waterfalls, *nāgas,* rocks, and cliffs. A case in point is the Kumano Fudō, a giant image that is one of the cliff engravings at Kumano on the Kunisaki peninsula in northern Kyūshū (see Figs. 3.23 and 3.24).

Fudō's role as the *honzon* of earth-quelling rituals is also surely due in part to the fact that his name alludes to the essential quality of the earth, firmness (as found in the name of the earth deity, Kenrō Jijin 堅牢地神). In a land prone to earthquakes there is of course a very real need to preserve this quality. This might explain in part the rigidity of Fudō representations in Japan, which stands in stark contrast to that of the Indian Acala, who is usually represented in dynamic posture.[142]

FIGURE 3.25. Sanbō Kōjin. Edo period. Sheet, ink on paper. University Art Museum, Kyoto City University of Arts. *BZS* 4090.

The *Kakuzenshō*, quoting the *Golden Light Sūtra*, states that Kichijōten, as "mother of all buddhas, is the immutable mind (*fudōshin*) of the earth deity (Kenrō Jijin)."[143] Kichijōten is the *honzon* of the *zōyaku goma* 増益護摩, a fire ritual performed to increase worldly benefits. She shares this function with the wish-fulfilling jewel and with the corresponding buddha, Hōshō 宝生 (Skt. Ratnasambhava).[144] Fudō is identified with Kenrō Jijin and Kichijōten, as well as with the wish-fulfilling jewel (*cintāmaṇi*), as a symbol of fertility and fecundity.

Fudō and Kōjin

In the foundational rites of esoteric Buddhism, the earth deity (Skt. Pṛthivī, J. Jiten 地天, Kenrō Jijin, or simply Jijin), in its manifestation as Kōjin 荒神, was often associated with Fudō (Fig. 3.25). In the *Hishō mondō* 祕鈔問答 by Raiyu 頼瑜 (1226–1304), the identity of Fudō with the earth deity of the lotus repository world (*kezō sekai* 華蔵世界) is said to be the reason he is often represented with a lotus on the crown of his head.[145]

As chief deity of the *goma* ritual, Fudō, immersed in his fire-producing *samādhi* (*kashō zanmai*) that burns all defilements, is closely related to the fire god Agni (J. Katen 火天), who also symbolizes Dainichi's fire of knowledge. This is why in subjugation rituals Fudō is represented inside a triangle, a shape that symbolizes fire. This symbolic element also links him to Kōjin, a deity associated with fire and purification. These linkages are reflected in the sequence of the *goma* ritual. After an initial series of visualizations, the fire is lighted, first for Katen (Agni), then for the *honzon,* Fudō. It is lighted one more time for the other deities of the Womb mandala, and finally, for the worldly deities.[146]

Fudō's commemorative day (*ennichi* 縁日) falls on the twenty-eighth of the month, and it is particularly important in the first, fifth, and ninth months. Significantly, this date is the same as that of Kōjin's *ennichi*. It is the day when people attempt to placate evil spirits and the spirits of the dead by offering them *kagura* 神楽 dance performances.[147] The same link appears in legends about Rōben 良弁 (689–722), the second patriarch of the Japanese Kegon school. In these stories, Rōben meets an old man who shows him where to build a temple dedicated to Fudō and asks to be worshiped as Sanbō Kōjin.[148]

Fudō was also associated with Shōten 聖天 (Kangiten 歡喜天), a deity that is identified with Kōjin. Fudō and Kangiten are both called "great saint" (daishō 大聖). The *Tenjin engi emaki* 天神縁起絵巻 (a text also known as *Kangiten reiken ki* 歡喜天霊験記), for instance, recounts how the Tendai priest Son'i officiated a nation-pacifying ritual centered on Fudō (Fudō *anchin kokka-hō* 不動安鎮国家法) to quell Taira no Masakado's rebellion.[149] An important passage, however, reports that during that ritual the Kangiten statuette worshiped at the side altar flew away like an arrow and Masakado's head dropped onto the main altar.[150] According to the *Minōji himitsu engi* 箕面寺秘密縁起, Mount Minō (near Osaka), the cultic site of both Shōten and Kōjin, was discovered by the ascetic En no Gyōja. This ascetic had been initiated by the bodhisattva Nāgārjuna and the goddess Benzaiten, who appeared to him in a vision. He subsequently had a vision of Fudō by the waterfall.[151] Vināyaka (Kōjin) was also perceived as a powerful demon king, whom only a few Buddhist deities can tame: namely, Gundari Myōō (Amṛtakuṇḍalin), Ususama Myōō (Ucchuṣma), Kongō Dōji 金剛童子 (Vajrakumāra), and, of course, Fudō. At any rate, Fudō's affinities with this demon reveal his deep ambivalence.

Fudō's Acolytes

Just as important as the image of a lone Fudō were the semiotic systems in which he occupied the central position. These included not only the cluster of five wisdom kings, but also many groups made up of his acolytes.[152] These acolytes tended to exhibit characteristics visible in Fudō *qua* servant (rather than in his role as tamer). Consequently, the image of Fudō with youthful acolytes (*dōji*) at his side can be seen as a representation of the full scope of Fudō's potential powers, the acolytes serving as a channel by which such potentialities could reemerge. Moreover, due to their position as separate yet associated figures, the acolytes revealed Fudō's dark side—and facilitated his harnessing of those powers—without seriously threatening their master's status as tamer, a status that Fudō acquired by concealing his previous identity.

With this in mind, there are two important points to notice with regard to the iconography discussed below. First, images in which Fudō's appearance exhibits *dōji*-like characteristics serve to remind us of this deity's former position. Such images also draw our attention to the fact that the two traditions, or two identities, of Fudō can never be fully disentangled. Second, depictions of Fudō and his entourage constituted an opportunity to personify Fudō's various attributes. Accordingly, one *dōji* will personify Fudō's compassion, while another will personify his ability to prolong life. With this in mind, let us turn to the details.

Unlike the other *myōō,* Fudō is usually accompanied by acolytes in varying numbers, usually two or eight (as in Fig. 3.26), but sometimes thirty-six.[153] They represent the elemental, untamed forces of nature, which the practitioner attempts to harness. Fudō and his acolytes brought about a shift whereby these elemental powers moved to the center of Buddhist rituals and theology. His two most common acolytes, Kongara 矜羯 羅 and Seitaka 制多迦, also appear as the last two in the list of eight great *dōji.* The first two in this list of eight constitute another couple, Ekō Dōji 慧光童子 (or Ekō Bosatsu 慧光菩薩, Skt. Matijvala) and Eki Dōji 慧喜 童子 (or Eki Bosatsu 慧喜菩薩, Skt. Matisādhu), who correspond to the east and the south, respectively.

FIGURE 3.26. Fudō's eight attendants. Edo period. Sheet, ink on paper. University Art Museum, Kyoto City University of Arts. *BZS* 2151.

According to Lokesh Chandra, rituals that mention the eight *dōji* were fabricated in China.[154] In Japanese representations, the eight companions of Fudō belong to two different categories: three *dōji*, looking very much like Fudō, and five servants, depicted in a kneeling position with their hands in prayer.[155] The eight *dōji* symbolize the eight directions, starting from the east, and were also subject to soteriological and embryological interpretations.[156]

The characteristics that Fudō exhibited as a servant were overshadowed by the apotropaic powers of the wrathful *myōō,* but they resurfaced in his acolytes, a development which in turn influenced the ever-changing image of Fudō. For example, in a thirteenth-century drawing preserved at the Nara National Museum, Fudō is represented as a handsome youth, seated, holding a sword and noose (see Fig. 3.17 above).[157]

Fudō's status is ambiguous: he is the master of his acolytes (in which case he represents the practitioner who ritually identifies himself with Fudō), but also their double (or, more accurately, their nondual origin). In this sense he represents the servant of the practitioner, the dark power that protects and follows him "like his shadow." Sōō, for instance, was said to be under the constant protection of Oto Gohō, a divine youth who was in fact an emanation of Fudō.[158] Legend has it that, on one occasion, Oto Gohō saved him from drowning when he tried to cross the flooding Kazura River.[159]

Kongara and Seitaka

Fudō was initially represented as a *dōji* but his image eventually split into those of Kongara (Skt. Kimkara) (Fig. 3.27) and Seitaka (Skt. Ceṭaka) (Fig. 3.28). As the *Keiran shūyōshū* puts it, "Kongara and Seitaka are Fudō's acolytes because they are transformations of him."[160] Their servile nature is reflected in their name (the Sanskrit *ceṭaka,* in particular, means "slave"). It is also symbolized by their topknots: the five hair tufts were the mark of banished people and slaves.[161]

The Secret Ritual of the Dhāraṇī of the Acolyte Acala (*Budong zhishe tuoluoni bimi fa* 不動使者陀羅尼秘密法) explains the appearance of the two youths and their names. Kongara is said to look like a fifteen-year-old boy with a white body (Fig. 3.29). His hands are usually joined in respect (*gasshō* 合掌) and he wears a monastic robe (*kesa* 袈裟).[162] Seitaka's body is red; he holds a *vajra* in his left hand and a *vajra* staff in his right (Fig 3.30). We are told that because of his evil nature he does not wear a *kesa.*[163] He is sometimes represented riding a horse or a lion.[164] Kongara and Seitaka are said to symbolize the Dharma-essence and ignorance, respectively, and to be in charge of good and evil—a terminology that links them to Jizō's acolytes, the "boys of good and evil" (*zen'aku dōji* 善悪童子) (Fig. 3.31).

FIGURE 3.27. Kongara on lion. *Kakuzenshō. DNBZ* 48: 299.   **FIGURE 3.28.** Seitaka on horse. *Kakuzenshō, DNBZ* 48: 301.

Fudō, who dwells in the spirit of beings, is said to pervade Kongara's obedient nature and Seitaka's disobedient nature; in other words, as symbol of nonduality, he transcends the moral dualism represented by his two acolytes.

In a remarkable painting depicting the two-headed Aizen (Ryōzu Aizen, a composite deity formed by Aizen and Fudō), Kongara and Seitaka appear riding an elephant and a lion—traditionally the mounts of Fugen and Monju (see Figs. 5.6 and 5.7 below). They are shooting arrows at a fox and a bird (perhaps a kite), respectively, a scene that suggests that the painting was used for an exorcism.[165] That they were invoked in such exorcisms is suggested by the *Kakuzenshō,* which describes a method to make Kongara appear on the night of the new moon.[166] (Here we are dealing not just with a visualization, but with a real apparition.) In Raiyu's *Hishō mondō,* Kongara is said to be a manifestation of the bodhisattva Kanjizai 観自在 (Kannon), and because the latter rules over the Lotus clan of the Womb mandala, Kongara holds a lotus. Seitaka is a manifestation of Vajrapāṇi,and therefore represents the Vajra clan. Fudō, of course, represents the Buddha clan.[167] Kongara and Seitaka are also said to be transformations of the dragon Kurikara (i.e., Fudō in his fundamental body).[168]

The representations of the two acolytes are color coded: green (corresponding to the eastern direction and the beginning of things) and red (corresponding to the southern direction and the developmental phase); in embryological terms, they correspond to the stages called *gararan* (Skt. *kalalaṃ*) and *abudon* (Skt. *arbudaṃ*), two of the five stages of fetal

FIGURE 3.29. Kongara, by Unkei. 1198. Color on wood. Kongōbuji, Kōyasan.

FIGURE 3.30. Seitaka, by Unkei. 1198. Color on wood. Kongōbuji, Kōyasan.

gestation; in soteriological terms, they symbolize the first two of the four gates that, in esoteric Buddhist and *shugen* practice, spatially define the ritual area and mark out the soteriological process.

In the *Chūgen hiteiki* 柱源秘底記, the two acolytes correspond to the Womb and Vajra realms, and to the two demonic acolytes of En no Gyōja. The first demon's green face symbolizes the water of compassion, his open mouth the letter *a;* the second demon's red face symbolizes the fire of knowledge, his closed mouth the letter *hūṃ*.[169] Accordingly, Fudō (or En no Gyōja) symbolizes the nonduality of the two mandalas,

FIGURE 3.31. Kongara and Seitaka as acolytes of the bodhisattva Jizō. Edo period. Sheet, ink on paper. University Art Museum, Kyoto City University of Arts. *BZS* 2114.

what in Tendai is called the Realization (*susiddhi*) realm. Because they "follow the person *like the shadow follows the body*," Kongara and Seitaka are said to correspond to the companion (*kushōjin*) and protecting (*gohō*) spirits of Buddhism, and to the helper spirits (*shikigami* 式神) of Onmyōdō.[170]

Ekō Dōji and Eki Dōji

While Kongara and Seitaka are the most famous of Fudō's eight acolytes, Ekō Dōji and Eki Dōji are actually considered the first two. Ekō's body is white, he wears a diadem, and holds a three-pronged *vajra* in his right hand and a lotus topped with a moon disk in his left hand (Fig. 3.32). Eki's body is red (like a red lotus, we are told), and he is compared to the light of the sun. He wears a golden diadem, and he holds a trident in his right hand, a wish-fulfilling jewel in his left (Fig. 3.33).[171] Following the cosmological schema of the five phases, Ekō corresponds to the eastern direction, Eki to the southern direction.

Oto Gohō and Tarōten

Oto Gohō was well known as a protecting deity of Mount Sefuri 背振 in northern Kyūshū (a mountain that owes its name, Trembling Back, to the belief that it is actually the back of a dragon). Scholars have been arguing whether this divine youth was a local Kyūshū deity brought to the Kinai region by Tendai monks, or the other way around. Koyama Satoko, in her recent work on the *gohō dōji*, thinks that he was more likely brought to Kyūshū by Hieizan monks.[172] At any rate, this deity calls to mind another youthful deity worshiped on the Kunisaki peninsula, Tarōten 太郎天. The Chōanji 長安寺 triad formed by Tarōten

FIGURE 3.32. Ekō Dōji. 13th century. Color on wood. Kongōbuji, Kōyasan.

FIGURE 3.33. Eki Dōji, by Unkei. 1198. Color on wood. Kongōbuji, Kōyasan.

and his two acolytes (Fig. 3.34) is strongly reminiscent of that formed by Fudō, Kongara, and Seitaka (see, for example, Fig. 3.35).[173] An inscription dated 1130 and a copy of Fudō's nineteen contemplations (*Fudō-son jūkyūkan* 不動尊十九観想) were found inside Tarōten's statue. Unlike Oto Gohō and other demonic *gohō,* however, Tarōten looks like one of those heavenly youths that were said to protect the believers of the *Lotus Sūtra,* and it is no coincidence that the date of the creation of its statue corresponds to the high point of the practice of sūtra burials in northern Kyūshū (in particular on Mount Kubote, Mount Hiko, and Mount Sefuri). This type of youth, with his hair forming two locks on the sides of his head, looks like the novices (*chigo*) of Buddhist temples, and in particular

FIGURE 3.34. Tarōten and two acolytes. 1130. Color on wood. Chōanji (Ōita prefecture).

like the young Shōtoku Taishi. In spite of their pleasant and elegant aspect, however, *dōji* were clearly identified with the wrathful Fudō. This same ambiguity is found in another youthful deity from Hie Shrine, Jūzenji 十禪師, who was well known for his habit of taking possession of children and using them as his mouthpiece.[174] Tarōten is also the name of the chief *tengu* of the nearby Mount Kubote. Thus, the Tarōten of Chōanji may represent a local variant of the Fudō cult, a return to the image of Fudō as a *dōji,* combined with a new conception of the *dōji* as a mixture of demonic and heavenly features.

Pushing the reasoning one step further, we come to see that, in such triads, the stable elements are the two acolytes Kongara and Seitaka, whereas the central figure (Fudō, Tarōten, or Jizō) can vary. Furthermore, the identity between Fudō and Tarōten, on the one hand, with the resemblance between Tarōten and Jūzenji (an emanation or trace of Jizō) on the other hand, has some interesting implications. As we will see, Jūzenji was perceived in the Tendai tradition as a placenta deity whereas Jizō was a protector of children—living, born dead, and yet-to-be-born children. All this reinforces the suggestion that Kongara and Seitaka have affinities with the companion spirits (*kushōjin*), and that the Fudō triad is a representation of the powers that protect individuals—before as well as after their birth.

The diversity of Fudō's acolytes expresses his multifaceted nature, his powers and virtues.[175] The fact that Fudō was initially described as a *dōji* (and a servant) accounts for a trajectory vastly different from that of the other *myōō.* Although theologically speaking Fudō is an emanation of the buddha Dainichi, his youthful appearance underscores the fact that he is (or was) himself an acolyte, an emissary (*shisha* 使者) or even a servant of the buddha Dainichi.[176] He is at the same time the "leader of all buddhas" because he symbolizes the thought or seed of awakening. This explains his ambiguity: while a double or servant of the practitioner, he also symbolizes the practitioner's true nature.

The dual nature of Fudō (and his acolytes) is also suggested by certain black magic–like rituals. One in particular—called Sending Back the

Live Spirits of King Fudō (*Fudō-ō ikiryōgaeshi*)—was performed for the purpose of exorcising a person possessed by an evil spirit. This ritual required the help of wild and powerful protector spirits or spirit servants (called *shikigami* 式神 or *shiki ōji* 式王子) who were hardly individualized, represented as they were by paper cutouts (*gohei* 御幣).[177]

Dualism

The third strand of symbolism at work in the representation of Fudō is his pairing with various deities. I shall address a number of these relationships, ending with a note on sexuality.

In the *Keiran shūyōshū,* the two guardians of the Buddha are Fudō and Bishamonten 毘沙門 天.[178] As the representative of the wisdom kings, Fudō plays the same role as Bishamonten's in representing the four deva kings. The medieval pairing of Fudō and Bishamonten, a common practice reflecting the values of a warrior society, epitomizes the association not only of two cosmological or spatial systems, but of two layers of apotropaic rituals. As we will see, the pairing also follows the logic of nondual polarities, a logic that led to the further pairing of Fudō and Aizen. The *Taiheiki,* for instance, speaks of the two youths (*dōji*) Fudō and Bishamon, who protect the devotees of the *Lotus Sūtra*. The *Keiran shūyōshū* likewise describes Fudō and Bishamonten 毘沙門天 as Dharma protectors (*gohō*) while contrasting them as representatives of esoteric and exoteric Buddhism: "Fudō is the wheel-commanding body of Dainichi, Tamon 多聞 (Bishamonten) the Dharma protector and acolyte of Shaka 釈 迦 (Śākya[muni]). This is why these two worthies are made to protect the true Dharma."[179]

Fudō was also paired with Daiitoku Myōō 大威徳明王 in the *Six-letter Sūtra* (*Rokujikyō* 六字経) mandala, in which both appear flanking a group formed by six spell deities (*susogami*) surrounding a jewel, below the Six Kannon that surround the main deity, Shaka Kinrin (Fig. 3.36).[180] The presence of these spell deities suggests that we are dealing with a subjugation ritual, used to counter curses and return them to their senders.

FIGURE 3.35. Fudō and two acolytes (Mitsume Fudō Myōō). Heian period. Kisshōji, Aritagawa-chō.

FIGURE 3.36.

Six-letter Sūtra mandala. Edo period. Sheet, ink on paper. University Art Museum, Kyoto City University of Arts. BZS 1050(1).

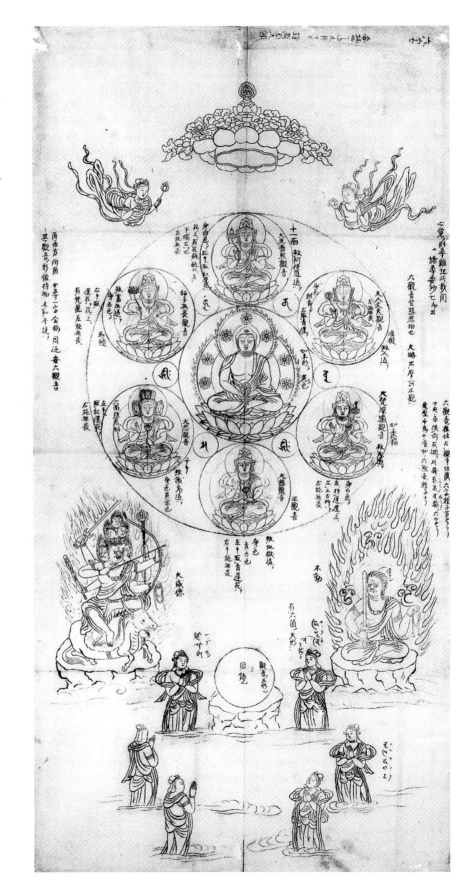

Fudō and Gozanze Redux

Fudō's prototype Acala was often associated (and occasionally identified) with Trailokyavijaya.[181] These two acolytes of Mahāvairocana are like two gatekeepers, and in a sense they are duplicates of Vajrapāṇi (like the wrathful "benevolent kings"—Niō 仁王—who are the guardians of monasteries). In the Womb mandala, they stand on both ends of the Vidyādhara Court (Jimyō-in 持明院), flanking the deified Prajñāpāramitā (Perfection of Wisdom), "Mother of the buddhas."[182] The scriptural source of this representation is the *Mahāvairocana Sūtra*, in which Acala and Trailokyavijaya are the only wisdom kings mentioned by name.[183] Trailokyavijaya is said to be the old king, Acala the young one, representing the beginning and completion of the virtue of perseverance.[184]

In Raiyu's *Usuzōshi kuketsu,* Gōzanze (Trailokyavijaya), who appears as a manifestation of Dainichi Nyorai 大日如来 in order to subjugate the demon king at the apex of the world of desire, is paired with Fudō, another Dainichi manifestation, who subjugates the demon king at the apex of the world of form.[185] In the Godai-in 五大院 section of the Womb mandala, Gōzanze appears twice: in one case, he is paired with Fudō, in the other, under the name Shōsanze, with Daiitoku Myōō. His importance is also reflected in the fact that in the ninefold Vajra Realm mandala, two assemblies or mandalas are devoted to him.[186] In other mandalas, we can see Acala sitting inside a fire triangle (symbolizing Agni), and Trailokyavijaya dancing wildly inside a moon crescent (or a half-moon) that symbolizes wind (and the god Vāyu), i.e., the element that complements fire.[187] Gōzanze is usually paired with Fudō in the so-called Sonshō and Miroku mandalas, in which both deities appear below the *honzon;* Fudō is seated in a triangular enclosure at the bottom right of the image while Gōzanze stands in a half-moon enclosure at the bottom left.

This pairing of Acala and Trailokyavijaya provides us perhaps with an epitome of the five wisdom kings grouping, a method of reduction common in Indian iconographic schemata.[188] In that sense, this pairing differs from the later association of Fudō with Aizen, which, as we will see, has a different symbolic meaning—referring essentially to sexuality and embryology—and undercuts the significance of the wisdom king pentad, since Aizen was never part of it (although in certain ways he is similar to Gōzanze). This representation is found for instance in a mirror supposedly owned by Myōe and preserved at Kōzanji 高山寺 on the outskirts of Kyoto. This mirror was created by the priest Genchō 玄朝 in 1224 for the funeral of his mother. The bodhisattva (and future Buddha) Miroku is carved on the mirrored bottom of the box, while Fudō (seated in a triangle) and Gōzanze (standing in a half-moon) are painted on the lateral doors of the mirror box.[189] Another interesting example is a portable shrine (*zushi* 厨子) from the Nara National Museum; the Siddhaṃ letter *a* lies at the center, Fudō and his two acolytes appear on the right door, and Gōzanze, trampling Daijizaiten (Maheśvara) and his consort (Uma), is portrayed on the left door.[190] In other words, the simplified set (reduced from five to two) takes on a new meaning: it is no longer a simplified mandala, but a representation of the widespread motif of the gatekeepers, well studied by Rolf Stein. This meaning would evolve further with the establishment of the Fudō-Aizen pairing. At any rate, the figure of Acala/Fudō, initially modeled after that of Trailokyavijaya/Gōzanze, came to overshadow the latter. While Fudō is often included in pairs, he comes to represent the third, nondual element. In the *Keiran shūyōshū,* for example, he represents the Dainichi of the Susiddhi (Realization) realm—the realm of the nonduality of the two mandalas in Tendai.[191]

Sexuality

Fudō's iconographic characteristics (such as the eyes, fangs, and other attributes) were interpreted allegorically to signify the polarity of his nature (and of all reality). The shift from duality to sexuality is explicit in marginal texts such as the *Fudōson gushō* 不動尊愚鈔. This relatively late work, influenced by the Tachikawa-ryū 立川流, elaborates on the symbolic meaning of Fudō's two fangs, which express various polarities: the upward-pointing left fang symbolizes the process of elevation toward awakening whereas the downward-pointing right fang represents the bodhisattva's descent to this world to teach sentient beings. The two fangs also symbolize the realms of sentient beings and buddhas, while the nonduality of these realms is expressed by Fudō's tightly closed lips. Furthermore, in a "personal" comment, the author notes that the two fangs correspond to heaven and earth, yang and yin, and male and female. Nonduality, he adds, is expressed (or achieved) by the sexual union of man and woman. Accordingly, the left fang points upward because the yin breath of woman, ascending to heaven, unites with the yang of man; while the right fang points downward because the yang breath of man, penetrating the earth, unites with the yin of woman. In sexual union, heaven and earth fuse and thoughts of desire and pleasure are cut off, revealing the singular taste of nonduality.[192]

Another factor reinforcing the sexual symbolism of Fudō was his identification with the earth in the five phases schema. By giving Fudō an association with the earth's fecundity, this cosmology fostered a symbolism that related Fudō not only to sexual fertility, but also to the role of protecting prenatal life. It is to the latter topic that we now turn.[193]

Embryology

Implicit in many theories and iconographic representations of Fudō is his embryological function, that is, his role in gestation. This function is described in a rather explicit manner in the *Fudōson gushō,* in which Fudō is said to represent the two drops of consciousness that fuse during sexual union. These two drops, one red and the other white, represent the yin and the yang and, more concretely, blood and semen.[194]

In Shugendō, practitioners identify themselves with Fudō through both ritual and attire. Entering the mountain, which is the central feature of Shugendō practice, is likened to gestation. Consequently, this religious process, like pregnancy, culminates with the identification of the practitioner with Fudō. For instance, the descent of the *shugenja* into a mountain cave is described as a descent into the belly of the wisdom king Fudō. With regard to attire, the Fudō robe (Fudō *kesa* 不動袈裟) worn by the *shugenja* not only identifies the practitioner as Fudō but also signifies his transformation into an embryo. In addition, this garment is said to represent Kurikara, the dragon manifestation of Fudō (identified in this context with the goddess Benzaiten).[195] The thick cord worn around the *shugenja*'s waist (*kai no o*) signifies the rope held by Fudō while also symbolizing an umbilical cord (*heso no o*). In the *Secret Traditions amid the Mountains* (*Buchū hiden* 峰中秘伝), a seventeenth-century Shugendō text, the ninth month of pregnancy is said to correspond to (and be protected by) Fudō.[196]

In the *Keiran shūyōshū,* Fudō is the deity who controls fetal gestation. Embryonic development and birth are the purview of Fudō, we are told, while the stages of childhood and adulthood constitute the domain of Dainichi.[197] Fudō also shares with the placenta deity (*enagami*) the function of protecting fetal gestation (and, by extension, the spiritual progress of the *shugenja,* perceived as a symbolic fetus).

Fudō is first on the list of thirteen buddhas that became a central feature of funerary rituals in the late medieval period. As such, he marks (or watches over) the beginning of the rebirth (or gestation) process, the phase of conception. Following medieval Japanese conceptions of gestation, it was thought that during the first seven-day period, which he controls, the liver, hands, and feet of the fetus all emerge. During the six other periods, ruled by Shaka, Monju, Fugen, Jizō, Miroku, and Yakushi, respectively, the rest of the body gradually takes shape.[198] This conception, a late medieval development, is found in Chikamatsu's play *Semimaru* 蝉丸 in a passage on the ten months of pregnancy: "In the first month a spirit takes form within the body. Its shape is just like a hen's egg. Originally this was one drop of seed. As regards its shape, the chaos has not yet been divided. As far as its name is concerned, it is called the Great Origin and the Great Beginning. . . . In Buddhism it is called the Original Vairocana; this is the original essence of the void. It is the responsibility of Fudō Myōō."[199]

When the womb is identified with the Pure Land, the nine months become the nine stages of the Pure Land. It is for this reason, explains the *Buchū hiden,* that there are nine caves at Mount Ōmine 大峰山. These caves constitute a replica of the Pure Land projected onto the Japanese landscape: "The nine-stage Pure Land is the Womb realm (*taizōkai*). The mother is Daishō Fudō Myōō. Because it is the Womb realm, [the fetus] remains there nine months; and so it is called the nine-stage Pure Land."[200]

The same embryological symbolism is developed in Fudō's acolytes. Ekō Dōji, for instance, symbolizes the first of the five stages of gestation, i.e., the moment of conception (called *gararan*). We are told that he is "the foundation where the life of all beings is tied." Eki Dōji corresponds to the second stage of gestation (*abudon*).[201] The *Fudō gushō* explains as follows the symbolism of the five-pronged *vajra* held by Ekō Dōji. The five prongs symbolize the union of man and woman. The upper four prongs and the center correspond to the five elements of the male root— the five knowledges of the Vajra realm. The lower four prongs and the center correspond to the five wheels of the female root—the five buddhas of the Womb mandala. The union of the two symbolizes the nonduality of yin and yang, the fusion of the red and white (i.e., the father's semen and the mother's blood).[202]

In the following chapters, I will mention repeatedly the embryological aspects of the medieval deities I discuss. Yet these remarks will remain as toothing stones. The importance of embryological discourse for medieval Japanese Buddhism is more fully treated in the companion volume, *Protectors and Predators*.

CODETTA

The grouping of the five wisdom kings resulted from a merging of Indian individual deities. Yet even after this development these deities continued to evolve individually within that framework. The unfolding of the Fudō cult constituted a gradual breaking away from the pentadic grid of the five *vidyārājas* toward a more individualized cult in which Fudō stood alone as a separate deity (*besson*). Nevertheless, two caveats are in order.

First, the introduction to Japan of an independent Fudō as the main deity in the fire ritual (*goma*) coincided with the introduction of the five wisdom kings. Therefore, rather than a linear evolution by which the individual emerged from the group, we have two distinct currents that developed simultaneously and in varying degrees of interaction. Complicating matters, the individual Fudō fluctuated between a singular and dual existence. While the individual Fudō did indeed come to great prominence at a certain point in Japanese history, this lone figure was soon reintegrated into a yin-yang duality by being paired with Aizen. This duality, expressed through Fudō's iconography, was further reinforced by the growing importance of his two main acolytes, Kongara and Seitaka. In addition, it set the stage for sexual and embryological readings of the deity, a trend that can also be witnessed in the treatment of the Fudō-Aizen coupling, where the motif of twinship resonated with Fudō's function as a substitute for (*mikawari*) and protector of the individual. The pair formed by Fudō and Aizen, however, never entirely replaced the single Fudō. Rather, the two models coexisted. It is important to note that Fudō's pairing with Aizen—the meaning of which was entirely different from Fudō's initial coupling with Gōzanze—represented a demotion: while their role was important, paired gatekeepers (like the Niō) do not have quite as exalted a status as the wisdom kings and deva kings.

Like Myōken, particularly in his capacity as the pole-star deity, the immobile (and unmovable) Fudō is elusive and unlocalizable. While rising to the top of the esoteric universe, he remains grounded in the earth. Whereas Myōken represents the center of the starry heaven, Fudō represents the center of earthly space. He has no special abode, apart from the mind of beings—or microcosm. On the doctrinal plane, he also symbolizes the universe—or macrocosm. He both founds and subverts the system. He represents both the center and a decentering force, the point of origin and the vanishing point. It is precisely through his immobility that Fudō mobilizes the energies of the individual, of the group, and of the state. As a figure of the origin and of the center, as the first motionless mover, and as the first of the thirteen buddhas, he acquires the embryological symbolism of conception.

To unravel this elusive Fudō requires a tangential, oblique reading of official mythology; it is only through such tangents that systems are undone and subsequently reconstitute themselves. I have therefore mentioned the traditional topoi of art history simply for good measure. In the five wisdom kings grouping, Fudō's immobility is negated (or supplemented) by the strange ballet of the four *myōō* around the central pivot formed by Fudō. Paradoxically, that figure emblematic of the center was eventually repositioned in a dual framework formed by Fudō and Aizen.

As we have seen, the classical Japanese Fudō was the result of the merging of two traditions: Fudō as servant and Fudō as powerful tamer. Yet even after merging, the two failed to fully synthesize and thereby remained in tension within a single figure. The contrast between the two forms of Fudō was initially represented via a juxtaposition of the two-armed Acala with the four-armed Acala. Besides this division between two types of Fudō, one can also distinguish between a symbolic Fudō (e.g., as found in the five phases schema) and a Fudō that, as symbol of the center, paradoxically resists symbolic appropriation: even though he maintains a position within the system's structure, he constantly implies (or refers to) that which is beyond the system's parameters. Similarly, the center is both one of the five points and the foundation of the four directions. Ironically, this renders it both internal and external to the very symbolic system of which it is the anchor and the vanishing point.

To recapitulate: Acala the *vidyārāja* was an evolution of Vajrapāṇi. In Japan Fudō appeared as the main deity of the Ninnōkyō and Anchin mandalas. First described as a servant of Dainichi, he eventually became a Dharma protector (*gohō*), essentially a protector of eminent monks. He is immovable and constitutes therefore a symbol of the center and of origins—hence his close relationship with the earth and the underworld, which in turn linked him to Jizō. Furthermore, his immovability lent itself to allegoric interpretations in which Fudō variously represented the fundamental mind, *bodhicitta,* the *ālaya-vijñāna*, and the *amala-vijñāna.*

In addition to his chthonian character, he symbolizes the highest (and most profound) reality: like Shaka Kinrin, he is often depicted dwelling at the top of Mount Sumeru, that is, the apex of the cosmos. He is the ruler of the five wisdom kings but also of the twelve devas. In his capacity as a tamer (and less often as a gatekeeper), he is associated—and sometimes identified—with Gōzanze (and later with Aizen). He is the main deity of *goma* rituals and (essentially) the subduer of Māra.

An important feature of Fudō's development can be seen in his acolytes—two, eight, or thirty-six in number—who served as a channel through which Fudō's previous attributes as a servant could be personified and united with Fudō *qua* tamer. In addition, Kongara and Seitaka—and, to an even greater extent, Ekō Dōji and Eki Dōji—played an important symbolic role in Buddhist embryology and Fudō's role in that arena.

Throughout this chapter there have been basically three recurring images of Fudō: as servant; as subduer; and as symbol of the center, in which capacity Fudō is essentially a pivot or a representation of the unlocalized mind. These three images combine, then separate, only to combine once again, resulting in different types of Fudō of varying character and function (e.g., the embryological and protective Fudō, modeled after the *kushōjin*). It is by this process that the figure of Fudō acquired its diversity.

4

LUST BUT NOT LEAST

Aizen Myōō

In terms of popularity, the only wisdom king that can vie with Fudō is Aizen Myōō 愛染明王 (Skt. Rāga-vidyārāja) or King Aizen (Aizen-ō 愛染王, Skt. Rāgarāja). Like Fudō, he is the personification of a *dhāraṇī,* and his scriptural source is the *Yuqi jing* (J. *Yugikyō* 瑜祇経), a text allegedly translated into Chinese by Vajrabodhi (671–741). In the first part of this chapter, I examine Aizen's official image as it reflects the explicit theology of Mikkyō. I begin with a discussion of the political context of the Aizen ritual, then proceed to discuss the god's official functions: love (*keiai*) and subjugation (*chōbuku*). After reviewing the main forms of Aizen's iconography, I dwell on some revealing details—among them his empty third left hand, holding the vital essence of beings. This leads, in the second part of the chapter, to an examination of the implicit theology of Aizen as it is disclosed, in particular, by his relations with other deities. This surprising network reveals in due course his embryological function, which complements his sexual and apotropaic functions and is perhaps just as important for understanding Aizen's rise into the pantheon of medieval Japan.

THE POLITICAL CONTEXT

The first Aizen ritual was reportedly performed at the time of Taira no Masakado's rebellion (940), following other subjugation rituals centered on Fudō and similar protectors.[1] Yet there is no actual record of that event. Hayami Tasuku has placed the development of Aizen rituals during the reigns of the retired emperors Go-Sanjō 後三条天皇 (r. 1068–1073) and Shirakawa 白河天皇 (r. 1073–1087), and he has identified Ningai 仁海 (951–1046), the founder of the Ono branch of Shingon, and his disciple Seison 成尊 (1012–1074) as the initiators of such practice.[2] While the ritual may have predated him, Ningai did compile rules about it and transmitted them to his disciples, some of whom were instrumental in the establishment of the Insei rule (1086–1192). The most active among them was Seison, who became the "protecting monk" (*gojisō* 護持僧)

FIGURE 4.6. Aizen seated on a vase. Edo period. Sheet, ink on paper. University Art Museum, Kyoto City University of Arts. *BZS* 2177.

FIGURE 4.7. Standing Aizen. Ryūsenji, Tokyo. Photo Bernard Faure.

have been efficient since she eventually produced an imperial heir. In the Edo period, Aizen was invoked as the Buddhist equivalent of the popular "Binding Kami" (*musubi no kami* 結びの神), as shown in the proverb "If a *kami,* it is the Binding Kami; if a buddha, it is Aizen Myōō."[26]

Not only was Aizen believed to cause desire, however, he was also able to transmute it into awakening. Another of his prototypes is the "bodhisattva of love" Ai Bosatsu 愛菩薩, one of the four emanations of Kongōsatta in the Ritual of the Five Mysteries centered on the Womb mandala. These bodhisattvas symbolize the four passions that produce one another: desire (Yoku Kongō Bosatsu 欲金剛菩薩, Skt. Iṣṭavajra), tactile pleasure (Soku Kongō Bosatsu 觸金剛菩薩, Skt. Kelikilavajra), amorous ardor (Ai Kongō Bosatsu 愛金剛菩薩, Skt. Rāgavajra), and arrogance (Man Kongō Bosatsu 慢金剛菩薩, Skt. Mānavajra).[27] They also symbolize the fact that beings, while externally soiled by passions, still inwardly preserve the seed of awakening (*bodhicitta*). In that way, the four passions acquire a positive value, illustrating the *hongaku* notion that "afflictions are none other than awakening" (*bonnō soku bodai* 煩悩即菩提).

Aizen's sexual connotations derive from the *Yuqi jing* (hereafter *Yugikyō*). The locus classicus is a passage in which the buddha Mahāvairocana enters the "horse penis *samādhi*" (J. *meonzō sanmaji* 馬陰蔵三摩地) to expound the ritual of Rāgarāja. This cryptic expression is glossed as "*samādhi* of the secret organ, hidden like that of the horse." The term *meonzō* itself refers to the so-called cryptorchidy of the Buddha, that is, the belief that his genitalia usually remain hidden. But what actually is this strangely named *samādhi,* out of which Aizen's *vidyā* (mantra) is said to emanate? The *Yugikyō chōmonshō* 瑜祇経聴聞抄 by Chōgō 澄豪 (1259–1350) provides two rather byzantine explanations. First, it argues that "horse penis" is used in reference to the eight horses that draw the cart of the sun deity (Nitten-shi 日天子), one of the twelve devas.[28] In other words, the term simply implies the identity between Aizen and the sun deity. The second explanation is even more far-fetched. This *samādhi,* we are told, is also called "*samādhi* that eliminates all defilements"—because "defilements are produced by ignorance and eliminated by awakening in the same way that the horse's penis appears at the time of coitus and disappears right after."[29] The *Yugikyō* also reports that when the Buddha entered this *samādhi,* his lion roar resounded like thunder. In texts attributed to the Tachikawa-ryū, this lion roar is interpreted as the cry emitted during sexual intercourse by the male Fudō and the female Aizen. According to the *Kakugenshō* 覚源抄 (ca. 1200), a record of the oral teachings of Kakukai 覚海 (1142–1223) and Yūgen 融源 (fl. 1160) by Rendō 蓮道, "This cry of bliss is far louder than that of ordinary [sexual] intercourse."[30] And it adds: "Because common people during sexual intercourse cry out of joy, [the practitioner] also utters the five lion cries."[31] Sexual union is also symbolized (or rather, enacted on a symbolic or spiritual plane) through combined mudrās and mantras. The priest forms a mudrā called "five-pronged *vajra*" or mudrā of the "human form," which symbolizes the union of principle and wisdom.[32] He first repeats the mantra *hūṃ* to empower the two—male and female—half-seals formed by his right and left hands; then, joining his two hands to symbolize sexual intercourse, he utters a double *hūṃ* to express the orgasmic realization of "great bliss" (Skt. *mahāsukha*).[33]

The expression "five-pronged seal" also refers to an actual five-pronged *vajra,* which is the *samaya* or symbolic form of Aizen.[34] This ritual object is also known as an "anthropomorphic *vajra*" (*ningyōsho* 人形杵), because it symbolizes the human body—its upper three prongs representing the head and arms, its lower two prongs the legs. This *vajra,* made

FIGURE 4.10. Aizen Myōō mandala. Kamakura period. Color on silk. Nezu Museum, Tokyo.

FIGURE 4.11. Detail of Aizen Myōō mandala. Kamakura period. Color on silk. Nezu Museum, Tokyo.

FIGURE 4.12. Incense case with Aizen. 13th century. Plain wood. Tōji, Kyoto.

FIGURE 4.13. Aizen Myōō mandala. Edo period. Sheet, ink on paper. University Art Museum, Kyoto City University of Arts. *BZS* 1067.

FIGURE 4.14. Aizen Myōō mandala. *Zuzō shūsei* 9: 10.

In the Ono lineage, Aizen is usually shown seated on or levitating above a tall vase, from which jewels come forth. This vase is the *samaya* form of the earth goddess (Jiten 地天, Skt. Pṛthivī), and it symbolizes prosperity and increase (*zōyaku* 増益, Skt. *pauṣṭika*).[40] Sometimes Aizen is shown seated on a lion, an image that calls to mind not only the usual representations of the bodhisattva Mañjuśrī (Monju), but also that of Bishamonten in the so-called Inari mandala preserved at Fushimi Inari Shrine. The lion also appears in Aizen's headgear as a lion head intended to scare evildoers.[41] One source interprets Aizen's appearance as follows: "The lion diadem means subjugation. The five-pronged hook means captation (*kōshō* 勾召). The three eyes mean wrath. Dwelling in the solar wheel means the *bodhi*-mind. The red body color means seduction (*keiai*), like the red lotus."[42]

Aizen's most conspicuous attributes are his bow and arrows. In the representation known as *Aizen Pointing His Bow at the Sky* (Tenkyū Aizen 天弓愛染), the god holds his weapon "as if he were aiming at the brightness of all the stars" (Fig. 4.15).[43] An oral tradition explains that Aizen is shooting at evil stars that symbolize false thinking, and he manifests himself as a solar disk to dissipate the night's darkness. This is why he is called the "king of stars" (*shō-ō* 星王), a name that he shares with Sonjōō 尊星王, i.e., Myōken.[44] Therefore his shooting at the stars emphasizes his role in maintaining order by subduing demonic astral deities.[45]

Aizen's crimson red color links him not only with the sun, but also with blood and life, and with human passions (hence his name).[46] This characteristic gives him precedence over other gods in matters of seduction (*keiai*, love subduing) rituals. Furthermore, his wrathful aspect designates him as a god of subjugation (*chōbuku*), and his association with jewels qualifies him for rituals of increase (*zōyaku*).[47] While the gods of the esoteric pantheon are polyvalent and can in principle become the *honzon* of the four or five types or esoteric ritual, this polyvalence is more marked in Aizen's case. With Fudō, it is expressed mainly by his acolytes, but for Aizen it is expressed essentially by his attributes. Their variety marks him as a god who responds to all desires. In this, of course, he is not alone. He does so, however, with a relative economy of means that contrasts with the symbolic proliferation shown, for example, by the Thousand-armed Avalokiteśvara (Senju Kannon 千手観音). Indeed, Aizen's iconology represents an elegant solution to the problem of representing functional polyvalence. The six-armed Aizen is not simply a polysemic deity, however. While the iconography of other deities tends to constitute a closed semiotic system, the endless potentiality opened by Aizen's closed fist represents a surplus of meaning that transcends any semiotic system.

The Third Left Hand

The six-armed Aizen holds specific attributes in five of his hands (lotus bud, bow and arrow,

FIGURE 4.15. Tenkyū Aizen (Aizen shooting at the stars). 12th century. Color on wood. Kongōbuji, Kōyasan.

vajra and *vajra* bell). His third left hand is at first glance empty, as if waiting for an object to hold. This object is left to the devotee to visualize in symbolic (*samaya*) form, depending on his or her wishes. Being left to the worshiper's imagination, it becomes a source of endless possibilities. Its mysterious content is referred to simply by a deictic pronoun, "*That*" (kare 彼).[48] While "That" usually remains invisible (or nonactualized) in many Aizen statues, such is not the case in drawings and paintings. Accordingly, this hand is also called the "hand of realization" (*jōju shu* 成就手). Yet there is more in it (or "That") than meets the eye, and this "more" needs to be visualized with the mind's eye. It allows interpretations to shift to a higher register. With "That," one enters the realm of implicit theology (supplemented by oral traditions). Constituting the essence of the Aizen ritual, it reveals (or hides) an important religious aspect of medieval kingship.

The sources give many conflicting interpretations about the nature and meaning of that elusive object (or nonobject). The types of objects (mentally) placed in Aizen's hand vary with the types of ritual performed.[49] The list is at first glance bewildering: it can be a sun disk, a ball or some other "red and round thing," a piece of paper with the name of an individual (the enemy) or a Siddhaṃ letter written on it, or again, a wish-fulfilling jewel.[50] The *Kakuzenshō* states: "The images in the diagrams of the Great Tang are not identical. At times [Aizen] holds a jewel, at other times a human head . . . or again, a hook, a wheel, a piece of armor, a moon disk."[51] Another source elaborates: "There are several levels of meanings as to what Aizen holds in his [third] hand. At the first level, it is the object of one's wishes. At another level, [it can be] a sun disk or a ball of flesh. At the most secret [level, however,] it is the human heart."[52]

But it is not easy—perhaps not even possible—to disentangle all these notions, although they all clearly obey the same underlying logic. The root metaphor is that Aizen holds in his hand the root of life or vital principle of all beings. Let us consider some of these symbols in more detail. One source reports that the Aizen icon in the Uji Repository (Byōdō-in) held the sun disk in its left hand. The same is true of the icon transmitted to retired emperor Shirakawa and enshrined in the Octagonal Hall of Hosshōji.[53] Both images, incidentally, were attributed to Kūkai. Likewise, the Aizen icon that the priest Dōkyō saw at Henchi-in in 1230 "was holding a sun disk with a three-legged crow in it."[54] The motif of the crow is said to derive from the shape of the seed-syllable *hūṃ,* Aizen's symbol. The Fujiwara regents emphasized Aizen's solar symbolism by putting a "red bird" in his hand.[55] In Chōgō's *Yugikyō chōmonshō,* the priest must visualize a three-legged bird inside a sun disk. This sun disk represents the sun goddess Amaterasu and the Buddhist sun god Nittenshi 日天子, while the "red bird" is also an allusion to the ruler.[56] In this fashion, the image of Aizen reinforces the identification between the ruling emperor, Amaterasu, and the sun god Nittenshi.

The disk held by Aizen also represents the vital principle of beings. This principle appears in other forms—as a human head, as the *hun* 魂 (spirit), as the heart or liver, or as a "ball of flesh" (the heart). In the *Besson zakki* 別尊雑記, for instance, Aizen is represented holding a human head in his left hand. This representation obviously corresponds to a subjugation ritual.[57] In his commentary on the *Yugikyō,* Chōgō writes: "Sometimes 'That' is a human head called *hitodama* 人玉 (man-jewel)."[58] According to the Tendai priest Kōgei 皇慶 (var. Kōgyō, 977–1049): "Know that the ball of flesh (the heart), the human head, and the sun disk are identical. If you can realize that, [Aizen's] holding the heart and the *hun* is the same as [his holding] the sun disk; in reality [the latter] is not the sun disk."[59] The *Hishō mondō* 祕鈔問答 by Raiyu 賴瑜 (1226–1304) specifies: "'That' is the liver [i.e., the essence] of the practitioner."[60] What the text calls "ball of flesh" symbolizes the consciousness of beings, which is also called "human king" (or "human yellow"). It equates these various notions (sun disk, ball of flesh, human yellow) with the seed-letter *a* and the wish-fulfilling jewel, both symbolizing the *fons et origo* of all things. Yet the same *Hishō mondō* offers another, more negative interpretation of the content held in Aizen's hand. A gloss on the passage *In his lower left [hand] he holds "That"* reads as follows: "'To hold' means 'to empower' (*kaji* 加 持). 'That' represents the sworn enemy, the defilements." Another passage is more specific: "'That' refers to the obstacles produced by one's own nature. 'To hold' [it] means to cut [these obstacles] and realize [the truth]. By holding [it] one destroys it."[61] In the Ono branch, the human yellow symbolizes fundamental ignorance, that is, the obstacles caused by one's own nature. Likewise, in the *Kakuzenshō,* "That" designates evil people or the defilements arising from ontological ignorance. As we will see, the notion of "obstacles produced by one's own nature" or "inborn obstacles" (*kushō shō* 倶生障, literally "born at the same time as the individual") is closely linked to the belief in companion spirits (*kushōjin*), that is, spirits born at the same time as a person and reporting on that person's actions to the ruler of human destiny, King Yama. In the Ono branch, these inborn obstructions are symbolized by the mysterious substance called "human yellow."

The Human Yellow

Probably the most important element in Aizen's subjugation ritual is the human yellow (*ninnō* 人黄), a term designating not only inborn obstructions but also, more generally, the elusive essence or life force of humans, which *ḍākinīs* and other demons try to steal from them.[62] Depending on the case, it can refer to the vital principle of Aizen's devotee, who requires the god's protection by literally placing himself/herself in his hand (Fig. 4.16); or the vital principle of the devotee's sworn enemy, which he or she asks Aizen to crush.[63]

Like the "ox yellow" (*goō* 牛黄) or bezoar found in cows and other ruminants, the human yellow was conceived of as a substance within the human body that constituted its vital principle. This notion traces back to Yixing's *Commentary on the Mahāvairocana Sūtra.* The Shingon priest Ningai (951–1046) is quoted as saying that: "The human yellow is the true *samaya* form of Aizen."[64] He is also said to have equated this vital essence with the "eightfold flesh ball," a metaphor for the human heart.[65] This substance, also identified with the wish-fulfilling jewel, came to be perceived as the essence of kingship. According to an oral tradition from Kajūji 勧修寺: "Inside oxen there is the ox yellow, inside deer, the deer yellow, and inside humans, the human yellow."[66] The *Kakuzenshō* states: "The human yellow is also said to be the letter *a* inside the human body. This letter is red when one is deluded, white when one is enlightened."[67] Being the essence of the human yellow, the letter *a* is also the seed-letter of the jewel.[68] The *Hishō mondō* emphasizes the homonymy and semantic drift between "human yellow" and "human ruler" (*ninnō* 人王): "The human ruler of a man is his fleshly heart and liver. To prevent the vital breath from being stolen is to hold that man's ruler. You must know that ruler means 'yellow.'"[69]

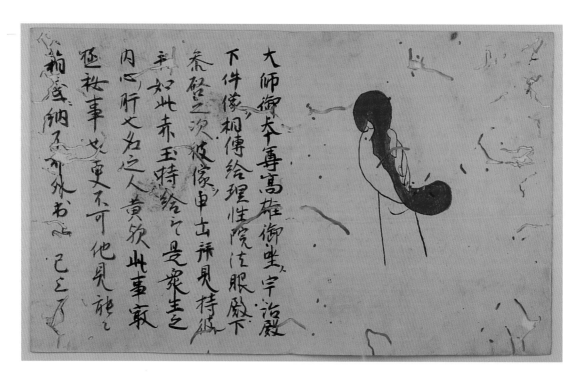

FIGURE 4.16. Human yellow. *Shōgyō.* Kanazawa bunko.

What, then, is this mysterious substance, and where is it found? While the prevalent theory is that the human yellow resides in a person's liver or heart, textual variants describe it as consisting of five, six, seven, or ten grains or drops located on the crown of a person's head. According to Iyanaga Nobumi, these interpretations are based on a misreading of the work of the Tendai master Annen 安然 (b. 841), who wrote that the human yellow consists in seven drops located at the top of the head.[70] The five grains are said to correspond to the five consciousnesses (J. *shiki* 識, Skt. *vijñāna*). The seven grains are already mentioned in the work of the Chinese master Jizang 吉蔵 (549–623), who says that the loss of one or two of these grains causes headaches; three, heartache; five or more, death.[71] According to the *Yugikyō chōmonshō:* "On the top of the head is something called the 'human jewel.' It is formed of seven dew drops."[72] The six grains are described in the *Kakuzenshō* and similar sources that reiterate Annen's localization: "Above the cross on the human head are six grains of human yellow, they are like the ox yellow."[73] They are also said to be protected by five dragons.[74] The ten grains, on the other hand, are said to designate the three *hun* and seven *po* (spirits) that constitute the vital principle of humans in Chinese conceptions. Whatever the number of grains, the point is that their gradual loss leads to sickness and death: "The six grains are the six consciousnesses of the mind-king. Or again: There are seven drops. When one of them disappears, one gets sick. When the six are gone, one dies."[75] As we will see, the human yellow was a coveted delicacy, which various demons—most notably the *ḍākinīs*—tried to steal.[76] The ingestion of that substance was said to bring ultimate realization.[77]

The human yellow also received a political interpretation that illustrates the relationship of Aizen with kingship (and regentship).[78] Since "human yellow" was also written at times "human king" (*ninnō*), the fact that Aizen holds the human king in his hand was interpreted by some as meaning that the Fujiwara regent, who controlled the Aizen ritual, held the Japanese sovereign in his hand and ruled over Japan. A similar interpretation was given to Aizen's holding the sun (symbol of the ruler). This reading is also linked to the fact that Fujiwara no Yorimichi 藤原頼通 (992–1074), the founder of Byōdō-in, saw Aizen as a "king of equality" (*Byōdō-ō*) who rules over all beings—a transparent metaphor for the regent himself.

The Wish-fulfilling Jewel

We have noted above the ambiguity of the vital principle as source of both prosperity and destruction. The same ambiguity is found in the deities who control that vital principle—beginning with Aizen, but also Dakiniten, Shōten 聖天, and related "gods of obstacles." This ambivalence is above all that of the wish-fulfilling jewel, which provides the common element between these deities. Aizen's third left hand often holds a golden sphere or a tripartite jewel, which is said to represent the vital principle of beings or their innermost consciousness, the so-called storehouse consciousness or *ālaya-vijñāna*.[79]

A vow found in a reliquary shaped like a five-wheel stūpa recommends that Aizen's seed-letter *hūṃ* be copied 84,000 times. This symbolic number calls to mind King Aśoka's legendary 84,000 stūpas and suggests that Aizen was identified with the Buddha's relics (*śarīra*).[80] Indeed, some sources expressly declare that "the Buddha's relics become Aizen."[81] The jewel is the emblem of Aizen's power, his symbolic or *samaya* form; it is also said to correspond to the eighth *vijñāna*, the storehouse consciousness. Interestingly, the human yellow as well came to be identified with the Buddha's relics, judging from a report in the *Hishō* 祕鈔 (by Shōken 勝賢 and Shukaku 守覚) that someone buried Śākyamuni's human yellow at the Shingon-in of Tōdaiji.[82]

Aizen's image lends itself to a wide variety of interpretations. Its dominant feature is the wish-fulfilling jewel, not only because it is Aizen's symbolic form, but also because the jewel is able to produce the myriad things that constitute a kingdom's wealth. This is probably why King Aizen rules over the four oceans and delegates his power to his earthly representatives (the emperor and the regent).

Thus, several registers overlap in the image of Aizen: subjugation—either through seduction (*keiai*) or subjugation (*chōbuku*); sexuality and

Yama, he holds a head in his left hand."[90] The passage continues with a discussion of the meaning of the title "king of equality": "King Yama dwells in the two realms of *saṃsāra* and nirvāṇa; he records good and evil and reveals heavy and light [offences]. King Aizen is the essence and the revealed marks of the eighth *vijñāna*. It is the general consciousness of defilement and purity, of true and false. Because they are both manifestations of the eighth *vijñāna*, Enma and Aizen are both called 'king of equality.' What King Raga (Aizen) holds in his hand is the eighth *vijñāna*. The lapis-lazuli mirror of King Yama also symbolizes the eighth *vijñāna*." Charles Malamoud points out that, already in Hindu scriptures such as the *Śatapatha Brāhmaṇa,* King Yama was said to dwell in the sun disk.[91] The sun is not just the source of life, it is also death, because it rules over beings whose life span is limited. As such, Yama is the ruler of the earth.[92]

In his *Sōjishō* 總持抄, Chōgō writes: "King Yama is the mind-king of the eighth *vijñāna*. In this eighth *vijñāna,* all dharmas, tainted and pure, dwell."[93] As to the staff that Enma holds: "*Daṇḍa* means banner with human head. The fact that in his right hand he holds a human-head banner means the life-root of all beings. Likewise, when one cuts the head of people, their life is destroyed. Thus, to hold a head means to hold the beings of the *dharmadhātu*. . . . All beings are born from the eighth consciousness, and they all return to it. Consequently, to hold a human head means to hold the karma of transmigration of false thoughts. It is the perfect and bright essence of the eighth *vijñāna*."[94]

A tradition from Kōryūji 広隆寺 states: "As king of equality, the love bodhisattva (Ai Bosatsu, Aizen's prototype) transforms into King Enma, his right hand holding the *daṇḍa* seal, his left hand holding the 'human king' (read: human yellow). The color of his body is that of red flesh, and he sits on a water buffalo. This king wards off in particular the obstacle of death."[95] The *Kakuzenshō* declares that the title of king of equality is applied to both because King Yama is in charge of the life span of beings, while Aizen controls the "heart-king." As we will see, the identity between Aizen and King Enma as rulers of human destiny came to be interpreted in embryological terms.

Myōken

The apotheosis of Aizen as ruler of destiny is reflected in his identification with the god of the pole star, Myōken, and in his association with the seven stars of the Northern Dipper.[96] The relation between Aizen and Myōken is implicit in the *Kojidan* (ca. 1212–1215) by Minamoto no Akikane 源顯兼 (1160–1215). In a section entitled "Go-Sanjō Tennō Prays to the Pole Star," we are told that Go-Sanjō's enthronement was the result of the Aizen ritual performed by the Shingon priest Seison.[97] In Chōgō's *Sōjishō,* we read that Myōken is one with the Buddha's relics and with

Ichiji Kinrin: "Myōken, in reality, is the relics of all the buddhas. He is the seed-letter *bhrūṃ* of Ichiji Kinrin. The numinous place of Myōken is none other than the Jingūji 神宮寺. This is where the image made by Dengyō Daishi 伝教大師 [Saichō] is enshrined. Apart from the followers of the Sanmon [Mount Hiei], no one knows this equal body."[98] The same text explains that Myōken, as Ichiji Kinrin, is identical with Aizen and that he rules over the seven planets, Rāhu (J. Rago-sei 羅睺星), and Ketu (J. Keito-sei 計都星).[99] Aizen's identity with Ichiji Kinrin and Myōken may also explain his connection with astrological divination through the lunar mansions, and his iconographic association with the seven stars of the Northern Dipper and with the baleful stars Rāhu, Ketu, and Saturn.[100]

The link between Aizen and Myōken brings the astral nature of Aizen's rituals to the forefront. The *Kakuzenshō,* for instance, mentions an exorcism in which the priest puts an image of the nine baleful planets into the mouth of Aizen's lion. By the same token, he puts the image under the power of the Lion constellation (one of the twelve zodiacal signs), ensuring that no obstacle will arise because of astral influences. This method is referred to as the "essential secret method of the three nines" (*sankū hiyō-hō* 三九祕要法), a term referring to three lunar mansions known as life mansion (*mei-shuku* 命宿), karma mansion (*gyō-shuku* 業宿), and womb mansion (*tai-shuku* 胎宿).[101] We recall that Aizen was said to destroy the "inborn obstacles" of people. He holds these obstacles in his fist, as if to crush them. Because these obstacles are the result of past actions, the Aizen chapter of the *Kakuzenshō* mentions another method, a star ritual consisting in offerings to the karma mansion.[102] The *Keiran shūyōshū* also quotes the *Xiuyaojing* 宿曜経 regarding the cult of Aizen to be performed on the day of the constellation Demon (Gui 鬼, Skt. Puṣya), because that constellation is particularly auspicious among the twenty-eight lunar mansions.[103]

Butsugen and Kinrin

Aizen is said to represent the union of Butsugen and Kinrin. Whereas the former symbolizes the Womb mandala and corresponds to Fudō, the latter symbolizes the Vajra Realm mandala and corresponds to Aizen.[104] Aizen is also said to be born from Ichiji Kinrin. His solar symbolism is reinforced by his identification with the form of Ichiji Kinrin known as Shijōkōbutsu 熾盛光仏 (Skt. Tejaprabhā), the sun buddha whose blazing light makes all other stars and deities pale.[105] The expression "blazing light" (*shijōkō*) is often used to describe the wheel of flames that surrounds Aizen. The Blazing Light ritual performed on Mount Hiei was presented as the Tendai equivalent of the Aizen ritual in Shingon. In many representations, however, Aizen is distinct from Ichiji Kinrin, and contrasted with the couple formed by Kinrin and Butsugen.[106] Like Aizen, Butsugen is often represented wearing a lion head as diadem (see Fig. 4.17).

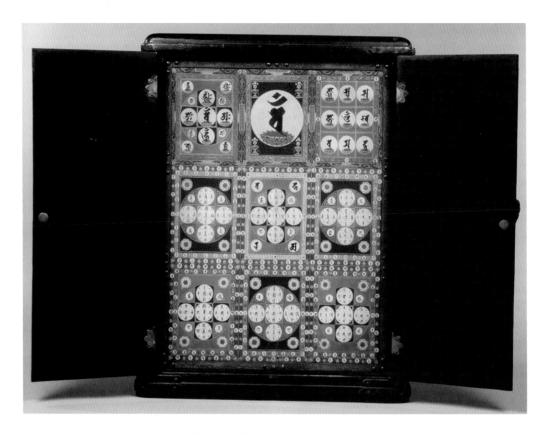

FIGURE 4.19. Vajra Realm and Aizen seed-letter mandalas. Interior detail (*right*) of the *August Body of the Ise Shrine* [*Deities*] portable shrine. Kamakura period. Lacquered wood with polychromy. Saidaiji, Nara.

The mediation of the images of Jūichimen Kannon and Nyoirin Kannon also facilitated that relation. In the *Tenshō nenju hikuketsu* 天照念誦秘口訣, for instance, we read that Jūichimen enters the Aizen *samādhi,* which represents the union of the nondual Womb and Vajra realms. Consequently, Aizen becomes the counterpart of Jūichimen, and Jūichimen's entering the Aizen *samādhi* is described as a sexual union that symbolizes the union of the two mandalas.[116] Another symbol of the two-realm mandalas is the coupling of Kinrin and Butsugen. It is also a way of expressing the nonduality of the "red" and "white" (blood and semen). In his *Yugikyō chōmonshō,* Chōgō explains that the union of Kinrin and Butsugen gives birth to the universe.

A fragmentary illustrated scroll dated 1350 and preserved at Myōhō-in 妙法院 in Kyoto describes a genesis of the world in which a demiurge named Amaterasu manifests itself in the form of the six-armed Aizen.[117] In the Miwa-ryū tradition, Jūichimen Kannon, the *honji* of Amaterasu, is also described as identical with Aizen. The *Ise daijingū mi[shō]tai nikki* 伊勢大神宮御体日記, for example, states: "Amaterasu is the Jūichimen Kannon of the sun disk, and she has six arms."[118] The *Daijingū no honnen* 大神宮の本然 likewise describes a six-armed deity named Kinrin-ō 金輪王 (Golden Wheel King) who bequeathes Japan to the *kami* Izanami 伊邪那美 (var. 伊弉冉) and Izanagi 伊邪那岐 (var. 伊弉諾). This deity, born from the "two dharmas of principle and knowledge," is clearly modeled after Aizen.[119] It splits into two "half-wheels, red and white." The red and white are identified with principle and knowledge in commentaries on the *Yugikyō* like the *Yugikyō kuketsu nukigaki* 瑜祇経口決抜書 (1312) by the Tendai priest Kōshū—the author of the *Keiran shūyōshū*—and the *Yugikyō chōmonshō* by the Shingon priest Chōgō, in relation to Aizen's dual nature (as Aizen and Zen'ai). The golden wheel is said to encompass the sun, the moon, and the five planets, and to correspond to the Yin-Yang deities Izanami and Izanagi.

A Ninnaji tradition traced back to the sixth-century Chinese master Baozhi (J. Hōshi 宝誌) records that Amaterasu is the *honzon* of the Ōsashihyō 奥砂子平 ritual performed at Murōzan, and that her *honji* is Jūichimen Kannon (identified with Ichiji Kinrin).[120] In the *Bikisho*'s 鼻歸書 discussion of that same ritual, Amaterasu is identified with Kūkai, who must be visualized seated in the sun palace on a jeweled wheel, on which Aizen's seed-syllable *hūṃ* is inscribed inside a moon disk. Although the jeweled wheel is usually Ichiji Kinrin's seed-letter *bhrūṃ,* here it symbolizes Amaterasu. This representation symbolizes (again) the fusion of the two—red and white—drops, the sexual union of man and woman, the sun and the moon.[121]

Another oral tradition traced back to Baozhi and to the Japanese statesman Kibi no Makibi 吉備真備 (Kibi Daijin 吉備大臣, 695–775) states that the *honji* of Amaterasu (or the sun deva, Nittenshi 日天子) is either Dainichi or Jūichimen Kannon, and that the two shrines—Inner and Outer—of Ise correspond to the Vajra Realm mandala (represented by a male deity, the moon deva Gatten 月天) and the Womb mandala (represented by a female deity, the sun deva Nitten 日天), respectively. A tradition attributed to Hanjun regarding the jewel ritual identifies Aizen with Kannon, Daishō Kongō 大聖金剛, Ichijin Kinrin, and Amaterasu—all deities linked by the same solar symbolism.[122]

Nyoirin Kannon

Both Aizen and Nyoirin are depicted as the *honji* of the Inari deity—an association that was probably made possible through the intermediary of Dakiniten. Inari and Aizen are both gods of love.[123] In the apocryphal *Ugajin darani kyō* 宇賀神陀羅尼経, the snake deity Ugajin 宇賀神 appears as Dakiniten, Shōten (Kangiten), and Aizen. His *honji* is Nyoirin Kannon.[124] The *Tenchi reikaku hishō* 天地霊覚祕鈔, a Ryōbu shintō text, states that: "King Aizen and Nyoirin Kannon share the same essence. When the buddhas, bodhisattvas, etc., want to benefit beings, they all do so by becoming Kannon. At that time, they become one with Nyoirin Kannon. The latter dwells in the sun disk, which is none other than King Aizen. Now, in that sun disk dwells a three-legged red crow. (It means ignorance. It means greed, anger, and stupidity)."[125] The *Miwa-ryū shintō-hen* 三輪流神道編 declares: "Like the sun deva (Nitten), all gods take the crow as their emissary. It is the three-legged crow that dwells in the sun. Its three legs mean 'One buddha, two wisdom kings'; they symbolize the tripartite wish-fulfilling jewel."[126] *The Matter of the Provisional Manifestation Seiryō* (*Seiryō Gongen onkoto* 清瀧権現御事) specifies that Aizen and Fudō are the manifestations of the Dainichi of the two mandalas, and that the formula "One buddha, two *myōō*" refers either to the triad formed by Nyoirin, Aizen, and Fudō or to the three jewels (both being essentially the same). The golden jewel between the red and white jewels represents their nonduality, just as Nyoirin represents the nonduality of Aizen and Fudō, that is, of the two-realm mandalas. I will return to this point in my discussion of the Joint Ritual of the Three Worthies.[127]

Aizen and the Three Devas

Dakiniten

The affinities between the rituals of Aizen and of Dakiniten, as rituals protecting imperial power and in particular the power of the retired emperors of the Insei period, are probably due to the fact that both rituals developed within the Ono branch of Shingon. Seison is credited with an enthronement ritual (*sokui kanjō* 即位灌頂) centered on Dakiniten, first performed at the time of Go-Sanjō's accession to the throne. Because of its homophony with *ḍākinī*, the name Takki (J. Taki 吒枳), sometimes used for Aizen, may have brought the two deities closer.[128] The main symbolic link between them, however, is probably the wish-fulfilling jewel.[129] The *Kakuzenshō* declares: "*Ḍākinīs* steal men's vital breath. To prevents this, [Aizen] holds [in his fist] the human yellow, that is, the root of life." Aizen is also said to strike at *ḍākinīs* and other demons with the lotus stem that he holds in his right hand. In this interpretation, he protects the vital essence of humans against the *ḍākinīs* intent on ravishing it. In this protecting role, he is comparable to Mahākāla (and Fudō). Kakuzen quotes the story according to which the Buddha Mahāvairocana, in his wrathful manifestation as Mahākāla (J. Daikoku 大黒), punished the *ḍākinīs* and decreed that they could only eat the heart of dying humans, that is, the human yellow.[130] Other sources suggest Aizen's ambiguity.[131] He is said, for instance, to be the *honzon* of exorcisms aimed at taming the so-called three foxes (*sanko* 三狐).[132] Yet he is sometimes described as one of them—for example, in the *Tamakisan gongen engi* 玉置山権現縁 起: "The heavenly fox is Haguro Gongen. . . . The earthly fox corresponds to the three fox deities of Kumano. . . . The human fox is King Aizen."[133]

Shōten

The elephant-headed deity Shōten 聖天 (a.k.a. Kangiten 歓喜天) is sometimes presented as an avatar of Kongōsatta 金剛薩多 (Skt. Vajrasattva), like Aizen. In the *Keiran shūyōshū,* Aizen is identified with Shōten.[134] In the *Shōten-hō zatsushū* 聖天法雑集, we also read: "The deva [Shōten] is identical with King Aizen. Among the four types of *vināyakas* (in the external court of the Vajra Realm mandala), the one with bow and arrows is none other than King Aizen. When respect and love (*keiai* 敬愛) are nondual, everything unites harmoniously, without obstacles. All dharmas are born from that stage."[135]

In the *Miwa-ryū shintō-hen,* the dual-body Kangiten is identified with King Aizen.[136] Also worth mentioning in this context is the triad formed by Aizen and two *vināyakas*—one white and female, the other red and male. These two elephant-headed deities stand for a series of polarities like the embryological "red and white," which are also expressed by the dyad formed by Aizen and Fudō. The triad they form with Aizen is reminiscent of other triads, most notably those formed by the Three Worthies (*sanzon* 三尊) and the Three Devas (*santen* 三天). In the Joint Ritual of the Three Worthies (Sanzon gōgyō-hō 三尊合行法), Aizen and Fudō enter into a relationship with the jewel or Nyoirin Kannon. In the Joint Ritual of the Three Devas (Santen gōgyō-hō 三天合行法), Aizen does not appear. Instead, he is replaced by one of the Three Devas (Shōten, Dakiniten, and Benzaiten). His intimate relationship with these three devas, however, suggests that, as a fundamental jewel deity, he is their common denominator.[137] Aizen is not simply the jewel's protector, he is the jewel himself. The same can be said, however, of several other deities— beginning with Ugajin.

Benzaiten

Significantly, the author of the *Keiran shūyōshū* includes a good part of his discussion of Aizen in the Benzaiten section of his work. In that section, Aizen and Fudō represent life and death, or spiritual and material dharmas. In Yamamoto Hiroko's view, the relation between Aizen and Benzaiten presupposes the fecundity/fertility symbolism of the wish-ful-filling jewel: "In the powerful magnetic field of embryology, Aizen has come closer to Benzaiten, through the intermediary of the *cintāmaṇi,* and has himself taken the form of a snake."[138] The *Keiran shūyōshū* alludes to Benzaiten's identity with Fudō and Aizen. Although it does not develop the associations, the fact that the discussion of Aizen and Fudō is placed at the beginning of the Benzaiten chapter is significant. In the *Omokage monogatari,* dated from the Muromachi period, Aizen takes Benzaiten as his wife.[139] In the *Kinpusen himitsuden* 金峰山秘密伝 by Monkan, the triad formed by the Three Worthies (Nyoirin, Aizen, and Fudō) is replaced by another, formed by Tenkawa Benzaiten 天河弁才天, Kumano Gon-gen 熊野権現, and Zaō Gongen 蔵王権現. This triad is projected on the geographical triangle formed by Tenkawa (at the top or center), Kumano, and Yoshino.

Aizen is also identified with Daikokuten and Ugajin. In his manifes-tation as Aizen, Ugajin is said to provide love and bliss and to help people to reach supreme awakening. As Iyanaga Nobumi points out, Aizen served as a link (or common denominator) between these devas.[140] In the apoc-ryphal *Ugaya daranikyō* 宇賀耶陀羅尼経, Uga Benzaiten is linked with Amaterasu (or Nichirin, the solar wheel), Dakiniten, Shōten, and Aizen. Another source identifying Aizen and Benzaiten is the so-called Peasant Aizen (Denpu Aizen 田夫愛染) ritual, already mentioned, in which Aizen appears in the form of a green snake whose shape evokes Benzaiten's seed-letter *oṃ.*[141] I will return to that form of Aizen in the next chapter.

THE EMBRYOLOGICAL GOD

Aizen's five-pronged *vajra* (a.k.a. *vajra* of the human form) symbolizes, among other things, the child in utero. In the *Towazu monogatari* 問わず物語, for example, Go-Fukakusa Tennō 後深草天皇 tells Lady Nijō: "I dreamed that you received a five-pronged *vajra* from Ariake. . . . It was made of silver and had belonged to the late emperor Go-Saga. Seeing this, I said that I would receive it as mine." Soon after, Lady Nijō finds that she is pregnant from her lover Ariake (a.k.a. Ariake no Tsuki, "Dawn Moon"; d. 1281), a Ninnaji priest of imperial blood.[142] This symbolism brings us one step closer to the implicit theology of Aizen, to which we now turn.

The Aizen ritual played an important part in the elaboration of a Buddhist spiritual embryology centered on the five stages of gestation.[143] Aizen's embryological ritual also revolves around the "five-pronged seal"(mudrā) and its counterpart, the five-pronged *vajra.* The symbolism of the five stages applies not only to the five fingers, but also to the five-mudrā sequence and the five mantras accompanying it. An example of this symbolism is found in an ordination certificate transmitted by the Daigoji priest Jakuen 寂円 (d.u.) to the prelate Gonkaku 厳覚 (1056–1121).

This document shows that esoteric initiation was based on the model of sexual intercourse followed by fetal gestation.[144] It began with three mudrās symbolizing a lotus blossom, a stūpa, and a five-pronged *vajra,* respectively. The lotus and the stūpa represent the female and male genitalia, but the stūpa also symbolizes the womb. The five-pronged *vajra* can represent the sexual union of man and woman but also the embryo resulting from that union. At any rate, the three symbols clearly symbolize the gestation process. In Chōgō's view, the five hand gestures that compose the sequence of the "five-pronged mudrā" symbolize the five stages of gestation. The first gesture also symbolizes the wish-fulfilling jewel as source of fecundity, while the last one represents "Aizen coming out of the womb." Here it is Aizen himself who is identified with the human fetus.[145]

Related to this ritual is an image of Aizen called the "five-finger-high Aizen" (*goshiryō* Aizen 五指量愛染)—that is, a statuette whose size is five times the width of the middle finger—which pregnant women kept as an amulet in their sash.[146] The five finger-widths symbolize the five stages of fetal gestation (*tainai goi* 胎内五位), while the fact of hiding the image in one's sash symbolizes the lodging of the embryo inside the womb.[147]

The red color of Aizen's body is interpreted following an embryological code in Chōgō's *Yugikyō chōmonshō* 瑜祇経聴聞抄; for instance, "Aizen is the form of the worthy inside the womb. His red color is the color inside the womb, it symbolizes the fetus."[148] Even Aizen's standing hair, usually interpreted as the sign of his wrath, is said to connote "the form inside the womb."[149] Aizen's size (five finger-widths), said to be equivalent to three inches (*sansun* 三寸), is precisely that of the "three-inch Fudō" (Sansun Fudō 三寸不動) and of the Buddha's relic buried on Mount Murō.[150] I will shortly return to these two figures, which play a prominent role in the so-called Joint Ritual of the Three Worthies.

Much of the embryological discourse of esoteric Buddhism revolves around the notion that the two "drops," red and white—symbolizing female blood and male semen—merge to produce the initial stage or entity called *gararan* (Skt. *kalalaṃ*), in which "consciousness" appears or is produced. In medieval commentaries on the *Yugikyō,* this consciousness corresponds to the "nondual golden wheel of red and white."[151] It is none other than the *ālaya-vijñāna,* itself equated with Aizen.[152]

The *Sanjūshichison haiishō* 三十七尊配位鈔 (1553) by Kyōga 教雅, a monk of the Sanbōin-ryū, explicitly links this embryological notion with, on the one hand, cosmological notions in which the red and the

FIGURE 5.5. Two-headed Aizen mandala. 14th century. Color on silk. Nara National Museum.

Aizen and Fudō symbolize the sun and moon, respectively, but also the "red" and "white" drops—that is, female blood and male semen.[23] Therefore, their union in one (two-headed) body is a symbol of conception.[24] In the *Fudōson gushō* 不動尊愚鈔, an anonymous text in the lineage of the Tachikawa-ryū, it is Fudō himself who represents the two drops of consciousness (red and white, yin and yang) as they exist in sexual union. In that state, they symbolize the seed-syllable *aḥ,* which is therefore called "unmovable."[25] The color code is also at work in the appearance of Fudō's acolytes, the white Kongara and the red Seitaka (see Fig. 5.5–5.6). The text interprets two other acolytes of Fudō, Ekō Dōji and Eki Dōji, as symbols of the first two stages of fetal gestation, the so-called *gararan* (Skt. *kalalaṃ*) and *abudon* (Skt. *arbudaṃ*).[26] It adds that the monk's robe (*kesa* 袈裟), also known as the "robe of the field of merits" (*fukuden-e* 福田衣), symbolizes Ekō and the initial stage of gestation. The *kesa* was also used as a symbol of the placenta, with Fudō and Aizen controlling the beginning and the end of the gestation process.[27]

The principle of double ambivalence is equally at work in the case of Aizen, who represents both the union of the opposites and one of the opposites (as in the pairs Aizen and Zen'ai, or Aizen and Fudō).[28] As Rolf Stein has shown, such polarities are characteristic of the gatekeepers motif, and Aizen and Fudō are indeed often represented as guardians on the doors of portable altars or reliquaries. In the *Tenjin engi* 天神縁起, the two-headed Aizen is associated with other dual deities such as Kangiten, the dual-bodied Bishamon (Sōshin Tamonten 双身多聞天), the *dōso-dōgyōjin* 道祖道行神, and King Enma's acolytes, Shimei 司命 and Shiroku 司禄.[29]

AIZEN AND GŌZANZE

The pairing of Aizen and Fudō seems to derive from that of Trailokyavijaya (J. Gōzanze) and Acala (J. Fudō). In the Sonshō mandala and Miroku

FIGURE 5.6. Detail of the Two-headed Aizen mandala. 14th century. Color on silk. Nara National Museum.

mandala, Gōzanze, on the bottom left, is still represented dancing wildly inside a half-moon (or a lunar crescent), while Fudō, on the bottom right, stands motionless in a triangle of fire.[30] When Aizen superseded Gōzanze in that dual structure, the coupling of Aizen and Fudō was based, above all, on embryological symbolism.[31]

The importance of the dyad is evident in the fact that Nichiren himself, who was otherwise rather critical of the wisdom kings' efficacy, chose Fudō and Aizen as protectors of his mandala.[32] As Lucia Dolce has shown, these two deities play an important role in Nichirenshū 日蓮宗 iconography.[33] In a letter to his female follower Nichinyo 日如, Nichiren explains that "Fudō and Aizen take up their station at the two directions, south and north," of the Nichiren mandala.[34] Their presence is all the more significant given the fact that, while Fudō played a role in certain exegeses of the *Lotus Sūtra,* Aizen is conspicuously absent from such texts and from the group of five myōō.

Nichiren associates Aizen and Fudō in an early document, the so-called *Fudō Aizen kankenki* 不動愛染感見記 (1254), in which he recollected his visions of the two wisdom kings.[35] The illustrations are quite detailed: Aizen, for instance, is riding a horse and has eight arms—instead of the usual six.[36] Fudō is shown in this document with his right foot lifted. In medieval iconographic compendia, Fudō is usually trampling the Indian god Śiva (known by the Buddhists as Daijizaiten) and his wife Umā when he is portrayed in such a position, but they do not appear in Nichiren's text.[37] The *Fudō Aizen kankenki* also identifies Aizen with the sun, and Fudō with the moon. The same symbolism is found

FIGURE 5.10. Wish-fulfilling Jewel mandala. 15th century. Hanging scroll, ink and color on silk. Mimurotoji, Uji.

does not appear in the Mimurotoji scroll: on the upper right stands a human-faced monster reminiscent of the mythical Hakutaku 白沢 (Ch. Baize 'White Marsh').[45]

Another interesting connection of Fudō and Aizen with dragons is found in the rain ritual at Shinsen'en 神泉苑, as analyzed by Steven Trenson. In this ritual structure, the rain master visualizes the central dragon-banner deity on top of the roof, identified with Kurikara (i.e., Fudō), which has to be unified with the earth dragon at the center of the platform, identified with Aizen.[46] Or, alternatively, the visualization has Kinrin on the rooftop and Butsugen on the platform—in other words, the deity on top of the roof (Kinrin, Fudō) is the buddha born from the "buddha-mother" (*butsumo* 仏母, i.e., Butsugen) on the great platform.[47]

Also worth mentioning is the representation—known by only a few exemplars, among them a scroll from Kongōbuji 金剛峰寺 on Mount Kōya, and another from the Nara National Museum—of a two-headed Aizen flanked by two acolytes (Kongara riding an elephant, and Seitaka riding a lion). Aizen is shooting his arrow toward the sky while Kongara aims at a demon above him, and Seitaka at a fox running below.[48] This representation nicely illustrates Ouwehand's principle of double ambivalence: the polarity symbolized by the two-headed Aizen is replicated in the two acolytes. One could also point to the structural equivalence between the bipolar Aizen and the bodhisattvas Monju 文殊 and Fugen 普賢 (suggested by the lion and the elephant).[49]

In the Kongōbuji scroll, two representations of Dainichi are above Aizen, symbolizing the Womb and Vajra Realm mandalas in red and white circles that represent the sun and the moon, but also perhaps, in an embryological context, the two opposites (blood and semen) that merge at the moment of conception.[50]

The scroll from the Nara National Museum, dated to the fourteenth century, slightly differs from that of Kongōbuji. The two youths are surrounded by a halo of flames, and one of them shoots at a fox, the other at a bird. A five-pronged *vajra* has been placed in the mouth of the lion,

FIGURE 5.11. Jewel guarded by Fudō and Aizen. Detail of the Wish-fulfilling Jewel mandala. 15th century. Hanging scroll, ink and color on silk. Mimurotoji, Uji.

which is represented frontally, and in a stylized, almost caricatural fashion. Above the two-headed Aizen, the two Dainichi have been replaced by an eight-armed Monju seated on an eight-lion seat (on the left) and a triangle (on the right), with two jewels at the base and top, flanking the seven stars. This disposition suggests an influence from the Monju cult in the Shingon Ritsu 真言律 school.[51]

Despite their quite distinct origins and trajectories, Fudō and Aizen literally became two birds of the same feather. In the *Secret Record of Mount Kōya* (*Kōyasan hiki* 高野山秘記), we are told that when Kūkai was about to enter his final *samādhi,* two birds came and sang a melodious song, to which Kūkai responded with a verse. These birds were none other than Aizen and Fudō. In a variant, they become the two emissaries of Amaterasu, and they are called the "provisional manifestations of the two [Ise] shrines."[52] Another bird associated is the three-legged crow in the sun—a very ancient Chinese image that came to symbolize the Joint Ritual of the Three Worthies—to which we now turn.[53]

THE JOINT RITUAL OF THE THREE WORTHIES

In this section, I examine the Joint Ritual of the Three Worthies (Sanzon gōgyō-hō 三尊合行法) as it is described in various documents preserved in the archives of Shōmyōji 称名寺 at Kanazawa bunko 金沢文庫 (Yokohama prefecture) and of Shinpukuji 真福寺 at Ōsu bunko 大須文庫 (Nagoya).[54] The term *sanzon gōgyō* appears by the twelfth century in several documents from Kanazawa bunko. In his *Great Matter of the Testament* (1327), Monkan traces the ritual back to a passage in Kūkai's apocryphal *Testament* (*Goyuigō* 御遺告, dated to the tenth century) and explains that Kūkai transmitted the ritual to his disciple Shinga 真雅 (801–879).[55] Transmitted from one generation to another, the ritual eventually reached Shōkaku 勝覚 (1057–1129), the founder of the Sanbōin lineage, and his disciple Shōken. Monkan credits Shōkaku with the image of the triad centered on the five-wheel stūpa. Shōken is in turn credited for developing the ritual by replacing the stūpa with Nyoirin and calling it the Rite of Nyoirin and the Three Buddhas (Sanbutsu Nyoirin no hō 三仏如意輪の法).[56] The ritual was further developed by Dōjun 道順 (fl. 1321), and by Monkan (1278–1357), who is credited with several commentaries beginning with the *Great Matter of the Testament*.[57]

Thus, Monkan did not create the ritual from scratch, he merely systematized its interpretation in order to provide ideological and ritual support to Emperor Go-Daigo against the bakufu. Monkan's works on the Sanzon gōgyō ritual were all written shortly before or during Go-Daigo's Kenmu Restoration (1333–1336).[58] Go-Daigo was not only the sponsor but also an occasional participant in this ritual. A case in point is the report that Monkan and Go-Daigo, in 1324, together fabricated jewels to bring about the fall of the shōgunate.[59] This does not mean that Monkan and his predecessors were cynical and manipulative (in the psychological sense). They lived in a world of political, emotional, and ontological lability, in which the rulers and their allies felt constantly threatened by military and spiritual aggression, and trusted the life-and-death powers unleashed by the ritual to protect them from their enemies.

This Sanzon gōgyō-hō was a multilayered and multipurpose ritual, having both apotropaic and soteriological functions. Since its initiatory or soteriological function has been already well described by Lucia Dolce and Gaétan Rappo, I will emphasize here its apotropaic function. Regarding the soteriological function, it may suffice to point out that the *Great Matter* introduces three levels of Dharma transmission in quasi-algebraic progression: on the first level, the practitioner uses two mudrās (*in,* 印) and two mantras (*myō* 名, hence the two *myōō*); on the second level, one mudrā and two mantras (hence the two-headed *myōō*); on the third level, one mudrā and one mantra.

In the *Goyuigō hiketsu,* for instance, the ritual is interpreted both as a three-step unction (*kanjō,* Skt. *abhiṣeka*) and as a method to cure the three poisons. The *hongaku* nonduality of defilements and awakening leads to the equation of Aizen, Fudō, and Nyoirin (or Daiitoku Myōō) both with the three poisons and with their cure: Fudō tames anger, Aizen desire, and Nyoirin stupidity.[60]

Iconography of the *Great Matter*

The *Great Matter* contains a series of nine drawings that represent transformations of the triad formed by Nyoirin, Aizen, and Fudō (and its symbolic expressions as jewels and dragons) in relation to the emblematic figure of Kūkai (Kōbō Daishi 弘法大師). It presents this triad as an illustration of the formula "One buddha, two *myōō*," and traces it back to the mythical Iron Tower in southern India (Nanten tettō 南天鉄塔).[61]

Since I discuss in the next chapter the illustrations related to Kūkai, I focus here on the representations of Fudō and Aizen. Fig. 5.12 shows two figures side by side, each surrounded by an aura of flames, inside a white circle.[62] The blue deity on the right, who looks like Fudō and holds a sword and a Dharma wheel (instead of a noose, Fudō's characteristic attribute), is called the "Snake-repelling Worthy" (Hija-son 避蛇尊). The flesh-colored deity on the left wears a three-pronged tiara, holds a jewel in its right hand, and a small snake on the palm of its left hand. It is called the "White Snake [holding] Worthy" (Byakuja-son 白蛇尊). While it is clearly related to Aizen, it has a serene, bodhisattva-like appearance.[63] Not surprisingly, these two deities, like other Mikkyō pairs, are said to symbolize the two realms and related polarities (compassion and wisdom, principle and knowledge). They correspond to the first of the three initiatory stages (expressed by two mudrās and two mantras), that of the initial duality, not yet mediated by the jewel (Nyoirin).

Fig. 5.13 shows a pink-colored, two-headed deity (patterned after Aizen), seated on a lotus inside a red circle. It is called the Worthy of the Ōsashihyō [ritual] 奥砂子平尊. It wears a tiara and holds a sword and a (larger) snake, thus combining the attributes of the two figures in the previous picture. It illustrates the second initiatory stage, expressed by one mudrā and two mantras.

Fig. 5.14 shows a five-colored five-wheel stūpa (*gorintō* 五輪塔) on a lotus pedestal, flanked by Fudō and Aizen. On the right, Fudō is seated on a pedestal, surrounded by a halo of flames. He holds a sword in his right hand and a Dharma wheel in his left hand. On the left, Aizen is seated on a jewel vase, itself standing on a lotus, inside a red circle. He holds a bow and arrows in his lower hands (rather than in his upper hands, as in usual representations). The two wisdom kings are said to symbolize the Womb mandala and the Vajra Realm mandala, respectively, while the stūpa (i.e., the jewel, symbol of Nyoirin) at the center represents their nonduality.[64]

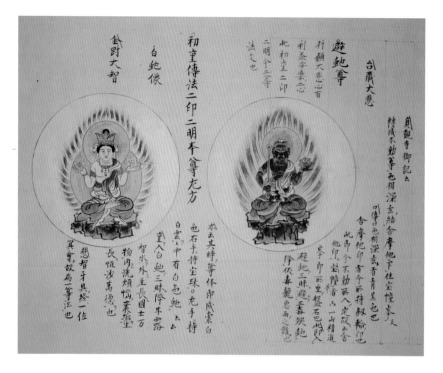

FIGURE 5.12. (*Left*) Worthies of the Hija and Byakuja rituals. 14th century. Color on paper. *Goyuigō daiji.* Ninnaji, Kyoto.

FIGURE 5.13. (*Right*) Two-headed deity. 14th century. Color on paper. *Goyuigō daiji.* Ninnaji, Kyoto.

This stūpa and its Buddha relics, identified with the wish-fulfilling jewel, are said to symbolize Nyoirin Kannon, a deity identified, among others, with the sun goddess Amaterasu and with Kūkai. The latter is presented as a reincarnation of Shōtoku Taishi 聖徳太子, himself an avatar of Nyoirin Kannon.[65]

The *Oral Teachings on the Origin of the Mysteries* (*Himitsu gentei kuketsu* 秘密源底口決) gives three different interpretations of these worthies. In the first interpretation, the five-finger-high (*goshiryō*) Aizen symbolizes the five clans of the Vajra Realm mandala, while the three-inch Fudō symbolizes the three clans of the Womb mandala, and the jewel represents the enlightened mind.[66] In the second interpretation, based on the *hongaku* identity of afflictions and awakening (*bonnō soku bodai*), the three deities are equated with the three poisons, which are ultimately identical with perfect awakening (Skt. *saṃbodhi*, J. *sanbodai* 三菩提) and with Vairocana's three mysteries (Nyoirin corresponding to the mystery of speech, Aizen to that of mind, and Fudō to that of body).[67] The third interpretation considers the Three Worthies in terms of Kūkai's image and of *kami* worship, and it emphasizes the identity between Nyoirin (the stūpa) and Amaterasu.[68]

In spite of the ritual's complexity, its generating schema is fairly simple: it emphasizes the jewel as symbol of nonduality, that is, as the third element (or the first, depending on the viewpoint) that transcends and encompasses all dualities. But perhaps to reduce a ritual to its generating schema is to miss the point, since its efficacy is supposedly a function of the context and of the practitioner's inner state.

Given a hierarchical triad of the type one plus two ("One buddha, two *myōō*"), one can choose to focus on the triadic structure of the whole or on the dyadic structure represented by the two acolytes. In the present case, it seems that the triadic structure derives from the dyadic structure by adding the unity—rather than the opposite (the dyad resulting from the bipartition of the monad). Both readings, however, remain possible. The appeal of both types of structures explains why singular deities like Nyoirin, Fudō, and Aizen were brought together in the Sanzon gōgyō ritual.[69] In fact, the *honzon* of this ritual becomes the triad itself, not just its central deity; thus, Fudō and Aizen seem to become more than acolytes—although a degree of hierarchy between them and the jewel (Nyoirin)

FIGURE 5.14. The Three Worthies. 14th century. Color on paper. *Goyuigō daiji*. Ninnaji, Kyoto.

FIGURE 5.15. The Three Worthies (Nyoirin Kannon, Aizen, and Fudō). 14th–15th century Hanging scroll, ink and color on silk. Nezu Museum, Tokyo.

remains. At any rate, this "composite" triad (two-one) differs from a genuine triad (of the kind represented by the Borromean knot—exemplified by the Three Devas that I will discuss in *Protectors and Predators*.[70]

Commenting on the *Testament,* the *Ben'ichizan hiki* explains that the *honzon* of the Mount Murō ritual is made up of the jewel (enshrined in or symbolized by a stūpa), Aizen, and Fudō, following the tripartite structure expressed by the formula "One buddha, two *myōō.*" Kūkai allegedly brought this *honzon,* transmitted from the legendary Iron Tower in southern India, to Japan and buried it on Mount Murō. Regarding this, Monkan's *Himitsu gentei kuketsu* (Kōyasan collection) contains an oral tradition concerning the belief that the "Joint Ritual of the Three Worthies [is] worthy of being the *honzon* of the state." Although not technically a buddha, Nyoirin is the *honzon* here.[71] As noted earlier, the central figure in the triad is actually the five-wheel stūpa that is said to contain two "jewels," i.e., relics, which transform into Nyoirin. The two wisdom kings (Aizen and Fudō) who guard the jewel symbolize the Vajra Realm mandala and the Womb mandala. The ritual opens with a secret mudrā, called "seal of the lotus and the jewel," which unites these two planes and expresses the jewel's essence. Then the Three Worthies are visualized as representing the essence of illusion and awakening. Fudō and Aizen symbolize the three poisons and they are paired with Nyoirin, the emblem of awakening; in other words, the group they form expresses the identity of one's afflictions and awakening (*bonnō soku bodai* 煩悩即菩提), which constitutes the main tenet of the Mahāyāna teaching. At this point in the ritual, Nyoirin is identified with the Golden Wheel King (Kinrin-ō 金輪王)—in other words, with the ruler, who is himself an avatar of the sun goddess Amaterasu. This ritual was apparently used during the enthronement ceremony and it constituted a centerpiece of imperial ideology.

The Byakuja and Ōsashihyō Rites

Let us now turn to the ritual segments that enter into the combination of the Three Worthies. The ritual in question culminates with two rites, the Hija (var. Byakuja) 避蛇 and Ōsashihyō (var. Ōsashihei) 奥砂子平 rites, centered on Fudō and Aizen, respectively.[72] Their combination seems to be a relatively late addition, however. The *Secret Record of Mount Ben'ichi* (*Ben'ichizan himitsuki* 宀一山秘密記, dated to the Kamakura period) already speaks of a ritual combining the Three Worthies but it does not mention the Hija and Ōsashihyō rites.[73] Yet these two rites were already mentioned side by side in the last three articles (23–25) of Kūkai's *Testament.* The reason they are singled out is not clear. While their content varies with each school, both are variants of the jewel rituals performed in the Daigoji and Kajūji lines. They form part of a series of seven secret rituals centered on the wish-fulfilling jewel (among them the Latter Seven Day ritual of Tōji). Both were fundamentally exorcisms, but the

Hija/Byakuja ritual, performed on the first day of each month, is described as more general in scope, while the Ōsashihyō ritual was an exorcism aimed at particular enemies, and performed at specific times. As we have seen, one of these enemies, in the case of Go-Daigo, was the bakufu.[74]

In his *Testament* (art. 23), Kūkai advocated the performance of the Hija/Byakuja ritual on the first three days and nights of each month, at the place of practice established by his disciple Kenne 堅慧 (d. ca. 860).[75] The latter is said to have performed this ritual on the first day of each month. Kūkai's admonition was interpreted differently by Shingon lineages. In the Ono branch, the rite was identified with the end-of-the month ritual, whereas in the Hirosawa branch it was seen as a variant of the Latter Seven Day ritual (*mishichiho*). The ritual's alternate name (Byakuja-hō 白蛇法, White Snake Ritual) implies that it was a snake exorcism, but it is only one of the code names that the Shingon tradition relishes.[76] According to Kōzen's 興然 *Four Scrolls* (*Shikan* 四巻, 1194), *hija* 避邪 (discarding the false) means *byakuja* 白蛇 (white snake), and this ritual was used against a "pervert god" (*jashin* 邪神). The reference to snakes is based on the homophony between *ja* 蛇 (snake) and *ja* 邪 (falsehood, heterodox teaching). The reading "white snake" is therefore a figurative reading, and the snake was probably added afterward to the picture. Yet, as we will see, the snake/dragon motif is overdetermined—since one of Fudō's emanations is a dragon, and Aizen also manifests himself as a snake—and it clearly influenced the image of the deity of the Byakuja ritual holding a black snake in his hand.

Byakuja is defined as a protecting deity, a snake or dragon king dwelling near Mount Murō. In the *Great Matter*, Monkan identifies it with Fudō. He also states: "The letter *vaṃ* is called the essence of watery nature. It transforms and becomes the body of Byakuja Myōō. It can make the sweet rain of the Dharma fall. Outside, it gives birth to all the things of the land; inside, it produces all the virtues of the One-Mind."[77] In the iconographic representation, as we have seen, the two meanings (*hija/byakuja*) refer to two different deities (see Fig. 5.12 above). Byakuja-son (White-snake Worthy) is represented as a bodhisattva-like figure, while Hija-son (Snake-repelling Worthy) is described as a wrathful figure.

For the time being, however, the dragon is the enemy. The Hija ritual is described as an exorcism aimed at driving away the evil dragon that attempts to steal the jewel transmitted by Kūkai and buried on Mount Murō. Thus, the Hija/Byakuja rite was not simply a "white snake" ritual, but a rite aimed at *driving away* the snake/dragon (*hija* 避蛇). Both meanings—*hija* (*hekija*) 'discarding the false', and *byakuja* 白蛇 'white snake'—fuse in the story of the "heretic" priest Shubin (var. Shuen), Kūkai's unfortunate rival who, because of his *perverse mind* (*jashin* 邪心), turned into a *dragon* intent on stealing Mount Murō's famous jewel. The Osashihyō rite, centered on the jewel, was also a ritual taming of a snake. According to the *Great Matter:* "The essence of the light of Great Knowledge transforms into the body of the Wisdom-king Ōsa, who kills the snake of the Three Poisons. The nefarious snake dies in the Garden of the Four Mandalas and the Three Mysteries, thereby bringing peace (*hyō*). Hence the name Ōsashihyō ("Nefarious snake dead, peace"). The Three Poisons here are both embodied and overcome by the divine triad.[78]

The *Testament* explains that the Ōsashihyō rite was first used in southern India to defeat a "fiendish brahmin" who disturbed the "flowering garden of the esoteric teaching." Kūkai is said to have transmitted that rite to his disciple Kenne, who buried it (or rather, the ritual text) in a box on Mount Murō. Ironically, this motif, mentioned by Monkan in his commentaries on the *Testament,* was reactualized as a criticism of Monkan in Yūkai's *Hōkyōshō* 寶鏡鈔: "Long ago, there was an evil brahman in India in the South who destroyed the secret flower garden. To subdue him, the Ōsashihyō ritual was performed. Now in Tōji, there is an alien presence who brings disgrace on the post of religious affairs." In superb hypocritical fashion, Yūkai affirms that he does not mean to slander that person.[79]

In spite of these different interpretations, both rituals were centered on the jewel. Yet they do not seem to have used Aizen's image initially, as was the case in the Joint Ritual. The text entitled *Mount Ben'ichi* (*Ben'ichizan* 宀一山), for example, links both rites without mentioning Aizen. Early documents about the Byakuja ritual mention only Fudō. The *Kakugenshō,* for instance, mentions Fudō but not the jewel. The same is true in a Kanazawa bunko text entitled *Byakuja-hō.*[80] Yet the Daigoji tradition emphasizes that both the jewel and Fudō's icon were buried on Mount Murō (Ben'ichi). An oral tradition quoted in the *Kōyasan hiki* states that "the three-inch Fu [*sic*] is the worthy Fudō. Kongōsatta gave this three-inch Fu to the bodhisattva Nāgārjuna, together with the wish-fulfilling jewel. These [two things] were transmitted through six generations of masters and disciples down to Kūkai, who gave them to Kenne."[81] Here only Fudō and the jewel are mentioned, while Aizen is conspicuously absent. Yet the icon used in this exorcism is a hand-sized Aizen.[82] Aizen seems to have been added later in the Byakuja ritual, when the jewel was described as his *samaya* form. Eventually he became the protector of the jewel (and an acolyte of Nyoirin/Amaterasu).

The addition of Aizen to the ritual mix may reflect an influence of the Kajūji lineage despite the fact that this lineage downplayed or denied the central role of the Mount Murō jewel. In documents about the Octagonal Hall of Hosshōji, only Aizen and the jewel are mentioned. The jewel was reportedly hidden inside the hand-sized Aizen. This tradition reflects the growing importance of the Nyohō Aizen rite, which, as we recall, was traced back to the Shingon priest Hanjun (1038–1112). In Raiyu's *Hishō mondō,* the Nyohō Aizen ritual was transmitted as an Ōsashihyō rite. Eventually, because of his identification with the jewel, Aizen was paired with Fudō, and this pairing paved the way to what became the Joint Ritual of the Three Worthies.

Even in the Ōsashihyō rite, Aizen is not always mentioned directly. In the Miwa-ryū tradition, the main deity of the Ōsa (abbreviation for Ōsashihyō 奥砂子平) rite of Mount Murō is Amaterasu. This deity, however, is described as a six-armed, eleven-faced (Jūichimen) Kannon who dwells in the solar wheel—in other words, it is identical with Aizen.[83] In his *Testament,* Kūkai states that the wish-fulfilling jewel and the two rites (or "ritual texts") were buried in a cavern under Shōjin Peak on Mount Murō.[84] Certain oral traditions state that these two rites and their deities were buried by Kenne, together with the jewel, in the "dragon hole" of Mount Murō.[85] Sources vary as to what was actually buried on Mount Murō: the jewel alone, or a ritual text (*hō*); and if the latter, which rite: the Byakuja or the Ōsashihyō? To clarify that point, the *Ben'ichizan himitsuki* declares that what was buried was the Sanzon gōgyō ritual (text) and its triad, thus bringing together the jewel and the ritual.[86] In particular, it claims that the crystal reliquary in the dragon hole is flanked by a three-inch Fudō in silver and a hand-sized Aizen in gold.[87]

Embryological Deities

The images of Aizen and Fudō used in the two rituals (and in the Sanzon gōgyō ritual that combines them) are very specific. They are two statuettes of about 10 cm, the so-called three-inch Fudō and the five-finger-high Aizen in sandalwood or silver.

These two figures have been interpreted in embryological terms based on a wordplay involving *sanzon* 三尊 (three worthies) and *sansun* 三寸 (three inches, as in three-inch Fudō). Three inches is said to be the size of the practitioner's body (conceived as a fetus in the womb), whereas "three worthies" describe the three phases of conception: the "red" and the "white" (that is, female blood and male semen, woman and man, female love and male anger, Aizen and Fudō) coming together to produce the golden jewel (the child, Nyoirin).[88] As noted earlier, Aizen's five finger-widths also symbolize the five stages of gestation.[89] They further express the five sections of the Vajra Realm mandala, while Fudō's three inches symbolize the three sections of the Womb mandala. Thus, the Sanzon gogyō ritual represents (or actualizes) the fusion of the Womb and Vajra realms, principle (Aizen) and knowledge (Fudō), and yin and yang. This union is compared to the sexual act by which man (Aizen) and woman (Fudō) engender a child (the jewel, or Nyoirin).[90] The white sandalwood of the hand-sized Aizen is also said to symbolize the mother's milk.[91]

Fudō, Aizen, and Kōjin

Aizen is linked with another deity that is closely related to the "companion spirits" (*kushōjin*), namely, Kōjin 荒神 (see Fig. 5.16).[92] The *Kōjin engi* explains that Kōjin's acolytes are Fudō and Aizen, who form with him a triad very similar to that of the Sanzon gogyō ritual. Indeed, Kōjin's acolytes are none other than the five-finger-high Aizen and the three-inch Fudō.[93] Furthermore, the text explains the identity between Kōjin and the relics, and there are records of its being copied at Murōji. The influence of Aizen's image is also visible in the jewel vase on which the form of Kōjin known as Nyorai Kōjin is seated.[94]

There are several extant representations of the triad formed by Kōjin, Aizen, and Fudō. The triad of the image in Boston's Museum of Fine Arts is a classical representation of Nyorai Kōjin with the two *myōō*. Another one is the *Sanbō Kōjin mandara* 三宝荒神曼荼羅 of Tokurajuji 徳楽寺 (Iga City, Mie prefecture). Dated to the Muromachi period, it shows Nyorai Kōjin 如来荒神 in the form of Kongōsatta (Skt. Vajrasattva), with Aizen and Fudō and twelve attendants.[95] A similar triad apparently existed at Murōji.

FIGURE 5.16. Nyorai Kōjin and two attendants. Late 14th century. Hanging scroll, ink, color, and gold on silk. Art Gallery of New South Wales, Sydney.

Although we do not know enough about the ritual context of such images, it is important to note that Kōjin is elsewhere described as a placenta deity that protects the fetus inside the womb. His association with Aizen and Fudō reinforce this embryological interpretation.[96]

FUDŌ AND AIZEN AT ISE

The name of the Ōsashihyō rite of Mount Murō is often abbreviated as Ōsa, and in this case it designates an enthronement ritual (*sokui kanjō*) whose *honzon* is Amaterasu.[97] Yet this deity is said to look like Aizen and it is identified with Jūichimen Kannon.[98] With this ritual, the emphasis shifts from Nyoirin to Jūichimen and Amaterasu.

FIGURE 5.17. Memyō
Bosatsu. Color on silk.
Private collection.

The triad formed by Amaterasu, Fudō, and Aizen has been studied by Lucia Dolce, who argues that it served to give visual, tangible form to the process of individual empowerment.[99] On the doctrinal level, its triadic structure was also a way to emphasize the ultimate nonduality behind (and beyond) the dual pattern formed by Aizen and Fudō. The triad is represented in several paintings that depict the *Shintō kanjō* 神道灌頂 or *Iwato kanjō* 岩戸灌頂, a ritual reenactment of Amaterasu's retreat into the Heavenly Rock Cave (Ama no Iwato 天岩戸).[100] This cave is identified with the Iron Tower in southern India, the matrix from which all the teachings of esoteric Buddhism emanated, as well as with the wish-fulfilling jewel that became their symbol.[101] It is also pregnant with embryological symbolism, inasmuch as both the stūpa and the cave are symbols of the womb.[102] Somewhat surprisingly, Amaterasu is represented here riding a horse, holding a scale in her right hand, a solar disk in her left hand (see Figs. 5.17 and 5.18). Some of these representations refer to the horse-riding deity as the "bodhisattva Horse Neigh" (Memyō Bosatsu 馬鳴菩薩, Ch. Maming Pusa), a name that usually designates the Buddhist poet and thinker Aśvaghoṣa, but in Chinese Buddhist mythology designates a sericultural deity who wears a white dress and rides a white horse. This deity emerged from its mythological cocoon in the late Tang period under the name "Lord of Silk."[103] The Tantric master Vajrabodhi compiled a short ritual text centered on it and aimed at the prosperity of sericulture.[104]

In his study on the feminization of the bodhisattva Avalokiteśvara (Guanyin) in East Asia, Rolf Stein has shown that the relation between the horse and silkworms can be traced back to a Chinese legend from the fourth century in which a father has to go to war, leaving his daughter alone at home with a horse.[105] The girl promises the horse that she will marry it if it brings her father back. The horse manages to do so, and asks for his reward; but when the father hears about his daughter's fateful promise, he kills the poor animal in his anger. The ungrateful girl rejoices at the horse's death and tramples on its skin, which suddenly wraps itself around her and takes her away through the air. She is later discovered hanging from the branches of a tree, transformed into a silkworm, the horsehide having become a cocoon. A legend from the Tang period says that women in Sichuan worshiped a horse-headed goddess of silkworms, Matouniang 馬頭娘, who was represented as wearing a horse skin. She was eventually superseded by the bodhisattva Maming, whose name is reminiscent of that of Hayagrīva (J. Batō 馬頭), a wrathful form of the bodhisattva Avalokiteśvara. In Japan, Hayagrīva came to be worshiped, under the name Batō Kannon, as a protector of silkworms, horses, and oxen.[106]

The popularity of Memyō Bosatsu in medieval Japan is attested by the fact that this bodhisattva appears in several Japanese iconographic collections and ritual texts.[107] He is often represented as a six-armed deity who rides a horse and holds a scale in his upper right hand (Fig. 5.20). He is surrounded by four attendants. Three of them, called Sanshitsu 蚕室 (Silkworm-raising Room), are youths wearing Chinese robes; the fourth one, called Sanmei 蚕命 (Silkworm Life), usually holds the reins of the horse. He is usually a curly-haired youth resembling Fudō's acolytes, but he can also be an older man with a beard and a horse head above his head. In addition, one worshiper is shown in prayer in front of the deity.[108]

FIGURE 5.18. Memyō Bosatsu. 12th century. *Besson zakki*, fig. 48.

According to the *Zuzōshō* 図像抄, Memyō Bosatsu "can transform into a 'silkworm room' (for nurturing beings). From his mouth a silken thread emerges, coursing round a thousand realms."[109] Memyō Bosatsu has also been linked with a sericulture deity known in eastern Japan as Oshirasama オシラ様, who is represented as a young woman riding a white horse.[110]

Whereas in China the male deity called Maming Pusa 馬鳴菩薩 came to replace an earlier female silkworm goddess, in Japan Memyō Bosatsu (a.k.a. Makari Myōjin) is clearly female and is also called Ōhirume 大日靈貴 (var. 大日女貴, another name of Amaterasu). This deity holds a scale in her right hand and a solar disk in her left hand. Unlike her Chinese counterpart, she is usually flanked by two acolytes, Aizen and Fudō. In the *Iwato honzon Memyō* scroll, the two wisdom kings are called Rock Cave acolytes (Iwato kyōshi).[111] In the scroll *The Central Worthy within the Rock Cave* (*Iwato chūson* 岩戸中尊), they are represented inside two circles that symbolize the sun and the moon.[112]

FIGURE 5.19. Memyō Bosatsu. Edo period. Sheet, ink on paper. University Art Museum, Kyoto City University of Arts. *BZS* 2122.

FIGURE 5.20. Memyō Bosatsu. *Sho Monju zuzō,* fig. 18.

In Japan sericulture was from early on associated with Korean immigrant groups.[113] In that respect, Memyō Bosatsu is akin to Kokūzō Bosatsu 虚空蔵菩薩, another deity related to sericulture and to Korea.[114] Kokūzō may even have been confused with Memyō Bosatsu in the iconography, because both are represented riding a horse.[115]

In the Miwa-ryū, an oral tradition criticizes the act of calling Amaterasu by the name Memyō Bosatsu.[116] Another source, quoting Buddhist sūtras, claims that Memyō Bosatsu is a reincarnation of Amaterasu.[117] In the *Tenchi reikiki* 天地麗氣記, it is Izanagi who is linked to that bodhisattva: "Izanagi represents the Vajra realm, and his profane form is that of a man. Like Memyō Bosatsu, he is riding a white horse. He holds a scale in his hand, to weigh the good and evil of all beings. Izanami represents the Womb realm, and her profane form is that of a woman. . . . She stands on a lotus leaf and preaches the Dharma for the benefit of beings."[118]

The *Oral Traditions on the Heavenly Rock Cave* (*Ama no sekkutsu kuketsu* 天石窟口決, 1673), a late compilation of Miwa-related rituals, identifies Amaterasu (Ōhirume no Mikoto) with Memyō Bosatsu and argues that "this bodhisattva is a reincarnation of the esoteric sun god (Nisshin 日神)."[119] The image of Amaterasu (Ōhirume) riding a horse is interpreted allegorically in terms of Yin-Yang cosmology.[120] In esoteric Buddhism, however, Fudō and Aizen are interpreted as symbolizing the two realms (Taizōkai and Kongōkai), the moon and the sun, knowledge and concentration, the seed-letters *a* and *ban* (*vaṃ*), and man and woman.[121] The scale is said to symbolize the weighing of the good and evil actions of people. In her function as judge of human actions, Amaterasu is also linked or identified with Enmaten, Taizan Fukun, and Bonten 梵天 (Skt. Brahmā). The sun disk in Amaterasu's left hand is said to be her *samaya* form.

The *Ama no sekkutsu kuketsu* provides a circumvoluted attempt to explain the fact that Amaterasu is riding a horse, connecting this to Amaterasu's femaleness through a complex exegesis of the second hexagram of the *Yijing* 易経 (where a horse, or rather a mare, appears as a yin symbol). [122] In so doing, it discards an entire mythological strand that links Memyō Bosatsu and Amaterasu, as silkworm deities, to the horse. This type of explanation reflects a later rationalizing tendency, and it may indicate that the relations of Amaterasu with sericulture and weaving, which were so important during the Nara and Heian periods, had grown dim by the beginning of the Edo period, when this text was compiled. That these relations were not entirely lost, however, is evident from the fact that the *Ama no sekkutsu kuketsu* also draws from the *Nihonshoki* episode in which the raging god Susanoo throws a flayed horse into his sister's weaving room, causing the accidental death of one of the distraught weaving maidens. Yet the strong gender-coded meaning of the horse in that context is almost entirely erased by the transformation of the Japanese mythological horse into the *Yijing*'s emblematic mare.

Regarding the exegesis of Fudō and Aizen, the text also strives to explain the contradiction between Chinese cosmology (in which the moon is a yin or female symbol, and the sun a yang or male symbol) and Japanese mythology (in which the moon god, Tsukiyomi 月読, is a male deity, and the sun goddess a female deity—like the central deity of the Amaterasu triad, but unlike Aizen, Fudō's counterpart). The yin-yang polarity, which fits very nicely with the dualism of esoteric Buddhism, is harder to reconcile with the data of Japanese mythology. The text resorts to the classical Buddhist hermeneutical trick that explains away contradictions by resorting to the two levels of truth (conventional and ultimate): "on the surface," the male god Tsukiyomi appears as Fudō, a yin deity of the Womb realm; at a deeper level, Fudō is actually male, yang. The opposite is true of Aizen, and that is why the latter is identified with the female deity

Amaterasu. This interpenetration of opposites also has the advantage of transforming what would otherwise appear as a dualistic opposition into a nondual polarity (like that of the yin and the yang).

An oral tradition explains the apparent inversion of the usual yin-yang symbolism—the moon's being on the yang side, and the sun on the yin side—by the fact that these two symbols are not understood here in their traditional cosmological sense, but as symbolizing Amaterasu's two acolytes.[123] This unusual disposition is also said to represent the nonduality of the Womb and Vajra realms, i.e., by placing Fudō, symbol of the Womb realm, inside a lunar disk (Vajra realm) and Aizen, symbol of the Vajra realm, inside a solar disk (Womb realm).[124] In contrast, I would suggest a more persuasive embryological reading in which the white moon connotes male semen, and the red sun female blood.

As Dolce points out, the two complementary figures of Fudō and Aizen interpenetrate like yin and yang, or like "red" and "white." Inasmuch as their nonduality is already implicit in their interpenetration, there seems to be no need of a third, mediating figure to express it. Perhaps we have here a compromise between the esoteric teachings of Shingon and Tendai, which expressed nonduality through binary and ternary models, respectively. From a superficial standpoint, Fudō symbolizes the Womb mandala and the Inner Shrine, Aizen the Vajra Realm mandala and the Outer Shrine. At a deeper level, however, it is the opposite: Fudō comes to symbolize the Vajra Realm mandala and the Outer Shrine, Aizen the Womb mandala and the Inner Shrine. The sun and the moon are said to be Aizen and Fudō in their "living body" (*shōjin* 生身).[125] Dolce points out that the concreteness of this expression implies an actual visualization practice, or a vision of the type recorded by Nichiren in his *Fudō Aizen kankenki*. Finally, the *Bikisho* identifies the triad formed by Aizen, Fudō, and Amaterasu with another—cosmological—triad consisting of the sun, the moon, and the stars.

Yet the *Ama no sekkutsu kuketsu* steps back from the Chinese cosmological model to return to a more Japanese, classical mythological interpretation. It argues that Fudō in the moon (yin) disk and Aizen in the sun (yang) disk are not to be taken as cosmological symbols but as acolytes of Amaterasu, and that this disposition is determined by the traditional representation of the two *kami* that accompany the goddess. Takuhatachiji-hime 栲機千々姫, on the left, has a sword as her "divine body" (*shintai*) and is therefore equated with Fudō, while Tajikarao 手力雄, on the right, has a bow as his *shintai* and is therefore identified with Aizen.[126]

The *Miwa-ryū dōjō kuketsu* explains that the Miwa relic ritual took as its *honzon* the triad formed by Nyoirin, Fudō, and Aizen, in front of which were placed the Buddha's relics, identical with the *cintāmaṇi*. Nyoirin is the *honji* of Amaterasu, while Fudō corresponds to Ame no Koyane 天児屋,

and Aizen to Takemikazuchi 武甕槌—the two *kami* who, in classical mythology, pulled Amaterasu out of the heavenly cave.[127]

Fudō and Aizen symbolize the two mandalas and the corresponding seed-letters, *a* (Womb mandala) and *vaṃ* (Vajra Realm mandala). The priest must visualize the letter *vaṃ* turning into a wish-fulfilling jewel that becomes Toyouke, the *kami* of the Outer Shrine; and the letter *a* turning into a *yata* mirror that becomes Amaterasu, the *kami* of the Inner Shrine. On each side are two *seed-letters,* which become the *kami* Ame no Koyane and Ame no Futodama 天太玉, respectively. Then the priest must visualize the seven stars, the nine luminaries, the twelve palaces, and the twenty-eight lunar mansions descending onto the altar, surrounded by myriads of gods.[128]

According to Dolce, the identification of Fudō and Aizen with two rather subaltern *kami* represents a departure from the earlier model, as represented for instance in the *Bikisho.* In this text, more in accordance with Ryōbu shintō, Fudō and Aizen correspond to the two Ise shrines, respectively. But here too, the text explains the discrepancy between Chinese notions of yin and yang and the symbolic connotations of Fudō and Aizen by resorting to the two truths theory. The triad formed by the two wisdom kings and Nyoirin is also identified with the three imperial regalia—Nyoirin corresponding to the divine mirror, Fudō to the divine sword, and Aizen to the wish-fulfilling jewel, that is, the divine seal.[129]

This image of Amaterasu (or Memyō Bosatsu) also brings to mind that of Taga Myōjin 多賀明神, the deity of Taga Shrine, who is usually represented as a woman riding a white or black horse, holding a sword in her right hand and a sūtra box in her left hand, with the sun and the moon above her (Fig. 5.21).[130] She is shown frontally, however, whereas Memyō Bosatsu and Amaterasu are usually facing toward the left (with one exception). While the main deities of Taga Shrine are said to be Izanami and Izanagi, Taga Myōjin is described as a manifestation of Amaterasu as ruler of the underworld. The *Tenshō daijin kuketsu* 天照大神口訣, for instance, declares: "Generally speaking the great deity [Amaterasu], from the standpoint of the Kusha 倶舎 (Skt. *Abhidharmakoṣa*) [school], corresponds to Bonten (Brahmā) and Taishakuten 帝釈天 (Indra), and from the Shingon standpoint to Shōten (Vināyaka). Because she is straightforward, when she dwells within beings she corresponds to their companion spirits (*kushōjin*). Because she witnesses the good and evil they commit, she corresponds to King Enma in the netherworld. Although all these deities are one, it is more particularly Taga Myōjin who corresponds to the infernal judge in that case. In his commentary on the *Nakatomi harae,* the great master [Kūkai] therefore interpreted her as the great deity of the five paths (Godō daijin 五道大神). She is the fundamental deity that controls the two dharmas of life and death."[131] The identification of Amaterasu with King Enma and the companion spirits provides another link with Fudō

FIGURE 5.21. Taga Myōjin. Edo period. Sheet, ink on paper. University Art Museum, Kyoto City University of Arts. *BZS* 4079.

and Aizen in their function as Dharma protectors and placenta deities.

THE OPHIDIAN AIZEN

The dyad formed by Aizen and Fudō reappears in a series of secret traditions related to the so-called Peasant Aizen (Denpu Aizen 田夫愛染) ritual. We recall that this ritual was transmitted by Ningai, who himself allegedly received it from his master reincarnated in the person of a peasant. Its *honzon,* Aizen, is represented in the form of a green snake wearing a jewel on its "neck" (Fig. 5.23).[132] In the two-headed snake representation of the Daigoji protector, Seiryō Gongen 清瀧権現, the two heads are said to represent Aizen and Fudō. In the Ise *kanjō* 伊勢灌頂, an unction ritual performed in the Ise tradition, the priest visualizes a five-wheel stūpa at the Outer Shrine. This stūpa changes into two snakes, which transform into Aizen.[133] Another text gives specific details: "At the Inner Shrine, one builds an eight-petaled lotus with stones, on which is a live golden-colored snake. At the Outer Shrine, one builds a five-degree stūpa, on the space-wheel of which is a live white-colored snake. From remote antiquity till the present they have always dwelt there, without change. They are called the body (or bodies) of Raga (i.e., Aizen)."[134] In other words, the golden snake symbolizes Amaterasu, the white snake Toyouke 豊受 (that is, Ugajin)—and both are manifestations of Aizen.[135]

Among various texts mentioning that ritual, the *Oral Tradition Concerning the Peasant Ritual* (*Denpu-hō kuketsu* 田夫法口訣) offers an excruciatingly elaborate discussion of the symbolism surrounding the seed-letter *hūṃ* (J. *un*).[136] The term *denpu* 田夫 is said to express the

FIGURE 5.22. Aizen's snake-like seed-letter. 14th century. Color on silk. Kanazawa bunko.

FIGURE 5.23. Denpu Aizen. 16th century. Color on paper. Ninnaji, Kyoto.

nonduality between the two realms and between the two wisdom kings Fudō and Aizen, and its two characters are explained in reference to the earth and its power to make things grow. In medieval exegesis, the character *den* 田 (field) is often described as a graphic variant of the swastika (*manji* 卍), itself a symbol of the seed-letter *a,* that is, the source of all things. It also alludes to the mind-ground, the source of all mental and physical phenomena. It is therefore equivalent to the wish-fulfilling jewel. The grains produced by the earth, in particular rice, are also identified with the Buddha's relics and consequently with the jewel. They are the source of life for all beings, and correspond to the buddha-nature in beings and to the gods' body. The character *den* (i.e., the letter *a*) is also identical with Fudō, whereas the character *fu/pu* 夫 (male, father) is equated with Aizen in his function as compassionate father of all beings. Yet the etymological speculation does not stop here. The seed-letter *hūṃ,* Aizen's seed-letter, is said to be composed of four elements (the syllables *a, ha, u,* and *ma.* The syllable *a,* being "unborn," does not appear. The syllable *ha* forms the phonic substance, modified by vocalization (*u,* the dot below), and the nasalization (*ma,* the dot, or *kūten* [Skt. *anusvāra*], "space-dot"). The shape of the letters *ha* and *u* evokes that of a snake, and *u-ha* signifies the snake deity Ugajin. The dot symbolizes the *cintāmaṇi* jewel. The seed-letter *hūṃ* is therefore a symbol of both the snake and the jewel, and the form of the snake evokes that of the *kami* (and of Benzaiten/ Ugajin). The text also quotes the *Testament* and links the syllables *a* and *hūṃ*—and the two wisdom kings Fudō and Aizen—to breathing. Opening the mouth to breathe out and form the sound *a* corresponds to Fudō, closing it to breathe in and form the sound *hūṃ* corresponds to Aizen. The text then identifies the old peasant who transmitted that secret ritual to Ningai with Amaterasu, whom it describes as a primordial deity, the origin of all the gods. After describing the mantras and mudrās of the ritual, it gives a rather far-fetched interpretation of the character *sun,* Aizen's emblem,

FIGURE 5.24. Blue snake (Denpu Aizen). Color on paper. Saidaiji, Nara.

FIGURE 5.25. Snake on *vajra* (Denpu Aizen). Color on paper. Saidaiji, Nara.

in terms of the five buddhas and the five knowledges. It also explains all the attributes of Aizen's image as expressions of the nonduality of Fudō and Aizen. The three eyes of Aizen operate a shift from the binary to the ternary model—the seed-letters *a, vaṃ,* and *hūṃ* representing the Womb and Vajra realms and their resolution into the Susiddhi realm. These three letters are also interpreted in terms of the earth's fertility: the letter *a* (Dainichi, the sun buddha, symbolizing fire), allied to the letter *vaṃ* (rain, water), produces *hūṃ* (vegetal growth). The text takes off in all kinds of tangents, but the main point remains its discussion of nonduality through Aizen's seed-letter *hūṃ* and the pair formed by Aizen and Fudō. The sudden apparition of Amaterasu suggests that one of the goals of the text was to link the medieval theory of the identity of Aizen and Amaterasu with the secret Aizen ritual (Denpu Aizen-hō 田夫愛染法).[137]

In another variant, the seed-letter *hūṃ* is equated with the sixth consciousness or mind consciousness (Skt. *mano-vijñāna*), and with one of the five knowledges, the so-called *myōkanzatchi* 妙観察知 (Skt. *pratyavekṣaṇā-jñāna*) or knowledge of differences within the undifferentiated totality, which brings the practitioner to buddhahood.[138] This snake-like letter represents Aizen in his ophidian form.[139] In an illustration preserved at Kanazawa bunko, Aizen is shown as a snake, on the head of which a yellow jewel emits a red light that becomes the *kūten* (space-dot). The ensemble forms the seed-letter *oṃ*—rather than Aizen's usual seed-letter, *hūṃ*.[140] This exorcism was actually part of a ritual centered on the "live body of Benzaiten"—probably because the snake is also the form of Ugajin (Daikokuten), Benzaiten's manifestation and husband.[141]

CODETTA

Despite their separate origins and apotheosis as *honzon* of their respective *besson* mandalas, Fudō and Aizen were ultimately forced back into a dual structure. By the same token, they seem to regress from their exalted position to the subaltern rank of acolytes and Dharma protectors (*gohō* 護 法)—but also to combine in a dual figure (the two-headed Aizen) that perhaps paved the way to the notion of the Three Worthies (*sanzon* 三尊). As one member of a dyad, Fudō in particular appears to be functionally similar to his acolytes Kongara and Seitaka. Actually, the two wisdom kings are not merely protectors, but the image of a bipolar yet nondual *totality*, as aspects of the wish-fulfilling jewel. The embryological symbolism may have played a role in this evolution. It also reminds us that unity and duality are never static but always caught in a twofold process of emanation and reabsorption, as an image of division or union. In the triad, the third element is conceived as either the source of the two members of the dyad or the result of their union: the one producing the two, or being produced by the two. Concretely, the triadic representation means either that the two acolytes are two aspects of the central figure, or that the latter is the result of the union of the two opposite elements (red and white, yin and yang) they represent.[142] Regarding Tantric binary thinking, and the way it came to work essentially as a formal principle of classification like yin and yang, one is reminded of Georges Dumézil's reflections on the couple formed in Indo-European ideology by Mitra and Varuṇa:

> Did the "sovereign concepts" couple evolve, like yin and yang, toward a sexed interpretation, toward a "male-female" pairing? If we take the Indo-European world as a whole, it appears not. . . . But the most precociously philosophical of the Indo-European regions, India, did indeed set out along the path of the sexed couple, and did so, it appears, like the Chinese, under the influence of their powerful hierogamic representation of heaven and earth: is Varuṇa not "the other world" and also, albeit not in a stable way, heaven, whereas Mitra is "this world"?[143]

In this sense, the semantic and symbolic values of these deities become ancillary to the classificatory purpose. As in the case of Mitra and Varuṇa as analyzed by Dumézil, once Aizen and Fudō become a pair, one can no longer provide a strict definition of their respective functions; at the most one can provide samples and say, for instance, that one of the two components (the Aizen side) covers a symbolic field related to love, desire, fertility, fecundity, solar symbolism, and life, whereas the other (Fudō) covers a field related to the dark side, anger, lunar symbolism, and death. But, as Dumézil points out, "it would be futile to start from one element in these lists of 'contents' in the hope of deducing the others from it."[144] Yet the attributes and functions of Fudō and Aizen, unlike those of Mitra and Varuṇa, are not fixed, and can at times be inverted. Aizen can at times symbolize anger, Fudō embryological gestation. Nevertheless, the conceptual couple they compose resembles that of Mitra and Varuṇa in the sense that it evolved, *like yin and yang, toward a gendered interpretation, a male-female pairing.* Perhaps under the influence of the powerful Chinese hierogamic representation of heaven and earth, Fudō came to represent "the other world" in this pairing whereas Aizen stood for "this world."[145] At the same time the shift from this binary model to the ternary model of the Three Worthies may reflect the kind of double opposition described by Lévi-Strauss: "In the first instance, it consists primarily in the opposition between a ternary and a binary organization, one asymmetrical, the other symmetrical; and in the second instance, in the opposition between social mechanisms, some of which are based on reciprocity, others on hierarchy."[146]

For the *Keiran shūyōshū,* the triadic structure formed in Tendai doctrine by the addition of the Susiddhi realm to the Womb and Vajra realms corresponds to the triad formed by Fudō and his two acolytes, Kongara and Seitaka.[147] Likewise, in the *Himitsu gentei kuketsu* 秘密源底口決 (1327–1334), regarding the formula "One buddha, two *myōō,*" the Joint Ritual of the Three Worthies is said to be the source and foundation (*gentei* 源底), the essence (*kanjin* 肝心, lit. "liver and heart") of that school.[148] This triadic structure is so basic that it gave its name to the Sanbō-in (Three Jewels Pavilion) school of Shingon.[149] Like the crystal of the jewel, it replicates itself in ever larger units. That logic is perfectly illustrated by the *Goyuigō daiji,* where the three jewels are superimposed on the various triads, above all those formed by Kūkai and his two disciples Jitsue and Shinga on the one hand, and by the jewel (Nyoirin), Aizen, and Fudō on the other.

The symbolism of the tripartite jewel resurfaces in the famous dream that the Tendai prelate Jien 慈円 (1155–1225) had in 1203, in which the Three Regalia (sword, mirror, and jewel) become Fudō, Butsugen, and Dainichi (symbolizing the sovereign, his consort, and the crown prince), respectively.[150] Here, however, Aizen has been replaced by Fudō, whose sword conveniently symbolizes the sovereign's virility. In an instruction given to his disciple Jiken in 1205, three years after this dream, Jien uses the same sexual metaphor, which he presents as a "deep secret," involving Aizen as the female this time and Vajrasattva.[151] Although the protagonists of Jien's dream do not exactly overlap with those of the Sanzon gōgyō ritual, the triadic structure is already solidly in place. The *Keiran shūyōshū* gives a further spin to that logic by turning any pairing of acolytes and Dharma protectors into companion spirits (*kushōjin*).[152]

Mikkyō clearly delights in numerological symbolism. It relentlessly imposed its binary and ternary schemas on reality, whether in ritual, doctrinal, or mythological fashion. This must be seen as an ideological attempt to impose order on reality, to domesticate the natural and social chaos. It cannot be taken simply as a soteriological technique to overcome duality through ternary structures pointing to transcendental unity. On the contrary, it contributed to reinforcing oppressive social structures. Nevertheless, this profusion of binary and ternary symbols had an unexpected effect, namely, the emergence of new patterns that linked deities in a radically original fashion and contributed to the extension of the divine network—in a way that both reinforced and undermined Mikkyō's grip on reality.

Despite his symmetry with Fudō, Aizen, probably because of his stronger association with the wish-fulfilling jewel, came to be identified with Nyoirin and Amaterasu. Next to the dual Aizen, a mere cipher of nonduality, the singular emerges (or survives)—a much more unpredictable and complex complex, related in obscure ways to demonic deities like Shōten and Dakiniten. In this sense, the Sanzon gōgyō ritual prefigured the Santen gōgyō ritual, the Joint Ritual of the Three Devas (Shōten, Dakiniten, and Benzaiten), to which I will return. Yet the former, centered on one bodhisattva (Nyoirin) and two wisdom kings (Aizen and Fudō), remains closer to the explicit theology of Mikkyō than the latter, centered on three devas. They also differ structurally: the hierarchy constituted by the combination of the main deity (Nyoirin) with a dyad is replaced by a genuine triadic structure where the three devas, having the same status, are interchangeable and can in turn occupy the central position.

The case of the triad formed by Amaterasu, Aizen, and Fudō reveals that the triad is actually formed by two dyads: Aizen and Fudō on the one hand, and Aizen and Amaterasu on the other. Indeed, Aizen, like Amaterasu and unlike Fudō, represents the solar principle and the jewel; we have also seen that he came to be identified with Amaterasu. The same seems to be true in the case of the Sanzon gōgyō triad.

In other words, it isn't simply a dialectic fusion of two binary opposites to form or produce a third transcendent term. One of the binary opposites (Aizen) is replicated in transcendent fashion (Amaterasu). If one follows that logic with regard to the jewel, one could say that the relation between Aizen and Amaterasu is the same as that between the two jewels of the Shingon tradition (conditioned and unconditioned, *shosa* and *nōsa*).

The metaphysical transformation of Amaterasu—from a local deity into a transcendent *kami*—also has two rather different meanings. On the one hand, in the explicit pantheon it represents an ideological attempt to identify a transcendental absolute, the counterpart of the absolute represented by Dainichi—the *clé de voûte* or keystone of Shingon and Ryōbu shintō theology. On the other hand, this system, as we noted, readily deconstructs itself, leading to an implicit mythology in which Amaterasu diffuses to all levels of the pantheon, exchanging attributes (and fusing natures) not only with her rival brother, the *kami* Susanoo (a paradigmatic *kōjin* figure), but also with various forms of the bodhisattva Kannon (beginning with Nyoirin), as well as with the wisdom king Aizen, the astral deity (and "bodhisattva") Myōken, the devas Yama, Dakiniten, and Benzaiten, and embryological deities like Kōjin and the *kushōjin*. In other words, the alleged nondualism of Shingon Buddhism led, in practice, to an orgy of binary structures. Even the triadic structures discussed above can be reduced upon analysis to dyadic structures. In contrast, the threefold structure of Tendai thinking may represent a more genuine ternary model.

In a book on the mysteries of the trinity, Dany-Robert Dufour opposes binary and ternary thinking as two fundamental and antagonistic epistemological structures of thought, and describes how, in Western culture, the ternary thinking that structured premodern mind and society (the three Dumézilian functions being just one example) has been gradually superseded by binary thinking—the world of logic, and of the excluded third, that has formed computers and come to dominate our minds. While Dufour's arguments take place in a radically different context, and some of them are unconvincing, I wonder if his analysis of ternary and binary models might not be heuristically useful to describe what I see as the opposition, within medieval Buddhism, of different generating schemes. The models available in Shingon and Tendai to overcome the duality they have created remain essentially ideological. In Shingon, the two-realm mandalas are said to fuse with one another (a nondual duality), while in Tendai they fuse in a third element, the Susiddhi. This ternary model, however, is no different from the Shingon model offered by Monkan with his Sanzon gōgyō ritual.

As Dolce and others have pointed out, much of Mikkyō doctrine and practice aims at overcoming duality. Dolce discusses in particular the performative nature of the triad based on the Aizen/Fudō dyad, which is developed as different stages of the union of opposites in specific ritual practice.[153] The unity is thus embodied in a third deity—Nyoirin, Amaterasu, or Kūkai.

Under the guise of nondualism, however, we witness a proliferation of binary thinking, an avatar of the *pensée par couples,* as this dualism spread from Mikkyō to nascent Shintō (Ryōbu shintō). Yet this binary thinking does not really "think," it merely divides and duplicates, like an algorithm. The final fusion always implies a loss or an exclusion. The third that is included implies an excluded third.[154] In this sense, even the ternary pattern of the Three Worthies is just an augmented variant of dualism. Incidentally, this pattern is a ritual one, not a mythological one: there is no myth of the Three Worthies, even if we find mythical fragments for Aizen and Fudō. Here the opposition (and complementarity) that Lévi-Strauss established between myth and ritual—the former structuring the world into polarities, the latter trying in vain to bridge the gap caused by mythical thinking and restore a primordial oneness—seems to break down: both myth and ritual remain essentially dualistic, even when they claim the contrary.[155]

However, next to such binary/ternary patterns, more genuine ternary structures (open triads) emerged in Tendai theology and in the rituals and iconology influenced by it. My contention is that such triads (for instance, that of the Three Devas, to which I will return) radically subverted the closure of the binary model. One may of course argue that this evolution from a closed to an open triad is merely a replay of the ancient Indian predilection for triads, modeled upon a ternary cosmos. But perhaps it actually points toward a site *beyond the triad,* beyond what Abel Bergaigne called the "mythological arithmetic." While the first type of triad remains part of an ideological discourse in the service of political ambitions (those of Monkan and Go-Daigo, for instance), the second type seems more attuned to the elusive nature of phenomenological experience and the proliferation of meaning that derives from it. While the first type reinforces the spell of the yin-yang paradigm on our minds, the second tries to dispel it. I feel therefore compelled to examine this second type of triad in more detail in the next volume, *Protectors and Predators.*

6

THE HIDDEN JEWEL
The Wish-fulfilling Jewel

*(What this meant / Nobody cared); the point is that
 the three
Chambers, then bound by you and her and me,
Now form a tryptich or a three-act play
In which portrayed events forever stay.*

VLADIMIR NABOKOV, *PALE FIRE*

The wish-fulfilling jewel (*cintāmaṇi*) played a cru-
cial role in the medieval Japanese *imaginaire*. Operating at the junction
between esoteric Buddhism (mainly Shingon) and imperial power, it
became an important part of ritual technology.[1] One essential aspect of
this development was the cult of Nyoirin, a form of Kannon that was
specifically associated with the wish-fulfilling jewel. The two cults reinforced each other and became so intertwined that it is impossible to study
one without the other. They are two faces of the same phenomenon,
the ritual and mythological poles of the same spectrum. Through such
symbols and objects, we discover another facet of medieval Japan, and
another Buddhism—quite different from ordinary accounts of the "new"
Kamakura Buddhism.

This chapter focuses on the cult of the wish-fulfilling jewel, leaving the cult of Nyoirin and related jewel deities for the next chapter. I
first describe the process through which the relics of the Buddha became
identified with the wish-fulfilling jewel, particularly in the Sanbō-in and
Kajūji branches of Shingon, as well as at Saidaiji, with Eison and his
disciples. This process went hand in hand with the ascension of jewel
deities like Aizen, Ichiji Kinrin, Butsugen, and Nyoirin Kannon (to name
just a few) and was further related to Buddhist efforts to back up imperial power. I discuss the nature of the jewel and the distinction between
its two types—the invisible or "generative" and the visible or "generated"—as well as the dynamics of secrecy that sustained the former.

At the center of this development were the jewel of Mount Murō and the legend of Kūkai as it developed with his apocryphal *Testament* (*Goyuigō*). The instrumental role played by his disciple Kenne in the spread of that local tradition, and the role of dragons in it, are then considered, together with the apotheosis of Kūkai and his identification with the jewel, as reflected in the work of the priest Monkan. As the cult of the jewel disseminated from Mount Murō, other jewels appeared on Mount Kōya and other sites, paving the way to the theory of the three imperial regalia. I reexamine this Japanese tradition in the light of possible continental influences, particularly from the Liao kingdom in northeastern China, before concluding with a look at the triadic structure that underlies the jewel symbolism.

THE CULT OF THE WISH-FULFILLING JEWEL

The Buddha's Relics and the Jewel

The wish-fulfilling jewel gained its full symbolic dimension in Japan by becoming linked to the Buddha's relics. The Buddha's relics had long been the focus of a thriving cult—indeed, practically since the time of his *parinirvāṇa*.[2] In due course they came to be deposited in stūpa-reliquaries throughout Asia, following the model of King Aśoka. In China and Japan, rulers disseminated such stūpas as symbols of legitimacy.[3] In Japan, a major change took place with the performance of the state-sponsored Ritual of the Latter Seven Days (Goshichinichi mishiho 後七日御修法), so named because it was held during the second week after New Year. Because relics were seen as the fusion point of the Womb and Vajra realms, a reliquary was placed in the center of the altar between the two mandalas.[4] Consequently, reliquaries became the focus and pivot of the esoteric teaching.

Kūkai was purportedly the first to perform this ritual, which was centered on the eighty grains of relics that he had brought back from China, believed to have come from the mythical Iron Tower in southern India—the *fons et origo* of the esoteric Buddhist teaching.[5] It was aimed at insuring the protection of the nation and the health of the emperor. Because it was the monopoly of Shingon, it was within this school that this particular relic cult initially developed, but a number of other rituals centered on the Buddha's relics soon developed.[6] Relics were credited with increasingly broad powers, from eliminating calamities to the salvation of beings in the final age of the Law. Owing to their supernatural aura as substitute bodies of the Buddha, they were seen as capable of granting all wishes. From that standpoint, they were functionally similar to the wish-fulfilling jewel, and thus they were eventually identified with it. The locus classicus for the establishment of this identity was the following passage of the *Da zhidu lun* 大智度論: "The jewel comes from the relics. When the Dharma disappears, the relics of the Buddha will all turn into *cintāmaṇi*. Likewise, after a thousand years, ice will turn into crystal pearls."[7] Ironically, this prediction was to come true in medieval Japan, perhaps under foreign influence, and owing to the agency of a handful of Shingon priests.

By the end of the Heian period, various texts—Kūkai's apocryphal *Testament* (*Goyuigō*), for instance, and the writings of Jichiun 実運 (var. Jitsuun, 1105–1160) and Shōken 勝賢 (1138–1198)—stated that the jewel was derived from the relics of the Buddha.[8] As the relics merged with the jewel, the *honzon* of relic rituals became the jewel itself or a deity related to it (for instance, Ichiji Kinrin, Aizen Myōō, or Nyoirin Kannon). In addition, by merging with beliefs and practices centered on the five-wheel stūpa (*gorintō*), the relics inherited the latter's cosmological symbolism and came to be associated with the five esoteric elements that constitute all physical and metaphysical phenomena, the human body and the body of the cosmic buddha Dainichi—or rather the human body *as* Dainichi's body.[9] In this way the relics were equal to Dainichi himself, the buddha in his transcendent dharma-body. This conception implies a radical departure from the old belief that the relics were merely actual fragments of the physical body of the "historical" Buddha. Reconceptualized as the wish-fulfilling jewel, they came to be perceived as the essence of various jewel deities (most notably Nyoirin Kannon). This conceptual innovation brought about major changes in ritual practice. After the Heian period, the Buddha's relics, released from the confines of stūpas, became the focus of rites aimed at protecting the State and the well-being of individuals.

New types of portable reliquaries appeared in the form of stūpas, lotuses, even jewels, their variety reflecting the diversity of the cult.[10] Increasingly miniaturized, these reliquaries were set in the middle of altars. Like embers glowing beneath ashes, the relics radiated spiritual warmth toward all who approached, and contained the potential of an all-consuming fire (represented notably by deities such as Aizen).

The cult of the wish-fulfilling jewel emerged in this setting. Relying on Japanese documents that trace its origins to Kūkai, scholars like Naitō Sakae have described this emergence as a purely Japanese development.[11] Recent archeological evidence, discussed by Kamikawa Michio and Kim Youn-mi, suggests otherwise.[12] It seems in particular that Hanjun, one of the Shingon priests who were instrumental in the creation of jewel rituals, was influenced by esoteric rituals from the Liao kingdom in northeastern China. I will return to that point shortly.

While the Buddha's relics and the jewel were believed to fulfill all wishes, they themselves became the object of intense desire. Indeed, thefts of relics became the talk of the capital during the medieval period.[13] Although the historical record is not always sufficiently explicit, such

Realization (Susiddhi) realm, the symbolic (*samaya*) form of which is the central stūpa.[25]

Relics as Seed-Syllables

Let us now turn to Ichiji Kinrin 一字金輪, the so-called Golden Wheel Buddha of the Single Letter. Toward the end of the Heian period, as relic worship grew increasingly detached from the physical reality of the object, relics came to be considered the equivalent of the seed-letter *bhrūṃ* (J. *boron*), the source of all things and symbol of the cosmic buddha Kinrin. The basis of this conception was the discrimination of three types of relics in accordance with the three bodies of the Buddha. The relics of the dharma body (Skt. *dharmakāya,* J. *hosshin* 法身) corresponded to physical dharmas; those of the reward body (*sambhogakāya, hōshin* 報身), to mental dharmas; while those of the transformation body (*nirmāṇakāya, ōjin* 応身) were verbal acts (in this case, the seed-syllable *bhrūṃ*).[26] They also corresponded to the three mysteries (*sanmitsu* 三密) of Dainichi's body, mind, and speech.

Furthermore, to explain why *bhrūṃ* was the supreme secret of the relics ritual, the *Keiran shūyōshū* states that after the Buddha entered *parinirvāṇa,* out of compassion he transformed himself into this seed-syllable that encapsulates the three bodies of the Buddha and is the source of all stars, devas, and *kami*.[27] In a sense, then, all mantras, beginning with the seed-syllable *bhrūṃ,* are relics of a higher order, and that is why they appear in reliquaries in place of (or next to) physical relics. At the same time, the *Keiran shūyōshū* elevates Śākyamuni (Kinrin) to the supreme rank, together with his local manifestation, the Sannō deity, which becomes the "global body" of all gods. In the final analysis, "Kinrin is none other than the relics"—that is, the relics, in their transcendental form, are none other than Kinrin (or the pair formed by Kinrin and Butsugen).[28]

Relic Worship

Relics became the focus of rain rituals—those performed by Kūkai at Shinsen'en, for instance, and those of Mount Murō. This tradition drew on the cult of *nāgas* (or dragons) and the belief that those water deities had received a portion of the Buddha's relics.[29] The early Kamakura period saw the development of new forms of reliquaries and *dhāraṇīs* associated with the relics. Among them was the Hōkyōin-tō 宝篋印塔, a miniature stūpa containing the Treasure-casket Seal (Hōkyōin) darani. This incantation, whose recitation was said to be as meritorious as the worship of the relics of all the buddhas, was first disseminated in China by the last ruler of Wuyue 呉越, Qian Hongchu 銭弘俶 (r. 947–978), who, emulating King Aśoka, commissioned the production of 84,000 small stūpas, all of them, so it was said, containing this *dhāraṇī*. These reliquaries, after being introduced in Japan around the middle of the tenth century, came to be used as grave markers.[30]

The relic cult developed and diversified particularly in the Ono branch of Shingon, centered on Daigoji and Kajūji.[31] The main difference between the two monasteries in this respect was that relics and the jewel were identical for Daigoji monks, whereas Kajūji monks saw them as the objects of two distinct realities.[32] At Kajūji, the relic ritual took Ichiji Kinrin (or more precisely, Shaka Kinrin) as its *honzon.* Since relics and seed-letters were perceived as identical, the Kajūji relic ritual was transformed into one for Ichiji Kinrin. Now the nonduality of Kinrin's two aspects (as Shaka Kinrin and Dainichi Kinrin) elevated relics to the status of the dharma body—a transcendent reality—without having to borrow the jewel's identity. While traditional relics, in their materiality, signified the Buddha in his transformation body as the "historical" Śākyamuni, these new esoteric relics became the visible form of the Buddha in his dharma body, as Dainichi. This shift was permitted by the equivalence between Shaka Kinrin and Dainichi Kinrin, two aspects of Ichiji Kinrin, the Golden Wheel Buddha emanating from the ultimate seed-letter *bhrūṃ.* According to Jichiun's *Hizō konpōshō* 祕藏金寶鈔, the officiating priest during the relic ritual hung an image of Ichiji Kinrin and placed a reliquary-stūpa (*sharitō* 舍利塔) in the middle of the altar while reciting the seed-letter *bhrūṃ.* The *Da tuoluoni mofa zhong yisi shenzhou jing* 大陀羅尼末法中一字神呪経, which served as the scriptural basis of this rite, states that the relics transform into this seed-letter, bringing salvation to all.[33]

Several esoteric Buddhist sources cite the *Sūtra on the Flower of Compassion* (Skt. *Karuṇāpuṇḍarīka-sūtra,* Ch. *Beihua jing* 悲華経, J. *Hikekyō*) as stating that even after the Buddha's *parinirvāṇa,* his relics would spread to benefit sentient beings. In fact, such a passage does not appear in the text in question, but the idea seems implicit.[34] The Buddha's relics were incorporated into the three mysteries of Shingon, corresponding to the mystery of the Buddha's body (*shinmitsu* 身密), while Buddhist scriptures and Japanese *kami* were linked to the mysteries of the Buddha's mind and speech, respectively. This allowed an incantation (*dhāraṇī*)—the quintessence of the scriptures—to substitute for the relics.[35]

The Buddha's relics eventually became a kind of absolute referent, no longer needing the (departed) Buddha to justify their existence. In turn, the jewel also became an absolute source of power, controlling the prosperity and fertility of the entire world, beginning with Japan and its ruler. At the same time, paradoxically, it became more concrete with the creation of artificial jewels, the main components of which were the relics. Eventually the relics and the jewel merged entirely—at least in Shingon currents such as the Daigoji-ryū 醍醐寺流, and among Ritsu priests such as Chōgen and Eison.

Because they constituted the "essence" of buddhahood, relics also came to be perceived as the "original ground" (*honji*) of the *kami* in the so-called Shintō mandalas. A case in point is a series of reliquaries from Kasuga Shrine (see Fig. 5.9 above).[36] In some of them, the relic is mounted on the image of a deer, the animal emblematic of Kasuga;[37] in others, the Kasuga mandala is carved on the wall of the reliquary.[38] In all cases, they were in one way or another identified with the Kasuga deity. Other examples, which I will come back to in more detail, include relics identified with Amaterasu and Hachiman.

The Symbolism of the Jewel

It is not easy to separate the cult of relics proper from that of the wish-filling jewel, even though the two cults followed their own dynamics. One must also distinguish between the conceptual and the ritual levels: in certain cases the relics merged with the jewel at the conceptual level, but not always; rituals sometimes took the jewel as their *honzon,* but relics were often used.

The wish-fulfilling jewel is usually represented in the form of a radiant drop-shaped sphere.[39] It was perceived as a transformation of the Buddha's relics and the *samaya* form of various buddhas and deities. It is a source of prosperity, the Asian equivalent of the horn of plenty or cornucopia. Its symbolism is particularly rich in Japan, where the word *tama* 玉 (jewel) is homonymous with *tama* 魂/霊 (soul, spirit). These symbolic values reintroduce ancient motifs into Buddhist theology, motifs reminiscent of the economic function in Dumézil's trifunctional theory—a function that covers notions such as fecundity and fertility.[40] Things are not so simple, however. This symbol also involves the notion of power, characteristic of the second or martial function, while its links to the three imperial regalia point toward the first or priestly function. The jewel was originally only one of the seven treasures of the *cakravartin* king, but it eventually eclipsed all the others. The *Jikaku daishi hiketsu* 慈覚大師秘決 reinterpreted the seven treasures by describing seven kinds of jewels—four mundane and three supramundane.[41] It emphasized the generative power of the jewel, which came to be a dominant feature of the Shingon jewel as well. By the Nara and Heian periods, several traditions already existed, which paved the way to the emergence of a medieval discourse related to the wish-fulfilling jewel. Important precursors to these traditions concerning the jewel(s) were the Hachiman cult and the legend of Empress Jingū 神功.[42] However, the text that contributed the most to establishing the identity of relics and the jewel toward the end of the Heian period is Kūkai's apocryphal *Testament* in twenty-five articles, to which we will return.[43]

Gradually, the jewel gained an absolute, timeless value. It was no longer just a relic—although the same, paradoxically, was also true for the relics themselves—but the source of all things and the emblem of the nonduality of mind and matter. It was no longer just the symbolic or *samaya* form of a specific buddha, but the mother of all buddhas: the cosmic egg out of which the entire world—beginning with Japan—emerged. This assertion has a recursive ring. In the *Record of the Origins of Mount Kinpu* (*Kinpusen engi yuraiki* 金峰山縁起由来記), for instance, when a monk objects that the jewel could not possibly be the source of Japan because it had been introduced to the country by Kūkai, the master counters that the jewel, being identical to Dainichi's mind, is eternally present in the three worlds. It is only for the benefit of beings that it appeared in this world through the Buddha's skillful means, first in India and eventually in Heian Japan.[44]

Twin Jewels

The question regarding the number of wish-fulfilling jewels existing in medieval Japan is a vexing—and perhaps futile—one. In Kūkai's *Testament,* the passage regarding the jewel gave rise to various interpretations, reflecting the rivalry between the Daigoji, Kajūji, and Hirosawa lineages. The *Testament* itself, perceived as a secret text, was both the proof of the jewel's authenticity and also a kind of textual equivalent: both were deposited at Shōkōmyō-in and provided legitimacy to the retired emperors of the Insei period. The *Testament* sets up a series of polarities that do not always overlap perfectly: between the "natural" jewel transmitted from India and the "artificial" jewel fabricated by Kūkai, the "generative" and "generated" jewel, the secret, invisible jewel and the manifest, visible jewel. The main distinction is that between the natural jewel hidden on Mount Murō and the artificial jewel fabricated by Kūkai from the Buddha's relics. In principle, only the former deserves to be called "generative" whereas the latter belongs to the category of "generated." Yet sometimes the artificial jewel is also labeled generative, and the distinction gets blurred.[45] The notion of generative (associated with the idea of incubation and embryological symbolism) implies latency, darkness, secrecy, concealment, invisibility, pure potentiality; whereas generated implies actualization, manifestation, full visibility, the plenitude of effects.

Burying the jewel, as Kūkai or his disciple Kenne allegedly did, meant not only to return it to the earth—from which it drew its generative power—but also to radically boost its power, by turning it into pure, transcendent potentiality. The elusive nature of the jewel(s) is related to the power of secrecy—a prominent feature of esoteric Buddhism.[46] In the *Testament,* the bodhisattva Vajrasattva explains to his disciple Nāgārjuna the importance of the esoteric teaching by comparing it to, or rather equating it with, the wish-fulfilling jewel. This is because "while we hear the name [of Mahāvairocana], its actual form is like that of the wish-fulfilling jewel which does not appear, yet produces jewels that benefit all sentient beings."[47] Like the esoteric teaching, the jewel is "both secret and beneficial to beings," or rather, it benefits beings precisely because it remains secret.

While the "high path" on Mount Murō ended in an unknown place with a "hidden" jewel, other Shingon lineages took a different path to power by emphasizing the manifest, "created" jewel that had been offered by Hanjun to retired emperor Shirakawa.[48] In a report to the court in 1192, Shōken argues that this jewel could be seen and worshiped whereas the Mount Murō jewel remained unseen and its immediate effects were by no means obvious.[49]

The theoretical distinction between two types of jewel soon became a concrete difference between two specific jewels, both traced back to Kūkai: one buried on Mount Murō, the other offered by Hanjun to retired emperor Shirakawa. Owing to its (relative) visibility, it was the latter that moved to the forefront in sectarian debates that opposed not only the Ono and Hirosawa branches, but also, within the Ono branch itself, the Kajūji and Sanbōin (Daigoji) lineages.

The *Keiran shūyōshū* quotes a Shingon priest's assertion that the generative (*nōsa* 能作) jewel was transmitted in the Ono branch, while the generated (*shosa* 所作) jewel was transmitted in the Hirosawa branch. Another source claims just the opposite. Obviously, each branch claimed to have the higher, generative jewel rather than the generated jewel.[50]

Kajūji monks, intent on developing relations with the ruler through the intermediary of concrete rituals, downplayed the jewel and put forward the traditional relic rituals. According to them, the jewel transmitted from the Chinese master Huiguo 惠果 (746–805) to Kūkai, and eventually from Hanjun to Shirakawa, was the only real one—no other jewel was ever buried on Mount Murō—and it was distinct from the relics. This jewel was eventually deposited at the Hall of Victorious Radiance (Shōkōmyō-in 勝光明院), the treasure house of retired emperor Go-Toba.[51] In other words, for the Kajūji lineage, the claims related to Mount Murō coming from Daigoji were false. This was a direct criticism of the *Testament.* Yet that text was also transmitted at Kajūji, along with the jewel deposited at Shōkōmyō-in.

While the Kajūji line initially claimed to be the legitimate possessor of the jewel, and specialized in jewel rituals such as the Nyohō Aizen-hō and the Nyohō Sonshō-hō initiated by Hanjun at the request of Shirakawa, other branches and lineages of Shingon actually performed these rituals as well.[52] After Kanjin 寛信 (1084–1153), the Kajūji line lost ground to the Daigoji line in that respect. It is with Shōken that Daigoji imposed itself in matters related to the jewel. Although Shōken was the founder of the Sanbō-in line at Daigoji, he also inherited the Kajūji rituals through Kanjin and Jichiun. He is singled out, with Kūkai and Hanjun, as one of the three men in Japan who "fabricated" jewels. One of these jewels— described as a ball containing nine kinds of precious substances—was allegedly inserted between the eyes of the Great Buddha of Tōdaiji after its restoration by Chōgen.[53] It seems that Shōken took several of the relics contained in Go-Shirakawa's jewel to put them into the jewel that he manufactured for Chōgen.[54] In the process, he may have damaged Go-Shirakawa's jewel, which perhaps explains why he was reluctant to return it. Another version has it that Shōken's jewel was inserted inside the torso (*tainai*) of the Great Buddha, not between its eyebrows.[55]

Shōken and the Sanbō-in line actually recognized two jewels (or types of jewels): the jewel buried on Mount Murō and the one transmitted by Hanjun (which passed in this way from the Kajūji to the Daigoji line). In a document written at the time of his returning the latter jewel to Shōkōmyō-in, Shōken distinguishes between the Mount Murō jewel and the "jewel" constituted by the two vases of relics at Tōji. Whereas the former was to be forever invisible and shrouded in mystery, the latter could be viewed by certain laymen (the ruler and his circle) in order for them to establish karmic links with Buddhism (and for the monks to establish karmic links with the court).[56]

The distinction between the two jewels overlapped with that between the two levels of truth, and in principle the Mount Murō jewel preserved its higher status. In the end, however, the visible or artificial jewel gained precedence. Yet that jewel itself remained hidden during and after its fabrication, despite Shōken's plea that it should be seen by all. Shōken argued that the two methods of producing the jewel (the traditional one, traced back to Kūkai, and the "contemporary" one—his own method), or rather the two views regarding the jewel (as regards its essential invisibility or visibility), were equally valid. In fact he privileged the latter, going so far as to criticize those who, relying only on the *Testament,* emphasized the hidden nature of the jewel. The target of his criticism was the Kajūji line, which emphasized the "Indian" jewel over the fabricated one.

Tōji monks adopted an intermediate position. For them, the relics of Tōji were literally a symbol, standing for something else—namely, the jewel on Mount Murō. They visualized that jewel during their relic rituals and faced toward the southeast, the direction of Mount Murō. They could also face southward, because in the symbolism of the mandala the southern direction corresponded to the jewel section. Their symbol was a potent one: the relics in the two bottles of the Tōji Repository were said to increase in number in response to the ritual, an undeniable effect of the jewel's generative power.[57]

Artificial Jewels

Since natural jewels could not be "invented," they had to be created, crafted out of bits and pieces. Here again the Shingon school took the first step, and this creation of an artificial (and procreative) jewel, like so many other new religious developments, was attributed to Kūkai.[58] The method of fabrication described by the *Testament* requires nine ingredients (among them rosewood, sandalwood, tree aloes, mulberry aloes, peach tree aloes, scented Chinese wood aloes, and Chinese peach aloes), which are crushed with a mortar and mixed into a ball, into which thirty-two grains of relics are inserted. The jewel is then to be put into a cypress box, which should be wrapped in a Buddhist robe (*kesa*) and kept out of sight.[59]

One exemplar, shown in the *Busshari to hōju* catalogue (fig. 8), is a blackish ball 7.2 cm in diameter. Another exemplar, used in a Nyohō Aizen ritual, was found at Shōkaiji 性海寺 (Aichi prefecture) in a wooden stūpa-reliquary dated to 1278 (fig. 106). This type of artificial jewel was at the center of the rituals performed at the turn of the twelfth century by Hanjun and his disciples on behalf of Shirakawa, and by Shōken during the Genreki era (1184–1185) on behalf of Go-Shirakawa.[60]

According to the *Keiran shūyōshū*, the jewels manufactured by Kūkai, miraculously obtained by Kyōkai 経海, abbot of the Bishamon Hall (in Yamashina, Kyoto), had a diameter of 7–8 inches 七八寸 (!) and were buried or enshrined in seven places: on Mount Kōya, Mount Mani 摩尼, Mount Inari, and Nyoi Peak, and at Ise, at Ninnaji, and in the Toba repository (Toba Hōzō 鳥羽宝蔵, that is, Shōkōmyō-in). The omission of Tōji and Murōji from that list suggests that it was based on the Hirosawa tradition. At any rate, the Ono current played the leading role in that cult. Manufactured jewels of this type were already being used in Nyoirin and Aizen rituals by the late eleventh century.[61]

Medieval authors naturally wondered about the number, types, origins, and whereabouts of the miraculous jewels. In his diary, the regent Kujō Kanezane 九条兼実 (1149–1207) ruminates on the history of the two jewels: one brought from China by Kūkai and buried on Mount Murō; the other created by Kūkai, transmitted to Hanjun, and offered to retired emperor Shirakawa before being finally placed inside the Aizen statue at Hosshōji. To this he adds the jewel of Shōkōmyō-in, which in other sources is simply Hanjun's jewel, removed from Hosshōji.[62]

In his *Record of the Jewel* (*Hōju ki* 宝珠紀), Shōken mentions two methods for making a wish-fulfilling jewel, one going back to Kūkai, the other more recent (that of Hanjun). He describes the artificial jewel as comprised of several relic grains placed in silver and gold flasks, linked by threads of five colors. These flasks were in turn placed in golden boxes, also linked by threads of five colors. Kujō Kanezane, who was able to see the content of the jewel box when Shōken returned it to the court in 1192, describes it as containing various precious objects, including bone fragments.[63] According to another account by Yoshida Tsunefusa 吉田経房 (1142–1200), the box also contained, apart from the jewel itself, one hundred grains of relics.[64] Shōken distinguishes between the two jewels as follows: "The production of [Hanjun's] jewel differs from the ritual instructions of the Great Master [Kūkai] in his *Testament,* with several grains of Buddha relics enshrined in a silver vase, with a five-colored string to string them together."[65] Other descriptions of this eminently elusive object make it seem to resemble a rosary made up of several spheres (seven in all). Shōken also contrasts the *Testament*'s dictum that "one must never look at the relics" with what he calls the "contemporary" method, according to which: "When yourself and others want to see the relics, you take them out and worship them."[66] *A chacun sa vérité.*

Shōken argues that the relics contained in the "A" and "B" urns of Tōji's repository are the equivalent of the Mount Murō jewel. These relics were used as *honzon* in various rituals. Indeed, "clerics and laity take them out and worship them at the time of the final vows [during such rituals], all the people looking at them—not at all an esoteric ceremony."[67] Shōken emphasizes the worldly benefits provided by the jewel while presenting himself as an advocate of "ritual gazing for all."

Imperial Claims

With Shōken, the Ono (Daigoji) branch came to the forefront. Yet by transmitting secret jewel rituals to his disciple the princely monk Shukaku (Shukaku Hōshinnō 守覚法親王, 1150–1202), a son of Go-Shirakawa and the abbot of Ninnaji, Shōken also prepared the rise of the Hirosawa branch (and its Ninnaji Omuro line 仁和寺御室). Owing to Shukaku, the Ninnaji line was able to establish privileged relationships with the retired emperor and to expand its ritual activity and prestige.

It could be argued, however, that the real shift of power had occurred much earlier, when the Kajūji monk Hanjun offered the jewel to retired emperor Shirakawa. In fact, it was not simply a shift within Shingon— from the Kajūji line to the Daigoji line of the Ono branch, and then to the Hirosawa branch—but also a shift from the inner circles of Shingon to the imperial court. By offering the jewel (and a copy of the *Testament*) to Shirakawa, Hanjun had aimed at increasing his lineage's prestige. But in so doing he also lost his monopoly on the jewel. Henceforward, the sectarian rivalry within Shingon was both exacerbated and complicated by the latent rivalry between that school and the retired emperor regarding possession of the jewel. That rivalry reveals itself in the way in which Shōken, then abbot of Daigoji, attempted to keep the jewel that Go-Shirakawa has given him in 1191 to perform a subjugation ritual against Minamoto no Yoshitsune 源義経 (1159–1189). After Go-Shirakawa's death, he was asked to return it to the court.[68]

The imperial claim on the jewel can be traced to the increasingly frequent imperial requests that the Tōji relics be brought to the palace to be viewed and counted, as the alleged increase in their number would be seen as a good omen and a proof of the jewel's efficacy. Eventually the requests included the condition that some of the relics be distributed among members of the nobility. For the retired emperor Shirakawa, the jewel became a family heirloom, which he kept in his private treasure house, the Shōkōmyō-in. The building of that treasure house, following the model of the Fujiwara regent's treasure house at Byōdō-in in Uji, had been part of an attempt to shift the center of power from the regents to the retired emperor.

Thereafter, the Shōkōmyō-in repository took on a powerful symbolic value as a device that allowed the retired emperor to transform his private collection of memorabilia into regalia.[69] This treasure house contained all kinds of precious things—sacred texts, ritual objects, weapons, musical instruments, statues, and paintings—in particular, the famous Aizen statue and the image of Hachiman as a monk, both attributed to Kūkai. All of the objects deposited therein became quasi-regalia. Among them, however, the jewel was by far the most precious. This symbolic moment marks the emergence of a model of the ruler—as sacred monarch—quite different from the one elaborated by the Ritsuryō state.

After the Insei period (1086–1192), with the rise of the Kamakura bakufu, this model underwent an eclipse, and the jewel now lent its fecundating power to rituals of easy childbirth and other worldly benefits. It was only during the Kenmu 建武 period (1333–1336), with Go-Daigo's attempt at restoring imperial power, that the jewel returned to center stage, as it was needed to create a surplus of legitimacy and as a ritual weapon against the bakufu. It was to that effect that Monkan wrote a series of texts centered on the jewel and on Kūkai, among them the *Great Matter of the Testament* (*Goyuigō daiji*), to which we will return. Another expression of that theological development is the painting, attributed to the same Monkan, of Go-Daigo as a "buddha in the flesh" (*sokushinbutsu* 即身仏) and a reincarnation of Kūkai. In this image, the emperor is shown wearing a Buddhist robe and imperial headgear while holding a *vajra* and a *vajra* bell (Aizen's attributes). Above him are three inscriptions referring to the three deities (Amaterasu, Kasuga Myōjin, and Hachiman Daibosatsu) that were allegedly reunited in his person—all three being perceived as identical with the jewel.[70]

It was at this point that the theory of the Three Regalia reached its full development, and the jewel, which had initially vied with the imperial regalia as symbols of legitimacy, came to be included among them. Unlike the other regalia, however, it was not merely a symbol but a powerful weapon. It was because of its presumed efficacy that Monkan used it in rituals such as the Joint Ritual of the Three Worthies, aimed at defeating the bakufu.[71]

THE JEWEL CULT OF MOUNT MURŌ

The theme of the Mount Murō jewel, as it appears in the *Testament* and its commentaries, set into place the various elements that would establish the jewel at the center of medieval religious activity. In other words, it is the text that connects a multitude of elements in a single narrative network, including legends about Kūkai, the jewel, and the relics; about Mount Murō and its dragon, and about Kenne. A complex network emerged, involving not only myths and legends, but real people, deities, ritual objects (reliquaries, *vajras,* stūpas), sacred sites, monasteries, and so on—together with their social, economic, political, and artistic dimensions. But then, after sparking a discursive proliferation that extended far beyond its original setting, the "narrative" jewel of Mount Murō, having fulfilled its role—just like the "real" jewel supposedly buried there—vanished from sight, although other jewels appeared in its place (and in other places as well).

Evidence for the emergence of a jewel cult at Murōji 室生寺 on Mount Murō (also known as Mount Ben'ichi)[72] can be traced to the last three articles (23 to 25) of Kūkai's *Testament.* Article 24 explains the origins of the jewel, while articles 23 and 25 mention two rituals centered on the jewel that were performed on Mount Murō.[73] By combining a dragon cult and its jewels, on the one hand, with the jewel from the Iron Tower on the other, this text signaled the convergence of two traditions, folkloric and esoteric.

Kenne's Role

There was another factor contributing to the meteoric rise of the Mount Murō jewel, namely, the role of Kūkai's disciple Kenne 堅慧 (d. ca. 860).[74] In his *Testament,* Kūkai declares: "The generative (*nōsa*) wish-fulfilling jewel that the great master of the Tang [Huiguo 惠果] gave me has crossed over to the great land of Japan and has already been specially buried in an excellent site on the celebrated mountain. This site is the peak to the east of the cavern on Shōjin Peak, where the Dharma master Kenne performed austerities."[75] The precedence of Kenne over Kūkai's two great disciples Shinga 真雅 and Jitsue 実慧 (var. Jichie), who appear in the *Goyuigō daiji* and other similar texts, may come as a surprise. Clearly, the aim was to exalt Kenne and his community on Mount Murō. But who was Kenne to deserve such praise from the anonymous author(s) of Kūkai's *Testament?* Kenne was known as the founder of Butsuryūji 仏立寺, a temple located some 4 km southwest of Murōji, but he was also credited with the founding of Murōji itself, a belief prompted by his importance in the *Testament.*[76]

Actually, contrary to what this text and the subsequent tradition claim, it's doubtful that Kenne was even a disciple of Kūkai; he likely belonged to the Tendai lineage of Saichō, Kūkai's rival.[77] Only after being driven away from Mount Hiei did he settle on Mount Murō. Quite possibly, the impact of the passage from the *Testament* had to do in part with the conspicuously occult nature of that tradition—in particular, the fact that Kenne and his legendary box are designated in coded terms. The title "Dharma master Kenne" (Kenne *hōshi*) is read with only the Chinese characters' radical, which gives Doshin suishi 土心水師 (Earth's Heart, Water's Master), an appropriate sobriquet that complements Kūkai's name (lit. "Sky and Sea"). For better or worse, these linguistic games play an important role in the esoteric tradition.

Under the authority of Kūkai's *Testament,* Kenne almost took precedence over Kūkai himself (at least in some circles). We are told for instance that Huiguo, Kūkai's Chinese master, had predicted that he would be reborn in Japan as Kūkai's disciple, with the clear implication that Kenne is Huiguo's reincarnation.[78] Just like Kūkai on Mount Kōya, Kenne is said to have entered *samādhi* on Mount Murō to wait for the advent of the future buddha Maitreya. His alleged mummification in a cave on Mount Murō replicates Kūkai's mummification at the Oku-no-in of Mount Kōya, but also, allegorically, the burial of the jewel. In other words, Kenne (like Kūkai in other sources) is identified with the jewel. The *Jindaikan hiketsu* cites an oral tradition concerning the jewel, according to which: "The Buddha is [represented by] the relics, the Dharma by the mudrās and mantras, the Sangha by Kenne and Kūkai. Because these three treasures are buried in the great country of Japan, they constitute the seeds of the field of merit. . . . These three seeds, namely, the relics, Nyoirin, and Nyohō Aizen, are what one calls Sanbō-in."[79]

The *Record of the Mysteries of Mount Ben'ichi* (*Ben'ichizan himitsuki*) emphasizes the sacredness of Mount Murō, but it is more discreet about Kenne.[80] In the *Secret Record of Mount Ben'ichi* (*Ben'ichizan hiki*), Kenne is subsumed into the group of Kūkai's disciples and his secret name (Doshin suishi) is not even mentioned. Kenne's (or his disciples') claim was not well accepted by other branches of Shingon, which sometimes openly criticized the Mount Murō tradition.[81] In a Ryōbu shintō text entitled *Record of the Eastern Penetration of the Divine Nature* (*Shinshō tōtsūki* 神性東通記), we are told that Kūkai, as he was about to enter into *samādhi* (in other words, into an apparent death), chose Kenne as his successor over his two main disciples, Shinga and Jitsue. After Kūkai's death, Kenne enshrined an image of Maitreya at the Oku-no-in as a substitute for his master's "flesh body" and was about to take the latter to a cave on Mount Murō when thirty-two wrathful deities (again, the number of the relics in the jewel) appeared and flew away with Kūkai's body. The mummified Kūkai eventually landed in Ise, where he would wait for Maitreya's coming. The jewel is no longer mentioned in this account, and Kenne's plans are ruined. While he still provides the narrative impetus, his role is rather negative. The linking of Kūkai with Ise presupposes the theory of the identity between Kūkai and Amaterasu that became prevalent in Ryōbu shintō. A variant of that motif is found in the *Oral Traditions concerning the Great Deity Amaterasu* (*Tenshō daijin kuketsu*

天照大神口決) compiled in 1327 by Kakujō (1273–1363), a monk from the Saidaiji branch of the Shingon-Ritsu school.[82]

The Jewel

By remaining hidden, the jewel of Mount Murō preserved its metaphysical purity, and its status as the generative principle initially increased. At the same time, we are reminded that it was "composed" of thirty-two or eighty grains of relics—like the artificial jewels that we will soon discuss. It was therefore already different in form from the ideal jewel represented in the iconography. On the whole, it escaped the materiality that characterizes artificial jewels—as well as relics and reliquaries. The secret was eventually revealed, however, and a legend recounts that the relics were specifically buried in a stūpa on Mount Nyoi, southwest of Murōji's pagoda.[83] Several of these relics were then stolen by the Tōdaiji monk Kūtai 空諦 (a.k.a. Ban'ya 鑁也, 1149–1230), and one of them was even offered to Mount Kōya by the imperial consort Senyōmon'in 宣陽門院 (1181–1252), a daughter of Go-Shirakawa.[84] It would have been harder, of course, to steal a jewel that did not exist.

Various sources, beginning with the *Testament,* emphasize that this jewel is intrinsically different from the traditional jewels found in East Asian traditions: "The great matter of Tōji is to guard the wish-fulfilling jewel. . . . When we think of this jewel, since its origin, it has been neither [found] in the liver of the dragon-king nor in the brain of the phoenix. It is by nature a manifestation of the Tathāgata."[85] The text rejects as a mere fabrication the belief that wish-fulfilling jewels can be found in dragons or phoenixes, adding: "While there are many jewels in the treasury of the dragon-palace at the bottom of the ocean, the wish-fulfilling jewel is the emperor among them. Indeed, if you ask, it is the manifestation of the Buddha Śākyamuni."[86]

And yet it is obvious that the jewel is intrinsically connected to the dragon of Mount Murō, and certain sources even state that it is the dragon's "divine body." The *Ben'ichizan hiki* claims that the *cintāmaṇi* of Mount Murō was transmitted to Kūkai by Huiguo, and that it is the essence (lit. "heart and liver" 心肝) of Dainichi and the conventional form of all buddhas and bodhisattvas.[87] Yet other sources indicate that it was directly transmitted to Kūkai by the dragon king Zennyo (善如龍王). The *Tōyōki,* quoted by the *Kakuzenshō,* distinguishes between three levels of efficacy: the efficacy achieved naturally by the generative or fundamental jewel; the efficacy achieved by Kūkai's rituals; and the dragon's power.[88] In contrast with the *Testament,* which simply states that the generative jewel shares its virtue with other gems, here Kūkai's power is inserted between the generative jewel and the dragon's jewel. The *Ben'ichizan hiki* identifies the jewel of Mount Murō with Dainichi, and its "trace" (*suijaku*) in Japan with the great goddess Amaterasu.[89] In this way, Amaterasu's hiding in the heavenly cave became a metaphor for the jewel's encasement in its reliquary.

The essential feature of Mount Murō's jewel is its secrecy. No one knows where it was buried—although several texts claim to give its precise location. In his *Testament,* Kūkai admonishes his disciples as follows: "You must never reveal the place to future generations. Then the esoteric teaching will flourish for kalpas, and the number of believers will dramatically increase."[90] Another reason invoked in certain sources for hiding the jewel is the terrible cosmic disorder that might ensue from its theft. An example of this is found in the *Kakugenshō:* when a disciple of Chōgen, the Chinese monk Kūtai, stole relics (or a *cintāmaṇi* jewel) from Mount Murō, calamities struck the province of Yamato, causing many people to starve.[91] Like a nuclear core, the true jewel must remain deeply buried. Its invisibility is what allows it to be the source of all things. But this absolute invisibility also had its drawbacks, which some Shingon ideologues tried to avoid by resorting to the notion of relative invisibility—the notion that the jewel, while hidden most of the time, can be revealed at *certain* times to *certain* people.

Mount Murō

The sacralization of Mount Murō and its jewel were connected to the dragon cult. Mount Murō had long been known for its "dragon hole" (*ryūketsu* 龍穴) and its rain rituals.[92] State-sponsored rituals for rain at the dragon cave on Mount Murō are already mentioned in the *Nihon kiryaku* 日本紀略 for the year 818.[93]

Murōji was initially a Hossō 法相 temple, whose origins can be traced to a shrine-temple (*jingūji* 神宮寺) established near the Dragon Cave Shrine by the priest Shuen 修円 (771–835, var. 769–834).[94] According to local tradition, Murōji was founded by the Kōfukuji 興福寺 priest Kenkyō 賢璟 (d. 793) and his disciple Shuen—who is occasionally confused with Shubin 守敏 (d.u.), Kūkai's legendary rival.[95] It remained a subtemple of Kōfukuji until the seventeenth century, although in doctrinal terms it had passed over to Shingon long before, already by the fourteenth century. The "conversion" of Murōji to Shingon is reflected in the claim that the temple was "restored" by Kūkai, as well as in the legends in which the esoteric dragon king Zennyo 善女 replaces the local dragon Zentatsu 善達. The development of the esoteric jewel cult corresponds to the takeover of that temple by the Shingon branch of Tōji. These sectarian developments are fairly late, however, and the early Murōji community was probably more diverse in its composition—judging from the fact that Tendai monks like Kenne found shelter there. The dragon cult of Mount Murō also had a national dimension that is reflected in the courtly ranks given to the dragon king in recognition of his protection of the country.[96]

The *Ben'ichizan ki* reports that "in Jambudvīpa, the homeland of Dainichi, in Yamato province, Uda district, there is an excellent place called Mount Ben'ichi. It is also called the Peak of Energy (Shōjin no Mine 精進の峰). This mountain is a sacred site unequalled in the whole kingdom. It is the first sacred place of Japan." Mount Murō thus becomes the symbolic center of Japan, a local equivalent of Mount Sumeru: "Ben'ichi is the center of the land of Japan. This country has the form of a one-pronged *vajra*. This mountain corresponds to the center of this *vajra*."[97] The text adds that "because the jewel is also the source of the Three Regalia, it is guarded by all the gods and *nāgas* of that land.[98]

In this text's description of the sacred geography of Mount Murō and its dragon hole, the dragon king is assimilated to Kurikara, the dragon manifestation of Fudō. The dragon cave becomes a kind of initiatic circuit that symbolizes the stages of the bodhisattva's career. It contains several relics (thirty-six grains in all), supposedly from the buddhas Kāśyapa, Maitreya, and Śākyamuni, and it symbolizes Dainichi's three bodies. Ningai 仁海 (951–1046), a Shingon priest famous for his rain rituals, was said to be the only person to have entered this cave after Kūkai. Another case is recorded, however: that of Nittai 日對 (d.u.), who, after entering the dragon cave, heard the dragon's voice and was able, eventually, to catch a glimpse of its claw. This vision moved him to build the Ryūketsu 龍穴 (Dragon Hole) Shrine.[99] The *Ben'ichizan hiki* (*Goryū shintō*) also ranks Mount Murō as the most sacred site of Japan, protected as it is by 84,000 *vajra* youths (*kongō dōji* 金剛童子), all the devas and *nāgas,* and by Amaterasu and all the great and small *kami* of the country.[100]

In the *Origin Story of Murōji* (*Murōji engi* 室生寺縁起; copy dated to 1747), Mount Murō takes the shape of a mandala and it becomes the site of Amaterasu's heavenly cave. The text adds that Kūkai's generative jewel has been deposited in the dragon king's cave to ensure fertile crops. As more emphasis is laid on the dragon cave itself and on the Nyoirin statue in the Kanjō-dō, the jewel recedes to the background.[101]

The *Ben'ichizan mitsuki* explains that "because this jewel is the transformed body of Dainichi . . . , this country is named Dainichi's primordial land (Dainichi honkoku 大日本国, a word play on Dainippon-koku). In Shintō, the jewel's trace (*suijaku*) is Amaterasu, because she opened the gate of the Heavenly Rock Cave [on Mount Murō]. Many *kami* came out of the caves of Mount Ben'ichi in Uda district."[102]

Like Mount Kōya, Mount Murō was believed to be the abode of the future buddha Maitreya. Such was Mount Murō's reputation that Tōji monks, when they performed a relic ritual like the Latter Seven Days rite, had to face the southeast (the direction of Mount Murō) and visualize the jewel.[103]

Another important text that emphasizes the importance of the dragon cave and of the jewel is the *Secret Record of the Dragon Hole on Mount*

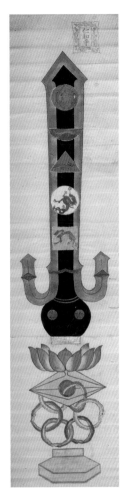

FIGURE 6.1. Sword with dragons. Muromachi period. Color on silk. Ninnaji, Kyoto.

FIGURE 6.2. Dragon protecting the jewel of Mount Murō. From Suzuki Chiben 1934.

Ben'ichi (*Ben'ichizan ryūketsu hiki*). It develops a complex mythical geography in which Japan is the land of the sun, India the land of the moon, and China the land of the stars; and the Shōjin Peak, where the jewel is buried, is the supreme sacred site of Japan. This jewel, which had manifested itself in India to benefit beings, had returned to its land of origin, Japan, once its mission was accomplished.[104]

The link (or identity) established between the jewel and the relics led also to a drift from the former to the latter. In certain texts, Mount Murō becomes the place where the 84,000 relics of the Buddha—the symbolic totality of his cosmic body—are buried.[105] The importance of relic worship at Murōji is shown by the discovery in 1953 of some 37,000 "rice-grain stūpas" (*momitō* 籾塔) under the main altar of the Maitreya Hall. These small wooden stūpas (9 cm high, like the three-inch Fudō) each contained a written *dhāraṇī* (the Hōkyōin darani 宝篋印陀羅尼) and one or two grains of rice.[106] In these sources, the relics take precedence over the jewel, which is hardly mentioned. The *Origin Story of the Transmission of Mount Murō's Relics* (*Murōzan goshari sōden engi* 室生山御舎利相伝縁起 , dated to the early fourteenth century), compiled by an abbot of Shōmyōji 称名寺 (Kanagawa prefecture), states for instance that Kūkai disseminated relics on Mount Murō.[107]

The Dragon

As Steven Trenson points out, the dragon (examples of which are shown in Figs. 6.1–6.4) was worshiped in Shingon as a variant of the Buddha's relics and the wish-fulfilling jewel. This belief seems to have influenced the performance of rainmaking rituals and rituals based on the divination board.[108] Because of their association with water, dragons were potent symbols of fertility, and the dragon god of Mount Murō was famous for its power to bring rain. While the symbolism of the *nāga*/dragon is too complex to fully unravel here,[109] one notable example occurred during a drought in the summer of 910, when the Tōji abbot performed a rain ritual at the dragon hole of Mount Murō. A heavy rain followed, which was attributed to the efficacy of the ritual and to the power of the dragon god, who subsequently received an official rank.[110]

According to the *Kojidan* 古事談 (ca. 1212–1215), the dragon cave on Mount Murō was the dwelling place of the dragon king Zentatsu, who had left his earlier abode in the Sarusawa 猿沢 Pond next to Kōfukuji after a maiden drowned in it.[111] This story, which suggests affinities between the dragon of Mount Murō and the Kasuga deity (who is described as a dragon in certain sources), probably goes back to a time when Murōji was still perceived as a subtemple of Kōfukuji.[112]

This perception changed when the dragon king of Mount Murō was reinterpreted as Zennyo, an Indian *nāga* king who had left his abode in Lake Anavatapta in northern India when Kūkai invited him to Shinsen'en

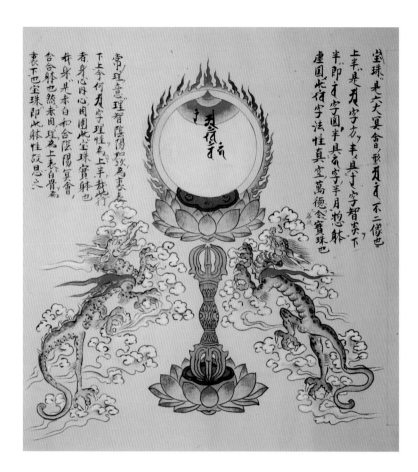

FIGURE 6.3. Dragons and jewels. 14th century. Color on paper. *Goyuigō daiji.* Ninnaji, Kyoto.

神泉苑 for a rain ritual.[113] This dragon king was depicted in both male and female forms, and it was this same Zennyo that Shingon monks, and in particular Shōkaku 勝覚 (1057–1129), worshiped at Daigoji as Seiryō Gongen 清瀧権現, a deity whose *honji* was said to be both Nyoirin and Jundei (var. Juntei) Kannon 准胝観音.[114] According to Trenson, the instructions regarding the jewel in Kūkai's *Testament* come from a monk who had the rain ritual in mind, and who saw Nyoirin as the *honji* of the dragon (as it was at Daigoji).[115]

Raiyu (1226–1304) argued that it was Zennyo, rather than the Chinese priest Huiguo, who had transmitted to Kūkai the jewel that insures the prosperity of Kongōbuji 金剛峰寺 (the Shingon headquarters on Mount Kōya).[116] This dragon king fused with Kurikara, the dragon manifestation of Fudō that protects Mount Kōya. In certain sources, he is identical with the jewel; in others, with the two dragon kings, Nanda and Upananda, who protect the jewel (and Mount Sumeru).[117] The dragon hole of Mount Murō was also functionally similar to the *nāga* palace where the relics of the Buddha and other sacra of Buddhism were preserved. Following the same logic, the treasure houses (*hōzō* 宝蔵) of Byōdō-in and

Shōkōmyō-in, built in 1069 and 1136, respectively, were assimilated to the *nāga* palace and became repositories for the jewels and other symbols of legitimacy.[118]

Beyond Mount Murō

Another development had the effect of multiplying the number of places where jewels (or parts of the single jewel) were thought to be buried. The very success of the theme of hiding the Mount Murō jewel paradoxically undermined the importance of both that jewel and Mount Murō's status as a sacred site. Kūkai was said to have produced no fewer than seven jewels and buried them in seven different places.[119] The Mount Kōya tradition, moreover, emphasized the fact that several jewels, of at least equal importance to that of Mount Murō, were buried on Mount Kōya.

Other sites that became associated with wish-fulfilling jewels include Tōji, Hosshōji 法性寺, Daigoji, and Kajūji (in Kyoto), Shōkōmyō-in 勝光明 and Byōdō-in (on the southern outskirts of Kyoto), Tōdaiji and Kōfukuji (in Nara), but above all Mount Kōya.[120] Indeed, the later development of the jewel theme underscores the importance of Mount Kōya. As noted above, the *Hachiman Daibosatsu* contains a criticism of Kenne's attempt to link Kūkai to Mount Murō: "People do not know the truth. [The place where] Kūkai [entered] *samādhi* is none other than Mount Kōya. What was buried on Mount Ben'ichi (Murō) was the box with the three robes and the jewel transmitted by the eight patriarchs. To say that Kūkai is [present] on Mount Murō reflects the fact that his 'spiritual essence' has been deposited on that mountain."[121] In the *Kōbō Daishi go-nyūjō kanketsu ki* 弘法大師御入定勘決記 by Saisen 済暹 (1025–1115), the emphasis is on Kūkai's awaiting the coming of the future buddha Maitreya to preserve the teachings of esoteric Buddhism.[122] The image of Kūkai immersed in permanent *samādhi* resonates with that of the jewel buried on Mount Murō. Both are waiting for the coming of Maitreya.

The *Kōyasan hiki* claims that after the two jewels buried on Mount Murō and Mani Peak, two more were buried on Mount Kōya, one near the Oku-no-in 奥の院, the other under the Great Pagoda.[123] The text also reports that Kūkai, before entering his final *samādhi* on Mount Kōya, told his disciple Jitsue 実恵 (786–847) that this place was a Pure Land and the abode of the dragon Kurikara (a manifestation of Fudō), whose "living body" was a wish-fulfilling jewel.[124] The Mieidō 御影堂 and the Great Pagoda of Mount Kōya are said to correspond to the head and tail of that dragon, respectively, and a jewel was supposedly buried in each place.[125]

Finally, not only did Kūkai bury jewels in several places (beginning with Mount Inari), but his example was then followed by En no Gyōja (although the latter had allegedly lived more than one century earlier): in the *Origin Story of the Provisional Manifestation of Mount Tamaki* (*Tamakisan gongen engi* 玉置山権現縁起), for instance, the legendary founder of Shugendō is reported to have buried one jewel on Mount Tamaki.[126] In a Shugendō tradition about Mount Hiko 英彦山 (northern Kyūshū), a character named Myōken tells the god Hachiman that another deity buried a jewel in a cavern on that mountain, and that if he retrieves it he will minister over all living beings. Hachiman then becomes the disciple of Hōren 法蓮, a hermit living on Mount Hiko, and eventually steals the jewel from him. When Hōren asks for the jewel back, Hachiman tells him: "Now, having acquired the precious jewel, I intend to protect the imperial lineage." Hōren finally resigns himself to parting with the jewel.[127]

It is difficult—and probably pointless—to follow any further the meandering trail of these various jewels. What is clear, however, is that their textual—if not always real—dissemination resulted from a discursive proliferation that reveals the intense competition that developed

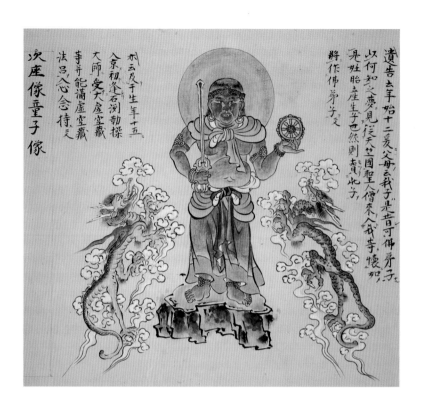

FIGURE 6.5. Kūkai as divine youth. 14th century. Color on paper. *Goyuigō daiji*. Ninnaji, Kyoto.

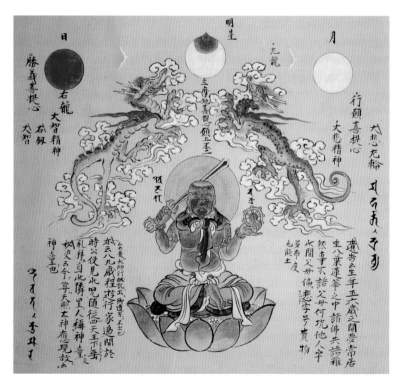

FIGURE 6.6. Kūkai as divine youth. 14th century. Color on paper. *Goyuigō daiji*. Ninnaji, Kyoto.

FIGURE 6.7. Aka Dōji. Color on silk. British Museum.

than to Kūkai, it is probably merely inspired in this case by the color of the divine youth's body. At any rate, this intriguing representation seems to have been fairly widespread till the Edo period.

The third drawing is supposed to represent Kūkai between the ages of twenty and twenty-two, at the time of his awakening.[143] The youth has now been replaced by the traditional representation of Kūkai as a monk, seated on a platform, holding a *vajra* and a rosary—but the representation of the jewels above him remains the same (Fig. 6.8). This image of Kūkai is interpreted in terms of the Three Worthies, with the top of his head corresponding to the jewel (Nyoirin), the five-pronged *vajra* in his right hand to Aizen, and the rosary in his left hand to Fudō.[144]

FIGURE 6.8. Kūkai with jewels and dragons. 14th century. Color on paper. *Goyuigō daiji.* Ninnaji, Kyoto.

In the fourth drawing, Kūkai is flanked by his two disciples Shinga and Jitsue, who are interpreted as his emanations and are identified with Aizen and Fudō, respectively (Fig. 6.9).[145] The triad they form overlaps with that of the three jewels.

A mandala recently discovered at Shinnō-in on Mount Kōya provides a global representation of the Joint Ritual of the Three Worthies. This mandala is centered on Kūkai. The Shingon master is seated, flanked by his two standing disciples. Compared to them, he appears larger than life, which suggests his divinization. Aizen and Fudō are represented at the bottom of the scroll, while their counterparts, Byakuja-son and Hija-son, are shown above Kūkai. The upper part of the image shows a wish-fulfilling jewel flanked by two dragons. This mandala, possibly dating from the Muromachi period, was clearly influenced by Monkan's *Great Matter of the Testament.*[146]

The point of these images was obviously to identify Kūkai with the wish-fulfilling jewel and the deities that represent it. The *Great Matter of the Testament* explicitly makes these identifications. It adds that Kūkai's *honji* is Aizen, and that the ritual's main deity, Nyoirin Kannon, is both Amaterasu's true nature and Kūkai's "fundamental body."[147] Kūkai is not only the "global body" of the three buddhas (Nyoirin, Aizen, and Fudō), he is also equated with the solar symbols Dainichi and Amaterasu, and with the astral symbol Kokūzō—through the legend of the young Kūkai swallowing the morning star (Venus) for his breakfast as a result of his practice of the Gumonji 求聞持 ritual.[148]

These symbolic identities found another concrete expression in certain portable shrines (*zushi*). For example, on the back of a black-lacquered reliquary shrine owned by the Fujita Museum of Fine Arts, the image of Kūkai is carved against the background of Mount Murō. Kūkai at the center is flanked by two dragons, which suggests that he *is* the wish-fulfilling jewel.[149] The dragons stand here for cosmic or psychic forces rather than for chthonian deities or *genii loci* like Zentatsu and Zennyo.[150] The two aspects are obviously related, but the point is that the dragons in question seem inscribed here in an alchemical and soteriological context representing the union of the male and female, or red and white, principles to produce a golden embryo that subsumes them—a kind of spiritual genetics. The male and female principles are symbolized by a red sun disk and a white moon disk, and by the red and white dragons; while their product (or their source, depending on the case) is represented by a bicolored jewel equated with the goddess Myōjō (a deification of the planet Venus) and with her *honji,* the bodhisattva Kokūzō.[151] On the psychic level, they represent the union of knowledge and wisdom that produces awakening.

FIGURE 6.9. Kūkai with his two disciples. 14th century. Color on paper. *Goyuigō daiji.* Ninnaji, Kyoto.

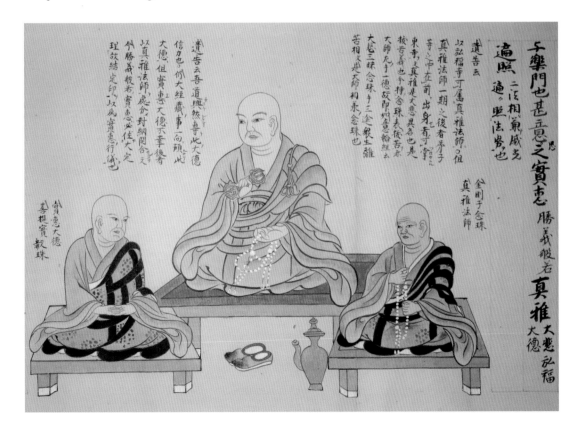

In a variant, the central jewel reproduces the triad in its own structure: it is in fact composed of three levels, corresponding to the three seed-syllables *a, vaṃ,* and *hūṃ;* in other words, it subsumes the three levels of reality into one. This text develops a complicated discourse on the three forms of *bodhi* and equates them with the three mysteries.[152] We have here a multilayered symbolism that articulates the cosmological, mythological, psychological, ritual (apotropaic and prosperity-promoting), soteriological, embryological, and sexual meanings into one complex network of meaning.

In the *Hachiman Daibosatsu* 八幡大菩薩, the jewel is said to symbolize Kūkai's body. The text also mentions Kūkai's visit to Ise. In his (apocryphal) prayer to the Ise deity Amaterasu, Kūkai quotes the topos according to which the first of the three mysteries (of Dainichi's mind, speech, and body) corresponds to the *kami* (represented by Amaterasu), the second to the Buddhist scriptures, and the third to the Buddha's relics.[153] But the text develops this motif by replacing the cosmic buddha Dainichi with Kūkai: now the *kami* (Amaterasu) expresses the mystery of Kūkai's mind, the divine incantations that of his speech, and the jewel that of his body.[154]

In the *Great Matter of the Testament,* Kūkai's well-known seated representation is glossed as embodying the ternary structure of the jewel and of the Womb mandala: the white light emanating from the crown of his head corresponds to the luminous aura of the jewel and to the Buddha clan in the Womb mandala, the rosary in his left hand corresponds to the Lotus clan, and the five-pronged *vajra* in his right hand to the Vajra clan. The three clans also correspond to Aizen, Fudō, and Nyoirin Kannon, respectively.[155] From the soteriological perspective, however, Kūkai (and the three deities he subsumes) are none other than the practitioner's body.[156]

The triadic structure of the jewel, as described by the *Goyuigō daiji,* lends itself to various kinds of iconographic identifications: with Nyoirin and her two acolytes Aizen and Fudō, for instance, or again with Kūkai and his two main disciples; but above all, it serves to express the logic of polarity resolving into nonduality, a logic supposed to guide the practitioner toward awakening. This nonduality, however, is not a mere *tertium quid.* Rather, it is akin to what Maurice Blanchot (followed by Roland Barthes) calls the *neutral,* an outplaying of the paradigm itself.[157]

The *Great Matter of the Testament* produces all sorts of substitutions on the basis of this ternary structure. First of all, it identifies Kūkai with the jewel. The Shingon master is shown flanked by his two disciples, and the triad they form overlap with the tripartite jewel (or the three jewels). These theoretical substitutions are found in concrete form in certain reliquaries, as in the previously mentioned black-lacquered shrine-reliquary (Fujita Museum of Fine Arts), where we see the image of Kūkai carved upon a background of Mount Murō, the sacred site of the jewel. He is flanked by two dragons that frequently appear as guardians of the jewel. Everything indicates that Kūkai and the jewel are one and the same. In a way, these triads express the reductionist tendency of esoteric theology. Yet the secret knowledge they disseminate makes these dualities more complex; or rather, while the dualities themselves reduce the diversity of reality, they also enable various links to be created through analogy.[158]

ANOTHER GENEALOGY?

Taking our cues from the textual tradition and from Japanese scholarship, we have traced the origins of the jewel tradition back to Kūkai, and beyond him to China and India. It is clear, however, that this genealogy is a fabricated one: the cult of the jewel did not originate with Kūkai, but much later, toward the eleventh or twelfth century. Most scholars, while accepting this view, still claim that it originated in Japan, within Shingon circles. Naitō Sakae, for instance, has described the evolution that led from the Japanese cult of the Buddha's relics to that of the jewel.[159] However, recent archeological excavations, done in the 1990s at the Chaoyang 朝陽 North Pagoda (1043–1044) in northern China (Liaoning province), have revealed the existence of architectural and ritual structures going back to the Liao Dynasty (916–1125) that are very similar to those of the Shingon jewel rituals performed by Hanjun and his disciples. Among the latter is the Nyohō sonshō ritual 如法尊勝法, centered on a miniature stūpa inside which was a jewel said to be the *samaya* form of Vairocana. The description of that pagoda in the *Kakuzenshō* seems remarkably similar to that of the Chaoyang pagoda, which contained an agate jewel of 4.3 cm in diameter.[160]

The earliest Nyohō sonshō ritual was allegedly performed in 1109 by Hanjun (or his disciple Genkaku 厳覚, 1056–1121) for retired emperor Shirakawa.[161] It was performed again in 1140 by Jichiun, and in 1143 and 1147 by Kanjin 寛信 (1084–1153), founder of the Kajūji-ryū, for retired emperor Toba (1107–1156). Hanjun is also said to have given Kūkai's jewel to Shirakawa, together with a copy of Kūkai's *Testament* and a text tracing the lineage of transmission from Kūkai, over ten generations, to himself.[162] In the 1109 ritual, that jewel is said to have been enshrined in a miniature pagoda. As we recall, Hanjun is also credited with the invention and performance of the Nyohō Aizen ritual, as well as the *Rokujikyō* (Six-Letter Sūtra) ritual. Yet the Nyohō Aizen ritual performed by Hanjun in 1080 does not seem to have used a jewel, so that the Nyohō sonshō ritual of 1109 would have been the first appearance of the jewel on the ritual stage.[163] Thus the Liao ritual of 1043 predates the Japanese ritual by half a century.

The Liao ritual could have been transmitted to Japan through Koryō or other routes. According to Kamikawa Michio, however, it was a Shingon monk named Myōhan 明範 who, after visiting the Liao in 1092, brought back new esoteric rituals to Japan. Kamikawa suggests that he was secretly sponsored by retired emperor Shirakawa.[164] The same Myōhan seems to have helped Hanjun prepare the Nyoshō sonshō and Nyohō Aizen rituals, and this would explain the Liao influence on Hanjun. From that time onward, it was the jewel allegedly handed down from Kūkai, and now owned by Shirakawa, that was used for the Nyohō sonshō ritual and other jewel rituals.[165]

All evidence seems to point to the conclusion that Hanjun fabricated the jewel that he had allegedly inherited from Kūkai and offered to Shirakawa. That jewel became the center of the new rituals he invented, perhaps with the help of Myōhan. In other words, the jewel and its rituals did not come from Kūkai, but from Liao Buddhism. Whether in the last analysis the Chaoyang North Pagoda and the date of 1043 remain their geographical and temporal origins is another question, which the current state of the documentation does not allow us to answer (while admitting that the question is valid).

The ulterior development of the jewel tradition, in which Kūkai's figure grew increasingly larger—achieving, in fact, a kind of apotheosis in Monkan's Joint Ritual of the Three Worthies—is therefore a purely ideological product that conveniently conceals the real nature of influences and relationships. One stage in that development was reached with the symbolic explosion surrounding the tradition of Mount Murō. Chronologically halfway between Hanjun and Monkan was Shōken. Hence the oral tradition, reported in Raiyu's *Hishō mondō,* that only three people had made a jewel: Kūkai, Hanjun, and Shōken.[166] That tradition is attributed to Jitsugen (1176–1249), a disciple of Shōken.

If the traditional Japanese genealogy of the jewel is not valid, why was the Liao connection so efficiently concealed by Hanjun and his circle? Hanjun probably fabricated that genealogy, linking himself directly to Kūkai, to claim legitimacy not only for himself but for the new rituals he had produced. This legitimacy was already questioned by the time of Shōken, who explained to the regent Kujō Kanezane in 1192 that Kūkai's jewel had been buried on Mount Murō, and that Hanjun's jewel had been produced by a different method from the one revealed in Kūkai's *Testament.*[167]

Shirakawa's motivations are of interest, too. His sending Myōhan on a mission to the Liao had to remain a secret, probably because the Liao were at war with the Song and he did not want to endanger Japanese diplomatic relations with their Chinese ally. Furthermore, the Liao were perceived as barbarians, in contrast to the civilized Chinese, and while they may have had some interesting Buddhist rituals to offer, displaying the Liao origins of those rituals would have done little to increase Shirakawa's legitimacy. Thus the retired emperor had good reason to draw upon the power of those rituals while concealing their dubious origins.

And, instead of tracing them back to esoteric Buddhist masters of Tang China, he chose to assert their Japanese origins—through the increasingly prestigious figure of Kūkai.[168]

There is no denying the agency of a few strongly motivated individuals, but the grafting of the jewel symbolism onto Kūkai's legend and the repertoire of Shingon rituals seems to obey a deeper reason. Having found in Japan a particularly rich terrain, this symbolism flourished in a way that neither Hanjun nor Shirakawa could have foreseen, or their personalities suffice to explain.

CODETTA

From all of the above, we can infer that the cult of the jewel developed first in Shingon (in the Sanbō-in lineage, in particular), then in Tendai, stimulated by sectarian rivalries and the desire for closeness to imperial power, before eventually becoming toward the fourteenth century a widespread symbol of prosperity and fortune.

This chapter may appear to be a departure from the preceding ones in that it focuses primarily on the wish-fulfilling jewel as an emblem of imperial power. This detour was necessitated by the fact that the jewel was another form of divine power, and it shows that the network of the gods was not simply an ideal or intellectual pantheon, but also involved objects as "marks" of the absolute.

In medieval Japan, the jewel became the fundamental symbol connecting the gods (and many other things) to people, but because it was, more specifically, the *samaya* form of some of those gods, it linked them into a special network and allowed them to become figures of the "general equivalent," the source of everything and (like Butsugen) the "mother of all buddhas."

The reliquary shrine is itself a symbolic and technical device that manifests the god in its material aspect (*deus ex machina*). The same is true for Buddhist statues that, having become repositories (of relics, sūtras, wishes, lists of all kinds, seed-letters and mantras, images and statuettes, and artificial viscera), can be described as transformative devices mediating the descent of the divine down to earth. The reliquary is as important as the relic, and it is sometimes difficult to distinguish the container from the contained: the artificial jewel is both a relic and a reliquary. Relics and jewels are put in boxes that in turn become mythical objects, such as the famous box that Kenne allegedly buried on Mount Murō. The mountain itself becomes a reliquary.[169] Here we have another example of the "logic of secrecy" that governs esoteric Buddhism.

The triadic structure of the reliquary or portable shrine defines (or produces) its own space. The two doors open this space horizontally. The *tengai* 天蓋, or lid, defines a vertical movement that symbolizes the emanation process from the first metaphysical principle (Dainichi) down to the physical world—a structure exemplified in the "precious stūpa" (hōtō 宝塔), one of the most common forms of reliquaries. This *tengai*, which in some cases can symbolize the placenta and its protecting deity, plays a particularly important role in certain relic rites, such as the Nyohō sonshō ritual.[170]

Like the pentadic structure of the five-wheel stūpa, this triadic structure of the reliquary is at the heart of the esoteric Buddhist ideology—and consequently of the imperial ideology (with the Three Regalia). In fact, it is a subliminal way of structuring the world, an a priori, generative schema akin to what Pierre Bourdieu calls a *habitus*, i.e., a vision or division of the world that implies power relations. This logic (be it dyadic, triadic, or pentadic) was concretely expressed through reliquaries and portable shrines, objects of varying forms that were liable to transform owing to their inner sanctums protected by two, four, and sometimes even sixteen doors (opening on one, two, or four sides), but also by virtue of their small detachable and reversible boards. In this way the reliquary or altar became a "material deity," or rather a three-dimensional pantheon or mandala. The explicit, orthodox theology of Mikkyō tried to reduce everything to the unity of a central principle (the jewel) by means of binary and ternary structures. Its implicit theology, however, multiplied transversal links, detours, and shortcuts.

It is worth noting, too, that in certain cases the jewel and its box were wrapped in a monastic robe (*kesa*). Thus, when the Daigoji abbot Shōken returned retired emperor Shirakawa's jewel to the palace, this jewel was placed in a lacquered box that was itself contained in a gold and copper box wrapped in a red *kesa*. Again, legend has it that when the jewel of Ninnaji was sent to Kamakura, a dragon tried to steal it but failed, because the jewel was wrapped in a *kesa*. We find here a kind of embryological symbolism in which the red *kesa* symbolizes the placenta, while the jewel is compared to the fetus.[171] This symbolism also applies to the *gorintō*-type reliquary, which represents the human body in gestation and the metaphysical body of the buddha Dainichi.

The triadic structure of the jewel and the reliquaries was determined by the prevalent symbolism of the center. The reliquary is identical to the Buddhist cosmic pillar and *axis mundi*, Mount Sumeru, which is guarded by the two dragons Nanda and Upananda. The same symbolism, in a simplified form, recurs in the image of the dragon Kurikara, the dual aspect of Fudō, and also in Dainichi's mudrā, the so-called Wisdom Fist, with its central axis (the index finger of one hand) surrounded by the five phases or elements (the five fingers of the other hand). Discussions about the symbolism of the center have admittedly an Eliadian ring, and Mircea Eliade's propensity to see such symbolism everywhere has been criticized by Jonathan Z. Smith and others.[172] However, Smith's criticism does not seem to apply here. Mount Sumeru is clearly an *axis mundi,* and the reliquary is clearly one with it. The symbolism of the center is undeniably at work in the notion of the reliquary, which is a kind of *mesocosm* in Paul Mus's sense, that is, an intermediary realm between two orders of reality.[173] Here the two realms are symbolized by the two great mandalas of Shingon, and the reliquary was placed precisely at their center during jewel rituals such as the Latter Seven Day ritual. One should keep in mind, however, that this parallelism is perhaps a false window, an artificial symmetry (textual and iconographic) that is often subverted by concrete, complex—even messy at times—practices.

We must also allow for the intrinsic dynamics of beliefs, which means that one may yield to them even when one is convinced of manipulating them. The jewel became both the stake and index of the sectarian struggles that divided the Shingon school during the twelfth century, caused by the desire of various monastic factions to draw closer to imperial power; and again during the fourteenth century, with Go-Daigo's attempt to restore that power. But it would be mistaken to see only this aspect, and to explain the development of that theme as a mere strategy on the part of Shingon priests such as Shōken and Monkan. The cult of the jewel crystallizes the idea of a power that is both beneficent and awe-inspiring. This power is an elusive reality that came to be objectified (and domesticated) in an object that some monks believed they could manufacture—a kind of philosopher's stone. But at the same time it is a power that overflows any objectification and imposes itself as *sui generis,* the source of all things and the mother of all buddhas and gods, to which one can only submit. It is only by taking into account the cast shadow of the jewel and of the deities that not only symbolize but actualize its power, in real time and space, that we can begin to understand its hold on medieval Japanese imagination and its rise to the center of all human relationships, the imperial throne. It is not by mere coincidence that it became the very symbol of the accession to the throne; it was itself that power that the ruler and the monks dreamt of obtaining. There is no denying the base nature of those power struggles that took the jewel as their stake, but such baseness is often the other side of the sublime, the acknowledgment of a dimension that escapes all human maneuvers. To neglect that dimension is to reduce esoteric Buddhism to a caricature, while to focus solely on it is to take Buddhist theology at face value. In either case, it is to fall short from understanding. Actually, the two levels of esoteric ideology require two—apparently contradictory— approaches, inasmuch as such symbolic proliferation cannot be reduced to a comfortable binary or ternary symbolism. This proliferation, in spite of its political and sectarian motivations, contributed to the philosophical vitality and the soteriological depth of medieval Japanese Buddhism.

It is difficult to imagine how a whole period of Japanese religious history could have been so obsessed with an imaginary object, the jewel

FIGURE 7.1. The bodhisattva Monju. Edo period. Sheet, ink on paper. University Art Museum, Kyoto City University of Arts. *BZS* 2060.

FIGURE 7.2. Monju crossing the sea. Edo period. Sheet, ink on paper. University Art Museum, Kyoto City University of Arts. *BZS* 2068.

example, the Monju statue of Hannyaji 般若寺 in Nara, for which Eison carried out the eye-opening ceremony in 1267, contained fifty-three grains of relics as well as various sūtras and mandalas—all meant to animate the statue.[1] The *Ben'ichizan hiki* identifies this jewel with Monju.[2] There are also a number of examples of reliquaries mounted on a lion (See, for example, Figs. 7.1 and 7.2) (which could be Monju's mount, but also that of Aizen).[3]

Monju was also associated with the bodhisattva Kokūzō (Skt. Ākāśagarbha). In the *Scripture on the Bodhisattva Ākāśagarbha* (*Xukongzang pusa jing* 虚空蔵菩薩経, translated by Buddhayaśas, ca. 403–413), the Buddha explains that Ākāśagarbha wears a jewel on his head as a "pure, bright sun of compassion, which enlightens the black darkness of ignorance."[4] The jewel is Ākāśagarbha *samaya* form. In China, Ākāśagarbha was often invoked in repentance rituals, whose goal was achieved when the practitioner had a vision of the bodhisattva stamping his forearm with a jewel seal.[5] The *Scripture on the Bodhisattva Ākāśagarbha* states: "When Ākāśagarbha manifests himself, his symbol, the jewel whose light eclipses all stars, appears in the West." Yixing, in his *Suyao yigui* 宿曜義軌 (*T.* 21, 1304), concurs: "The sun, the moon, and the stars are all manifestations of Ākāśagarbha." In Japan, Kokūzō was initially the *honzon* of the Gumonji-hō, a ritual made famous by Kūkai.[6] According to the *Keiran shūyōshū,* the jewel was an important element of that ritual, whose basic mudrā was the "seal for arranging everything by means of Kokūzō's jewel."[7] Kokūzō is usually represented holding a jewel on a white lotus flower in his left hand (Fig. 7.4). While the early Japanese cult of Kokūzō was focused on wisdom, the esoteric Kokūzō soon was invoked in rituals of increase and subjugation. From the end of the Heian period onward, in part due to the influence of Pure Land teachings, the Kokūzō cult became increasingly funerary, a development that reflected his function as a god of destiny. Indeed, Kokūzō was the *honzon* of divination rituals influenced by Onmyōdō conceptions.[8] Despite his theological origins, he became a popular deity of fortune, invoked in particular for the protection of silkworms.

The medieval period also saw the development of a Five Kokūzō ritual, whose *honzon* was five forms of Kokūzō riding different animals (Fig. 7.6). This ritual, which traces back to the Shingon master Ningai

FIGURE 7.3. The Eight-letter (Hachiji) Monju (Mañjuśrī). Kamakura period. MOA Museum of Art, Atami City (Shizuoka prefecture).

FIGURE 7.4. The bodhisattva Kokūzō (Ākāśagarbha). *Kongōkai kue daimandara,* fig. 284.

FIGURE 7.5. Dual-bodied Kokūzō. Edo period. Sheet, ink on paper. University Art Museum, Kyoto City University of Arts. *BZS* 2093.

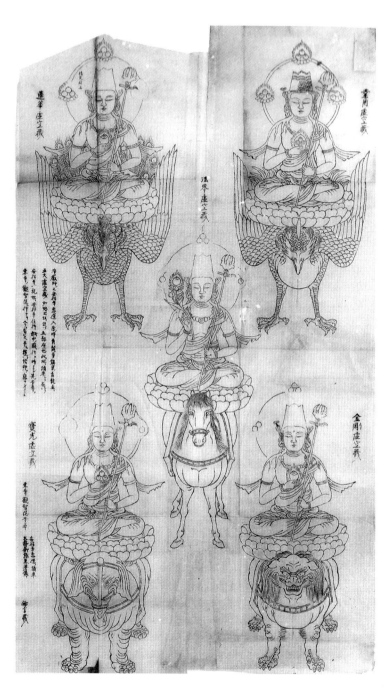

FIGURE 7.6. The Five Kokūzō. Edo period. Sheet, ink on paper. University Art Museum, Kyoto City University of Arts. *BZS* 2095.

FIGURE 7.7. Kokūzō and Myōjō tenshi (Venus) on dragon. 14th century. Color on silk. Nezu Museum, Tokyo.

(951–1046), was an exorcism against baleful stars.[9] These five Kokūzō—several of whom hold a jewel—were also introduced in the Latter Seven Day ritual of Tōji.[10]

Uhō Dōji and Amaterasu

Kokūzō is the *honzon* of Kongōshōji 金剛證寺 on Mount Asama (Asamagatake 朝熊ヶ岳) in Ise (Mie prefecture) (Fig. 7.8), a former Shingon temple now belonging to the Rinzai sect. As local tradition has it, Mount Asama is the place where the young Kūkai performed the Gumonji ritual. Kongōshōji was restored by the Zen priest Butchi 仏地 in 1392, allegedly on the basis of an oracle from Amaterasu. We are also told that a youth appeared to him and asked him to restore the temple. The youth was in fact a manifestation of the deity of Taga Shrine (not of Ise Shrine) and was known locally as Uhō Dōji 雨宝童子 (Rain Treasure Youth, var. Sekisei Dōji 赤精童子 or Red Essence Youth).[11]

In early documents, Uhō Dōji appears simply as a guardian of Mount Asama. In the *Uhō Dōji keibyaku* 雨宝童子啓白 attributed to Kūkai, he is said to be the red essence of all beings, the soul of all sentient and nonsentient beings, the *honji* of all gods, the creator of the sun, moon, and stars. In Japan, he is Amaterasu; in India, the buddhas Vairocana, Amitābha, and Śākyamuni; in China, Fu Xi, Shennong, and Huang Di. As the essence of Venus, he is also identified with Benzaiten (the essence of the sun) and Dakiniten (the essence of the moon).[12]

Uhō Dōji is also said to be a manifestation of Amaterasu at the age of sixteen. He is usually represented as a gigantic figure standing on a mountain top, wearing a small stūpa on his head, with his hair falling on his shoulder and a jewel above his eyebrows (Figs. 7.9–7.13). He holds a jewel in his left hand, a jeweled staff in his right hand.[13] According to the *Asamagatake giki* 朝熊ヶ岳義軌, a text attributed to Kūkai, "Amaterasu stroked the head of Sekisei Dōji and spat a five-jewel [stūpa,] which she put on his head. Kokūzō spat a golden jewel, which he hung at the neck of the youth. Then, from the red jewel held by the youth, Jizō appeared and preached the verse of deliverance for the beings on the six paths. From the youth's jeweled staff, Venus appeared and recited a verse explaining

FIGURE 7.8. Uhō Dōji. Kongōshōji, Ise City (Mie prefecture).

FIGURE 7.9. Uhō Dōji. 17th century. Color on wood. Kongōbuji, Kōyasan.

FIGURE 7.10. Uhō Dōji. Color on paper. Kongōbuji, Kōyasan.

the growth of the ten thousand things and the prosperity of heaven and earth."[14] Here Uhō Dōji is an emanation of both Amaterasu and Kokūzō, and his two attributes (the jewel and the jeweled staff) give birth to two further deities, the chthonian Jizō and the astral Venus. His cult reflects (and allows) the transition from Kokūzō to Amaterasu, and from Asama to Ise. Uhō Dōji is also said to be identical with Kūkai, probably owing to the latter's identification with Amaterasu.[15]

FIGURE 7.11. Uhō Dōji. Edo period. Sheet, ink on paper. University Art Museum, Kyoto City University of Arts. *BZS* 4018.

FIGURE 7.12. Uhō Dōji (a.k.a. Sansha Gongen, manifestations of the Three Shrines). Edo period. Sheet, ink on paper. University Art Museum, Kyoto City University of Arts. *BZS* 4022.

Let us now focus on some of the links that allowed the identification of Amaterasu (and her symbol, the mirror) with the wish-fulfilling jewel. There are several references to wish-fulfilling jewels having been enshrined at Ise. The *Keiran shūyōshū* makes reference to one having been enshrined there,[16] and a widespread tradition reports that Gyōki 行基 (668–749) had offered a relic to Ise Shrine on behalf of the sovereign.[17] Furthermore, during his pilgrimage to Ise, the Tōdaiji priest Chōgen is said to have received two jewels from Amaterasu—one red, the other white—which he later inserted into the head of the Great Buddha of Tōdaiji.[18]

In order to match the *kami* and the buddhas in accordance with the *honji suijaku* theory of Ryōbu shintō, it had been necessary to extract Amaterasu from her concrete mythological and cosmogonic context and to turn her into a higher principle symbolizing unity—while polarity was preserved with the two Ise shrines to avoid absolute monism. This model has obvious structural affinities with the ternary structure of the jewel, as we recall from our discussion of Aizen and Fudō.

A number of medieval sources identify Amaterasu with the jewel, and her acolytes—or the two jewels—with the Inner and Outer Ise shrines. She is also one with Kūkai who, we recall, asserted the identity of the *kami* and the Buddha's relics during his alleged visit to Ise.[19] In Monkan's *Goyuigō daiji,* Nyoirin Kannon (symbolized by a five-wheel stūpa) is said to be the *honji* of Amaterasu. In the *Kakuzenshō,* Kannon is referred to as the fire jewel among the twin (fire and water) jewels, and she is identical with Nittenshi 日天

FIGURE 7.13. Uhō Dōji and Marishiten. 19th century. Color on silk. Ichigami Shrine, Yōkaichi City (Shiga prefecture).

子 (or Nitten, Skt. Āditya), the Buddhist sun deity, who is itself identified with Amaterasu.

A document recently found in a five-wheel stūpa of Shōkaiji 性海 寺 (Aichi prefecture), and written by the abbot Jōin (fl. 1273–1283), says that its *honzon* (i.e., the jewel) is worshiped together with the two realms, Aizen and Fudō, the Inner and Outer shrines of Ise, the Upper and Lower shrines of Kamo, Kōbō Daishi, etc.[20] Jōin notes the existence of two jewels: the sun/fire jewel and the moon/water jewel, which, through "harmonious union" (*wagō,* a term usually connotating sexual intercourse), produce a space wheel. The color coding of the two jewels (red and white) allows again for a sexual or embryological reading.

During his pilgrimage to Ise, the Daigoji monk Tsūkai 通海 (1234–1305) also equated Nittenshi (Amaterasu) with Kūkai, the mirror, and the wish-fulfilling jewel.[21] Likewise, in the *Commentary on the Secret Traditions regarding the Relics* (*Dato hiketsushō* 駄頭秘決鈔), the Saimyōji priest Gatō (d. 1317) describes the goddess of Mount Kōya, Niu Myōjin 丹生明神, as a younger sister of Amaterasu and identifies the latter with Aizen, Nichirin (Nittenshi), and Kūkai.[22] In the *Reiki ki,* Amaterasu (or rather her symbol, the sacred mirror) is equated with the jewel.[23] The ten treasures of Shintō are said to be the two jewels of life and death, that is, the two wish-fulfilling jewels.[24] In the *Reiki kanjō* 麗気灌頂, Nyoirin and Jūichimen are said to be Amaterasu's *honji.*[25] By the fourteenth century, the equation between Amaterasu and the jewel had become commonplace (see, for example, Fig. 7.14). This is shown by various texts contained in the Shinpukuji archives at Ōsu Library in Nagoya.

In his *Kuji hongi gengi* 旧事本紀玄義 (Profound Meaning of the *Kuji hongi*), the Tendai priest Jihen 慈遍 (fl. 14th century) writes that the Yasakani no magatama 八尺瓊曲玉 (var. 八坂瓊曲玉) jewel, one of the three imperial regalia, is in its yang aspect a transformation of the relics of the ancient buddhas, whereas in its yin aspect it is the "sea jewel" of the dragon kings. The wish-fulfilling jewel, in his view, unites the yin and the yang, heaven and earth, and the powers of the two Ise shrines; it is therefore only transmitted to the descendants of the imperial line. Jihen also equates the regalia, the wish-fulfilling jewel, and the Buddha's relics.[26] The *Nihongi Miwaryū* 日本紀三輪流, in a section about the "Ōsa honzon" 奥砂本尊, declares that the *honzon* of the "jewel ritual" (Ōsa is read here as *hōju* 宝珠) of Mount Murō is none other than Amaterasu.[27] The *Keiran shūyōshū* goes one step further, arguing, on the basis of a Ninnaji tradition, that all the jewel rituals take in fact Amaterasu as their *honzon.*[28] In this way, Amaterasu and the Three Regalia, symbols of the ruler's legitimacy and sovereignty, came to be tied to the wish-fulfilling jewel. In this context, Ise and its deity, far from being emblems of Shintō nativism as they are usually perceived, were part and parcel of the imperial ideology developed by esoteric Buddhist priests such as Monkan.[29] An important aspect of that ideology was the identification of Amaterasu with the jewel, Nyoirin, and Aizen.

Hachiman

The symbolism of the jewel in Ryōbu shintō was not limited to Ise and Amaterasu, however; it permeated other major *kami* cults, most notably those of Kasuga and Hachiman.[30] I will focus here on the latter. Regarding Kasuga, let me simply mention the dragon jewel box owned by Kasuga Shrine: a nested box, on which are represented the Kasuga deities (together with the twelve signs of the Western zodiac) (Fig. 7.15).[31]

As noted above, jewels played an important role in the cult of Empress Jingū and of Hachiman (Fig. 7.16). In the tradition of Usa Hachiman Shrine—next to Kunisaki peninsula, a major Tendai stronghold—we see the emergence of an esoteric cult of the jewel inspired by that of Mount Murō.[32] This shrine played an important local and national role,

FIGURE 7.15. Nested boxes for the wish-fulfilling jewel, with outer box showing Kasuga deities and the twelve zodiacal signs. 14th century. Lacquered wood with polychromy. Nara National Museum.

same lines, Nyoirin was associated with the buddha Hōshō 宝生, one of the five directional buddhas of the Womb mandala, the one who rules over the southern quarter and the Jewel clan. Thus, Nyoirin ended up at the forefront (or rather the top) of the Six Kannon list; she is in fact presented as the "global body" of the Six Kannon, a *prima inter pares*.[69]

FIGURE 7.18. (*Opposite*) Daibutchō mandala. 12th century. Hanging scroll, ink and color on silk. Nara National Museum.

Functions

Although Nyoirin, like the wisdom kings, can be the primary icon of subjugation rites, as we have seen in the Sanzon gōgyō ritual, she is above all the *honzon* of increase (*zōyaku*) and seduction (*keiai*) rituals.[70] She showers upon beings earthly and heavenly jewels, foremost among which are the seven jewels of the universal monarch or "wheel-turning" (*cakravartin*) king and the jewel of ultimate reality.[71] Nyoirin was particularly popular for her love rituals, performed in both Tendai and Shingon.[72] When men (and in particular the ruler) were obsessed with sexual desire, she could turn into a "jade maiden" and guide them to salvation.[73] The *Kakuzenshō,* for example, says that a man who desires the love of a woman "must take one *gō* 合 (roughly 0.18 liter) of white sesame seeds and empower them (*kaji*) 108 times while reciting her name; he will then obtain a jade maiden." A similar ritual is described in the case where the supplicant is a woman.[74]

Iconography

Nyoirin is usually represented as a six-armed deity, seated in the so-called "royal ease" (*rājalilāsana*) position, with her left leg bent horizontally, her right leg vertical, and her head inclined in a pensive position, resting on her right arm (see Figs. 7.19–7.23).[75] Her attributes are the jewel and the wheel. The latter is similar to Viṣṇu's disk, a powerful weapon that enables him to vanquish all his enemies. It is also a symbol of the Buddhist teachings, as well as an emblem of kingship—the attribute *par excellence* of the *cakravartin* king. These two canonical attributes—the jewel and the wheel—define Nyoirin Kannon as a compassionate divinity who "grants the desire of beings and destroys their suffering"—or annihilates the demons that cause it.[76] Eventually, the jewel upstaged the wheel—though the latter remained important in subjugation rites.

Nyoirin's six arms symbolize the six Kannon and the six paths of rebirth.[77] Yet there are other forms of Nyoirin Kannon with two, four, ten, or twelve arms. The famous Nyoirin of Ishiyamadera, for instance, is a *two-armed* figure,[78] while the Nyoirin of Rokkakudō in Kyoto reportedly had six arms, and that of the Tsukiba Hall on Mount Hiei, four—but all three images were three inches (lit. "three *sun*" 三寸) in size, like the image of Fudō used in the Mount Murō ritual. As noted earlier, this detail is highly significant because this size was said to be that of the human fetus in the womb.

FIGURE 7.23. Nyoirin of Mount Shosha, with the priest Shōku and the divine youths Otomaru and Wakamaru. Muromachi period. Nezu Museum, Tokyo.

FIGURE 7.24. (*Top right*) Nyoirin Kannon. Edo period. Sheet, ink on paper. University Art Museum, Kyoto City University of Arts. *BZS* 2021.

FIGURE 7.25. Seated Nyoirin. Edo period. Sheet, ink on paper. University Art Museum, Kyoto City University of Arts. *BZS* 2024.

An interesting image shows a four-armed Nyoirin sitting on a rock in the midst of the sea. Her two upper hands hold a text and a jewel, respectively; her other two hands form mudrās. Above her is a cloud with seven buddhas in it (representing the seven Yakushi or the seven stars of the Northern Dipper); in front of her, emerging from the waves, are three anthropomorphic *nāga* deities and an elephant-headed *vināyaka*.[82] In another similar representation, she appears in a characteristic position with two of her hands joined above her head (Fig. 7.27), and she is flanked by Aizen and an unknown bodhisattva (Fig. 7.28). She resembles Rokuji Myōō 六字明王 (mentioned in Chap. 2), though unlike him she is not standing on one leg.[83] Of particular interest is the twelve-armed Nyoirin: she stands erect, held up from beneath by the earth goddess (like Bishamonten), holding the sun and the moon in two of her hands, thereby revealing her cosmic nature.[84]

Development

Images of Nyoirin began to multiply during the Heian period. In spite of the Tendai interest in her, her cult developed essentially within the Ono branch of Shingon, alongside rituals centered on the Buddha's relics and the wish-fulfilling jewel.[85] She became in particular the *honzon* of the "eighteen paths," a term designating the standard ritual sequence performed in esoteric temples.[86] The Nyoirin ritual was introduced as a ritual of imperial protection into the Three-altar Ritual (*Sandan no mishuho* 三壇の御修法), together with life-prolonging rituals centered on Fudō and

FIGURE 7.26. Nyoirin seated on a rock. Color on paper. *Shoson zuzōshū.* Kanazawa bunko.

Enmei Fugen 延命普賢. These rituals were performed by a protecting monk (*gojisō* 護持僧) at the Futama 二間, a room in the imperial palace adjacent to the emperor's bedroom, where two of the Three Regalia— the sword and the divine seal—were kept. The jewel eventually became identified with the latter. Theories regarding the identity of the Futama Kannon vary: at times she was identified with Shō Kannon, at other times with Jūichimen Kannon. The *Keiran shūyōshū* asserts that she was in fact Nyoirin.[87] One of the arguments that weigh in favor of this interpretation is the fact that Nyoirin was perceived as the *honji* of Amaterasu, the deity symbolized by the sacred mirror (the third member of the imperial regalia). Of course, the identity of that icon may have varied over time.

Around the end of the twelfth century, Nyoirin's cult merged with that of Shōtoku Taishi 聖徳太子, a development triggered by the belief that Shōbō 聖宝 (832–909), the founder of Daigoji 醍醐寺, was a reincarnation of Shōtoku and an avatar of Nyoirin.[88] In the *Mizu kagami* 水鏡, Kūkai is in turn presented as a reincarnation of Shōtoku Taishi and

FIGURE 7.28. Nyoirin standing on the earth deity. Color on paper. *Shoson zuzōshū.* Kanazawa bunko.

a manifestation of Nyoirin.[89] We have seen that the Sanzon gōgyō ritual identified Kūkai with both. Nyoirin was also the *honzon* of Rokkakudō 六角堂.[90] The link between Nyoirin and Shōtoku is made in *Shinran's Record of Dreams* (*Shinran muki* 親鸞夢記), where Nyoirin tells the young Shinran that she will appear to him as a jade maiden (*gyokunyo* 玉女).[91] In another famous dream, that of the Tendai prelate Jien 慈円 (1155–1225), the term "jade woman" designates the imperial consort, whom Jien identifies with Butsugen (Skt. Buddhalocanī), the Tendai equivalent of Nyoirin.[92] The link is explicitly made in a later text, the *Hokke betchō* 法華別帖, which argues in a rather tortuous fashion that the deity in Jien's dream was in fact Nyoirin: because the Japanese ruler is a golden wheel king (*kinrin-ō* 金輪王), the only form of Kannon worthy of him must be linked to the Dharma wheel.[93] At any rate, the implicit logic of this dream links Nyoirin with Butsugen as well as with Amaterasu.[94]

We have seen how, toward the end of the Heian period, with the Sanbō-in Ritual of the Three Buddhas and Nyoirin (Sanbutsu Nyoirin-hō 三仏如意輪法), and later, with the Nyoirin Flower Rituals (Nyoirin kehō 如意輪華法) performed by Eison and his disciples at Saidaiji, Nyoirin came to be associated with Aizen and Fudō, as well as with Kūkai and Amaterasu. Shōken used a five-wheel stūpa as *honzon,* while Eison used another *samaya* form of Nyoirin, known as the *Jewel of secret contemplation* (*mikkan hōju* 密観宝珠).[95] It is Shōken's model that was inherited by Monkan for his Sanzon gōgyō ritual.

While most sources on the Joint Ritual of the Three Worthies simply mention that its *honzon* is the jewel (or the five-wheel stūpa that contains it) and do not mention Nyoirin by name, Dōjun's *Seven Great Matters of the Testament* (*Goyuigō shichika daiji* 御遺告七個大事, 1321) states that the Byakuja ritual 避蛇法 is centered on Nyoirin.[96] The Sanbō-in lineage claimed that the sun deity's seed-letter, which produces all things, is called Nyoirin Kannon, another name for the jewel.[97] This deity (Nittenshi, but also Nyoirin Kannon) is identical to the Buddha's relics, but also to the sun goddess Amaterasu.[98] According to the *Jindaikan hiketsu,* Nyoirin Kannon is identical with Sonjōō (Myōken Bosatsu), Monju, Butsugen, and Kinrin—all merely different names for the same divine power: "It is called Butsugen Kinrin in the Sanmon (Mount Hiei), Nyoirin Kannon at Tōji, and Sonjōō Bosatsu at Miidera."[99]

The Seven-star Nyoirin

Under the name Seven-star Nyoirin (Shichishō—var. Shichisei—Nyoirin 七星如意輪), the bodhisattva took on a cosmic dimension (see Fig. 7.29). The link between Nyoirin and the seven stars had already been made in China, as shown by a set of relic boxes recently discovered at Famen Monastery 法門寺.[100] In Japan, Nyoirin was represented at the center of a wheel whose spokes, formed by *vajras,* delimit eight sections (Fig. 7.30). Seven of these sections are occupied by the stars of the Northern Dipper, while the eighth is occupied by the goddess Hārītī (J. Kariteimo 訶梨帝母).[101]

In the contemplation of the Seven-star Nyoirin's ritual area, the practitioner first visualizes the transformation of the seed-letters *hrīḥ, trāḥ,* and *trāḥ* into three jewels, which in turn morph into the twelve-armed (or six-armed) Nyoirin. Between the spokes of the wheel, the seed-syllable *ru* becomes the seven stars of the Northern Dipper and the goddess Hārītī.[102] This form of Nyoirin reigns over the celestial realm and brings harmony to the world by causing the spirits of the seven stars to descend from heaven, and Hārītī to arise from the earth.[103] A commentary quoted in the *Kakuzenshō* states that this mandala actually represents her subjugation of the five hundred demons that came down from heaven and of the chthonian deities that arose from the earth together with Hārītī.[104] Nyoirin controls all the devas and acts to prevent calamities caused by

FIGURE 7.29. Seven-star Nyoirin. 14th–15th century. Hanging scroll, color on silk. Nezu Museum, Tokyo.

lunar mansions and other astral deities. The *Tohyō Nyoirin shikihō* offers a description of the divination board (*shikiban*), with Nyoirin at the center, surrounded by a deity called "White Body" (White-robed Kannon?) in the east, Fukūkenjaku Kannon in the southeast, Tara in the southwest, Senju Kannon in the northwest, and Benji Myōō in the north; they are themselves surrounded by the twelve directional devas, the four deva kings, the seven planets, the twenty-eight mansions, and the thirty-six animals. The goddess Hārītī (J. Kariteimo, a.k.a. Kishimojin 鬼子母神 'Mother of the Demons') is also represented among them. The diagrams found in this and other texts show that Nyoirin's *shikiban* looked very much like a three-dimensional, rotating mandala (each court of the mandala becoming a ring of the *shikiban,* pivoting around its *honzon*).[114]

NYOIRIN'S NETWORK

Nyoirin's identity with the wish-fulfilling jewel led to her association with other jewel deities. As we have seen, she was often associated with Aizen and Fudō, as well as with Ichiji Kinrin. Like Aizen and Enmaten, she symbolized the storehouse consciousness. She was also identified with female divinities like Amaterasu and Benzaiten.[115] She was said, for example, to be an emanation of Amaterasu (and was therefore identified with the sacred mirror, Amaterasu's "divine body," while her acolytes in the Sanzon gōgyō ritual, Aizen and Fudō, were equated with the other two regalia).[116] In the *Record of the Mysteries of Mount Ben'ichi* (*Ben'ichizan himitsu ki*) and the *Record of Mount Ben'ichi* (*Ben'ichizan ki*), Amaterasu herself is described as a manifestation of the jewel.[117] In the *Oral Teachings of the Great Goddess Amaterasu* (*Tenshō daijin kuketsu*), her identification with the jewel is so complete that she becomes the primordial deity transmitted by Vajrasattva to Nāgārjuna in the Iron Tower in southern India.[118]

Benzaiten

Nyoirin also became one with Myōon Bosatsu 妙音菩薩, a bodhisattva who appears in the *Lotus Sūtra* but came to be linked with Benzaiten. Some texts also identify her with Monju (Skt. Mañjuśrī), a bodhisattva often represented as a divine youth and identified with the jewel. In addition, she is one of the *honji* of Jūzenji, the youthful deity of Hie 日吉 (present-day Hiyoshi) Shrine, and the *honji* of the Saintly Lady (Seijo 聖女), a manifestation of Dakiniten or Benzaiten worshiped at the Seijo-gū 聖女宮 on Mount Hiei.[119] Jūzenji is ordinarily presented as an avatar of the bodhisattva Jizō, another jewel-holding deity, himself perceived as identical with Nyoirin.[120]

The *Origin Story of Benzaiten* (*Benzaiten engi* 弁才天縁起) tells us that "dragons are the essence of the water element. This is why they dwell at the bottom of the sea. The jewel is produced by the water wheel; it is the source of all beings. This is why the *nāgas* take the essence of the relics as the spirit of water."[121]

The jewel is not only one of Benzaiten's attributes, it is more specifically her *samaya* form. In the *Keiran shūyōshū,* the three sacred sites of Benzaiten are represented as three jewels connected together in triangular fashion. The same text also contains a section on the identity of the *nāga* maiden and Benzaiten, which states that "the *nāga* maiden is Nyoirin Kannon."[122] In the *Lotus Sutra,* the *nāga* maiden offers a relic to the Buddha.[123] Benzaiten's *honji* is also Nyoirin,[124] who is said to have three bodies: the buddha Hōshō 宝性 (Ratnasambhava) in the southern quarter is her dharma body (*hosshin* 法身, Skt. *dharmakāya*); Nyoirin Kannon is her retribution body (*hōjin* 報身, Skt. *sambhogakāya*); the *nāga* maiden of the *Lotus Sūtra* is her transformation body (*keshin* 化身, Skt. *nirmāṇakāya*). These three bodies all take the wish-fulfilling jewel as their symbolic form. This wish-fulfilling jewel is the essence of the union between objects and wisdom.[125] The *Jindaikan hiketsu* adds that the exoteric *honzon* of the relic ritual is the bodhisattva Hōshō; at a deeper level it is Nyoirin Kannon, and at the ultimate secret level, the wisdom king Kongōyasha 金剛夜叉 (Skt. Vajrayakṣa).[126]

Another important jewel deity (and a jade maiden) connected with Nyoirin and Benzaiten was Kichijōten 吉祥天 (Skt. Śrī or Lakṣmī).[127] In most representations, this goddess holds a jewel in her left hand.[128] She is also a reliquary carrier, as shown by a statuette found at Famensi 法門寺 in China.[129] Like Nyoirin (and Benzaiten), she possesses a noticeable erotic aspect.[130] In her auspicious golden form, Kichijōten symbolizes the earth in its beneficial aspects (the earth's dark aspects are represented by her sister Kokuanten). Nyoirin's relation to Benzaiten also contributes to linking her with Ugajin (an ophidian deity with an old man's head, usually associated with Benzaiten) and with the astral fox (or "fox dragon," *shinko* 辰狐), Dakiniten's mount. In an apocryphal sūtra, we learn that Ugajin goes by the name of Nyoirin Kannon in the Sahā world and that his "live body," which resides in the solar wheel, is none other than Aizen. Nyoirin is also the essence of Ugajin, who manifests himself in the forms of various devas (including Shōten and Dakiniten). In the *Record of Inari* (*Inari ki* 稲荷記), Aizen and Nyoirin are described as the *honji* of the Inari deity (another deity related to Ugajin).[131] This deity was the protector of Tōji, and his shrine marks the site where Kūkai allegedly buried a wish-fulfilling jewel for the beings of the final period of the Law (*mappō*).

Nyoirin, Inari, and Ise

The deity worshiped at the Shrine of the Saintly Lady (Seijo-sha 聖女社) on Mount Hiei was also believed to be a manifestation of the Inari deity. The origin of that shrine is traced to a dream that the Tendai priest Son'i 尊意 had in 926. In this dream, he saw a lady of noble demeanor arrive in a magnificent cart to the Great Lecture Hall of Enryakuji. When he told her that the mountain was forbidden to women, she replied that she was no ordinary woman, and revealed her true nature as a manifestation of the Inari deity who had come to worship the Buddha's relics. She added that her *honji* was Nyoirin. Duly impressed by his dream, Son'i dedicated a shrine to her.[132]

Through Inari, Nyoirin was also identified with Dakiniten and her mount, the fox. In the *Keiran shūyōshū,* her identity with the fox is said to derive from that with Amaterasu. The image of Amaterasu in the Heavenly Rock Cave, we are told, is that of a fox shining in the darkness. This fox has a jewel on the tip of its tail, and it is said to be a manifestation of Nyoirin. His name, King Shindamani, expresses the belief that the wish-fulfilling jewel (*cintāmaṇi*) is its essence.[133] As noted above, Amaterasu's cave was also associated with the dragon cave of Mount Murō, inside which the jewel was hidden. The *Saimon of the Great Bright Deity Inari* (*Inari Daimyōjin saimon* 稲荷大明神祭文) states that "Da[kini]ten is a trace of the bodhisattva Monju. . . . Among the bodhisattvas, she corresponds to Jūichimen (Eleven-faced) Kannon and Nyoirin Kannon; among the wisdom kings, to the two wisdom kings Fudō and Aizen. The heavenly youths [that form the retinue] of Benzaiten, Shōten, Daikokuten, all are none other than Da[kini]ten."[134]

Nyoirin was also linked to Dakiniten through the jewel, as well as through accession rites (centered on secret mudrās) that drew on the same symbolism of the vitality and fecundity of the imperial body—radiating through the emperor (and his symbol, the jewel) to the entire kingdom. One of the five mudrās of the Dakiniten ritual used during the enthronement ceremony was the Jewel Seal, a gesture saturated with embryological symbolism.[135]

According to an illustrated scroll dated to 1350 and preserved at the Myōhō-in 妙法院 in Kyoto, Japan was the abode of a six-armed deity named Amaterasu who manifested itself in the forms of Nyoirin and Aizen. Here Aizen and Nyoirin are presented as the descendants of Amaterasu rather than her original ground (*honji*). In other texts, Nyoirin is the *honji* not only of various deities, but also of eminent monks and laymen. We recall that Shōtoku Taishi and Shōbō, the founder of Daigoji, were described as manifestations of this bodhisattva. Such was also the case with Ryōgen 良源 (a.k.a. Ganzan Daishi 元三大師, 912–985) in the Tendai tradition.[136]

Nyoirin and Dragon Deities

Nyoirin appears in some of the origin stories of famous Japanese temples. The Ishiyamadera tradition, for example, records that Shōmu Tennō 聖武天皇 (r. 724–749) invoked the aid of Nyoirin on the advice of Zaō Gongen 蔵王権現 (the tutelary deity of Kinpusen), asking her to help him find the gold needed to construct the Great Buddha of Tōdaiji.[137] Nyoirin's association with *nāgas* and dragons also figures in these legends. One example is the belief that the Nyoirin Kannon Hall of Nachi 那智 (in Wakayama prefecture) was erected on the head of a local dragon (Hirō Gongen 飛瀧権現) in order to pin down and control the unruly energies symbolized by the dragon.[138]

Shōbō, the founder of Daigoji and a patriarch of Shugendō, was also a promoter of the Nyoirin cult. The *Origin Story of Daigoji Temple* (*Daigoji engi*) records that he built two halls on Mount Kasatori 笠取 (in Uji) in 874, one dedicated to Jundei Kannon 准胝観音, the other to Nyoirin.[139] These halls were completed in 876, the official date of Daigoji's founding.[140] A few years later, in 902, the dragon maiden Seiryō Gongen 清瀧権現 is said to have appeared to him and revealed that she was a manifestation of *both* Jundei and Nyoirin, as well as the third daughter of the *nāga* king Sāgara (Fig. 7.32). She explained that she had formerly been the protector of Qinglong 清龍 (Blue Dragon) Monastery in Chang'an, where the Japanese master Kūkai studied under Huiguo. When Kūkai returned to Japan, she followed him and settled eventually on Mount Kasatori, changing her name from Qinglong (J. Seiryū 青龍) to Seiryō (Pure Waterfall).[141]

Seiryō Gongen appears at times as a beautiful woman holding a jewel, resembling Kichijōten, and at other times as a two-headed snake (whose heads symbolize Jundei and Nyoirin). This polarity is also interpreted as representing the esoteric complementarity between principle and knowledge, Aizen and Fudō, the red and the white (symbolizing female blood and male semen).[142] The *Daigoji shin'yō roku* (mid-Kamakura) declares that "the two buddhas Jundei and Nyoirin Kannon are the nondual body of the deity."[143] As Sarah Aptilon points out, this statement suggests that the "provisional manifestation" (*gongen*) takes precedence over the two bodhisattvas, becoming in fact their *honji*. It represents their nonduality, their union as higher principle.[144] The goddess appeared again in 1088, taking possession of the Daigoji abbot Shōkaku 正覚 (1057–1129), the son of Minamoto no Toshifusa 源俊房.[145] The *Daigo zōjiki* (late twelfth century) tells us that she appeared to Shōkaku in the form of

FIGURE 7.32. Seiryō Gongen. Edo period. Sheet, ink on paper. University Art Museum, Kyoto City University of Arts. *BZS* 4064.

Kichijōten, vowing her support of the Minamoto clan and requesting that a shrine be dedicated to her.[146] The shrine was built on the very same rock where Nyoirin/Seiryō Gongen had appeared to Shōbō. Significantly, while the two images enshrined in it were those of Jundei and Nyoirin (rather than of Seiryō Gongen), Nyoirin remained a "hidden buddha" (*hibutsu*)—like the jewel that is her true nature.

In 1204, the Daigoji priest Seigen 成賢 (1162–1231), a nephew of Shōken, offered a relic to Seiryō Gongen during a rain ritual, declaring that she was the daughter of the dragon king Sāgara.[147] A number of documents mention the identity of Nyoirin (or Jūichimen) Kannon and Amaterasu. Amaterasu was first identified with Jūichimen, the Eleven-faced Kannon. Avalokiteśvara (Ch. Guanyin) had already been interpreted as the sun deity (J. Nittenshi) in various Chinese apocrypha and in commentaries on the *Lotus Sūtra*. It was therefore easy to link one of her manifestations (Nyoirin) with the Japanese sun deity, Amaterasu, thereby drawing on the symbolic constellation that linked all these deities to the sun and the jewel.

Nyoirin and the Nun Nyoi

As we have seen, one of Kūkai's claims to fame was the efficacy of his rain rituals. Although the success of those rituals was usually attributed to the jewel and to the invocation of the Shinsen'en dragon, Kokan Shiren's 虎関師錬 *Chronicle of the Śākya Clan during the Genkō Era* (*Genkō shakusho* 元亨釈書, 1321–1326) suggests that it was mainly due to Kūkai's possession of a mysterious jewel box that had been transmitted to him by the jade woman.[148] Who is the jade woman? A passage in the *Sanbō ekotoba* 三宝絵詞, quoting a legend reported in Xuanzang's 玄奘 *Da Tang Xiyouji* 大唐西遊記, underscores the metaphorical associations between the jewel, the jade woman, and imperial power. The protagonist of that legend is a prince who, to improve his people's lives, goes to the palace of the dragon king in search of the wish-fulfilling jewel. He first meets a jade woman who guards the palace's gates, then the dragon king himself. In the *Da Tang Xiyouji*, this jade woman is called a "dragon woman," and she is the princess who watches over the wish-fulfilling jewel, which is said to be the relic of an old buddha.[149]

Let us turn now to the legend of the nun Nyoi 如意 as it is told in the *Genkō shakusho* against a background of tales related to Kūkai, Benzaiten, and the jewel.[150] It may seem strange at first glance to find this legend in the historiographic work of a Zen master like Kokan Shiren (1278–1346), but that impression recedes when we consider that Shiren was a contemporary of the Ritsu priest Monkan, one of the promoters of the cults of Nyoirin and Benzaiten, and that his work was presented to Emperor Go-Daigo to be included in the Buddhist canon.

As a young woman, we are told, Nyoi was the second consort of the emperor of the Tenchō 天長 era (824–834), that is, Junna Tennō 淳和 (r. 823–833). She is described as a kind of Daoist immortal who, without ever bathing or using aromatic plants, was always immaculate and fragrant. She is endowed with all the virtues of the perfect wife: she is beautiful, gentle, and submissive. Furthermore, she is a Buddhist paragon: she is generous, compassionate, and vegetarian. Like the emperor himself, she is a devotee of Nyoirin Kannon; actually, she is a manifestation of that bodhisattva—a fact revealed to the emperor in a dream. Several references to the number thirty-three (the traditional number of Kannon's avatars) appear in Nyoi's biography.

With all her fortune, however, the handsome Nyoi yearns to leave the palace to live a secluded life in the mountains. One day she receives a revelation from the goddess Benzaiten, who appears in the form of a heavenly woman riding a white dragon and tells her about a mountain called Nyoirin-mani 如意輪摩尼 (Nyoirin Jewel) in Settsu province. This fictitious mountain calls to mind Mount Murō, also known as Nyonin Kōya 女人高野 (Mount Kōya for Women).

Nyoi leaves the palace with two of her ladies-in-waiting. After some miraculous adventures, she discovers the mountain in question, where she is welcomed by the mountain's goddess, who reveals the existence of treasures hidden there—in particular, the jewels of Empress Jingū (Jingū Kōgō 神功皇后).[151] Meanwhile, the emperor, yearning after Nyoi, sends men to search for her. They eventually find her, but, no longer so submissive, she refuses to follow them. In the end, it is the emperor who has to come to her. When at length he returns to the palace without Nyoi, he claims that she has died in a fire, to protect her from the jealousy of his other consorts.

Having settled on the mountain, Nyoi invites Kūkai to perform a Nyoirin Kannon ritual there. Furthermore, having discovered a numinous tree, she asks the Shingon priest to carve an image of Nyoirin in her semblance. Once the icon is finished, it nods its head as a sign of approval.[152] With the help of Kūkai (and of Benzaiten), Nyoi goes on to tame a threatening, eight-faced and eight-armed deity living on the eastern peak of the mountain.

Kūkai also teaches Nyoi how to perform the Benzaiten ritual. Benzaiten then appears with her fifteen attendants (dōji 童子) and becomes the mountain's protecting deity. Under Kūkai's guidance, Nyoi then learns how to perform the ritual of the wish-fulfilling jewel. In 831, after completion of the Great Hall of Shinjuji 神呪寺 (Temple of Divine Incantations), Nyoi is ordained there with her two female companions. In 835, the year of Kūkai's death, and two years after Junna's death, she receives the visit of Ninmyō Tennō 仁明天皇 (r. 833–850). Soon afterward, she dies, aged 33, seated in lotus position and facing southward.

Nyoi's purported biography ends with a strange discussion related to her mysterious casket, which is said to have allowed Kūkai, in 824, to defeat his rival, the Kōfukuji priest Shubin 守敏, during a rain ritual aimed at ending a drought.[153] This object was identified as the Purple Cloud casket by a witness named Urashima no ko 浦島子, who claimed to have seen it in Penglai 蓬萊, the island of the immortals (associated here with the *nāga*/dragon palace). The casket was thought to give whoever possessed it power over the *nāgas*/dragons who preside over rain. Kūkai is said to have deposited it inside the Nyoirin icon he had just carved.

The mention of the Purple Cloud casket and the fisherman Urashima no ko deserves a few remarks.[154] As was well known, the fisherman known as Ura no Shimako entered folklore under the name Urashima Tarō. His legend was already written in the *Nihonshoki* (720), where, in the twenty-second year of the reign of Yūryaku Tennō (478), it is said: "A man from Tsutsukawa in the Yosa county of Tanba province, Ura no Shimako, had gone off to fish on his boat. He eventually caught a large tortoise, which transformed into a maiden. Urashima fell in love with her and married her. They went far out on the sea and reached Penglai Island, where they saw immortals." The *Nihonshoki* version ends there, but another version, that of the *Tango Fudoki* 丹後風土記 (ca. 715)—at least as cited by the *Shaku Nihongi* 釈日本紀 in the thirteenth century—is more prolix. It tells us that after three years of happiness in that Chinese Shangri-La, our Japanese Rip van Winkle became homesick and desired to return to his village. His wife then gave him a precious casket, telling him never to open it. Back in his village, he discovered that his parents had long been dead, and that to the villagers, his name only evoked the distant memory of a fisherman who had disappeared at sea three centuries earlier. He at once understood that he had been wrong to leave the island of the immortals. In his despair, he opened the casket, from which a purple cloud—his vital essence—escaped. He instantly took on the weight of his years and, according to the *Man'yōshū* 万葉集 version, died.[155]

The explicit correspondence between Penglai Island and the dragon palace only appears in later versions and is linked among other things to the belief that Benzaiten lives on an island called Hōrai (Ch. Penglai). Thus, in the *Tale of the Heike* (*Heike monogatari*), when the warrior Taira no Tsunemasa discovers the existence of Chikubushima Island on Lake Biwa, here is how he describes it:

> Even thus must have been the appearance of Mount Hōrai, the unattained goal of those boys, girls, and magicians dispatched by Shihuangdi and Wudi to seek the elixir of immortality, who frittered away their lives in ships on the vast ocean, pledged not to return without having reached their destination. A sutra says, 'In the world of men, there is a lake, and in that lake, emerging from the bowels

of the earth, there is a crystal isle where heavenly maidens dwell.' This was that very island.[156]

The notion of a *nāga*/dragon palace overlaps with that of the *tokoyo* 常世, a kind of other world located below or beyond the human world. A variant of the Urashima legend more directly linked to imperial mythology is that of Hoori no Mikoto 火遠理命, who journeyed to the palace of the sea god and married his daughter, Toyotama-hime 豊玉姫. When after three years he decided to return to the human world, he received from the sea king two jewels that controlled the sea tides. Wiser than Urashima, however, he took along his wife and her sister (Tamayori-hime玉依姫). The imperial line is said to have stemmed from his union with the two sisters.[157]

This myth was eventually connected with the famous story of the *nāga* princess in the *Lotus Sūtra*. In that text, the eight-year-old daughter of the dragon king Sāgara obtained awakening upon hearing the utterance of the bodhisattva Mañjuśrī, and offered a wish-fulfilling jewel to the Buddha. This jewel was in fact her vital essence, the source of her power. In medieval exegesis, the two daughters of the sea king, Toyotama-hime and Tamayori-hime, came to be seen as the sisters of that *nāga* princess and of other ophidian deities like Benzaiten. These Japanese sisters of the French Mélusine became by the same token the prototypes of the jade woman of imperial ritual.

The Zen historiographer Kokan Shiren follows up this tale with a strange discussion, apparently aimed at validating Urashima's legend (with its Daoist connotations) by inscribing it into an esoteric Buddhist context. He quotes an old story about the "men of the Way" of Penglai to assert the presence of Buddhist monks on the island of the immortals. By the same token, the casket becomes a Buddhist ritual implement that Urashima no ko could have recognized, although because he was not initiated into Buddhist esotericism he could not have known its content. Significantly, all later chronicles, while mentioning Nyoi's legend, pass over it quickly and focus either on Urashima no ko or on Kūkai.[158]

A PORTABLE DEITY

During the Kamakura period, relics were placed inside numerous statues, as well as within ritual instruments (for example, the five-pronged *vajra* used in Aizen rituals). Curiously, the material emphasis of the relic cults themselves, as well as the concrete evolution of reliquaries, came to influence a certain structural conception of Nyoirin in her relationships with the ritual objects and their substitutes. We can examine this phenomenon by delving into the rich catalogue of an exhibition held at the Nara National Museum in 2001 under the title "The Buddha's Relics and the Jewel" (*Busshari to hōju* 仏舎利と宝珠) (see, for example, Figs. 7.34–7.36).[159]

FIGURE 7.33. Portable shrine with Nyoirin (and Dainichi Kinrin on the other side of the central board) flanked by Aizen and Fudō. 14th century. Lacquered wood with polychromy and ink and color on silk. Nezu Museum, Tokyo.

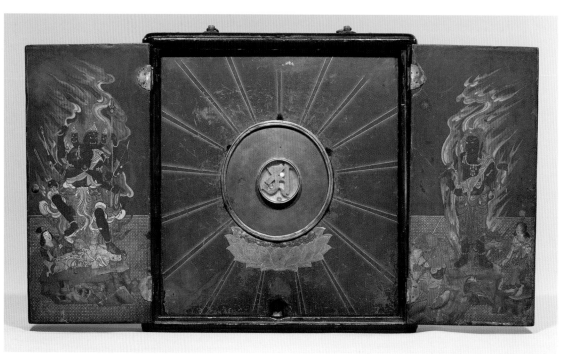

FIGURE 7.34. *Dato shuji mandara* portable shrine, with reliquary flanked by Gōzanze and Fudō. 1387. Lacquered wood with polychromy. Nara National Museum.

FIGURE 7.35. Seed-letter Vajra Realm mandala on the back of the central board. Detail of *Dato shuji mandara*. 1387. Lacquered wood with polychromy. Nara National Museum.

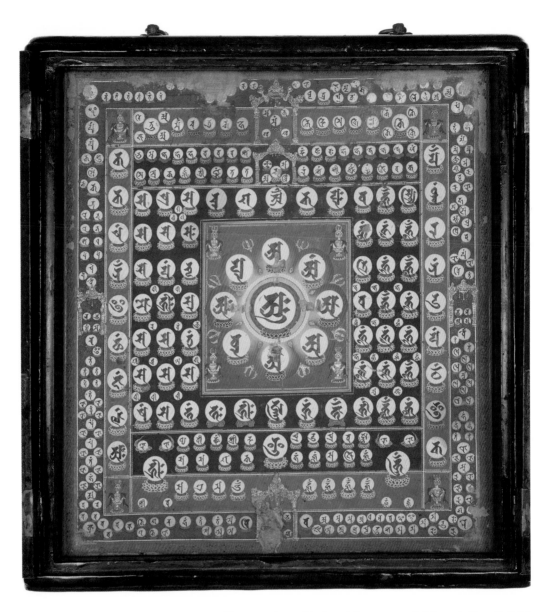

FIGURE 7.36. Seed-letter Womb mandala (revealed upon removal of the central board). Detail of *Dato shuji mandara*. 1387. Lacquered wood with polychromy. Nara National Museum.

Nyoirin's *Samaya* Form

The origin of the jewel ritual centered on Nyoirin can be traced to the monk Shōkaku 勝覚 (1057–1129), founder of the Sanbō-in, a subtemple of Daigoji. This ritual, which can be seen as a precursor of Monkan's Joint Ritual, was actually centered on three worthies, namely, a five-wheel stūpa (*gorintō* 五輪塔) symbolizing Nyoirin, flanked by Fudō and Aizen.[160] Eison performed the same type of ritual at Saidaiji, during a Kannon Flower Ritual that first took place in 1260 and was repeated at each New Year thereafter. As Naitō Sakae points out, Eison can be credited (or held responsible) for the spread of that ritual, which had remained secret in the Sanbō-in tradition.[161]

The *honzon* of Eison's ritual was probably no longer a *gorintō* but an artifact that modern scholars have, somewhat misleadingly, called a "jewel of secret contemplation" (*mikkan hōju* 密観宝珠), because it was supposedly derived from esoteric visualizations of the type taking place during the contemplation of the ritual area.[162] In spite of its name, the *mikkan hōju* is not simply a jewel, but a vertical combination of different symbolic elements, including a lotus dais, a wheel, a one-pronged *vajra* stalk, a second lotus dais, and a jewel on top (see Fig. 7.37).[163] Eison's ritual was soon replicated in other Ritsu monasteries such as Jōdoji (in Hiroshima prefecture).[164] As a result, this symbolic form of Nyoirin—a jewel on a lotus, itself atop a *vajra*—can be seen in a great number of reliquaries, dating mostly from the Nanbokuchō to the Muromachi period (see Figs 7.38–7.42). A good sample can be found in the catalogue *Busshari to hōju*.[165]

FIGURE 7.37. Jewel of secret contemplation, the *samaya* form of Nyoirin. 13th century. Gilt bronze. Tokyo National Museum.

The reliquaries containing the *samaya* form of Nyoirin (or Butsugen) are usually protected by two dragons and/or by Aizen and Fudō. The portable shrine from Kōfukuji, for example, opens to reveal a reliquary flanked by Aizen and Fudō, but its back doors show Nyoirin surrounded by the four deva kings (*Busshari to hōju*, fig. 77). The symbolic identity of Nyoirin and the jewel in the *mikkan hōju* appears clearly in a portable shrine from Saidaiji (fig. 78), where a *gorintō* is flanked by Aizen and Fudō; when the central board is removed, however, it is Nyoirin who appears at the center, seated on a lotus on a vertical one-pronged *vajra*.[166] The reliquary from Fukudenji 福田寺 in Hyōgo prefecture (fig. 79) also shows a *gorintō* on the front, flanked by two bodhisattvas, while the back reveals Nyoirin flanked by Aizen and Fudō.

A portable shrine in Tōkyō National Museum shows another variant of the *mikkan hōju;* here the reliquary reveals a mandala of the seed-letter *a* (equated with the jewel) inside a sphere on a lotus mounted on a vertical *vajra* (*Busshari to hōju,* fig. 81).[167] The reliquary from Murōji (fig. 74),

FIGURE 7.38. Nyoirin's *samaya* form with seed-letter. Edo period. Sheet, ink on paper. University Art Museum, Kyoto City University of Arts. *BZS* 1084.

FIGURE 7.39. Jundei Kannon. Edo period. Sheet, ink on paper. University Art Museum, Kyoto City University of Arts. *BZS* 2028.

FIGURE 7.40. Jundei Kannon. Edo period. Sheet, ink on paper. University Art Museum, Kyoto City University of Arts. *BZS* 2031.

FIGURE 7.41. Kōharishiki (Scarlet Glass) Amida. Ink on paper. Tokyo National Museum.

described as "Amaterasu's divine body" (Daijingū mishōtai 大神宮御正体), contains a mirror, on the back of which is carved the image of a *mikkan hōju*. This setup suggests the identity of Nyoirin and Amaterasu.[168] In the reliquary from Nezu Museum (fig. 113), the main icon, flanked by Aizen and Fudō, is Dainichi Kinrin seated on a lion inside an eight-spoke wheel; or, if one turns the board over, it is Nyoirin (see Fig. 7.33 above).[169] As we can see, the identity of the two divinities, sometimes explicitly formulated in texts like Monkan's *Great Matter of the Testament,* is suggested here by the positions of the central board (flipped over or removed), preserving the same triadic structure formed by the *honzon* and its two acolytes, usually Aizen and Fudō.[170]

THE TRIADIC STRUCTURE REDUX

Though several deities came to be identified with the wish-fulfilling jewel (*nyoi hōju*), Nyoirin's very name marked her as the archetypal jewel deity. Like Aizen, she served as a bridge toward a whole group of deities that included, to name just a few, Amaterasu, Kichijōten, Benzaiten, Ugajin, and Dakiniten. We recall that the Sanzon gōgyō ritual also linked Nyoirin with Amaterasu, Aizen, and Fudō. From a certain point onward, the jewel is no longer simply Nyoirin's attribute or *samaya* form. Indeed, it is Nyoirin who is perceived as an emanation of the jewel—or of the incantation that constitutes its verbal expression, in the same way that Aizen Myōō was an emanation of the Cintāmaṇi Dhāraṇī.

CODETTA

We have seen how dualistic epistemological structures tended to reassert themselves by turning a singular deity into a dyad. Furthermore, this dyad, coupled with the nonduality that is both its principle (*arché*) and its goal (*telos*), yielded a triadic structure exemplified among others by the Sanzon gōgyō ritual. It is a robust structure, since it remains even when

FIGURE 7.42. Amida Nyorai. Muromachi period. Color on silk. Nezu Museum, Tokyo.

its components (Nyoirin, Kinrin and Butsugen, Aizen and Fudō) change or trade places.

Material culture cannot be dissociated from spiritual culture. The procreative power connoted by Nyoirin Kannon was not simply objectified in the form of an esoteric goddess, it was also "objectalized" as an imaginary object—the wish-fulfilling jewel—and as a concrete, transformative device, the reliquary. At the same time, the jewel was deified and came to replace the traditional image of the deity at the center of the altar. This ritual technology was not merely a marginal development in medieval Japanese religious history; it was literally "instrumental" in the development of a new form of religiosity centered on different types of deities. The cult of Nyoirin is the paradigmatic case of a type of worship that derives from innovations in material culture. It is essential to grasp this new technology, together with the older technologies of the mandala and the divination board (*shikiban*), to understand the extraordinary development of the esoteric Buddhist pantheon. Mikkyō ideology and mythology were not simply the products of freewheeling mental permutations, they were also generated by the concrete permutations realized through portable altars and divination boards. The recent emphasis on Buddhist material culture is particularly welcome, as Buddhist Studies have for too long neglected the ritual and technological sides of Mikkyō.[171]

The quasi-obsession of medieval Japanese Buddhists with nonduality and with the ways to express (or reach) it through binary and ternary models may seem hopelessly reductionistic, but paradoxically, owing to its swerve, just the opposite may (at times) be true. Its apparently endless repetition of the same basic motifs and its linking of various dyadic, triadic, and pentadic patterns resulted in a kind of "swarm thinking" that allowed emergent patterns to appear, like a rich tapestry created by the interweaving of the same basic colored threads. While there is no denying the role of individual agency and of the sociohistorical context, these patterns, reflecting the partial actualization of Mikkyō's implicit theology, subverted and deconstructed the well-ordered system they were initially supposed to reinforce. Like the wish-fulfilling jewel that became Mikkyō's emblem, they proliferated and disseminated beyond the wildest dreams of those who had conceived them.

CODA

At the beginning of this book, I acknowledged the provisional usefulness of the notions of structure and function proposed by Lévi-Strauss and Dumézil before suggesting that, in a constantly evolving Buddhist practice, those notions are always at play and yet constantly subverted. For instance, the cult of deities like Aizen and Fudō reflects not only the relentless effort of medieval Buddhists to impose a dual structure on all kinds of religious ideas and practices, but also the way in which that duality was constantly supplemented, not simply by ternary structures but also by a more fluid dissemination that defies all attempts at unification. We need here to go beyond traditional cultic, cosmic, and mythic models. The discursive field has become dis-cursive, dis-located, inter-located—in the sense that all those deities that were conveniently forgotten or silenced by Buddhist and Shintō orthodoxies have become interlocutors whose voices must be heard. Lévi-Strauss tended to reduce the multiplicity of myth to a binary system of structures, a tendency also at work in esoteric Buddhist thought. We need on the contrary to *deconstruct* that logic and tease out the multiplicity of the networks it masks.

The gods are only segments of a patterned, heterogeneous network or *meshwork* composed of myths and rituals, but also of human and divine bodies, objects, institutions, techniques, images, and feelings.[1] Unlike Lévi-Strauss's mental structures, this meshwork, which encompasses both the mental and the material, is akin to the networks analyzed by the actor-network theory. Medieval Japanese gods were enmeshed in a tangle of relationships, they did not so much exist as they occurred. In spite of our fixation with stable iconography, they were identified not by attributes or features but by their trajectories, their transformations, their ever-changing stories, the ebb and flow of their efficacy. They were not caught in a finite, closed, all-encompassing system of synchronic connections, a structure or stricture. They constantly forged ahead, overflowing any systematic attempt to hold them accountable. In our attempts to unravel that tangle, that dense interweaving of rituals and stories and the (un)like, we can no longer simply pigeonhole them into taxonomies and hierarchies. The gods are not pigeons or doves, but hawks, kites, eagles, dragon-snakes, flying foxes, and flying elephants.

Take the case of Aizen: he is at the same time an individual and plural deity, a bundle of relationships and functions, one of the poles of a dual or ternary structure, and a nodal point in a mythological constellation that includes Fudō and the other wisdom kings, as well as deities as diverse at first glance as Myōken, Enmaten, and Amaterasu. Furthermore, he is a knot or node in a broader material and symbolic meshwork including the Buddha's relics, wish-fulfilling jewels, and the portable reliquaries that contained them, as well as subjugation rituals centered on the vital essence or "human yellow"; the emperors and regents, esoteric Buddhist monks, shrines and temples, buddhas, *kami* and "wild gods" (*kōjin*), human and divine sexuality, apotropaic rituals, beliefs centered on the placenta and the fetus—all this and so much more. Aizen does not occupy a single location in that network, he is constantly moving or rather transforming (which implies a different type of movement) along it, as well as transforming it. He is an elusive, fractional object or fractured subject that is at once "more than one and less than many."[2] Paradoxically, he has been used to bring closure to a triad, but, like the two other members of that triad, his fractal nature is precisely that which ensures the impossibility of any kind of closure.

Likewise Myōken, the very symbol of the solitary center, is caught in a star-shaped web, beginning with the seven stars of the Northern Dipper and extending to a multitude of beings. The wish-fulfilling jewel, another symbol of the fundamental source of everything, proliferates, crowding the mandalas of Aizen and related deities (Benzaiten, Dakiniten, and Bishamonten, to name a few). Thus these deities, which initially symbolize the solid foundation, the fundamental, the central transcendence, become part of a network that signifies precisely the opposite. They deconstruct themselves, and the system that produced them.

Although the context of the present work is quite different from the sociological setting of Bruno Latour and John Law's study of scientific practices, the patterns they describe are surprisingly resonant with those found in my analysis of deity networks: something circulates, which is made out of semantic and symbolic associations and which constitutes other (social) associations. This network emerges against a nonsymbolic (and nonsocial) background or *hinterland*.[3]

Our passage through these deity networks took us to strange places, uncharted lands where dragons and other fantastic beasts live, across and beyond the territories known as Buddhism, Onmyōdō, or Shugendō, which turned out to exist only as abstractions both produced and cancelled by these networks. The networks connect practices (objects, techniques, and, almost incidentally, individuals and institutions) rather than monolithic (or even plural) entities like esoteric Buddhism and Shintō, or even Tendai and Shingon. Yet, while remaining aware of the hypostatic danger they represent, I have continued to use those terms as shorthand. In the end, as suggested at the beginning, "the centre does not hold," and infinite variations on Fudō and Myōken correspond to what one may call "the mobile immobile," or the "fluctuating centre."

DUO À TROIS

The paradigmatic case of the pair formed by the half-brothers Gaṇeśa and Skanda, studied by Rolf Stein, shows the extent to which the initial structural duality symbolized in their role as gatekeepers ends up reasserting itself in very different cultural contexts.[4] At the same time, this duality tends to obscure concrete transformations and historical tensions: in this particular case, it hides the rivalry and fight between the two siblings and the fact that Gaṇeśa eventually superseded Skanda (at least in northern India);[5] it also glosses over their negative, demonic aspects. The same is true for Buddhist and non-Buddhist gatekeepers and other pairs of guardians like the companion spirits (kushōjin) and crossroad deities (Dōsojin). It is therefore necessary to question the binary thinking (pensée par couples) that constitutes the basic structure of structuralism and of Mikkyō.

Triads and Ternary Structures

Binary structures tend to develop into triadic structures in which the third term usually constitutes either the synthesis of the first two (as we have seen in the case of Aizen, Fudō, and Nyoirin) or their very source (in which case it is actually the first term).[6] The triadic structure was so pregnant in medieval Japan that, even in cases where the symmetry and the spatial symbolism produced a tetrad (as in the case of Dakiniten's four acolytes), one still ends up with a combination of three plus one (three females, one male).[7] The same gender polarity obtains in the triadic structure itself (two plus one). In the case of the Joint Ritual of the Three Worthies, for instance, the formula "One buddha, two wisdom kings" hides the fact that the "buddha" (or bodhisattva) in question, Nyoirin Kannon, is a female. Rolf Stein has suggested that this triadic symbolism, which also appears in the case of the stove god (or stove deities, kamadogami 竃神), should be perceived against a background of technologies centered on the stove or hearth.[8] The best example may be that of Sanbō Kōjin, the protector of the Three Jewels, who is also identified with the stove deity. In other words, material culture—the triangular shape of the earth or the three stones, soon deified, supporting the cauldron—may have contributed (if not singlehandedly produced) ternary mental structures. These mental structures may also be more fundamental, reflecting the basic linguistic situation of human beings.[9]

The "equality" between two and three in what the Vedic scholar Abel Bergaigne called "the mythological arithmetic" also derives from a common structure described by David Knipe as "the imagery of 'X plus one.'"[10] In this case, "three is of course the dyad plus one, and therefore a totality *succeeding* duality."[11]

Likewise, the dyadic symbolism derives naturally from technologies like weaving (the warp and the woof).[12] Weaving has inspired mythologies across cultures. At any rate, scholars should not uncritically accept this *more geometrico* approach, for it is too often a facade behind which vastly more complex exchanges go on, stable or fugitive combinations and transformations that reveal the infinite powers of imagination. The reading of the gods (and other similar realities) in the cosmological terms of yin and yang amounts to a philosophical domestication.[13] Dyadic, triadic (and pentadic) schemas are also a way to structure the experience, to objectify it through cosmological models, even if (or precisely because) the latter are unable to account for the infinite wealth of practices (and of reality).

This formidable structure comes apart at the seams, however. Gods are always dis-located, fragmented, they never stay put. Even the unmovable Fudō cannot keep still, as if taken by Saint Vitus' dance. As Robert Cooper points out: "Taxonomies, hierarchies, systems and structure represent the instinctive vocabulary of institutionalised thought in its subordinating of movement and transformation. [Whitehead] called this the principle of simple location in which clear-cut, definite things occupy clear-cut, definite places in space and time. There is movement—of a kind: the simple movement of definite things from one definite place to another. But it's a form of movement which denies the restlessness of transformation, deformation and reformation. Simple location reconstitutes a world of finished subjects and objects from the flux and flow of unfinished, heteromorphic 'organisms.'"[14]

Confronted with the phenomenal (in both senses) multiplicity of the gods, Buddhist theology attempted to elaborate a comprehensive taxonomy, organized along the lines of dual or ternary structures, which themselves point to a nondual reality. Mutual identifications, based on various types of analogies, led to a system based on a kind of metaphysical monism. The paradigmatic and most encompassing grid structure was that of the twin mandalas of Shingon, around which Ryōbu shintō theology developed. But this taxonomic tendency was not limited to esoteric Buddhism, and it can be found practically everywhere in medieval Japan.

These cosmological and ritual taxonomies—and analogical thought in general—were also aimed at producing presence (or at least a semblance of presence). Japanese religiosity relies on divine presence—whether that presence is seen as ontologically primary or emergent, as a privileged experience or a cultural creation. I agree with Jan Assmann that this divine presence should not be seen as having its roots in the privileged experience of the individual, but rather that it implies the primacy of ritual activity and the collective religious experience that emerged from it.[15] Yet I do not see the deities as mere social or cultural creations; or rather, I believe that, as "emergent properties," they came to have their own agency—even if this agency was itself an effect "generated by a network of heterogeneous, interacting, materials."[16] Whether individual or collective, human agency too is limited, dis-located, disseminated, traversed by other agencies; consequently, ritual mastery over the gods remains elusive, indeed it belongs essentially to the domain of wishful thinking.

The elusive presence of the divine is what is at stake in this endless textual, ritual, and iconographic proliferation. To apprehend this presence, traditional methodologies—whether those of religious history, Buddhology, folklore studies (*minzokugaku*), or structuralism—prove inadequate. Their specific insights must be duly recognized and preserved, but too often these methodologies are one-sided, reducing the analysis to the sociohistorical, economic, ideological, or mythological levels, depending on the case. They also are by nature and necessity objectivist, bypassing the gods in the process, or at best reducing them to cyphers for human intentionality. While claiming to respect people's beliefs, they refuse to lend any credence to the gods' existence and agency, which these beliefs presuppose.

By contrast, my heuristic model is resolutely multidimensional, emphasizing as it does the importance of "hybrids," yet ultimately questioning the very notion of hybridity.[17] I contend that, in order to understand the gods' oracles, we have to take them and their followers seriously—which does not necessarily mean at face value. We may have to adopt here what Daniel Dennett calls the "intentional stance"—endowing the gods with an intentionality that sometimes contradicts human intentions. In a first phase, I attempt to retrieve the implicit, submerged, or hidden dimensions of a small sample of gods—for instance, their embryological function or their *doppelgänger* nature—and I emphasize their structural links with other deities, their shifting position in a continuously changing network. It is worth noting that the analogical or correlative nature of medieval Japanese religion, instead of simply combining two individualized deities, correlates specific qualities and features common to a number of them. It constitutes a rhizome-like network that connects "a thousand plateaus"— myths, rituals, images, and other cultic objects; buddhas, gods, and demons; people (in particular religious specialists) and socioreligious movements (subsumed under such names as Mikkyō, Onmyōdō, Shugendō); ideas, fears, and desires; and types of knowledge. This network contrasts with the nested hierarchy of the pantheon, where the "original nature" (*honji*) and its "traces" (*suijaku*)—buddhas, bodhisattvas, *myōō,* devas, and *kami*—are nested within each other like Russian or Daruma dolls.[18]

This book's trajectory can be characterized as a succession of *écarts* (discrepancies or departures): vis-à-vis the "naive" phenomenological approach, that of the believers (or of the theologians who operate within the limits of their structure/culture); vis-à-vis the naive "objective" approach under its multiple guises: historicist (focusing on ideologies and political motivations), anthropological (focusing on "beliefs"), and structuralist ("structures"). There is no denying the degree of reality and the richness of analyses produced at each of these levels, but in the end they all seem to fall short. Thus, I felt the need to reintroduce a pinch of phenomenology, to acknowledge the importance of the lived experience of the Buddhists and of the scholars, and the transference between both, who in spite of cultural differences bump up against the same epistemological limits: those of language (Wittgenstein) and the "blinding proximity of the real."[29] Starting from a methodological individualism, I used some features of structural analysis that seemed to account for the "already structural" aspect of medieval mythology. Yet Lévi-Strauss tends to reduce the multiplicity of myth to the binary logic of structures, a tendency that is also at work in esoteric Buddhist mythology (for instance, in binary structures such as the Aizen/Fudō pair). What I have tried to do, instead, is to deconstruct that logic to reveal the underlying multiplicity of networks that it attempted to hide.

What do all these associations mean from a philosophical or soteriological standpoint? Are they merely mindless combinations that repeat themselves ad nauseam, and should we therefore stick to the explicit theology? If not, do we have the means today to reconstitute the implicit theology that underpinned it, a quasi Lévi-Straussian deep structure? Lévi-Strauss would have found himself in good company with esoteric Buddhist monks in their almost obsessive coupling of everything in terms of yin and yang, from the Womb and Vajra Realm mandalas to Aizen and Fudō, and on to infinity. Yet, and this is one thing that perhaps neither Lévi-Strauss nor his clerical precursors foresaw, binary oppositions also allow the creation of lateral associations, the dissemination of symbols, the spreading of a rhizome, the extension of a network. Each deity (or node) becomes richer, albeit temporarily, from the values of its connections. Lévi-Strauss's structures look like forgotten landscapes, natures as dead as those accumulations of clouds and putti in classical Western art, whose pictorial beauty still moves us when its symbolic urgency has long since left us. A whole continent has sunk into oblivion, from which only opaque, enigmatic images remain—even when art historians and other iconologues claim to decipher them. Iconology—and even discussions of the "sublime"—miss the essential.

To be fair, perhaps Lévi-Strauss had foreseen this, almost in spite of himself. According to Viveiros de Castro, his work reveals two different concepts of structure: as transcendental principle of unification, formal law of invariance; and as operator of divergences, modulator of continuous variations; structure as closed grammatical *combinatoire* or as open differential multiciplicity.[30] In other words, we are confronted with two forms of duality: a closed, perfect one, and an open, imperfect one; the former is the duality between equal twins, the other between unequal twins. My point has been, precisely, that Aizen and Fudō are unequal twins, and that this difference (and others) is not, as Lévi-Strauss would have it, what insured the smooth functioning of the system; but rather that it paved the way to a kind of Derridean *différance*, which prevented esoteric Buddhism (in spite of its theologians) from ever becoming a closed, combinatory system. The same argument can be applied to the triadic structures we have discussed.

What I have tried to do amounts to a kind of archeology of Japanese religions. The quasi-structures that I bring to light (or reconstruct) are reminiscent of the networks of the Roman land registry, still visible in the outline of fences and the layout of the paths and roads in contemporary landscapes. These structures still lend rhythm to our life in strange ways. Along the same lines, the apparent randomness of distribution of some villages over the French landscape is a result of the distance that a Roman legion could travel in one day, whereas other villages may have their origins in prehistoric settlements.[31] Similarly, rituals may be "islands of time" barely emerging from the sea of modern life. Like an archeological palimpsest, myths and rituals are a constant repetition (and transformation, reinscription, or rather re-transcription, through the working of cultural memory). Thus, these structures are not *the* deep structures of structuralism, and I don't even claim that they have an objective reality. I merely propose a reading, one view among others that are necessarily contextual, moving in constant disarray and reorganization; in other words, not a "key" to Japanese mythology, but a mere idiosyncratic "re-mythologizing"; not another map of the invisible world, even less the annexation of a new territory, but a mere hike along the multifarious ridges of Japanese religion.

There is no going beyond "conventional" truth in this bookish format; all we can do is admit that we always miss the essential. I naively thought that, with every new book, I would get closer to it. This asymptotic model of reality, I am told, is no longer valid (at least among scientists). Yet I persist in believing that a description of medieval Japanese religion in concrete (iconographic, mythological, ritual) terms is closer (more inclusive, more efficient) to its reality than a philosophical approach. A mythico-ritual expression of ambivalence and nonduality is more efficient than a doctrinal expression of *hongaku* thought, even if the two are fundamentally complementary.

Acknowledging failure is perhaps the only way to articulate the pure disorder of raw experience with the sterile order of ideological discourse;

to partly restore the symbolic profusion or proliferation without falling back into the unspeakable or the unreadable—which remains the divine presence as multiplicity (not to be confused with the mystic experience of Oneness—at least so I presume). In the end, I am not sure that writing a scholarly book on Japanese religion is any better than writing something like "The Folklore Studies of Professor Munakata" (a manga series by Hoshino Yukinobu).[32] My lingering doubt could be expressed as follows: is a scholarly book like this one just another form of storytelling, and one that can never hope to reach the fascinating efficiency, the mediated immediacy and appeal of popular culture? (As any Google search makes clear, the current vogue of Japanese gods has to do less with scholarly publications than with the popularity of manga and video games.)

Starting from not just one, but two conventional symbols of the center and nonduality (Myōken and Fudō), I argued that these symbols are highly mobile and open to a myriad of interpretations. Myōken's origin was in Daoism and in divination, while Fudō, originating in esoteric Buddhism, became the main deity of Shugendō, and his divinatory aspects also brought him close to Onmyōdō. The same is true regarding the duality represented by Fudō and Aizen, or the triad they form with Nyoirin Kannon. Wittgenstein is said to have once noted that "if you wrap up different kinds of furniture in enough wrapping paper, you can make them all look the same shape."[33] This is what happens with Buddhist gods: by adding layer after layer of symbols and functions, they become more complex, yet they also look increasingly similar. The multiplication of dual and ternary models amounts to wrapping up different deities in all kinds of bands, or to covering them with horoscopes (*omikuji*) and silver paper (as in popular practices), so that their specific shapes eventually disappear and they all look the same. From there to the notion of a synthetic deity, there is only one small step, which was sometimes taken.

The worst reductionism is perhaps the kind of dualism that reduces everything to the same irenistic, abstract yin-yang polarity. Even so, taking our cue from auto-organization theory, we may surmise that the endless replication of the same dual structure in nonideal conditions of transmission or communication leads to a proliferation of minor differences and to a "noise" that augments the complexity of the global system. The same polarity that seems simplifying and reductionist (for instance, the interpretive grid of *honji suijaku*) may also translate into an increased complexity. All dyads (and triads) seem to overlap, but in practice never quite do so. This obsession with triads may (or may not) have something to do with the three-step methodology I have adopted here:

1) I started from the historical emergence of medieval deities; while the conditions of that emergence often remain obscure, the questions raised at this level (which is that of most studies

on the question) seem relatively straightforward—not to say trivial.[34]

2) At the structural level, I tried to tease out some underlying schemas—for instance, the embryological symbolism shared by Myōken, Fudō, and Aizen. This symbolism also connects various levels of the macrocosm and microcosm into a multilayered structure: heaven, the underworld, and the female womb, for example.

3) I eventually departed from structuralist objectivism in order to: a) reintroduce a more complex, less naive phenomenological approach; b) emphasize the hybrid nature of the deity; and c) point toward the "unsaid," the "mystical" (in the Wittgensteinian sense).[35] In so doing, I am aware of leaving the theoretical Garden of traditional scholarship, but it is a risk well worth taking. The fact remains that even if the major part of the analysis takes place in a structuralist framework, it overflows that framework in at least two ways:

    —By taking into account the "ontological" experience (real or perceived as such, which is practically the same thing) of the absolute.

    —By criticizing the ideological aspects of the way in which that experience is always already recuperated, inasmuch as it has to express itself in and through language games.

In this book, I have discussed the "dualistic" aspects of the analogical thought of medieval Mikkyō, which attempted to prevent the dissemination of practices and to reduce them to a quasi-Hegelian ternary structure. However, the proliferation of symbols such as the wish-fulfilling jewel proved too great to remain caught for long in such reductionist discourses.

Without downplaying the importance of the doctrine, what I have tried to do was, on the one hand, to reveal behind those geometrical figures the teeming multiplicity of the network at the very heart of the ritual and of its *honzon;* and on the other hand, for lack of access to the lived reality of human actors, to attempt to retrieve at least the *perspective* that inspired them and that still obliges us to take them seriously—if not always at their word.

Owing to their transductive nature, myth and ritual take us always further afield, beyond the traditional rubrics of Japanese religion (buddhas, bodhisattvas, and *kami*), introducing new actors like the wisdom kings, devas, and "bright" deities (*myōjin*) and creating new links between them. In this way, the watertight sealing of the pantheon's compartments is breached. Of course, anyone who has read a *saimon* or any other ritual invocation—where one moves smoothly from the buddhas and bodhisattvas to the devas, the underworld deities, and the *kami*— knows this, but Buddhist scholarship has long been blind to the evidence. These texts still belong to the explicit, hierarchical theology, whereas in actual practice even that hierarchy is subverted. In spite of the evidence, we continue to be blinkered by a traditional model that shows us what to see (doctrinal Buddhism and Shintō) and hides the rest (the reality of beliefs and practices).

This book was intended as a first step in that direction. As a second step, in *Protectors and Predators,* I focus my attention on the devas—which played such an important role in Mikkyō—and the *myōjin,* who provide a bridge between Buddhism and local cults. I attempt to show, for instance, how one passes, through the mediation of the snake, from Aizen to Daikokuten and to the resurgence of ancient snake cults. In so doing, I emphasize the ambivalent nature of those deities and their role as *pharmaka* (remedy and/or poison), particularly in their functions as gods of obstacles and controllers of human destiny. Thus, the story has no epilogue, in large part because the identities of its characters have changed along the way. Toward the beginning of our journey through the *terra incognita* of medieval Japanese religion, a "land where dragons live," I discussed the case of Myōken.[36] We recall how this deity is sometimes represented riding a dragon, with snakes emerging from his hair. In *Protectors and Predators,* I attempt to show the affinities that link him to the dragon maiden Benzaiten, the fox-riding maiden Dakiniten, the ophidian Ugajin, and the elephant-headed Shōten—to name just a few. But that journey is not for the faint at heart.

ABBREVIATIONS

BDJ	*Bukkyō daijiten*
BEFEO	*Bulletin de l'École française d'Extrême-Orient*
BZS	*Bukkyō zuzō shūsei*
CEA	*Cahiers d'Extrême-Asie*
DNBZ	*Dai Nihon bukkyō zensho*
DZ	*Daozang*
GR	*Gunsho ruijū*
IBK	*Indogaku bukkyōgaku kenkyū*
JJRS	*Japanese Journal of Religious Studies*
KST	*Shintei zōho kokushi taikei*
KT	*Shinpen kokka taikan*
MN	*Monumenta Nipponica*
NKBT	*Nihon koten bungaku taikei*
NKBZ	*Nihon koten bungaku zenshū*
NSBS	*Nihon shomin bunka shiryō shūsei*
NSSS	*Nihon shomin seikatsu shiryō shūsei*
NST	*Nihon shisō taikei*
SNKBT	*Shin Nihon koten bungaku taikei*
SNKBZ	*Shinpen Nihon koten bungaku zenshū*
ST	*Shintō taikei*
SZ	*Shingonshū zensho*
T	*Taishō shinshū daizōkyō*
TASJ	*Transactions of the Asiatic Society of Japan*
TSZ	*Tendaishū zensho*
TZ	*Taishō shinshū daizōkyō zuzō*
ZGR	*Zoku gunsho ruijū*
ZNKZ	*Zoku Nihon koten zenshū*
ZST	*Zoku shintō taikei*
ZSZ	*Zoku Shingonshū zensho*
ZTZ	*Zoku Tendaishū zensho*
ZZGR	*Zokuzoku gunsho ruiju*

15. Among works in English influenced by Kuroda, see McMullin 1984 and 1987; Grapard 1992; Stone 1999; and Adolphson 2000 and 2007.

16. See Amino 1993. See also Amino 1978 and 2007; and Yamamoto 1998a.

17. For a good discussion, see Iyanaga 2002–2003.

18. Hayami Tasuku (1975a and 1998), for instance, has described the development of apotropaic rituals in the late Heian and Kamakura periods.

19. These themes have been insightfully analyzed by Iyanaga Nobumi (1981–1985 and 1996–1997). See also Davidson 1991 and Stein 1995.

20. On *chūsei shinwa* 中世神話, see Saitō 2006.

21. See Kuroda's seminal essay, "Shintō in the History of Japanese Religion" (Kuroda 1980b). See also Teeuwen and Rambelli 2003a; Breen and Teeuwen 2000 and 2010.

22. See Itō Masayoshi 1972. More recently, see Teeuwen and Rambelli 2003a; and Iyanaga 2006–2007.

23. See Durkheim 1995: 28: "[There] are great religions from which the idea of gods and spirits is absent, or plays a secondary and inconspicuous role. This is the case of Buddhism."

24. This view has recently been challenged, in the case of early Buddhism, by Robert DeCaroli (2004).

25. The field of Chinese religion has produced a number of significant works on Chinese deities. See for instance Katz 1995a; Yü 2000; and Kleeman 1994. While there are some similar Japanese studies (e.g., Yamamoto 1993a and 1998b; Iyanaga 2002a and 2002b and Suzuki Masataka 2001), they have not yet had much impact on Western scholarship. An early and significant exception is the work of Cornelius Ouwehand on the catfish deity (1964). Although Ouwehand, strongly influenced by Yanagita Kunio's ethnocentric approach, tends to leave Buddhism out of the catfish picture, it is so far the only English-language monograph that deals with a "deity of obstacles," a category to which I shall return. Also worth mentioning in this respect is the work of Hartmut Rotermund on the cult of smallpox deities (1991).

26. For a critique of the functionalist approach, see Favret-Saada 1980; de Castro 2009; and Latour 2010. The social scientists' "respect" of the natives' beliefs reminds me of Ishmael's show of tolerance in *Moby Dick:* "I cherish the greatest respect towards everybody's religious obligations, never mind how comical, and could not find it in my heart to undervalue even a congregation of ants worshipping a toad-stool" (Melville, *Moby Dick,* chap. 17).

27. See Mauss 2001.

28. See Hubert and Mauss 1981; on this question, see also Malamoud 1996a.

29. See Lévi-Strauss 1987; and Siegel 2006.

30. Calvino 1997: 45.

31. See Hornung 1996: 238.

32. Latour 2005: 217.

33. Latour 1996: 372.

34. Latour 2005: 46.

35. On this question, see Eco 1989.

36. See Kuroda Toshio 1989: 152.

37. See Kyoto shiritsu geijutsu daigaku geijutsu shiryōkan 2004.

38. See Dumézil's argument in *Le problème des Centaures* (1929); and Stein 1995.

39. Similar *kirigami* came to be used in other Buddhist schools (for instance in Sōtō Zen), as well as in Shugendō and in artistic traditions. For the *kirigami* of the Sōtō Zen tradition, for instance, see Ishikawa 2001.

40. *T.* 76, 2410. In references to the Taishō edition of the Buddhist canon, or *Taishō shinshū daizōkyō*, the first number is the volume number, the second that of the work in the general catalogue. Out of the 300 original fascicles (*kan* 巻), only 116 remain. While the work originally covered exoteric and esoteric Buddhism, Vinaya, and "documents" (*ki* 記), what remains is essentially Mikkyō. The preface by Kōshū is dated to 1318. According to Tanaka Takako, an important section of this work—dealing with the devas—was actually compiled by Kōshū's disciple Unkai 雲海. See Tanaka Takako 2003: 105–131.

41. A similar question has been raised recently by Bruno Latour in *An Inquiry Into Modes of Existence* (2013: 181–206).

42. Lévi-Strauss 1969: 3.

43. In this sense, Japanese mythology looks more like Joyce's *Finnegan's Wake* than like Lévi-Strauss's *Mythologiques*.

44. Early research is represented by the monographs of Marinus De Visser (1913, 1914, 1931); Robert van Gulik (1935); and Noël Péri (1916 and 1917). For India, we have the work of Georges Dumézil on the Gandharvas/Centaurs (1929) and of Wendy Doniger (O'Flaherty) on Śiva (1973). Rolf A. Stein is the author of a seminal essay on the "gatekeepers" (1991b), to which I will often refer. Worth mentioning on the Chinese side are recent monographs by Paul Katz (1995) and Chün-fang Yü (2000). For Japan, the traditional monographic approach is still found in the work of Sasama Yoshihiko (1988, 1991, and 1993). Also worth mentioning is a series of edited volumes entitled Minshū shūkyōshi sōsho 民衆宗教史叢書, and the pioneering work of Kida Sadakichi (1976). The research on gods and demons remains largely the province of folklore studies (*minzokugaku*), art history, and Shintō scholarship. Recent work by Yamamoto Hiroko (1993a and 1998b), Tanaka Takako (1993), Suzuki Masataka (2001), Iyanaga Nobumi (1994, 2002a, and 2002b), Kawamura Minato (2007 and 2008), and Itō Satoshi (2011) has begun to break these disciplinary boundaries. There is still little in Western languages; apart from the dated monographs by U. A. Casal (1956 and 1959), one should mention the interesting combination of structuralism and folklore studies by Cornelius Ouwehand, in particular his classic *Namazu-e and Their Themes* (1964). Also worth mentioning are the recent monographs of Ingrid Fritsch (1996) and Catherine Ludwik (2007) on Benzaiten, and the doctoral dissertations of Sarah Aptilon on Nyoirin Kannon 如意輪観音 (2008) and of Benedetta Lomi on Batō Kannon 馬頭観音 (2011).

45. For a critique of that approach, see Faure 1986b.

46. Latour 2005: 121.

47. See Mus 1988; and Satō Hiroo 1998 and 2003.

48. Law 2004: 62.

49. Souriau 2009: 151–154.

50. See Serres 1980.

51. Detienne 2009: 94.

52. Wittgenstein 1987: 8e.

53. Quoted in Poirier 1968: 1069.

54. I borrow this metaphor from Marcelle Lalou (1946: 97).

55. On this question, see Como 2005 and 2009.

56. Lévi-Strauss 1969: 4.

57. Ibid.

58. While it would be better for the sake of coherence to give only the Sanskrit or Japanese name of the deities, I have found it necessary to give both, or either, depending on the context: it makes no sense to speak of Sarasvatī in the context of medieval Japan, where Benzaiten has departed so significantly from her Indian prototype—but it would be anachronistic to use the name Benzaiten when I am dealing with the Indian river goddess. Similarly, it seems difficult to speak of Yama when most medieval Japanese only knew Enma (as king or deva). In the case of Aizen Myōō, it is misleading to speak of Rāgarāja, since this deity hardly had any existence (under this name at least) in India.

59. See Deleuze and Guattari 1987; Latour 1993, 1996, and 2005; and Law 2004.

60. Stengers and Latour 2009: 21.

CHAPTER 1: TWISTS AND TURNS

1. Coleridge, quoted in Sacks 1996: 288–289.

2. Przyluski 1923: 309.

3. Greek mythology is usually presented as the perfect example of a classificatory pantheon in which gods have a clear identity. Yet this has more to do with the type of sources used—essentially narratives. As Marcel Detienne has shown, when one looks at rituals instead, things are no longer so clear, and even the classical Nietzschean distinction between Apollonian and Dionysian religion falls apart: Apollo, whom Dumézil too quickly called "the most moral of all gods," is caught with a knife in his hand, and he shares several attributes and functions, and even features such as madness, with Dionysos. See Dumézil 1982; and Detienne 2009. In Japan, attempts were made to organize the demonic world as well, but the demons resisted, as one might expect. Perhaps the attempt was doomed from the start, inasmuch as a pandemonium is precisely the contrary of a pantheon.

4. On this point, see Bourdieu 1990. See also actor-network theorists like John Law (1992, 2004) and Michel Callon (1986).

5. Tarabout 1993: 55.

6. Vernant 1982: 110.

7. David Kinsley (1986), for instance, describes a gallery of distinct goddesses (like Lakṣmī, Parvatī, and Radha) on the basis of a narrative (mythological) corpus, and downplays the (ritual) interpretation that sees them all as figures of *the* Goddess (Devī).

8. The four traditional types of Tantric rituals, for example, imply a radical modification or modulation in the nature of a single deity.

9. According to Gilles Tarabout, these fields (referential, cultic, initiatic, narrative) are interdependent: a cult (corresponding to the cultic field) unfolds spatially in relation to a reference system (referential field); it generates powers by resorting to "secret" formulas and mental representations (initiatic field); it honors deities whose myths are otherwise known (narrative field). Nevertheless each field is partly autonomous in its organization, that is, in its possible coherence. See Tarabout 1993: 48 and 68.

10. Tarabout 1993: 61.

11. Tarabout 1993: 67. See also Bhattacharya 2000. In the case of Vedic India, at least, the demonic troupe is more hierarchized than a pandemonium—and the pantheon less hierarchized than one would think.

12. Descola 2005: 163–180.

13. In the case of medieval Japan, one seems to have passed from an ontology that was by and large animist or shamanistic to an analogical ontology influenced by esoteric Buddhism and Chinese cosmology.

14. Descola 2005; Viveiros de Castro 2004 and 2009.

15. Dantec 2006: 302.

16. I need to cite the relevant passage *in extenso:* "[Explicit] mythology and implicit mythology are two different modes of an identical reality: in both cases we are dealing with mythic representations. The error of contemporary theoreticians arises from the fact that they do not distinguish between these two modes of existence of mythology, or do so only incidentally. So, instead of taking as a whole the problems raised by mythic representations, whether explicit or implicit, and making a separate study of ritual, they draw the dividing line between explicit mythology on the one hand, arbitrarily reserving the name 'mythology' for it, and, on the other hand, the glosses or commentaries on ritual, which belong to the category of myth, but which they link up with, and confuse with, ritual proper. . . . By endeavouring at the outset to give a specific definition of ritual distinguishing it from mythology, they leave in the former all sorts of elements which rightly belong to the latter, and get everything thoroughly confused." Lévi-Strauss 1981: 669.

17. See Mus 1975; Bouillier and Toffin 1993: 18–19.

18. Borgeaud 2004a: 210.

19. Malamoud 1996: 3.

20. Wittgenstein 1960: 17.

21. See Starobinski 1979.

22. Unlike the French *porte-manteau,* from which it derives, the English portmanteau has the two meanings of "coat-hanger" and "suitcase" (hence, again, the French *mot-valise* to designate the same phenomenon).

23. Bourdieu 1990: 261. For an interesting discussion of "analogical" epistemology, see Descola 2005: 280–320.

24. According to Bourdieu: "It is no accident that the difficulties of the Greek and Chinese exegetes began when they tried to construct and superimpose *series.* . . . When one tries to push the identification of the different series beyond a certain degree of refinement, behind the fundamental homologies all sorts of incoherences begin to appear. True rigor does not lie in an analysis which tries to push the system beyond its limits, by abusing the power of the

discourse that gives voice to the silences of practice, exploiting the magic of the writing that tears practice and discourse out of the flow of time, and above all by putting the essentially mandarin questions of coherence or logical correspondence to the most typically practical of practices" (1990: 261). Bourdieu quotes Granet who, in *La pensée chinoise,* offers "examples of the would-be impeccable, but merely fantastic, constructions produced by the effort to resolve the contradictions arising from the hopeless ambition of giving an intentionally systematized form to the objectively systematic products of analogical reason" (Bourdieu 1977: 230). A case in point is the Chinese theory of the "five phases" (*wuxing* 五行), which was also prevalent in medieval Mikkyō and Onmyōdō. The notion of "correlative thinking" owes much to Granet, and Lévi-Strauss, among others, was influenced by it.

25. For instance, if the wish-fulfilling jewel (*a*) is equated with Aizen (*b*) and with Benzaiten (*c*), Aizen comes to be equated with Benzaiten. On this point, see Pinnington 1994:132.

26. The attribution of an original substance (*honji*) to a *kami* is perhaps not only a way to enroll that god into the Buddhist pantheon but also a way to insure that, behind that dangerous power, is hidden another, more powerful, and benevolent one, and thus, that there is a rationality behind the demonic hubris. It is perhaps also a way for the faithful to elevate their god by giving it the prestige of a buddha, a nominal prestige that takes nothing away from its agency. While it amounts to paying tribute to Buddhism, it does not mean that the buddhas have the last word in local affairs.

27. As when, for instance, the mountain god becomes the rice field god, or the rough spirit (*aramitama*) of a *kami* becomes, through ritual process, a benign spirit (*nigimitama*). A similar process is sometimes expressed in Buddhism as the conversion of a demon, indicated by a partial identity of names (Bhairava becoming Vajra-Bhairava). To say that *a* is *b*, however, is not the same as saying that there is only *a* in different forms. It is also to say that *a* is not (quite) *b*, it is *b* under a certain relation.

28. As Derrida points out, the function of the copula or the "grammatical mark of equivalence" is absolutely distinct from the full-fledged use of the verb "to be" (1985: 240). According to Émile Benveniste, "the two have coexisted and will always be able to coexist since they are completely different. But in many languages they have merged." (Quoted in Derrida 1980b: 114.) The two functions actually coexist in our medieval Buddhist texts, where an identity is at times fully ontological, at other times merely classificatory.

29. Malamoud 2002: 122.

30. Riffaterre 1982: 111.

31. On this technique, known as *allegoresis,* see Klein 2002: 13–40. In the name of Kasuga Myōjin 春日明神, for instance, the compound Kasuga 春日, decomposed in its elements (two 二, great 大, sun 日), is interpreted as a reference to the two 二 Dainichi 大日 of the Womb and Diamond realms.

32. A case in point is the way the Tendai priest Kōshū 光宗 (1276–1350) collects information about Benzaiten in two fascicles of his *Keiran shūyōshū.* By weaving together homophonies, metonymies, and spatial and numerological symbolism (for instance the ternary symbolism of Tendai), he is able

to link Benzaiten to astral deities (Kokūzō, Myōken, Aizen), water deities (Suiten, the *nāga* princess), and to various local or chthonian deities. Yet the Benzaiten section is pulled into two opposite directions: the abstract tendency of Tendai doctrine and the concrete dissemination of local cults. This feature is characteristic of the "chroniclers" (*kike*), a group to which Kōshū belonged and which was straddling two traditions: cosmological (with the five phase theory of Chinese cosmology) and mythological (with an emphasis on concrete ethnographic cases).

33. An example of partial "homo-graphy" is that between *shin/kami* 神 and *saru* 申 (monkey), from which is derived the status of monkeys of Mount Hiei as messengers of the Sannō deity.

34. See n. 31. A case in point is the writings of the "chroniclers" (*kike*) in the Tendai tradition. On this question, see Kuroda Toshio 1989.

35. On the *imaginaire* and its dimensions, see Faure 1996: 10–13.

36. Stein 1991a: 120–121.

37. See Stein 1976.

38. Stein 1991a.

39. Stein 1991b.

40. See Shiga kenritsu Azuchijō kōko hakubutsukan 2011: 5, fig. 15; and *BZS* 1: 217, fig. 2093.

41. See Littleton 1974. In the field of Japanese studies, the two types of structuralism are represented by Cornelius Ouwehand and Yoshida Atsuhiko, respectively. Ouwehand, a student of Yanagita Kunio, is the author of a seminal study on the myth of the catfish (*namazu*). See Ouwehand 1964. Yoshida is a disciple of Dumézil who, in spite of his master's caution that the three functions may not be found outside the Indo-European sphere, searched for and found them in classical Japanese mythology. See Yoshida 1961–1962; Lyle 1982; Littleton 1981; and Macé 2009. For a Lévi-Straussian reading of Buddhist mythology, see Stein 1986, 1991a, and 1991b; and Iyanaga 2002a and 2002b; for structuralist readings of Japanese mythology, see Macé 1989 and Rocher 1997.

42. Lévi-Strauss 1992. For a discussion of Lévi-Strauss's affinities with Buddhism, see Strenski 1980.

43. Lévi-Strauss 1976: 135.

44. Ibid.

45. Lévi-Strauss and Eribon 1991: 128.

46. See Yoshida Atsuhiko 1977.

47. See for instance Lévi-Strauss 1992, chap. 5. On the influence of Dumézil in Japan, see Macé 2009.

48. The most important have been made by Derrida 1980b, Favret-Saada 1980, Deleuze and Guattari 1987, and Bourdieu 1977 and 1990.

49. In Western scholarship, very little has changed under the sun and its goddess, at least since Frazer and E. B. Tylor. See the latter's description of the relation between Amaterasu and her brother Susanoo, whose "purely nature-descriptive nature is evident." Amaterasu is reduced to a mythological expression of the sun, while Susanoo becomes the "god of winds." In the myth of the Heavenly Rock Cave, consequently, "it is evident that we have really here, in a very clear and perfect form, the nature-myth of the sun driven into

hiding by the storm and peeping out from her cloud-cave, when presently the great cloud is rolled away like a rock from a cave's mouth. Following out the same course of ideas, we read of the wind god descending to earth and slaying the eight-headed and eight-tailed serpent, who is about to destroy the 'lady of the young rice field.' The monster is known to the Japanese as being an eight-mouthed river, so the story seems really that of the wind and the flood." Tylor 1877: 56–57. For a different approach, see Isomae Jun'ichi 2010.

50. See Saitō Hideki 1996, Yamamoto Hiroko 1998b, Satō Hiroo 2000, Itō Satoshi 2011; and Teeuwen and Rambelli 2003b.

51. Spivak 2001: 123.

52. See Detienne 1971.

53. On this question, see Borgeaud 2004a: 209.

54. For instance, Detienne has shown how specific details could reveal a contrast between Athena and Poseidon in their relation with horses, or how Apollo's knife could serve as a reagent, revealing an entirely different aspect of the god. He writes: "These various situations in which Athena and Poseidon appear in opposition in regard to horses are indicative of the different way used by religious traditions to denote the differences and similarities between two powers intervening in the same domain, but with different means of action. . . . The remaining case . . . will show us a fourth way of delimiting the respective spheres of the two powers in regard to their action on a single concrete object." See Detienne 1971: 181; see also Detienne 1986b, 1999, 2001, and 2009.

55. Detienne 2008: 69.

56. Such is the case of the Buddhist Sarasvatī (J. Benzaiten), who in Japan no longer has the nature of a river goddess that she had in India; even if she is still related to water, she has become increasingly chthonian, while her earlier relationship with Speech and Music still predominates in her manifestation as Myōon Benzaiten. On this question, see Vol. 2, *Protectors and Predators*, chaps. 4–5.

57. Detienne and Hamonic 1995: 5.

58. See Arasse 1996.

59. See Didi-Huberman 1998.

60. Arthur Rimbaud, "The Drunken Boat," trans. Samuel Beckett.

61. Lévi-Strauss 1987.

62. Lévi-Strauss 1969: 12.

63. Lévi-Strauss and Eribon 1991: 139.

64. Ibid.

65. Lévi-Strauss and Eribon 1991: 142.

66. See Descombes 1979.

67. Lévi-Strauss 1969: 10–14.

68. See Geertz 1988: 48; and Evans-Pritchard 1969.

69. Geertz may have a point when he argues that Lévi-Strauss's books "seem to exist behind glass, self-sealing discourses into which jaguars, semen, and rotting meat are admitted to become oppositions, inversions, isomorphisms" and reproaches him for forgetting the "moods and motivations" that reinforce the cosmology of a given people. See Geertz 1988: 48.

For all his *esprit de finesse,* however, he himself perhaps lacks the *esprit de géométrie* that he criticizes in Lévi-Strauss. Furthermore, neither the cosmology of a people nor its moods and motivations are as monolithic as Geertz seems to think. Contrary to his view, I think that moods and motivations, far from always reinforcing cosmology, tend at times to deconstruct it.

70. Tim Ingold also criticizes Lévi-Strauss's plan for drawing up an inventory of all human societies, past and present, as being "surely the closest thing to butterfly collecting ever encountered in the annals of anthropology," and concludes that, unsurprisingly, given its ambition, the plan came to nothing. This is certainly an overstatement, and any reader of Nabokov knows that collecting butterflies can be a passion that engages a person's life as totally as anthropological scholarship. See Ingold 2011: 235.

71. Lévi-Strauss and Eribon 1991: 113–114. On Lévi-Strauss's ambivalence, see Viveiros de Castro 2009: 171–194.

72. See Maillet 1998: 1129.

73. Lévi-Strauss 1981: 670–680.

74. Ibid.

75. Lévi-Strauss 1981: 679.

76. See Blondeau and Schipper 1995; and Bell 1992.

77. Deleuze and Guattari 1987: 237.

78. Deleuze and Guattari 1987: 238.

79. Viveiros de Castro 2009: 79–80.

80. For a discussion of that problem, see Viveiros de Castro 2004; and Latour 2010.

81. Favret-Saada 1980.

82. Law 1992: 385–386.

83. Law 1992: 389.

84. For an application of that model to Japanese Buddhism, see Iyanaga 2003.

85. See Doniger 1998.

86. Blanchot 1993: 157.

87. Eliot 1958: 3.

88. Latour 2005: 37–42.

89. Latour 2005: 60.

90. Deleuze and Guattari 1987: 78–80.

91. See Tim Ingold on the "real" encounter, not between man and god, but between man and deer (Ingold 2000: 111–131).

92. For a discussion of this question, see Favret-Saada 1980.

93. "Jeder Angel ist schrecklich." Rilke's "First Elegy," in Rilke 1993.

94. See Latour 1993, 2010, and 2013; Favret-Saada 1980; Descola 2005; Ingold 2000; Viveiros de Castro 2009.

95. Significant in this regard is the debate that opposed Eliade to De Martino. See Angelini 2001: 126–139; and Mancini 1999.

96. See Ingold 2000: 107.

97. Atlan 1979: 48–51.

98. The Nō playwright Konparu Zenchiku 禪竹 (1405–ca. 1470), for instance, had the intuition of such a symbolism, even if he stretched it a bit

to fit his own agenda and that of his artistic tradition. See his *Meishuku shū* 明宿集, in Omote and Katō 1974.

99. On this point, see Viveiros de Castro 2009.

100. I borrow this image from Henri Miller: "Grass only exists between the great non-cultivated spaces. It fills in the voids. It grows between—among other things. The flower is beautiful, the cabbage is useful, the poppy makes you crazy. But the grass is overflowing, it is a lesson in morality." *Sexus,* cited in Deleuze and Parnet 1977: 30.

101. People in Lilliput cracked their soft-boiled eggs at the small end, while in the rival kingdom of Blefoscu, they cracked theirs at the big end. This trivial difference led to a hundred-year war between the two kingdoms.

CHAPTER 2: UNDER THE GAZE OF THE STARS

1. Souriau 1952: 13.

2. The case of the Inari deity is a little peculiar in the sense that it was always double—male and female. This allowed the Meiji fundamentalists to downplay or drive out the female component (identified with Dakiniten) without modifying the structure of the Inari shrines. Gozu Tennō, on the other hand, had to give way to the "classical" Shintō god Susanoo (an ironic development given the fact that the latter had long been an outcast in the divine world). As in the case of Myōken and Hachiman, the initial process of identification turned into the highjacking, and eventually the replacement of one god by another.

3. *TZ* 9, 3190: 463a.

4. On this question, see Faure 2012a.

5. See *Kakuzenshō, DNBZ* 53: 147b. According to another commentary: "The Blazing Light [Buddha] is the form under which Śākyamuni, from the top of Mount Sumeru, commands all devas." *Asabashō, TZ* 9: 52a.

6. Both are, technically speaking, referred to as *butchō* 佛頂, that is, figures personifying (or emanating from) the Buddha's crown. In other words, they are manifestations and symbols of the wisdom of the Buddha (the five knowledges). On Dainichi Kinrin, see *Kakuzenshō, DNBZ* 53: 204c; on Shaka Kinrin, see *Toluoni xi jing* 陀羅尼集経, *T.* 18, 901: 790. According to the *Hokuto kuden* 北斗口伝, the two Kinrin are identical and correspond to the two mandalas of Shingon. It is Shaka Kinrin, however, who is the source or "original ground" (*honji*) of all stars. See Morita 1941, 2: 4.

7. Quoted in Morita 1941, 2: 22.

8. See *Hokushin bosatsu daranikyō* 北辰菩薩陀羅尼経, in *Shugen seiten,* 50–51; Miyake 1971: 209. See also *Hokushin Myōken Bosatsu reiōhen* 北辰妙見菩薩霊応編, in Hayakawa 2000: 433; Yoshida Mitsukuni 1970: 239–257; Ariga Shō 2000; and Hayashi 1997, a special issue of *Nihon no bijutsu* on Myōken.

9. On Buddhist star worship, see Morita 1941; and Sano 1994a and 1994b. On Tantric astronomy/astrology and the *Sukuyō kyō,* see Yano 1986.

10. The locus classicus is in *Shiji* 27.1291 ("Tianguan").

11. *Lunyu* 2.17. In D. C. Lau's translation, this reads: "The rule of virtue can be compared to the Pole star which commands the homage of the

multitude of stars without leaving its place" (1979: 63). See also *Wuxing dayi* 五行大義, in Kalinowski 1991: 367. On Taiyi, see Harper 2001:1–13; and Little 2000: 242–243.

12. See *BDJ* 5: 4784–4785; Izumi 1990; Frank 1991: 241–246, 2000a: 103–108, and 2000b: 123–127.

13. Xuanwu is represented as a being with a composite body, part tortoise, part snake.

14. On Zhenwu, see Major 1986; Little 2000: 113 and 291–308; Chao 2002; and De Bruyn 2010: 87–137. Although Myōken's image is clearly indebted to that of Xuanwu 玄武 (Zhenwu), the two figures did not completely merge: thus, the Genbu (Xuanwu) Shrine on Funaoka Hill (Kyoto) duplicates the Myōken temple farther north. On Myōken and the Xuanwu/Zhenwu cult, see Yoshioka 1966–1967. See also *BZS* 4116 (Fig. 2.10 above).

15. This representation of Zhenwu surrounded by seventy-two talismans is reminiscent of esoteric mandalas. It is said to "protect against abnormalities in the shape of pigs, cats, dogs, or all those who eat their own young," as well as against "old trees that turn into sprites." See Little 2000: 308–309; and Boltz 1987: 86–91.

16. See *T.* 21, 1332: 546c. See also *Kakuzenshō, DNBZ* 50: 2a; and *Chintaku reifujin engi shūsetsu*: 335.

17. *T.* 79, 2535: 278b.

18. *DNBZ* 55: 283b.

19. See *Hishō mondō, T.* 79, 2536: 543c, quoted in Hayashi 1997: 47. See also the *Shijūjō ketsu* 四十帖決, a record made by the Tendai monk Chōen 長宴 (1016–1081) on the basis of oral explanations from his master Kōgei (977–1049): "The Northern Chronogram (Hokushin) is Myōken. . . . He is also called Sonjōō." *T.* 75, 2408: 880a. See also *Shikan, T.* 78, 2500: 816c.

20. See for instance *Kakuzenshō, DNBZ* 50: 4a; and *Byakuhō kushō, TZ* 7: 265c-266a. Regarding the problematic definition of Myōken as "auxiliary star," see Iwahara 1988: 42–43. In the Shingon tradition, Tenposei and Myōken are related yet distinct, as shown by the Nikkō legend in which they appear as two jewels in the basin of Takinoo 瀧尾 waterfall in Nikkō after Kūkai performed the Butsugen 佛眼 and Kinrin 金輪 rituals at this waterfall for one week.

21. More specifically, Hosei stands near Mugoku 武曲, the second star in the dipper's tail (see Figs. 2.13–2.15 below). In her female form, this deity is also identified with Venus (Myōjō Tenshi 明星天子). In Sannō shintō, the auxiliary star is identified with Matarajin 摩多羅神, a god that is often represented with the seven stars above him. See Takafuji 2001: 33–34. It is also linked with Sekizan Myōjin 赤山明神, a protector of Mount Hiei, and with the underworld deity Taizan Fukun. It was known as the Star of Emoluments and Longevity (Fukuroku-sei 福禄星), a name that brings to mind one of the seven gods of fortune, Fukurokuju 福禄寿.

22. The full title is *Secret Instructions for Prolonging Life from the Purple Court of the Seven Principles of the Northern Emperor* (*Beidi qiyuan ziting yangshen bijue* 北帝七元紫庭延生秘訣). See Mollier 2009: 162.

23. *Kakuzenshō, DNBZ* 50: 10b.

24. *Kakuzenshō*, *DNBZ* 50: 2–3; and Morita 1941, 1: 418.

25. *T.* 79, 2536: 543c.

26. *DNBZ* 86, Jishi-bu 4: 79a–b.

27. See Misaki 1992: 250–251. See also *Hokuto shichishō goma hiyō giki*, quoted in Iwahara 1988: 44; and *Tenge kōtaijin honnen*, in *Ryōbu shintō shū*: 515. The *Onjōji denki* also states that "in the moon-wheel of the heart is the letter *bhrūṃ,* which transforms into Kinrin Butchō; on the heart-moon of [Kinrin] Butchō is the letter *sei* 正 [i.e., *bhrūṃ*], which transforms into the seven stars. The auxiliary star is the ruler, the six other [stars] are its subordinates." Here Myōken is identified with Kinrin, Hosei, Hokushin, *and* Rokuson.

28. See *Jakushōdō kokkyōshū*, *DNBZ* 149: 215a; *Kakuzenshō*, *DNBZ* 50: 2b; and *Henkushō*, *T.* 78, 2496: 697b.

29. See Nojiri 1971: 13.

30. On the Daoist cult, see Franke 1990; Orzech and Sanford 2000: 383–395; Mollier 2009: 134–173; and Bumbacher 2012.

31. See Mollier 2009: 140; and Bumbacher 2012.

32. See Sørensen 1995.

33. Schafer 1977: 157. Another example is a sword preserved at Yatsushiro Shrine in Yatsushiro City (Kyūshū).

34. On the seven stars and the seven Hie shrines, see Arichi 2006. Another example is that of Mount Hiko, a major Shugendō center in northern Kyūshū; on which, see Grapard (forthcoming).

35. This evolution is particularly visible in Korean Buddhism, where the seven stars have almost completely superseded the pole-star deity.

36. The *Chintaku reifu engi shūsetsu*, an Edo-period work documenting (and promoting) the Myōken cult, mentions two successive "descents" of Myōken on Mount Hikami 氷上 (Suō province), which led to the founding of a Star Hall (Seidō 星堂) on that mountain. The organizer of the cult was said to be a fifth-generation descendant of Prince Imseong, Shigemura Ason 茂村朝臣. See also the *Myōken gūsha ki* 妙見宮社記: "The coming of the god Myōken took place in the ninth year of Hakuō (680) under Tenmu Tennō. This god, through a divine transformation (*jhinpen* 神変), turned into the three deities Mebuka 目深 (Deep Eyes), Tenaga 手長 (Long Arms), and Ashinaga 足長 (Long Legs), and from the ford of Mingzhou (Ningpo) . . . , riding a tortoise-snake (*kida,* i.e., Xuanwu), he landed in Japan . . . in the province of Yatsushiro." See *Yatsushiro-shi shi* 八代市史, quoted in Dewa 2004: 155. On the giants Tenaga and Ashinaga, characters borrowed from the *Shanhai jing,* see Ōwa 2009: 50–60.

37. On this question, see Ueno 2010.

38. See Hayakawa 2000: 453.

39. See *NKBT* 70: 152–154, 330–331, and 410–412; and Kyoko Nakamura 1973: 149, 229, and 266.

40. A case in point was the eye disease of retired emperor Toba, cured by a Myōken ritual performed at Byōdō-in 平等院 by the Taimitsu priest Shōshō 聖照 (fl. ca. 1060); see *Asabashō*, *TZ* 9: 462b.

41. See *Gonki* 権記, s.v. Chōbo 1 (999)/12, in *Zōho shiryō taisei,* 4: 95.

42. We have for instance the text of the *Hokushin saimon* 北辰祭文 read in 1113 by retired emperor Shirakawa. See also the *imayo* 今様 on Myōken by Go-Shirakawa in *Ryōjin hishō* 梁塵秘抄, in Kim Yung-hee 1994: 61.

43. Nojiri 1971: 12.

44. See Nojiri 1971: 5–8.

45. On this question, see for instance Tsuda 1988b. The popularity of the seven stars of the Northern Dipper among warriors may have been due in part to the name of the seventh star, Hagun 破軍 (Army Destroyer). Hagun was also associated with Marishiten 摩利支天 (Skt. Marīcī), another deity that has affinities with Myōken. On Marishiten as a warrior deity, see Hall 2013; Wada 1918; and Shimaji 1931.

46. See Rabinovitch 1986. Other traditions argue that Masakado's defeat was the result of the subjugation rituals centered on Fudō, Kangiten, and Daii-toku Myōō which Shingon monks performed on behalf of the court. On the historical background of Masakado's rebellion, see Friday 2007.

47. See Miyahara 1999.

48. The term *tenshi* 天子, qualifying Sonjōō, can mean either Son of Heaven (in the imperial ideology that constituted one of the interpretations of astral cults in China) or Son of Deva (*devaputra*), in a more Tantric reading. Miidera monks consciously played with that double-entendre.

49. See Misaki 1992: 226–228.

50. *TZ* 10: 1160b. In the *Tenge Kōtaijin honnen* 天下皇太神本縁, we are told that Myōken, in the form of Sonjōō, becomes the sun deity during the day, the moon deity at night, and that as these two aspects unite they give birth to Venus. See *Ryōbu shintō shū*: 515.

51. The Sonjōō ritual was more probably created against a background of Sanmon-Jimon rivalry and modeled after the Blazing Light Ritual of the Sanmon. It was one of the four imperial rites traditionally performed at Mii-dera and its *monzeki* 門跡 temples and was performed thirty-six times between 1161 and 1335, usually on behalf of nobles. See *Asabashō, TZ* 9: 462b; see also Misaki 1992: 226–227. The *Jitokushū* 寺徳集 (1344) by the Miidera priest Suishin 水心 claims that it is a secret ritual for the protection of the state, and that the "secret image of Sonjōō" has been handed down through the lineage of the Qinglonsi 青龍寺 priest Fachuan 法全 (Enchin's Chinese master). See Misaki 1992: 228–229; 1974: 163–167; and Tsuda 1998a. On Rokuji Myōō, see Mikkyō gakkai 1970, 5: 2314–2315; and Tsuda 1998c.

52. See *Mii zokutō ki* 三井続灯記, in *DNBZ*, Denki sōsho: 232–247. On the Sonjōō ritual at Miidera, see Misaki 1992: 226–261.

53. *DNBZ* 50: 5a. Here again, the female nature of Sonjōō alludes to that deity's identity with Kichijōten 吉祥天.

54. *DNBZ* 55: 279b. Sonjōō is said to manifest himself as the bodhisattvas Kannon and Seishi in the heavenly realm, Nikkō 日光 and Gakkō 月光 in the land of the buddha Ashuku 阿閦, and as the sun and moon devas in the Jambudvīpa. He nurtures and benefits all beings. Furthermore, Kichijōten and Sonjōō are interpreted as two manifestations of Dainichi—Kichijōten being the highest, and Sonjōō the "second" dharma body. Thus, the pairing of two images of Myōken, the one sitting on a lotus, the other riding a dragon,

reflects this hierarchy of aspects or manifestations. The same distinction is found in the two images on the two faces of the Gotō-in 後唐院 mirror mentioned below. See Misaki 1992: 239.

55. *Asabashō*, *TZ* 9: 462c. See also Misaki 1992: 255–257.

56. On the twelve names of Kichijōten, see *T.* 21: 253a. Indeed, according to the *Zuzō* 図像, the mantra used in the Myōken ritual, namely, *oṃ mahā śriye dṛve* [= *devī*] *svāha*, is clearly about Kichijōten (Śrī *devī*). See Misaki 1992: 256.

57. See *Higo kokushi* 肥後国志 169. It is located on a hill near Yatsushiro Shrine (originally Yatsushiro Myōken-dō 八代妙見堂). In spite of the denial of the current shrine priest, the proximity of the two shrines suggests that they were once part of the same compound.

58. Today, the Myōken Festival of Yatsushiro, on November 22–23, is one of the three great annual festivals of Kyūshū.

59. It is no coincidence that the name *tatara*, which seems of Korean origin, designates the traditional furnace for smelting iron and steel, and in particular for manufacturing swords. As Michael Como has shown, Korean immigrants brought with them continental technologies. Swords were among the most appreciated of these technological products, and Myōken and the seven stars were closely associated with these new technologies. Prince Rinshō is said to have offered a similar sword to his Japanese counterpart, Prince Shōtoku.

The name Tatara is found all over Japan, usually in relation with mining areas. A case in point is Tatara in Bōsō peninsula, a region well known for Myōken worship. According to Inoue Takao (1994), the cults of Myōken and Kokūzō developed in relation to metallurgy, through the Hata lineage and Shōtoku Taishi, with an emphasis on the lineage of Rinshō Taishi and his elder brother Asa Taishi 阿佐太子. Although the coming of the latter to Japan is even less documented than that of Rinshō, he is said to have resided for seven years at Kannoji 神野寺 (Suō province) and to have died there in 600.

60. The town and its shrine (Kudamatsu jinja, a.k.a. Myōken Shrine) draw their name from the legend according to which a star (Myōken) fell on this site and continued to shine on the branch of a pine tree. During the repression of Buddhism at the beginning of the Meiji period, the Myōken statue enshrined there was moved to the nearby Jutōji, and Myōken was replaced by Ame no Minakanushi 天之御中主 as *saishin* 祭神 (main deity) of the shrine. Another site linked to that legend is the Kanawa 金輪 Shrine in Hokuto-chō (Northern Dipper district), whose name seems to preserve a trace of its former *saishin*, the buddha Kinrin (identified with Myōken).

61. See Higuchi 1976; and Miyahara 1999.

62. In the twelfth century, retired emperor Nijō 二条 (r. 1158–1165), on the basis of an oracle of Hachiman at the Tsurugaoka Hachiman 鶴岡八幡 Shrine, introduced Myōken's cult to Kamakura. On the relationship between Myōken and Hachiman, see Marui 2013: 38–41.

63. These documents and others related to Myōken have been edited by the Chiba shiritsu kyōdo hakubutsukan and studied by Marui Keiji, Miyahara Satsuki, and others.

64. Myōken's relation with horses brings him closer to Batō Kannon and Memyō Bosatsu, deities also linked to sericulture.

65. See Nauman 1959: 246. On Myōken and horses, see also Yanagita 1990b: 184, 208, and 220; and Miyahara 1999: 21–24.

66. The icon of Nose Myōken (Fig. 2.26) was conceived by Nikken in the image of Yoritsugu: it looks like a warrior making the sword mudrā with his left hand and holding a sword above his hand with his right hand, in a defensive position. Another, less well-known Nose Myōken image is that of the Oku-no-in 奥の院 of Shinnyoji 真如寺: the god holds a sword in his right hand, a snake in his left hand—perhaps in imitation of Suiten, who holds a snake noose. On the rim of his halo are seven disks, symbolizing the seven stars. See Frank 1991: 242–244.

67. The story is still spread by the temple today in the form of a manga. On Shuten Dōji, see Komatsu 1997; and Lin 2003.

68. Kanezashi criticizes the *Chintaku reifu engi shūsetsu* for confusing Chintaku Reifujin and Myōken, and denounces as a fabrication of the *onmyōji* the link between the Chintaku Reifujin of Yatsushiro and the Korean prince Rinshō. He implies that the *onmyōji* sought to capitalize on Myōken's prestige, but of course the reverse might also be true. See Kanezashi 1974:172–173.

69. This hall looks rather like a tumulus or a kind of artificial cave. Faithful to Nittō Shōnin's vision, the stone image inside represents Myōken standing on a tortoise, holding a sword in his right hand and a white snake in his left hand, with the seven stars above his head. The acolyte on his right, the White Cloud Benzaiten, holds a *biwa* and is said to have come from the imperial palace.

70. See Hayakawa 2000: 335. Another edition has been published under the title *Chintaku reifujin;* see Yamagishi 1929.

71. Sekimori 2006: 219.

72. On Hokusai and Myōken, see Frank 2000b: 137–138.

73. For example, Ame no Minakanushi is worshiped at the Myōken Shrine of Tokushima 徳島 (Shikoku), a shrine founded by the tenth Muromachi shōgun, Ashikaga Yoshitane (1466–1523). On Myōken and Ame no Minakanushi, see Komine 2007: 95–98.

74. Morita 1941, 2: 229–240.

75. See Ueno 2010: 241–260.

76. See for instance *Shike shō zuzō,* figs. 203–206, *TZ* 3: 900.

77. See for instance the exemplars of the MOA Museum and the Sylvan Barnett and Bill Burto collection (Figs. 2.6 and 2.7 above). For a detailed description of that mandala, see *Kakuzenshō, DNBZ* 50: 4ab.

This image brings to mind the primordial god of Orphic cosmology, Phanes, who is usually represented as a handsome winged youth, surrounded by the zodiacal signs and wrapped in a serpent's coils. See Panofsky 1976: 109, and figs. 36–37.

78. *TZ* 3: 588, fig. 264.

79. See *TZ* 7: 663–686, figs. 21 and 25.

80. A fourth moon disk appears on the head of the dragon that serves as Myōken's mount: it is the moon on which Myōken is standing. See

Kakuzenshō, DNBZ 50: 5a; and *Byakuhō kushō, TZ* 7: 266c; *Shoson zuzō, TZ* 3: 735, figs. 86–87; *Shike shō zuzō, TZ* 3: 899, fig. 202; and *Myōken bosatsu zō, TZ* 7, fig. 25, which adds the diagrams of constellations. See also Misaki 1992: 235.

81. The *Shiragisan Myōken Daibosatsu engi*, for instance, explains that Myōken landed in Higo province riding a tortoise, in 680 (under the reign of Tenji Tennō 天智天皇). See *ST*, Jinja-hen 45, Hizen Higo: 444–445. The *Myōken-gū jitsuki* 妙見宮実記, on the other hand, traces the origin of the Myōken Shrine in Yatsushiro to the arrival, that same year, of three men who crossed over from Mingzhou 明州 in China on the back of a tortoise.

82. On Zhenwu, see Little 2000: 291–295. Compare with the painting of Zhenwu preserved at Tōji. The god appears in martial attire, flanked by two attendants, one of which holds a box, the other a banner. (See Fig. 2.11 above.)

83. See Little 2000: 308. These talismans are said to go back to the time of the Chinese emperor Xiao Wendi 孝文帝 (r. 471–499), and to have been introduced in Japan by Rinshō Taishi.

84. See also Morita 1941.

85. Morita 1941, 2: 241.

86. See Nikaido 2012.

87. Ibid.

88. In certain representations, Zaō Gongen 蔵王権現 makes the same gesture, as does Rasetsuten 羅刹天 (Skt. Nirṛti), one of the twelve directional devas. See Frank 1998: 175 and 2000b: 134–135.

89. On this question, see Schafer 1977. See also *Besson zakki, TZ* 3: 585, 587; and *Myōken Bosatsu zuzō* 妙見菩薩図像, *TZ* 7: 673, 682, and 684.

90. See Anderson 1989.

91. See the *Jing'you dunjia fuying jing zan* 景祐遁甲符応経纂 (comp. 1034–1037), quoted in Tsuda 1998a: 77. On this question, see also Schafer 1977; Tsuda 1998a and 1998c. The Pace of Yu was also used in village rituals influenced by Shugendō, and is still used today during the Ōgi Festival in Kurokawa, near Mount Haguro. See Martzel 1982: 98, 103.

92. *Asabashō, TZ* 9: 462c.

93. On this deity and its ritual, see Lomi 2011.

94. See Tsuda 1998a and 1998c.

95. We know that the Kasuga deities were associated with the stars from the decoration of one of the treasures of Kasuga Shrine, a jewel box, one side of which represents the fourth Kasuga deity (Shinomiya 四宮), a goddess who holds symbols of the sun and moon, and the Wakamiya 若宮, a child deity; both are riding a deer, with the symbolic representation of the twelve cyclical signs below them. See Fig. 6.1 below. Yet there is no direct link between Myōken and these two deities. A more likely relation might be with the second Kasuga deity (Ninomiya 二宮), the Katori 香取 god, whose *honji* is the Healing Buddha Yakushi. In the *Kasuga gosha gohonji narabini gotakusenki* 春日御社御本地并御託宣記, a list of the twelve spirit generals of Yakushi 薬師 contains the following passage: "On the left is the controller of destiny King Enma, on the right the controller of destiny Myōken

Bosatsu, the Northern Dipper" (*ST*, Jinja-hen 13, Kasuga: 38). The deer may also indicate a connection with immortality, as it is often associated with Chinese immortals. Alternatively, Myōken's association with the deer in the *Konjaku monogatari shū* shows that this animal was from early on perceived as Myōken's messenger. See *Konjaku monogatari shū* 1.34, 3.5, and 3.32; translated in Kyoko Nakamura 1973: 149, 229, and 266–267. See also Dykstra 1998–2003, 2: 67–68.

96. See the *Shakusun gaeshi no saimon*, quoted in Suzuki 2001: 165–170.

97. The term "musk" (from the Skt. *muṣkā* 'testicle') derives from the fact that the gland that secretes this scent is located near the stag's genitals. In the West, musk has long been reputed to be an aphrodisiac.

98. See fig. 92 in the *Shoson zuzō, TZ* 3: 738. In the Northern Dipper ritual of the *Kakuzenshō*, Saturn is also placed at the center, because it is the "earth-star" and the earth is at the center of the spatiotemporal diagram of the five phases (Ch. *wuxing*). This central "co-incidence" creates a link between Saturn and Myōken. See *DNBZ* 50: 24a. See also the representations of Saturn and Mars from the Metropolitan Museum in Rosenfield and ten Groetenhuys 1980: 109 and 111, figs. 28 and 29.

99. *Besson zakki, TZ* 3: 532.

100. Note, however, that in at least one case, the animal head above Myōken's head is that of a boar (like Marishiten), not that of a deer.

101. The god is also called Tamer of the Three Worlds (Gōzanze 降三世), and he is the deity that subdues the Eastern Barbarians. See *ST*, Ronsetsu-hen 1, Shingon shintō 1: 203.

102. In the *Zuzōshō* 図像抄, an iconographic compendium by the Shingon priest Ejū 恵什 (ca. 1135), Myōken's two acolytes—one of which looks like a bodhisattva, the other like a *yakṣa*—hold paper and brush, respectively. See TZ 3, 3006.

103. On this notion, see below. We find again here the *hongaku* notion of the identity of awakening and defilement—which already informed the concepts of the dual nature of Sonjōō (as both "pure" and "lewd") and the nonduality of Sonjōō and Kichijōten (and of the back-to-back representations of Sonjōō).

104. This image of the seven snakes evokes representations of the *nāga* king Nanda. The image is reminiscent of Caravaggio's *Head of Medusa* at the Uffizi in Florence. It also brings to my mind a distant echo of Racine's play *Andromaque* (act 5, sc. 5), whose verses every French child had to memorize. Oreste, addressing the daughters of hell, asks: "Pour qui sont ces serpents qui sifflent sur vos têtes?" This passage is often admired as an example of alliteration—here the initial *s*, evoking the hissing of the snakes.

105. See *Kakuzenshō, TZ* 5: 511, and 511b–512, fig. 366. See also the *Byakuhō kushō, TZ* 7: 164c; and the *Jūniten keizō, TZ* 7: 585, fig. 4.

106. See *Asabashō, TZ* 9: 463a. See also Misaki 1992: 233–234; and Ariga Shō 2000: 55. There is a confusion here between the Byōdō-in of Miidera and that of Uji. Yorimichi, the founder of the latter, was also a powerful patron of Miidera. Incidentally, he is said to have become the dragon of the

Uji River after his death, in order to protect Byōdō-in. See Kuroda Hideo 2003: 138–139.

107. Marui 2013: 203–205.

108. On Urashima and Penglai, see the discussion of Nyoirin in Chap. 7 below.

109. *Besson zakki*, *TZ* 3: 524b; *Byakuhō kushō*, *TZ* 7: 266bc; and Misaki 1992: 243.

110. At times there is only one attendant, the *yakṣa*-like acolyte, who holds an inkstone for Myōken's brush.

111.   *T.* 21, 1306: 425a. The *kōshin* day was the day in the sexagenary cycle of the Chinese calendar when the Three Worms (or Corpses 三尸) would ascend to heaven to report on the misdeeds of people. This belief led to the observance of the Kōshin Watch (Kōshin-machi 庚申待ち), a night-long watch aimed at preventing those baleful spirits from leaving their human hosts. On this question, see Kohn 1993–1995.

112. See *Kakuzenshō*, *DNBZ* 50: 62a.

113. *TZ* 9: 452c.

114. Like Myōken, Bishamonten was often identified with the Northern Dipper, and he is the *honzon* of some star mandalas (*hoshi mandara* 星曼荼羅). See *Yuzu nenbutsu engi* (Anrakuji, Nara), in Hayashi 1997: 178, fig. 104. See also Takeda 1995.

115. See Miyahara 1993.

116. Raiyu's *Hishō mondō* 秘鈔問答 (*T.* 79, 2536) mentions two theories regarding Myōken's *honji:* Kannon and Yakushi. It also quotes the *Qifo bapusa suoshuo da tuoluoni shenzhou jing* (*T.* 21, 1332), according to which Yaoshi enters Miaojian (Myōken)'s *samādhi.* Quoted in Morita 1941, 2: 9.

117. See Marui 2013: 217–222.

118. Quoted in Morita 1941, 2: 401.

119. Mollier 2009: 159.

120. An interesting case is that of the Bungo kokubunji 豊後国分寺 near Okayama, where, next to the Yakushi Hall, is an impressive five-degree pagoda whose central beam is said to represent Dainichi, framed by four statues of the same buddha riding various animals. That ensemble calls to mind the Five Kokūzō.

121. Likewise, the Kongōjuji in Chiba was built after the death of the rebel Taira no Tadatsune 平忠常 (975–1031), and its first abbot was Tadatsune's son Kakusan 覚算.

122. On this question, see Chap. 4 below; and Vol. 2, *Protectors and Predators.*

123. See Morita 1941, 2: 21.

124. On the Tendai cult of Yakushi, see Suzuki 2012: 45–123.

125. See the *Qifo bapusa suoshuo da tuoluoni shenzhou jing, T.* 21, 1332. The seven Yakushi appear, under slightly different names, in the *Yaoshi liuliguang qifo benyuan gongde jing* 薬師瑠璃光七仏本願功徳経, translated by Yijing 儀浄 (*T.* 14, 451: 409). Yakushi was also said to be the *honji* of one of the seven stars, the seventh one, Hagun 破軍 (Army Destroyer). See also Morita 1941, 1: 408–409.

126. See Suzuki 2012: 103–123.

127. *T.* 21, 1205: 36, quoted in Morita 1941, 2: 24.

128. See *Kakuzenshō, TZ* 5: 399b; *DNBZ* 50: 7b. See also Misaki 1992: 240–242.

129. "Chishō Daishi (Enchin) explained that Myōken is Kichijōten. . . . Kichijō is a northern goddess. The fact that the Northern Chronogram (Hokushin) is also said to have a female form may have led to this statement" (*Asabashō, TZ* 9: 462c). See also *Kakuzenshō, DNBZ* 50: 2. The *Asabashō* refutes this tradition as heterodox.

130. See Yamashita 1999. Myōken is also described as an avatar of Kannon. Sonjōō and Kichijōten are identified with each other in the *Asabashō, TZ* 9: 462b; in *Kakuzenshō, TZ* 5: 397c; and also in *Onjōji denki, DNBZ* 127: 7.

131. See *TZ* 10: 1160b–c. Kichijōten's mirror is also identified with the sacred mirror, one of the Three Regalia, and the divine body of the sun goddess Amaterasu. See also Misaki 1992: 239–240; and Tōkyō kokuritsu hakubutsukan et al. 1990, fig. 57.

132. See *Kakuzenshō, DNBZ* 50: 2a; and *Byakuhō kushō, TZ* 7: 264c.

133. On this form of Nyoirin, see Chap. 7 below. The *Jindaikan hiketsu* 神代巻秘訣, quoting the origin story of Shitennōji 四天王寺 (in Ōsaka), identifies the dragon-riding Nyoirin of the Shitennōji pond with Myōken, and further links Sonjōō (Myōken) with Ichiji Kinrin, Butsugen, and Monju. Sonjōō is said to be the Miidera equivalent of Butsugen and Kinrin for the Sanmon (Mount Hiei) and of Nyoirin for Tōji (Shingon). *ST,* Ronsetsu-hen, Shūgō shintō: 178.

134. See *Fomu dakongqiao mingwang jing* (Skt. *Mahāmāyūrī*), *T.* 19, 982: 618c.

135. See Frank 1991: 237.

136. Here is how the Persian Muslim scholar Al Bīrūnī (11th century) presents them in his description of India: "The head of the dragon is called Rāhu, its tail Ketu. The Indians use only the head of this dragon and have recorded nothing about its tail. Generally speaking, one calls Ketu all the comets that appear in the sky." Al-Bīrūnī, *India*, quoted in Yano 1986: 157–158.

137. *TZ* 7: 772b.

138. In China and in Japan, Taiyi (J. Tai'ichi, Tai'itsu) was worshiped as a water god. The main instance is found in a text known as *Taiyi sheng shui* 太一生水 (*Taiyi Generates Water*), discovered at Guodian (Hubei province). On Taiyi, see Harper 2001. In Onmyōdō, however, Tai'ichi became a threatening ambulatory deity requiring directional taboos. See Frank 1998: 126–132. At Ise, the deity of the Outer Shrine, Toyouke, was identified with Taiyi. See Teeuwen 2006b. Yoshino Hiroko, however, argues that the symbolism of the ritual implements reveals that the Inner Shrine at Ise was associated with Taiyi, the Outer Shrine with the Northern Dipper. See Yoshino 1975 and 2000: 84. This confusion may result from the rivalry between the two shrines.

139. See Teeuwen 2006b.

140. See also in *Asabashō* a representation of Suiten as Myōken, standing on a dragon. *TZ* 9, fig. 93.

141. The *Kakuzenshō*, for example, notes that Myōken (or the Northern Chronogram) and Mercury are the same. See *DNBZ* 50: 3b. See also *Byakuhō kushō*, *TZ* 7: 265b. The same *Kakuzenshō* offers a variant that claims that Myōken and Suiyō are distinct. See *DNBZ* 50: 3b. On Mercury, see also the *Fantian huoluo tu* 梵天火羅図, *TZ* 7: 714, fig. 3. The water star is represented as a female deity wearing a diadem, and holding a brush and a register. See also *Kuyō tō zuzō*, TZ 7: 740, fig. 3; *Kuyō-sei zuzō*, *TZ* 7: 752, fig. 3; and *Kuyō hireki*, *TZ* 7: 770bc.

142. See Frank 1991: 237.

143. See Frank 1991: 244. Incidentally, Suiten is associated not with the northern direction (which in India, unlike in China, is auspicious), but with the western direction.

144. *Kakuzenshō*, *DNBZ* 50: 237–239. See also *Shoson zuzō*, *TZ* 3: 728, fig. 74. Despite his bodhisattva status, Myōken (Sonjōō) is classified under the deva (*tenbu* 天部) rubric in these iconographic works. See Komine 2007: 85.

145. The all-seeing eyes of Myōken call to mind Varuṇa, a Vedic water deity already linked with Myōken through water symbolism (see the preceding section on water deities). Varuṇa (J. Suiten) was also perceived as a constant presence, watching over human actions and serving as silent witness to contracts. On the Vedic Varuṇa, see Hillebrand 1981, 2: 1–33. See also Dumézil 1988. In Japan, as Satō Hiroo has shown, "punishing gods" were also invoked as witnesses in oaths. See Satō 2003.

146. *T.* 78, 2496.

147. *T.* 21, 1304: 423a.

148. *T.* 78, 2476: 185. Taizan Fukun is said to have become in heaven the "auxiliary star" (Hosei) that helps the seven stars, a function also attributed to Myōken. He is also identified with Siming (J. Shimei 司命), the controller of destiny, one of Myōken's Chinese precursors. In Japan, he became identified with Sekizan Myōjin, one of the protectors of Mount Hiei, and with the *kami* Susanoo. On Taizan Fukun, see Nasu 2004.

149. *Yaoshi ben'yuan jing* 薬師本願経, *T.* 14, 449: 415; and Takeda 1995: 136–137.

150. See for instance the catalogue *Shinjung* 신중 神衆 (*Buddhist Guardian Deities of Late Joseon*) (Seoul: National Museum of Korea, 2013): 7–16.

151. See Frank 2000b: 99–104.

152. The locus classicus is the *Sitianwang jing*, *T.* 15, 590: 118b.

153. See *Sanbōe ryakuchū*, ed. Yamada Yoshio (Tokyo: Hōbunkan, 1951): 217–218.

154. *T.* 54, 2127: 304c.

155. See Kawaguchi 1965: 115. The name Tsuno Daishi 角大師 refers to the Tendai monk Ryōgen (912–985), who is said to have been reborn as a demon.

156. See Komatsu 1986: 67.

157. On Kōshin, the classical work remains that of Kubo Noritada (1961, 1996). See also Kohn 1993–1995.

158. See Frank 1990 and 2000b: 100–101; and Kyburz 2007.

159. Quoted in Kanezashi 1974: 247.

160. *ZGRJ* 28, 1: 16; Misaki 1992: 228–229.

161. See *Onjōji denki, DNBZ* 86: 59. Another esoteric deity associated with Mount Zhongnan is the "Great General Deep Sands" (Shensha Dajiang 深沙大将, J. Jinja Daishō), who was also perceived as a manifestation of Bishamonten and identified with Taizan Fukun. Here again, the northern direction plays a significant role. On Jinja Daishō, see Strickmann 1996.

162. See Misaki 1992: 229–232; Morita 1941, 2: 20; and Ueno 2010: 261–280.

163. *Keiran shūyōshū, T.* 76, 2410: 527b.

164. Hōshuku 法宿 is another name of Ōmiya 大宮 (Ōkuninushi 大国主), a name that suggests the stellar nature of that god.

165. See Yamagishi 1929: 21–22.

166. In Daoism, Taishan Fujun is the rector of human destinies. Dwelling in the lower realms of Taishan—one of the five peaks, and the site of the Feng 封 and Shan 禅 rituals—he is said to be the essence of the pole star, i.e., the divinization of the ultimate principle Taiyi. He is in that sense identical with Myōken. On the cult of Taishan, see Chavannes 1910.

167. Yamagishi 1929: 40–41.

168. *Chintaku reifu engi shūsetsu*, 341b. The same passage is found a propos Jūzenji 十禅師, a god of Hie Shrine, at the foot of Mount Hiei. Incidentally, the seven sanctuaries of Hie Shrine were said to correspond to the seven stars of the Northern Dipper.

169. This passage does not appear in Kūkai's apocryphal *Goyuigō* (*T.* 77, 2431), and the title must refer to another Testament.

170. On this deity, see Hall 2013.

171. See Chiba shiritsu kyōdo hakubutsukan 1995.

172. See Hayakawa 2000: 338a.

173. *Shiragisan Myōken Daibosatsu engi, ST,* Jinja-hen 45, Hizen, Higo: 444.

174. According to Hayashi On, Myōken is also linked to Uhō Dōji 雨宝童子, the Buddhist form or prototype of Amaterasu. The renowned Uhō Dōji of Kongōshōji 金剛證寺 on Mount Asama 朝熊山, a famous Buddhist site in Ise (Mie prefecture), is said to be in fact a representation of Kichijōten 吉祥天 (who, as we recall, is identified with Myōken in the Miidera tradition). Amaterasu and Hokushin 北辰 were also identified, and Mount Asama became the cultic center of another astral deity, Kokūzō Bosatsu 虚空蔵菩薩. This suggests that it was from very early on a cultic center of the Northern Chronogram (Hokushin, i.e., Myōken), and that, after its takeover by Shingon, it retained its astral features by passing them over to Kokūzō. See Hayashi 1997: 47.

175. See Miyahara 1994.

176. See Kawaguchi 1999: 359–361.

177. See *Yanagita Kunio zenshū* 15: 7–200.

178. In Daoism, Taiyi was believed to provide the essence of both the womb and the embryo, and to be the "mother of birth." See *Dongshen badi*

miaojing jing 洞神八帝妙精経 (*Scripture of the Wondrous Essence of the Eight Emperors of the Storehouse for Divinity*), in *Zhengtong daozang* 640: 4ab. I am indebted to Dominic Steavu for this reference.

179. As noted earlier, Shimei is said to ascend to heaven on the *kōshin* day. See *Kakuzenshō*, Seishuku-hō, *DNBZ* 50: 62a.

180. See "La conscience," in *La légende des siècles* (Hugo 1859).

CHAPTER 3: THE ELUSIVE CENTER

1. The translation of *vidyā* by the Chinese *ming* 明 (J. *myō*), and of *vidyārāja* by *mingwang* 明王 (J. *myōō*), leads to a further meaning, that of "bright kings." This is also due to the fact that these deities, as described in the Womb mandala, "radiate with splendor for the benefit of beings." See Tajima 1959: 84; and Soymié 1987: 17–23.

2. See Orzech 1998: 179.

3. *T.* 20, 1092: 271b.

4. *T.* 18: 7b. See also Tajima 1992: 84; and Snodgrass 1988: 270–275.

5. In that sense, Richard Payne's comparison of Fudō with Śiva's phallic symbol (*lingam*) seems obvious. See Payne 1987 and 1988. Yet the theory of a relation between Fudō and Śiva, once popular, has been questioned by recent scholarship. This does not mean that there are no links between Śiva and Fudō (indeed, Śiva casts a long shadow on the entire esoteric pantheon); simply, that they are neither as direct nor as exclusive as Payne suggests.

6. Agni, "the most excellent among the *yakṣas*," is identified with Rudra. Fudō is also an emanation of the earth deity Pṛthivī (J. Jiten 地天), and as such, he is also closely related to *nāgas* and dragons (as his manifestation as the dragon Kurikara 倶梨伽羅 attests).

7. Originally a mere attendant of the Buddha, Vajrapāṇi became the personification of the Buddha's triumph over Māra. See Linrothe 1999: 28. In that function, both Vajrapāṇi and Acala can be seen as manifestations of the earth deity.

8. Lamotte 1966: 149, translated in Linrothe 1999: 7. See also Lalou 1956 and 1961.

9. Lamotte 1966: 149.

10. In Indian mythology, the *guhyakas* (from the Sanskrit *guhya* 'hidden, secret') are usually the attendants of the god of wealth, Kubera (Vaiśravaṇa), and the guardians of his treasures.

11. Lamotte 1966: 116.

12. In the *Mahāparinirvāṇa Sūtra,* for instance, Vajrapāṇi explodes the head of an "impure" young man who had crept into the *poṣadha* ceremony. Asked about this, the Buddha replies that both Vajrapāṇi and the young man are magical creations used for didactic purpose. See *T.* 374: 380c; *T.* 375: 620; and Lamotte 1966: 120. Vajrapāṇi also frightens the six "heretical masters." See Lamotte 1966: 124–126.

13. Lamotte 1966: 126–127, and 130.

14. See *Apidamoxi yimen zulun* 阿毘達磨集異門足論, *T.* 26, 1537: 471–475.

15. Contrary to Sawa's point, Vajrapāṇi plays from the outset the two roles of a servant and a bully that frightens heretics. The pair formed by the sweet-looking Ānanda and the quasi-demonic Vajrapāṇi calls to mind the motif of the companion spirits (*kushōjin*) of the Japanese tradition (and in particular Fudō's acolytes, Kongara and Seitaka).

16. Lamotte 1966: 117.

17. Lamotte 1966: 148.

18. Lamotte 1966: 151. It is a similar symbol, the jewel—and more specifically the wish-fulfilling jewel or *cintāmaṇi*—that will be one of the keys of the success of the devas.

19. See Lamotte 1966: 153.

20. Linrothe 1999: 26.

21. See *DNBZ* 48: 280.

22. Tang images of Acala, very similar to those that were diffused in Japan on the basis of the Womb mandala and the sculptural program of Tōji, have been found in excavations in Xi'an (Chang'an).

23. *T.* 39: 679a. The scene takes place at the time of Buddha's enlightenment, when he wants to include all beings in his mandala. The *Kakuzenshō* notes the discrepancy, pointing out that in the *Mahāvairocana Sūtra* Acala is said to tame the asura (Maheśvara), whereas in the *Yuqi jing* 瑜祇経 (better known by its Japanese title, *Yugikyō*), it is Trailokyavijaya. Various solutions are offered, which shows that the point was problematic. In one source, Acala summons Maheśvara, while Trailokyavijaya tames (actually kills) him. The solution is found in the identity between the two wisdom kings, but the *Kakuzenshō* points out that, in certain circles at least, the two remained distinct. See *Kakuzenshō, DNBZ* 48: 278–280.

24. In the scriptures of the *Vajraśekhara* lineage, which Yixing must have studied under Vajrabodhi, it is Vajrapāṇi who tames Maheśvara.

25. *DNBZ* 48: 279. There is a similar illustration of Fudō trampling on Daijizaiten and his consort in the *Besson zakki* (Fig. 3.12).

26. See Linrothe 1990.

27. See Annen, *Fudō myōō ryūin giki shugyō shidai taizō gyōhō* 不動明王立印儀軌修行次第胎蔵行法 (a commentary on Amoghavajra's *Budong liuyin gui* 不動立印軌, *T.* 21, 1199), in *Nihon daizōkyō* 48: 150; and the *Yōson dōjōkan* 要尊道場観 by Shunnyū (890–953), *T.* 78, 2468: 43–44; see also Frank 2000a: 290.

28. See for instance *Shiojiri* 53, in *Nihon zuihitsu taisei* 10: 61.

29. Murayama 1997: 108.

30. The *Budong anzhen fa* (*T.* 21, 1203, translated into Chinese by Vajrabodhi) was brought to Japan by the Shingon monk Shūei 宗叡 (var. Sōei, 809–884) and also allegedly transmitted by Kūkai. According to the *Besson zakki*, it does not appear in the catalogues of the latter because it was held secret and later was reintroduced in Japan by Shūei. See *Besson zakki, TZ* 3: 485.

31. The *Budong zhentuo zhen'yan* was brought to Japan by the Tendai priest Ennin 円仁 (794–864).

32. Murayama 1997: 110.

33. In both rituals, the deities of the eight directions are (starting from the east) Taishakuten 帝釈天 (Skt. Indra), Katen 火天 (Agni, southeast), Enmaten 閻魔天 (Yama, south), Rasetsuten 羅刹天 (Nairṛti, southwest), Suiten 水天 (Varuṇa, west), Fūten 風天 (Vayu, northwest), Tamonten 多聞天 (Vaiśravaṇa, north), and Jizaiten 自在天 (Maheśvara, northeast). See Misaki 1992: 172.

34. The same disposition is found in other rituals such as the Offering to the Twelve Devas (Jūniten-ku 十二天供) or the Offering to the Seventy Devas (Shichijūten-kū 七十天供). In the latter, as performed in the Shijōkō ritual, next to the devas of the eight directions, one placed the four great wisdom kings (the four-armed Gōzanze, Mudō Myōō 無動明王, the four-armed Munōshō 無能勝, and the four-armed Dairiki Ususama Kongō 大力烏枢沙摩金剛). It is not clear why, in ulterior Shijōkō rituals, one kept only Fudō.

35. *Shijūjō ketsu, T.* 75, 2408: 901c.

36. Misaki 1992: 180. Fudō himself is said to be an emanation or "trace" of Dainichi, Shaka, and Vajrapāṇi. See *DNBZ* 48: 278a. In his *Usuzōshi kuketsu,* Raiyu 頼瑜 states: "Does Fudō open his two eyes or only one? When he opens his two eyes, he is Dainichi Fudō; when he opens only one, he is Shaka Fudō" (*T.* 79, 2535: 252c). See also Raiyu's *Hishō mondō* (*T.* 79, 2536: 470a).

37. Such is the case of the Yojiri Fudō (Writhing Fudō) by the Buddhist painter Yoshihide 良秀 (Ryōshū), who is said to have learned how to paint vivid flames while watching his house burning. In a painting based on Ryōshū's model, dated 1195, the flames come out of Fudō's body and his sword. See Nakano Genzō 1986.

38. See also *BZS,* fig. 2143.

39. *Kakuzenshō, DNBZ* 48: 280a.

40. Sawa 1955: 71.

41. The *Sheng Wudongzun anzhen jiaguo dengfa* 聖無動尊安鎮家国等法 (translated by Vajrabodhi; *T.* 21, 1203) takes as its main deity a four-armed Acala. This ritual was transmitted to a layman named Wang Guang at a time when monks were forbidden to perform it. The two-armed Fudō was then perceived as more orthodox, as shown by the following passage in Raiyu's *Usuzōshi kuketsu:* "—Which image of Fudō has the deepest meaning, the two-armed or the four-armed one? —It is the one-faced, two-armed one" (*T.* 79, 2535: 252c). On the "much maligned monsters" of Hinduism, see Mitter 1992.

42. Sawa 1955: 84–85.

43. In typical fashion, Sawa sees this Fudō as a representative of *zōmitsu* 雑密 (mixed esotericism). As noted above, this notion, which takes for granted the existence of a "pure esotericism"—that of Kūkai and of the Shingon school—has long outlived its usefulness.

44. Sawa 1955: 80.

45. Sawa 1955: 76–77.

46. Sawa 1955: 74.

47. See for instance the *Shijō hiketsu* 四帖秘訣, in *ZTZ,* Mikkyō 3: 352: "Furthermore, the Earth-goddess is the Worthy Fudō. When [the Buddha] was about to reach awakening under the bodhi-tree, King Māra of Sixth Heaven

tried to cause him obstacles. At that point, the Buddha took the Earth-goddess as his witness; she appeared and presented that swastika to him. Then she transformed into Fudō and tamed King Māra."

48. See *T.* 76, 2410: 610a.

49. Ibid.

50. See Linrothe 1999: 153.

51. *Mahāvairocana Sūtra, T.* 18, 848: 13b-c.

52. In his protective and exorcistic function, Fudō is also related to the cult of the Buddha's relics and of the wish-fulfilling jewel (*cintāmaṇi*).

53. See *T.* 76, 2410: 614c. On "induced possession" (Skt. *aveśa*, J. *abi-sha* 阿尾舍, 阿尾奢, 阿毘舍), see *Hōbōgirin* 1: 7; and Strickmann 2002: 204–218 and 228–238. This is perhaps what the *Keiran shūyōshū* means when it states: "When one takes as model the Fudō ritual, one takes a plump boy." *T.* 76, 2410: 863c.

54. *GR* 4: 530.

55. Komatsu 1994: 198.

56. See *ST,* Jinja-hen 5, Yamato: 40.

57. See *Soga monogatari,* translated in Cogan 1987: 189–193. See also Mack 2006a: 205. Lady Nijō quotes that story in her diary as an example of abnegation and concludes: "The debt I owed His Majesty was far greater than the debt Shōkū owed his teacher. Why then had my offer been fruitless?" See Brazell 1975: 246–247.

58. In the *Mahāvairocana Sūtra* 7, for instance, Acala's mudrā and mantra are used for closing the ritual area and excluding evil influences. See Linrothe 1999: 24. The *Mahāvairocana Sūtra* gives an allegorical ("inner") interpretation of Acala's destruction of "outer" obstacles and expulsion of outer demons. Linrothe 1999: 152.

59. The term *gohō* 護法 (protecting the Dharma) actually refers to the protection of an individual (usually a priest) that upholds the Dharma. But it also has an embryological connotation: as we will see, it was related to figures like the *kushōjin,* companion spirits "born at the same time as the individual, and who protect the latter." On this question, see Faure 2009.

About the *gohō,* see Koyama 2003; and Lin 2003; about *shugenja* and *gohō,* see Miyake 1985: 475–478; about *gohō* and possession, see Miyake 1985: 478–482; about the position of the *gohō* in the *shugen* pantheon, see Miyake 1985: 482–484.

60. Tradition has it that when opponents attacked his temple on Mount Kōya, Kakuban sat meditating in front of a Fudō statue in the Mitsugon-in 密厳院. When the monks forced their way into the monastery, they saw only two statues of Fudō. As they pierced both figures to determine which one was the real Fudō, both began to bleed and the voice of Fudō resounded, saying that Kakuban was under his protection. The monks did not insist, and Kakuban escaped. See van der Veere 2000: 153–157.

61. The *Keiran shūyōshū* gives a list of eminent monks and their protectors (*gohō*), in which Sōō and Fudō occupy a prominent place. *T.* 76, 2410: 783c.

62. Snodgrass 1988: 272.

63. The *Kakuzenshō* explains that Fudō eats food leftovers. After his meals, the practitioner must empower his leftovers by reciting Fudō's mantra seven times or twenty-one times and place them into a pure place as offerings to Fudō. *DNBZ* 48: 307b. Fudō, not unlike the demonic *ḍākinīs*, is said to devour the impregnations brought on by ignorance, the cause of future karma. See *Asabashō, TZ* 9: 325a, 334c-335c. See also Mack 2006a: 31.

64. See Stein 1972–1973; on the Brahmanic notion of "remainder," see also Malamoud 1996b. Familiarity breeds contempt. Nakano Genzō mentions weird (*igyō* 異形) or humorous images of Fudō described in the *Keiran shūyōshū:* Fudō in the lavatory with diarrhea, Fudō holding his nose because of his acolytes' smell, Fudō wiping his rear with his sword, Fudō in the form of a woman, Fudō chasing after his youths. Nakano 1986: 65–66, without references, as quoted in Mack 2006a: 36. I have not found these descriptions in the *Keiran shūyōshū,* however, and at first glance they seem to reflect the spirit of a later period. Nakano simply says that, according to the *Keiran shūyōshū,* the "weird" Fudō painted by Toba Sōjō 鳥羽僧正 (1053–1140) looks as if he were in the privy suffering from diarrhea.

65. He also devours evil dragons; despite his affinities with dragons, his relationship with the bird-like *garuḍas,* the mortal enemies of dragons, is symbolized by the *garuḍas* in his flaming mandorlas.

66. See *Heike monogatari,* as translated in McCullough 1988: 179.

67. See *Hikosan ruki* 彦山流記, in Gorai 2000, 2: 466b.

68. See *Eigaku yōki* 叡岳要記, in *GSRJ* 24: 546.

69. In this image of the *mikawari* Fudō, two (mytho)logical threads intertwine: that of the popular *mikawari* (in which the compassionate god or bodhisattva chooses to suffer on behalf of his follower); and that of the identification of the Mikkyō practitioner with the *honzon* of the ritual, which gives him the powers and invulnerability of that deity.

70. See Iyanaga 1981–1985.

71. See *Kōshinshō* 幸心鈔, *T.* 78, 2498: 724b.

72. On Fudō's life-prolonging ritual, see also *Sōjishō, T.* 77, 2412: 83.

73. See *Kakuzenshō, DNBZ* 48: 326b.

74. See *Usuzōshi, T.* 79, 2495: 251c.

75. *Kakuzenshō, DNBZ* 48: 326a. See also *Asabashō, TZ* 9: 311b; and *Usuzōshi kuketsu, T.* 79, 2535: 256a.

76. See for instance the *Miwaryū kanjō injin hiketsu* 三輪流灌頂印信秘決, in *ST,* Ronsetsu-hen 2, Shingon shintō 2: 315.

77. The seal looks like a red jewel on a lotus, with a five-branched star on it. It can be seen on a painting preserved at Shinnyodō 真如堂, known as *Abe no Seimei's Return to Life (Abe no Seimei sosei zu* 安倍晴明蘇生図). On this painting, the famous *onmyōji* is shown unconscious, with King Yama and Fudō on the right, Yama's two acolytes in front, and several demons drawing the deceased in front of the mirror of destiny. See also fig. 135 in Ōsaka shiritsu bijutsukan 2009.

78. The incident is translated in Seidensticker 1978, 2: 617–618.

79. On Fudō, see Sawa 1955 and 2006; Nakano Genzō 1986; Tanaka Hisao 1993a; Takai 1941; and Miyasaka 2006. In English, see Mack 2006a.

On the spread of Fudō's cult, see Tanaka Hisao 1993b: 31–46; and Ariga Yoshitaka, 1993. On Sōō, see Kageyama Haruki 1993. On Fudō and Shugendō, see Miyake 1993; on Fudō and Onmyōdō, see Iwata 1993; and Sawa 1955: 35–139.

80. The Miidera mandala shows Miroku 弥勒 at the center, surrounded by Yellow Fudō (in the northeast), Shinra Myōjin 新羅明神 (in the east), the good deities that protect the Dharma, or gohō zenshin 護法善神 (in the southeast), Sannō Gongen (in the south), Chishō Daishi 智証大師, i.e., Ennin (in the southwest), Mio Myōjin 三尾明神 (in the west), the eighteen myōjin (in the northwest), and Sonjōō 尊星王, i.e., Myōken, the god of the Polar Star (in the north). See Kageyama 1973a.

81. On the latter, see Moran 1961.

82. In the Keiran shūyōshū, Fudō himself explains his golden color to Enchin as follows: among his three bodies, the golden body is revealed to advanced practitioners, the white one to practitioners of medium capacities, the blue/black one to practitioners of lower capacities. Enchin is consequently praised as a being of superior quality. T. 76, 2410: 612b. See also Kakuzenshō, DNBZ 48: 290. The yellow color in this case is also related to the symbolism of the five elements, and it is no coincidence that it refers precisely to the element earth. Indeed, as noted earlier, Fudō was reputed for his efficacy in rituals for placating the earth deity. There were also representations of Fudō in the other four colors. Several of them were worshiped in Edo, and, among the five Fudō temples that protected the capital, two have left their names to their neighborhood: Meguro 目黒 (black-eyed Fudō) and Mejiro 目白 (white-eyed Fudō).

83. The Konjaku monogatari shū elaborates with a description of "anthropophagous" indigenes carrying spears. Then, as the wind returned, owing to the apparition of Fudō, Enchin's boat finally reached the China coast. In his message to the throne upon his return to Japan, Enchin reports that his ship, following a Korean ship, reached China on the sixteenth of the seventh month. This is perhaps a development of the tradition that he was able to leave the Ryūkyū owing to Fudō's apparition. See Konjaku monogatari shū, NKBZ 22: 69–70; and Dykstra 1998–2003, 1: 43.

84. Mack 2006a: 266–267.

85. The importance of Mudōji is clear from Kōshū's remark, in the Keiran shūyōshū, that its founding on the southern slope of Mount Hiei can be compared to Nāgārjuna's discovery of the Iron Tower in southern India, the legendary source of the esoteric Buddhist tradition. See T. 76, 2410: 713b.

86. Legend has it that the main deity of Enryakuji's central hall, the buddha Yakushi, had told Sōō to circumambulate the three pagodas of Mount Hiei while meditating on Fudō. This was the origin of the kaihōgyō practice, still performed today. See Tendai Nanzan Mudōji konryū oshōden 天台南山無動寺健立和尚伝, in GSRJ 4; quoted in Rhodes 1987: 186.

87. Indeed, Fudō's cult developed mainly among shugenja, whose honzon he became (together with a derived figure, Zaō Gongen 蔵王権現).

88. See Kazuragawa engi, ZGR 1: 119–120; Uji shūi monogatari, NKBT 42: 386–388, translated in Mills 1970: 429; and Kojidan, KT 18: 56–57.

89. See Mack 2006a: 286. This local deity, still worshiped today at the Jishū Shrine, seems to have been initially a god of the Kazura River. His relation with Fudō, a god related to the chthonian powers, is not coincidental. After Myōō-in was turned into a Tendai temple (*betsuin* 別院), the Jishū jinja 地主神社 came to enshrine the seven deities of Sannō. See Kageyama 1993: 74–78 and 1973a: 442.

90. On this occasion, Fudō's statue is said to have turned its back to Sōō. Asked for the reason for that behavior, Fudō revealed to him that the possessing spirit was that of the Shingon priest Shinzei 真済 (800–860), whom he had in the past vowed to protect; therefore he could not subdue him. In the Nanto-bon version of the *Heike monogatari,* we read that, after being defeated by the priest Eryō 恵亮 (791–859) in a ritual contest at the time of the succession quarrel between Princes Koretaka 惟喬 and Korehito 惟仁, Shinzei fasted and performed the Fudō rite with the aim of becoming a vengeful spirit (*onryō* 怨霊). But Fudō tells Sōō that he can exorcise that spirit by invoking Daiitoku Myōō 大威徳明王 (the same deity which Eryō had invoked to defeat Shinzei). This is the first recorded five-altar ritual. On this episode, see Faure 1998a: 162–63; Mack 2006a: 299, and Tanaka Takako 1993: 95. On Sōō, see also Mack 2006a: 276–288 and 296–299.

91. Mack 2006a: 272–299.

92. On that legend, see Tanaka 1993: 95.

93. See for instance *Iizuna Daimyōjin engi,* in Gorai 2000, 1: 470; and Sasama 1988: 95–114.

94. See Stramigioli 1973.

95. Kanjō, a grandson of Uda Tennō 宇多天皇 (r. 887–897), founded Shinshōji (at the time of Masakado's revolt in 940) and enshrined the statue of Fudō there, performing a twenty-one-day subjugation ritual. Yet Masakado was eventually deified. Interestingly, the parishioners of Honshōji (Chiba prefecture), a temple dedicated to him (as shown by the character "Shō" 正 in its name, the same as "Masa" in Masakado), refuse to this day to visit Shinshōji because they hold Fudō responsible for Masakado's defeat. Likewise, the parishioners (*ujiko* 氏子) of Kanda Myōjin 神田明神, a shrine dedicated to the deified Masakado, consider Fudō an enemy to this day.

96. These rituals fall into the same categories as state rituals, namely, subjugation (*chōbuku*), elimination of calamities (*sokusai*), increase (*zōyaku*), and captation (*keiai*).

97. The description in *Murasaki Shikibu no nikki* is translated in Bowring 1996: 51; for *Eiga monogatari* 栄華物語, see the translation in McCullough and McCullough 1980: 270–271. See also Mack 2006a: 175–176.

98. See *Heike monogatari,* translated in McCullough 1988: 96–98. Similar rituals were allegedly performed on behalf of Go-Daigo's consort, but they were in fact subjugation rituals aimed at the bakufu. See *Taiheiki,* translated in McCullough 1979: 12–14.

99. McCullough 1988: 97.

100. Fudō was also invoked to induce voluntary possession. See Fudō's "Method for *Aveśa*" (*abisha-hō* 阿尾捨法) in *Keiran shūyōshū, T.* 76, 2410: 614c.

101. Although this Red Fudō is said to be the one painted by Enchin after his vision of the god near the waterfall on the Kazura River, it more likely is dated to the Kamakura period. According to legend, Enchin knocked his head against a rock and painted the image with the blood flowing from his wound. An interesting specimen is found at the Myōō-in on Kōyasan, in which a dragon is coiled around Fudō's sword (a rare conflation of Fudō's *samaya* or symbolic form as Kurikara and the "live" Fudō). See *TZ* 7, 3137. On the Red Fudō, see also Mack 2006a: 39.

102. See McCullough 1979: 35.

103. The name Kurikara comes from the Sanskrit Kulika (Kṛka), originally the name of a *nāga* king. The *Keiran shūyōshū* explains that *kuri* is the Sanskrit term for sword, and *kara* for dragon. See *T.* 76, 2410: 612a. The Kurikara motif, in which the dragon swallows the tip of the sword, is said to represent the polarity of yin and yang, and other derived polarities.

104. The association between Fudō and the dragon or *nāga* suggests that he is also a figure of autochthony. On the central place of Fudō in Shugendō, see Miyake 1985: 417–425. Until the middle of the medieval period, the main *shugen* deity was Zaō Gongen. As Shugendō absorbed esoteric conceptions (in particular those related to the Two Realm mandalas, Zaō Gongen gradually gave way to Fudō, the emanation of the cosmic buddha Dainichi.

105. This sword was said to be the Kusanagi 草薙 sword of the god Susanoo, and it therefore links Fudō to Susanoo and to classical Japanese mythology. A local legend reports that a Korean monk named Dōgyō attempted to steal it, but the sword, wrapped in a monastic robe (*kesa*), flew back to Atsuta. The Korean king, angered, sent seven Fudō from India to retrieve it, but to no avail. See *Shinsen hiketsu shū,* in Atsuta jingū gūchō 2006, 1: 107–108. See also *Atsuta kōshiki,* in Abe Yasurō 2005: 48. This legend is reminiscent of that of Mount Atago 愛宕山, which developed during the Muromachi period. In that legend, Fudō is sent by the Korean king to bring back the Korean general Nichira 日羅, who had defected to Japan and retired on Mount Atago. As it happens, Fudō is defeated and converted by the bodhisattva Jizō (the *honji* or true nature of Nichira) in his martial form as Shōgun Jizō 将軍地蔵. On this legend, see Bouchy 1979.

106. See Morrell 1985: 116. On the identity between Jizō and Fudō, see *Keiran shūyōshū, T.* 76, 2410: 615b.

107. Significantly, Shinshōji erected subtemples dedicated to Shōten and Myōken Bosatsu, two other deities involved in Masakado's rebellion. The latter was and still is popular in eastern Japan, particularly in Chiba prefecture.

108. On Acala, see also Heller 2001: 209–228. On Fudō, see Frank 1991: 148–153; Nakano 1986; Tanaka Hisao 1993a; and Brinker 1990.

109. See for instance *Daigo-bon Shoson zuzō, TZ* 4, 3015; *Usuzōshi kuketsu, T.* 79, 2535: 283c; and *Keiran shūyōshū, T.* 76, 2410: 864a. See also Chandra 1999–2005, 1: 63.

110. This work, found in the Goryū sonsō Collection, is quoted in Miyake 1971: 209.

111. See *Hakusan ōkagami* 白山大鏡, in Uemura 2000: 31, 94.

147. On Fudō and Kōjin, see Miyake 1971: 242n68.

148. See "Daizanji engi," in Gorai 2000, 1: 305. Another story is found in the *Daizanji engi emaki:* After Rōben practiced austerities for a long time in front of a pond, a huge snake appeared. It told Rōben that it had been a *kōjin* for a long time, but now, delivered by his sermon, it would at long last be reborn in Tuṣita heaven. See Gorai 2000: 367.

149. Nanri 1996: 35–46.

150. This icon, incidentally, was the one that Ennin received in China and placed in front of his boat when he returned to Japan in 847, in order to placate demons that conjured obstacles to his return. It was eventually enshrined at Zentō-in 前唐院 on Mount Hiei. The Shinshōji 新勝寺 of Narita-san 成田山, a monastery whose *honzon* is the Fudō statue that was used to subdue Masakado, is also popular for its Shōten temple. Vajrapāṇi (J. Shūkongōjin 執金剛神), Fudō's prototype, is also credited with that subduing. Another composite deity related to both Kōjin and Fudō is Izuna 飯綱 (var. Iizuna) Daimyōjin, represented standing on a white fox (the usual mount of Dakiniten) and holding Fudō's attributes, the sword and the noose, with which he subdues the gods of obstacles and famine (like Kōjin). See "Izuna Daimyōjin engi" in Gorai 2000, 1: 470–471.

151. See Gorai 2000, 2: 275–277.

152. On Fudō's acolytes, see Manabe 2000–2001, 2: 526–536.

153. The eight acolytes of Fudō, beginning with Ekō and Eki, and ending with Kongara and Seitaka, are said to be the emanations of eight seed-syllables (*bīja*). Regarding these acolytes, the *Kakuzenshō,* quoting an oral tradition, states: "Because Fudō is the wheel-commanding body of Dainichi, he takes the four knowledges and the four perfections (*pāramitā*) as his retinue." *DNBZ* 48: 293b and 362c–363a. See also *Keiran shūyōshū* (*T.* 76, 2410: 612a), which compares them to the eight buddhas born from the Buddha's crown (*butchō* 仏頂). The eight *dōji* seem to have replaced the eight wisdom kings, whose cult, while popular in China, was never widespread in Japan. On the iconography, see also Chandra 1999–2005, 1: 34.

154. Chandra 1999–2005, 1: 64.

155. See for instance *Besson zakki, TZ* 3, fig. 163, and *TZ* 18: 416–417; and two exemplars belonging to Enryakuji and Miidera, respectively (see Nakano Genzō 1986, figs. 10 and 110). Actually, the latter five look rather like slaves, subdued, as if begging for mercy. In a series of representations of the five wisdom kings, several of them have demon heads or animal heads. See Kyōto kokuritsu hakubutsukan 1998: 96.

156. The statues of the eight *dōji* in the Fudō Hall on Mount Kōya were allegedly carved by Unkei 運慶 (d. 1223) at the time this building was constructed, in 1197 or 1198. In the *Tales from Times Now Past,* the Ōhara priest Chōen has a vision of the eight *dōji* at Katsuragi. See Dykstra 1983, 1: 201.

157. See also Nara kokuritsu hakubutsukan 1978: 284, fig. 45.

158. This Oto Gohō is often coupled with Nyaku Gohō 若護法, and sometimes with Seitaka Dōji, one of Fudō's acolytes. He is also identified with Sensha Dōji 船車童子, one of Benzaiten's fifteen acolytes; see *Keiran shūyōshū, T.* 76, 2410: 783ab.

159. *T.* 76, 2410: 259–260.

160. *T.* 76, 2410: 613a.

161. See Lalou 1930: 67. In Mañjuśrī's case, the paradox of a supreme god with a servant's appearance merges the kingly nature of the bodhisattva riding his majestic lion, symbol of wisdom, with the lowly nature of elemental spirits. Mañjuśrī is also the awesome power that lurks behind the threatening figure of Yamāntaka (Daiitoku Myōō).

162. Kongara's *kesa* is called the "robe of the field of merits" (*fukuden-e* 福田衣). It symbolizes Ekō Dōji, the *gararan* or initial stage of embryological gestation, and the eastern direction. He wears on his crown the water of knowledge of the Sanskrit letter *Vam,* which means that he advances to the stage of buddhahood where the action of the *abudon* stage of gestation takes place, corresponding to the southern direction. The two pairs formed by Kongara/Seitaka and Ekō/Eki are closely related, even practically interchangeable.

163. See *Asabashō, TZ* 9: 337b. On Seitaka, see also *Kakuzenshō, DNBZ* 48: 298–300 and 318b; and *Bukkyō daijiten,* 3: 2895.

164. See *Kakuzenshō, DNBZ* 48: 299, 301; and *Asabashō, TZ* 9: 337a.

165. See the Kongōbuji exemplar (Kamakura period) in Kōyasan Reihōkan 2001, fig. 31; and the Jimyō-in exemplar (Kamakura period) in Ōsaka shiritsu bijutsukan 2004, fig. 145.

166. *DNBZ* 48: 319a.

167. *T.* 79: 470b.

168. See *Kakuzenshō, DNBZ* 48: 302. Seitaka is said to symbolize the mental practice of the skillful means of the perfection of action, as well as the ritual to eliminate calamities (*sokusai*). On the five topknots of Seitaka, see *DNBZ* 48: 300. On Kongara, see *DNBZ* 48: 296 and 319a. See also Manabe Shunshō 2000–2001, 2: 526–536.

169. *ST,* Jinja-hen 50, Aso, Hikosan 2: 83.

170. See *Keiran shūyōshū, T.* 76, 2410: 864a.

171. *Kakuzenshō, DNBZ* 48: 293. See also Nara kokuritsu hakubutsukan 2000: 168, fig. 36.

172. Koyama 2003.

173. On this question, see Kondō 2006. See also the Heian-period triad of Kisshōji 吉祥寺 (Aritagawa-chō), formed by Fudō and his two acolytes, Kongara and Seitaka (who look like those of Tarōten), in Wakayama kenritsu hakubutsukan 2012: 141, fig. 103; and in this book, fig. 3.35.

174. Incidentally, both Oto Gohō and Tarōten are called "Daigyōji" 大行事, a name that evokes the Hie Shrine deity Daigyōji, a monkey-faced god closely associated with Jūzenji. See Kondō 2006: 60–61.

175. Sawa 1955: 64.

176. See for instance *Gyōrinshō, T.* 76: 360ab.

177. Komatsu 1994: 198.

178. *T.* 76, 2410: 782b.

179. *T.* 76, 2410: 782b.

180. See Nakano Genzō 1986, fig. 85.

181. See *Kakuzenshō, DNBZ* 48: 280; but the same source also explains that the two are distinct.

13. There are some exceptions, in which Aizen replaces Fudō in a slightly different grouping of the five myōō.

14. Full title: *Jingangfeng louge yiqie yujia yuqi jing* 金剛峰楼閣一切瑜伽瑜祇経 (Scripture of All Yogas and Yogīs of the Vajra-top Pavilion), *T.* 18, 867. Vanden Broucke argues that it is rather a collection of Indian fragments edited by Vajrabodhi, and perhaps by Amoghavajra as well. See Vanden Broucke 1994.

15. See also *Keiran shūyōshū, T.* 76, 2410: 615c.

16. See Goepper 1993. See also Henrik Sørensen's review (1991–1992).

17. See the Rite of the Supreme Mantra of Butsumo and Aizen, translated by Amoghavajra, and quoted in the *Keiran shūyōshū, T.* 76, 2410: 615c. On Aizen as warrior deity, see Okuda 2005.

18. The subjugation ritual involved a kind of mimicry, in which the name of the enemy was placed under the foot of the statue in order to be crushed, or in the mouth of the lion (either the mount or the headgear) to be devoured. A source quoted by Murayama Shuichi says that one should write the name of one's enemy and trample on it—with one's left foot for a woman, one's right for a man—while performing a series of 108 empowerments (*kaji* 加持, Skt. *adhiṣṭhāna*). See Murayama 1990: 372. A similar procedure was followed when the *honzon* of the ritual was Fudō. See for instance, in the *Miyadera enji shō,* in *ZGRJ* 1: 351, the passage concerning an affiliated shrine (*massha* 末社) called Tsurugi no Gozen 剣御前 (Sacred Site of the Sword): "Its main deity is a sword whose *honji* is Fudō. When he was still a crown prince, the future emperor Go-Sanjō buried this symbol of Fudō [here], together with a spell against Go-Reizei."

19. *Keiran shūyōshū,* T. 76, 2410: 569bc.

20. See *Yugikyō kaishin shō,* 164.

21. *TZ* 7: 113b; translated in Goepper 1993: 133.

22. On love-subduing rituals, see *T.* 20, 1125, and *Kakuzenshō, DNBZ* 48: 255a–275a.

23. In that passage, it is not clear if the mouth is that of Aizen, his lion, or the practitioner. In subjugation rituals, the name of the person to be subdued is written on a piece of paper and placed in the lion's mouth, and the same is probably the case here as well. See Jichiun's *Hizō konpōshō, T.* 78, 2485: 355. See also Goepper 1993: 14 and 134; Murayama 1990: 373; and Okuda 2005: 28.

24. Quoted in Murayama 1990: 372.

25. On the popularity of Aizen among warriors, see Okuda 2005.

26. In Japanese: "Kami naraba musubi no kami, hotoke naraba, Aizen myōō." Quoted in Frank 2000b: 82.

27. See Astley-Kristensen 1988a and 1988b. This disposition can also be found in medieval portable altars (*zushi*). In his mandala, Aizen is surrounded by four wisdom kings: Batō Kongō 馬頭金剛 in the northeast, Gōzanze Kongō 降三世金剛 in the southeast, Daiitoku Kongō 大威徳金剛 in the southwest, and Munōshō Kongō 無能勝金剛 in the northwest. See Duquenne 2003: 1037.

28. See *Yugikyō chōmonshō*: 283c–284a. See also Yamamoto 1993a: 311.

29. See *Yugikyō chōmonshō*: 283c–284a; and *T.* 18, 867, ch. 2.

30. The text adds: "Man is called Kongōsatta (Vajrasatta), Woman King Aizen." *SZS* 36: 342–343.

31. *SZS* 36: 342; translated in Goepper 1993: 116, slightly modified.

32. Chōgō's *Yugikyō chōmonshō* explains: "The left half-seal is . . . the female form. The right half-seal is . . . the male form. By uniting them one produces the five-pronged *vajra,* thereby uniting principle and wisdom into a single nondual reality." See *Yugikyō chōmonshō*: 302.

33. See *Besson zakki, TZ* 3: 453. This double *hūṃ,* written *hhūṃ,* is also analyzed as a combination of the two syllables *hoḥ* and *hūṃ.* Such is also, as we will see shortly, the meaning of the two-headed (Ryōzu) Aizen.

34. Sexual intercourse is also suggested by the two attributes of Aizen, the *vajra* (symbolizing the male organ) and the *vajra* bell (symbolizing the female organ). See *Kakugenshō, SZ* 36: 342–343.

35. Here is how the *Fudōson gushō* describes this *vajra:* "In what is called the five-pronged [*vajra*], the upper four prongs and the upper central prong represent the five wisdoms of the Vajra realm, the five great elements of the male sexual organ. The lower four prongs and the lower central prong are the five buddhas of the Womb realm, the five *cakras* of [the sexual organ of] the woman. Upper and lower parts are identical, yin and yang are nondual, the red and white [drops] unite harmoniously, the two "thoughts" (*nen*) fuse into one: such is the true meaning." See Moriyama 1965: 139–140.

36. *SZS* 36: 342–343; Goepper 1993: 116.

37. On the Aizen mandala, see *T.* 76, 2410: 568 and 616ab. See also Nedachi 1997; and Manabe 2000–2001, 1: 280–293.

38. See Nedachi 1997, fig. 117; and *Kakuzenshō, DNBZ* 49: 40b and 41. See also Goepper 1993: 73, fig. 33; and *BZS,* fig. 1067 (see Fig. 4.13). Another exemplar shows Aizen surrounded by Daikokuten, Bishamonten, Daiitoku Myōō, and Sanbō Kōjin (at the four corners). See Nedachi 1997, fig. 131.

39. The robe's color connotes the type of ritual performed: white for appeasement (*sokusai* 息災), yellow for increase (*zōyaku* 増益), black for exorcism (*gōbuku* 降伏), and red for love subduing (*keiai* 敬愛) or captation (*kōchō* 鉤召) rituals. Because Aizen's robe is red, it symbolizes more specifically the *keiai* rituals.

40. "The jewel vase has two small openings on its sides, because otherwise, since Aizen sits on it, the jewels could not come out." See *Shōgo shū,* *T.* 78, 2479: 212b.

41. Two other deities wearing a lion headgear are the Gandharva King (Kendatsuba-ō 乾闥婆王), a protector of children who is sometimes associated with Fudō; and Butsugen.

42. *T.* 78: 698c.

43. See Goepper 1993: 43; and *Besson zakki, TZ* 3: 462, fig. 185. Like the two-headed Aizen, this form of Aizen has no canonical origin and seems to have appeared toward the end of the Kamakura period. It is represented in an interesting portable shrine from the late Kamakura period known as the Aizen Myōō triad (Aizen Myōō sanzonbutsu 愛染明王三尊仏), in which

also *Minakata Kumagusu zenshū* 2 (1971): 167–168. On the human yellow and *ḍākinīs,* see *T.* 8, 901: 876b; and Strickmann 1993: 72–73; and Iyanaga 2002a: 858a.

63. *Kakuzenshō, DNBZ* 49: 50a-b.

64. See *Yugikyō kaishinshō,* 166.

65. Ibid.

66. See *Hishō mondō, T.* 79: 500c. On the ox yellow, see also *Kakuzenshō, DNBZ* 47: 251. On the "yellow" in humans, oxen, and deer, see *Kakuzenshō, DNBZ* 49: 51a.

67. *DNBZ* 49: 50b.

68. *Kakuzenshō, DNBZ* 49: 50b. See also *SZ* 35: 293a; and *T.* 78: 733a.

69. *T.* 79, 2536: 501a.

70. Iyanaga, personal communication. See *T.* 75, 2397: 457c.

71. See *T.* 34, 1721: 630b.

72. Iyanaga 1999: 99.

73. See *DNBZ* 49: 50b.

74. *Hishō mondō, T.* 79, 2536: 501a.

75. See also *Kakuzenshō, DNBZ* 45: 90.

76. On this question, see *T.* 8, 901: 876b; Strickmann 1993: 72–73; and Iyanaga 2002a: 858.

77. See Gray 2005.

78. On this question, see Yamamoto 1993a: 316–319.

79. See Nara kokuritsu hakubutsukan 2000, figs. 64 and 66.

80. See Nara kokuritsu hakubutsukan 2001, fig. 106. Similarly, in fig. 82, a crystal jewel containing relics is set on top of a vase that looks like Aizen's vase. This suggests that this jewel and the relics it contains are identical with Aizen, and that it was used in a ritual of Nyohō Aizen. The object shown in fig. 83 is a box with a statuette of Aizen and, on the cover, an Aizen mandala, at the center of which are three jewels and relics. Again, this suggests an identity between Aizen and the relics. Likewise, in the portable shrine with a *cintāmaṇi* mandala seen in fig. 84 (private collection), the *cintāmaṇi* is drawn on the door while an image of Aizen is placed inside. This portable shrine too was probably used during a Nyohō Aizen ritual. Judging from its small size, this ritual may have been a private and widespread one. See Nara kokuritsu hakubutsukan 2001: 182.

81. See for example *Hishō mondō, T.* 79, 2536: 338c.

82. *Hishō, T.* 78, 2489: 563b. I am indebted to Iyanaga Nobumi for this reference.

83. See Dolce 2002: 328; and Ogawa 2014: 74–117. The Nyohō Aizen ritual is said to have been transmitted from Gihan 義範 (1023–1088) and Hanjun 範俊 (1038–1112) to Shōkaku 勝覚 (1057–1129), Kanjin 寛信 (1084–1153), Genkai 元海 (1093–1157), and Shukaku 守覚 (1150–1202).

84. See *Tōchō daiji* 東長大事, in Nara kokuritsu hakubutsukan 2001: 183; and Chap. 6 below.

85. As part of the explicit network, duly mentioned in textual commentaries on Aizen, we find Mahāvairocana, Vajrasattva, Daishō Kongō 大勝金剛, Takki Rāja, Gōzanze Myōō, and Fudō Myōō.

86. On Aizen as Byōdō-ō, see also Goepper 1993: 56. That title is also the name of one of the ten kings of hell (the sixth). While Yama is only one of the ten kings (the fifth, therefore the central one), these figures can be seen as his facets or emanations. On the ten kings, see Teiser 1994 .

87. In the Hannyaji 般若寺 tradition, Aizen holds a skull in his left hand.

88. *Keiran shūyōshū, T.* 76, 2410: 579b. On this much-debated notion, see Weinstein 1964; and Schmitthausen 2007.

89. *T.* 76, 2410: 579b, 799c.

90. *T.* 76, 2410: 579b. Chōgō's *Sōjishō,* which quotes this passage verbatim, adds: "This is the so-called human-head banner." *T.* 77, 2412: 87c.

91. See Śatapatha Brāhmaṇa X, 5, 2, 13, quoted in Malamoud 2002: 15.

92. See Malamoud 2002: 15 and 26. As we will see, Yama is also identified with Amaterasu.

93. See *Sōjishō, T.* 77, 2412: 87b. This duality brings to mind the figure of the "twin devas" (*kushōjin*), on which see Faure 2009.

94. The same interpretation is given for the mirror of King Yama: "Question: 'What is the essence of the crystal mirror?'—Answer: 'It is the perfectly bright essence of the eighth consciousness.'" *T.* 77: 87c.

95. *Atsuzōshi, T.* 78, 2483: 272.

96. A similar process can be discerned in the case of deities like Dainichi or Matarajin, although the latter are not stellar deities like Myōken Bosatsu.

97. See *Kojidan* 古事談 1: 56, quoted in Tanaka Takako 1993: 240.

98. *Sōjishō, T.* 77, 2412: 83a.

99. *Sōjishō, T.* 77, 2412: 82c.

100. *Kakuzenshō,* in *DNBZ* 49: 46. On Aizen and the seven stars, see the drawing in *Kakuzenshō, DNBZ* 49: 44. The *Kakuzenshō* section on Aizen includes representations of the three baleful stars Saturn, Rāhu, and Ketu, and an explanation of the "method of the three nines."

101. *Kakuzenshō, DNBZ* 50: 46. The life mansion is said to correspond to the day of birth, the karma mansion to the day of birth in a past life (when the individual began to accumulate karma), and the womb mansion to the day when the individual's consciousness entered the mother's womb. See Ōyama 1956: 481–483.

102. *DNBZ* 50: 47a.

103. *T.* 76, 2410: 567c.

104. In Shukaku's *Tsuiki* 追記, Butsugen Myōō 仏眼明王 and Kinrin Myōō 金輪明王 (*sic*) are compared to the father and mother, and their compassion unites to produce *dato* (Skt. *dhātu*). *Dhātu* is a polysemic term written here in Siddhaṃ script, meaning "element," "realm," or "relic," and designating by extension the wish-fulfilling jewel, i.e., Aizen. See *Tsuiki, T.* 78, 2494: 618c; *Usuzōshi kuketsu, T.* 79, 2535: 182c; and *Keiran shūyōshū, T.* 76, 2410: 644a.

105. On this buddha, see Russell-Smith 2006.

106. As noted earlier, Butsugen and Kinrin are usually represented as a couple. See for instance *Keiran shūyōshū, T.* 76, 2410: 644c.

107. See Itō Satoshi 1993. See also Andreeva 2006b: 365–367.

108. On Aizen and Butsugen in the *Daijingū mishōtai zushi,* see Abe 1985b: 338–346. See also Kondō Yoshihiro 1985.

109. *T.* 76, 2410: 621c; see also Iyanaga 2002a: 595. The central face symbolizes their nonduality (that is, the source of the dual powers or aspects of reality represented by Kinrin and Butsugen, but perhaps also the product of their union).

110. See *Keiran shūyōshū, T.* 76, 2410: 567b.

111. *T.* 76, 2410: 615c.

112. See for instance *Shikan, T.* 78, 2500: 778b; and Goepper 1993: 49. In Aizen's case, this is probably because Aizen's mantra itself is called "mother of the buddhas."

113. *Atsuzōshi, T.* 78, 2483: 272a.

114. This series of associations is hierarchically structured, from the cosmic buddha of esoteric Buddhism in his two fundamental aspects (represented by the Womb and Vajra Realm mandalas); to its two most powerful emanations, Fudō and Aizen; to the deva king of the realm of form, Brahmā; to King Yama, the ruler of hell; and finally to his human manifestation, Kōbō Daishi (Kūkai). See Teeuwen and Rambelli 2003b: 48–49.

115. See Ruppert 2000: 190–191.

116. See Ōmiwa jinja shiryō henshu iinkai 1983: 44.

117. See Murayama 2000: 330.

118. Ōmiwa jinja shiryō henshu iinkai 1983: 39–40.

119. See Ogawa Toyoo 2007: 9. The same passage appears in the *Nichii hongi* 日諱貴本紀, a Ryōbu shintō text anterior to 1350; see Itō 2011: 631.

120. The *Miwa-ryū shintō-hen* records that the Aizen ritual performed at the time of retired emperor Shirakawa was performed conjointly with that of Jūichimen Kannon. This secret ritual was to be performed on Murōzan. See Ōmiwa jinja shiryō, 6: 641.

121. See *Bikisho*, in *ST,* Ronsetsu-hen 2, Shingon shintō 2: 141. On the identity of Kūkai with Amaterasu, see *Miwa-ryū shintō sho daiji kuketsu*, in *ST,* Ronsetsu-hen 2, Shingon shintō 2: 409.

122. *Miwa-ryū shintō-hen,* in Ōmiwa jinja shiryō, 6: 641b.

123. See *Inari ki* 稲荷記, in Yamaori 1999: 360. See also Iyanaga 2002a: 598.

124. Kida 1976: 41.

125. *Tenchi reikaku hishō,* in *Ryōbu shintō shū,* 406.

126. Ōmiwa jinja shiryō, 6: 642a.

127. *ST,* Ronsetsu-hen 2, Shingon shintō 2: 538.

128. See *Kakuzenshō,* in *DNBZ* 49: 38a, and 40a; and *Keiran shūyōshū, T.* 76, 2410: 568b. Takki-rāja is also one of the names of Gōzanze Myōō. On this question, see Goepper 1993: 58–62.

129. On this point, see Tanaka Takako 1993: 246.

130. *DNBZ* 49: 49b–50a.

131. See Iyanaga 2002a: 598.

132. *ST,* Jinja-hen, Yamato no kuni: 522–523. On the three foxes, see *Kakuzenshō, DNBZ* 46: 330; and Strickmann 2002: 266.

133. *Tamakisan gongen engi,* in Gorai 2000, 2: 151.

134. *T.* 76, 2410: 642b.

135. See *Byakuhō shō, TZ* 10, 3191: 1123a; *Byakuhō kushō, TZ* 7:

185c–187a; and Iyanaga 2002a: 597. An Edo period text, the *Sangai isshin ki* 三界一心記, explains: "In Shingon, the harmonious union of man and woman [is symbolized by] Shōten and Aizen." See Washio 1930: 503–540.

136. *Miwa-ryū shintō-hen,* in Ōmiwa jinja shiryō, 6: 641a. Daishō Kongō also appears in the *Yugikyō.* See Duquenne 2003.

137. See Iyanaga 2002a: 613; Yamamoto 1998a: 478; and Kida 1976: 73–74. More generally, Aizen becomes a kind of "general equivalent." In the *Miwaryū jingi kanjō injin kuketsu,* for example, we read that "Raga (Aizen) is the *honji* common to all the gods." *ST,* Ronsetsu-hen 2, Shingon shintō 2: 458.

138. Yamamoto 1998a: 418–419.

139. See Tanaka Takako 1993: 61; and Iyanaga 2002a: 598.

140. *T.* 76, 2410: 634c. Sometimes the link is provided by another deity like Daikokuten.

141. See Yamamoto 1998a : 418–419; Itō Satoshi 2011: 396–419.

142. See Brazell 1973: 127. Another imperial prince of Ninnaji was Shukaku 守覚 (1150–1202), who has left important writings on esoteric Buddhist rituals. See Abe and Yamazaki 1998.

143. See Yamamoto 1993a: 320; Sanford 1997.

144. See Sanford 1997: 6.

145. See *Yugikyō chōmonshō*: 302; and Yamamoto 1993a: 321. See also *Jindaikan hiketsu* 5: "Although [the fetus] is compared to the five-finger-high Aizen in the *Yugikyō,* scholars of esoteric Buddhism ignore this." *ZST,* Ronsetsu-hen, Shūgō shintō: 95–96.

146. For a discussion of that measure, see *Kakuzenshō, DNBZ* 51: 241b; *Byakuhō shō, TZ* 10: 1049; *Keiran shūyōshū, T.* 76, 2410: 568a–b; *Yugikyō chōmonshō*: 300b; Kanagawa kenritsu Kanazawa bunko 2011: 48; and Goepper 1993. Incidentally, Kūkai, who is sometimes credited with carving the first *goshiryō* Aizen, is also said to have carried it constantly on him.

147. See *Yugikyō kuketsu nukigaki,* in *ZTZ,* Mikkyō 2, Kyōten chūsha-kurui 1: 241b; and Yamamoto 1993a: 321. For more on these Buddhist conceptions of conception and gestation, see Faure 2003a. The "hand-sized" (*goshiryō*) Aizen was also used in exorcisms.

148. *Yugikyō kuketsu nukigaki*: 295b. In the same source, the jewel is described as "Aizen within the womb" (p. 302).

149. See *Yugikyō kuketsu nukigaki*: 295b; and Ogawa Toyoo 2007: 14. This embryological symbolism is prevalent in Shugendō, where the five stages of gestation are said to correspond to the five-finger-width Aizen. See for instance *Jindaikan hiketsu,* in *ZST,* Ronsetsu-hen, Shūgō shintō: 93–98.

150. *Goyuigō hiketsu* 御遺告祕決, attributed to Jichiun 実運 (1105–1160); quoted in Fujimaki 2001: 5–6.

151. See Ogawa Toyoo 2007: 19.

152. See *Keiran shūyōshū, T.* 76, 2410: 579b. Similar notions were found in Zen, as shown by the record of the oral teachings of Chikotsu Daie 痴兀大慧 (Buttsū Zenji 仏通禅師, 1229–1312), a disciple of Enni Ben'en 円爾弁円 (1202–1280); see Ogawa 2007: 25

153. Quoted in Ogawa 2007: 18–19.

154. *Jindaikan hiketsu, ZST,* Ronsetsu-hen, Shūgō shintō: 96.

155. See Adolphson 2007.

CHAPTER 5: FEARFUL SYMMETRY

1. See *Kakuzenshō, DNBZ* 49: 54b. In the *Asabashō,* the two-headed Aizen is also represented by a *vajra*. See *TZ* 9: 303c. See also *Kōyō shūi* 紅葉拾遺, in *Tanzan jinja shiryō:* 244; Iyanaga 2002a: 599; and Tanaka Hisao 1993a: 219–223.

2. Iyanaga 2002a: 597. Iyanaga points out the resemblance between the two-headed Aizen and the dual-body Kangiten. I would like to add that in both cases, apart from a purely sexual reading, an embryological reading is also possible. I will return to that point.

3. See *Kakuzenshō, DNBZ* 49: 47a.

4. *Keiran shūyōshū, T.* 76, 2410: 616c.

5. See Nara kokuritsu hakubutsukan 2001: 108–109, figs. 83 and 84. Another case in point is the mandala of the two-headed Aizen (Ryōzu Aizen mandara) of Kongōbuji, dated to the Kamakura period. See Kōyasan Rei-hōkan 2001: 47, fig. 3; and Nara kokuritsu hakubutsukan 2001, fig. 70. Another Ryōzu Aizen mandala (fig. 71) shows a two-headed Aizen with a buddha and a circle with a triangle in the middle above him. A secret tradition from Tōdaiji claims that the two-headed Aizen is the fire deity Katen (Skt. Agni). See *Asabashō, TZ* 9: 303a.

6. These two faces symbolize various doctrinal paradigms such as concentration and wisdom, or defilement and purity. See *Keiran shūyōshū, T.* 76, 2410: 570b; *Gyōrinshō, T.* 76, 2410: 402b; and Goepper 1993: 46. Nothing in Aizen's look suggests that we are dealing with a female deity, however.

7. On conflicting theories regarding the identity *or* distinct nature of the two deities, see *Keiran shūyōshū, T.* 76, 2410: 570b; and *Kakuzenshō, DNBZ* 49: 55–56. See also Uchida Keiichi 2012b: 237–241.

8. Although Goepper thinks that the two-headed Aizen must be regarded as a "later speculative form," the *Yuqi jing* already mentions Zen'ai and Aizen. Goepper 1993: 40 and 46–53.

9. See *T.* 867; and *Hōbōgirin,* 1: 16. See also *Kakuzenshō, DNBZ* 49: 47a. On Aizen and Zen'ai as male and female, see for instance the *Yugikyō chōmonshō*: 283b and 295c.

10. *Henkushō, T.* 78, 2469: 698c. See also *Usuzōshi kuketsu, T.* 79, 2535: 247a.

11. One such representation by Enkei 円慶 is said to have been used in rituals for black magic, love magic, prolongation of life, and easy childbirth. See Goepper 1993: 46–53. See also *Ryōzu happi Aizen-ō ki* (1297) by Enkai, and another work of same title by the second Shōmyōji abbot, Kenna 釼阿 (1261–1338).

12. See *Bikisho, ST,* Ronsetsu-hen 2, Shingon Shinto 2: 506–507. This color coding is strongly reminiscent of the *kushōjin* or "companion spirits" (lit. "born at the same time [as the individual]"). See Faure 2009.

13. Shōbō was also instrumental in promoting the cult of Nyoirin Kannon, a figure closely associated with the two wisdom kings. Aizen and Fudō were already "logically" paired in Kūkai's *Goyuigō,* but the latter is an apocryphal text probably ulterior to Shōbō's time. On Ryōzu Aizen, see also Frank 1991: 157. On the use of that figure by Nichiren, see Frank 1991 and Dolce 2002: 316–335. See also *Jindaikan hiketsu*: 217–220.

14. See *SZ* 36: 342–343, and Moriyama 1965: 141, translated in Goepper 1993: 52.

15. See *Usuzōshi, T.* 79, 2535: 251b. The obstacle of afflictions is the delusion of discrimination born at the same time as the individual (*kushō* 倶生).

16. See *Keiran shūyōshū, T.* 76, 2410: 616c. A similar symbolism is reflected in popular rituals. For instance, in the New Year exorcism at Tennenji 天然寺 on the Kunisaki 国東 peninsula (Kyūshū), two apotropaic demons—the red demon who eliminates calamities (*saibarai oni* 災払い鬼) and the black "wild demon" (*ara oni* 荒鬼), identified with Aizen and Fudō, respectively—expel ordinary demons by running nine times around the temple's gallery. A similar exorcism takes place at Rozanji, on the eastern side of the imperial palace in Kyoto. On New Year rituals, see Caillet 1981b: 107–109.

17. See Goepper 1993: 1233.

18. The same is true of their attributes: Aizen's bow and arrows become Fudō's sword and noose, and conversely. See Abe Yasurō 1983: 107–110. I am indebted to Elizabeth Tinsley for drawing my attention to that text.

19. Abe Yasurō 1983: 106–107. The two guarding lions are differentiated in name and gender because one is actually the tamer of the other. The text also mentions that both Aizen and Fudō are standing and comments that a standing Aizen has never been seen before (p. 107). Indeed, representations of Aizen standing are practically unheard of; the only one I know is the Aizen statue in the Fudō Hall of Meguro (Tokyo) (see above, fig. 4.7).

20. See *Busshari to hōju*: 166, bottom. The snake seems to derive from Fudō's noose, and gives its name to the Hija 避蛇 (snake exorcism) ritual.

21. See Chap. 5 below, and Fig. 5.13; in this representation, however, the two faces are red.

22. See Mizuhara 1931: 172–215; and Strickmann 1996: 286–289.

23. See *Bikisho,* in *ST,* Ronsetsu-hen 2, Shingon shintō 2: 506.

24. See for instance *Reikiki kuketsu,* in *Miwa-ryū shintō-hen,* 646; and *Byakuhō kushō,* quoted in Goepper 1993: 52.

25. Strickmann 1996: 287.

26. The five stages of gestation were interpreted according to the pentadic system of esoteric Buddhism, and the two acolytes are therefore described here as "wheel-commanding bodies" (*kyōryōrinshin* 教令輪身) of the buddhas Jewel Pennant (Skt. Ratnaketu, J. Hōdō 宝憧) and Opening Flower King (Skt. Saṃkusumitarāja, J. Kaifukeō 開敷華王), two of the five buddhas of the Womb mandala who correspond to the eastern and southern directions and to the gates of the initial thought of awakening (*hosshin-mon*) and of practice (*shugyō-mon*). More specifically, Eki Dōji's red color, said to symbolize love subduing (*keiai*), is reminiscent of Aizen. See Strickmann 1996: 229.

27. See Matisoff 1978: 268–271, and Chap. 3 above.

28. Cornelius Ouwehand, borrowing from Matsudaira Narimitsu 松平齊光 (*Matsuri: honshitsu to shosō,* 1946), sees the principle of double ambivalence at work when two elements of a deity (for instance the *aramitama* and the *nigimitama*), "independently developing and manifesting themselves in separate deities, appear to be once more ambivalent" (1964: 113).

29. The term *dōso-dōgyōjin* apparently refers to a specific notion of the crossroads deities (Dōsojin 道祖神) as "deities that accompany travelers." See Akiyama 1943: 38–62; and *Kokka* 594, 1940: 140–143.

30. See Duquenne 2001: 368–369; and Dolce 2002: 324–326.

31. Gōzanze (Skt. Trailokyavijaya 'Conqueror of the Three Worlds') is a Buddhist transformation of Śiva Tripurāntaka, the "exterminator of the three cities" (in which the demons of pride, anger, and lust had entrenched themselves). He is considered superior to Śiva (Maheśvara), whom he subdues in a famous mythical episode. On this question, see Iyanaga 1981–1985. In a variant of that myth, it is Acala (Fudō) who subdues the Hindu god and his consort.

32. As Lucia Dolce points out, in his *Letter on the Kings of our Divine Land* (*Shinkokuō gosho* 神国王御書), Nichiren describes two failed attempts made by the court to "subdue the Kantō [warriors]." The first occurred in 1185, when Emperor Antoku (who was still a child) allegedly sponsored the performance of rituals centered on Fudō and on the Sonshō Dhāraṇī 尊勝陀羅尼 on Mount Hiei in order to defeat Minamoto no Yoritomo. It was a five-altar ritual, led by the chief abbot Myōun 明雲 (1115–1183) and three thousand monks of Enryakuji. The second ritual took place during the Jōkyū disturbance (1221): a fifteen-altar ritual and a Nyohō Aizen ritual were performed at the imperial palace in the fifth month. The fifteen-altar ritual took as its *honzon* deities such as Ichiji Kinrin, the four deva kings, Fudō, Daiitoku, Tenpōrin 転法輪, Nyoirin, Aizen, Butsugen, Rokuji Myōō 六字明王, Kongō Dōji 金剛童子, Sonjōō (Myōken), and Daigensui Myōō 大元帥明王. Nichiren claimed that these rituals failed and actually caused the exile of the emperor and the coming of warrior armies to Kyoto. Yet contemporary diaries and records show no mention of such rituals. See Dolce 2002: 329–331. Another example often mentioned by Nichiren is the Fudō ritual performed by the Tendai priest Sōō (831–918) to exorcize Empress Somedono. On this question, see Faure 1998a: 167–168.

33. See Dolce 2002: 316–335.

34. *Nichinyo gozen gohenji*: 1375, quoted in Dolce 2002: 318.

35. Dolce 2002: 322–327. On this text, see also Takamori 2001: 98–102.

36. Dolce 2002: 322–323.

37. Dolce 2002: 325. On Fudō and Daijizaiten, see Chap. 3 above.

38. See *ZTZ* 3: 403a; and Dolce 2002: 326.

39. Dolce 2002: 334. See also *Jindaikan hiketsu* in *ZST,* Ronsetsu-hen, Shūgō shintō: 217–231. The *Fudō Aizen kankenki*'s cosmological symbolism has recently given rise to nationalist ramblings on the part of Honmon 本門 (Nichiren) Buddhism. The official website of the sect quotes a talk allegedly given by Einstein at Tōhoku University in 1922, in which he declared that a

messianic ruler of Japan will emerge to save the world. The talk ends with these words: "World culture began in Asia and must return to Asia, that is, to Asia's peak, Japan. We are grateful to God for this. Heaven created such a noble country, Japan, for us." Q.E.D.

40. See Fujimaki 2003: 113a.

41. The catalogue *Busshari to hōju* contains many representations of Fudō and Aizen as keepers of reliquaries, with Nyoirin Kannon or another jewel deity at the center. See for instance figs. 76–79, 80, 113, 121, and 128 in Nara kokuritsu hakubutsukan 2001. See also Manabe 2000–2001, 1: 280–293.

42. Among the examples found in *Busshari to hōju,* see in particular figs. 66, 85, 87, 113, and 121–123.

43. See Nara kokuritsu hakubutsukan 2001: 93, fig. 66. Mimurotoji was an important monastery of the Jimon 寺門 (Miidera) branch of Tendai.

44. This three-headed, six-armed deity holds the sun and the moon in two of its hands, a monk's staff (*shakujō*) and a jewel in two others. It looks like the goddess Marishiten, but the five-wheel stūpa below is the usual symbol of Butsugen. On *cintāmaṇi* and female figures, see Manabe 2000–2001, 1: 416–431. In Shukaku's *Tsuiki* 追記, the pair formed by Fudō and Aizen is said to represent Kujaku Myōō 孔雀明王. In other words, Kujaku Myōō (like Nyoirin Kannon) symbolizes the nonduality of Fudō and Aizen. "Kujaku" designates Fudō, "Myōō" designates Aizen. See *Tsuiki, T.* 78, 2494: 618c.

45. On that deity, see Harper 1985; and Matsumoto Eiichi 1956.

46. Trenson 2013: 121–122.

47. See in particular fig. 6 on Trenson 2013: 120, representing a five-dragon mandala dated to the late twelfth or early thirteenth century, with Aizen at the center. Originally published in Asano 1967: 120, fig. 125.

48. Murayama Shūichi suggests that the three figures may be shooting at the so-called three foxes (only one of which is actually represented as a fox). See Murayama 1990; see also Uchida Keiichi 2012b: 244. This image may be linked to that of Rokuji Myōō, who is also associated with the three foxes.

49. In one representation, at least, relics appear mounted on a lion. See *Busshari to hōju*: 114, figs. 90 and 91. It has been suggested that in that instance the relics symbolize Monju. However, the lion here is more probably related to Aizen. See the discussion in *Kōyō shūi* 紅葉拾遺, a Tōnomine document, in *ST,* Jinja-hen 5, Yamato no kuni: 244.

50. See Nedachi 1997, fig. 15. In a variant from Kōsanji 耕三寺 (Hiroshima prefecture), the lion and elephant are shown running in a fashion that is strongly reminiscent of the foxes in the Dakiniten mandala. The two Dainichi above are now symbolized by their respective seed-letters, *a* and *vaṃ,* while jewels are scattered around the two-headed Aizen. See Nedachi 1997, figs. 110–113. On this question, see also Iyanaga 2002a: 597; and Strickmann 1996: 282–285. On Dakiniten mandalas, see the companion volume, *Protectors and Predators.* In one source at least, the foxes are said to be those of Dakiniten, at which Aizen is aiming his arrows. See *Ryūkyōshō*, in Shōmyōji shōgyō, box 73, 13, quoted in Uchida Keiichi 2012b: 251.

51. See Nara kokuritsu hakubutsukan 2000, fig. 71; and Kanagawa kenritsu Kanazawa bunko 2011, fig. 13.

52. See Abe Yasurō 1999b 359; see also Abe Yasurō 1983. The birds are described as "emissaries" of the deity, like the crows of Kumano. On birds as emissaries of Amaterasu, and the ties between Kōya and Ise, see *Henmyōin daishi myōjin gotakusen ki*. The same idea is found in Tsūkai's record of his pilgrimage to Ise (*Daijingū sankei ki* 大神宮参詣記), where we are told that two birds from the Oku-no-in 奥の院 on Mount Kōya came to perch on the torii of Ise Shrine, and that Kūkai spread esoteric Buddhism in Japan as an emissary of the *myōjin*. See Abe Yasurō 1999b: 360. In the *Nichigyō shidai* 日行次第 (Jingū bunko, colophon dated 1310), the form of Aizen's seed-letter *hūṃ* is used to explain why the messengers of Ise are crows (designated by a character said to derive from *hūṃ*), and that the gods all transform into snakes. As we have seen in the previous chapter, an oral tradition known as Peasant Aizen states that the form of Aizen's seed-letter is that of a snake. The *Sankaku kashiwa denki* 三角柏伝記 discusses the relation between Kūkai and the two birds of Ise, and the golden bird that protects Mount Kōya. See *Ryōbu shintō shū*: 367.

53. See *Mantokuji-bon,* in *Chūsei sentoku chosakushū*: 623.

54. These texts, probably all written by Monkan just before or during the Kenmu 建武 Restoration (1333–1336), include the *Great Matter of* [Kūkai's] *Testament* (*Goyuigō daiji* 御遺告大事), the *Oral Teachings on the Origins of the Mysteries* (*Himitsu gentei kuketsu* 秘密源底口決, 1327–1334) in *Chūsei sentoku chosakushū*: 485–498; the *Secret Ritual Combining the Three Worthies* (*Sanzon gōgyō hi shidai* 三尊合行秘次第) in *Chūsei sentoku chosakushū*: 351–400; the *Treatise on the Ultimate Mystery* (*Saigoku himitsu shō,* 1337), in Abe Yasurō 2010a: 133–138 (a fragmentary variant of which, from Mantokuji, therefore known as the *Mantokuji-bon* 万徳寺本 or *Itsudai kuketsu* 逸題口訣, was edited in *Chūsei sentoku chosakushū*; see n. 53 above); the *Secret Teachings on Combining the Three Worthies* (*Sanzon gōgyō hiketsu* 三尊合行秘訣, 1349), Ōsu bunko, no. 60.6, edited in Rappo 2010b: 189–192. Abe Yasurō recently discovered three texts entitled *Ritual of the Testament* (*Yuigō-hō* 遺告法), and two mandalas representing the whole ritual, preserved at Shinnō-in and Ryūkoku-in (2013: 247–248). I am indebted to Gaétan Rappo for drawing my attention to these documents.

For more details, see Abe Yasurō 1989, 2006c, and 2013: 242–253; Itō Satoshi 1995; Manabe 2000–2001; Fujimaki 2002c, 2003, 2004, and 2005; Makino and Fujimaki 2002; Dolce 2006–2007, 2008, and 2010; and Rappo 2010b and 2014: 195–320.

55. This passage is found in *Goyuigō, T.* 77, 2431: 412a–414a. For a diagram of the ritual area, see *Miwa shintō dōjō shitaku shiki,* in *ST,* Ronsetsu-hen 2, Shingon shintō 2: 464.

56. See Naitō 2010: 115–116.

57. Until recently, Dōjun was believed to be the author of the *Goyuigō daiji* (a.k.a. *Tōchō daiji* 東長大事, "Great Matter of the Tōji Abbot"), but this text is now considered to be the work of Monkan. Introduced very early on by Mizuhara Gyōhei (1925: 12–43, and figs. 16–22), it has only recently become the object of scholarly discussion, owing to its publication in the Nara National Museum catalogue *Busshari to hōju* (2001). It is known by several

recensions: the one from Jigenji in Gunma prefecture, published by the Nara National Museum, is incomplete; another from the Yamagishi Library of Jissen joshi daigaku (published in Makino and Fujimaki 2002: 1–38); and a third one from Ninnaji (yet unpublished). See Abe Yasurō 2013.

58. See Abe Yasurō 2010b: 124–125.

59. It is perhaps on that occasion that the famous representation of Go-Daigo as an esoteric Buddhist master, mentioned in Chap. 4 (see n. 10), was painted. See the scroll from Shōjōkōji 清浄光寺 (Kanagawa pref.) in Nara kokuritsu hakubutsukan 2007, fig. 177. See also Rappo 2014.

60. See also the *Sanzon gōgyō hiketsu:* "Beings, in the midst of ignorance and stupidity, produce innumerable defilements, which translate as love and anger. Love takes the form of Aizen, anger that of Fudō. Buddhas, immerged in the great formless concentration, produce countless buddha-wisdoms, which translate as knowledge and wisdom. Wisdom takes the form of Fudō, compassion that of Aizen. This is why these two worthies are the source of all virtues." *Sanzon (Sam suraṃ) higyō kuketsu,* 2a–b, cited in Dolce 2008: 67.

Another related image is a scroll preserved at Shinnō-in, the Daishi shinzō mandara, in which Kūkai is shown seated on a high chair, flanked by his two standing disciples, Jitsue on the left and Shinga on the right. Below Jitsue is Aizen, below Shinga, Fudō; above Jitsue is Hija-son 避蛇尊, above Shinga, Byakuja-son 白蛇尊. Above Kūkai is Ōsa[shihyō]-son (Ōja-son 殃蛇), and at the top of the scroll is a jewel flanked by two dragons, representing the *bodhi*-mind. See Mizuhara 1925: 21–24 and fig. 15.

61. See Fujimaki 2003: 113b. The *Jindaikan hiketsu* mentions that Kūkai added a hand-sized Aizen to the jewel and, in what sounds like an anachronistic slip, states that he gave these to retired emperor Shirakawa, who had them buried under the altar of the Octagonal Hall of Hosshōji. See *ZST,* Ronsetsu-hen, Shūgō shintō: 281. On the identity between the Iron Tower and Amaterasu's Heavenly Cave (Ama no Iwato), see Fujimaki 2002a : 131. On Shōken's role and the potential influence of Liao Buddhism on medieval Japanese relic worship, see Kamikawa 2008a; and Kim Youn-mi 2010.

62. This image and the next two are from a work preserved in the Ninnaji archives. An almost similar document from Shinnō-in was published a long time ago by Mizuhara Gyōhei. See Mizuhara 1925, figs. 19, 20, and 22; and pp. 33–43. The images in the *Tōchō daiji* from Jigenji (Gunma prefecture) are more elegant but basically similar. The accompanying text can be found in Naitō 2010: 116–118. It describes two different triads, one by Shōken, the other by Shōkaku (1057–1129), the founder of the Sanbōin-ryū. Shōkaku is said to have conceived a portable shrine, with a five-wheel stūpa flanked by Aizen and Fudō. On the ceiling above the stūpa is a mandala of Butsugen (not Nyoirin), symbolizing nonduality, while the Womb and Vajra Realm mandalas are painted above Fudō and Aizen, respectively.

63. Makino and Fujimaki 2002: 25–26.

64. Makino and Fujimaki 2002: 32–33.

65. See fig. 68 in *Busshari to hōju* (Nara kokuritsu hakubutsukan 2001: 95). See also Manabe 2000–2001, 1: 103–104; and Mizuhara 1981, 2: 40–41.

It is of course a moot point whether the tripartite jewel symbolizes the divine triad or the other way around. Nyoirin is also linked with the bodhisattva Kokūzō: for example, in the Kanazawa bunko drawing representing a *gumonji* ritual altar, whose *honzon* (Kokūzō) is also a five-wheel stūpa identified with the three-inch Kūkai (and by extension Fudō). See Manabe 2000–2001: 116.

66. See Watanabe 1999: 121ab.

67. Watanabe 1999: 123–124. There seems to be a discrepancy here: Nyoirin (not Aizen) at the center should correspond to the mystery of Vairocana's (that is, the practitioner's) nondual mind.

68. Watanabe 1999: 125–127. Several portable shrines of the thirteenth century already show the same disposition. Kōzen 興然 (1121–1204), in his *Shikan,* mentions that Shūi 宗意 (1074–1148) had performed a jewel ritual centered on Nyoirin, and in the form of a Byakuja ritual (*T.* 78, 2500: 802b). See also Rappo 2014: 204.

69. This ritual is described in a number of texts, among them the *Goyuigō hiketsu,* the *Ben'ichizan himitsuki,* the *Sanzon gōgyō hiketsu,* the *Himitsu gentei kuketsu* (1327–1334), and the *Mantoku-bon* by Monkan. See Kokubungaku kenkyū shiryōkan 2006: 501–511 and 619–624. On this question, see also Fujimaki 2002a: 147–149; Abe Yasuro 2006c , 2010a; and Rappo 2010b. The Three Worthies are identified with the Amida triad (Amida, Kannon, and Seishi) and the Shaka triad (Shaka, Monju, and Fugen). The former is presented as Indian, the second as Japanese. See *Sanzon gōgyō hiketsu,* in Rappo 2010b: 190c.

70. The Borromean rings are three intersecting circles that were used in the coat of arms of the Borromeo family, representing three islands in Lake Maggiore in northern Italy: Isola Bella, Isola Madre, and Isola Superiore. The image would fit well with the three main cultic sites of Benzaiten (three islands represented by three jewels). The symbol already appears in Buddhist art in Gandhara around the second century (*vide* Wikipedia).

71. See Abe Yasurō 1989: 152–153.

72. The reading *byakuja* seems more common in the Sanbō-in tradition. The *Ben'ichizan* claims that Kūkai asked Kenne 堅慧 to bury on Mount Murō the three-inch Fudō and the jewel that had been transmitted from the Iron Tower, and to perform the Byakuja and the Ōsa[shihyō] rites on that mountain. The same text adds that, according to a secret tradition of the Ono school, Mount Murō is a Pure Land where the nonduality of the two realms is realized, and it is there that the Byakuja ritual is performed at the Dharmatā Stūpa, on the island of the dragon palace. On this question, see Fujimaki 2002a: 139. The *Nihongi Miwa-ryū* also provides references to the Ōsa ritual.

73. Fujimaki 2002a.

74. See *Takushō* 沢抄 by Kakujō 覚成 (1126–1198), *T.* 78, 2488: 477a; and Kōzen's *Shikan, T.* 78, 2500: 802b. However, the author of the *Kita-in gyōki* 北院御記 strongly disagrees with this identification. See also *Henkushō, T.* 78, 2496: 697b, which states that the Hija-hō is a jewel rite, while the Ōsashihyō-hō is a wheel-turning rite whose *honzon* is at times Gōzanze, at others Fudō. See also the *Goyuigō hiyōshō* 御遺告秘要鈔: 108–113; *Kakugenshō, SZ* 36: 364; and *Takushō, T.* 78, 2488: 476c, which distinguishes two

levels: a superficial level, where the Hija-hō is a subjugation ritual, and a deeper level, where it is a jewel ritual.

Regarding the Ōsashihyō ritual, the *Mikkyō daijiten* gives several possible etymologies: Ōsa may be a coded reading for Aca (i.e., Acala, or Fudō), or Ōsashi for Gōzanze. An even more far-fetched explanation decomposes the name into Ō = *onzō* (hidden sex organ); *sa* (śarīra, relic); *shi* (*shitei,* disciples); and *hyō* (peace). Shihyō would thus mean "peace for the disciples"—as if Kūkai had had a premonition that his disciples would fight over this! See also Vanden Broucke 1992: 78.

75. See Ruppert 2000: 150–151. On the Byakuja ritual, see also Ueda 1986, 2: 252–254.

76. In the Ono branch, *hija is* a coded term for *hisha,* an abbreviation of *abisharokya* (Skt. *abhicaraka,* subjugation). The *Anryū denju kiyō* 安流伝授紀要 argues that the pronunciation *byakuja* was specific to the Anryū 安流 lineage. This lineage claims to offer a synthesis between the various sectarian interpretations of that ritual. See *SZ* 35: 480.

77. See Rappo 2014: 225.

78. Quoted in Rappo 2014: 229. We find a similar representation in the case of the Peasant Aizen (Denpu Aizen), whose seed-letter, *hūṃ,* symbolizes the three poisons and has the shape of a snake. See "The Ophidian Aizen" section below.

79. See Van den Broucke 1992: 26. In a variant, the exorcism is directed at an evil old couple, which perhaps refers to the Hindu deities Maheśvara (Śiva) and his consort Uma. See *Goyuigō,* art. 25, *T.* 77: 414a; and Mikkyō bunka kenkyūjo 1978, 8: 92. See also *Shikan, T.* 78, 2500: 802b; and *Henkushō, T.* 78, 2496: 697b.

80. See Fujimaki 2002a: 151.

81. See Kokubungaku kenkyū shiryōkan 1999c: 272. Kenne's box, designed by the not-so-cryptic characters 竹木目 (which turn out to be the components of the word *hako* 箱, box), was said to contain the jewel that Kūkai received from the dragon king Zennyo. Eventually, the story of the transmission by Zennyo, which conflicted with that of the transmission from the Iron Tower, was abandoned. See Fujimaki 2002a.

82. This particular icon, together with the three-inch Fudō, came to play an important role in certain exorcisms of the Shingon school. For a discussion of the meaning of Aizen's *goshiryō* (five finger-widths) size, see *Keiran shūyōshū, T.* 76, 2410: 568ab; *Byakuhō shō, TZ* 10: 1049b-c; Goepper 1993; and Kanagawa kenritsu Kanazawa bunko 2011: 48.

83. See also *Miwa-ryū shintō-hen,* 6: 641.

84. *T.* 77, 2431: 413a.

85. These two rituals are the last in a series of seven mentioned in the *Goyuigō shichika hihō* 御遺告七固秘法 (*Seven Secret Rites of the* Last Testament), a Kajūji-ryū text transmitted by Shinkei 真慶 (fl. mid-Kamakura)—the others being the Tsugomori gonenju 晦御念誦, the Goshichinichi mishiho 後七日御修法, the Goya nenju 後夜念誦, the Jūhachinichi Kannon-ku 十八日観音供, and the *cintāmaṇi* ritual proper (Nyoi hōju-hō). See Fujimaki 2002a: 143. The *Goyuigō shichika hihō* argues that, while these rituals were

109. *Zuzōshō, TZ* 3: 24ab; quoted in Birnbaum 1983: 112.

110. See Naumann 1959: 207. See also Kindaichi 1933. One further link is with Batō Kannon, another protector of silkworms. On the theme of the horse and the silkworm, see Stein 1986: 61–63. Benzaiten, wearing a blue silk robe, was also worshiped as a protector of silkworms, as was one of her fifteen acolytes or children, called San'yō Dōji 蚕養童子 (Silkworm-nourishing Lad). Benzaiten's symbolic animal and manifestation, the snake, may also have contributed to this perception, since snakes feed on mice, one of the worst enemies of silkworms. See Takano 1959: 32–33.

111. See Gangōji bunkazai kenkyūjo 1999: 14. In one example (*TZ* 6: 112), Memyō Bosatsu has four arms, and he holds a scale and a twig in his upper hands while his lower hands hold the reins of his horse. See also *Mandara shū, TZ* 4: 184–185.

112. See Ōmiwa jinja shiryō henshu iinkai 1983: 289–290. In the *Reikiki*, instead of Aizen and Fudō, we find eight bodhisattvas. But the number coding (five plus three) still suggests the five-finger-high Aizen and the three-inch Fudō. Incidentally, Fudō himself was worshiped as a protector of silkworms. See Takano 1959: 33.

113. On this question, see Como 2009: 155–192; and Ōwa 1993: 325–338.

114. Kokūzō is occasionally linked with Shinra Myōjin, the protector of Miidera. See Kimura 1991; see also *Kokūzō-dō engi,* in *Yamagata-shi shiryō* 16.

115. Kokūzō was associated with Nyoirin and Amaterasu in certain variants of the jewel ritual. See for instance the *Goyuigō hiketsu* (Hikone Library, Kondō Collection).

116. *Miwa-ryū kanjō shodaiji kuketsu*: 291.

117. *ST,* Ronsetsu-hen 4, Tendai Shintō 2: 410. See also *Reikiki, shintaizu,* in *ST,* Ronsetsu-hen 1, Shingon shintō 1: 95.

118. *Tenchi reikiki,* in *ST,* Ronsetsu-hen 1, Shingon shintō 1: 29.

119. See *Miwa-ryū shintō kanjō hoshin shō*: 137.

120. Ibid. For a discussion of these hexagrams, see Dolce 2006–2007: 131–136. Other far-fetched explanations invoke Aizen's "horse penis *samādhi*" (*meonzō sanmaji* 馬陰蔵三摩地), and the notion that Aizen is identical with Nittenshi (Sūrya or Aditya, the sun deva), who is visualized on a cart drawn by eight horses. See *Yugikyō chōmonshō*: 229a. The horse penis remains hidden, and therefore the horse penis *samādhi* is also a metaphor for the *samādhi* of nonduality from which everything springs forth; in this sense it is identical with the wish-fulfilling jewel, and consequently with Amaterasu. Another link has to do with the fact that both Aizen and Amaterasu are identified with Ichiji Kinrin, who counts the horse as one of his seven treasures. Last but not least, in Chinese cosmology the horse, as one of the twelve cyclical animals, corresponds to the south, and therefore to the element fire and the sun. In Nichiren's *Fudō Aizen kankenki* and in the Mimurotoji scroll, Aizen rides a galloping horse, perhaps another dynamic symbol of the sun. As we can see, the symbolism is overdetermined, if not entirely convincing.

121. *Miwa-ryū shintō kanjō hoshin shō*: 137.

122. Although the horse is a yang symbol, the *Yijing* actually uses the mare as a yin symbol of the earth. On this point, see Dolce 2006–2007: 131–132.

123. Ōmiwa jinja shiryō henshu iinkai 1983: 292. See also *Bikisho*: 506.

124. See Dolce 2006–2007: 133–137.

125. *ST,* Ronsetsu-hen, Ise shintō 2: 506–507. See also *Miwa-ryū shintō kanjō hoshin shō*: 138. The inversion of the yin-yang symbolism is followed by a description of the five stages of gestation that form the content of the "one-night" *kanjō.*

126. *Miwa-ryū shintō kanjō hōshin shō*: 137–138.

127. In the *Reiki kanjō*, a ritual paired in the *Miwa-ryū shintō kanjō juyoshiki* with the Iwato daiji, the three Buddhist deities are said to be the "traces" (*suijaku*) of the three *kami,* and the two divine sets are symbolized in turn by the three imperial regalia: Tenshō daijin (Amaterasu)/Nyoi-rin corresponding to the mirror, Ame no Koyane/Fudō to the sword, and Takemikazuchi/Aizen to the bow and arrows (the bow here, as Rambelli suggests, being probably identified with the curved jewel or *magatama* 勾玉). See *Miwa-ryū shintō kanjō juyoshiki*: 74–78. As Rambelli puts it, these triads "are envisioned as sub-species of the most important sacred object, i.e., the combination of Buddha relics and the wish-fulfilling jewel" (2002: 288–289). The text adds that the relics *qua* jewel are the original form or *honji* of Kunitokotachi, the primordial *kami.* Note that here, it is this *kami,* rather than Amaterasu, who is equated with the primordial buddha Mahāvairocana (Dainichi). Yet the point of the ritual is to identify the mind of the initiate with Amaterasu.

128. Ōmiwa jinja shiryō henshu iinkai 1983: 307.

129. *ST,* Ronsetsu-hen 2, Shingon shintō 2: 130. See also the *Oral Instruction on the Heavenly Cave, ST,* Ronsetsu-hen 2, Shingon shintō 2: 136–137; and Ōmiwa jinja shiryō henshu iinkai 1983: 171 and 193–194.

130. See Shiga kenritsu Biwako bunkakan 1990, figs. 1–4. In fig. 1, Taga Myōjin appears as an old man riding a black horse, with his *honji* Amida and the latter's two acolytes, Kannon and Seishi 勢至. But this is a rare representation, and in the numerous talismans (*ofuda*) of Taga Shrine, the deity is usually a female figure. A missionary source quoted by Michael Cooper declares: "There are many sects among the pagans. . . . They have a god called Taga-daimyōjin to whom they pray for a long life." See Cooper 1982: 300.

131. *ST,* Ronsetsu-hen 2: Shingon shintō 2: 502. Although Fudō and Aizen do not appear here, Fudō was very important at Taga Shrine, since the monks of Fudō-in, one hall in the shrine-temple complex (*jingūji* 神宮寺) of Taga, were in fact administering the shrine. Fudō and Aizen were also worshiped—albeit separately—at Atsuta Shrine. On Godō Daijin, see Dudbridge 1996–1997.

132. See *Yugikyō kuketsu nukigaki*: 243. See also Kanagawa kenritsu Kanazawa bunko 2011, figs. 68 and 69. In the first of the two paintings from Saidaiji (Fig. 5.24), the snake is blue with a white belly; in the second (Fig. 5.25), its back is black, its belly red, and it is on a three-pronged *vajra.* See also Ogawa 2014: 347.

133. Goepper 1993: 114. The *Bikisho* mentions the existence of two snakes, green and white (assimilated to the two dragons that guard Mount Sumeru) under the Heart Pillar of Ise. See *ST,* Ronsetsu-hen 2: Shingon shintō 2: 518. On Aizen as a snake, see Yamamoto 1998a: 410–419; and Itō Satoshi 2011: 396–418.

134. Kushida 1979: 326.

135. The identity between Aizen and Amaterasu is also expressed in the *Ise kanjō* and the *Ise Daijingū mishōtai* 伊勢大神宮御御正躰 (The August Body of [the deity of] Ise Shrine)—a document from Kanazawa bunko. The *Ise kanjō* "featured Amaterasu as Aizen Myōō and as a snake carrying the wish-fulfilling gem on its head. In rituals of this kind, Amaterasu appeared both as a 'real kami' (a witch animal) and, at the same time, as the ultimate embodiment of original enlightenment: the Three Poisons themselves." See Teeuwen and Rambelli 2003b: 35.

136. See Itō Satoshi 2005: 821–840.

137. For a discussion of this text and its context, see Itō Satoshi 2005. See also Ogawa Toyoo 2003: 42–45, where the triad formed by Amaterasu, Tsukuyomi and Toyouke is equated with the three seed-syllables *a, vaṃ, hūṃ,* and with the three "placenta deities."

138. See Yamamoto 1998a: 413.

139. See the *Miwa-ryū jingi kanjō injin kuketsu,* in *ST,* Ronsetsu-hen 2: Shingon shintō 2: 458, which explains that all *kami* have a reptilian body and all are Aizen's spiritual essence.

140. Yamamoto 1998a: 418.

141. On the *kami* as snake, see *Keiran shūyōshū, T.* 76, 2410: 866a. See also Ogawa 2003: 47c; and "Shintō injin," in Abe Yasurō 2000: 78b.

142. See for instance the notion of the Three Devas. The semiotic system of the two mandalas is omnipresent. See the interpretation of Yoshino and Kumano as the two mandalas, with Ōmine at the center representing the fusion or non-duality of both.

143. Dumézil 1988: 178.

144. Ibid.

145. Ibid.

146. See Lévi-Strauss 1973b: 196.

147. *T.* 76, 2410: 864a.

148. On the oral traditions of the Sanbōin-ryū and the *Sanzon gōgyō* ritual, see Fujimaki 2002a: 137–159.

149. See *Goyuigō hiketsu,* Hikone-jō Archives, Kondō Collection.

150. See *Bizeibetsu,* in *ZTZ,* Mikkyō 3, Kyōten chūshakurui 2: 231b–232a. This dream has been copiously commented upon in recent scholarship. See for example Akamatsu 1957: 318–322; Tanaka Takako 1993: 75–93; Faure 1998a: 128–129; and Grapard 2002–2003: 134–143.

151. Yamamoto 1993a: 309.

152. *T.* 76, 2410: 783.

153. Dolce 2006–2007: 122. See also Rappo 2014.

154. See Serres 1991.

155. See the "Finale" in Lévi-Strauss 1981.

CHAPTER 6: THE HIDDEN JEWEL

1. On this question, see Ruppert 2000.

2. See Faure 2004; and Strong 2004. Tradition has it that some relics (hair and nails) were worshiped even while the Buddha was still alive.

3. See Faure 2002.

4. See Naitō 2001a. The same structure is found in the Shijōkō-in on Mount Hiei, where the Blazing Light Ritual (Shijōkō-hō), a Tendai counterpart of the Shingon Mishiho, was performed. See also Nara kokuritsu hakubutsukan 2001, figs. 87, 88, and 106.

5. On the Mishiho and Kūkai, see Naitō 2010: 20–25; on the identity between the Buddha's relics and the jewel in that ritual, see pp. 40–41.

6. In various reliquaries, the Buddha's relics were placed between the two mandalas painted on their doors, whose transcendental unity they symbolize. See Nara kokuritsu hakubutsukan 2001, figs. 87 and 88.

7. See *T.* 25: 134a; and Lamotte 1949–1976, 2: 600. For a description of the *cintāmaṇi* and other jewels, see Lamotte, op. cit., 1: 499.

8. See for instance *Kakuzenshō, DNBZ* 51: 105.

9. The association between relics and the five-wheel stūpa may also derive from the term *dhātu* (J. *dato*), meaning both "relic" or "element" and (Dharma)dhātu, the latter itself being symbolized by the five elements and seed-syllables.

10. See Naitō 2001a: 178–180.

11. See Naitō 2001a.

12. See Kamikawa 2004, 2006, 2007, and 2008a; and Kim Youn-mi 2010.

13. On relic theft in medieval Japanese Buddhism, see Faure 2014.

14. See Ruppert 2000.

15. While these aspects are most notable in Chinese cases of self-immolation or self-mutilation in front of the Buddha's relics, they are not entirely absent in Japan. On the Chinese cases, see Faure 1991, Kieschnick 1997, and Benn 2007.

16. Some texts interpret this expression as meaning "rituals in accordance with the rules"—as if all rituals were not supposed to be so. Or perhaps what is meant here are *special* rules for the preparation of the ritual. See *Henkushō* 遍口鈔, *T.* 78, 2496: 693b; and Goepper 1993: 144–151. In the present context, *nyohō* is in fact a coded term and an abbreviation for "nyoi hōju," and the expression simply qualifies rituals centered on the *cintāmaṇi* jewel. See *Sanbōin-ryū dōsen sōjō kuketsu* 三宝院流洞泉相承口決, *SZ* 34: 158a, 159b. The *Keiran shūyōshū* specifies that the term is applied to the Butsugen, Sonjō, Hokke, and Hokuto rituals; *T.* 76, 2410: 784c. In the Edo period, however, the term *nyohō* as applied to the monastic robe (*nyohō kesa*) does indeed mean a return to a "correct" method of fabricating the robes, more in accordance with the intrinsically nonviolent Dharma. See Faure 1995. On the Nyohō sonshō ritual, see Kim Youn-mi 2010. In one commentary, *nyohō* means to perform by making the *honzon* enter the jewel *samādhi.*

17. The Nyohō sonshō ritual was initially centered on the Sonshō Dhāraṇī 尊勝陀羅尼. On the evolution of that ritual from the Liao kingdom in northern China to Heian and Kamakura Japan, see Kim Youn-mi 2010.

18. On the cult of Butsugen by the Tendai abbot Jien, see Misaki 1994: 545–563. On relic worship in Tendai (in particular at Chūsonji in Hiraizumi), see Naitō 2010: 289–314.

19. *T.* 76, 2410: 554b. On the horse penis *samādhi* as pure potentiality, identical with the wish-fulfilling jewel, see *Hachiman Daibosatsu,* in *Chūsei Nihongi shū,* 492b–493a. In the *Zassho* 雑書 (a text in the Kanazawa bunko archives, 43.4; quoted in Trenson 2013: 123), Aizen and Butsugen are said to be one and the same.

20. It may be because of this ritual's highly secretive character that Butsugen's image remained more abstract than that of Nyoirin. While it may not have exercised the seductive power of Nyoirin's image, it was not completely lacking in emotional affect, however, judging from the famous story in which the Kegon priest Myōe 明恵 (1173–1232) cuts off his ear in front of an image of Butsugen.

21. *T.* 76, 2410: 555b–556a. If Butsugen's seed-letter *khaṃ* and Ichiji Kinrin's seed-letter *bhrūṃ* express the yin-yang polarity, the former also represents the nonduality of the two Shingon mandalas; see *T.* 76, 2410: 644a. And yet, paradoxically, it is Kinrin who represents the absolute aspect of reality, and Butsugen its relative aspect; see *T.* 76, 2410: 722c. Lucia Dolce (2006a) argues that the Hokke mandala corresponds to the Susiddhi mandala.

22. *T.* 76, 2410: 621c. The jewel is also associated with Aizen's famous horse penis *samādhi,* another expression of nonduality. Both images evoke hiddenness, and therefore pure potentiality and fertility. On this *samādhi,* see Chap. 4 above.

23. It also contained the five buddhas symbolizing the five knowledges (or the five eyes of the Buddha, subsumed by the fifth, named, precisely, Buddha's Eye or Butsugen). See *Keiran shūyōshū, T.* 76, 2410: 858b.

24. *Keiran shūyōshū, T.* 76, 2410: 550b, 622a, and 865a. This theory reflects Chinese conceptions regarding the two types of 'soul' that constitute the individual, the *hun* and the *po*—the former having a heavenly nature, the latter an earthly nature.

25. *T.* 76, 2410: 622a. This stūpa is also said to represent the Iron Tower in southern India, where Kūkai's jewel originated. As an emblem of nonduality, it represents the supreme reality. At the same time, its three degrees symbolize the fundamental destiny of the emperor (top), of the members of the state apparatus (middle), and of the common people (bottom), respectively. Kōshū emphasizes that the common people were not forgotten in this distribution of benefits. *T.* 76, 2410: 622a.

26. *T.* 76, 2410: 556b. See also *Kakugenshō, SZ* 36: 361b. On relics and Ichiji Kinrin, see Naitō 2010: 82–85.

27. After his *parinirvāṇa,* the Buddha is also said to have remained in this world in three forms: physical (the relics proper), verbal (the canonical doctrine), and mental (mantras). See *T.* 76, 2410: 557a.

28. Ibid. The ternary model applies quite naturally to the three imperial regalia: the "divine seal"—sometimes described as a curved jewel (*magatama*), at other times as a map of Japan—was said to represent the form of

the Buddha; the precious sword, his symbolic or conventional (*samaya*) form; and the divine mirror, his seed-letter. Likewise, Amaterasu is said to have three ranks or aspects, corresponding to the three Buddha bodies and specific deities: at the higher level, she is identical with the dharma body; at the intermediary level, with the reward or enjoyment body and with the demiurgic god Bonten (Skt. Brahmā); and at the lower level, with the transformation or correspondence body and with the Ise goddess (namely, Amaterasu herself). See *T.* 76, 2410: 557b.

29. On this legend, see Strong 1983. On rain rituals, see Ruppert 2002b; and Trenson 2002–2003.

30. See *Kakuzenshō, DNBZ* 46: 383–388; and Groner 2001: 132.

31. Monks from Nara, such as Chōgen 重源 of Tōdaiji and Eison 睿尊 of Saidaiji, also contributed to this process.

32. See Naitō 2001a.

33. See Naitō 2010.

34. The passage in question might have been quoted from another, apocryphal text with the same title, no longer extant. On this point, see Misaki 1992: 279–280; and Imahori 1990: 88–102.

35. See *Keiran shūyōshū, T.* 76, 2410: 556b. See also Misaki 1988: 576–583; Misaki 1992: 278–287; and Takahashi Yūsuke 2005. To give just one example, a miniature five-wheel stūpa-*cum*-reliquary (*gorintō* 五輪塔) in quartz and a copy of the *Hikekyō* were placed in the head of the Shaka statue at Saidaiji, the headquarters of the Shingon-Ritsu school. The upper part of the torso also contained various scriptures, written vows (*ganmon*), and a roster of no fewer than 6,670 names. Groner 2001: 125.

36. For other representations of the Kasuga mandala flanked by Aizen and Fudō, see figs. 121 (Tokyo National Museum), 122 (private collection), and 123 (Kōfukuji) in the catalogue *Busshari to hōju* (Nara kokuritsu hakubutsukan 2001). On the identity between the relics and Japanese deities, most notably Amaterasu, see Takahashi Yūsuke 2005. In the Miwa tradition, the pair of *kami* formed by Takemikazuchi and Ame no Koyane flanking Amaterasu—whom they have just tricked out of the Heavenly Rock Cave—is also said to be the manifestations of Aizen and Fudō flanking Nyoirin. See Chap. 5 above.

37. See Nara kokuritsu hakubutsukan 2001, figs. 118, 119, and 125.

38. Another example is a portable shrine from Shōjūraigōji 聖衆来迎寺 in Ōtsu (Shiga prefecture) (ibid., fig. 128) representing a Sannō mandala with eight buddhas and bodhisattvas on an eight-petaled lotus, flanked by Fudō and Bishamonten (at the front), Aizen and Daiitoku (at the back), and the four Tendai patriarchs (Zhiyi 智顗, Saichō 最澄, Ennin 円仁, and Ryōgen 良源) on the four doors. The total number of deities represented is twenty-one, symbolizing the twenty-one shrines of Hie Shrine.

39. This is also the shape of the fifth element in the model of the five-wheel stūpa, corresponding to space. However, the relics are usually placed in the second element, the sphere of water—perhaps owing to their affinities with the *nāgas* (but also because of the symbolism of the circular shape of the jewel).

40. Dumézil's trifunctional hypothesis postulated that ancient Indo-European ideology was reflected in three main social categories: priests, warriors, and commoners. See Dumézil 1968.

41. Quoted in Murayama 1987b: 188.

42. Jewels were also said to appear at the spot where lightning struck, and were thus related to the dragon as a god of rain and thunder.

43. See *Goyuigō, T.* 77, 2431; and Mizuhara 1925: 24–31, and figs. 16–19.

44. See for instance the *Kinpusen engi yuraiki,* in Gorai 2000, 2: 664b.

45. Note the ambiguity of the expression usually used to designate that jewel, *nōsa hōju* 能作宝珠, where *nōsa* means both "that which one can produce"—therefore artificial—and "that which can produce" (as distinct from the passive form *shosa,* "that which is produced," i.e., the artificial jewel). This ambiguity is probably due to semantic drift through which *nōsa* came to be interpreted as "generable" or "producible" and to designate the generated, artificial jewel. The distinction between "generative" (*nōsa*) and "generated" (*shosa*) is reminiscent of that between "uncreated" or "unconditioned" (*musa* 無作 'absolute') and "created" or "conditioned" (*usa* 有作 'relative'). It brings to mind the Western scholastic distinction between *natura naturans* and *natura naturata,* or, in Derrida's terms, the difference between *differance* (*sic*—the power of pure differentiation) and *differences.* On the *nōsa* jewel, see Naitō 2010: 69–73.

46. See Scheid and Teeuwen 2006; Faure 1999 and 2006.

47. See *Goyuigō*: 412b; and Ruppert 2000: 149–150.

48. I use the term "emperor" in this case precisely because possession of the jewel legitimated imperial ideology.

49. See "Hōju no koto" (About the Jewel) in *Hishō mondō, T.* 79, 2536: 518; see also Ruppert 2002a: 12.

50. *T.* 76, 2410: 545b. The polarity was also expressed in terms of heaven and earth. The *Keiran shūyōshū* links the jewel with the ox king, and contrasts the two notions of ox king and deer king in terms applicable to two jewels associated with earth and space. On the various conceptions of the jewel found in the three branches of the Ono school, see Naitō 2010: 79–82.

51. See Faure 1999; and Ruppert 2000: 157–169. Another theory claims that it was buried under the altar of the Octagonal Hall of Hosshōji, together with a statuette of Aizen Myōō.

52. On the Nyohō Sonshō rite for state protection, see Kim Youn-mi 2010.

53. The Great Buddha had been destroyed by the fire that ravaged Tōdaiji in 1180 during the fight between the Taira and the Minamoto. On Chōgen and relic worship, see Naitō 2010: 230–250.

54. See for instance the *Hishō kuketsu* by Kyōshun: "The late Shōken made a jewel on request of Daibutsu Shōnin (Chōgen), and this jewel was placed between the eyebrows of the Great Buddha of Tōdaiji." Quoted in Itō Satoshi 2002a: 16.

55. See the *Daisōjō onbō onmonogatari ki* 大僧正御房御物語記, a compilation of oral teachings of Jōken 成賢 (1024–1100) by his disciple Jōhen 静

遍 (1166–1224), quoted in Itō Satoshi 2002a: 20–21. The *Keiran shūyōshū* mentions an oral tradition from the Hieizan priest Gyōnin 行忍 about the importance of the *ūrṇā* and *uṣṇīṣa* for the relics: the white spot between the eyebrows and the red flesh protuberance on the top of the Buddha's head are secret affairs of the relic ritual. Why? Because the former emits a white light and the latter is red, which symbolizes the Kongōkai and Taizōkai, the fact that the practitioner's nondual body is the secret essence of the relics (*T.* 76, 2410: 544c).

56. Another view, represented by monks such as Seigen (1162–1231) and Raiyu (1226–1304), is that the jewel transmitted by Hanjun had been deposited at Shōkōmyō-in whereas Kūkai's jewel, initially transmitted at Tōji, ended up at Hosshōji. For the Daigoji tradition, the jewel was also the divine body of the dragon god, as well as the *samaya* form of the bodhisattvas Nyoirin and Jundei. In his *Hishō mondō,* Raiyu summarizes as follows the various sectarian positions: The Daigoji branch argues that there is one jewel on Mount Murō and another at Tōji. The Kajūji branch claims that there is no jewel on Mount Murō, only a text. The Sanbō-in branch added Aizen and Fudō to the jewel to constitute the Joint Ritual of the Three Worthies, arguing that this ritual was initially performed on Mount Murō.

57. On this question, see Faure 1999; Ruppert 2000; and Abe Yasurō 1989: 126–127.

58. According to Kamikawa Michio, article 24 of the *Testament*—if not the whole section—may have been added by Hanjun himself (2008a: 281). See also Kim Youn-mi 2010.

59. See Ruppert 2000: 151–152, and Kim Youn-mi 2010. The number of relics (thirty-two) is the same as that of the marks on the body of the Buddha, which suggests the equivalence between the jewel and the Buddha. Another document, an apocryphal scripture entitled *Ruyi baozhu zhuanlun bimi xianshen chengfo jinlun zhuwang jing* 如意宝珠転輪秘密現身成仏金輪呪王経 (*T.* 19, 961) describes the method for manufacturing a jewel in very similar fashion, through the use of thirty-two relics of the Buddha and ten other precious substances. See Ruppert 2000: 131.

60. The jewel used by Shōken was eventually returned to the palace, in 1192, in a lacquered box three inches in depth (a size that calls to mind that of Fudō's statuette, mentioned earlier), which was itself placed in a chest of gilt bronze, together with a small stūpa, stones, drugs, and scented wood. Another significant detail is that the chest was wrapped in a red *kesa.* See also the case of the *cintāmaṇi* of a Daigoji priest, whose lotus-shaped reliquary was broken by a disciple after the master's death, revealing a clay *cintāmaṇi* containing relics. See *Keiran shūyōshū, T.* 76, 2410: 545c.

61. See *T.* 76, 2410: 545c; and Ruppert 2002a: 23. An actual *nōsa hōju* can be seen in *Busshari to hōju* (Nara kokuritsu hakubutsukan 2001: 129).

62. See *Gyokuyō,* s.v. Kenkyū 3 (1192)/4/8.

63. See *Reihō mokuroku,* quoted in Kadoya 1997:101. While Shōken defends the authenticity of Hanjun's jewel, Kanezane argues that it is not the same as the one that Hanjun gave to retired emperor Toba (the Shōkōmyō-in jewel). According to him, Hanjun transmitted two jewels: Kūkai's jewel,

which retired emperor Shirakawa received and enshrined in the Aizen statue of Hosshōji; and another, which he probably manufactured himself, and which was deposited at Shōkōmyō-in. See Ruppert 2000: 164–166.

64. See *Yoshibe hikunshō* 吉部秘訓抄, quoted in Abe Yasurō 1989: 130. See also Itō Satoshi 2002a .

65. Ruppert 2000: 162.

66. See "Hōju no koto," in *Dainihon shiryō* 大日本資料, sv. Kenkyū 3 (1292)/4/8; and *Hishō mondō*: 518c–519a.

67. Ruppert 2000: 162–163.

68. Shōken was asked to return the jewel to the court in 1192. On this occasion, the relic box was opened in his presence, and he recorded its appearance in his *Hōju ki* 宝珠記: several grains of relics placed in golden and silver bottles sealed by a five-colored thread, and placed into a wooden box sealed in the same fashion. This record is complemented by Kanezane's account in his *Gyokuyō* (s.v. Kenkyū 3 (1192)/4/8), which states that the jewel was eventually returned to the Shōkōmyō-in by Emperor Toba.

69. See Matsumoto Ikuyo 2004.

70. On this portrait, see Uchida 2010.

71. See *Himitsu gentei kuketsu,* in Watanabe 1999; and Abe Yasurō 1989: 152. In this ritual, Monkan identifies the "practitioner" (i.e., the ruler, Go-Daigo) with powerful symbols such as Shōtoku Taishi, Kūkai, and Nyoi-rin Kannon. Even after Go-Daigo's death, the relics were put to good use during the ensuing succession quarrel between the two courts. Thus, in 1371, thirty-two grains (the amount needed to make a jewel) were brought to the southern court to be used in a ritual of subjugation aimed at the bakufu. See *Tōji busshari kankei ki* 東寺仏舎利勘計記, quoted in Abe Yasurō 1989: 150.

72. Ben'ichizan 宀一山 (var. Men'ichizan, U'ichizan), a coded term for Mount Murō, is formed by taking the upper and lower stroke of the first and second Chinese characters of that toponym, respectively. See *Sanbōin-ryū Dōsen sōjō kuketsu, SZ* 34: 187.

73. The rituals are reminiscent of the Latter Seven Day ritual of Tōji and the Kannon offerings in the Futama room of the imperial palace. These three sections of the *Testament* were abundantly commented upon in the Sanbōin-ryū and other Shingon branches, and I discuss Monkan's commentary in the *Goyuigō daiji* below. See also Makino and Fujimaki 2002.

74. On Kenne, see Kadoya 1997.

75. See Ruppert 2000: 155; and Fowler 2005: 23. This passage is quoted in many sources: see for instance Kanezane's *Gyokuyō,* 1966: 806. See also *Tōyōki* (twelfth century), *ZGR* 26, 2: 413–414; and *Kōya kōhaiki, DNBZ* 120, quoted in Fowler 2005.

76. See *Ben'ichi hiki* and *Ainōshō* (1445), quoted in Fowler 2005: 23, 58. See also *Washū Murōzan kaizan Kenne daitoku den* 和州室生山開山堅慧大徳伝 (Kenne's "biography"), in *Kōbō Daishi zenshū,* vol. 10; and Ruppert 2000: 150, 155–156.

77. The *Daitōkoku Nihonkoku fuhō kechimyaku zu ki* 大唐国日本国付法血脈図記 gives this filiation as Saichō—Gishin (781–831)—Enshu—Kenne. See *Chishō daishi zenshū* 2, quoted in Kadoya 1997: 100b. On this

question, see also Fowler 2005: 54–58. On Mount Murō's shift to Mikkyō cosmology, see Fowler 2005: 59–61.

78. See for instance the *Ben'ichizan Yamashinadera kankei hōkyō* 山階寺寛継法橋, cited in Kadoya 1997: 99–100. This document from Kanazawa bunko quotes Huiguo's alleged inscription.

79. *Jindaikan hiketsu,* in ZST, Ronsetsu-hen, Shūgō shintō: 281.

80. On the *Ben'ichizan himitsuki,* see Abe Yasurō 1989; Tsuji 1979: 142–149; Itō Satoshi 1995; Kadoya 1997; and Fujimaki 2002a: 117–122, and 2002b.

81. See for instance *Hachiman Daibosatsu* 八幡大菩薩, in Kokubungaku kenkyū shiryōkan 1999b: 429–430.

82. See *Ryōbu shintō shū*: 459–460. The text is written in archaic language (a mixture of *man'yōgana* and Siddhaṃ), which renders its reading difficult but underscores its secret nature. On Kakujō, see Itō Satoshi 2011: 619–631.

83. See Fowler 2005: 25.

84. Ibid.

85. Ruppert 2000: 151.

86. Ruppert 2000: 153.

87. See Fujimaki 2003, and Naitō 2001a: 181.

88. See *Kakuzenshō, DNBZ* 51: 129b.

89. In the *Miwa-ryū shintō-hen,* the *cintāmaṇi* is identified with the primordial *kami* Kunitokotachi 国常立. See Ōmiwa jinja shiryō, 10: 249.

90. Ruppert 2000: 151, slightly modified.

91. See *Kakugenshō, SZ* 36: 363a (39a). The text adds that the whereabouts of the jewel are not known, and that its container as well, Kenne's mysterious box, is no longer on Mount Murō. On Kūtai, see Fowler 2005: 24–25; and Ruppert 2000: 183–185. The legend is still alive: according to local informants, a Murōji priest who had opened the jewel's cache mysteriously died not so long ago.

92. See Fujimaki 2000; and Fowler 2005. On the dragon hole, see Naitō 2010: 42–43.

93. See *Nihon kiryaku, KT* 5: 430, quoted in Fowler 2005: 17.

94. On Murōji see Fowler 2005. On the burial of relics on Mount Murō, see Fowler 2005: 21–36.

95. On the rivalry between Kūkai and Shubin during the rain ritual at Shinsen'en 神泉苑, see *Taiheiki,* translated in McCullough 1979: 374–378. On the origins of Murōji, see Fowler 2005: 44–52.

96. See for instance the *Ben'ichizan nenbun dosha* 宀一山年分度者, quoted in Fowler 2005: 15–16.

97. Quoted in Tsuji 1970: 125–126. See also Fowler 2005: 59.

98. See *Ben'ichizan ki* 宀一山記, in *DNBZ, Jishi sōsho* 3; and *ZGR* 27: 299. In the *Keiran shūyōshū,* Japan is represented with the form of a *vajra,* but the *vajra*'s center is Lake Biwa. See *T.* 76, 2410: 626b.

99. See *Kojidan, KT* 21: 102–103; and Fowler 2005: 17–18.

100. See Fujimaki 2003: 113.

101. Fowler 2005: 75. On the *Murōji engi,* see pp. 74–83.

102. Fowler 2005: 60 (slightly modified).

103. See *Keiran shūyōshū, T.* 76, 2410: 543c.

104. See Fujimaki 2004: 76. See also *Ben'ichizan hiki,* in Fujimaki 2003: 110a.

105. See *Ben'ichizan ryūketsu anchi shari no koto* 宀一山龍穴安置舎利事 (added title), quoted in Kadoya 1997:101. According to this text, near the dragon hole was a five-wheel stūpa, in which was hidden a box (Kenne's box) that contained a vase full of relics and an exemplar of the *Lotus Sūtra*—but no jewel.

106. On this question, see Fowler 2005: 27–34.

107. See *ZGR* 27: 299. Kūtai, a Chinese disciple of Chōgen, reportedly stole seven grains of relics from Murōji and was subsequently arrested at Kōfukuji. Yet he came to be known as "the saint who spread the relics of Mount Murō." In 1272, a group of Shingon priests also obtained some of these relics and disseminated them in Kantō. See *Azuma kagami* 11, s.v. Ken-kyū 2 (1191)/7/23. See also Nōtomi 1985; and Tsuji 1970: 90.

108. See Trenson 2013, and Ruppert 2002b.

109. On this question, see Kuroda Hideo 2003. On relics and dragons in China, see Naitō 2010: 46–50.

110. See *Kakuzenshō, TZ* 4: 600. On rain rituals and *nāgas*/dragons, see De Visser 1913 and, more recently, Ruppert 2002b and Trenson 2013. On the role of relics in such rituals, see Naitō 2010: 43–46.

111. *Kojidan, KT* 21: 102–103. See also Fowler 2005: 17–18; De Visser 1913: 168–169; and Royall Tyler 1990: 150. On Zentatsu, see Royall Tyler 2007.

112. On the dragon god of Kasuga, see Morrell 1982.

113. On this episode, see *Konjaku monogatari shū* 14.41. On Shin-sen'en, see De Visser 1913: 159–168; Ruppert 2000: 134–135; and Ruppert 2002b. This change reflects the fact that Mount Murō came under the juris-diction of Kōfukuji, which worshiped Zennyo as its protector. When Murōji passed over to Shingon, however, new stories were produced.

114. On Zennyo's male and female forms, see Fowler 2005: 34–37.

115. Trenson 2013: 127.

116. See Fujimaki 2002a: 97–98.

117. See the *Mani hōju mandara* 摩尼宝珠曼荼羅 of Mimuroto-ji (Fig. 6.5), and the dragons protecting the jewel in the *Goyuigō daiji.* We find here again the ternary symbolism of the jewel (identified with Mount Sumeru) and the two dragons.

118. See Faure 1999 and 2004.

119. See *Keiran shūyōshū, T.* 76, 2410: 545c.

120. See map in Ruppert 2000: 159.

121. *Chūsei Nihongi shū*: 437a.

122. Nakamura Honnen 2005a: 64.

123. Nakamura Honnen 2005a: 67.

124. See *Chūsei Kōyasan engishū,* quoted in Nakamura Honnen 2005a: 73.

125. Abe and Yamazaki 1999: 264b.

126. *ST,* Jinja-hen 5, Yamato no kuni: 524; and Gorai 2000, 2: 151–152.

127. See Grapard 1986: 40–42. On Hōren and Usa Hachiman, see Miyake 2007: 265–281.

128. See Riffaterre 1983.

129. *SZ* 35: 477a.

130. In Kokan Shiren's *Genkō shakusho,* we read of Kyōen's performance of a thousand-day austerity on Mount Murō, at the end of which he met a noblewoman who asked him for the mudrā to become a buddha in this body. After he gave it to her, she revealed herself as the dragon king Zennyo 善女 and disappeared, showing a long claw. The episode is reminiscent of Nittai's encounter with the dragon god Zentatsu. See also De Visser 1913: 168. Kyōen is further credited with meeting manifestations of Kōjin and of Māra, the ruler of the sixth heaven. See *Miwa-san Byōdōji Kyōen shōnin betsuden* 三輪山平等寺慶円上人別伝, in *ST,* Ronsetsu-hen 2, Shingon shintō 2: 483–495.

131. This triad was perhaps also influenced by stove symbolism, which came in turn to be linked to Jingū Kōgō 神功皇后 worship. Rolf Stein argues that the three stones that constituted the earliest and simplest form of the stove were deified, and their triad may have formed the prototype of later triads. See Stein 1970. In one version of the Jingū Kōgō legend, her sister goes to the *nāga* palace and returns with the two tide-controlling jewels Kanju 干珠 (ebb-controlling jewel) and Manju 満珠 (flow-controlling jewel). In the *Origin Story of Shidoji Temple* (*Shidoji engi* 志度寺縁起), a courtesan named precisely Kanju 貫主 dives to recover a Chinese wish-fulfilling jewel that had been stolen by a dragon. The jewel is eventually brought to Usa Hachiman 宇佐八幡 Shrine. See Royall Tyler 2007: 73–75. In the same *engi,* the Chinese jewel, stolen by the dragon king Zentatsu, is brought back from the dragon palace by a sea-woman, who eventually dies from her wounds. The jewel is finally placed between the eyebrows of the Shaka statue that is the *honzon* of Kōfukuji. Zentatsu wants it so badly that he moves to Sarusawa Pond near Kōfukuji to watch over it. See Royall Tyler 2007: 67.

132. Kokubungaku kenkyū shiryōkan 1999b: 428–429. In the *Goyuigō daiji* (a.k.a. *Tōchō daiji*), the "three dots" (of the Siddhaṃ letter *i*) correspond to the sun, moon, and the planet Venus, respectively. On the symbolic interpretation of these three dots, see Faure 1991: 197.

133. See *T.* 76, 2410: 519c, 625a, and 864b. On this symbolism, see Kikuchi 2011. (I am indebted to Gaétan Rappo for this reference.)

134. See *T.* 78, 2476: 147a; *T.* 2484: 359c; *T.* 78, 2488: 441c; *T.* 79, 2536: 424a; and *DNBZ* 47: 163a. Sometimes it is simply the seed-syllables *a* or *hūṃ* that play this eidetic role, transforming, depending on the case, into a stūpa, a *cintāmaṇi,* or a wheel—all of which are conventional forms of Nyoirin. See *Kakuzenshō, DNBZ* 47: 168–169. On this structure, called the "jewel of secret contemplation" (*mikkan hōju* 密観宝珠), see Naitō 2010: 98–109.

135. Perhaps because he perceived Monkan as a representative of the "heterodox" Tachikawa-ryū 立川流, Mizuhara Gyōhei did not recognize the *Goyuigō daiji* as Monkan's work and attributed it instead to Dōjun. See Mizuhara 1981: 23–41; and Abe Yasurō 2010b. Yet this text and its companions reveal the extent of Monkan's creativity and orthodoxy as Shingon theoretician.

136. See Mizuhara 1981: 11–43 and figs. 16–19; Manabe Shunshō 2000–2001, 1: 101–117; Makino and Fujimaki 2002: 14–21; and Dolce 2010. Since I have already discussed in the previous chapter the representations of Aizen and Fudō in relation to the wish-fulfilling jewel, I will focus here on the representations of Kūkai.

137. In the *Goyuigō hiketsu,* Kūkai becomes the "global body" (*sōtai* 惣体) of these three buddhas.

138. See Makino and Fujimaki 2002: 11.

139. For the relevant passages in the *Testament,* see Bohner 1946: 300–301.

140. See Makino and Fujimaki 2002: 14 and 16. See also the *Sanzon gōgyō hiketsu,* in Rappo 2010b: 192b. The same representations appear in a document recently discovered on Mount Kōya, the *Saigoku himitsu shō* 最極秘密鈔; see Abe 2013: 248–249. The standing youth is said to represent both Kūkai and Kokūzō. Manabe Shunshō (2000–2001, 1:110) thinks that it is a representation of Kokūzō based on the *Daikokuzō bosatsu shomon kyō.* Kokūzō is also identified with the jewel and Nyoirin, and his presence in Monkan's commentary is not surprising. Being the *honzon* of Kongōshōji 金剛證寺 on Mount Asama in Ise, he is also closely related with Amaterasu. On this question, see also Rappo 2014: 257.

The same motif, including the jewel, the sun, the moon, and the two dragons, is found in an Edo period scroll preserved at Rinnōji 輪王寺 (Nikkō). In this painting, the youth appears above a lion-riding Tohachi Bishamon 刀八毘沙門. The tiled floor is reminiscent of certain Dakiniten representations. The presence of two guardian foxes below (or in front of) the youth reinforces this impression. See fig. 37 in Tochigi kenritsu hakubutsukan 1996: 50.

141. The *Himitsu gentei kuketsu* describes the red youth as a manifestation of Aizen's attribute of love subduing, and as symbolizing stupidity. See *Chūsei sentoku chosakushū*: 494b. These two images are also found in a fragmentary text from Mantokuji, which contains a section on "Daishō Nyoi Kongō Dōji" 大聖如意金剛童子. The youth is here assimilated to the Vajra Youth (Kongō Dōji), also known as Kibutsu (Precious Thing), and is identified with the Mount Murō jewel. He symbolizes the three poisons, yet is identical with the three buddhas Nyoirin, Aizen, and Fudō. His red color symbolizes the fire and the sun, and the solar symbolism links him to deities like Aizen, Ichiji Kinrin (Dainichi), Amaterasu, and Hachiman. The triadic structure is also emphasized through the image of the three-legged crow within the sun. See *Chūsei sentoku chosakushū*: 622–624.

142. *Chūsei sentoku chosakushū*: 622a. This tradition is said to go back to Gihan (1023–1088). The Mantokuji-bon focuses on the image of Kūkai as a divine youth incarnating the three poisons (greed, anger, and stupidity). The commentary emphasizes the red color of the youth's body, which is said to symbolize both love subduing (*keiai*) and the anger involved in subjugation (*chōbuku*), two aspects of Aizen and Fudō, respectively. The color code allows the youth's identification not only with Aizen, but also with other solar deities such as Dainichi, Amaterasu, and Hachiman. In his *Himitsu gentei kuketsu,* Monkan also identifies Kūkai with Amaterasu. This identification is already

found in Tsūkai's *Record of a Pilgrimage to Ise,* or in Eison's *Requests to the Great Ise Shrine* (*Daijingū keihaku*), a record of Eison's probably spurious visit to Ise.

143. See Mizuhara 1981, fig. 19.

144. The Three Worthies are also said to correspond to the three mysteries of the Buddha's body, speech, and mind: Nyoirin represents the mystery of speech, Aizen that of the mind, and Fudō that of the body. See also *Miwa-ryū shintō-hen,* 5: 587.

145. See Makino and Fujimaki 2002: 19 and 21.

146. See Abe 2013: 250, fig. 9–5; and Rappo 2014: 250–251

147. See Mizuhara 1981: 40. Although the Mount Murō jewel is usually identified with Nyoirin, in some cases it is identified with Aizen. In the *Sansun Fu*[*dō*] from Kanazawa bunko, for instance, we read: "The wish-fulfilling jewel is the body of King Aizen. You must realize that King Aizen was transmitted from the Iron Tower under his *samaya* form." Raiyu's *Shinzoku zatsuki mondōshō* 雑記問答鈔 also includes the following exchange: "Question: What does it mean to bury the jewel and [the icon of] Fudō? —Answer: It is said in the *Mokuban kuketsu* 木幡口訣: 'The three-inch Fudō is the jewel; the form of the worthy is Fudō, his *samaya* form is King Aizen.'" This oral tradition is traced back to the Shingon priest Shinkū 真空 (a.k.a. Mokuban Shōnin 木幡上人, 1204–1268), the founder of Daitsūji 大通寺 in Kyoto. On the identity of Kūkai and Amaterasu, see *Jingi hishō,* in *ST,* Ronsetsu-hen 1, Shingon shintō 1: 208.

148. See *Goyuigō hiketsu.* See also *Himitsu gentei kuketsu,* in *Chūsei sentoku chosaku shū*: 492–496; and *Mantokuji-bon,* in *Chūsei sentoku chosaku shū*: 622–24. In the *Bikisho* 鼻帰書 (1326), Kūkai is presented as a manifestation of both Amaterasu and Kasuga Myōjin 春日明神. See *ST,* Ronsetsu-hen 1, Shingon shintō 2: 509–510.

149. For representations of the jewel flanked by the two dragons Nanda and Upananda, see figs. 63 (Ninnaji, Kyoto), 64 (Tokyo National Museum), 65 (private collection), and 66 (Mimurotoji) in *Busshari to hōju* (Nara kokuritsu hakubutsukan 2001: 91–93).

150. On the theft of the wish-fulfilling jewel by the dragon-king Zentatsu, see the *engi* of Shidoji (in Shikoku), in Tyler 2007: 65–67.

151. See also in the *Reikiki shintō zu* 麗気記神道図 the diagrams of the three jewels, with the captions "star light" (golden color), Womb realm (blue), and Vajra realm (black)—and the diagram of the tripartite jewel. *ST,* Ronsetsu-hen 1, Shingon shintō 1: 105–108. Here, the "star light" diagram refers to Venus, the other two diagrams correspond to the sun and the moon.

152. On this question, see Dolce 2008; and Rappo 2014.

153. On this topos, see Takahashi 2005.

154. *Hachiman Daibosatsu,* in *Chūsei Nihongi shū*: 427–428.

155. In the *Sanzon gōgyō hiketsu,* the crown of Kūkai's head is said to correspond to Aizen, and his two eyes to Kinrin and Butsugen. See Rappo 2010b: 192c.

156. See *Goyuigō hiketsu.*

157. See Manabe 2000–2001, 1: 101–116; Dolce 2006–2007, 2008, and 2010; and Rappo 2010b. See also Blanchot 1993; and Barthes 2002.

158. In his *Kinpusen himitsuden,* Monkan establishes another structurally similar triad, with Tenkawa Benzaiten (representing nonduality) at its center, between Kumano Gongen and Zaō Gongen. See Abe Yasurō 2010b: 124.

159. Naitō 2001a and 2010.

160. See *Kakuzenshō, TZ* 4, 3022: 168a. The following account is indebted to Kim Youn-mi's dissertation (Kim 2010).

161. See *Atsuzōshi, T.* 78: 269–70. However, one source at least claims that it can be traced back to the Ninnaji priest Kakui 覚意 (1052–1107). See *Kakuzenshō*, TZ 4: 547, cited in Naitō 2010: 77–78.

162. See Kanjin's *Ono ruihi shō*: 18–19. Kamikawa Michio suggests that Hanjun wrote article 24 of Kūkai's *Testament,* if not the whole text (2008a: 281).

163. On the Nyohō sonshō ritual, see also Nakano Genzō 2008.

164. Kamikawa 2008a; see also Kim Youn-mi 2010: 271–275.

165. Kamikawa 2006b.

166. *T.* 79, 2536: 520b.

167. The two methods are described in Kim Youn-mi 2010: 322–323.

168. Kamikawa 2008a: 256–261.

169. This also brings to mind Kūkai's "purple box" in the legend of the nun Nyoi 如意. That box, whose importance Kokan Shiren emphasizes in his *Genkō shakusho,* is the esoteric equivalent of the mythological box of Urashima no ko 浦島の子, brought back from the undersea palace of the dragon king, which contains Urashima no ko's vital breath. See Faure 2002–2003.

170. On this ritual, see Kim Youn-mi 2010: 114–186.

171. On the embryological symbolism of the *kesa* (Skt. *kāṣāya*), see Faure 1995.

172. See Smith 1982.

173. Mus 1998. In Mus's model, these two orders of reality are the microcosm and the macrocosm, while here they are the Womb and Vajra realms, but the basic schema remains the same.

CHAPTER 7: LIVING JEWELS

1. On the animation of statues, see Faure 1991 and 1996. On Monju's statue in particular, see Quinter 2007.

2. A reliquary in the Nezu Museum collection shows Ichiji Kinrin on a lion, flanked by Aizen and Fudō. When one removes the board, Nyoirin appears in its place, still flanked by the two wisdom kings. See Fig. 5.10 above.

3. See fig. 91 in the catalogue *Busshari to hōju* (Nara kokuritsu hakubutsukan 2001), a reliquary found at Kongōji 金剛寺 (Ōsaka).

4. De Visser 1931: 23.

5. De Visser 1931: 30.

6. As we recall, Kūkai's performance of the Gumonji ritual led to his identification with Kokūzō in the *Goyuigō daiji*. In the *Himitsu gentei kuketsu,* this image of Kūkai as a young immortal represents the fusion of Fudō and Aizen, but also of Nyoirin and Kokūzō in Amaterasu. See *Chūsei sentoku shū*: 495b.

7. De Visser 1931: 40.

8. These rituals used a symbolic device composed of two elements, a heavenly board (*tenban*) and an earthly board (*chiban*). At the center of the heavenly board, the Five Kokūzō were represented together with the seven stars, surrounded by various astral deities (the twelve zodiacal constellations, etc.) on the earthly board. The same disposition on other boards centered on Nyoirin, Dakiniten, and Shōten led naturally to the equation of their central deities. On these divination boards, see the catalogue *Onmyōdō kakeru mik-kyō* (Kanazawa kenritsu Kanazawa bunko 2007b).

9. In the current disposition at Tōji, the horse-riding Kokūzō is at the center whereas in the traditional disposition, because of the yang symbolism of the horse, it was in the southern direction. On the Five Kokūzō, see Naitō 2010: 194–198; and Pedersen 2010.

10. See Izumi 1998.

11. There is also a Sekisei Dōji among Benzaiten's fifteen attendants.

12. Tanaka Takako, 2000: 133. Uhō Dōji's association with these two devas brings to mind the triad formed by Dakiniten, Benzaiten, and Shōten and suggests that he is functionally similar to Shōten.

13. Nishiyama Masaru 1999. In the Kōyasan scroll (see Fig. 7.10 below), he is represented with a red sun disk and a white moon disk, in which the three-legged solar crow and the white moon hare are visible. This ternary structure, reminiscent of the images in the *Goyuigō daiji,* points to Uhō Dōji's identity with the *tertium quid,* the jewel. In various representations, he is shown flanked by the Red Youth (Aka Dōji, the protector of Kasuga Shrine) and Hachiman in the guise of an old monk. See the Sansha Gongen, *BZS* 4021 (Fig. 7.12). Aka Dōji's red color, as well as the red sun disk above Hachiman, contrast with the white color of Uhō Dōji's robe and point to the embryological symbolism of the red (blood) and white (semen). Again, the combination of the jewel he holds and the wheels that form the motif of his robe suggest a link with Nyoirin, the Kannon with the jewel (*nyoi*) and the wheel (*rin*). In more recent representations, he appears flanked by two deities in official dress, which may be the two *kami* that pulled Amaterasu out of the Rock Cave.

14. Nishiyama 1999: 89.

15. In a reliquary shrine from a private collection, the relics in a central stūpa are flanked by Fudō and Kūkai. Above Fudō are the five buddhas of Kasuga, while above Kūkai stands Uhō Dōji. A red sun disk also appears above Kūkai's head. See Nara kokuritsu hakubutsukan 2007, fig. 198. At Saidaiji, Uhō Dōji is associated with Aizen in a large portable shrine. At Hasedera, he is, with the dragon king, one of the two acolytes of Kannon.

16. *T.* 76, 2410: 519a.

17. See *Genkō shakusho, DNBZ* 62, 470: 160c (1973 reprint).

61. See *Hokke ryakugi, T.* 56, 2192: 200a.

62. See *Taizō kongō bodaishingi ryaku mondō shō* 胎蔵金剛菩提心義略問答抄, *T.* 75, 2397: 482b. In this model, Nyoirin corresponds to the highest realm, that of the devas.

63. *T.* 79, 2536: 424b. The new list, however, can already be found in the work of the Shingon master Kyōyū (890–953). See Hayami 2000: 297–298.

64. See *Keiran shūyōshū, T.* 76, 2410: 584bc; and Hayami 2002: 122–125. See also Chandra 1999–2005, vol. 2: 427–428.

65. For an image of the Six Kannon (surrounding Ichiji Kinrin, with Daiitoku Myōō and Fudō Myōō as guardians below), as used in the Six Letters Ritual, see *Kakuzenshō, DNBZ* 47: 316a.

66. See *T.* 77, 2411: 28a; and *Kakuzenshō, DNBZ* 46: 324b. On this ritual, see also Strickmann 2002: 265.

67. In this ritual, the priest burns various offerings, as well as figurines of the emblems of evil known as the three foxes—namely, the heavenly fox (actually a kite), the earthly fox (an actual fox), and the human fox (a woman, who perhaps represents the witch against which this ritual is performed). In the Rokuji mandala 六字曼荼羅 (a seed-letter or *bīja* mandala), Nyoirin Kannon is represented on top of the picture; then we have (clockwise): Jūichimen, Jundei, Batō (at the bottom), Shō, and Senju. See *Kakuzenshō, DNBZ* 46: 316.

68. *T.* 76, 2410: 797c. Elsewhere, Nyoirin is simply the sixth *vijñāna* (*mano-vijñāna*). See *T.* 76, 2410: 587b.

69. See *T.* 76, 2410: 587b–c.

70. See *Shikan, T.* 78: 811c; 812b.

71. *Kakuzenshō, DNBZ* 47: 155.

72. Literary sources like the *Hōgen monogatari* 保元物語 imply that a love ritual was the reason for the favors that the Hossō priest Dōkyō 道鏡 obtained from Empress Kōken (Shōtoku) in 761. See Tanaka Takako 1992: 71–72.

73. *Kakuzenshō, DNBZ* 47: 181–182. This is, for instance, what Nyoirin is said to have done for the young Shinran 親鸞 (1173–1263). On Shinran's dream, see Faure 1998a: 122–123, and 2003a: 206–210. On the jade maiden in Jien's dream, see Faure 2003a: 206–208.

74. *Kakuzenshō, DNBZ* 47: 182a.

75. For an explanation of the six arms, see *Gobu darani mondō gesan shūhi ron* 五部陀羅尼問答偈讃宗秘論 by Kūkai, *T.* 78, 2464: 14b; and *Shōgo shū* 勝語集, *T.* 78, 2479: 211a.

76. *Byakuhō shō, TZ* 10: 847.

77. See *Kakuzenshō, DNBZ* 47: 174b; *Keiran shūyōshū, T.* 76, 2410: 587ab; and *Besson zakki, TZ* 3: 164, where the deity coming out of the earth is described as a bodhisattva. For a representative example, see the Nyoirin Kannon of Daigoji, fig. 128 in the catalogue *Shinbutsu shūgō* (Nara kokuritsu hakubutsukan 2007).

78. On the Ishiyamadera Kannon, see *Kakuzenshō, DNBZ* 47: 185; and *Keiran shūyōshū, T.* 76, 2410: 852c. For an analysis of that icon, see Aptilon 2008: 78–106.

79. *Kakuzenshō, DNBZ* 47: 186–187.

80. *Kakuzenshō, DNBZ* 47: 188–189.

81. *Kakuzenshō, DNBZ* 47: 189–191.

82. *Kakuzenshō, DNBZ* 47: 189.

83. *Kakuzenshō, DNBZ* 47: 191. See also *Zuzō shō, TZ* 3, figs. 62.2 and 64.4; and *Besson zakki, TZ* 3: 159–178.

84. See *Kakuzenshō, DNBZ* 47: 189; *Zuzōshō (Jikkanshō), TZ* 3, fig. 62; *Besson zakki*: 166–167, figs. 58–59; and *TZ* 3: 222–223. The two deities in the pond are the bodhisattvas Kongōzōō 金剛蔵王菩薩 and Gundari 軍荼利菩薩. Both are represented seated: the former holds a lotus stalk with a *vajra* on top, and a white fly whisk (*hossu* 払子); the latter holds a wheel and a *vajra* in his upper hands, and forms a specific mudrā with his two crossed arms. The textual description differs somewhat from the image. An almost similar image is found in *Kakuzenshō, DNBZ* 47: 192: Nyoirin has twelve arms and is standing on a lotus with two *apsaras* above her. She is flanked by a standing, wrathful Zaō and a dancing Gundari Myōō.

85. See Ruppert 2000: 157.

86. *T.* 76, 2410: 701a.

87. See *Keiran shūyōshū, T.* 76, 2410: 511c. In another passage, however, the author explains that the three jewels of the Futama Hall corresponded to Shō Kannon (center), Jūichimen (left), and Nyoirin (bottom); see *T.* 76, 2410: 797c.

88. See for instance Shukaku Hōshinnō's *Gyōki, T.* 78, 2493: 616a. On Nyoirin and Shōtoku Taishi, see also Aptilon 2008: 196 ff. In the *Shōtoku taishi denryaku*, Shōtoku is perceived as a manifestation of Guze Kannon 救世観音, but the latter was soon identified with Nyoirin. Already in the *Asabashō*, Shōtoku Taishi becomes a manifestation of Nyoirin, and the latter becomes the *honzon* of Rokkakudō 六角堂 (in Kyoto). The *Asabashō* also quotes the *Rokkakudō engi*, in which Nyoirin appears to Shōtoku Taishi and tells him that she has protected him during his past seven lifetimes. See *TZ* 9: 194b. (In the *Ishiyamadera engi*, she protects Shōtoku Taishi during two lifetimes only; see *DNBZ* 117: 179a.) In the *Keiran shūyōshū*, Shōtoku is also described as a manifestation of Amaterasu. See *T.* 76, 2410: 789bc. On Shōbō as a reincarnation of Nyoirin, see *Gyōki, T.* 78, 2493: 616a.

89. See Inoue Ichinen 1992: 43b.

90. See for instance *Keiran shūyōshū, T.* 76, 2410: 852c.

91. Iyanaga 2002b: 577.

92. See Mizukami 2008: 468–472. On Jien's dream, see pp. 491–508. On Nyoirin as symbol of the fusion of kingly law (ōbō 王法) and Buddha dharma (*buppō* 仏法), see pp. 539–547.

93. See *ZTZ*, Mikkyō 3: 287; and Itō Satoshi 2011: 230–233.

94. As Iyanaga Nobumi points out, Kannon's vow to Shinran, in which she declares that she would become a jade maiden to fulfill his sexual desires, calls to mind Jūichimen Kannon's vow to the elephant-headed demon Vināyaka (2002b: 578–579). On Nyoirin as jade maiden, see pp. 577–591.

95. On this question, see Naitō 2010: 120–128.

96. Cited in Fujimaki 2001: 4b.

97. See the section on Shōtoku Taishi in the *Jindaikan hiketsu*, in *ZST*, Ronsetsu-hen, Shūgō shintō: 177–183.

98. *Jindaikan hiketsu*, *ZST*, Ronsetsu-hen, Shūgō shintō: 177.

99. *ZST*, Ronsetsu-hen, Shūgō shintō: 178–179. On the identity between Nyoirin and Myōken, see also *Keiran shūyōshū*, *T.* 76, 2410: 789c. On the identity between Nyoirin and Monju, see *T.* 76, 2410: 582b.

100. See Aptilon 2008: 16.

101. This mandala was reportedly drawn by the Shingon priest Jitsue 実慧 (var. Jichie, 786–847) under Kūkai's directions, based on the *Secret Essential Scriptures of the Seven-star Nyoirin* (*Qixing Ruyilun bimi yaojing* 七星如意輪秘密要経, J. *Shichishō Nyoirin himitsu yōkyō*) (*T.* 20, 1091: 224). See also *TZ* 4: 876; *Betsugyō* 別行 by Kanjō (1057–1125), *T.* 78, 2476: 182b; *Shōgo shū*, *T.* 78: 210b; *Shikan*, *T.* 78, 2500: 780b; and Takeda 1995: 25.

102. See *Bukkyō daijiten*, 2: 1904b; *Mikkyō daijiten*, 2: 971–972; and *Takushō*, *T.* 78, 2488: 441c. The same seed-letters were visualized during the contemplation of the ritual area of the Nyoirin Flower Ritual (Nyoirin kehō 如意輪華法) as practiced at Saidaiji among the New Year rituals. In that ritual, however, Nyoirin was flanked by Aizen and Fudō, not by the seven stars and Hārītī. See Naitō 2010: 76–77 and 128–132.

103. *Kakuzenshō*, *DNBZ* 47: 195. See also *Bukkyō daijiten*, 2: 1904. This calls to mind the union of the two stars in the formation of individual destiny, one coming down from heaven, the other emerging from the earth, to fuse in the human body that both help to form. See the discussion of Kinrin and Butsugen (the Tendai equivalents of Nyoirin), in *Keiran shūyōshū*, *T.* 76, 2410: 622a.

104. A variant of that ritual, called Ritual of the Union of Heaven and Earth (Tenchi wagō hō 天地和合法), states that the five hundred demons and Hārītī descend from heaven while all the earth deities come out from the earth. See *Kakuzenshō*, *DNBZ* 47: 187.

105. This ritual, described in Seigen's *Usuzōshi*, implies a series of visualizations: the practitioner first visualizes seven jeweled wheels (or a seven-spoke wheel) on the altar; at their center is a lotus, on which he visualizes a seed-syllable (*hrīḥ*) flanked by two other seed-syllables (*traḥ*). The latter transform into a *cintāmaṇi*, which transforms in turn into a red-bodied Nyoirin, with twelve (or six) arms, holding various precious objects. Or again, in the spaces between the eight spokes, he visualizes syllables that become the seven stars of the Northern Dipper and Mother Hārītī—surrounded by the bodhisattvas of the Lotus section, the nine luminaries, the twelve palaces, and the twenty-eight mansions. See *T.* 78, 2495: 661c.

106. *Shikan*, *T.* 78, 2500: 812c.

107. See *Asabashō*, *TZ* 9: 199c.

108. See *Jūhachidō kuketsu* 十八道口決, *T.* 79, 2529: 812b; and *Kakuzenshō*, *DNBZ* 50: 2a.

109. Tendai monks also performed a Nyoirin Offering (Nyoirin Kannon kashō ku) in which Nyoirin was worshiped together with the nine luminaries.

110. In one Nyoirin Kannon mandala, Saturn is depicted just below the main deity (as he is also in the Myōken mandala and in the *Karazu* centered

on Monju). See also *Henkushō, T.* 78, 2496: 691a, on the Nyoirin rite to control the comet Ketu.

111. *Mudai ki, ZST,* Ronsetsu-hen, Shūgō shintō: 514. In the *Jindaikan hiketsu,* the five assemblies of the Womb and Vajra realms are interpreted as symbols of the human body. See *ZST,* Ronsetsu-hen, Shūgō shintō: 131 and 149–150. See also p. 400, where the seven stars are identified with the seven generations of earthly *kami.* The positive value attributed here to the northeastern direction, which in Chinese cosmology is the "gate of demons," reflects the influence of Indian cosmology.

112. *ZST,* Ronsetsu-hen, Shūgō shintō: 515. See also *Gojikkan shō, SZ* 30: 544–546. On Tohyō Nyoirin as the sun, see Miyake 1971: 198.

113. For a description of the two boards, see *Gojikkan shō,* in *SZ* 30: 145–147; and Trenson 2013. A concrete example has recently been found among the documents of Kanazawa bunko; see Nishioka 2007: 14. The Kajūji priest Kōzen 興然 (1121–1203), the master of Kakuzen 覚禅 (1143–ca. 1213) and author of the *Gojikkan shō* 五十卷抄, already mentions divination boards centered on Fudō, Kokūzō, and Nyoirin. Similar divination boards centered on Fudō, Dakiniten, or Shōten are also known. On Fudō, see *Gojikkan shō, SZ* 30: 680. On Tohyō Nyoirin Kannon, Dakiniten, and Shōten, see Kanagawa kenritsu Kanazawa bunko 2007b: 38–71; and Nishioka 2008: 38–47.

114. See *Tohyō Nyoirin shikihō* in Nishioka, 2008: 43–44, fig. 41; and Nishioka 2013: 151–152. We have here what Paul Mus, speaking of the Borobudur stūpa, called "kinetic symbolism." We tend to forget that mandalas, frozen in their representation, are in fact dynamic, kinetic structures. See Mus 1998: 236–237. One text clearly associates the mandala and the *shikiban.* It is the *Himitsu shū* 秘密集 (Kanazawa bunko 84.13, fasc. 2), in which we find a passage on the Hokuto mandala, whose gist is as follows: Kinrin sits at the center, surrounded by the various star deities whom he controls, thereby preventing calamities. This mandala looks like the celestial board (*tenban*). The celestial board is used by astrologers, the earthly board by Yin-Yang masters. (I am indebted to Steven Trenson for bringing my attention to this passage.)

115. On this question, see Aptilon 2008: 158–177.

116. See *Miwa-ryū shintō-hen,* 5: 587–588.

117. See Fujimaki 2000: 109; Fujimaki 2002b: 108; and Takahashi Yūsuke 2005.

118. *ST,* Ronsetsu-hen 2, Shingon shintō 2: 503.

119. *Keiran shūyōshū, T.* 76, 2410: 865a.

120. See for instance *T.* 76, 2410: 854b.

121. Yamamoto 1993a: 275.

122. *T.* 76, 2410: 590, 622. See also p. 863c.

123. On this topos, see Faure 2003a: 91–106.

124. This identification appears in various sources. See for instance *Minoodera himitsu engi* 箕面寺秘密縁起, in Gorai 2000, 2: 279. See also *Keiran shūyōshū, T.* 76, 2410: 625c.

125. *Shingon hiōshō,* quoted in Yamamoto 1993a: 280.

126. *ZST,* Ronsetsu-hen, Shūgō shintō: 230.

127. Nyoirin is attended by Kichijōten (who also holds a *cintāmaṇi*), flanked by Baso Sennin (Skt. Vasu Ṛṣi) and Taishakuten (Śakra, i.e., Indra), in a Japanese painting dated to the twelfth century. See Chapin 1932: 29–43; and Manabe 2000–2001, 1: 416–432.

128. In the Famensi reliquary, the goddess holds in front of her a relic of the Buddha (in this case a finger bone). This scene actually represents an *abhiṣeka* ritual, as shown by the presence of an elephant above her, suggesting the bath of the newborn Śākyamuni. In the *Kakuzenshō* and other iconographic sources, Kichijōten appears standing, holding a jewel in her hand, against a mountain background, but the elephant is still there, on a rock promontory above her.

129. See Wu and Han 1998: 273–275. See also fig. 18 (Yakushiji, Nara) in Nara kokuritsu hakubutsukan 2007.

130. In an amusing story found in the *Nihon ryōiki* 日本霊異記, a monk falls in love with a statue of Kichijōten, going so far as to suck its (her) breast. See Kyoko Nakamura 1973: 178; and Faure 1998a: 123.

131. See *ST,* Jinja-hen, Inari: 15. See also Iyanaga 2002a: 598.

132. The tradition regarding the Seijo-sha already appears in the *Kongō himitsu Sannō denju daiji* 金剛秘密山王伝授大事, a record of oral traditions by Chūson 忠尊 (1046–1138), which gives this simple description of the Seijo-sha deity: "Female form; Inari Daimyōjin; Nyoirin Kannon." From this we can infer that her *honji* is Nyoirin. See *TZ* 12: 26. This theory must have been transmitted as part of the Sannō shintō by the chroniclers of Mount Hiei, and it also appears in the *Wakō dōjin riyaku kanjō* 和光同塵利益灌頂, *TZ* 12: 186. In his *Tenchi jingi shinchin yōki,* Jihen also declares: "The Saintly Lady is Ugajin; she is also Toyouke." Again: "This Saintly Lady is also identical with Inari. . . . If you ask about her *honji,* she is identical with Nyoirin Kannon." See *TZ* 12: 217–218. The equivalence between the goddess and Nyoirin is clearly asserted in the Sannō mandala. See for instance Ōtsu-shi rekishi hakubutsukan 2006: 24, 26, and 34; and fig. 189 in the catalogue *Saichō to Tendai no kokuhō* (Kyōto kokuritsu hakubutsukan 2005: 221). Equally significant is one of the Sannō reliquaries that represents the eight-petaled lotus of the Womb mandala, with the relics in a small glass container at the center and Nyoirin Kannon (as the Saintly Lady) on one of the eight petals. See Kyōto kokuritsu hakubutsukan 2005: 38.

133. *Keiran shūyōshū, T.* 76, 2410: 520c and 867b. See also the mandalas of Benzaiten and Dakiniten, which depict running foxes carrying jewels. The identity of the divine fox and Nyoirin is asserted in a Japanese apocryphon, the *Shinko Nyoirin kyō* 辰狐王如意輪経 (mentioned in Moriyama 1965: 585).

134. Nanami 1986: 77.

135. See Abe Yasurō 1989: 145–146.

136. See Wakabayashi 1999: 495.

137. See Ruppert 2000: 146; and Kamens 1988: 328.

138. See *ST,* Jinja-hen, Kumano: 65; and Nikō 1981: 244. This motif recalls that of the *kaname-ishi* 要石 used to pin down the giant catfish (*namazu* 鯰) that lives under the Japanese archipelago. On this question, see Ouwehand 1964.

139. Jundei (Ch. Zhunti) is the converted form of an ogress, Cundī (or Cundā, a name associated with lower caste women in India), who was known for her power to subdue snakes. She is often represented seated on a lotus throne held up by the *nāga* kings Nanda and Upananda (an image reminiscent of the *cintāmaṇi*) and was worshiped in particular for easy childbirth (like Nyoirin in Japan). See figs. 7.38 and 7.39. See also Gimello 2004.

140. See *Daigoji engi, DNBZ* 117: 246a–252b; and Aptilon 2008: 51.

141. *DNBZ* 117: 247b–248a. Sāgara's second daughter was the famous *nāga* princess of the *Lotus Sūtra.* My account of Seiryō Gongen relies on Aptilon 2008.

142. See *Seiryō gongen daiji,* 18–20. Shōmyōji archives, boxes 340.79 and 418.37. I am indebted to Steven Trenson for this reference.

143. *Daigoji shin'yōroku,* 1: 397; cited in Aptilon 2008: 61.

144. Aptilon 2008: 61. In a sense, the Seiryō Gongen figure inverts the traditional formula "One buddha, two wisdom kings" into "One *gongen,* two buddhas." The resulting image is reminiscent of the Tenkawa Benzaiten, a three-snake-headed figure. Although we are not told in the latter case what (or whom) the three snake heads symbolize, the deity seems to stand for a higher truth. At any rate, its ternary symbolism is clearly related to the jewel. We will return to Tenkawa Benzaiten when we consider the Three Devas. See also Nara kokuritsu hakubutsukan 2007, fig. 120.

145. Shōkaku is also known as the founder of the Sanbō-in (1115), which became an imperial temple and the headquarters of the Tōzan-ha, one of the two main branches of Shugendō. Aptilon 2008: 64–70.

146. Daigoji zōjiki, 41–42; cited in Aptilon 2008: 65.

147. See Ruppert 2000: 204.

148. *Genkō shakusho* 18.6, in *DNBZ* 62, 470: 160–161.

149. See *Sanbō ekotoba* 1.4; translated in Kamens 1988: 118–120.

150. On Nyoi and the jade woman, see also Faure 2002–2003: 209–210.

151. See *Jinnō shōtōki:* "While she was at sea, Empress Jingū obtained a wish-fulfilling jewel (*nyoi no tama*), owing to which she was able to postpone until her return to Kyūshū the birth of her son, the future emperor Ōjin." Quoted in Varley 1980: 102.

152. It is that image that is said to be preserved today at Saidaiji in Nara. When I saw it a few years ago, it was accompanied by a recent and noteworthy caption. The anonymous author accused Nyoi of having left her imperial husband to live with a monk, and reproached Kūkai for giving Nyoirin the slightly erotic features of Nyoi. All this, according to him, reeked (lit. "stinks of the flesh," *niku-kusai*), suggesting a somewhat unhealthy relationship between the priest and the lady. When I saw it again in 2012, the caption had disappeared.

153. See Ruppert 2002b: 152–159.

154. See *Urashima-ga-ko den,* in *GSRJ* 135, 6: 468; and Shigematsu Akihisa 1981: 40–46. See also Faure 2002–2003: 177–196.

155. See *Man'yōshū,* verse 1740, in *From the Country of Eight Islands: An Anthology of Japanese Poetry,* trans. Satō Hiroaki and Burton Watson (Seattle: University of Washington Press, 1981).

156. McCullough 1988: 226.

157. See Philippi 1968: 150–158.

158. See for instance its treatment in the *Honchō kōsōden* 本朝高僧伝 (*DNBZ* 431), where, after mentioning the legend of Urashima no ko from Tango province, the text adds: "At that time, in the same region, lived a woman named Nyoi who had obtained a Purple Cloud casket. People could not see her face. She became the consort of Emperor Junna. She received from Kūkai the Nyoirin ritual. Climbing on Mount Takekura, she performed that ritual and was able to complete her practice of incantations. Kūkai carved an image of Nyoirin and deposited the casket inside." The author then adds his commentary: "Some say that Kūkai, having obtained the Purple Cloud casket, prayed to make the rain fall and end a drought. [The said casket] was probably a *secret realization* of the Mystery vehicle, and not an instrument of immortals. I for one think that the latter view is erroneous. Kūkai inherited from Huiguo and obtained the true secret of [the buddha] Dainichi. What use could he have had for an object governed by the power of karma? There are many objects of that kind among the specialists in divination. Thus, Su Dan of the Later Han obtained the technique of Dao and ascended to heaven. Leaving a casket behind, he said: 'If one desires to cultivate oneself, one must strike it.' His mother did as he had said, and the objects of her desires appeared. Still in doubt, she opened the casket and looked inside. After that, there was no response. Can we still then speak of a mysterious realization? Kūkai's Dharma heirs, when they prayed for rain, obtained it. . . . This [efficacy] is entirely due to Kūkai himself. Why should one doubt this?" See also *Jakushōdō kokkyōshū* 寂照堂谷響集, in *DNBZ*, 37–38.

159. See Nara kokuritsu hakubutsukan 2001.

160. See Naitō 2001a: 182–183.

161. Naitō 2010: 77.

162. It has been traced to a visualization described in the *Muryōju nyorai kuyō sahō shidai* 無量寿如来供養作法次第 (in *Kōbō Daishi zenshū*, 2: 512). However, as Naitō points out, the ritual artifact in question is complex and variable in its structure, and cannot be traced to any particular source. It seems at any rate to derive from Nyoirin's *samaya* form.

163. The lotus and the *vajra* traditionally represent the female and male aspects of reality, while the jewel represents their nonduality. It is also sometimes identified with the *vajra*. On this form, see Naitō 2010: 98–141.

164. Naitō 2010: 77.

165. See for instance the exemplars in figs. 71 (Tokyo National Museum), 72 (Saidaiji), 75 (Hannyaji), and 76 (Kongōsanji) in Nara kokuritsu hakubutsukan 2001.

166. Note that the relics are placed in the sphere in the middle of the *gorintō,* which corresponds to the water element, probably due to the association with the *nāgas.*

167. Also noteworthy is a triptych from Jōdoji (Hiroshima prefecture) formed by three painted scrolls (*Busshari to hōju,* fig. 80), with a five-petaled jewel (symbolizing Nyoirin) on a lotus dais at the center, atop a standing *vajra;* the two lateral scrolls represent Aizen and Fudō, respectively, the latter flanked by his two acolytes. On this representation, see Naitō 2010: 77; and Rappo 2014.

168. In this type of representation, the back of the mirror reveals the identity of the Buddhist deity who is the true nature (*honji*) of the *kami* symbolized by the mirror's face. This is somewhat paradoxical, since the empty mirror, as symbol of formlessness, should be identified with the highest reality, i.e., the Buddhist deity, rather than its *kami* manifestation. See also fig. 174 in *Shinbutsu shūgō* (Nara kokuritsu hakubutsukan 2007). Another portable shrine with the same name, but quite different in form, was preserved at Saidaiji (Nara). See Chap. 4 above; and *Shinbutsu shūgō,* fig. 175. On this question, see Abe Yasurō 1985b: 338–346.

169. See Naitō 2010: 111–112.

170. On the identity between Nyoirin and Dainichi, see *Keiran shūyōshū, T.* 76, 2410: 676b.

171. Significant exceptions are Kieschnick 2003 and Rambelli 2007a. Unfortunately, neither book deals with divination. For a survey of divination in East Asia and beyond, see Strickmann 2005.

CODA

1. See Law 1992: 380; Ingold 2011: 63–65; and Viveiros de Castro 2009: 80. I borrow the notion of "meshwork" from Tim Ingold.

2. Law 2004: 62.

3. On the hinterland, see Law 2004; Latour calls this the *plasma* (Latour 2005).

4. See Stein 1991b.

5. See Krishan 1999.

6. Knipe mentions another possibility, in which the third element does not represent a transcendent entity, but a subordinate or interstitial one; this, however, does not seem to be the case with our esoteric triads. See Knipe 1972: 35.

7. Or perhaps it is the other way around: starting from three, we add a fourth element that symbolizes transcendence or the "remainder." See Derrida 2002; and Malamoud 1996b. Knipe writes that "each of the basic triadic, tetradic and pentadic series makes a unique statement. 'Three' is the vertical cosmos, the cosmos envisioned in elevation. . . ; 'four' is the horizontal cosmos, the cosmos in plan, stretching to the four points of space; and 'five' is quite simply both at once and therefore the most complete expression of all, all that provides transcendent closure to the world view." Knipe 1972: 35.

8. See Stein 1970.

9. In a monograph on the topic, Dany-Robert Dufour writes: "The trinity that I take as object is anterior to all beliefs, it is inscribed in our condition of speaking being" (1990: 17).

10. See Bergaigne 1933, 2: 115–156, quoted in Knipe 1972: 32.

11. Knipe 1972: 35.

12. On the introduction of weaving to Japan and its relation to Japanese mythology, see Como 2009.

13. On this point, see Žižek 2003: 71.

14. Cooper 1998: 108, quoted in Law 2004: 104.

15. Assmann 2001: 7.

16. Law 1992: 384.

17. On the notion of *hybrids*, see Latour 1993: 41–43.

18. On the notion of network, see Latour 2005: 128–133; and Law 1992.

19. Deleuze and Guattari 1987: 20. Viveiros de Castro offers the following comment: "Dualisms are real, not imaginary. . . . If one has to undo them, it is first of all because they have really been done. To undo them, however, it is important to avoid the circular trap that would consist in negating or contradicting them; we have to come out of them 'in a calculated fashion,' that is, aways through a tangent — through a vanishing line or point" (2009: 88).

20. See Atlan 1979: 14–25. Michel Serres also explains that noise is *productive* and creative: "The noise, through its presence and absence, the intermittence of the signal, produces the new system" (1982: 52).

21. See Sokal 1996.

22. Goffman 1959.

23. I use this expression in tribute to Stephen Jay Gould (see 1996).

24. Law 2004: 6.

25. Souriau 2009: 159; see also Latour 2013.

26. See Latour 2013: 181–206.

27. Still subscribing to a Christian worldview, however, Latour tries to distinguish between the "beings of metamorphosis" and the "beings of religion," arguing that their ontology cannot be the same. Thus, he would like "to reserve the name *divinities* for the powers of transaction through which one addresses the beings that bear psyches, reserving the name *gods* for the beings with whom no transaction is possible, the ones that come not to treat but to save" (2013: 309). In my opinion, that unfortunate distinction is one of the polarities that Latour himself has been trying to undermine, and it reproduces the assymetrical views of the Moderns that he has so eloquently criticized. In an earlier work, Latour characterizes the gods by the neologism *factish*, by which he means a cross between "fact" and "fetish." While the word "fact" seems to refer to an external reality, the word "fetish" points to the mistaken beliefs of the subject. By contrast, a factish is a type of action that does "not fall into the comminatory choice between fact and belief." In other words, it is neither an independent reality nor a projection. See Latour 2009: 53, and 1999: 306.

28. Keller 2014.

29. I borrow this expression from Bitbol 1999.

30. See Viveiros de Castro 2009: 181. Derrida (1980a) had already pointed out the ambivalence of Lévi-Strauss's notion of structure.

31. See Olivier 2008.

32. Hoshino Yukinobu 星野之宣, *Munakata kyōju denkikō* 宗像教授伝奇考 (Tokyo: Shogakkan).

33. This remark is often quoted but without reference, and I have been unable to locate it. It does sound like vintage Wittgenstein.

34. In his study of Saint Guinefort (the Holy Greyhound), Jean-Claude Schmitt provides a model of historical-*cum*-structural analysis. See Schmitt 1983.

35. See Wittgenstein 1997, 6.522.

36. See Kuroda Hideo 2003.

BIBLIOGRAPHY

PRIMARY SOURCES

Ainōshō 塵嚢鈔 (1445). By Gyōyō 行誉. In *Jinten ainōshō, Ainōshō* 塵添塵
  嚢鈔. 塵嚢鈔, ed. Hamada Atsushi 濱田敦 and Satake Akihiro 佐竹昭広
  (Kyoto: Rinsen shoten, 1971).

Aji hishaku 阿字祕釋. By Kakuban 覺鑁 (1095–1143). *T.* 79, 2512.

Amano zatsuki 天野雑記. *ST,* Ronsetsu-hen 1, Shingon shintō 1: 379–409.

Amida shaku 阿弥陀釋. By Kakuban 覺鑁 1095–1143). *T.* 79, 2522.

Anryū denju kiyō 安流伝授紀要. By Zuihō 瑞宝. *SZ* 34: 257–460; 35: 5–552.

Asabashō 阿娑縛抄. By Shōchō 承最 (1205–1282). *T.* 93–94 (*TZ* 8–9), 3190.

Asama-san engi 朝熊山縁起. In *Jisha engi* 寺社縁起, *NST* 20: 77–88.

Atsuta-gū hishaku kenmon 熱田宮秘釈見聞. In *Chūsei Nihongi shū,* 357–360.
  Also in *ST,* Jinja-hen 19, Atsuta: 30–33.

Atsuta kōshiki 熱田講式. *ST,* Jinja-hen 19, Atsuta: 21–29.

Atsuzōshi 厚造紙. Ed. Genkai 元海 (1094–1157). *T.* 78, 2483.

Azuma kagami 吾妻鏡 (or 東鑑). Anon. *KST* 32–33. Also in *Zenshaku Azuma
  kagami,* ed. Nagahara Keiji and Kishi Shōzō, 6 vols. (Tokyo: Shinjinbutsu
  ōraisha, 1976–1979).

Bankyō honnen shinrei zuiki ki 萬鏡本縁神靈瑞器記. *ST,* Ronsetsu-hen 1, Shingon shintō 1: 60–63.

Beidi qiyuan ziting yansheng bijue 北帝七元紫庭延生秘訣. Attr. Ge Xuan 葛玄
  (164–244). *Zhentong daozang* 1002.

Beidou qixing houmo biyao yigui 北斗七星護摩秘要儀軌. Trans. Amoghavajra.
  T. 21, 1306.

Beidou qixing houmo fa 北斗七星護摩法. By Yixing 一行 (673–727). *T.* 21,
  1310.

Beidou qixing niansong yigui 北斗七星念誦儀軌. Trans. Vajrabodhi. *T.* 21, 1305.

Beihua jing 悲華経 (*Karuṇāpuṇḍarīka-sūtra*). Trans. Tanwuchan 曇無讖. *T.* 3,
  157.

Ben'ichizan hiki 宀一山秘記. *DNBZ* 119. See also *ZGR* 27.

Ben'ichizan hiki 宀一山秘記. In Fujimaki 2003: 108–117.

Ben'ichizan himitsuki 宀一山秘密記. Ms. Naritasan Library.

Ben'ichizan ki 宀一山記. *ZGR* 27: 2.

Ben'ichizan ki (*Goryū shintō*) 宀一山記 (御流神道). In Fujimaki 2003: 113.

Ben'ichizan ryūketsu hiki 宀一山記龍穴秘記. In Fujimaki 2004: 75–80.

Besson zakki 別尊雑記 (*Gojikkanshō* 五十巻抄). By Shinkaku 心覚 (1117–
  1180). *TZ* 3, 3007: 57–674.

Betsugyō 別行. By Kanjo 寛助 (1052–1125). *T.* 78, 2476.

Bikisho (var. *Hanagaerisho*) 鼻帰書 (1326). By Chien 智円. *ST,* Ronsetsu-hen 2,
  Shingon shintō 2: 505–522.

Bizeibetsu. By Jien 慈円 (1155–1225). In *ZTZ,* Mikkyō 3, Kyōten chūshakurui 2: 212–256.

Bonkan dōmyō shakugi 梵漢同名釈義. In *Ryōbu shintō shū* 両部神道集, 487–491.

Bonten karazu kuyō 梵天火羅図九曜. *TZ* 7: 705–736.

Buchū hiden 峰中秘伝. In *Shugendō shoso* 修験道章疏 1.

Buchū himitsu ki 峰中秘密記. *ST,* Ronsetsu-hen 17, Shugendō 修験道: 441–458.

Budong liuyin gui 不動立印軌.Trans. Amoghavajra. *T.* 21, 1199.

Bukkyō daijiten 仏教大辞典 (*BDJ*). Ed. Mochizuki Shinkō 望月信亨. 10 vols. Kyoto: Sekai seiten kankō kyōkai, 1960.

Bukkyō zuzō shūsei 仏教図像聚成 (*BZS*). In Kyoto shiritsu geijutsu daigaku geijutsu shiryōkan 2004.

Bukong juansuo shenbian zhen'yan jing 不空羂索神変真言経 (Skt. *Amoghapāśa-kalparāja-sūtra,* J. *Fukukenjaku kyō*) (ca. 707–709). Trans. Bodhiruci. *T.* 20, 1092.

Buppō shintō ki 仏法神道記. *ST,* Ronsetsu-hen 1, Shingon shintō 1: 84–90.

Bussetsu chijin kyō 仏説地神経. In *Shugen seiten* 修験聖典, 53–54.

Bussetsu daikōjin seyo fukutoku enman darani-kyō 佛説大荒神施与福徳圓満陀羅尼經. Transl. attr. Amoghavajra. In *Shugen seiten,* 51–53.

Busshari kankei ki 仏舎利勘計記. By Genpō 賢宝 (1333–1398). In Kageyama 1986: 229–257.

Busshari to hōju 仏舎利と宝珠. See Nara kokuritsu hakubutsukan 2001.

Busshin ittai kanjō shō 佛神一躰灌頂鈔. Eizan bunko archives.

Butsuga shariki 仏牙舎利記. *GR* 24: 443.

Byakuhō kushō 白宝口鈔. By Ryōson 亮尊. *TZ* 6–7, 3119.

Byakuhō shō 白宝鈔. By Chōen 澄円 (1218–ca.1290). *TZ* 10, 3191.

Chikubushima engi 竹生島縁起. In Gorai 2000, 2: 26–29. Also in *GR* 25: 616–620.

Chintaku reifu engi shūsetsu 鎮宅霊符縁起集説. By Takuryō 沢了. *ST,* Ronsetsu-hen 16, Onmyōdō: 243–294. Also as *Chintaku reifujin engi shūsetsu,* in Hayakawa 2000: 335–364.

Chishō daishi zenshū 智証大師全集. Ed. Onjōji 園城寺. Ōtsu: Onjōji jimusho, 1918. Reprint, Kyoto: Dōhōsha shuppan, 1978.

Chōgōroku 徴業録 (1775). By Yūsei Genmyō 祐誠玄明 (n.d.). In *Shugendō shoso,* 3: 291–304.

Chōshū ki 長秋記 (1015–1036). By Minamoto no Morotoki 源師時. In *Zōho shiryō taisei* 増補資料大成, vols. 16–17.

Chūgen hiteiki 柱源秘底記. *ST,* Jinja-hen 50, Aso, Hikosan 阿蘇,英彦山 2: 69–102.

Chūin-ryū daiji kikigaki 中院流大事聞書. By Yūkai 宥快 and Seiō 成雄. *T.* 78, 2506.

Chūin-ryū no koto 中院流事. By Yūkai and Seiō. *T.* 78, 2505.

Chūin-ryū shido kuden 中院流四度口伝. By Yūkai. *T.* 78, 2504.

Chūsei Nihongi shū 中世日本紀集. Ed. Abe Yasurō and Yamazaki Makoto. Shinpukuji zenpon sōkan, 2nd ser., vol. 7. See Kokubungaku kenkyū shiryōkan 1999b.

Chūsei sentoku chosaku shū 中世先徳著作集. Ed. Abe Yasurō and Yamazaki Makoto. Shinpukuji zenpon sōkan, 2nd ser., vol. 3. See Kokubungaku kenkyū shiryōkan 2006.

Chūyū ki 中右記. By Fujiwara no Munetada 藤原宗忠 (1062–1141). In *Zōho shiryō taisei,* vols. 8–14.

Daigo-bon Fudō Myōō zuzō 醍醐本不動明王図像. *TZ* 6: 179–200.

Daigo-bon Yakushi jūni shinshō zu 醍醐本薬師十二神将図. *TZ* 7: 405–472.

Daigo-bon zuzō 醍醐寺本図像. *TZ* 4: 45–50.

Daigoji engi 醍醐寺縁起. *DNBZ* 117. Also in *GR* 24: 430.

Daigoji shin'yōroku 醍醐寺新要録 (mid-Kamakura). Ed. Daigoji bunkazai ken-kyūjo. 2 vols. Kyoto: Hōzōkan, 1991 (1941).

Daigoji zōjiki 醍醐寺雑式. By Kyōen 慶円 (fl. 1158–1186). *GR* 25.

Daijingū gosōden kesa ki 大神宮御相伝袈裟記. *GR* 427: 604–605.

Daijingū no honnen 大神宮の本然. In *Kanazawa bunko no chūsei shintō shiryō* 金沢文庫の中世神道資料, ed. Kanagawa kenritsu Kanazawa bunko (1996).

Daijingū sankei ki 大神宮参詣紀 (a.k.a. *Tsūkai sankei ki* 通海参詣記). By Tsūkai 通海 (1234–1305). Jingibu. *ZGR* 28: 927–949.

Dai Nihon bukkyō zensho 大日本仏教全書 (*DNBZ*). Ed. Suzuki Gakujutsudan. 100 vols. Tokyo: Suzuki Gakujutsu Zaidan, 1970–1973. Earlier edition published 1912–1919 by Bussho kankōkai.

Dai Nihonkoku kaibyaku honnen jingi himon. In Kokubungaku kenkyū shiryōkan 1999a: 466–476.

Dai Nihon zokuzōkyō 大日本続蔵経. Ed. Nakano Tatsue. 150 vols. Kyoto: Zōkyō shoin. 1905–1912. Reprint, Taibei: Xinwenfeng, 1968–1970.

Daisōjō Gobō onmonogatari ki 大僧正御房御物語記. By Jōhen 静遍 (1166–1224). Copy dated 1325. Shinpukuji archives. *Daitōkoku Nihonkoku fuhō kechimyaku zu ki* 大唐国日本国付法血脈図記. In *Chishō daishi zenshu,* vol. 2.

Daitōkoku Nihonkoku fuhō kechimyaku zu ki. In *Chishō daishi zenshū* 智証大師全集, vol. 2.

Dankai 譚海. By Tsumura Shōkyō (Masayuki) 津村正恭. Tokyo: Kokusho kankōkai, 1970.

Daozang 道蔵 (*DZ*). 36 vols. Beijing: Wenwu chubanshe; Shanghai: Commercial Press, 1926. See *Concordance du Tao-tsang: titres des ouvrages,* ed. K. M. Schipper, Publications de l'École Française d'Extrême-Orient 104 (Paris: École Française d'Extrême-Orient, 1975).

Dato hiketsu shō 駄都秘決鈔. By Gahō 我宝 (d. 1317). *SZ* 22: 179–293.

Da tuoluoni mofa zhong yisi xinzhou jing 大陀羅尼末法中一字心呪経. Trans. Ratnacinta (Ch. Baosiwei 宝思惟). *T.* 19, 956.

Dazhidu lun 大智度論. Attr. Nāgārjuna. *T.* 25, 1509.

Denbō kanjō shiki 伝法灌頂私記. By Kyōjun 教舜. *T.* 78, 2499.

Dengaku ki 田楽記. *ST,* Ronsetsu-hen 4, Tendai shintō 2: 617–618.

Dengyō daishi zenshū 伝教大師全集. Vol. 5. Tokyo: Nihon Bussho kankōkai, 1926; repr. 1975.

Denju shū 傳受集. By Kanjin 寬信 (1084–1153). *T.* 78, 2482.

Denpu-hō kuketsu 田夫法口決. Kanazawa bunko archives.

Dokyo shō 土巨抄. Oral teachings of Shinken 深賢 (d. 1261), comp. Shinkai 親快 (1215–1276). In Itō Satoshi 2002a: 12–13.

Dubiao Ruyilun niansong fa 都表如意輪念誦法 (J. *Tohyō Nyoirin Kannon nenju-hō*). *T.* 20, 1089.

Eigaku yōki 叡岳要記. *GR* 24: 504–562.

Eiga monogatari 栄華物語 (ca. 1092). *NKBT* 75–76, ed. Matsumura Hiroji 松村博司 and Yamanaka Yutaka 山中裕. English translation in McCullough and McCullough 1980.

Eizan daishi den 叡山大師傳. By Ninchū (n.d.). *ZGR* 8: 2.

Engishiki 延喜式. Comp. Fujiwara no Tadahira 藤原忠平 (880–949). *ST,* Koten-hen 12, ed. Torao Toshiya (1991–1993).

En no gyōja hongi 役行者本記. In *Shugendō shōso,* 3: 245–257.

Fantian huoluo jiuyao 梵天火羅九曜. By Yixing 一行 (673–727). *T.* 21, 1311.

Fomu dakongqiao mingwang jing 仏母大孔雀明王経 (Skt. *Mahāmāyūrī*). Trans. Amoghavajra. *T.* 19, 982.

Fudō Aizen kankenki 不動愛染感見記 (1254). By Nichiren. In *Shōwa teihon Nichiren shōnin ibun* 昭和定本日蓮上人遺文, 1: 16. See Risshō daigaku Nichiren kyōgaku kenkyūjo 1989. English translation in *Writings of Nichiren Shonin,* vol. 5, ed. Jay Sakashita (Honolulu: University of Hawai'i Press, 2008).

Fudō giki 不動儀軌. *TZ* 12: 1057–1108.

Fudoki 風土記. *NKBT* 2, ed. Akimoto Kichirō (1958).

Fudō mandara 不動曼荼羅. *TZ* 6: 201–204.

Fudōson gushō 不動尊愚鈔. Anon. In Hiroya 1925: 222–234.

Fusō ryakki 扶桑略記. *KST* 12, 1965.

Gangōji garan engi 元興寺伽藍縁起. In *Jisha engi* 寺社縁起, *NST* 20: 7–22.

Genji monogatari 源氏物語. *NKBZ* 12–17, ed. Abe Akio et al. (1970–1976). Also *NKBT* 14–18 (1958–1963).

Genkō shakusho 元亨釈書 (1322). By Kokan Shiren 虎関師錬 (1278–1346). *DNBZ* 62, 470. (Vol. 101 in Bussho kankōkai edition.)

Genpei seisuiki 源平盛衰記. Published 1932 by Kokumin bunko kankōkai. Also published 1988 by Shinjinbutsu Ōraisha, ed. Mizuhana Hajime; and 1918 by Hakubunkan in *Kokubun sōsho,* 3rd ed., vol. 8, ed. Ikebe Yoshitaka.

Genpishō 玄祕抄. By Jichiun 実運 (1105–1160). *T.* 78, 2486.

Genzu reikiki ki 現図麗気記. *ST,* Ronsetsu-hen 1, Shingon shintō 1: 81–83.

Gobu darani mondō gesan shūhi ron 五部陀羅尼問答偈讃宗秘論. By Kūkai, *T.* 78, 2464.

Gochinza shidaiki shō. ST, Ronsetsu-hen 6, Ise shintō 2.

Godaikokūzō yō 五大虚空蔵様. *TZ* 6: 81–93.

Godaikokūzō zakyo sho zuzō 五大虚空蔵座居諸図像. *TZ* 6: 69–80.

Godaikokūzō zuzō 五大虚空蔵図像. *TZ* 6: 63–68.

Godai myōō zuzō 五大明王. *TZ* 6: 157–168.

Godaison zō 五大尊像. *TZ* 6: 123–130.

Godaison zuzō 五大尊図像. *TZ* 6: 131–146.

Gōdanshō 江談抄. By Ōe no Masafusa (1041–1111). Comp. Fujiwara no Sanekane 藤原実兼 (1249–1322). In *Kōhon gōdan shō no kenkyū* 校本江談抄の研究, ed. Kōda Toshio 甲田利雄, vols. 1–2 (Tokyo: Zoku gunsho ruijū kanseikai, 1988). Also in *GR* 17.

Gogyō rokkon shugo saimon. In Gorai 2000, 1: 483–485.

Gojikkanshō 五十巻鈔. By Kōzen 興然 (1120–1203). *SZ* 29–31.

Gōke shidai 江家次第. By Ōe Masafusa 大江匡房 (1041–1111). *ST,* Chōgi saishi-hen 朝儀祭祀編 4.

Goma kuketsu 護摩口決. By Raiyu 賴瑜 (1226–1304). *T.* 79, 2532.

Gong'yang shier daweidetian baoen pin 供養二大威徳天報恩品. Trans. Amoghavajra. *T.* 21, 1297.

Gonjinshō 厳神抄. *ZGR,* Jingi-bu 49: 636–653.

Gonki 權記. By Fujiwara no Yukinari 厳神抄 (972–1027). In *Dai Nihon kiroku,* vols. 4–5.

Gorin kujimyō himitsu shaku 五輪久字明祕密釋, by Kakuban 覺鑁 (1095–1143). *T.* 79, 2514.

Goyuigō 御遺告 (a.k.a. *Nijūgokajō goyuigō* 二十五固条告). Attr. Kūkai (774–835). *T.* 77, 2431.

Goyuigō daiji 御遺告大事 (var. *Tōchō daiji* 東長大事). By Monkan 文観 (1278–1357). Ms. Ninnaji (Kyoto). See Makino and Fujimaki 2002.

Goyuigō hiketsu 御遺告秘決. Attr. Jichiun 実運 (1105–1160) but probably by Monkan. *ZSZ* 26: 3–7. See also ms. in Hikone Library, Kondō Collection.

Goyuigō hiyō shō 御遺告秘要鈔. Kanazawa bunko shiryō zensho 金沢文庫資料全書, Butten 仏典 6: Shingon-hen.

Goyuigō shakugi shō 御遺告釈疑鈔. *ZSZ* 26.

Goyuigō shaku yōshō. Kanazawa bunko shiryō zensho Butten 金沢文庫資料全書, Butten 仏典6: Shingon-hen 真言篇 1.

Goyuigō shichika daiji 御遺告七箇大事. Ms. Chishaku-in, Kyōto. In Rappo 2014, docs. 13: 75–86.

Goyuigō shichika hihō 御遺告七箇秘法. Colophon by Shingyō 真慶 (fl. mid-Kamakura). In Fujimaki 2002a: 140–142.

Gōzanze myōō zōshū 隆三世明王像集. *TZ* 12: 1109–1130.

Gukanshō 愚管抄. By Jien 慈円 (1155–1225). Ed. Okami Masao 岡見正雄 and Akamatsu Toshihide 赤松俊秀. Tokyo: Iwanami shoten, 1967.

Gumonji Kokūzō bosatsu 求聞持虚空蔵菩薩. *TZ* 6: 62–63.

Gunsho ruijū 群書類従 (*GR*). 25 vols. Zoku gunsho ruijū kanseikai, 1959–1960.

Gyōki 御記 (ca. 1180). By Shukaku Hōshinnō 守覺法親王 (1150–1202). *T.* 78, 2493.

Gyokuyō 玉葉. By Kujō Kanezane 九条兼実 (1149–1207). Ed. Ichishima Kenkichi 市島謙吉. 3 vols. Tokyo: Kokusho kankōkai, 1907. See also the 1966 edition published by Sumiya shobō.

Gyokuyō wakashū 玉葉和歌集. In *Gyokuyōshū sōsakuin* 玉葉集総索引, ed. Takizawa Sadao 滝沢貞夫 (Tokyo: Meiji shoin, 1988).

Gyōrinshō 行林抄. By Jōnen 静然 (fl. 1154). *T.* 76, 2409.

Hachiman Daibosatsu 八幡大菩薩. In *Chūsei Nihongi shū*, 423–440.

Hachiman gudōkun 八幡愚童訓. By Kaigen (d. 1469) and Urabe Kanetomo (d. 1511). *ZGR* 30, Jingi-bu: 49–109. Also in *Jisha engi* 寺社縁起, *NST* 20: 169–206 (A) and 207–274 (B).

Hachiman kō hishiki 八幡講秘式. By Raijo 頼助(1246–1297). In Funata 2011: 348–350.

Hachiman Usa-gū gotakusen shū 八幡宇佐宮御託宣集 (1313). By Jin'un 神吽 (1230–1314). *ST,* Jinja-hen 47, Usa 宇佐: 13–206.

Hakusan no ki 白山の記. In *Jisha engi* 寺社縁起, *NST* 20: 291–304.

Hakusan ōkagami 白山大鏡. In Uemura 2000: 14–49.

Haru no miya Sonjōō go-saimon. NSSS 17: 325.

Heike monogatari 平家物語 (Kakuichi-bon 覚一本) (late 12th–early 13th c.). Anon. *NKBT* 32–33, ed. Takagi Ichinosuke et al. 1960.

Henkushō 遍口鈔. By Seigen 成賢 (1162–1231), ed. Dōkyō 道教 (1200–1236). *T.* 78, 2496.

Henmyōin daishi myōjin gotakusen ki 遍明院大師明神御託宣記. In *Chūsei Kōyasan engi no kenkyū* 中世高野山縁起の研究, ed. Abe Yasurō (Nara: Gangōji bunkazai kenkyūjo, 1983), 103–112.

Hie hongi (1235). By Kenchū (d.u.). *ST,* Ronsetsu-hen, Tendai shintō 2: 543–586. See also *ZGR,* Jingi-bu 52: 707–749.

Hie Sannō ben 日吉三王辨. In *ST,* Ronsetsu-hen 4, Tendai shintō 2: 1073–1084.

Hie Sannō gongen chishinki 日吉山王權現知新記. By Gōkan 豪觀. *TSZ* 12: 43–179.

Hie Sannō gongen ki 日吉三王權現記. By Kakushin 覚深. *ZTZ,* Shintō 1, Sannō shintō 1: 400–410.

Hie Sannō hiden ki 日吉山王祕傳記. By Gigen 義源. *ZTZ,* Shintō 1, Sannō shintō 1: 211–221.

Hie Sannō ki 日吉山王. *ZTZ,* Shintō 1, Sannō shintō 1: 270–296.

Hie Sannō rishōki 日吉山王利生記. *ZGR* 2, Jingi-bu 50: 654–706. Also *ST,* Jin-ja-hen 29, Hie: 649–695.

Hie Sannō sansha shidai 日吉三王參社次第. *ST,* Ronsetsu-hen 4, Tendai shintō 2: 675–686.

Hie Sannō sansha shidai, shiki 日吉三王參社次第　私記. *ST,* Ronsetsu-hen 4, Tendai shintō 2: 653–674.

Hie Sannō shinki. 日吉三王新記. By Kakuo 覺雄. *ZGR* 52: 751–772.

Hie Sannō zatsuki 日吉三王雜記. *ZTZ,* Shintō 1, Sannō shintō 1: 324–354.

Hie-sha shintō himitsu ki 日吉三王神道秘密記. *GR* 18: 441–469.

Hie shinkō gonyūraku kenmon ryakki 日吉神輿御入洛見聞畧記. *GR* 18: 470–472.

Higashiyama ōrai 東山往来 (1086). *ZGR* 359. Translated in Waley 1932: 531–562.

Higo kokushi 肥後国誌. Comp. Gotō Zezan 後藤是山. 2 vols. Kumamoto: Kyūshū Nichinichi Shinbunsha Insatsubu, 1916–1917. Reprint, Kumamoto: Seichōsha, 1972.

Hikekyō 悲華経. See *Beihua jing.*

Hikosan rūki 彦山流記 In Gorai 2000, 2: 463–473.

Hikosan shugendō hiketsu kanjō no maki 彦山修験道秘訣灌頂巻. In *Shugendō shōso,* 2: 556–570.

Hikosan shugen saihi injin kuketsu shū 彦山修験最秘印信口決集. In *Shugendō shōso,* 2: 519–555.

Hikyō shō 秘経抄. By Jien 慈円 (1155–1225). *ZTZ* 3, Kyōten chūsakurui 2: 1–31.

Himitsu gentei kuketsu 秘密源底口決 (1327–1334). In *Chūsei sentoku chosaku shū,* 485–498. See Kokubungaku kenkyū shiryōkan 2006. See also Watanabe 1999.

Himitsu shugen yōhō shū 祕密修験要法集. *ST,* Ronsetsu-hen 17, Shugendō: 515–542.

Hinoo kuketsu 檜尾口決. By Jichie 實慧. *T.* 78, 2465.

Hishō 祕鈔. By Shōken 勝賢 (1138–1196). Ed. Shukaku Hōshinnō 守覚法親王 (1150–1202). *T.* 78, 2489.

Hishō mondō 祕鈔問答. By Raiyu 頼瑜 (1226–1304). *T.* 79, 2536.

Hizō konpō shō 祕藏金寶鈔. By Jichiun 實運 (1105–1160). *T.* 78, 2485.

Hōbutsu shū 宝物集. Attr. Taira no Yasuyori 平康頼 (fl. 1190–1200). *ZGR* 32: 2. See also *Hōbutsu shū, Kankyo no tomo, Hirasan kojin reitaku* 宝物集 閑居友 比良山古人霊託, ed. Koizumi Hiroshi 小泉弘 et al. *SNKBT* 40.

Hōgen monogatari 保元物語. Ed. Takadashi Sadaichi 高橋貞一. Tokyo: Kōdansha, 1952. English translation in Wilson 2001.

Hōju ki 宝珠紀. By Shōken 勝堅 (1138–1196).

Hōju no koto 宝珠事. By Shōken 勝堅 (1138–1196). Daigoji Sanbō-in shōgyō archives, 268.3.

Hōki naiden ホキ内伝. Attr. Abe no Seimei. *ST,* Ronsetsu-hen 16, Onmyōdō: 27–86. Also *ZGR* 31a: 347–414.

Hokishō ホキ抄. In *Nihon koten gisho sōkan* 日本古典偽書総観, ed. Fukazawa Tōru 深沢徹, vol. 3 (Tokyo: Gendai shichō shinsha, 2004), 163–195.

Hokke betchō 法華　別帖. By Jien 慈円 (1155–1225). *ZTZ,* Mikkyō 3, Kyōten chūshakurui: 257–290.

Hokke ryakugi 法華略儀 (full title: *Nyū shingonmon jū nyojitsuken kōen hokke ryakugi* 入真言門住如実見講演法華略儀). By Enchin. *T.* 56, 2192.

Hokushin saimon 北辰祭文. *NSSS* 17: 321.

Hokuto bosatsu darani kyō 北斗菩薩陀羅尼經. In *Shugen seiten,* 50–51.

Hokuto mishihō saimon 北斗御修法祭文. *NSSS* 17: 325–326.

Hōkyōin daranikyō wakai hiryakushaku 宝篋印陀羅尼経和解秘略釈. In Hiroya 1925: 124–181.

Hōkyōshō 寶鏡鈔. By Yūkai 宥快 (1346–1416). *T.* 77, 2456. In *Tachikawa jakyō to sono shakaiteki haikei no kenkyū* 立川邪教とその社会的背景の研究, ed. Moriyama Shōshin 守山聖真 (Tokyo: Rokuyaon, 1965), 572–581.

Honchō jinja kō 本朝神社考. *NSSS* 26: 79–180.

Honchō kōsōden. 本朝高僧伝. *DNBZ* 431.

Honchō monzui 本朝文粹. *NKBT* 27; *KST* 29: 2.

Honchō shinsenden 本朝神仙伝. *NST* 7; *ZGR* 8.

Honmyō-ku saimon 本命供祭文. *NSSS* 17: 327.

Hyakurenshō 百錬抄. Anon. (late 13th c.). *KST* 2.

Ichijitsu shintō ki 一實神道記. *ST,* Ronsetsu-hen 4, Tendai shintō 2: 871–994.

Ichi ni sun [Sanzon] gōgyō hi shidai 一二寸合行秘次第. In *Chūsei sentoku chosaku shū,* 351–402 and 501–511.

Inari Daimyōjin engi 稲荷大明神縁起. In *Inari shinkō jiten* 稲荷信仰辞典. See Yamaori 1999: 380–394.

Inari Daimyōjin ruki 稲荷大明神流記. In *Inari shinkō jiten.* See Yamaori 1999: 372–379.

Inari ki 稲荷記. *ST,* Jinja-hen 9: Inari, 7–22. See also Yamaori 1999: 359–368.

Inari ki hiku kikigaki 稲荷記祕口聞書. *ST,* Ronsetsu-hen 2, Shingon shintō 2: 701–706.

Inryōken nichiroku 蔭凉軒日録. *DNBZ* 75–78, 596.

Ise nisho kōtaijin gochinza denki 伊勢二所皇太神御鎮座伝記. *ST,* Ronsetsu-hen 5, Ise shintō 1: 11–32.

Ise nisho kōtaijin gochinza denki shō 伊勢二所皇太神御鎮座伝記鈔. *ST,* Ronsetsu-hen 6, Ise shintō 2: 25–68.

Ise shintō shū 伊勢神道集. In Kokubungaku kenkyū shiryōkan 1999b.

Ishiyamadera engi 石山寺縁起. *DNBZ* 86, 791: 269–278.

Ishiyama shichishū 石山寺七集. By Shunnyū 淳祐 (890–953). *TZ* 2, 2924.

Ison shō 異尊抄. By Shukaku Hōshinnō 守覺法親王. *T.* 78, 2490.

Jakushōdō kokkyōshū 寂照堂谷響集. By Unshō 運敞 (1614–1693). *DNBZ* 149: 1–381.

Jikaku daishi den 慈覚大師伝. *ZTZ, shiden* 続天台宗全書、史伝, 2: 58–76, ed. Tendai shūten hensanjo (1990).

Jikkanshō 十巻抄. See *Zuzōshō* 図像抄. *TZ* 3, 3006.

Jikki shō 實歸鈔. By Jinken 深賢 (d. 1261). *T.* 78, 2497.

Jimon denki horoku 寺門伝記補録. By Shikō 志晃 (1662–1730). *DNBZ* 127, 787: 108–157.

Jindaikan hiketsu 神代巻秘決. *ZST,* Ronsetsu-hen, Shūgō shintō 習合神道: 41–406.

Jindaikan shikenmon 神代巻私見聞. By Ryōhen 良遍 (n.d.). *ST,* Ronsetsu-hen 3, Tendai shintō 1: 559–594.

Jingangfeng louge yiqie yujia yuqi jing 金剛峯楼閣一切瑜伽瑜祇経. Trans. Vajrabodhi. *T.* 18, 867.

Jingi dōryō fuin 神祇道靈符印. *ST,* Ronsetsu-hen 9, Urabe shintō 卜部神道: 145–163.

Jingi hishō 神祇秘抄. *ST,* Ronsetsu-hen 1, Shingon shintō 1: 175–208. See also *Chūsei Nihongi shū,* 375–401.

Jingi keizu 神祇系図. By Ryōhen 良遍 (n.d.). *ST,* Ronsetsu-hen 3, Tendai shintō 1: 595.

Meishuku shū 明宿集. By Konparu Zenchiku 金春禅竹 (1405–ca. 1470). In Omote and Katō 1974. Also in *Konparu kodensho shūsei* 金春古伝書集成, ed. Omote Akira and Itō Masayoshi 伊藤正義 (Tokyo: Wan'ya shoten 1969).

Mii zokutō ki 三井続灯記. *DNBZ, Denki sōsho,* 232–247.

Mippō sōjō shinron yōshō 密法相承審論要抄. By Jihen 慈遍 (fl. 14th c.). *ST,* Ronsetsu-hen 3, Tendai shintō 1: 475–514.

Mitsugon jōdo ryakkan 密嚴淨土略觀. By Kakuban 覺鑁 1095–1143). *T.* 79, 2515.

Miwa daimyōjin engi 三輪大明神縁起. *ZGR* 46: 536–543.

Miwa-ryū kanjō injin hiketsu 三輪流灌頂印信秘決. *ST,* Ronsetsu-hen 2, Shingon shintō 2: 227–322.

Miwa-ryū kanjō shodaiji kuketsu 三輪流灌頂諸大事口決. In Ōmiwa jinja shiryō henshu iinkai 1983.

Miwa-ryū shintō-hen 三輪流神道篇. In Ōmiwa jinja shiryō 大神神社資料, vols. 5–6.

Miwa-ryū shintō-hen (zokuzoku) 三輪流神道篇 (続々). In Ōmiwa jinja shiryō 大神神社資料, vol. 10.

Miwa-ryū shintō kanjō denju roku 三輪流神道灌頂伝授録. *ST,* Ronsetsu-hen 2, Shingon shintō 2: 363–382.

Miwa-ryū shintō kanjō hoshin shō 三輪流神道灌頂補真鈔. *ST,* Ronsetsu-hen 2, Shingon shintō 2: 125–150.

Miwa-ryū shintō kanjō juyoshiki 三輪流神道灌頂授与式. In Ōmiwa jinja shiryō 大神神社資料, 5: 74–78.

Miwa-san Byōdōji Kyōen Kan shōnin betsuden 三輪山平等寺慶円観上人別伝. *ST,* Ronsetsu-hen 2, Shingon shintō 2: 483–496.

Miwa shōnin gyōjō shō 三輪上人行状抄. *ST,* Ronsetsu-hen 2, Shingon shintō 2: 21–24; also Miwa shintō-hen, 16–17.

Miyadera enji shō 宮寺縁事抄. *ST,* Jinja-hen 7, Iwashimizu: 1–676.

Mohezhiguan 摩訶止観. By Zhiyi 智顗 (538–597). *T.* 46, 1911.

Mudai ki 無題記. *ZST,* Ronsetsu-hen, Shūgō shintō: 407–540. Also in *Inari taisha yushoki shūsei, Shinkō chosaku-hen* 稲荷大社由緒紀集成―信仰著作篇 (Kyoto: Fushimi Inari sha).

Murasaki Shikibu nikki 紫式部日記. In *Murasaki shikibu nikki Sarashina nikki* 紫式部日記・更級日記, ed. Tamai Kōsuke 玉井 幸助, *Nihon koten zensho* 26 (Tokyo: Asahi shinbunsha, 1948).

Murōji engi 室生寺縁起. Copy dated to 1747. See Fujimaki 2003.

Murōzan goshari sōden engi 室生山御舎利相伝縁起 (1302). By Sōmyō 宗明 (n.d.). *ZGR* 27: 2.

Myōken bosatsu zō 妙見菩薩像. *TZ* 7: 663–692.

Myōō-bu zuzō 明王部図像. *TZ* 6: 241–276.

Nichiiki hongi 日諱貴本紀. In *Ryōbu shintō shū,* 493–506.

Nichinyo gozen gohenji 日如御前御返事. In *Shōwa teihon Nichiren shōnin ibun* 昭和定本日蓮聖人遺文 2 (256): 1375–1376. See Risshō daigaku Nichiren kyōgaku kenkyūjo 1989.

Nihongi ichiryū no daiji 日本紀一流の大事. *ST,* Ronsetsu-hen 2, Shingon shintō 2: 523–536.

Nihongi Miwaryū. In *Chūsei Nihongi shū,* 457–486.

Nihon kiryaku 日本紀略. In *Kokushi taikei,* ed. Kokushi taikei kankōkai, vols. 10–11 (Tokyo: Kokushi taikei kankōkai, 1929; repr. 1988).

Nihon koten bungaku taikei 日本古典文学大系 (*NKBT*). 100 vols. Tokyo: Iwanami shoten, 1957–1967.

Nihon koten bungaku zenshū 日本古典文学全集 (*NKBZ*). 60 vols. Tokyo: Shōgakkan, 1970–1976.

Nihon ryōiki 日本霊異記 (ca. 823). By Keikai 景戒 (fl. 9th c.). *NKBT* 70, ed. Endō Yoshimoto 遠藤嘉基 and Kasuga Kazuo 春日和男.

Nihon shisō taikei 日本思想大系 (*NST*). 67 vols. Tokyo: Iwanami shoten, 1970–1982.

Nihon shoki 日本書紀 (720). By Toneri Shinnō 舎人親王 (676–735) et al. *NKBT* 67–68, ed. Sakamoto Tarō 坂本太郎 et al. (1967).

Nihon shoki kan daiichi kikigaki 日本書紀巻第一聞書. By Ryōhen 良遍. *ST,* Ronsetsu-hen 3, Tendai shintō 1: 515–558.

Nihon shomin bunka shiryō shūsei 日本庶民文化資料集成 (*NSBS*). 16 vols. Tokyo: San'ichi shobō, 1973–1978.

Nihon shomin seikatsu shiryō shūsei. 日本庶民生活資料集成 (*NSSS*). Ed. Miyamoto Tsuneichi 宮本常一 et al. 31 vols. Tokyo: San'ichi shobō, 1968–1984.

Nijūhachibu narabini Jūni shinshō zu 二十八部并十二神将図. *TZ* 7: 479–522.

Nijūhasshuku zuzō 二十八宿図像. *TZ* 7: 775–800.

Nikkōsan engi 日光山縁起. In *Jisha engi* 寺社縁起, *NST* 20: 275–290.

Nisho daijingū reiki ki 二所大神宮麗氣記. *ST,* Ronsetsu-hen 1, Shingon shintō 1: 3–6.

Nyorai shishari denrai 如来歯舎利伝来. By Shin'yu 信瑜. *ZGR* 25: 716.

Omokage monogatari おもかげ物語. In *Muromachi jidai monogatari taisei* 室町時代物語大成, ed. Yokoyama Shigeru 横山重 and Matsumoto Ryūshin 松本隆信, vol. 3 (Tokyo: Kadokawa shoten, 1973–1985).

Ōmiwa jinja shiryō 大神神社資料. Ed. Ōmiwa jinja shiryō henshū iinkai 大神神社資料編修委員会. 10 vols. Sakurai: Ōmiwa jinja shiryō henshu iinkai, 1968–1991.

Onjōji denki 園城寺伝記. *DNBZ* 86, 786: 56–107.

Ono rokujō 小野六帖. By Ningai 仁海 (951–1046). *T.* 78, 2473.

Ono rui hishō 小野類祕鈔. By Kanjin 寛信. *SZ* 36: 3–92.

Oto Gohō kōshiki 乙護法講式. *ST,* Jinja-hen 50: Aso, Hikosan 阿蘇, 英彦山, 258–262.

Putixin lun 菩提心論. Trans. attr. Amoghavajra. *T.* 32, 1665.

Qifo bapusa soshuo da tuoluoni shenzhou jing 七仏八菩薩所説大陀羅尼神呪経. *T.* 21, 1332.

Qixing Ruyilun bimi yaojing 七星如意輪秘密要経 (J. *Shichishō Nyoirin himitsu yōkyō*). Trans. Amoghavajra. *T.* 20, 1091.

Reiki kanjō (shi) 麗氣灌頂私. *ST,* Ronsetsu-hen 2, Shingon shintō 2: 25–36.

Reiki ki 麗氣記. *ST,* Ronsetsu-hen 1, Shingon shintō 1: 1–118. *ZGR* 59: 92–136.

Reikiki gu'an shō 麗氣記愚案鈔. *ST,* Ronsetsu-hen 1, Shingon shintō 1: 327–352.

Reiki kikigaki 麗氣聞書. *ST,* Ronsetsu-hen 1, Shingon shintō 1: 211–274.

Reikiki shō 麗氣記抄. *ST,* Ronsetsu-hen 1, Shingon shintō 1: 275–326.

Reikiki shūi shō 麗氣記拾遺鈔. *ST,* Ronsetsu-hen 1, Shingon shintō 1: 167–174.

Reiki seisaku shō 麗氣記制作抄. *ST,* Ronsetsu-hen 1, Shingon shintō 1: 151–166.

Renwang jing shu 仁王経疏. By Wonchok 円測. *T.* 33, 1708.

Renwang niansong yigui 仁王念誦儀軌. Trans. Amoghavajra. *T.* 19, 994.

Rokugō kaisan Ninmon bosatsu hongi 六郷開山仁聞大菩薩本記. In *Jisha engi* 寺社縁起, *NST* 20: 305–325.

Ruijū jingi hongen 類従神祇本源. In Kokubungaku kenkyū shiryōkan 1999c.

Ruyi baozhu zhuanlun bimi xianshen chengfo jinlun zhouwang jing (J. *Nyoi hōju tenrin himitsu genshin jōbutsu kinrin shuō kyō*) 如意宝珠転輪秘密現身成仏金輪呪王経. Trans. Amoghavajra. *T.* 19, 961.

Ryōbu shintō shū 両部神道集. Ed. Abe Yasurō and Yamazaki Makoto. Shinpukuji zenpon sōkan 真福寺善本叢刊, 2nd ser., vol. 6. See Kokubungaku kenkyū shiryōkan 1999a.

Ryōgū keimon shinshaku 両宮形文深釈. In *Ryōbu shintō shū* 両部神道集, 429–441.

Ryōin ketsu 了因決. By Ryōe 了惠 (n.d.). *T.* 77, 2414.

Ryōzu happi Aizen-ō ki 両頭八臂愛染王記 (1297). By Enkai 円戒 (n.d.). Kanazawa bunko archives, no. 292.

Ryōzu happi Aizen-ō ki 両頭八臂愛染王記. By Kenna 劔阿 (1261–1338). Kanazawa bunko archives, inv. 307 (971).

Saidaiji Eison denki shūsei 西大寺叡尊傳記集成. Ed. Nara kokuritsu bunkazai. kenkyūjo 奈良国立文化財研究所. Kyoto: Hōzōkan, 1977.

Saigoku hiden 最極秘伝. In *Chūsei sentoku chosaku shū*, 491–492.

Saigoku hi kanjō 最極秘灌頂. Kanazawa bunko archives.

Saigoku himitsu shō 最極秘密鈔 (1337). By Monkan 文観 (1278–1357). In *Monkan Kōshin chosaku no kenkyū: Sanzon gōgyo-hō kankei shōgyō shiryō-shū*, ed. Abe Yasurō (Nagoya: Nagoya daigaku, 2011), 133–138.

Saishōōkyō 最勝王経. See *Jinguangming zuishengwang jing.*

Sakei ki 左京記. By Minamoto Tsuneyori 源経頼 (985–1039). In *Zōho Shiryō taisei* 増補資料大成, vol. 6.

Saki 左記. By Shukaku Hōshinnō 守覺法親王. *T.* 78, 2492.

Sanbōe kotoba 三宝絵詞. By Minamoto no Tamenori 源為憲 (d. 1010). In *Sanbōe ryakuchū* 三宝絵繪略注, ed. Yamada Yoshio 山田孝雄 (Tokyo: Hōbunkan, 1951). English translation in Kamens 1988.

Sanbōin-ryū dōsen sōjō kuketsu 三宝院流洞泉相承口決. By Dōchō 動潮, Unjo 運助, and Ryūō 隆応. *SZ* 33: 11–400; 34: 15–256.

Sange sairyakki 山外最略記. *ZTZ*, Shintō 1, Sannō Shintō 1: 149–166.

Sange yōryakki 山外要略記 by Kenshin 顕真. *ST*, Ronsetsu-hen 4, Tendai shintō 2: 1–362. Also *ZTZ*, Shintō 1, Sannō Shintō: 1–148.

Sangyō sōō Miwa Sannō 三業相應三輪山王. *ST*, Ronsetsu-hen 4, Tendai shintō 2: 523–527.

Sanjūshichison haiishō 三十七尊配位鈔 (1553). By Kyōga 教雅. Ms. Kyoto University Library.

Sankaku kashiwa denki 三角柏伝記. In *Ryōbu shintō shū*, 361–368.

Sanmon dōsha ki 山門堂舎記. In *Shugendō shiryō shū* 2: 47–75.

Sanmon shibun kiroku ryakki 山門四分記録略記. *ZTZ*, Shintō 1, Sannō shintō: 149–166.

Sannō hiki 山王秘記. *ST*, Ronsetsu-hen 4, Tendai shintō 2: 587–602; and *ZTZ*, Shintō 1, Sannō shintō: 222–234.

Sannō hiyō ki 山王秘要記. *ST*, Ronsetsu-hen 4, Tendai shintō 2: 529–541.

Sannō ichijitsu shintō hiroku. ST, Ronsetsu-hen 4, Tendai shintō 2: 693–870.

Sannō ichijitsu shintō ki. ST, Ronsetsu-hen 4, Tendai shintō 2: 995–1056.

Sannō mitsuki 山王密記. *ZTZ*, Shintō 1, Sannō shintō: 235–269.

Sannō mitsuki (bonji) 山王密記 (梵字). *ZTZ*, Shintō 1, Sannō shintō: 181–188.

Sannō yurai 山王由来. *ST*, Ronsetsu-hen 4, Tendai shintō 2: 603–612.

Sanshū shingi narabi ni shintō himitsu 三種神祇并神道秘密. In *Chūsei Nihongi shū*, 441–456.

Sansun Fu[dō] 三寸不 [動]. Kanazawa Bunko archives.

Santō mindan shū 三島民譚集. In *Yanagita Kunio zenshū*, 5: 55–484.

Sanzon gōgyō hiketsu 三尊合行秘決 (1349). Shinpukuji archives, Ōsu bunko, no. 60.6. In Rappo 2010b: 189–193.

Sanzon gōgyō hi shidai (shiki) 一二寸合行秘次第私記. In *Chūsei sentoku chosaku shū*, 499–512.

Sasagimon 些々疑文. By Enchin 円珍. In *Chishō daishi zenshū* 智証大師全集, 3: 1038–1070.

Seiryō gongen onkoto 清瀧権現御事. *ST,* Ronsetsu-hen 2, Shingon shintō 2: 537–538.

Sekizan Myōjin engi 赤山明神縁起. *ST,* Ronsetsu-hen 4, Tendai shintō 2: 623–626.

Shasekishū 砂石集. By Mujū Ichien 無住一円 (1226–1312). *NKBT* 85.

Sheng Wudongzun anzhen jiaguo deng fa 聖無動尊安鎮家国等法. *T.* 21, 1203.

Shichisha ryakki 七社略記. By Zonshin 存心. *TZS* 12 : 225–232.

Shidoji engi 志度寺縁起. In *Setouchi jisha engi shū* 瀬戸内寺社縁起集, ed. Wada Shigeki 和田茂樹 (Hiroshima: Hiroshima chūsei bungaku kenkyū, 1967).

Shiertian gong 'yang yigui 十二天供養軌. *T.* 21, 1298.

Shigisan engi 信貴山縁起. In *Jisha engi* 寺社縁起, *NST* 20: 23–28.

Shijō hiketsu 四帖秘決. Oral teachings of Jien 慈円 (1155–1225), recorded by Jiken 慈賢. *ZTZ,* Mikkyō 3, Kyōten chūshakurui: 291–423.

Shijūjō ketsu 四十帖決. By Chōen 長宴 (1016–1081). *T.* 75, 2408.

Shikan 四巻. By Kōzen 興然 (1120–1203). *T.* 78, 2500.

Shikanshō 四巻抄. By Shunzen 俊然. *SZ* 31: 215–372.

Shike shō zuzō 四家鈔図像. *TZ* 3: 749–916.

Shiku 師口. By Yōzen 榮然 (1172–1259). *T.* 78, 2501.

Shin bongo ki. 神梵語記. *ST,* Ronsetsu-hen 1, Shingon shintō 1: 54–59.

Shinchū ki. 心柱麗氣記. *ST,* Ronsetsu-hen 1, Shingon shintō 1: 50–53.

Shingō ki. 神號記. *ST,* Ronsetsu-hen 1, Shingon shintō 1: 64–73.

Shingonshū zensho. Ed. Shingonshū zensho kankōkai. 44 vols. Kōyasan: Shingonshū zensho kankōkai, 1933–1939.

Shinkeichū reiki ki 神形注麗気記. *ST,* Ronsetsu-hen 1, Shingon shintō 1: 74–76.

Shinkokuō gosho 神国王御書. By Nichiren 日蓮. In *Shōwa teihon Nichiren Shōnin ibun* 昭和定本日蓮聖人遺文, 1: 877–893. See Risshō daigaku Nichiren kyōgaku kenkyūjo 1989.

Shin Nihon koten bungaku taikei 新日本古典文学大系 (*SNKBT*). 100 vols. Iwanami shoten, 1989–.

Shinnyokan 真如観. In *Tendai hongakuron* 天台本覚論. *NST* 9.

Shinpen kokka taikan 新編国歌大観 (*KT*). 20 vols. Kadokawa shoten, 1983–1992.

Shinpen Nihon koten bungaku zenshū 新編日本古典文学全集 (*SNKBZ*). 88 vols. Tokyo: Shōgakkan, 1994–.

Shinra ryakki 新羅略記. *ST,* Ronsetsu-hen 17, Shugendō: 319–358.

Shinsen hiketsu shū. In *Atsuta kōshiki,* 107–108.

Shinshō tōtsūki 神将東通記. In Itō Satoshi 2011: 269–270.

Shinshō tōtsūki, Daijingū ontakusen ki 神将東通記, 大神宮御託宣記. In *Ryōbu shintō shū* 両部神道集, 457–464.

Shintai zu 神体図. *ST,* Ronsetsu-hen 1, Shingon shintō 1: 91–118.

Shintei zōho kokushi taikei 新訂増補国史大系 (*KST*). 60 vols. Tokyo: Yoshikawa kōbunkan, 1929–1964.

Shintō daiji 神道大事. Ms. Kyōtō University Library.

Shintō kanjō seiki 神道灌頂清軌. *ST,* Ronsetsu-hen 2, Shingon shintō 2: 183–210.

Shintō kan'yō 神道簡要. In *Ise shintō shū* 伊勢神道集, 681–696.

Shintō shū 神道集. *ST,* Bungaku-hen, Shintō shū.

Shintō taikei 神道大系 (*ST*). 123 vols. Ed. Shintō taikei hensankai 神道大系編纂会. Tokyo: Shintō taikei hensankai, 1977–1994.

Shintō zatsuzatsushū 神道雑々集. Ms. Tenri Library, Yoshida bunko 吉田文庫.

Shinzoku tekkin ki 真俗擲金記 (1265). Attr. Shukaku Hōshinnō 守覚法親王. Sonkyōkaku Bunko 尊経閣文庫 archives.

Shinzoku zatsuki mondōshō 真俗雑記問答鈔. By Raiyu 頼瑜 (1226–1304). *SZ* 37: 3–482.

Shiojiri 塩尻. By Amano Sadakage 天野信景. In *Nihon zuihitsu taisei*日本随筆大成, 3rd ser., vols. 9–10 (Tokyo: Yoshikawa kōbunkan, 1930; repr. 1995–1996).

Shirushi no sugi しるしの杉. By Ban Nobutomo 伴信友 (1775–1846). *ST,* Jinja-hen, Inari 稲荷: 375–436; *NSSS* 26: 673–704.

Shōgo shū 勝語集, by Ejū 慧什. *T.* 78, 2479.

Sho Monju zuzō 諸文殊図像. *TZ* 6: 95–113.

Shōmonki 将門記. Ed. Hayashi Rokurō 林陸朗. Tokyo: Gendai shichōsha, 1975. English translation in Rabinovitch 1986.

Shoryū kanjō 諸流灌頂. *ST,* Ronsetsu-hen 2, Shingon shintō 2: 3–20.

Shoson yōshō 諸尊要抄. By Jichiun 實運 (1105–1160). *T.* 78, 2484.

Shoson zuzō 諸尊図像. By Shinkaku 心覺. *TZ* 3, 3008: 675–748.

Shōyūki 小右記. By Fujiwara no Sanesuke 藤原実資. In *Zōho shiryō taisei,* vols. 1–3.

Shozan engi 諸山縁起. In *Jisha engi* 寺社縁起, *NST* 20: 89–140.

Shugen buchū hiden 修験峰中秘伝. In *Shugendō shōso,* 1: 557–584.

Shugendō shiryō shū 修験道資料集. See Gorai 2000.

Shugendō shōso 修験道章疏. Ed. Nihon daizōkyō hensankai 日本大蔵経編纂会. 4 vols. Tokyo: Nihon daizōkyō hensankai, 1916–1919. Reprint, Tokyo: Kokusho hakkōkai, 2000.

Shugendō shuyō hiketsu shū 修験道修要秘決集. *ST,* Ronsetsu-hen 17, Shugendō: 242–318.

Shugen hiokushō 修験祕奥鈔. By Kyokuren 旭蓮. In *Shugendō shōso,* 1: 385–432.

Shugen seiten 修験聖典. Ed. Shugen seiten hensankai 修験聖典編纂会. Tokyo: Sanmitsudō shoten, Daigakudō shoten, 1927.

Shugen shūshi sho 修験宗旨書. *ST,* Ronsetsu-hen 17, Shugendō: 1–46.

Soga monogatari 曽我物語 (ca. 1399). *NKBT* 88, ed. Ichiko Teiji 市古貞次 and Ōshima Tatehiko 大島建彦 (1966). English translation in Cogan 1987.

Sōjishō 總持抄. By Chōgō 澄豪 (1259–1350). *T.* 77, 2412.

Song gaoseng zhuan 宋高僧伝. By Zanning 賛寧. *T.* 50, 2061.

Suidai ki 水台記. In *ST,* Jinja-hen 9, Inari: 23–66.

Suxidi jieluo jing 蘇悉地羯羅経. Trans. Śubhakarasiṃha (Ch. Shanwuwei 善無畏). *T.* 18, 893.

Suyao jing 宿曜経. By Amoghavajra (Ch. Bukong 不空). *T.* 21, 1299.

Suyao yigui 宿曜儀軌. By Yixing 一行 (673–727). *T.* 21, 1304.

Taiheiki 太平記. Vols. 1–2: *NKBT* 35–36, ed. Gotō Tanji 後藤丹治 and Kamata Kisaburō 釜田喜三郎 (Tokyo: Iwanami shoten, 1961). Vol. 3: Ed. Yamashita Hiroaki (Tokyo: Shinchosha, 1983). English translation in McCullough 1979.

Taishō shinshū daizōkyō 大正新脩大蔵経 (*T*). Ed. Takakusu Junjirō 高楠順次郎 and Watanabe Kaigyōku 渡邊海旭. 85 vols. Tokyo: Issaikyō kankōkai and Daizō shuppan, 1924–1932.

Taishō shinshū daizōkyō zuzōbu 大正新修大蔵経続 (*TZ*). Ed. Takakusu Junjirō 高楠順次郎 and Watanabe Kaigyōku 渡邊海旭. 12 vols. Tokyo: Taishō issaikyō kankōkai, 1924–1935.

Taizan Fukun saimon 泰山府君祭文. *NSSS* 17: 324–327.

Taizō kongō bodaishingi ryaku mondō shō 胎蔵金剛菩提心義略問答抄. By Annen 安然. *T.* 75, 2397.

Taizō nyūri shō 胎蔵入理鈔. By Raiyu 賴瑜 (1226–1304). *T.* 79, 2534.

Takakura zōtō hishō 高倉蔵等秘抄. In *Ryōbu shintō shū* 両部神道集, 369–378.

Tamakisan gongen engi 玉置山権現縁起. In Gorai 2000, 2: 148–154.

Takao kuketsu 高雄口決. By Shinzei 眞濟. *T.* 78, 2466.

Takushō 澤鈔. By Kakujō 覺成 (1126–1198). *T.* 78, 2488.

Tankai 談海. By Tsumura Masayuki 津村正恭 津村正恭. Tokyo: Kokusho kankōkai, 1970.

Tanzan jinja shiryō 談山神社資料. *ST*, Jinja-hen 5, Yamato no kuni: 157–316.

Tenchi reiki furoku 天地麗氣付録. *ST*, Ronsetsu-hen 1, Shingon shintō 1: 119–150.

Tenchi jingi shinchin yōki 天地神祇蕃鎮要記. By Jihen 慈遍 (fl. 14th c.). *ST*, Ronsetsu-hen 3, Tendai shintō 1: 403–474. See also *TSZ* 12: 187–224.

Tenchi kaibyaku chijin dai daranikyō 天地開闢地神大陀羅尼経. *NSSS* 17: 121–123.

Tenchi reiki ki. 天地麗氣記 Anon. *ST*, Ronsetsu-hen 1, Shingon shintō 1: 28–35. Also in *Chūsei shintō-ron, NST* 19.

Tenchi reikaku hishō, Sengū himon 天地霊覚秘書 仙宮秘文. In *Ryōbu shintō shū*, 381–417.

Tenchi reikiki. 天地麗氣記. *ST*, Ronsetsu-hen 1, Shingon shintō 1: 28–35.

Tendai Nanzan Mudō-ji konryū oshōden 天台南山無動寺建立和尚伝. *GR* 4.

Tendaishū zensho 天台宗全書 (*TSZ*). Ed. Tendai shūten kankōkai (1935–1937). Reprint, Tokyo: Daiichi shobō, 1974.

Tenge kōtaijin honnen 天下皇太神本縁. In *Ryōbu shintō shū*, 507–521.

Tenshō daijin giki 天照大神儀軌 (*Hōshi oshō den* 宝誌和尚伝). In *Kanazawa bunko no chūsei shintō shiryō* 金沢文庫の中世神道資料, vols. 24–25.

Tenshō daijin gotakusen ki (var. *Amaterasu ōmikami gotakusen ki*) 天照大神御託宣記. *ST*, Ronsetsu-hen 2, Shingon shintō 2: 585–592.

Tenshō daijin kuketsu 天照大神口決 (1327). By Kakujō 覚成 (1273–1363). *ST*, Ronsetsu-hen 2, Shingon shintō 2: 497–504.

Tenshō kōtaijin giki 天照皇太神儀軌. In *Ryōbu shintō shū*, 355–360.

Tenshō kōtaijingū chinza shidai 天照皇太神宮鎮座次第. *ST*, Ronsetsu-hen 1, Shingon shintō 1: 36–42.

Tōbō ki 東宝記. By Gōhō 杲宝 (1306–1362). *ZZGR* 12: 1–164.

Tōdō shinshikimoku 当道新式目. *NSSS* 17: 241–247.

Tōdō yōshū 当道要集. *NSSS* 17: 229–241.

Tōji-bon Fudō Myōō zuzō 東寺本不動明王図像. *TZ* 6: 205–240.

Tōryū saigoku hiketsu 當流最極秘決. Ms. Shinpukuji, Ōsu bunko archives.

Toyoashihara hongi 豊葦原本紀. By Jihen 慈遍 (fl. 14th c.). *ST*, Ronsetsu-hen 3, Tendai shintō 1: 341–359.

Tōyōki 東要記 (12th c.). Anon. *ZGR* 26: 2.

Tsuiki 追記. By Shukaku Hōshinnō 守覺親王. *T.* 78, 2494. Also *GR* 25: 444.

Tsūkai sankei ki 通海参詣記. In *Jinja engi* 神社縁起. *NSSS* 26: 451–474. See also *ZGR* 3.

Uji shūi monogatari 宇治拾遺物語 (ca. 1210–1220). *NKBT* 27, ed. Watanabe Tsunaya 渡邊 綱也 and Nishio Kōichi 西尾光一 (1960).

Uki 右記. By Shukaku Hōshinnō 守覺法親王. *T.* 78, 2491.

Ususama kongō shusen reiyō roku 烏樞沙摩金剛修仙靈要錄. *ST*, Ronsetsu-hen 16, Onmyōdō: 295–358.

Ususama Myōō zuzō 烏樞沙摩明王図像. *TZ* 6: 277–296.

Usuzōshi 薄雙紙, by Seigen 成賢 (1162–1231). *T.* 78, 2495.

Usuzōshi kuketsu 薄草子口決. By Raiyu 頼瑜 (1226–1304). *T.* 79, 2535.

Wagō saimon 和合祭文. *NSSS* 17: 347–349.

Wakan sansai zue 和漢三才圖絵 (1712). By Terajima Ryōan 寺島良安 (n.d.). 2 vols. Tokyo: Wakan sansai zue kankō iinkai, 1970.

Wakō dōjin riyaku kanjō 和光同塵利益灌頂. *ST*, Ronsetsu-hen 4, Tendai shintō 2: 505–522. Also *TSZ* 12: 179–187.

Washū Murōzan kaizan Kenne daitoku den 和州室生山開山堅恵大徳伝. In *Kōbō Daishi zenshū* 弘法大師全集, vol. 10. See Mikkyō bunka kenkyūjo 1978.

Wuchuse mingwang yigui fanzi 烏芻沙摩明王儀軌. *T.* 21, 1226.

Xukongzang pusa jing 虚空蔵菩薩経. Trans. Buddhayaśas (ca. 403–413). *T.* 13, 405.

Xukongzang pusa jiuwenqifa 虚空蔵菩薩求聞持法. Trans. Śubhakarasiṃha. *T.* 21, 1145.

Xukongzang pusa tuoluoni jing 虚空蔵菩薩陀羅尼経. *T.* 21, 1147.

Yako kaji hihō 野狐加持秘法. In Yamaori 1999: 395–402.

Yakon kuketsu shō 野金口決鈔. By Raiyu 賴瑜 (1226–1304). *T.* 79, 2530.

Yakushi jūni shinshō zu 薬師十二神将図. *TZ* 7: 385–404.

Yamatohime no mikoto seiki 倭姫命世記. *ST,* Ronsetsu-hen 5, Ise shintō 1: 71–108. See also *ZGR,* Jingi-bu 3: 48–65.

Yatai kuketsu shō 野胎口決鈔. By Raiyu 賴瑜 (1226–1304). *T.* 79, 2531.

Yizi foding lunwang jing 一字仏頂輪王経 (J. Ichiji butchō rinnōkyō). Trans. Bodhiruci. *T.* 19, 951.

Yoshibe hikunshō 吉部秘訓鈔. Ms. Waseda Library.

Yōsonbō 要尊法. By Yōgen 永嚴 (Eigon) (1075–1151). *T.* 78, 2478.

Yōson dōjōkan 要尊道場観. By Shunnyū (890–953). *T.* 78, 2468.

Yōtenki 耀天記 (1223). Anon. *ST,* Jinja-hen 29, Hie: 7–96. See also *ZGR,* Jingi-bu 48: 581–635.

Yugi kyō. See *Yuqi jing.*

Yugikyō chōmonshō 瑜祇経聴聞抄. By Chōgō 澄豪 (1259–1350). *ZTZ,* Mikkyō 2, Kyōten chūshakurui 1: 257–355.

Yugikyō hiyōketsu 瑜祇経秘要決. By Shōshin 性心. *SZ* 5: 137–434.

Yugikyō kaishin shō 瑜祇経開心鈔. In *Kanazawa bunko shiryō zensho* 金沢文庫資料全書 6, *Shingon-hen.* See Kanagawa kenritsu Kanazawa bunko 1974.

Yūgikyō kenmon 瑜祇経見聞. By Enni Ben'en 円爾弁円 (Shōichi kokushi 聖一国師, 1202–1280). *ZTZ,* Mikkyō 2, Kyōten chūshakurui 1: 205–216.

Yugikyō kuketsu nukigaki 瑜祇経口決抜書. By Kōshū 光宗 (1276–1350). *ZTZ,* Mikkyō 2, Kyōten chūshakurui 1: 217–256.

Yugikyō sho 瑜祇経疏. By Annen 安然 (9th c.). *T.* 61, 2228.

Yunji qiqian 雲笈七籤 (ca. 1029). By Zhang Junfang 張君房 (ca. 961–1042). In *Zhengtong daozang* 正統道藏 (Ming edition), no. 1632, ed. Zhang Yuchu 張宇初 (1361–1410) and Zhang Yuqing 張宇清 (d. 1426).

Yuqi jing (J. *Yugi kyō;* abbr. of *Jingangfeng louge yiqie yujia yuqi jing* 金剛峯楼閣一切瑜伽瑜祇經). Trans. attr. Vajrabodhi. *T.* 867.

Zatsuzatsu kikigaki 雑々聞書. *ST,* Ronsetsu-hen 2, Shingon shintō 2: 593–604.

Zōho shiryō taisei 増補資料大成. Ed. Zōho shiryō taisei kankōkai 増補資料大成刊行会. 48 vols. Kyoto: Rinsen shoten, 1965.

Zoku gunsho ruijū 続群書類従 (*ZGR*). Ed. Hanawa Hokiichi 塙保己一. 37 vols. and 3 supplementary vols. Zoku gunsho ruiju kanseikai, 1959–1960. Earlier edition published 1902–1912 by Keizai zashisha, 19 vols.

Zoku Nihon koten zenshū 続日本古典全集 (*ZNKZ*). Tokyo: Gendai shinchōsha, 1979–1981.

Zoku shintō taikei 続神道体系 (*ZST*). Ed. Shintō taikei hensankai 神道体系編纂会. Tokyo: Shintō taikei hensankai.

Zoku Tendaishū zenshū 続天台宗全書 (*ZTZ*). Tendai shūten hensanjo 天台宗典編纂所. Tokyo: Shunjūsha, 1987–.

Zokuzoku gunsho ruijū 続続群書類従 (*ZZGR*). Ed. Kokusho kankōkai 国書刊行会. 16 vols. Tokyo: Kokusho kankōkai, 1906–1909. Reprint, Kosho hozonkai 古書保存会, Tokyo: Zoku gunsho ruijū kanseikai, 1978.

Zuzōshō 図像抄 (a.k.a. *Jikkanshō* 十巻抄). By Ejū 慧什 (fl. 1135). *TZ* 3, 3006.

Zuzō shū 図像集. *TZ* 4, 3020.

REFERENCES

Abé, Ryūichi. 1999. *The Weaving of Mantra: Kūkai and the Construction of Esoteric Buddhist Discourse.* New York: Columbia University Press.

Abe Yasurō 阿部泰郎. 1980. "'Iruka' no seiritsu"「入鹿」の成立. *Geinō kenkyū* 藝能研究 69: 16–38.

———, ed. 1983. *Chūsei Kōyasan engi no kenkyū* 中世高野山縁起の研究. Nara: Gangōji bunkazai kenkyūjo.

———. 1984. "Jidō setsuwa no seiritsu" 慈童説話の成立. *Kokugo kokubun* 600–601, 1–29: 30–56.

———. 1985a. "Chūsei ōken to chūsei Nihongi: Sokuihō to sanshū shinki-setsu o megurite" 中世王権と中世日本紀ー即位法と三種神器説をめぐりて. *Nihon bungaku* 365: 31–48.

———. 1985b. "Shintō mandara no kōzō to shōchō sekai" 神道曼荼羅の構造と象徴世界. In Sakurai Yoshirō 桜井好郎, ed., *Kami to hotoke: bukkyō juyō to shinbutsu shūgō no sekai* 神と仏ー仏教受容と神仏習合の世界, 311–357. Tokyo: Shunjūsha.

———. 1989. "Hōju to ōken: chūsei to mikkyō girei" 宝珠と王権ー中世と密教儀礼. *Iwanami kōza tōyō shisō 16: Nihon shisō 2* 岩波講座東洋思想 16ー日本思想 2, 115–169. Tokyo: Iwanami shoten.

———. 1990. "Jien to ōken: Chūsei ōken shinwa o umidashita mono" 慈圓と王権ー中世王権神話を生み出したもの. In *Tennōsei, rekishi, ōken, daijōsai.* Special issue, *Bessatsu Bungei,* 111–119. Tokyo: Kawade shobō shinsha.

———. 1999a. "'Nihongi' to iu undō"「日本紀」という運動. *Kokubungaku: kaishaku to kanshō* 814: 6–17.

———. 1999b. "*Chūsei Kōyasan engishū* kaidai"「中世高野山縁起集」解題. In Abe and Yamazaki 1999: 345–388.

———, ed. 2000. "Ninnaji shiryō (Shintō-hen) shintō kanjō injin" 仁和寺資料 (神道篇) 神道灌頂印信. *Nagoya daigaku hikaku jinbungaku kenkyū nenpō* 2. Nagoya: Nagoya daigaku.

———. 2001. "Shinpukuji Ōsu bunko: chūsei jiin no chiteki taikei kenkyū no shoten" 真福寺大須文庫ー中世寺院の知的体系探究の拠点 (特集 文庫のドラマをよむ). *Bungaku* 2, 3: 51–54.

———. 2002a. "Ise ni mairu hijiri to ō: *Tōdaiji shuto sankei Ise daijingū ki* o megurite" 伊勢に参る聖と王ー「東大寺衆徒参詣伊勢大神宮記」をめぐりて. In Imatani Akira 今谷明, ed., *Ōken to jingi* 王権と神祇. Tokyo: Shibunkaku shuppan.

———, ed. 2002b. "Ninnaji shiryō daisanshū: Engi-hen" 仁和寺資料第三集 (縁起篇). *Nagoya daigaku hikaku jinbungaku kenkyū nenpō.* Nagoya: Nagoya daigaku.

———, ed. 2005. *Shinpukuji Ōsu bunko jingi shozuroku* 真福寺大須文庫神祇書図録. Special issue, *Nagoya daigaku hikaku jinbungaku kenkyū nenpō.* Nagoya: Nagoya daigaku.

———. 2006a. "Chūsei shinbutsu bunka no ten to sen" 中世神仏文化の点と線. *Shintō shūkyō* 202: 1–106.

———. 2006b. "Chūsei shintō to chūsei Nihongi" 中世神道と中世日本紀. *Shintō shūkyō* 202: 4–43.

———. 2006c. "*Himitsu gentei kuketsu, Sanzon gōgyō hi shidai shiki* kaidai「秘密源底口決」「一二寸合行秘次第私記」解題. In Kokubungaku kenkyū shiryōkan 2006: 598–611.

———. 2006–2007. "Shintō as Written Representation: The Phases and Shifts of Medieval Shintō Texts." *CEA* 16: 91–117.

————. 2010a. "Monkan chosaku shōgyō no saihakken: Sanzon gōgyō no tekusuto fuchi to sono isō" 文観著作聖教の再発見—三尊合行法のテクスト布置とその位相. In Abe Yasurō, ed., *Chūsei shūkyō tekusuto taikei no fukugenteki kenkyū: Shinpukuji shōgyō tenseki no saikōchiku,* 121–144. Nagoya: Nagoya daigaku daigakuin bungaku kenkyūka.

————. 2010b. "Medieval Japanese Liturgical Texts and Performance: The World of Buddhist Ritual as Religious Text." In Matsuo Koichi, ed., "Religious Texts and Performance in East Asia," 11–23. Sakura-shi, Chiba-ken: Kokuritsu rekishi minzoku hakubutsukan.

————. 2011. "Hōju no katadoru ōken: Monkan-bō Kōshin no sanzon gōgyō-hō shōgyō to sono zuzō" 「宝珠の象る王権—文観房弘真の三尊合行法聖教とその図像」. In Naitō Sakae 2001b: 80–93.

————. 2013. *Chūsei Nihon no shūkyō-tekusuto taikei* 中世日本の宗教テクスト体系. Nagoya: Nagoya daigaku shuppankai.

Abe Yasurō and Yamazaki Makoto 山崎誠, eds. 1998. *Shukaku Hōshinnō to Ninnaji goryū no bunkengaku-teki kenkyū* 守覚法親王と仁和寺御流の文献学的研究. Tokyo: Benseisha.

————, eds. 1999. *Chūsei Kōyasan engi shū* 中世高野山縁起集. Shinpukuji zenpon sōkan 9. Tokyo: Rinsen shoten.

Adolphson, Mikael S. 1997. "Enryakuji: An Old Power in a New Era." In Jeffrey P. Mass, ed., *The Origins of Japan's Medieval World: Courtiers, Clerics, Warriors, and Peasants in the Fourteenth Century.* Stanford, CA: Stanford University Press.

————. 2000. *The Gates of Power: Monks, Courtiers, and Warriors in Premodern Japan.* Honolulu: University of Hawai'i Press.

————. 2007. *Teeth and Claws of the Buddha: Monastic Warriors and Sōhei in Japanese History.* Honolulu: University of Hawai'i Press.

Aikō Shōkan 愛甲昇寛. 1992. "Inazawa-shi Shōkaiji no gorintō nōnyū shiryō" 稲沢市性海寺の五輪塔納入資料. *Bukkyō geijutsu* 仏教藝術 204: 106–123.

Akamatsu Toshihide 赤松俊秀. 1957. *Kamakura bukkyō no kenkyū* 鎌倉仏教の研究. Kyoto: Heirakuji shoten.

Akima Toshio. 1993. "The Myth of the Goddess of the Undersea World and the Tale of Empress Jingū's Subjugation of Silla," *JJRS* 20, 2–3: 95–185.

Akiyama Teruo 秋山光夫. 1943. *Nihon bijutsushi ronkō* 日本美術史論攷. Tokyo: Daiichi shobō.

Allen, N.J. 1987. "The Ideology of the Indo-Europeans: Dumézil's Theory and the Idea of a Fourth Function." *International Journal of Moral and Social Studies* 2: 28–39.

————. 1998. "Varnas, Colours and Functions." *Zeitschrift für Religionswissenschaft* 6: 163–177.

Amino Yoshihiko 網野良彦. 1978. *Muen, kugai, raku: Nihon chūsei no jiyū to heiwa* 無縁・公界・楽一日本中世の自由と平和. Tokyo: Heibonsha.

————. 1980. *Nihon chūsei no minshūzō* 日本中世の民衆像. Iwanami shinsho 136. Tokyo: Iwanami shoten.

————. 1993. *Igyō no ōken* 異形の王権. Heibonsha raiburarii. Tokyo: Heibonsha.

————. 1995. "Les Japonais et la mer." *Annales HSS* 50, 2: 235–358.

————. 2007. "Medieval Japanese Constructions of Peace and Liberty: *Muen, Kugai,* and *Raku.*" *International Journal of Asian Studies* 4, 1: 3–14.

Anderson, Poul. 1989. "The Practice of Bugang," *CEA* 5: 15–53.

Andreeva, Anna. 2006a. "On the Crossroads of Esoteric Kami Worship: Mount Miwa and the Early Beginnings of Miwa (ryū) Shintō." PhD diss., University of Cambridge.

———. 2006b. "Saidaiji Monks and Esoteric Kami Worship at Ise and Miwa." *JJRS* 33, 2: 349–377.

———. 2006–2007. "The Origin of the Miwa Lineage." *CEA* 16: 71–89.

———. 2010. "The Karmic Origins of the Great Bright Miwa Deity: A Transformation of the Sacred Mountain in Premodern Japan." *Monumenta Nipponica* 65, 2: 245–296.

Angelini, Pietro. 2001. *L'uomo sul tetto: Mircea Eliade e la 'storia delle religioni'.* Turin: Bollati Boringhieri.

Aptilon, Sarah Fremerman. 2008. "Divine Impersonations: Nyoirin Kannon in Medieval Japan." PhD diss., Stanford University.

Arai Daisuke 新井大祐. 2008. "*Sannō shintō hiyō* shū no seiritsu ni kansuru ichi shiron: *Shintō zatsuzatsushū* kenkyū no tame no oboegaki to shite no" 『山王神道秘要集』の成立に関する一試論ー『神道雑々集』研究のための覚書としての. *Shintō shūkyō* 212: 49–82.

Araki Hiroshi 荒木浩, ed. 2007a. *Ono Zuishin-in shozō no mikkyō bunken, zuzō chōsa o kiban to suru sōkanteki, sōgōteki kenkyū to sono tankyū* 小野随心院所蔵の密教文献・図像調査を基盤とする相関的・総合的研究とその探求. Osaka: Osaka daigaku.

———. 2007b. *Ono Zuishin-in shozō no bunken, zuzō chōsa o kiban to suru sōkanteki, sōgōteki kenkyū to sono tenkai* 小野随心院所蔵の文献・図像調査を基盤とする相関的・総合的研究とその展開. Vol. 2. Osaka: Osaka daigaku.

Arasse, Daniel. 1996. *Le détail: Pour une histoire rapprochée de la peinture.* Paris: Flammarion.

Arichi, Meri. 2006. "Seven Stars of Heaven and Seven Shrines on Earth: The Big Dipper and the Hie Shrine in the Medieval Period." In Dolce 2006b: 195–216.

Ariga Shō 有賀匠. 2000. "Hoshi mandara to Myōken bosatsu no zuzōgakuteki kenkyū" 星曼荼羅と妙見菩薩図象学的研究. *Mikkyō bunka* 204: 25–63.

Ariga Yoshitaka 有賀祥隆. 1993. "Fudō shinkō: funnu-zō ni motometa sukui" 不動信仰—忿怒像に求めた救い. In Tanaka Hisao 1993a: 5–29.

Artaud, Antonin. 1968 (1925). *Umbilical Limbo.* Trans. V. Corti. Vol. 1 of *Collected Works.* London: Calder & Boyars.

Asano Nagatake 浅野長武. 1967. Daigoji 醍醐寺. Vol. 8 of *Hihō* 秘宝. Tokyo: Kōdansha.

Assmann, Jan. 1996. "The Mosaic Distinction: Israel, Egypt, and the Invention of Paganism." *Representations* 56: 48–67.

———. 2001. *The Search for God in Ancient Egypt.* Ithaca, NY: Cornell University Press.

———. 2006. *Religion and Cultural Memory: Ten Studies.* Stanford, CA: Stanford University Press.

———. 2008. *Of God and Gods: Egypt, Israel, and the Rise of Monotheism.* Madison: University of Wisconsin Press.

Astley-Kristensen, Ian. 1988a. "An Example of Vajrasattva in the Sino-Japanese Tantric Buddhist Tradition." *Studies in Central and East Asian Religions* 1: 67–87.

———. 1988b. "The Five Mysteries of Vajrasattva: A Buddhist Tantric View of the Passions and Enlightenment." *Temenos* 24: 7–27.

———. 1994a. "The Study of the Esoteric Buddhist Tradition of Japan." In Ian Astley, ed., *Esoteric Buddhism in Japan,* 1–15. SBS Monographs 1. Copenhagen and Aarhus: Seminar for Buddhist Studies.

————. 1994b. "An Annotated Translation of Amoghavajra's Commentary on the *Liqu jing* (*Rishūkyō*)—Part 1." *Studies in Central and East Asian Religions* 7: 27–53.

Aston, W. G., trans. 1972 (1956). *Nihongi: Chronicles of Japan from the Earliest Times to A.D. 697.* Rutland, VT: Charles E. Tuttle Company.

Atlan, Henri. 1979. *Entre le cristal et la fumée: Essai sur l'organisation du vivant.* Paris: Éditions du Seuil.

————. 1986. *À Tort et à raison: intercritique de la science et du mythe.* Paris: Seuil.

Atsuta jingū gūchō, ed. 熱田神宮宮庁. 2006. *Atsuta jingū shiryō: Engi yuisho-hen* 熱田神宮資料—縁起由緒編. Nagoya: Atsuta jingū gūchō.

Augé, Marc. 1988. *Le dieu-objet.* Paris: Flammarion.

Baltrušaitis, Jurgis. 1981. *Le Moyen Age fantastique: antiquités et exotismes dans l'art gothique.* Paris: Flammarion.

————. 1986. *Formations, déformations: La stylistique ornementale dans la sculpture romane.* Paris: Flammarion.

Barthes, Roland. 2002. *The Neutral: Lecture Course at the Collège de France (1977–1978).* Trans. Rosalind E. Krauss and Denis Hollier. New York: Columbia University Press.

Bell, Catherine. 1992. *Ritual Theory, Ritual Practice.* New York: Oxford University Press.

Benn, James. 2007. *Burning for the Buddha: Self-Immolation in Chinese Buddhism.* Honolulu: University of Hawai'i Press.

Benveniste, Émile. 1969. *Le vocabulaire des institutions indo-européennes.* 2 vols. Paris: Éditions de Minuit.

Bergaigne, Abel. 1933 (1878). *La religion védique d'après les hymnes du Rig-Véda.* Paris: F. Vieweg.

Berthon, Jean-Pierre, Anne Bouchy, and Pierre F. Souyri, eds. 2001. *Identités, marges, médiations: Regards croisés sur la société japonaise.* Etudes Thématiques 10. Paris: EFEO.

Bhandarkar, R. G. 1965 (1913). *Vaiṣnavism, Śaivism and Minor Religious Systems.* Varanasi: Indological Book House.

Bharati, Agehananda. 1965a. *The Tantric Tradition.* London. Reprint, New York: Doubleday, 1970.

Bhattacharya, Narendra Nath. 2000. *Indian Demonology: The Inverted Pantheon.* New Delhi: Manohar Publishers.

Bialock, David T. 2002–2003. "Outcasts, Emperorship, and Dragon Cults in *The Tale of the Heike.*" *CEA* 13: 227–310.

————. 2007. *Eccentric Spaces, Hidden Histories: Narrative, Ritual, and Royal Authority from The Chronicles of Japan to The Tale of the Heike.* Stanford, CA: Stanford University Press.

Biardeau, Madeleine. 1991a (1981). "The *Yūpa* (Sacrificial Post) in Hinduism." In Bonnefoy 1991: 37–39.

————. 1991b. "The Mythologies of Hindu India." In Bonnefoy 1991: 34–36.

————. 1991c. "Rudra/Śiva and the Destruction of the Sacrifice." In Bonnefoy 1991: 39–43.

————. 1991d. "Deva/Asura: Celestial Gods and 'Demons' in Hinduism." In Bonnefoy 1991: 52–53.

————. 1991e. "Gaṇapati." In Bonnefoy 1991: 90–92.

————. 1991f. "Skanda, a Great Sovereign God of South India." In Bonnefoy 1991: 92–95.

————. 1991g. "Devī: The Goddess in India." In Bonnefoy 1991: 95–99.

————. 1991h. "Symbols of the Earth in Indian Religion." In Bonnefoy 1991: 99–101.

Birnbaum, Raoul. 1979. *The Healing Buddha.* Boulder, CO: Shambhala.

————. 1980. "Introduction to the Study of T'ang Buddhist Astrology: Research Notes on Primary Sources and Basic Principles." *SSCR Bulletin* 8: 5–19.

————. 1983. *Studies on the Mysteries of Mañjuśrī: A Group of East Asian Maṇḍalas and their Traditional Symbolism.* Society for the Study of Chinese Religions Monograph 2. Boulder, CO: Society for the Study of Chinese Religions.

Bitbol, Michel. 1999. *L'Aveuglante proximité du réel.* Paris: Flammarion.

Blanchot, Maurice. 1993. *The Infinite Conversation.* Trans. Susan Hanson. Minneapolis; London: University of Minnesota Press.

Blondeau, Anne-Marie, and Kristofer Schipper, eds. 1995. *Essais sur le rituel.* 2 vols. Louvain/Paris: Peeters.

Boedeker, Deborah. 1983. "Hecate: A Transfunctional Goddess in the Theogony?" *Transactions of the American Philological Association* 113: 79–93.

Bogel, Cynthea J. 2002. "Canonizing Kannon: The Ninth-Century Esoteric Buddhist Altar at Kanshinji." *Art Bulletin* 84, 1: 30–64.

————. 2009. *With a Single Glance: Buddhist Icon and Early Mikkyō Vision.* Seattle: University of Washington Press.

Bohner, Hermann, 1946. "Kōbō Daishi." *Monumenta Nipponica* 6, 1–2: 266–313.

Boltz, Judith. 1987. *A Survey of Taoist Literature: Tenth to Seventeenth Centuries.* China Research Monograph. Berkeley, CA: Center for Chinese Studies.

Bonnefoy, Yves, ed. 1991. *Asian Mythologies.* Trans. Wendy Doniger. Chicago: University of Chicago Press.

————. 1992. *L'Improbable et autres essais.* Paris: Gallimard.

Boon, James. 1991. *Affinities and Extremes.* Chicago: University of Chicago Press.

Borgeaud, Philippe. 2004a. *Aux origines de l'histoire des religions.* Paris: Seuil.

————. 2004b. *Exercices de mythologie.* Geneva: Labor et Fides.

Borges, Jorge Luis. 1962. *Labyrinths: Selected Stories and Other Writings.* New York: New Directions.

Bouchy, Anne-Marie (Anne). 1979. "Comment fut révélée la nature véritable de la divinité du Mont Atago." *Cahiers d'études et de documents sur les religions du Japon* 1: 9–48.

————. 1997. "Silences et rituels devant les Dragons: réflexion sur l'ascèse de la cascade au Japon." In Jacqueline Pigeot and Hartmut O. Rotermund, eds., *Le Vase de béryl. Études sur le Japon et la Chine—en hommage à Bernard Frank,* 137–147. Paris: Éditions Philippe Picquier.

————. 2000. "La cascade et l'écritoire: Dynamique de l'histoire du fait religieux et de l'ethnologie du Japon: le cas du shugendō." *BEFEO* 87: 341–366.

Bouillier, Véronique, and Gérard Toffin, eds. 1993. *Classer les dieux? Des panthéons en Asie du Sud. Puruṣārtha* 15. Paris: Éditions de l'EHESS.

Bourdieu, Pierre. 1977. *Outline of a Theory of Practice.* Cambridge: Cambridge University Press.

————. 1990. *The Logic of Practice.* Trans. Richard Nice. Stanford, CA: Stanford University Press.

Bowring, Richard, trans. 1996. *The Diary of Lady Murasaki.* Penguin Classics. New York: Penguin.

Brazell, Karen, trans. 1975. *The Confessions of Lady Nijō.* London: Peter Owen.

Breen, John, and Mark Teeuwen, eds. 2000. *Shinto in History: Ways of the Kami.* Honolulu: University of Hawai'i Press.

———. 2010. *A New History of Shinto.* Oxford: Wiley-Blackwell.

Brinker, Helmut. 1990. "Gemalt aus Vertrauen auf Fudō Myōō: Serienbilder der Zen-Mönche Ryūshū Shūtaku (1308–1388) und Chūan Bonshi (1346–nach 1437)." *Asiatische Studien/Études asiatiques* 44, 2: 267–347.

Brown, Delmer M., and Ishida Ichirō, trans. *The Future and the Past: A Translation and Study of Gukanshō, an Interpretive History of Japan Written in 1219.* Berkeley: University of California Press.

Bryson, Megan. 2010. "The Transformation of Baijie Shengfei: Gender and Ethnicity in Chinese Religion." PhD diss., Stanford University.

Bumbacher, Stephan Peter. 2012. *Empowered Writing: Exorcistic and Apotropaic Rituals in Medieval China.* St. Petersburg, FL: Three Pines Press.

Callon, Michel. 1986. "Some Elements of a Sociology of Translation: Domestication of the Scallops and the Fishermen of St Brieuc Bay." In John Law, ed. *Power, Action and Belief: A New Sociology of Knowledge,* 196–233. London: Routledge & Kegan Paul.

Calvino, Italo. 1997. *Invisible Cities.* Trans. William Weaver. New York: Vintage.

Casal, U. A. 1956. "Far Eastern Monkey Lore." *Monumenta Nipponica* 12, 1–2: 13–49.

———. 1959. "The Goblin Fox and Badger and Other Witch Animals of Japan." *Folklore Studies* 18: 1–94.

Chamberlain, Basil Hall, trans. 1982. *The Kojiki: Records of Ancient Matters.* Rutland, VT: Charles E. Tuttle Company.

Chandra, Lokesh. 1999–2005. *Dictionary of Buddhist Iconography.* 15 vols. Satapitaka Series. New Delhi: Aditya Prakashan.

Chao, Shin-yi. 2002. "Zhenwu: The Cult of a Chinese Warrior Deity from the Song to the Ming Dynasty (960–1644)." PhD diss., University of British Columbia.

Chapin, Helen B. 1932. "A Study in Buddhist Iconography." *Ostasiatische Zeitschrift* 8: 29–43.

Chavannes, Édouard. 1910. *Le T'ai chan: Essai de monographie d'un culte chinois.* Paris: Librairie Ernest Leroux.

Chen Jinhua. 2009. *Legend and Legitimation: The Formation of Tendai Esoteric Buddhism in Japan.* Mélanges Chinois et Bouddhiques 30. Brussels: Institut Belge des Hautes Études Chinoises.

Chiba-shi bijutsukan 千葉市美術館, ed. 1999. *Bōsō no kami to hotoke* 房総の神と仏. Chiba: Chiba-shi bijutsukan.

Chiba shiritsu kyōdo hakubutsukan 千葉市立郷土博物館, ed. 1995. *Chiba Myōken daiengi emaki* 千葉妙見大縁起絵巻. Chiba: Chiba shiritsu kyōdo hakubutsukan.

Chisan kangaku kai 智山勧学会, ed. 2005. *Chūsei no bukkyō: Raiyu sōjō o chūshin to shite* 中世の仏教—頼瑜僧正を中心として. Tokyo: Seishi shuppan.

Chou Yi-liang. 1944–1945. "Tantrism in China." *Harvard Journal of Asiatic Studies* 8: 241–332.

Cogan, Thomas G, trans. 1987. *The Tale of the Soga Brothers.* Tokyo: University of Tokyo Press.

Como, Michael. 2005. "Silkworms and Consorts in Nara Japan." *Asian Folklore Studies* 64: 111–131.

———. 2009. *Weaving and Binding: Immigrant Gods and Female Immortals in Ancient Japan.* Honolulu: University of Hawai'i Press.

Cooper, Michael. 1982. *They Came to Japan.* Berkeley: University of California Press.

Cooper, Robert. 1998. "Assemblage Notes." In Robert C. H. Chia, ed. *Organized Worlds: Explorations in Technology and Organization with Robert Cooper,* 108–129. London: Routledge.

Dantec, Maurice. 2005. *Cosmos Incorporated.* Paris: Albin Michel.

Davidson, Ronald M. 1991. "Reflections on the Maheśvara Subjugation Myth: Indic Materials, Sa-skya-pa Apologetics, and the Birth of Heruka." *Journal of the International Association of Buddhist Studies* 14, 2: 197–225.

———. 2002. *Indian Esoteric Buddhism: A Social History of the Tantric Movement.* New York: Columbia University Press.

———. 2006. "The Problem of Secrecy in Indian Tantric Buddhism." In Scheid and Teeuwen 2006: 60–77.

De Bruyn, Pierre-Henri. 2010. *Le Wudang Shan: Histoire des récits fondateurs.* Paris: Les Indes savantes.

DeCaroli, Robert. 2004. *Haunting the Buddha: Indian Popular Religions and the Formation of Buddhism.* Oxford: Oxford University Press.

de Certeau, Michel. 1992. *The Mystic Fable: The Sixteenth and Seventeenth Centuries.* Chicago: University of Chicago Press.

De Ferranti, Hugh. 2009. *The Last Biwa Singer: A Blind Musician in History, Imagination and Performance.* Ithaca, NY: Cornell University Press.

De Groot, J. J. M. 1892–1910. *The Religious System of China: Its Ancient Forms, Evolution, History and Present Aspects; Manners, Customs, and Social Institutions Connected Therewith.* 6 vols. Taipei: Literature House.

Deleuze, Gilles. 2004 (1968). *Difference and Repetition.* Trans. Paul Patton. New York: Continuum.

Deleuze, Gilles, and Félix Guattari. 1987. *A Thousand Plateaus: Capitalism and Schizophrenia.* Trans. Brian Massumi. Minneapolis: University of Minnesota Press.

———. 1996. *What Is Philosophy?* Trans. Hugh Tomlinson and Graham Burchell. New York: Columbia University Press.

Deleuze, Gilles, and Claire Parnet. 1977. *Dialogues.* Trans. Hugh Tomlinson and Barbara Habberjam. New York: Columbia University Press.

Delumeau, Jean. 1990. *Sin and Fear: The Emergence of a Western Guilt Culture, 13th–18th centuries,* New York: St. Martin's Press.

de Mallmann, Marie-Thérèse. 1948. *Introduction à l'étude d'Avalokiteçvara.* Paris: Civilisations du Sud.

———. 1963. *Les enseignements iconographiques de l'Agni-purāṇa.* Annales du Musée Guimet, Bibliothèque d'Études 67. Paris: Presses Universitaires de France.

———. 1964a. *Étude iconographique sur Mañjuśrī.* Paris: École Française d'Extrême-Orient.

———. 1964b. "'Dieux polyvalents' du tantrisme bouddhique." *Journal Asiatique* 252, 3: 365–377.

———. 1964c. "Divinités hindoues dans le tantrisme bouddhique." *Arts Asiatiques* 10: 67–86.

De Martino, Ernesto. 1967 (1948). *Il mondo magico: Prolegomena a una storia del magismo.* Turin: Editore Boringhieri.

———. 1999. *Oeuvres, tome 1: Le monde magique.* Trans. Marc Baudoux. Paris: Les Empêcheurs de Penser en Rond.

Derrida Jacques. 1980a. "Structure, Sign, and Play in the Discourse of the Human Sciences." In Jacques Derrida, *Writing and Difference,* 278–294. Trans. Alan Bass. Chicago: University of Chicago Press.

———. 1980b. "The Supplement of Copula." In Josué V. Harrari, ed., *Textual Strategies: Perspectives in Post-Structuralist Criticism.* Ithaca, NY: Cornell University Press.

———. 1983 (1972). "Plato's Pharmacy." In Jacques Derrida, *Dissemination,* 67–186. Trans. Barbara Johnson. Chicago: University of Chicago Press.

———. 1985. *Margins of Philosophy.* Trans. Alan Bass. Chicago: University of Chicago Press.

———. 1998 (1976). *Of Grammatology.* Trans. Gayatri Chakravorti Spivak. Baltimore: Johns Hopkins University Press.

———. 2002. "Reste—le maître, ou le supplément d'infini." In Lyne Bansat-Boudon and John Scheid, eds., *Le Maître et ses disciples: pour Charles Malamoud,* 25–63. Paris: Seuil.

Descola, Philippe. 2005. *Par-delà nature et culture.* Paris: Gallimard.

Descombes, Vincent. 1979. "L'équivoque du symbolique." *MLN* 94, 4: 655–675.

Detienne, Marcel. 1971. "Athena and the Mastery of the Horse." Trans. A.B. Werth. *History of Religions* 11, 2: 161–184.

———. 1986a. "Apollo's Slaughterhouse." *Diacritics* 16, 2: 46–53.

———. 1986b. "Du polythéisme en général." *Classical Philology* 81, 1: 47–55.

———. 1986c. *The Creation of Mythology.* Chicago: University of Chicago Press.

———. 1999. "Experimenting in the Field of Pantheism." *Arion* 7: 127–149.

———. 2001. "Forgetting Delphi between Apollo and Dionysus." *Classical Philology* 96, 2: 147–158.

———. 2008. *Comparing the Incomparable.* Trans. Janet Lloyd. Stanford, CA: Stanford University Press.

———. 2009. *Apollon le couteau à la main: une approche expérimentale du polythéisme grec.* Paris: Gallimard.

Detienne, Marcel, and Gilbert Hamonic, eds. 1995. *La Déesse Parole: quatre figures de la langue des dieux.* Idées et Recherches. Paris: Flammarion.

De Visser, Marinus Willem. 1913. *The Dragon in China and Japan.* Amsterdam: J. Müller.

———. 1914. *The Bodhisattva Ti-tsang (Jizō) in China and Japan.* Berlin: Oesterheld.

———. 1931. *The Bodhisattva Ākāśagarbha (Kokūzō) in China and Japan.* Amsterdam: Koninklijke Akademie van Wetenschappen.

Dewa Hiroaki 出羽弘明. 2004. *Shiragi no kamigami to kodai Nihon: Shiragi jinja no kataru sekai* 新羅の神々と古代日本 ： 新羅神社の語る世界. Tokyo: Dōseisha.

Didi-Huberman, Georges. 1998. *Phasmes: Essais sur l'apparition.* Paris: Editions de Minuit.

Dobbins, James C., ed. 1996. "The Legacy of Kuroda Toshio." *JJRS* 23, 3–4: 217–232.

———. 2002. *Jōdo Shinshū: Shin Buddhism in Medieval Japan.* Honolulu: University of Hawai'i Press.

Dodds. E. R. 1965. *Pagan and Christian in an Age of Anxiety: Some Aspects of Religious Experience from Marcus Aurelius to Constantine.* Cambridge: Cambridge University Press.

Dolce, Lucia. 2002. *Esoteric Patterns in Nichiren's Interpretation of the Lotus Sutra.* PhD diss., Leiden University.

————. 2006a. "Reconsidering the Taxonomy of the Esoteric: Hermeneutical and Ritual Practices of the *Lotus Sūtra*." In Scheid and Teeuwen 2006: 130–171.

————, ed. 2006b. "The Worship of Stars in Japanese Religious Practice." Special issue, *Culture and Cosmos* 10, 1–2.

————. 2006c. "The Worship of Celestial Bodies in Japan: Politics, Rituals and Icons." In Dolce 2006b: 3–43.

————. 2006–2007. "Duality and the Kami: The Ritual Iconography and Visual Constructions of Medieval Shintō." *CEA* 16: 119–50.

————. 2008. "Girei ni yori seisei-sareru kanzen-naru shintai: chūsei mikkyō ni 'hiseitōteki zuzō' to shuhō o megutte" 儀礼により生成される完全なる身体ー中世密教の"非正統的図像"と修法をめぐってー. In Abe Yasurō, ed. *Nihon ni okeru shūkyō tekusuto no shoisō to tōjihō* 日本における宗教テクスト諸位相と統辞法 , 58–71. Nagoya: Nagoya daigaku daigakuin bungaku kenkyūka.

————. 2010. "Nigen-teki genri no gireika: Fudō, Aizen to chikara no hizō" 二元的原理の儀礼化ー不動、愛染と力の秘像. In Dolce and Matsumoto 2010: 159–206.

Dolce, Lucia, and Matsumoto Ikuyo 松本郁代, eds. 2010. *Girei no chikara: chūsei shūkyō no jissen sekai* 儀礼の力ー中世宗教の実践世界. Kyoto: Hōzōkan.

Doniger (O'Flaherty), Wendy. 1973. *Ascetism and Eroticism in the Mythology of Śiva.* London: Oxford University Press.

————, trans. 1975. *Hindu Myths: A Sourcebook.* Harmondsworth: Penguin.

————. 1980. *Women, Androgynes, and Other Mythical Beasts.* Chicago: University of Chicago Press.

————. 1998. *The Implied Spider: Politics and Theology in Myth.* New York: Columbia University Press.

Dudbridge, Glen. 1996–1997. "The General of the Five Paths in Tang and Pre-Tang China." *CEA* 9: 85–98.

Dufour, Dany-Robert. 1990. *Les mystères de la Trinité.* Paris: Gallimard.

Dumézil, Georges. 1929. *Le problème des Centaures: Étude de mythologie comparée indo-européenne.* Annales du Musée Guimet. Paris: Paul Geuthner.

————. 1968. *Mythe et épopée: 1. L'idéologie des trois fonctions dans les épopées des peuples indo-européens.* Bibliothèque des sciences humaines. Paris: Gallimard.

————. 1977. *Les dieux souverains des Indo-européens.* Paris: Gallimard.

————. 1982. *Apollon sonore et autres essais: vingt-cinq esquisses de mythologie.* Paris: Gallimard. Reprint, Collection Quarto, Gallimard, 2005.

————. 1985. "D'une coupe à quatre, de quatre bols à un." In Georges Dumézil, *L'Oubli de l'homme et l'honneur des dieux,* 192–210. Paris: Gallimard. Reprinted in Georges Dumézil, *Esquisses de mythologie,* 708–726. Collection Quarto, Gallimard, 2005.

————. 1988. *Mitra-Varuna: An Essay on Two Indo-European Representations of Sovereignty.* Trans. Derek Coltman. New York: Zone Books.

Dumont, Louis. 1953. "Définition structurale d'un dieu populaire tamoul: AiyaNār, le Maître." *Journal Asiatique* 241: 255–270.

Duquenne, Robert. 1979. "Chūtai" 中台. *Hōbōgirin* 5: 527–551.

————. 1983a. "Dai" 大. *Hōbōgirin* 6: 585–592.

————. 1983b. "Daigensui (Myōō)" 大元帥 (明王). *Hōbōgirin* 6: 610–640.

————. 1983c. "Daiitoku Myōō" 大威徳明王. *Hōbōgirin* 6: 652–670.

————. 1994. "Dairiki-daigo-myōhi" 大力大護明妃. *Hōbōgirin* 7: 947–953.

———. 2001. Review of Rob Linrothe, *Ruthless Compassion: Wrathful Deities in Early Indo-Tibetan Buddhist Art,* Boston: Shambhala, 1999. *BEFEO* 88: 366–372.

———. 2003. "Daishō Kongō" 大勝金剛. *Hōbōgirin* 8: 1035–1041.

Durkheim, Emile. 1995 (1912). *The Elementary Forms of Religious Life.* Trans. Karen Elise Fields. New York: Simon and Schuster.

Durkheim, Emile, and Marcel Mauss. 1963. *Primitive Classification.* Trans. Rodney Needham. Chicago: University of Chicago Press.

Dykstra, Yoshiko K. 1976. "Tales of the Compassionate Kannon: The *Hasedera Kannon kenki.*" *Monumenta Nipponica* 31, 2: 113–143.

———, trans. 1983. *Miraculous Tales of the Lotus Sūtra from Ancient Japan: The* Dainihonkoku Hokekyōkenki *of Priest Chingen.* Honolulu: University of Hawai'i Press.

———, trans. 1998–2003. *The Konjaku Tales, Japanese Section (Honchō-hen) from a Medieval Japanese Collection.* 3 vols. Osaka: Kansai Gaidai University.

Eco, Umberto. 1989. *The Open Work.* Trans. Anna Cangogni. Cambridge, MA: Harvard University Press.

Eliot, T. S. 1958. *The Waste Land and Other Poems.* Harvest Paperback. New York: Harcourt.

Epprecht, Katharina, ed. 2007. *Kannon: Divine Compassion—Early Buddhist Art from Japan.* Zürich: Museum Rietberg.

Evans-Pritchard, E. E. 1937. *Witchcraft Oracles and Magic among the Azande,* Oxford: Clarendon Press.

———. 1969. *The Nuer: A Description of the Modes of Livelihood and Political Institutions of a Nilotic People.* London: Oxford University Press.

Faure, Bernard. 1986a. "The Concept of One-Practice *Samādhi* in Early Ch'an." In Peter N. Gregory, ed., *Traditions of Meditation in East Asian Buddhism,* 99–128. Honolulu: University of Hawai'i Press.

———. 1986b. "Bodhidharma as Textual Paradigm." *History of Religions* 25, 3: 187–198.

———. 1991. *The Rhetoric of Immediacy: A Cultural Critique of Chan/Zen Buddhism.* Princeton, NJ: Princeton University Press.

———. 1995. "Quand l'habit fait le moine: The Symbolism of the *kāṣāya* in Sōtō Zen." *CEA* 8: 335–369.

———. 1996. *Visions of Power: Imagining Medieval Japanese Buddhism.* Princeton, NJ: Princeton University Press.

———. 1998a. *The Red Thread: Buddhist Approaches to Sexuality.* Princeton, NJ: Princeton University Press.

———. 1998b. "The Buddhist Icon and the Modern Gaze." *Critical Inquiry* 24, 3: 768–813.

———. 1999. "Relics, Regalia, and the Dynamics of Secrecy in Japanese Buddhism." In Eliot R. Wolfson, ed., *Rending the Veil: Concealment and Secrecy in the History of Religions,* 271–287. New York: Seven Bridges Press.

———. 2000. "Japanese Tantra, the Tachikawa-ryū, and Ryōbu Shintō." In David G. White, ed., *Tantra in Practice,* 543–556. Princeton, NJ: Princeton University Press.

———. 2002. "Les cloches de la terre: un aspect du culte des reliques dans le bouddhisme chinois." In Catherine Despeux, ed., *Bouddhisme et lettrés dans la Chine médiévale,* 25–44. Paris-Louvain: Éditions Peeters.

———. 2002–2003. "Une perle rare: la 'nonne' Nyoi et l'idéologie médiévale." *CEA* 13: 177–196.

———. 2003a. *The Power of Denial: Buddhism, Purity, and Gender.* Princeton, NJ: Princeton University Press.

———. 2003c. "Dato" 駄都. *Hōbōgirin* 8: 1127–1158.

———. 2004. "Buddhist Relics and Japanese Regalia." In David Germano and Kevin Trainor, eds., *Embodying the Dharma: Buddhist Relic Veneration in Asia,* 93–116. Albany, NY: SUNY Press.

———. 2006. "The Elephant in the Room: The Cult of Secrecy in Japanese Tantrism." In Scheid and Teeuwen 2006: 255–268.

———. 2009. "Vers une nouvelle approche de la religion japonaise: le cas du Japon médiéval." *Historia religionum* 1: 105–113.

———, ed. 2012a. *CEA* 21.

———. 2012b. "Relic Theft in Medieval Japan." In Rebecca Redwood French and Mark A. Nathan, eds., *Buddhism and Law: An Introduction.* Cambridge: Cambridge University Press.

Favret-Saada, Jeanne. 1980. *Deadly Words: Witchcraft in the Bocage.* Cambridge: Cambridge University Press.

Filliozat, Jean, and Louis Renou. 1985 (1947–1953). *L'Inde classique: Manuel des études indiennes.* 3 vols. Paris: École Française d'Extrême-Orient.

Fowler, Sherry D. 1989a. "Nyoirin Kannon: A Chronological Analysis of Six-armed Sculptural Examples from the Ninth through the Fourteenth Century." MA thesis, University of Washington.

———. 1989b. "Nyoirin Kannon, Stylistic Evolution of Sculptural Images." *Orientations* 20, 12: 58–65.

———. 1997a. "Setting Foot on the Mountain: Mt. Murō as a Women's Alternative to Mt. Kōya." *Asian Journal of Women's Studies* 3, 4: 52–73.

———. 1997b. "In Search of the Dragon: Mt. Murō's Sacred Topography." *JJRS* 24, 1–2: 145–161.

———. 2000–2001. "Shifting Identities in Buddhist Sculpture: Who's Who in the Murōji Kondō." *Archives of Asian Art* 52: 83–104.

———. 2005. *Murōji: Rearranging Art and History at a Japanese Buddhist Temple.* Honolulu: University of Hawai'i Press.

Frank, Bernard. 1981–1982. "Résumé de cours et travaux: Civilisation Japonaise." In *Annuaire du Collège de France,* 587–611. Paris: Collège de France.

———. 1986. "Vacuité et 'corps actualisé': le problème de la présence des 'Personnages Vénérés' dans leurs images selon la tradition du bouddhisme japonais." In *Le Temps de la réflexion: Corps des dieux,* 7: 141–170. Reprinted in *Journal of the International Association of Buddhist Studies* 11, 2 (1988): 53–86.

———. 1990. "Les *deva* de la tradition bouddhique et la société japonaise: l'exemple d'Indra/Taishakuten." In Alain Forrest, Eiichi Katō, and Léon Vandermeersch, eds., *Bouddhisme et sociétés asiatiques: clergés, sociétés et pouvoirs,* 61–74. Paris: Éditions L'Harmattan. Reprinted in Frank 2000b.

———. 1991. *Le panthéon bouddhique au Japon: Collections d'Émile Guimet.* Paris: Réunion des Musées Nationaux.

———. 1998 (1958). *Kata-imi et kata-tagae: Étude sur les interdits de direction à l'époque Heian.* Paris: Collège de France, Institut des Hautes Études Japonaises.

———. 2000a. *Dieux et Bouddhas au Japon.* Paris: Éditions Odile Jacob.

———. 2000b. *Amour, colère, couleur: Essais sur le bouddhisme au Japon.* Paris: Collège de France, Institut des Hautes Études Japonaises.

Franke, Herbert. 1990. "The Taoist Elements in the Buddhist *Great Bear Sūtra* (Pei-tou ching)." *Asia Major* 3, 1: 75–111.

Friday, Karl. 2007. *The First Samurai: The Life and Legend of the Warrior Rebel, Taira Masakado.* London: Wiley.

Fritsch, Ingrid. 1996. *Japans blinde Sänger: im Schutz der Gottheit Myōon-Ben-zaiten.* Munich: Iudicium Verlag.

Fujimaki Kazuhiro 藤巻和宏. 2000. "Hatsuse no ryūketsu to 'nyoi hōju': Hase-dera engi no tenkai, 'Ben'ichizan' o meguru gensetsugun to no kōsa" 初瀬の龍穴と〈如意宝珠―長谷寺縁起の展開・「宀一山」をめぐる言説群との交差. *Kokubungaku kenkyū* 130: 102–112.

———. 2001. "Ben'ichizan to nyoi hōju-hō o meguru Tōmitsu-kei kuden no tenkai: Sanbōin-ryū sanzon gōgyō-hō o chūshin to shite" 如意宝珠をめぐる東密口伝の展開―三宝院流三尊合行法を中心として. *Muromachi* 5: 1–15.

———. 2002a. "Hasedera engi no keisei to tenkai" 長谷寺縁起の形成と展開. PhD diss., Waseda University.

———. 2002b. "Nyoi hōju o meguru Tōmitsu-kei kuden no tenkai to Ben'ichizan engi-rui no seisei: '*Ben'ichizan himitsuki*' o chūshin to shite" 如意宝珠をめぐる東密口伝の展開と宀一山縁起類の生成―「宀一山秘密記」を中心として. *Kokugo kokubun* 71, 1: 1–17.

———. 2002c. "Jissen joshi daigaku fuzoku toshokan Yamagishi bunko zō '*Goyuigō daiji*' ichijiku kaidai, keiin" 実践女子大学付属図書館山岸文庫蔵「御遺告大事」一軸解題，影印. *Jissen joshi daigaku bungakubu kiyō* 44: 1–38.

———. 2003. "Hōju o meguru hisetsu no kengen: Zuishin-in zō '*Ben'ichizan hiki*' no shōkai ni yosete" 宝珠をめぐる秘説の顕現―随心院 随心院蔵「宀一山秘記」の紹介によせて. *Koten isan* 古典遺産 53: 103–117.

———. 2004. Zuishin'in zō '*Ben'ichizan ryūketsu hiki*' to Anzenji kyūzō shōgyō-gun" 随心院蔵「宀一山龍穴秘記」と安禅寺旧蔵聖教群. *Zuishin-in seikyō to jiin nettowāku* 1: 71–80.

———. 2005. "Kinsei no Kūkai *Goyuigō* chūshakusho, Zuishin-in zō *Goyuigō hishaku* ni tsuite (jō): Ken-kan hankoku to Zuishin-in no Yuigō kankei shiryō" 近世の空海御遺告注釈書：随心院蔵「御遺告秘釈」について（上）―乾巻翻刻と随心院の遺告関係資料. *Zuishin-in seikyō to jiin nettowāku* 2: 80–112.

Funata Jun'ichi 船田淳一. 2011. *Shinbutsu to girei no chūsei* 神仏と儀礼の中世. Kyoto: Hōzōkan.

Gangōji bunkazai kenkyūjo 元興寺文化財研究所, ed. 1983. *Chūsei Kōyasan engi no kenkyū* 中世高野山縁起野の研究. Nara: Gangōji.

———, ed. 1999. *Shintō kanjō: wasurareta shinbutsu shūgō no sekai* 神道灌頂―忘られた神仏習合の世界. Nara: Gangōji.

Geertz, Clifford. 1977. *The Interpretation of Cultures.* New York: Basic Books.

———. 1988. *Works and Lives: The Anthropologist as Author.* Stanford, CA: Stanford University Press.

George, Christopher S., ed. and trans. 1974. *The Caṇḍamahāroṣaṇa-Tantra, Chapters I-VIII.* New Haven, CT: American Oriental Society.

Germano, David, and Kevin Trainor, eds. 2004. *Embodying the Dharma: Relic Veneration in Asia.* Albany, NY: SUNY Press.

Gimello, Robert. 2004. "Icon and Incantation: The Goddess Zhunti and the Role of Images in the Occult Buddhism of China." In Phyllis Granoff and Koichi Shinohara, eds. *Images in Asian Religions,* 225–256. Vancouver: University of British Columbia Press.

Girard, Frédéric.1990. *Un moine de la secte Kegon à l'époque de Kamakura, Myōe (1173–1232) et le "journal de ses rêves."* Paris: École Française d'Extrême-Orient.

———. 1994. "Note critique de lecture: Misaki Ryōshū. *Taimitsu no ronri to jissen* 台密の論理と実践." *BEFEO* 81: 425–444.

———. 2004. "Quête et transmission des reliques de la Chine au Japon." In Philippe Borgeaud and Youri Volokhine, eds. *Les objets de la mémoire— Pour une approche comparatiste des reliques et de leur culte,* 149–180. Bern: Peter Lang.

Godelier, Maurice. 2012. *The Mental and the Material.* New York: Verso.

Goepper, Roger. 1979. "Some Thoughts on the Icon in Esoteric Buddhism of East Asia." In Wolfgang Bauer, ed., *Studia Sino-Mongolica: Festschrift für Herbert Franke,* 245–254. Wiesbaden: Steiner.

———. 1983a. *Das Kultbild im Ritus des esoterischen Buddhismus in Japan.* Opladen.

———. 1993. *Aizen-myōō: The Esoteric King of Lust: An Iconological Study.* Artibus Asiae. Zurich: Museum Rietberg.

———. 2001. "Maṇḍala Speculations in Shingon Buddhism based on the *Hizōki* and its Commentaries." In Rob Linrothe and Henrik H. Sørensen, eds., *Embodying Wisdom: Art, Text and Interpretation in the History of Esoteric Buddhism,* 37–56. SBS Monographs 6. Copenhagen: Seminar for Buddhist Studies.

Goffman, Erving. 1959. *The Presentation of Self in Everyday Life.* New York: Anchor Books.

Gonda, Jan. 1974. "Dumézil's Tripartite Ideology: Some Critical Observations." *Journal of Asian Studies* 34, 1: 139–149.

Gorai Shigeru 五来重, ed. 2000 (1983–1984). *Shugendō shiryō shū* 修験道史料 集. 2 vols. Tokyo: Meicho shuppan.

Gossaert, Vincent. 2004. "Les reliques en Chine." In Philippe Borgeaud and Youri Volokhine, eds. *Les objets de la mémoire—Pour une approche comparatiste des reliques et de leur culte,* 180–191. Bern: Peter Lang.

Gould, Stephen Jay. 1996. *Full House: The Spread of Excellence from Plato to Darwin.* New York: Three Rivers Press.

Goux, Jean-Joseph. 1990. *Symbolic Economies: After Marx and Freud.* Trans. Jennifer Curtis Gage. Ithaca, NY: Cornell University Press.

Granet, Marcel. 1999 (1934). *La pensée chinoise.* Paris: Albin Michel.

Grapard, Allan G. 1982. "Flying Mountains and Walkers of Emptiness: Toward a Definition of Sacred Space in Japanese Religions." *History of Religions* 21, 3: 195–221.

———. 1986. "Lotus in the Mountain, Mountain in the Lotus: *Rokugō kaizan Nimmon daibosatsu hongi.*" *Monumenta Nipponica* 41, 1: 21–50.

———. 1987. "Linguistic Cubism: A Singularity of Pluralism in the Sannō Cult." *JJRS* 14: 211–234.

———. 1992. *The Protocol of the Gods: A Study of the Kasuga Cult in Japanese History.* Berkeley: University of California Press.

———. 1998. "*Keiranshūyōshū:* A Different Perspective on Mt. Hiei in the Medieval Period." In Payne 1998: 55–69.

———. Forthcoming. *Mountain Mandalas.* New York: Bloomsbury Publishing.

Gray, David B. 2005. "Eating the Heart of the Brahmin: Representations of Alterity and the Formation of Identity in Tantric Buddhist Discourse." *History of Religions* 45, 1: 45–69.

Grinstead, Erik, trans. 1994. "The Sūtra of the Eleven-headed Avalokiteśvara Bodhisattva." In Henrik K. Sørensen, ed., *The Esoteric Buddhist Tradition,* 97–125. SBS Monographs 2. Copenhagen: Seminar for Buddhist Studies.

Groner, Paul. 2000. *Saichō: The Establishment of the Japanese Tendai School.* Honolulu: University of Hawai'i Press.

———. 2001. "Icons and Relics in Eison's Religious Activities," In Sharf and Sharf 2001: 114–150.

———. 2002. *Ryōgen and Mount Hiei: Japanese Tendai in the Tenth Century.* Kuroda Institute Studies in East Asian Buddhism 15. Honolulu: University of Hawai'i Press.

Gülberg, Niels. 1999. *Buddhistische Zeremoniale (Kōshiki) und ihre Bedeutung für die Literatur des japanischen Mittelalters.* Münchener ostasiatische Studien 76. Stuttgart: Franz Steiner Verlag.

Guth (Kanda), Christine M. E. 1985. *Shinzō: Hachiman Imagery and Its Development.* Cambridge, MA: Harvard University Press.

Hadot, Pierre. 2006. *The Veil of Isis: An Essay on the History of the Idea of Nature.* Trans. Michael Chase. Cambridge, MA: Harvard University Press.

Hall, David A. 2013. *The Buddhist Goddess Marishiten: A Study of the Evolution and Impact of Her Cult.* Leiden: Brill.

Hara Katsuaki 原克昭. 2012. *Chūsei Nihongi ronkō: chūshaku no shisōshi* 中世二本紀論考一注釈の思想史. Kyoto: Hōzōkan.

Harper, Donald. 2001. "The Nature of Taiyi in the Guodian Manuscript *Taiyi sheng shui:* Abstract Cosmic Principle or Supreme Cosmic Deity?" *Zhongguo chutu shiliao yanjiu* 中国出土資料研究 5: 1–13.

Hasegawa Makoto 長谷川誠. 1966. "Saidaiji Aizen Myōō-zō to sono zengo" 西大寺愛染明王像とその前後. *Bukkyō geijutsu* 63: 141–155.

Hatta Yukio 八田幸雄. 1984. "Miwaryū shintō no shinbutsu shūgō shisō: shintō kanjō shiki mandara o chūshin to shite" 三輪流神道の神仏習合思想―神道灌頂敷曼荼羅を中心として. *Mikkyōgaku kenkyū* 16: 100–122.

———. 1985. "Miwaryū shintō to Rishūkyō mandara: *Shintō kanjō seiki* o chūshin to shite" 三輪流神道と理趣経曼荼羅―「神道灌頂清軌」を中心として. *Mikkyō bunka* 151: 10–28.

———. 1991. "Murō, Hase, Ōmiwa jinja no shinbutsu shūgō no genryū" 室生・長谷・大神神社の神仏習合の源流. *Chisan gakuhō* 智山学報 40: 53–67.

Hattori Nyojitsu 服部如実, ed. 1972. *Shugendō yōten* 修験道要典. Tokyo: Sanmitsudō shoten.

Hayakawa Junzaburō 早川純三郎, ed. 2000 (1915). *Shinkō sōsho* 信仰叢書. Tokyo: Hachiman shoten.

Hayami Tasuku 速水侑. 1970. *Kannon shinkō* 観音信仰. Tokyo: Hanawa shobō.

———. 1975. *Heian kizoku shakai to bukkyō* 平安貴族社会と仏教. Tokyo: Yoshikawa Kōbunkan.

———, ed. 1982. *Kannon shinkō* 観音信仰. Tokyo: Yūzankaku.

———. 1987. *Jujutsu shūkyō no sekai* 呪術宗教の世界. Tokyo: Hanawa shobō.

———. 1998. *Insei-ki no bukkyō* 院政期の仏教. Tokyo: Yoshikawa kōbunkan.

———, ed. 2000. *Kannon shinkō jiten* 観音信仰事典. Tokyo: Ebisu kōshō shuppan.

———. 2002. *Kannon shinkō* 観音信仰. Tokyo: Hanawa shobō.

———, ed. 2006. *Nihon shakai ni okeru hotoke to kami* 日本社会における仏と神. Tokyo: Yoshikawa kōbunkan.

Hayashi On 林温, ed. 1997. "Myōken bosatsu to hoshi mandara" 妙見菩薩と星曼荼羅. *Nihon no bijutsu* 日本の美術 377. Tokyo: Shibundō.

———. 2002. "Besson mandara" 別尊曼荼羅. *Nihon no bijutsu* 日本の美術 433. Tokyo: Shibundō.

Heller, Amy. 2001. "On the Development of the Iconography of Acala and Vignāntaka in Tibet." In Rob Linrothe and Henrik H. Sørensen, eds., *Embodying Wisdom: Art, Text and Interpretation in the History of Esoteric Buddhism,* 209–228. SBS Monographs 6. Copenhagen: Seminar for Buddhist Studies.

Higuchi Seitarō 井口清太郎. 1976. "Chūsei buke shakai ni okeru shugojin shinkō: Chiba ichizoku no Myōken shinkō shinwa" 中世武家社会における守護神信仰−千葉一族の妙見信仰神話. *Kokugakuin daigaku daigakuin kiyō* 8: 267–288.

Hillebrand, Alfred. 1981 (1891–1902). *Vedic Mythology.* Trans. Sreeramula Rajeswara Sarma. 2 vols. Delhi: Motilal Banarsidass.

Hiltebeitel, Alf. 1974. "Dumézil and Indian Studies." *Journal of Asian Studies* 34, 1: 129–137.

Hiraizumi Takafusa 平泉隆房. 1986. "Ise shintō he no shingon kyōgi no eikyō: Nakatomi harae tenjin norito o chūshin to shite" 伊勢神道への真言教義の影響−中臣祓天神祝詞を中心として. *Shintō-shi kenkyū* 34, 1: 39–54.

Hirasawa Takuya 平沢卓也. 2004. "Kaike ni okeru Sannō-setsu" 戒家における山王説. *Waseda daigaku daigakuin bungaku kenkyūka kiyō* 9, 1: 85–97.

———. 2005. "Sannō no jukai: chūko Tendai ni okeru jingi-kan no ippan" 山王の受戒—中古天台における神祇観の一班. *Tōyō no shisō to shūkyō* 22: 93–120.

Hiroya Yutarō 廣谷雄太郎, ed. 1925. *Kinsei bukkyō shūsetsu* 近世佛教集説. Tokyo: Hiroya Kokusho kankōkai.

Hōbōgirin: Dictionnaire encyclopédique du bouddhisme d'après les sources chinoises et japonaises. 1927–. Vols. 1–8. Paris: Adrien Maisonneuve.

Hornung, Erik. 1996. *Conceptions of God in Ancient Egypt: The One and the Many.* Trans. John Baines. Ithaca, NY: Cornell University Press.

Hubert, Henri, and Marcel Mauss. 1981. *Sacrifice: Its Nature and Functions.* Trans. W. D. Halls. Chicago: University of Chicago Press.

Hugo, Victor. 1859. *La légende des siècles.* Paris: Michel Lévy Frères.

Huntington, John C. 1975. "The Tendai Iconographic Model Book *Shosonzuzō,* Dated 1858." *Studies in Indo-Asian Art and Culture* 4: 121–424.

———. 1981. "Cave Six at Aurangabad: A Tantrayāna Monument?" In Joanna Williams, ed. *Kalādarśana: American Studies in the Art of India,* 47–55. Leiden: E. J. Brill.

Ihara Shōren 伊原照蓮. 1984. "Yugikyō to buttō" 瑜祇経と仏塔. In Taishō daigaku shingongaku Chizan kenkyūshitsu 大正大学真言学智山研究室, ed. *Bukkyō shisō ronshū: Nasu Seiryū hakushi beiju kinen* 仏教思想論集−那須政隆博士米寿記念, 225–238. Narita: Shinshōji.

Imahori Taitsu 今堀太逸. 1990. *Jingi shinkō no tenkai to bukkyō* 神祇信仰の展開と仏教. Tokyo: Yoshikawa kōbunkan.

Inaya Yūsen 稲谷祐宣. 1993. *Shingon shintō shūsei* 真言神道集成. Osaka: Seizansha.

Ingold, Tim. 2000. *The Perception of the Environment: Essays in Livelihood, Dwelling and Skill.* London: Routledge.

———. 2011. *Being Alive: Essays on Movement, Knowledge and Description.* London and New York: Routledge.

Inoue Ichinen 井上一稔, ed. 1992. "Nyoirin Kannon zō, Batō Kannon zō" 如意輪観音像・馬頭観音像. *Nihon no bijutsu* 312. Tokyo: Shibundō.

Inoue Takao 井上孝夫. 1994."Bōsō chiiki no sangaku shūkyō ni kansuru kisōteki kōsatsu" 房総地域の山岳宗教に関する基礎的考察. *Chiba daigaku kyōiku gakubu kenkyū kiyō* 千葉大学教育学部研究紀要 42, 1: 197–211.

———. 1995. "Bōsō chiiki no seitetsu bunka ni kansuru kisōteki kansatsu" 房総地域の製鉄文化に関する基礎的考察. *Chiba daigaku kyōiku gakubu kenkyū kiyō* 千葉大学教育学部研究紀要 43, 2: 1–12.

Ishikawa Rikizan 石川力山. 1983. "Chūsei Sōtōshū kirigami no bunrui shiron (2): Ryūtaiji shozō 'Bukke ichidaiji yawa' ni tsuite" 中世曹洞宗切紙の分類試論（二）一竜泰寺所蔵〔仏家一大事夜話」について. *Komazawa daigaku bukkyō gakubu ronshū* 14: 123–155.

———, 2001. *Zenshū sōden shiryō no kenkyū* 禅宗相伝資料の研究. 2 vols. Kyoto: Hōzōkan.

Ishizaki Tatsuji 石崎達二. 1936. *Tōfukuji Bishamon Tennō* 東福寺毘沙門天王. Kyoto: Tōfukuji Bishamondō Shōrin-an.

Isomae Jun'ichi. 2010. *Japanese Mythology: Hermeneutics on Scripture*. Trans. Mukund Subramanian. Nichibunken Monograph series 10. London: Equinox.

Itō Masatoshi 伊藤正敏. 2008. *Jisha seiryoku no chūsei: muen, uen, imin* 寺社勢力の中世一無縁、有縁、移民. Chikuma shinsho 734. Tokyo: Chikuma shobō.

Itō Masayoshi 伊藤正義. 1970. *Konparu Zenchiku no kenkyū* 金春禅竹の研究. Tokyo: Akao shobundō.

———. 1972. "Chūsei *Nihongi* no rinkaku: *Taiheiki* ni okeru Urabe no Kanekata setsu o megutte" 中世日本紀の輪郭一太平記における卜部兼員説をめぐって. *Bungaku* 40, 10: 28–48.

———. 1981. "Jidō setsuwa kō" 慈童説話考. *Kokugo kokubun* 49, 11: 1–32.

Itō Satoshi 伊藤聡. 1993a. "Yoshida bunko shozō no Benzaiten kankei gikyō ni tsuite: sono hankoku to shōkai." 吉田文庫所蔵の弁財天関係偽経について一その翻刻と紹介. *Muromachi* むろまち 2: 40–46.

———. 1993b. "Ise no shintō-setsu no tenkai ni okeru Saidaiji-ryū no dōkō ni tsuite" 伊勢の神道説の展開における西大寺流の動向について. *Shintō shūkyō* 153: 70–105.

———. 1995. "Tenshō Daijin, Kūkai dōtai-setsu o megutte: toku ni Sanbōin-ryū o chūshin to shite" 天照大神・空海 同体説を巡って. *Tōyō no shisō to shūkyō* 12: 112–131.

———. 1996a. "Chūsei shintō setsu ni okeru Tenshō Daijin: toku ni Jūichimen Kannon to no dōtaisetsu o megutte" 中世神道説における天照大神—特に十一面観音との同体説を巡って. In Saitō Hideki, ed., *Amaterasu shinwa no henshinfu*, 251–290. Tokyo: Shinwasha.

———. 1996b. "I-Se niji o megutte: Kokonchū・Ise-chū to mikkyō-setsu・shintō-setsu no kōshō" 伊勢二字を巡って一古今注・伊勢注と密教説・神道説の交渉. In Sugahara Shinkai 菅原信海, ed., *Shinbutsu shūgō shisō no tenkai* 神仏習合思想の展開, 77–122. Tokyo: Kyūko shoin.

———. 1998. "Chūsei shinwa no tenkai: Chūsei kōki no dairokuten Enma-ō dan o megutte" 中世神話の展開一中世後期の第六天閻魔王談を巡って. *Kokubungaku: kaishaku to kanshō* 811: 68–76.

———. 2001d. "Futama Kannon to Tenshō Daijin" 二間観音と天照大神. *Nihon bukkyō gakkai nenpō* 67: 219–234.

———. 2002a. "Chōgen to hōju" 重源と宝珠. *Bukkyō bungaku* 仏教文学 26: 10–26.

———. 2002b. "Dai Nihon ni okeru taiyō shinkō: tokuni Amaterasu ōmikami to Aizen Myōō no shūgō o megutte" 大日本における太陽信仰—特に天照大神と愛染明王の習合を巡って. In Matsumura Kazuo 松村一男 and Watanabe Kazuko 渡辺和子, eds., *Taiyōshin no kenkyū* 太陽神の研究, 1:191–208.

———. 2003a. "Tenshō Daijin = Dainichi nyorai shūgō-setsu o megutte (jō)" 天照大神＝大日如来習合説をめぐって（上）. *Ibaraki daigaku gakubu kiyō 'Jinbun gakka ronshū'* 39: 65–81.

———. 2005. "Denpu Aizen-hō o megutte" 田夫愛染法をめぐって. In Fukui Fumimasa hakushi koki taishoku kinen ronshū kankōkai 福井文雅博士古稀・退職記念論集刊行会, ed., *Ajia bunka no shisō to girei* 博士古希退職記念論集刊行会, 821–840. Fukui Fumimasa hakushi koki kinen ronshū. Tokyo: Shunjūsha.

———. 2011. *Chūsei Tenshō daijin shinkō no kenkyū* 中世天照大神信仰の研究. Kyoto: Hōzōkan.

Iwahara Taishin 岩原諦信. 1988. *Hoshi to Shingon mikkyō* 星と真言密教. Osaka: Tōhō shuppan.

Iwata Masaru 岩田勝. 1993. "Gohō ni kanjō-sareru busshin no henbō" 五方に勧請される仏神の変貌. In Tanaka Hisao 田中久夫, ed., *Fudō shinkō* 不動信仰, 341–348. Minshu shūkyōshi sōsho 25. Tokyo: Yūzankaku.

Iyanaga Nobumi 彌永信美. 1983. "Daijizaiten (Maheśvara)" 大自在天. *Hōbōgirin* 6: 713–765.

———. 1981–1985. "Récits de la soumission de Maheśvara par Trailokyavijaya—d'après les sources chinoises et japonaises." In Strickmann 1981–1985, 3: 633–745.

———. 1994. "Daikoku-ten" 大黒天. *Hōbōgirin* 7: 839–920.

———. 1996–1997. "Le Roi Māra du Sixième Ciel et le mythe médiéval de la création du Japon." *CEA* 9: 323–396.

———. 1999. "Dākinī et l'Empereur: Mystique bouddhique de la royauté dans le Japon médiéval." *Versus: Quaderni di studi semiotici* 83–84: 41–111.

———. 2002a. *Daikokuten hensō: bukkyō shinwagaku 1* 大黒天変相 一仏教神話学 1. Kyoto: Hōzōkan.

———. 2002b. *Kannon hen'yōdan: bukkyō shinwagaku 2* 観音変容談一仏教神話学 2. Kyoto: Hōzōkan.

———. 2002–2003. "Tantrism and Reactionary Ideologies in Eastern Asia: Some Hypotheses and Questions." *CEA* 13: 1–34.

———. 2003. "*Honji suijaku* and the Logic of Combinatory Deities: Two Case Studies. In Teeuwen and Rambelli 2003a: 145–176.

———. 2006. "Secrecy, Sex, and Apocrypha: Remarks on Some Paradoxical Phenomena." In Scheid and Teeuwen 2006: 204–228.

———. 2006–2007. "Medieval Shintō as a Form of 'Japanese Hinduism': An Attempt at Understanding Early Medieval Shintō." *CEA* 16: 263–303.

Izumi Takeo 泉武夫. 1990. "Sonjōō to chintaku reifushin" 尊星王と鎮宅霊符神. In "Miidera no bukkyō bijutsu: Kenkyū happyō to zadankai" 三井寺の仏教美術一研究発表と座談会, 1–4. Ed. Bukkyō bijutsu kenkyū Ueno kinen zaidan josei kenkyūkai hōkokusho 仏教美術研究上野記念財団女性研究会報告書 20. Kyoto: Bukkyō bijutsu kenkyū Ueno kinen zaidan josei kenkyū kai.

———, ed. 1998. "Kokūzō bosatsu zō" 虚空蔵菩薩像. *Nihon no bijutsu* 日本の尾術 380. Tokyo: Shibundō.

———. 2001. "Sentai Aizen-ō gakan to tasūson no seisaku" 千体愛染王絵巻と多数尊の制作. In "Inseiki no sakuzen to bijutsu: Kenkyū happyō to zadankai" 院政期の作善と美術一研究発表と座談会, 12–21. Ed. Bukkyō bijutsu kenkyū Ueno kinen zaidan josei kenkyūkai 仏教美術研究上野記念財団女性研究会. Kyoto: Bukkyō bijutsu kenkyū Ueno kinen zaidan josei kenkyūkai.

Kadoya Atsushi 門屋温. 1993. "Ryōbu shintō shiron: *Bikisho* no seiritsu o megutte" 両部神道試論：「鼻帰書」の成立をめぐって. *Tōyō no shisō to shukyō* 東洋の思想と宗教10: 80–96.

———. 1997. "'Ben'ichizan Doshinsuishi' o megutte" 「宀一山土心水師」をめぐって. *Setsuwa bungaku kenkyū* 説話文学研究32: 96–105.

———. 2002. "'Shinki, shinpō' kō: Shintō zuzōgaku no kokoromi" 「神器・神宝」考―神道図像学の試み. *Nihongaku kenkyū* 日本学研究 5: 1–31.

———. 2006. "Myths, Rites, and Icons: Three Views of a Secret." In Scheid and Teeuwen 2006: 269–283.

———. 2007. "On the Formation of Shintō Icons." *CEA* 16: 151–182.

Kageyama Haruki 影山春樹. 1962. *Shintō bijutsu no kenkyū* 神道美術の研究. Tokyo: Yamamoto Koshū shashin kōgeibu.

———, ed. 1967. "Shintō bijutsu" 神道美術. *Nihon no bijutsu* 日本の美術 18. Tokyo: Shibundō.

———. 1971. *Shintai-san: Nihon no genshi shinkō o saguru* 神体山―日本の原始信仰を探る. Tokyo: Gakuseisha.

———. 1973a. *Shintō bijutsu: sono shosō to tenkai* 神道美術―その諸相と展開. Tokyo: Yūzankaku Shuppan.

———. 1973b. *The Arts of Shinto*. Trans. Christine Guth. New York: Weatherhill/Shibundo.

———. 1975a. *Hieizan* 比叡山. Kadokawa sensho 75. Tokyo: Kadokawa shoten.

———. 1980. *Hieizan to Kōyasan* 比叡山と高野山. Rekishi shinsho 29. Tokyo: Kyōikusha.

———. 1981. "Tendai shugen to bijutsu: Sannō mandara o chūshin ni" 天台修験と美術―山王まんだらを中心に. In Gorai Shigeru 五来重, ed., *Shugendō no bijutsu, geinō, bungaku* 修験道の美術、芸能、文学 (2), 16–38. Sangaku shūkyōshi kenkyū sōsho 15. Tokyo: Meicho shuppan.

———. 1986. *Shari shinkō: sono kenkyū to shiryō* 舎利信仰―その研究と資料. Tokyo: Tōkyō bijutsu.

———. 1993. "Fudō-son to himitsu shuhō" 不動尊と秘密修法. In Tanaka Hisao 1993a: 59–82.

Kakuzenshō kenkyūkai 覚禅鈔研究会, ed. 2004. *Kakuzenshō no kenkyū* 覚禅鈔の研究. Wakayamaken Itogun Kōyachō: Shinnōin gyōei bunko.

Kalinowski, Marc. 1991. *Cosmologie et divination dans la Chine ancienne: Le Compendium des Cinq Agents* (*Wuxing dayi, VIe siècle*). Paris: École Française d'Extrême-Orient.

Kamens, Edward, trans. 1988. *The Three Jewels: A Study and Translation of Minamoto Tamenori's Sanbōe*. Ann Arbor, MI: Center for Japanese Studies, University of Michigan.

Kamikawa Michio 上川通夫. 1990. "Accession Rituals and Buddhism in Medieval Japan." *JJRS* 17, 2–3: 243–280.

———. 2004. "Nyoi hōju-hō no seiritsu" 如意宝珠法の成立. In Kakuzenshō kenkyūkai 覚禅鈔研究会, ed. *Kakuzenshō no kenkyū* 覚禅鈔の研究, 379–402. Kōyasan: Shinnōin gyōei bunko.

———. 2006a. "Kakuzenshō Nyohō sonshō-hō kaidai" 「覚禅鈔」「如法尊勝法」解題. In Kokubunkagu kenkyū shiryōkan 2006: 577–597.

———. 2006b. "Nihon chūsei bukkyō no seiritsu" 日本中世仏教の成立. *Nihonshi kenkyū* 日本史研究 522: 3–21.

———. 2007. *Nihon chūsei bukkyō keiseishi-ron* 日本中世仏教形成史論. Tokyo: Azekura shobō.

———. 2008a. *Nihon chūsei bukkyō shiryō-ron* 日本中世仏教資料論. Tokyo: Yoshikawa kōbunkan.

———. 2008b. "Nyohō sonshō-hō shōgyō no seisei" 如法尊勝法聖教の生成. In Abe Yasurō, ed., *Nihon ni okeru shūkyō tekusuto no shoisō to tōjihō: tekusuto fuchi no kaishakuteki kenkyū to kyōiku* 日本における宗教テクストの諸位相と統治法―テクスト布置の解釈的研究と教育, 74–80. Nagoya: Nagoya daigaku daigakuin bungaku kenkyūkai.

Kanagawa kenritsu Kanazawa bunko 神奈川県立金沢文庫, ed. 1952–1964. *Kanazawa bunko komonjo* 金沢文庫古文書. 19 vols. Yokohama: Kanagawa kenritsu Kanazawa bunko.

———, ed. 1974. *Kanazawa bunko shiryō zensho* 金沢文庫資料全書. Yokohama: Kanagawa kenritsu Kanazawa bunko.

———, ed. 2004. *Mihotoke to goriyaku* みほとけとごりやく. Yokohama: Kanazawa bunko.

———, ed. 2007a. *Benzaiten: sono sugata to riyaku* 弁財天―その姿と利益. Yokohama: Kanazawa bunko.

———, ed. 2007b. *Onmyōdō kakeru mikkyō* 陰陽道×密教. Yokohama: Kanazawa bunko.

———, ed. 2011. *Aizen Myōō: Ai to ikari no hotoke* 愛染明王―愛と怒りのほとけ. Yokohama: Kanazawa bunko.

Kanezashi Shōzō 金指正三. 1974. *Hoshi-uranai hoshi-matsuri* 星占い星祭り. Tokyo: Seiabō.

Kasahara Kazuo 笠原一男, ed. 2001. *A History of Japanese Religion.* Trans. Paul McCarthy and Gaynor Sekimori. Tokyo: Kosei Publishing Co.

Katsumata Shunkyō 勝又俊教, ed. 1968–1973. *Kōbō Daishi chosaku zenshū* 弘法大師著作全集. 6th ed. 3 vols. Tokyo: Sankibō busshorin.

Katz, Paul R. 1995. *Demon Hordes and Burning Boats: The Cult of Marshal Wen in Late Imperial Chekiang.* Albany, NY: SUNY Press.

Kawada Sadamu 河田貞, ed. 1989. "Busshari to kyō no shōgon" 仏舎利と経の荘厳. *Nihon no bijutsu* 280. Tokyo: Shibundō.

Kawaguchi Kenji 川口謙二. 1965. *Wasurareta shinbutsu* 忘られた神仏. Tokyo: Kinseisha.

———, ed. 1999. *Nihon no kamigami yomitoki jiten* 日本の神々読み解き事典. Tokyo: Kashiwa shobō.

Kawamura Minato 川村湊. 2007. *Gozu Tennō to Somin Shōrai densetsu: ke-sareta ijin tachi* 牛頭天王と蘇民将来伝説―消された異神たち. Tokyo: Sakuinsha.

———. 2008. *Yami no Matarajin: hengen-suru ijin no nazo o ou* 闇の摩多羅神―変幻する異神の謎を追う. Tokyo: Kawade shobō shinsha.

Keller, Catherine. 2014. *The Cloud of the Impossible: Theological Entanglements.* New York: Columbia University Press.

Kida Teikichi [Sadakichi] 喜田貞吉. 1976. *Fukujin* 福神. Ed. Yamada Norio. Tokyo: Hōbunkan.

Kieschnick, John. 1997. *The Eminent Monk: Buddhist Ideals in Medieval Chinese Hagiography.* Honolulu: University of Hawai'i Press.

———. 2003. *The Impact of Buddhism on Chinese Material Culture.* Princeton, NJ: Princeton University Press.

Kikuchi Hiroki 菊池大樹. 2007. *Chūsei bukkyō no genkei to tenkai* 中世仏教の原型と展開. Tokyo: Yoshikawa kōbunkan.

———. 2011. "Shūson no hen'yō to itabi no shintai: 'Guhariki-shikki Amida' itabi o megutte" 主尊の変容と板碑の身体ー「紅頗梨色阿弥陀」板碑をめぐって. In Fujizawa Fumihiko 藤澤典彦, ed., *Sekizōbutsu no kenkyū: Bukkyō bunbutsu no shosō* 石造物の研究ー仏教文物の諸相, 125–150. Tokyo: Kōshi shoin.

Kim Youn-mi. 2010. "Eternal Ritual in an Infinite Cosmos: The Chaoyang North Pagoda (1043–1044)." PhD diss., Harvard University.

Kim Yung-Hee, trans. 1994. *Songs to Make the Dust Dance: The Ryōjin Hishō of Twelfth-Century Japan.* Berkeley: University of California Press.

Kimura Hirokazu 木村博. 1991. "Yōsan goshin to shite no Kokūzō bosatsu" 養蚕護神としての虚空蔵菩薩. In Sano Kenji, ed., *Kokūzō shinkō,* 85–91. Tokyo: Yūzankaku shuppan.

Kindaichi Kyōsuke 金田一京助. 1933. "Kantō no Oshirasama" 関東のオシラ様. *Minzokugaku* 5: 944–958.

Kinsley, David. 1986. *Hindu Goddesses: Vision of the Divine Feminine in the Hindu Religious Tradition.* Berkeley: University of California Press.

Kishi Shōzō 貴志正造, ed. 1967. *Shintōshū* 神道集. Tōyō bunko 94. Tokyo: Heibonsha.

Kitagawa Masahiro 北川真寛. 2004. "*Keiran shūyōshū* ni miru Tō-Tai ryōmitsu no kōryū" 「渓嵐拾葉集」にみる東台両密の交流. *Mikkyōgaku kenkyū* 密教学研究 36: 65–80.

Kleeman, Terry F. 1994. *A God's Own Tale: The Book of Transformations of Wenchang, the Divine Lord of Zitong.* Albany, NY: SUNY Press.

Klein, Susan Blakeley. 2002. *Allegories of Desire: Esoteric Literary Commentaries of Medieval Japan.* Harvard-Yenching Institute Monograph Series 55. Cambridge, MA: Harvard University Press.

Knipe, David M. 1972. "One Fire, Three Fires, Five Fires: Vedic Symbols in Transformation." *History of Religions* 12: 28–41.

Kobayashi Sachio 小林幸夫. 2009. "Shukushin to shite no Myōken dōjo-zō: Watarai-shi no sosen saishi to ena no matsuri" 宿神としての妙見童女像ー度会氏の祖先祭祀と胞衣の奉り. Tōkai gakuen gengo, bungaku, bunka 東海学園言語文学文化 9: 1–11.

Kobayashi Taichirō 小林太一朗. 1951. "Shikkongōjin to Fudō-son" 執金剛神と不動尊. *Bukkyō geijutsu* 13: 53–81.

———. 1974b. *Kobayashi Taichirō chosakushū,* vol. 7: *Shūkyō geijutsu-ron* 宗教芸術論 I. Tokyo: Tankōsha.

Kohn, Livia. 1993–1995. "Kōshin: A Taoist Cult in Japan." Pts. 1–3. *Japanese Religions* 18, 2 (1993): 113–139; 20, 1 (1995): 34–55; 20, 2 (1995): 123–142.

———. 2000. "Doumu: The Mother of the Dipper." *Ming Qing yanqiu* 21: 149–196.

Kojima Yasuko 小島裕子. 1998. "Insei-ki ni okeru Aizen-ō mishihō no tenkai: Ninnaji Shukaku hōshinnō sōden 'Kōbuyō' o kiten to shite" 院政期における愛染王御修法の展開ー仁和寺守覚法親王相伝「紅薄様」を起点として. In Abe Yasurō and Yamazaki Makoto 1998: 319–387.

Kokubungaku kenkyū shiryōkan 国文学研究資料館, ed. 1999a. *Ryōbu shintō shū* 両部神道集. Shinpukuji zenpon sōkan 真福寺善本叢刊, 2nd ser., vol. 6. Tokyo: Rinsen shoten.

———, ed. 1999b. *Chūsei Nihongi shū* 中世日本紀集. Shinpukuji zenpon sōkan, 2nd ser., vol. 7. Tokyo: Rinsen shoten.

———, ed. 1999c. *Chūsei Kōyasan engi shū* 中世高野山縁起集. Shinpukuji zenpon sōkan, 2nd ser., vol. 9. Tokyo: Rinsen shoten.

———, ed. 2006. *Chūsei sentoku chosaku shū* 中世先徳著作集. Shinpukuji zenpon sōkan, 2nd ser., vol. 3. Tokyo: Rinsen shoten.

Komatsu Kazuhiko 小松和彦. 1986. *Oni no tamatebako: Minzoku shakai to no kōkan* 鬼の玉手箱—民族社会との交感. Tokyo: Seigensha.

———. 1994. *Hyōrei shinkō ron* 憑霊信仰論. Kōdansha gakujutsu bunko 1115. Tokyo: Dentō to gendaisha.

———. 1997. *Shuten Dōji no kubi* 酒呑童子の首. Tokyo: Serika shobō.

Komine Chigyō 小峰智行. 2007. "Myōken Bosatsu no shinkō to tenkai" 妙見菩薩の信仰と展開. *Mikkyōgaku kenkyū* 39: 85–101.

Kondō Yoshihiro 近藤喜博. 1985. "Ise jingū mishōtai zushi: Eison no Ise sangū to Mōko chōbuku no inori ni kanren shite" 伊勢神宮御正体厨子—叡尊の伊勢参宮と蒙古調伏に関連して. In Hagiwara Tatsuo 萩原龍夫, ed., *Ise shinkō 1*, 113–141. Minshū shūkyōshi sōsho 1. Tokyo: Yūzankaku.

Kondō Yuzuru 近藤譲. 2006. "Nyohōkyō shinkō to Ōita Chōanji Tarōten-zō" 如法経信仰と大分長安寺太郎天像. In *Bukkyō daigaku Ajia shūkyō bunka jōhō kenkyūjo kenkyū kiyō* 仏教大学アジア宗教文化情報研究所研究紀要 3: 21–73.

Koyama Satoko 小山聡子. 2003. *Gohō Dōji shinkō no kenkyū* 護法童子信仰の研究. Kyoto: Jishōsha shuppan.

Kōyasan Reihōkan 高野山霊宝館, ed. n.d. *Mandara to hoshi* 曼荼羅と星. Kōyasan: Kōyasan Reihōkan.

———. 1994. *Tenbu no shoson* 天部の諸尊. Kōyasan: Kōyasan Reihōkan.

———, ed. 2001. *Danjō garan to Oku-no-in* 壇上伽藍と奥の院. Kōyasan: Kōyasan Reihōkan.

———, ed. 2002. *Sacred Treasures of Mount Kōya: The Arts of Japanese Shingon Buddhism.* Kōyasan: Kōyasan Reihōkan.

Krishan, Yuvraj. 1999. *Gaṇeśa: Unravelling an Enigma.* Delhi: Motilal Banarsidass.

Kubo Noritada 窪徳忠. 1961. *Kōshin shinkō no kenkyū* 庚申信仰の研究. Tokyo: Nihon gakujutsu shinkōkai.

———. 1996. *Kōshin shinkō no kenkyū: Nitchū shūkyō bunka kōshō-shi* 庚申信仰の研究—日中宗教文化交渉史. 2 vols. Kubo Noritada chosakushū 1–2. Tokyo: Daiichi shobō.

Kubota Osamu 久保田収. 1959. *Chūsei shintō no kenkyū* 中世神道の研究. Kyoto: Shintōshi gakkai.

———. "Tenshō Daijin to Uhō Dōji: Asama-yama no shinkō o chūshin to shite" 天照大神と雨宝童子—朝熊山の信仰を中心として. In Hagiwara Tatsuo 萩原龍夫, ed., *Ise shinkō* 伊勢信仰 1, 142–158. Minshū shūkyōshi sōsho 1. Tokyo: Yūzankaku. Reprinted in Kubota Osamu, *Shintō-shi no kenkyu* 神道史の研究, 1973: 412–432.

———. 1973. *Shintōshi no kenkyu* 神道史の研究. Tokyo: Kōgakkan daigaku shuppanbu.

Kuo Li-ying. "Divination, jeux de hasard et purification dans le bouddhisme chinois: autour d'un *sūtra* apocryphe, le *Zhanchajing*." In Fukui Fumimasa and Gérard Fussman, eds., *Bouddhisme et cultures locales: Quelques cas de réciproques adaptations,* 145–224. Paris: École Française d'Extrême-Orient.

Kuroda Hideo 黒田日出男. 2003. *Ryū no sumu Nihon* 龍の棲む日本. Iwanami shinsho 831. Tokyo: Iwanami shoten.

Kuroda Toshio. 1975. *Nihon chūsei no kokka to shūkyō* 日本中世の国家と宗教. Tokyo: Iwanami shoten.

———. 1980a. *Jisha seiryoku* 寺社勢力. Tokyo: Iwanami shoten.

———. 1980b. "Shintō in the History of Japanese Religion." Trans. James C. Dobbins and Suzanne Gay. *Journal of Japanese Studies* 7, 1: 1–21.

———. 1989. "Historical Consciousness and *Hon-jaku* Philosophy in the Medieval Period on Mount Hiei." Trans. Allan Grapard. In George Tanabe and Willa Tanabe, eds., *The Lotus Sūtra in Japanese Culture,* 143–158. Honolulu: University of Hawai'i Press.

———. 1990. *Nihon chūsei no shakai to shūkyō* 日本中世の社会と宗教. Tokyo: Iwanami shoten.

———. 1996a. "The Development of the *Kenmitsu* System as Japan's Medieval Orthodoxy." Trans. James C. Dobbins. *JJRS* 23, 3–4: 233–269.

———. 1996b. "The Imperial Law and the Buddhist Law." Trans. Jacqueline Stone. *JJRS* 23, 3–4: 271–285.

———. 1996c. "The World of Spirit Pacification: Issues of State and Religion." Trans. Allan Grapard. *Japanese Journal of Religious Studies* 23, 3–4: 321–351.

Kuroita Katsumi 黒板勝美. 1929–1964. *Shintei zōho kokushi taikei* 新訂増補国史大系. 60 vols. Tokyo: Yoshikawa kōbunkan.

———. 1966. *Shoku Nihongi* 続日本紀. Vol. 2 of *Shintei zōho kokushi taikei* 新訂増補国史体系. Tokyo: Yoshikawa kōbunkan.

Kushida Ryōkō 櫛田良洪. 1979 (1964). *Shingon mikkyō seiritsu katei no kenkyū* 真言密教成立過程の研究. Tokyo: Sankibō busshorin.

Kyburz, Joseph. 2007. "Histoires d'amulettes: le Taishaku-ten de Shibamata." In Arnaud Brotons and Christian Galans, eds., *Japon pluriel 7: Actes de la Société française des études japonaises,* 335–342. Paris: Editions Philippe Picquier.

Kyōto kokuritsu hakubutsukan 京都国立博物館, ed. 1998. *Ōchō no butsuga to girei* 王朝の仏画と儀礼. Kyoto: Kyoto National Museum.

———, ed. 2004. *Kamigami no bi no sekai* 神々の美の世界. Kyoto: Kyoto National Museum.

———, ed. 2005. *Saichō to Tendai no kokuhō* 最澄と天台国宝. Kyoto: Kyoto National Museum.

Kyōto shiritsu geijutsu daigaku geijutsu shiryōkan 京都市立芸術大学芸術資料館, ed. 2004. *Rokkakudō Nōman'in butsuga funpon, Bukkyō zuzō shūsei* 六角堂 能満院 仏画 粉本·仏教 図像 聚成. 2 vols. Kyoto: Hōzōkan.

Lalou, Marcelle. 1930. *Iconographie des étoffes peintes* (paṭa) *dans le Mañjuśrīmūlakalpa.* Buddhica: Documents et travaux pour l'étude du bouddhisme. 1st ser., vol. 6. Paris: Paul Geuthner.

——— . 1946. "Mythologie indienne et peintures de Haute-Asie: 1. Le dieu bouddhique de la fortune." *Artibus Asiae* 9: 97–110.

———. 1956. "Four Notes on Vajrapāṇi." *Adhyar Library Bulletin* 20, 3–4: 287–293.

———. 1961. "A Fifth Note on Vajrapāṇi." *Adhyar Library Bulletin* 25, 1–4: 242–249.

Lamotte, Étienne, trans. 1949–1976. *Le Traité de la grande vertu de sagesse de Nāgārjuna.* 4 vols. Louvain: Institut Orientaliste, Université de Louvain.

———. 1960. "Mañjuśrī." *T'oung Pao* 48, 1–3: 1–96.

———. 1966. "Vajrapāṇi en Inde." In Paul Demiéville, *Mélanges de Sinologie offerts à Monsieur Paul Demiéville,* 113–159. Paris: Presses Universitaires de France.

Latour, Bruno. 1993. *We Have Never Been Modern.* Trans. Catherine Porter. Cambridge, MA: Harvard University Press.

———. 1996. "On Actor-Network Theory: A Few Clarifications plus More Than a Few Complications." *Soziale Welt* 47: 369–381.

———. 1999. *Pandora's Hope: Essays on the Reality of Science Studies.* Cambridge, MA: Harvard University Press.

———. 2005. *Reassembling the Social: An Introduction to Actor-Network Theory.* Oxford: Oxford University Press.

———. 2010. *On the Modern Cult of the Factish Gods; followed by Iconoclash.* Durham: Duke University Press.

———. 2013. *An Inquiry into Modes of Existence: An Anthropology of the Moderns.* Cambridge, MA: Harvard University Press.

Lau, D. C., trans. 1979. *The Analects.* London: Penguin Books.

Law, John. 1992. "Notes on the Theory of the Actor-Network: Ordering, Strategy, and Heterogeneity." *Systems Practice* 5, 4: 379–393.

———. 2004. *After Method: Mess in Social Science Research.* London: Routledge.

Lévi-Strauss, Claude. 1969. *The Raw and the Cooked.* 1969. Mythologiques, vol. 1. Trans. John and Doreen Weightman. London: J. Cape.

———. 1973a. *From Honey to Ashes.* Mythologiques, vol. 2. Trans. John and Doreen Weightman. London: Cape.

———. 1973b (1955). *Tristes Tropiques.* Trans. John and Doreen Weightman. New York: Penguin Books.

———. 1976. *Structural Anthropology: Volume 2.* Trans. Monique Layton. Chicago: University of Chicago Press.

———. 1978. *The Origin of Table Manners.* Mythologiques, vol. 3. Trans. John and Doreen Weightman. London: Cape.

———. 1981. *The Naked Man.* Mythologiques, vol. 4. Trans. John and Doreen Weightman. Chicago: University of Chicago Press.

———. 1982 . *The Way of the Masks.* Trans. Sylvia Modelski. Seattle: University of Washington Press.

———. 1983 (1969). *The Raw and The Cooked.* Mythologiques, vol. 1. Trans. John and Doreen Weightman. New York: Harper and Row.

———. 1987. *Introduction to the Work of Marcel Mauss.* London: Routledge.

———. 1992. *The View from Afar.* Trans. Joachim Neugroschel and Phoebe Hoss. Chicago: University of Chicago Press.

Lévi-Strauss, Claude, and Didier Eribon. 1991. *Conversations with Claude Lévi-Strauss.* Trans. Paula Wissing. Chicago: University of Chicago Press.

Lin, Irene. 2003. "The Ideology of Imagination: The Tale of Shuten Dōji as a *Kenmon* Discourse." *CEA* 13: 379–410.

Linrothe, Rob. 1999. *Ruthless Compassion: Wrathful Deities in Early Indo-Tibetan Esoteric Buddhist Art.* Boston: Shambhala.

Linrothe, Rob, and Jeff Watt, eds. 2004. *Demonic Divine: Himalayan Art and Beyond.* New York: Rubin Museum of Art.

Linton, Ralph. 1970. *Tree of Culture.* New York: Vintage Books.

Little, Stephen, ed. 2000. *Taoism and the Arts of China.* Chicago: Art Institute of Chicago.

Littleton, Scott. 1974. "'Je ne suis pas . . . structuraliste': Some Fundamental Differences between Dumézil and Lévi-Strauss." *Journal of Asian Studies* 34, 1: 151–158.

———. 1981. "Susa-nö-wo versus Ya-mata nö woröti: An Indo-European Theme in Japanese Mythology." *History of Religions* 20, 3: 269–280.

Lomi, Benedetta. 2011. "The Precious Steed of the Buddhist Pantheon: Ritual, Faith and Images of Batō Kannon in Japan." PhD diss., School of Oriental and African Studies, University of London.

Loth, Anne-Marie. 2003. *Védisme et hindouisme: Images du Divin et des dieux.* Brussels: Éditions Chapitre douze.

Ludvik, Catherine. 2007. *Sarasvatī, Riverine Goddess of Knowledge: From the Manuscript-carrying* Vīṇā-*player to the Weapon-wielding Defender of the Dharma.* Leiden: Brill.

Lyle, Emily B. 1982. "Dumézil's Three Functions and Indo-European Cosmic Structure." *History of Religions* 22, 1: 25–44.

Macé, François. 1989. *Kojiki shinwa no kōzō* 古事記神話の構造. Tokyo: Chūōkōronsha.

———. 2009. "Dumézil et la mythologie japonaise." In Jean-Noël Robert and Jean Leclant, eds., *150e anniversaire de l'établissement des relations diplomatiques entre le Japon et la France,* 37–47. Paris: AIBL–Diffusion De Boccard.

Mack, Karen. 2006a. "The Function and Context of Fudō Imagery from the Ninth to Fourteenth Century in Japan." PhD diss., University of Kansas.

———. 2006b. "The Phenomenon of Invoking Fudō for Pure Land Rebirth in Image and Text." *JJRS* 33, 2: 297–317.

Maillet, Chantal. 1998. "Figures de rêve." In Boris Cyrulnik, ed. *Si les animaux pouvaient parler: Essais sur la condition animale,* 1126–1133. Paris: Gallimard.

Major, John S. 1986. "New Light on the Dark Warrior." *Journal of Chinese Religions* 13–14: 65–86.

Makino Kazuo 牧野和夫 and Fujimaki Kazuhiro 藤卷和宏. 2002. "Jissen joshi daigaku fuzoku toshokan Yamagishi bunko-zō 'Goyuigō daiji' ichijiku kaidai eiin" 実践女子大学附属図書館山岸文庫蔵『御遺告大事』一軸解題・影印. *Jissen joshi daigaku bungakubu kiyō* 44: 1–38.

Malamoud, Charles. 1992. "Histoire des religions et comparatisme: la question indo-européenne." *Revue de l'histoire des religions* 208, 2: 115–121.

———. 1996a (1989). *Cooking the World: Ritual and Thought in Ancient India.* Trans. David G. White. New York: Oxford University Press.

———. 1996b. "Remarks on the Brahmanic Concept of the 'Remainder.'" In Malamoud 1996a: 7–22.

———. 2002. *Le Jumeau solaire.* La Librairie du XXIe siècle. Paris: Seuil.

Manabe Shunshō 真鍋俊照. 1999. *Jakyō Tachikawa-ryū* 邪教立川流. Tokyo: Chikuma shobō.

———. 2000. "Shingon mikkyō to jakyō Tachikawa-ryū" 真言密教と邪教立川流. *Kokubungaku: kaishaku to kyōsai no kenkyū* 45, 12: 110–117.

———. 2000–2001. *Mikkyō zuzō to giki no kenkyū* 密教図像と儀軌の研究. 2 vols. Kyoto: Hōzōkan.

Mancini, Silvia. 1999. "Postface." In De Martino 1999: 285–584.

Markel, Stephen. 1990. "The Imagery and Iconographic Development of the Indian Planetary Deities Rāhu and Ketu." *South Asian Studies* 6: 9–26.

———. 1995. *Origins of the Indian Planetary Deities.* Lewiston, NY: Edwin Mellen Press.

Martzel, Gérard. 1982. *La fête d'Ōgi et le Nō de Kurokawa.* Paris: Publications Orientalistes de France.

Marui Keiji. 1993. "Chiba Myōken-gū no kodenshō to *Genpei tōsōroku*" 千葉妙見の古伝承と『源平闘争録』. In Chiba-shiritsu kyōdo hakubutsukan 千葉市立郷土博物館, ed., *Myōken shinkō chōsa hōkokusho* 妙見信仰調査報告書 2: 1–13.

———. 1994. "Bōsō de no Minamoto Yoritomo no dōkō ni kansuru ichi kōsatsu:

Chiba no Myōken kodenshō to Minamoto Yoritomo no dōkō" 房総での源頼朝の動向に関する一考察―千葉の妙見古伝承と源頼朝の動向. In Chiba-shiritsu kyōdo hakubutsukan 千葉市立郷土博物館, ed., *Myōken shinkō chōsa hōkokusho* 妙見信仰調査報告書 3: 17–49.

———. 2005. "Bōsō chihō no Myōken shinkō to seitetsu, kaji ni tsuite" 房総地方の妙見信仰と製鉄、鍛冶について. *Chiba-shiritsu kyōdo hakubutsukan kenkyū kiyō* 千葉市立郷土博物館研究紀要 11: 1–29.

———. 2013. *Chiba-shi to Myōken shinkō* 千葉氏と妙見信仰. Tokyo: Iwata shoin.

Matisoff, Susan. 1973. *The Legend of Semimaru, Blind Musician of Japan.* New York: Columbia University Press.

Matsumae Takeshi 松前健. 1978. "Origin and Growth of the Worship of Amaterasu." *Asian Folklore Studies* 37, 1: 1–11.

Matsumoto Eiichi 松本榮一. 1956. "Tonkōbon Hakutaku seikai zukan" 敦煌本白沢精怪図巻. *Kokka* 国華770: 135–147.

Matsumoto Ikuyo 松本郁代. 2004. "Toba Shōkōmyō-in zō 'Goyuigō' to hōju: Inseiki Onoryū no Shingon mikkyō 鳥羽勝光明院蔵の「御遺告」と宝珠一院政期小野流の真言密教. In Kakuzenshō kenkyūkai 覚禅鈔研究会, ed. 2004. *Kakuzenshō no kenkyū* 覚禅鈔の研究, 349–378. Wakayamaken Itogun Kōyachō: Shinnōin gyōei bunko.

———. 2005. *Chūsei ōken to sokui kanjō: shōgyō no naka no rekishi jojutsu* 中世王権と即位灌頂―聖教のなかの歴史叙述. Tokyo: Shinwasha.

———. 2006. "Two Mediaeval Manuscripts on the Worship of the Stars from the Fujii Eikan Collection." In Dolce 2006b: 125–144.

———. 2008. "Chūgū osan to mikkyō: 'Hōhiki' Sonjōō-hō mishuhō o megutte" 中宮御産と密教―『宝秘記』 尊星王法御修法をめぐって. In Abe Yasurō, ed., *Nihon ni okeru shūkyō tekusuto no shoisō to tōjihō,* 81–88. Nagoya: Nagoya daigaku daigakuin bungaku kenkyūkai.

———. 2009. "Chūsei Nihon ni okeru kanjō to higi denju: Kuge to jike ni yoru shinwa to mikkyō" 中世日本における灌頂と秘儀伝授―公家と寺家による神話と密教. In James Baskind, ed., *Scholars of Buddhism in Japan: Buddhist Studies in the 21st Century,* 179–193. Kyoto: International Research Center for Japanese Studies.

Matsumoto Kōichi 松本公一. 1991. "Go-Sanjō Tennō to jingi shinkō: tokuni Hieizan to Hie-sha o chūshin to shite" 後三条天皇と神祇思想―とくに比叡山と日吉社を中心として. *Jinbun kagaku* 11: 109–133.

Matsumoto Nobuhiro. 1928. *Essai sur le mythe japonais.* Paris: Paul Geuthner.

Matsunaga Yūkei 松長有慶. 1965. "Indian Esoteric Buddhism as Studied in Japan." In Kōyasan daigaku, ed., *Mikkyōgaku mikkyōshi ronbunshū* 密教学密教史論文集, 229–242. Kyoto: Naigai Press.

Mauss, Marcel. 2001 (1950). *A General Theory of Magic.* Trans. Robert Brain. London: Routledge and Kegan Paul.

McCullough, Helen Craig, trans. 1979 (1959). *The Taiheiki: A Chronicle of Medieval Japan.* Rutland, VT: Charles E. Tuttle Company.

———. 1988. *The Tale of the Heike.* Stanford, CA: Stanford University Press.

McCullough, William H., and Helen Craig McCullough, trans. 1980. *A Tale of Flowering Fortunes: Annals of Japanese Aristocratic Life in the Heian Period.* 2 vols. Stanford, CA: Stanford University Press.

McMullin, Neil. 1984. "The Sanmon-Jimon Schism in the Tendai School of Buddhism: A Preliminary Analysis." *Journal of the International Association of Buddhist Studies* 7, 1: 83–105.

———. 1987. "The Enryakuji and the Gion Shrine-Temple Complex in the Mid-Heian Period." *JJRS* 14, 2–3: 161–184.

———. 1988. "On Placating the Gods and Pacifying the Populace: The Case of the Gion 'Goryō' Cult." *History of Religions* 27: 270–293.

Mikkyō bunka kenkyūjo, ed. 1978. *Kōbō Daishi zenshū* 弘法大師全集. 8 vols. Kyoto: Dōhōsha.

Mikkyō gakkai 密教学会, ed. 1970 (1931). *Mikkyō daijiten* 密教大辞典. Kyoto: Hōzōkan.

Miller, Henri. 1970. *Sexus: The Rosy Crucifixion*. St. Albans: Panther.

Mills, Douglas Edgar, trans. 1970. *A Collection of Tales from Uji: A Study and Translation of 'Uji Shūi Monogatari'*. Cambridge: Cambridge University Press.

Minamoto Ken'ichirō 源健一郎. 2006. "Chiba Myōken no hontai, honji setsu: Genpei tōsōroku to Chiba Myōken-sha kankei shiryō to no aida" 千葉妙見の本体・本地説—源平闘争録と千葉妙見社関係資料との間. *Junreiki kenkyū* 巡礼記研究 3: 67–85.

Misaki Ryōshū 三崎良周. 1955. "Chūsei jingi shisō no ichi sokumen" 中世神祇思想の一側面. *Philosophia* 29: 54–76. Reprinted in Misaki 1992: 192–220.

———. 1956. "Gozu shinkō to mikkyō-teki yōso" 牛頭信仰と密教的要素. *IBK* 7, 1: 216–219.

———. 1960. "Sannō shintō to Ichiji kinrin butchō" 山王神道と一字金輪佛頂. *IBK* 8, 2: 251–254.

———. 1964. "Jichin wajō no Butsugen shinkō" 慈鎮和尚の仏眼信仰. *Mikkyō bunka* 密教文化 69–70: 60–76.

———. 1986. "Yakushi shinkō to Gozu Tennō" 薬師信仰と牛頭天王. *Tendai gakuhō* 29: 17–28.

———. 1988. *Taimitsu no kenkyū*. Tokyo: Sōbunsha.

———. 1992. *Mikkyō to jingi shisō* 密教と神祇思想. Tokyo: Sōbunsha.

———. 1994. *Taimitsu no ronri to jissen* 台密の論理と実践. Tokyo: Sōbunsha. (See review in Girard 1994)

Mitsuhashi Masashi 三橋正. 2006. "*Reikiki* no kōsō to 'shintaizu': mikkyō ni yoru kami no rironka to genshōka" 「麗気記」の構想と「神体図」—密教による神の理論化と図像化. In Hayami 2006: 248–284.

Miwa jinja shiryō henshu iinkai 大神神社資料編修委員会, ed. 1983. *Miwa-ryū shintō no kenkyū: Miwa jinja no shinbutsu shūgō bunka* 三輪流神道の研究—大神神社の神仏習合文化. Tokyo: Meicho shuppan.

Miyahara Satsuki 宮原さつき. 1993. "Chiba Myōken no honji o megutte" 千葉妙見の本地をめぐって. In Chiba-shiritsu kyōdō hakubutsukan 千葉市立郷土博物館, ed., Myōken shinkō chōsa hōkokusho 妙見信仰調査報告書 2: 14–51.

———. 1994. "Chiba Myōken o meguru shinbutsu" 千葉妙見をめぐる神仏. In Chiba-shiritsu kyōdō hakubutsukan, ed., Myōken shinkō chōsa hōkokusho 3: 50–86.

———. 1995. "Washi to Myōken" 鷲と妙見. *Chiba-shiritsu kyōdō hakubutsukan kenkyū kiyō* 千葉市立郷土博物館研究紀要 1: 26–31.

———. 1996. "Gozu Tennō ni tsuite (1): Chiba Myōken no kakawari o chūshin ni" 牛頭天王について (1) —千葉妙見の関わりを中心に. *Chiba-shiritsu kyōdō hakubutsukan kenkyū kiyō* 2: 44–58.

———. 1997. Gozu Tennō ni tsuite (2): Chiba Myōken no kakawari o chūshin ni" 牛頭天王について (2) —千葉妙見の関わりを中心に. *Chiba-shiritsu kyōdō hakubutsukan kenkyū kiyō* 3: 32–52.

———. 1999a. "Chiba-shi no Myōken shinkō to Bōsō no shinbutsu" 千葉市の妙見信仰と房総の神仏. In Chiba-shi bijutsukan 1999: 21–24.

———. 1999b. "Chiba shinai no yasashii hyōjō no Myōken-zō to josei no shinkō ni tsuite" 千葉市内の優しい表情の妙見像と女性信仰について. *Chiba-shiritsu kyōdō hakubutsukan kenkyū kiyō* 5: 24–28.

Miyake Hitoshi 宮家準. 1971. *Shugendō girei no kenkyū* 修験道儀礼の研究. Tokyo: Shunjūsha.

———, ed. 1984. *Yama no matsuri to geinō* 山の祭りと芸能. 2 vols. Tokyo: Hirakawa shuppansha.

———. 1985. *Shugendō shisō no kenkyū* 修験道思想の研究. Tokyo: Shunjūsha.

———. 1993. "Shugendō to Fudō Myōō" 修験道と不動明王. In Tanaka Hisao 1993a: 47–58.

———. 1995. "Shinbutsu shūgō ron: Shugendō o chūshin ni" 神仏習合論–修験道を中心に. In Takasaki Jikidō 高崎直道 and Kimura Kiyotaka 木村清孝 eds., *Nihon bukkyō-ron: Higashi Ajia no bukkyō shisō,* 3: 165–203. Higashi Ajia bukkyō 4. Tokyo: Shunjūsha.

———. 2002a. "Gozu Tennō shinkō to shugendō" 牛頭天王信仰と修験道. *Kokugakuin zasshi* 103, 11: 233–48.

———. 2002b. "Shinra Myōjin shinkō to En no gyōja zō" 新羅明神信仰と役行者像. *Shintō shūkyō* 188: 1–33.

———. 2007. *Shintō to shugendō: Minzoku shūkyō shisō no tenkai* 神道と修験道：民俗宗教思想の展開. Tokyo: Shunjūsha.

Miyasaka Yūshō 宮坂宥勝, ed. 1977. *Kōgyō daishi senjutsushū* 興教大師撰述集. Tokyo: Sankibō busshorin, 1977.

———, ed. 2006. *Fudō shinkō jiten* 不動信仰事典. Tokyo: Ebisu kōshō shuppan.

Mizuhara Gyōhei 水原堯栄. 1925. "Kōbō Daishi eizō zu kō" 弘法大師画像図考. Tokyo: Heigo shuppansha. Reed. in Nakagawa Zenkyō 中川善教, ed. *Mizuhara Gyōei zenshū* 水原堯栄全集, vol. 2. Tokyo: Dōbōsha, 1981.

———. 1931. *Jakyō Tachikawa-ryū no kenkyū* 邪教立川流の研究. Kyoto: Shibundō.

———. 1982. "Goyuigō o chūshin to shite arawaretaru Kōbō Daishi eizō hensen no shushusō" 「御遺告を中心として顯はれたる弘法大師影像変遷の種々相」. In Nakagawa Zenkyō 中川善教 ed., *Mizuhara Gyōei zenshū* 10: *Ronbunshū* 1 水原堯榮全集10 論文集 1, 46–75. Kyoto: Dōhōsha.

Mizukami Fumiyoshi 水上文義. 1995. "Sannō yurai ni miru shinwa to kuden" 「山王由来」に見る神話と口伝. *Shintō koten kenkyūjo kiyō* 神道古典研究所 1: 19–32.

———. 2004. "Jien no 'Musōki' to jingi shisō" 慈円の「夢想記と神祇思想. *Tendai gakuhō* 天台学報 47: 55–64.

———. 2008. *Taimitsu shisō keisei no kenkyū* 台密思想形成の研究. Tokyo: Shunjūsha.

Mollier, Christine. 2009. *Buddhism and Taoism Face to Face: Scripture, Ritual, and Iconographic Exchange in Medieval China.* Honolulu: University of Hawai'i Press.

Moran, Sherwood. 1961. "The Blue Fudō: A Painting of the Fujiwara Period," *Arts Asiatiques* 8: 281–310.

Mori Hiroko. 2001. "Les légendes de l'impératrice Jingū en terre de Kyūshū." In Berthon, Bouchy, and Souyri 2001: 53–67.

Morita Ryūsen 森田龍僊. 1941. *Mikkyō sensei hō* 密教占星法. 2 vols. Kōyasan daigaku shuppanbu. Reprint, Kyoto: Rinsen shoten, 1974.

Moriyama Seishin 守山聖真. 1965. *Tachikawa jakyō to sono shakai-teki haikei no kenkyū* 立川邪教とその社会的背景の研究. Tokyo: Kokusho kankōkai.

Morrell, Robert E. 1982. "Passage to India Denied: Zeami's *Kasuga Ryūjin.*" *Monumenta Nipponica* 37, 2: 179–200.

———. 1985. *Sand and Pebbles (Shasekishū): The Tales of Mujū Ichien, A Voice for Pluralism in Kamakura Japan.* Albany, NY: SUNY Press.

Morse, Anne Nishimura, and Nobuo Tsuji, eds. 1998. *Japanese Art in the Museum of Fine Arts, Boston.* 2 vols. Boston: Museum of Fine Arts. Tokyo: Kōdansha.

Murase, Miyeko. 2000. *Bridge of Dreams: The Mary Griggs Burke Collection of Japanese Art.* New York: Metropolitan Museum of Art.

Murayama Shūichi 村山修一. 1942. "Muromachi jidai no bukkyō kyōka to reki-shi ishiki" 室町時代の仏教教化と歴史意識. *Shina bukkyō shigaku* 支那仏教史学 6, 2: 60–82.

———. 1957. *Shinbutsu shūgō shichō* 神仏習合思潮. Sāra sōsho 6. Kyoto: Hei-rakuji shoten.

———. 1976. *Kodai bukkyō no chūsei-teki tenkai* 古代仏教の中世的展開. Kyoto: Hōzōkan.

———. 1979. "Nihon ni okeru kami to hotoke no kōshō" 日本における神と仏の交渉. *Bukkyō shisōshi* 仏教思想史 1: 225–253.

———. 1983. *Tenjin shinkō* 天神信仰. Tokyo: Yūzankaku.

———. 1984. "Gion-sha no goryōshin-teki hatten" 祇園社の御霊神的発展. In Shibata Minoru, ed., *Goryō shinkō* 御霊信仰, 207–215. Minshū shūkyōshi sōsho 5. Tokyo: Yūzankaku.

———. 1987a. *Nihon onmyōdō shiwa* 日本陰陽道史話. Asahi Culture Books 71. Osaka: Ōsaka shoseki.

———. 1987b. *Shugō shisō-shi ronkō* 習合思想史論考. Tokyo: Hanawa shobō.

———. 1990. *Henbō-suru kami to hotoke-tachi: Nihonjin no shūgō shisō* 変貌する神と仏たちー日本人の習合思想. Kyoto: Jinbun shoin.

———. 1994. *Hieizan shi: tatakai to inori no seiiki* 比叡山史ー闘いと祈りの聖域. Tokyo: Tōkyō bijutsu.

———. 1996. *Tenjin goryō shinkō* 天神御霊信仰. Tokyo: Hanawa shobō.

———. 1997. *Shugen, Onmyōdō to shaji shiryō* 修験・陰陽道と社寺資料. Kyoto: Hōzōkan.

———. 1998. "Goryō shinkō to wa" 御霊信仰とわ. *Kokubungaku: kaishaku to kanshō* 63, 3: 10–16.

———. 2000 (1981). *Nihon onmyōdō-shi sōsetsu* 日本陰陽道史総説. Tokyo: Hanawa shobō.

Murayama Shūichi et al., eds. 1993. *Onmyōdō sōsho* 陰陽道叢書. 4 vols. Tokyo: Meicho shuppan.

Mus, Paul. 1928. "Le Bouddha paré, son origine indienne, Çakyamuni dans le Mahayanisme moyen." *BEFEO* 28, 1–2: 153–280.

———. 1939. *La Lumière sur les Six Voies: Tableau de la transmigration boud-dhique.* Paris: Institut d'Ethnologie.

———. 1975. *India Seen from the East: Indian and Indigenous Cults in Champa.* Ed. Ian W. Mabbett and David P. Chandler. Trans. Ian W. Mabbett. Clayton: Monash University Centre of Southeast Asian Studies.

———. 1998 (1935). *Barabuḍur: Sketch of a History of Buddhism Based on Archaeological Criticism of the Texts.* Trans. Alexander W. Macdonald. New Delhi: Indira Gandhi National Centre for the Arts.

Naitō Sakae 内藤榮. 2001a. " 'Busshari to hōju' ten gaisetsu" 「仏舎利と宝珠」展概説. In Nara kokuritsu hakubutsukan 2001: 172–188.

———, ed. 2001b. "Shari to hōju" 舎利と宝珠. *Nihon no bijutsu* 日本の美術 539. Tokyo: Shibundō.

———. 2010. *Shari shōgon bijutsu no kenkyū* 舎利荘厳美術の研究.Tokyo: Seishi shuppan.

Nakahara Shōtoku 中原祥徳. 1998. "Ise jingū mishōtai zushi: Butsugen to Aizen no haitō keitai ni tsuite" 伊勢神宮御正体厨子—仏眼と愛染の配当形態について. *IBK* 46, 2: 285–287.

Nakamura Honnen 中村本然. 2005a. "Shingon mikkyō ni okeru hōju 'shinkō'" 真言密教における如意宝珠「信仰」. In Chisan kangaku kai 2005: 41–79.

———. 2005b. "Shingon mikkyō no shuhō to nyoi hōju" 真言密教の修法と如意宝珠. *Mikkyō bunka kenkyūjo kiyō* 密教文化研究所紀要 18: 1–29.

Nakamura Ikuo 中村生雄. 1994. *Nihon no kami to ōken* 日本の神と王権. Kyoto: Hōzōkan.

Nakamura, Kyoko Motomochi, trans. 1973. *Miraculous Stories from the Japanese Buddhist Tradition: The Nihon Ryōiki of the Monk Kyōkai.* Cambridge, MA: Harvard University Press.

Nakanishi Mochiyasu 中西用康. 2008. *Myōken shinkō no shiteki kōsatsu.* 妙見信仰の史的考察 Tokyo: Sagami shobō.

Nakano Genzō 中野玄三, ed. 1986. "Fudō Myōō zō" 不動明王像. *Nihon no bijutsu* 日本の美術 238. Tokyo: Shibundō.

———. 1997. "Godai myōō-zō" 五大明王像. *Nihon no bijutsu* 日本の美術 378. Tokyo: Shibundō.

———. 2008. "Shinpukuji-bon *Kakuzenshō*" 真福寺本「覚禅鈔」. *Bukkyō geijutsu* 仏教藝術 297: 71–86.

Nakano Hatayoshi 中野幡能. *Hachiman shinkō* 八幡信仰. Hanawa shinsho 59. Tokyo: Hanawa shobō.

Nakano Tasue 中野達慧 and Tomita Kōjun 富田学純, eds. *Kōgyō Daishi zenshū* 興教大師全集. Tokyo: Sesōken, 1936.

Nanami Hiroaki 名波弘彰. 1986. "Nantobon 'Heike monogatari' Tsunemasa Chikubushima mōde to Hie-sha Seijo-gū no biwa hōshi: Eizan shinkō-ken ni okeru Uga Benzaiten shinkō o megutte" 南都本「平家物語」経正竹生島詣と日吉社聖女宮の琵琶法師—叡山信仰圏における宇賀弁財天信仰をめぐって. *Bungei gengo kenkyū: bungei-hen* 文芸言語研究 文芸篇 11: 59–99.

Nanri Michiko 南里みち子.1996. *Onryō to shugen no setsuwa* 怨霊と修験の説話. Tokyo: Perikansha.

Nara kokuritsu bunkazai kenkyūjo 奈良国立文化財研究所, ed. 1997. *Saidaiji Eison denki shūsei* 西大寺睿尊伝記集成. Kyoto: Hōzōkan.

Nara kokuritsu hakubutsukan 奈良国立博物館, ed.1964. *Suijaku bijutsu* 垂迹美術. Tokyo: Kadokawa shoten.

———, ed. 1975. *Shaji engi-e* 社寺縁起絵. Tokyo: Kadokawa shoten.

———, ed. 1978. *Nihon bukkyō bijutsu no genryū* 日本仏教美術の源流. Narashi : Nara National Museum.

———, ed. 2000. *Myōō: ikari to itsukushimi no hotoke* 明王—怒りと慈しみの仏. Nara: Nara National Museum.

———, ed. 2001. *Busshari to hōju: Shaka o shitau kokoro* 仏舎利と宝珠—釈迦を慕う心. Nara: Nara National Museum.

———, ed. 2006. *Daikanjin Chōgen: Tōdaiji no Kamakura fukkō to aratana bi no sōshutsu* 大勧進重源—東大寺の鎌倉復興と新たな美の創出. Nara: Nara National Museum.

———, ed. 2007. *Shinbutsu shūgō: kami to hotoke ka orinasu shinkō to bi* 神仏習合—神と仏か織りなす信仰と美. Nara: Nara National Museum.

Ōsaka shiritsu bijutsukan 大坂市立美術館, ed. 1999. *En no gyōja to shugendō no sekai* 役行者と修験道の世界. Ōsaka: Ōsaka shiritsu bijutsukan.

———, ed. 2004. *Inori no michi: Yoshino・Kumano・Kōya no meihō* 祈りの道—吉野・熊野・高野の名宝. Ōsaka: Mainichi shinbunsha.

———, ed. 2009. *Dōkyō no bijutsu* 道教の美術. Ōsaka: Ōsaka shiritsu bijutsukan.

Ōsumi Kazuo 大隅和雄, ed. 1977. *Chūsei shintō-ron* 中世神道論. NST 19. Tokyo: Iwanami shoten.

———. 1999. "Jien no Nihongi ninshiki" 慈円の日本紀認識. *Kokubungaku: kaishaku to kanshō* 814: 51–57.

Ōtsu-shi rekishi hakubutsukan 大津市歴史博物館, ed. *Kaihōgyō to seichi Katsuragawa* 回峰行と聖地葛川. Ōtsu: Ōtsu-shi rekishi hakubutsukan.

———. 2006. *Tendai o mamoru kamigami: Sannō mandara no shosō* 天台を守る神々—山王曼荼羅の諸相. Ōtsu: Ōtsu-shi rekishi hakubutsukan.

Ouwehand, Cornelius. 1958. "Some Notes on the God Susa-no-o." *Monumenta Nipponica* 14: 138–161. Reed. in P. E. de Josselin De Jong, ed., *Structural Anthropology in the Netherlands,* 338–358. The Hague: Martinus Nijoff, 1977.

———. 1964. *Namazu-e and Their Themes: An Interpretive Approach to Some Aspects of Japanese Folk Religion.* Leiden: E. J. Brill.

Ōwa Iwao 大和岩雄. 1993. *Hata-shi no kenkyū: Nihon no bunka to shinkō ni fukaku kan'yoshita torai shūdan no kenkyū* 秦氏の研究—日本の文化と信仰に深く関与した渡来集団の研究. Tokyo: Yamato shobō.

———. 2009. *Jinja to kodai minkan saishi* 神社と古代民間祭祀. Tokyo: Hakusuisha.

Ōyama Kōjun 大山公淳. 1956. *Himitsu bukkyō Kōyasan Chūin-ryū no kenkyū* 秘密佛教高野山中院流の研究. Kōyasan: Ōyama kyōju kinen shuppankai.

———. 1975. *Shinbutsu kōshō-shi* 神仏交渉史. Kyoto: Rinsen shoten.

Ozeki Akira 尾関章. 2009. *Ryōmen no kishin: Hida no Sukuna denshō no nazo* 両面の鬼神—飛驒の宿儺伝承の謎. Tokyo: Mensei shuppan.

Padoux, André. 1988. *L'énergie de la parole: Cosmogonies de la parole tantrique.* Paris: Soleil Noir.

———, ed. 1990. *L'image divine: Culte et méditation dans l'hindouisme.* Paris: Editions du CNRS.

Pal, Pratapadita. 1976–1978. "The Iconology of Cintāmaṇicakra Avalokiteśvara." *Journal of the Indian Society of Oriental Art,* n.s. 2: 39–48.

Panofsky, Erwin. 1939. *Studies in Iconology.* Oxford: Oxford University Press.

———. 1955. "Iconography and Iconology: An Introduction to the Study of Renaissance Arts." In Erwin Panofsky, *Meaning in the Visual Arts,* 26–41. Chicago: University of Chicago Press.

———. 1967. *Essais d'iconologie: Les thèmes humanistes dans l'art de la Renaissance.* Paris: Gallimard.

Payne, Richard K. 1987. "Standing Fast: Fudō Myōō in Japanese Literature." *Pacific World* 3: 53–58.

———. 1988. "Firmly Rooted: On Fudō Myōō's Origins." *Pacific World* 4: 6–14.

———. 1991. *The Tantric Ritual of Japan. Feeding the Gods: The Shingon Fire Ritual.* Delhi: International Academy of Indian Culture and Aditya Prakashan.

———, ed. 1998. *Re-Visioning "Kamakura" Buddhism.* Kuroda Institute Studies in East Asian Buddhism 11. Honolulu: University of Hawai'i Press.

Pedersen, Hillary Eve. 2010. "The Five Great Space Repository Bodhisattvas: Lineage, Protection and Celestial Authority in Ninth-Century Japan." PhD diss., University of Kansas.

Peri, Noël. 1916. "Le dieu Wei-t'ouo." *BEFEO* 16, 3: 41–56.

———. 1917. "Hārītī la Mère-de-démons." *BEFEO* 17, 3: 1–102.

Philippi, Donald L., trans. 1968. *Kojiki*. Tokyo: University of Tokyo Press.

Piggott, Joan R. 1997. *The Emergence of Japanese Kingship*. Stanford, CA: Stanford University Press.

Pinnington, Noel J. 1994. "Strategies of Legitimation: An Approach to the Expository Writings of Komparu Zenchiku." PhD diss., Cambridge University.

Poirier, Jean, ed. 1968. *Ethnographie générale*. Encyclopédie de la Pléiade 24. Paris: Gallimard.

Przyluski, Jean. 1923. "Les Vidyārāja: contribution à l'histoire de la magie dans les sectes mahāyānistes." *BEFEO* 23: 301–318.

Quinter, David. 2007. "Creating Bodhisattvas: Eison, Hinin, and the 'Living Mañjuśrī." *Monumenta Nipponica* 62, 4: 437–458.

Rabinovitch, Judith N., trans. 1986. *Shōmonki: The Story of Masakado's Rebellion*. Monumenta Nipponica Monographs 58. Tokyo: Sophia University, Monumenta Nipponica.

Rambelli, Fabio. 1996. "Religion, Ideology of Domination, and Nationalism: Kuroda Toshio on the Discourse of *Shinkoku*." *JJRS* 23, 3–4: 387–426.

———. 2000. "Tantric Buddhism and Chinese Thought in East Asia." In David G. White, ed., *Tantra in Practice*, 361–380. Princeton, NJ: Princeton University Press.

———. 2002. "The Ritual World of Buddhist 'Shintō': The *Reikiki* and Initiations on Kami-Related Matters (*Jingi kanjō*) in Late Medieval and Early-Modern Japan. *JJRS* 29, 3–4: 265–297.

———. 2002–2003. "The Emperor's New Robes: Processes of Resignification in Shingon Imperial Rituals." *CEA* 13: 427–453.

———. 2003. "*Honji Suijaku* at Work: Religion, Economics, and Ideology in Pre-modern Japan." In Teeuwen and Rambelli 2003a: 255–286.

———. 2006a. "Secrecy in Japanese Esoteric Buddhism." In Scheid and Teeuwen 2006: 107–129.

———. 2006b. "Texts, Talismans, and Jewels: The *Reikiki* and the Performativity of Sacred Texts in Medieval Japan." In Richard K. Payne and Taigen Dan Leighton, eds., *Discourse and Ideology in Medieval Japanese Buddhism*, 52–78. London: Routledge.

———. 2006–2007. "Re-positioning the Gods: 'Medieval Shintō' and the Origins of a Non-Buddhist Discourse on the *Kami*." *CEA* 16: 305–325.

———. 2007a. *Buddhist Materiality: A Cultural History of Objects in Japanese Buddhism*. Stanford, CA: Stanford University Press.

———. 2007b. "Interactions between Buddhism and Local Cults: Considerations from the Perspective of Cultural Semiotics." *Sapporo daigaku sōgō ronsō* 札幌大学総合論叢 23: 35–55.

Rappo, Gaétan. 2010a. "*Tōryū saigoku hiketsu*: kaidai, hankoku" 「当流最極秘決」一解題・翻刻. In Abe Yasurō, ed., *Chūsei shūkyō tekusuto taikei no fukugenteki kenkyū: Shinpukuji shōgyō tenseki no saikōchiku*, 145–160. Nagoya: Nagoya daigaku daigakuin bungaku kenkyūka.

———. 2010b. "*Sanzon gōgyō hiketsu*: kaidai, hankoku" 「三尊合行秘決」一解題・翻刻. In Abe Yasurō, ed., *Chūsei shūkyō tekusuto taikei no fukugen-teki kenkyū: Shinpukuji shōgyō tenseki no saikōchiku*, 174–193. Nagoya: Nagoya daigaku daigakuin bungaku kenkyūka.

———. 2014. "Un ritualiste à la cour impériale—Itinéraire et oeuvre du moine Monkan (1278–1357)." PhD diss., Université de Genève.

Reis-Habito, Maria D. 1991. "The Repentance Ritual of the Thousand-armed Guanyin." *Studies in Central and East Asian Religions* 4: 42–51.

———. 1993. *Die Dhāraṇī des Grossen Erbarmens des Bodhisattva Avalokiteś-vara mit tausend Händen und Augen.* Sankt Augustin.

Reischauer, Edwin O. 1940. "The Thunder-Weapon in Ancient Japan." *Harvard Journal of Asiatic Studies* 5, 2: 137–141.

———. 1955a. *Ennin's Diary: The Record of a Pilgrimage to China in Search of the Law.* New York: Reginald Press.

———. 1955b. *Ennin's Travels in T'ang China.* New York: Reginald Press.

Renondeau, George. 1957. "Histoire des moines-guerriers du Japon." In *Mélanges publiés par l'Institut des Hautes Études Chinoises,* vol. 1. Paris: Collège de France.

Renou, Louis, and Jean Filliozat, eds. 1985 (1947). *L'Inde classique: Manuel des études indiennes.* 2 vols. Paris: Librairie d'Amérique et d'Orient.

Rhodes, Robert F. 1987. "The *Kaihōgyō* Practice of Mt. Hiei." *JJRS* 14, 2–3: 185–202.

Riffaterre, Michael. 1982. "L'illusion référentielle." In Roland Barthes et al. eds., *Littérature et réalité,* 91–118. Paris: Éditions du Seuil.

Rilke, Rainer Maria, 1993. *Duino Elegies; The Sonnets to Orpheus.* Trans. Robert Hunter. Cottage Grove, OR: Hulogosi.

Risshō daigaku Nichiren kyōgaku kenkyūjo 立正大学日蓮教学研究所, ed. 1989. *Shōwa teihon Nichiren shōnin ibun* 昭和定本日蓮上人遺文. 4 vols. Minobu: Minobusan Kuonji.

Robertson, Jennifer Ellen. 2005. *A Companion to the Anthropology of Japan.* London: Wiley-Blackwell.

Rocher, Alain. 1997. *Mythe et souveraineté au Japon.* Paris: Presses Universitaires de France.

Rosenfield, John M., and Elizabeth ten Groetenhuis. 1980. *Journey of the Three Jewels: Japanese Buddhist Paintings from Western Collections.* New York: Asia Society.

Rotermund, Hartmund O. 1991. *Hôsôgami ou la petite vérole aisément.* Paris: Maisonneuve et Larose.

Ruegg, David Seyfort. 1964. "Sur les rapports entre le bouddhisme et le 'substrat religieux' indien et tibétain." *Journal Asiatique* 252, 1: 77–95.

Ruppert, Brian. 2000. *Jewel in the Ashes: Buddha Relics and Power in Early Medieval Japan.* Cambridge, MA: Harvard University Press.

———. 2002a. "Pearl in the Shrine: A Genealogy of the Buddhist Jewel of the Japanese Sovereign." *JJRS* 29, 1–2: 1–33.

———. 2002b. "Buddhist Rainmaking in Early Japan: The Dragon King and the Ritual Careers of Esoteric Monks." *History of Religions* 42, 2: 143–174.

Russell-Smith, Lilla. 2006. "Stars and Planets in Chinese and Central Asian Buddhist Art in the Ninth to Fifteenth Centuries." In Dolce 2006b: 99–124.

Sacks, Oliver. 1996. *An Anthropologist on Mars: Seven Paradoxical Tales.* New York: Vintage.

Saitō Hideki 斎藤英喜, ed. 1996. *Amaterasu shinwa no henshinfu* アマテラス神話の変身譜. Tokyo: Shinwasha.

———. 2003. *Jujutsu no chi to tekunee: sekai to shutai no hen'yō* 呪術の知とテクネー―世界と主体の変容. Tokyo: Shinwasha.

———. 2006. *Yomigaerareta Nihon shinwa* 読み替えられた日本神話. Kōdansha gendai shinsho 1871. Tokyo: Kōdansha.

———. 2007. *Onmyōdō no kamigami* 陰陽道の神々. Kyoto: Bukkyō Daigaku tsūshin kyōikubu, Shinbunkaku shuppan.

———. 2011. *Amaterasu: saikōshin no shirarezaru hishi* アマテラス一最高神
の知られざる秘史. Gakken shinsho 88. Tokyo: Gakken paburisshingu.

Sakade Yoshinobu 坂出祥伸. 2010. *Nihon to dōkyō bunka* 日本と道教文化.
Kadokawa sensho 466. Tokyo: Kadokawa gakugei shuppan.

Sakuma Ruriko. 1995. "Visualization of Avalokiteśvara as the Divinity of Lust."
IBK 43, 2: 1013–1009 [*sic*].

Sakurai Tokutarō 桜井徳太郎, Hagiwara Tatsuo 萩原龍夫, and Miyata Noboru
宮田登, eds. 1975. *Jisha engi* 寺社縁起. *NST* 20. Tokyo: Iwanami shoten.

Sanford, James H. 1997. "Wind, Water, Stupas, Mandalas: Fetal Buddhahood in
Shingon." *JJRS* 24, 1–2: 1–38.

Sano Kenji 佐野賢治, ed. 1991a. *Kokūzō shinkō* 虚空蔵信仰. Minshu shūkyōshi
sōsho 24. Tokyo: Yūzankaku.

———. 1991b. "Hoshi to Kokūzō shinkō: Nihon hoshi shinkō-shi oboegaki: sono
ichi" 星と虚空蔵信仰—日本星信仰史覚書: その一. In Sano Kenji 1991a:
93–121.

———. 1992. "Myōken shinkō to Kokūzō shinkō: Nihon no hoshi shinkō
oboegaki" 妙見信仰と虚空蔵信仰一日本の星信仰覚書. In Chiba-shiritsu
kyōdō hakubutsukan 千葉市立郷土博物館, ed., *Myōken shinkō chōsa
hōkokusho* 妙見信仰調査報告書 1: 15–28.

———, ed. 1994a. *Hoshi no shinkō: Myōken, Kokūzō* 星の信仰一妙見・虚空
蔵. Tokyo: Hokushindō.

———. 1994b. "Nihon hoshi shinkō-shi gairon: Myōken, Kokūzō shinkō o
chūshin ni shite" 日本星信仰史概論一妙見・虚空蔵を中心にして. In
Sano Kenji 1994a: 3–53.

———. 1995. "Saigai to minkan shinkō" 災害と民間信仰. In Yamaori Tetsuo,
ed., *Nihon no kami, 2: Kami no hen'yō* 日本の神 2一神の変容, 87–119.
Tokyo: Heibonsha.

———. 1996a. *Kokūzō bosatsu shinkō no kenkyū* 虚空蔵菩薩信仰の研究.
Tokyo: Yoshikawa kōbunkan.

———. 1996b. "Ryōgyōshin to shite no Kokūzō Bosatsu: Hyōjakushin shinkō
no bukkyō minzokugaku-teki ichi shiron" 漁業神としての虚空蔵菩薩一
漂着信仰の仏教民俗学的一試論. In Liu Mengyuan 劉茂源, ed., Kokubu
Naoichi hakushi beiju kinen ronbunshū: Hito, mono, kotoba no jinruigaku 国
分直一博士米寿記念論文集一ヒト・モノ・コトバの人類学, 296–303.
Tokyo: Keiyusha.

Sasama Yoshihiko 笹間良彦. 1988. *Dakini shinkō to sono zokushin* ダキニ信仰
とその俗信. Tokyo: Daiichi shobō.

———. 1989. *Kangiten (Shōten) shinkō to zokushin* 歓喜天（聖天）信仰と俗
信. Tokyo: Yūzankaku.

———. 1991. *Benzaiten shinkō to zokushin* 弁才天信仰と俗信. Tokyo: Yūzankaku.

———. 1993. *Daikokuten shinkō to zokushin* 大黒天信仰と俗信. Tokyo: Yūzankaku.

Saso, Michael. 1991. *Homa Rites and Mandala Meditation in Tendai Buddhism.*
New Delhi: International Academy of Indian Culture and Aditya Prakashan.

Satō Hiroo 佐藤弘夫. 1998. *Kami, hotoke, ōken no chūsei* 神、仏、王権の中世.
Kyoto: Hōzōkan.

———. 1999. "Tenshō Daijin no henbō: 'Nihon kokushū Tenshō Daijin' kan no
keisei" 天照大神の変貌一「日本国主天照大神」観の形成. In Takagi
Yutaka 高木豊 and Komatsu Kuniaki 小松邦彰, eds., *Kamakura bukkyō no
yōsō* 鎌倉仏教の様相, 115–146. Tokyo: Yoshikawa kōbunkan.

———. 2000. *Amaterasu no henbō: Chūsei shinbutsu kōshō-shi no shiza* アマテ
ラスの変貌一中世神仏交渉史の視座. Kyoto: Hōzōkan.

———. 2003. "Wrathful Deities and Saving Deities." In Teeuwen and Rambelli 2003a: 95–114.

———. 2006. *Kishōmon no seishin-shi: Chūsei sekai no kami to hotoke* 起請文の精神史一中世世界の神と仏. Tokyo: Kōdansha.

———. 2007. "'Shinbutsu shūgō' ron no keisei no shiteki haikei" '神仏習合' 論の形成の史的背景. *Shūkyō kenkyū* 353: 211–234.

Satō Masato 佐藤真人. 1984. "Chūsei Hie-sha no fugeki ni tsuite" 中世日吉社の巫覡について. *Kokugakuin zasshi* 国学院雑誌 85, 8: 46–59.

———. 1985a. "Sannō shintō keiseishi no ippan: Sannō shichisha, Hokuto shichi-shō dōtaisetsu no seiritsu o megutte" 山王神道形成史の一班―山王七社、北斗七星同体説の成立をめぐって. *Shūkyō kenkyū* 宗教研究 266: 28–53.

———. 1985b. "Sannō shichisha no seiritsu" 山王七社の成立. *Shintōgaku* 神道学 125: 16–37.

Satō Torao 佐藤虎雄. 1966. "Kinpusen himitsuden no kenkyū 金峯山秘密伝の研究. *Tenri daigaku gakuhō* 天理大学学報 47, 1: 119–136.

Sauzeau, Pierre, and André Sauzeau. 2004. "La quatrième fonction: Pour un élargissement du modèle dumézilien." In "Mythe et mythologie dans l'Antiquité gréco-romaine," *Europe* 904–905: 231–253.

Sawa Ryūken 佐和隆研. 1955. *Mikkyō bijutsuron* 密教美術論. Kyoto: Benridō.

———, ed. 1972. *Omuro-ban Ryōbu mandara, Sonzō-shū* 御室版両部曼荼羅, 尊像集. Kyoto: Hōzōkan.

———. 2006. "Nihon ni okeru Fudō Myōō to sono tenkai" 日本における不動明王とその展開. In Miyasaka Yūshō 2006: 296–330.

Schafer, Edward H. 1977. *Pacing the Void: T'ang Approaches to the Stars.* Berkeley: University of California Press.

Scheid, Bernhard, and Mark Teeuwen, eds. 2006. *The Culture of Secrecy in Japanese Religion.* London: Routledge.

Schmithausen, Lambert. 2007. Ālayavijñāna: *On the Origin and the Early Development of a Central Concept of Yogācāra Philosophy.* Reprint with addenda and corrigenda, Tokyo: International Institute for Buddhist Studies.

Schmitt, Jean-Claude. 1983. *The Holy Greyhound: Guinefort, Healer of Children since the Thirteenth Century.* Cambridge: Cambridge University Press.

Schnell, Scott. 1999. *The Rousing Drum: Ritual Practice in a Japanese Community.* Honolulu: University of Hawai'i Press.

Schopen, Gregory. 1997. *Bones, Stones, and Buddhist Monks: Collected Papers on the Archaeology, Epigraphy, and Texts of Monastic Buddhism in India.* Honolulu: University of Hawai'i Press.

———. 2004. *Buddhist Monks and Business Matters: Still More Papers on Monastic Buddhism in India.* Honolulu: University of Hawai'i Press.

Seidel, Anna. 1983. "Imperial Treasures and Taoist Sacraments: Taoist Roots in the Apocrypha." In Strickmann 1983b, 2: 291–371.

———. 2003a. "Danda" 檀拏. *Hōbōgirin* 8: 1113–1125.

———. 2003b. "Datsueba" 奪衣婆. *Hōbōgirin* 8: 1159–1169.

———. 2003c. "Den'e" 傳衣. *Hōbōgirin* 8: 1171–1178.

Seidensticker, Edward, trans. 1978. *The Tale of Genji.* 2 vols. Rutland, VT: Charles E. Tuttle Company.

Seki Shōdō 関尚道, ed. 1987. *Waga kuni ni okeru Shōten shinkō* わが国における聖天信仰. Tokyo: Hirai Shōten Tōmyōji.

Sekimori, Gaynor. 2006. "Star Rituals and Nikkō Shugendō." In Dolce 2006b: 217–250.

Serres, Michel. 1980. *Hermes V: Le Passage du Nord-Ouest.* Paris: Éditions de Minuit.

———. 1982. *The Parasite.* Trans. Lawrence R. Schehr. Baltimore: Johns Hopkins University Press.

———. 1991. *Le Tiers-instruit.* Paris: François Bourin-Julliard.

Setsuwa to setsuwa bungaku no kai 説話と説話文学の会 ed. 2007. *Setsuwa ronshū, daijūrokushū: setsuwa no naka no zen'aku shoshin* 説話論集, 第16集: 説話の中の善悪諸神. Tokyo: Seibundō.

Seya Takayuki 瀬谷貴之. 2010. "Kanazawa Shōmyōji ni okeru yogen to chōbuku no katachi: Miroku to Aizen" 金沢称名寺における予言と調伏のかたち 一弥勒と愛染. In "Yogen to chōbuku no katachi." *Bukkyō bijutsu kenkyū Ueno kinen zaidan jojō kenkyūka hōkokusho* 37: 7–10.

Sharf, Robert H. 2000. *Coming to Terms with Chinese Buddhism: A Reading of the Treasure Store Treatise.* Honolulu: University of Hawai'i Press.

———. 2001. "Visualization and Mandala in Shingon Buddhism." In Sharf and Sharf 2001, 151–197.

Sharf, Robert H., and Elisabeth Horton Sharf, eds. 2001. *Living Images: Japanese Buddhist Icons in Context.* Stanford, CA: Stanford University Press.

Shibata Kenryū 柴田賢龍. 2010. "Aizen Myōō shinkō no kōryū to Shirakawa hōkō" 愛染明王信仰の交流と白河法皇. http://blog.goo.ne.jp/sarvasattva.

———. n.d. "Tōdaiji Shingon-in to Nyoi hōju" 東大寺真言院と如意宝珠. http://www.ab.auone-net.jp/~badra20/nyoihoushu.html.

Shiga kenritsu Azuchijō kōko hakubutsukan 滋賀県安土城考古博物館. 2011. *Busshō ga sugatta shinbutsutachi* 武将が縋った神仏たち. Hachiman-shi: Shiga kenritsu Azuchi kōko hakubutsukan.

Shiga kenritsu Biwako bunkakan 滋賀県立琵琶湖文化館, ed. 1990. *Taga shinkō to sono shūen* 多賀信仰とその周縁. Ōtsu: Shiga kenritsu Biwako bunkakan.

———. 1998. *Tenjōkai no hotoke-tachi* 天上界のほとけたち. Ōtsu: Shiga kenritsu Biwako bunkakan.

Shigematsu Akihisa 重松明久. 1981. *Urashimako den* 浦島子伝. *Zoku Nihon koten zenshū.* Tokyo: Gendai shichōsha.

Shimaji Daitō 島地大. 1931. "Marishiten ron" 摩利支天論. In Shimaji Daitō, ed., *Kyōri to shiron* 教理と史論, 151–174. Tokyo: Meiji Shoin.

Shishiō Enshin 獅子王円信. 1995. "Tani Ajari Kōgei no mikkyō ni tsuite: *Yonjūjō ketsu* o chūshin to shite" 谷阿闍梨皇慶の密教について一四十帖決を中心として. In Miyasaka Yūshō 宮坂宥勝, ed., *Nihon mikkyō* 日本密教 4: 119–134. Mikkyō taikei 7. Kyoto: Hōzōkan.

Siegel, James. 2006. *Naming the Witch.* Stanford, CA: Stanford University Press.

Silk, Jonathan A. 2006. *Body Language: Indic śarīra and Chinese shèlì in the Mahāparinirvāṇa-sūtra and Saddharmapuṇḍarīka.* Studia Philologica Buddhica 19. Tokyo: International Institute for Buddhist Studies.

Smith, Jonathan Z. 1982. *Imagining Religion: From Babylon to Jonestown.* Chicago: University of Chicago Press.

———. 1987. *To Take Place: Toward Theory in Ritual.* Chicago: University of Chicago Press.

Snellgrove. David L., ed. and trans. 1959a. *The Hevajra Tantra: A Critical Study.* 2 vols. London Oriental Series 6. London: Oxford University Press.

———. 1959b. "The Notion of Divine Kingship in Tantric Buddhism." In *The Sacral Kingship,* 204–218. Studies in the History of Religions 4. Leiden: E. J. Brill.

Snodgrass, Adrian. 1988. *The Matrix and Diamond World Mandalas in Shingon Buddhism.* 2 vols. New Delhi: Aditya Prakashan.

Sokal, Alan D. 1996. "A Physicist Experiments with Cultural Studies." *Lingua Franca* 6, 4 (May/June): 62–64.

Sørensen, Henrik K. 1991–1992. "Typology and Iconography in the Esoteric Buddhist Art of Dunhuang." *Silk Road Art and Archeology* 2: 285–349.

———. 1994. "Esoteric Buddhism in Korea." In Henrik K. Sørensen, ed., *The Esoteric Buddhist Tradition*, 73–96. SBS Monographs 2. Copenhagen: Seminar for Buddhist Studies.

———. 1995. "The Worship of the Great Dipper in Korean Buddhism." In H. Sørensen, ed., *Religions in Traditional Korea*, 71–103. SBS Monographs 3. Copenhagen: Seminar for Buddhist Studies.

Souriau, Étienne. 1952. "The Cube and the Sphere." *Education Theatre Journal* 4, 1: 11–18.

———. 2009 (1956). *Les différents modes d'existence*. Paris: Presses Universitaires de France.

Souyri, Pierre F. 2001. *The World Turned Upside Down: Medieval Japanese Society*. Trans. Käthe Roth. New York: Columbia University Press.

Soymié, Michel. 1987. "Notes d'iconographie bouddhique: Des Vidyārāja et Vajradhara de Touen-houang." *CEA* 3: 9–26.

Spivak, Gayatri Chakravorti. 2001. "Moving Devī." In Vidya Dehejia, ed., *Devī: The Great Goddess*, 181–200. Washington, DC: Smithsonian Institute.

Starobinski, Jean. 1979. *Words upon Words: The Anagrams of Ferdinand de Saussure*. New Haven, CT: Yale University Press.

Stein, Rolf A. 1970. "La légende du foyer dans le monde chinois." In Jean Pouillon and Pierre Maranda, eds., *Échanges et communications: Mélanges offerts à Claude Lévi-Strauss à l'occasion de son 60ème anniversaire*, 1280–1305. Paris: Mouton.

———. 1972–1973. "Étude du monde chinois: institutions et concepts." In *Annuaire du Collège de France*, 499–517. Paris: Collège de France.

———. 1975. "Étude du monde chinois: institutions et concepts." In *Annuaire du Collège de France*, 481–495. Paris: Collège de France.

———. 1976. "Étude du monde chinois: institutions et concepts." In *Annuaire du Collège de France*, 599–615. Paris: Collège de France.

———. 1986. "Avalokiteśvara/Kouan-yin, un exemple de transformation d'un dieu en déesse." *CEA* 2: 17–80.

———. 1988. *Grottes-matrices et lieux saints de la déesse en Asie Orientale*. Publications de l'EFEO 151. Paris: École Française d'Extrême-Orient.

———. 1990. *The World in Miniature: Container Gardens and Dwellings in Far Eastern Religious Thought*. Trans. Phyllis Brooks. Stanford, CA: Stanford University Press.

———. 1991a (1981). "Buddhist Mythology." In Bonnefoy 1991: 119–121.

———. 1991b (1981). "The Guardian of the Gate: An Example of Buddhist Mythology, from India to Japan." In Bonnefoy 1991: 122–136.

———. 1995. "La soumission de Rudra et autres contes tantriques." *Journal Asiatique* 283, 1: 121–160.

Stengers, Isabelle, and Bruno Latour. 2009. "Le sphynx de l'oeuvre." Introduction to Étienne Souriau, *Les différents modes d'existence*, 1–78. Paris: Presses Universitaires de France.

Stone, Jacqueline I. 1995. "Medieval Tendai Hongaku Thought and the New Kamakura Buddhism: A Reconsideration." *JJRS* 22, 2: 17–48.

———. 1999. *Original Enlightenment and the Transformation of Medieval Japanese Buddhism*. Kuroda Institute Studies in East Asian Buddhism 12. Honolulu: University of Hawai'i Press.

Stramigioli, Giuliana. 1973. "Preliminary Notes on the *Masakadoki* and Taira no Masakado Story." *Monumenta Nipponica* 28, 3: 261–293.

Strenski, Ivan. 1980. "Lévi-Strauss and the Buddhists." *Comparative Studies in Society and History* 22, 1: 3–22.

Strickmann, Michel. 1983. "Homa in East Asia." In Frits Staal, ed., *Agni: The Vedic Ritual of the Fire Altar,* 2: 418–455. Berkeley, CA: Asian Humanities Press.

———, ed. 1983–1985. *Tantric and Taoist Studies in Honour of R. A. Stein.* 3 vols. Brussels: Institut Belge des Hautes Études Chinoises.

———. 1993. "The Seal of the Law: A Ritual Implement and the Origins of Printing." *Asia Major,* 3rd Ser., 6 (2): 1–83.

———. 1996. *Mantras et Mandarins: Le bouddhisme tantrique en Chine.* Paris: Gallimard.

———. 2002. *Chinese Magical Medicine.* Ed. Bernard Faure. Stanford, CA: Stanford University Press.

———. 2005. *Chinese Poetry and Prophecy: The Written Oracle in East Asia.* Ed. Bernard Faure. Stanford, CA: Stanford University Press.

Strong, John S. 1979. "The Legend of the Lion-Roarer: A Study of the Buddhist Arhat Piṇḍola Bhāradvāja." *Numen* 26: 50–88.

———. 1983. *The Legend of King Aśoka: A Study and Translation of the Aśokāvadāna.* Princeton, NJ: Princeton University Press.

———. 2004. *Relics of the Buddha.* Princeton, NJ: Princeton University Press.

Strong, John S., and Sarah M. Strong. 1995. "A Tooth Relic of the Buddha in Japan: An Essay on the Sennyū-ji Tradition and a Translation of Zeami's Nō Play 'Shari.'" *Japanese Religions* 20, 1: 1–33.

Sueki Fumihiko 末木文美士. 1996. "A Reexamination of the *Kenmitsu Taisei* Theory." *JJRS* 23, 3–4: 449–466.

———. 2003. *Chūsei no kami to hotoke* 中世の神と仏. Tokyo: Yamakawa shuppansha.

———. 2008. *Kamakura bukkyō tenkai-ron* 鎌倉仏教展開論. Tokyo: Toransubyū.

Sugahara Shinkai 菅原信海. 1992. *Sannō shintō no kenkyū* 山王神道の研究. Tokyo: Shunjūsha.

———. 1996a. *Nihon shisō to shinbutsu shūgō* 日本思想と神仏習合. Tokyo: Shunjūsha.

———. 1996b. "The Distinctive Features of Sannō Ichijitsu Shintō." *JJRS* 23, 1–2: 61–84.

Sugihashi Takao 杉橋隆夫. 1970. "Shitennōji shozō 'Nyoi hōju mishuhō nikki' 'dō' shihai (Togashishi kankei) monjo ni tsuite" 四天王寺所蔵「如意宝珠御修法日記」・「同」紙背（富樫氏関係）文書について. *Shirin* 53, 3: 115–140.

Suzuki Chiben 鈴木智弁, ed. 1934. *Saiin-ryū Hakketsu narabini shigon* 西院流八結并ム言. Kyoto: Kōbō Daishi issen hyakunen onki jimukyoku.

Suzuki Masataka. 2001. *Kami to hotoke no minzoku* 神と仏の民俗. Nihon rekishi minzoku sōsho. Tokyo: Yoshikawa kōbunkan.

Suzuki, Yui. 2012. *Medicine Master Buddha: The Iconic Worship of Yakushi in Heian Japan.* Leiden: Brill.

Swanson, Paul L., and Clark Chilson, eds. 2006. *Nanzan Guide to Japanese Religion.* Honolulu: University of Hawai'i Press.

Tada Kōryū 多田厚隆 et al., eds. 1973. *Tendai hongakuron* 天台 本學論. Tokyo: Iwanami shoten.

Taira Masayuki. 1996. "Kuroda Toshio and the *Kenmitsu Taisei* Theory." *JJRS* 23, 3–4: 427–448.

———. 2005. "Tabous et alimentation carnée dans l'histoire du Japon." In Jean-Pierre Berthon, Anne Bouchy, and Pierre F. Souyri, eds., *Identités, marges, médiations: Regards croisés sur la société japonaise,* 165–182. Études Thématiques 10. Paris: École Française d'Extrême-Orient.

Tajima Ryūjun. 1959. *Les deux grands maṇḍalas et la doctrine de l'ésotérisme Shingon.* Tokyo: Nakayama shobō busshorin.

———. 1992. *Étude sur le Mahāvairocana Sūtra (Dainichikyō) avec la traduction commentée du premier chapitre.* Reprint, Paris: Adrien Maisonneuve. English translation in Alex Wayman and Tajima Ryūjun, *The Enlightenment of Vairocana.* Delhi: 1992.

Takafuji Harutoshi 高藤晴俊. 2001. "Nikkōzan ni okeru seishin shinkō ni tsuite no oboegaki" 日光山における星辰信仰についての覚書. *Sangaku shugen* 山岳修験 28: 27–36.

Takahashi Shūhei 高橋秀栄. 1984. "Sanbōji no Darumashū monto to rokuso Fugen shari" 三宝寺の達磨宗と六祖普賢舎利. *Shūgaku kenkyū* 宗学研究 26: 116–121.

Takahashi Yūsuke 高橋悠介. 2004. "Anshōji Seiryūsha to *Seiryū gongen saimon*" 安祥寺青龍社と「青龍権現祭文」. *Zuishin-in shōgyō to jiin nettowāku* 1: 60–70.

———. 2005. "Enman'i-za no shari to Zenchiku" 円満井座の舎利と禅竹. *Zeami: chūsei no geijutsu to bunka* 世阿弥—中世の芸術と文化 3: 124–185.

———. 2006. "Kōjin no engi to saishi" 荒神の縁起と祭祀. *Junreiki kenkyū* 巡礼記研究 3: 1–22.

———. 2012. "Kōjin no zuzō ni tsuite: Nyorai Kōjin o chūshin ni" 荒神の図像について一如来荒神を中心に. In Tsuda Tetsuei, ed., *Zuzōgaku* 図像学, 1: 334–349.

———. 2014. *Zenchiku nōgakuron no sekai* 禅竹能楽論の世界. Tokyo: Keio gijuku daigaku shuppankai.

Takai Kankai 高井観海. 1941. *Fudō-son to goma hihō.* 不動尊と護摩秘法. Tokyo: Fudō zenshū kankōkai.

Takamori Daijō 高森大乗. 2001. "Nichiren ibun *Fudō Aizen kanken ki* shōkō" 日蓮遺文『不動愛染感見記』小考. *IBK* 50, 1: 98–102.

Takano Nobuyoshi 高野進芳. 1959. "Bukkyō ni okeru sanjin shinkō" 仏教における蚕神信仰. *Bukkyō to minzoku* 仏教と民俗 5: 25–36.

Takeda Kazuaki 武田和昭. 1995. *Hoshi mandara no kenkyū* 星曼荼羅の研究. Kyoto: Hōzōkan.

Takei Shōgu 武井正弘. *Okumikawa hanamatsuri saimonshū* 奥三河花祭り祭文集. Tokyo: Iwata shoin 2010.

Takeuchi Rizō 竹内理三, ed. 1943–1944. *Nara ibun* 奈良遺文. Ed. Takeuchi Rizō 竹内理三. 2 vols. Tokyo: Tōkyōdō.

———, ed. 1947–1980. *Heian ibun* 平安遺文. 15 vols. Tokyo: Tōkyōdō shuppan.

———, ed. 1971–1997. *Kamakura ibun* 鎌倉遺文. 52 vols. Tokyo: Tōkyōdō shuppan.

Tanabe, George J., ed. 1999. *Religions of Japan in Practice.* Princeton, NJ: Princeton University Press.

Tanaka Hisao 田中久夫, ed. 1993a. *Fudō shinkō* 不動信仰. Minshu shūkyōshi sōsho 25. Tokyo: Yūzankaku.

———. 1993b. "Fudō-son shinkō no denpansha no mondai" 不動尊信仰の伝播者の問題. In Tanaka Hisao 1993a, 31–46.

Tanaka Takako 田中貴子. 1992. *"Akujo" ron* 「悪女」論. Tokyo: Kinokuniya shoten.

———. 1993. *Gehō to aihō no chūsei* 外法と愛法の中世. Tokyo: Sunakoya shobō.

———. 1994. *Hyakki yakō no mieru toshi* 百鬼夜行の見える都市. Tokyo: Shin'yōsha.

———. 2000. *Butsuzō ga kataru shirarezaru dorama* 仏像が語る知られざるドラマ. Tokyo: Kōdansha.

———. 2002. *"Keiran shūyōshū* ni okeru ōken to jingi: shinji no hako o meguru ichi setsuwa kara" 「渓嵐拾葉集」二おける王権と神祇一神璽の箱をめぐる一説話から. In Imatani Akira 今谷明, ed. *Ōken to jingi* 王権と神祇, 173–192. Tokyo: Shibunkaku shuppan.

———. 2003. Keiran shūyōshū *no sekai* 「渓嵐拾葉集」の世界. Nagoya: Nagoya daigaku shuppankai.

Tarabout, Gilles. 1993. "Quand les dieux s'emmêlent: Point de vue sur les classifications divines au Kérala." In Véronique Bouiller and Gérard Toffin, eds., *Classer les dieux? Des panthéons en Asie du Sud. Purusārtha* 15: 43–74.

Teeuwen, Mark J. 1996. *Watarai Shintō: An Intellectual History of the Outer Shrine in Ise.* CNWS Publications 52. Leiden: Research School CNWS.

———. 2000. "The Kami in Esoteric Buddhist Thought and Practice." In Breen and Teeuwen 2000: 95–116.

———. 2002. "From *Jindō* to Shinto: A Concept Takes Shape." *JJRS* 29, 3–4: 233–263.

———. 2006a. "Knowing vs. Owning a Secret: Secrecy in Medieval Japan, as Seen through the *sokui kanjō* Enthronement Unction." In Scheid and Teeuwen 2006: 172–203.

———. 2006b. "The Imperial Shrines of Ise: An Ancient Star Cult?" In Dolce 2006b: 79–98.

Teeuwen, Mark, and Fabio Rambelli, eds. 2003a. *Buddhas and Kami in Japan: Honji Suijaku as a Combinatory Paradigm.* London. Routledge Curzon.

———. 2003b. "Introduction: Combinatory Religion and the *Honji Suijaku* Paradigm in Pre-modern Japan." In Teeuwen and Rambelli, 2003a, 1–53.

Teeuwen, Mark J., and Hendrik van der Veere. 1998. *Nakatomi Harae Kunge: Purification and Enlightenment in Late-Heian Japan.* Buddhismus-Studien 1. Munich: Iudicium-Verlag.

Ten Grotenhuis, Elizabeth. 1999. *Japanese Mandalas: Representations of Sacred Geography.* Honolulu: University of Hawai'i Press.

Tochigi kenritsu hakubutsukan 栃木県立博物館, ed. 1996. *Nikkōsan Rinnōji no butsuga* 日光山輪王寺の仏画. Utsunomiya: Tochigi kenritsu hakubutsukan.

Toganoo Shōun 母尾祥雲. 1948–1949. *Shingonshū tokuhon* 真言宗読本. 3 vols. Kōyasan: Kōyasan shuppansha.

———. 1958 (1932). *Mandara no kenkyū* 曼荼羅の研究. Vol. 4 of *Toganoo Shōun zenshū* 母尾祥雲全集. Kōyasan: Kōyasan daigaku.

Tōji hōmotsukan 東寺宝物館, ed. 1993. *Tōji no tenbu-zō* 東寺の天部像. Kyotō: Tōji hōmotsukan.

Tōkyō daigaku shiryō hensanjo, ed. 1901–. *Dai Nihon shiryō* 大日本史料. 380 vols. Tokyo: Tōkyō daigaku shiryō hensanjo.

———. 1901–1940. *Dai Nihon komonjo* 大日本古文書. Tokyo: Tōkyō daigaku shuppankai.

———. 1955–1957. *Daigoji monjo* 醍醐寺文書. Vol. 19 of *Dai Nihon komonjo* 大日本古文書. Tokyo: Tōkyō daigaku shiryō hensanjo.

Tōkyō gakushi kaiin, ed. 1927. *Koji ruien* 古事類苑. Tokyo: Koji ruien sankei.

Tōkyō kokuritsu hakubutsukan 東京国立博物館 et al., ed. 1990. *Miidera hihōten* 三井寺秘宝展. Tokyo: Nihon keizai shinbunsha.

Tomishima Yoshiyuki 富島義幸. 2007. *Mikkyō kūkan shiron* 密教空間論. Kyoto: Hōzōkan.

Trainor, Kevin. 1997. *Relics, Ritual and Representation in Buddhism: Rematerializing the Sri Lankan Theravāda Tradition.* Cambridge Studies in Religious Traditions 10. Cambridge: Cambridge University Press.

Trenson, Steven. 2002–2003. "Une analyse critique de l'histoire du *Shōugyōhō* et du *Kujakukyōhō:* rites ésotériques de la pluie dans le Japon de l'époque de Heian." *CEA* 13: 455–495.

———. 2010. "Daigoji ni okeru kiu no kakuritsu to Seiryō-shin shinkō" 醍醐寺における祈雨の確立と清瀧神信仰. In Dolce and Matsumoto 2010: 231–270.

———. 2013. "Shingon Divination Board Rituals and Rainmaking." *CEA* 21: 107–137.

Tsuda Tetsuei 津田徹英. 1998a. "Uho, henbai to Sonjōō, Rokuji Myōō no zuzō" 禹歩、反閇と尊星王、六字明王の図像 . *Nihon shūkyō bunkashi kenkyū* 日本宗教分化史研究 2, 2: 75–83.

———. 1998b. "Jisha engi to bijutsu: Chūsei Chiba-shi ni yoru dōkyō no Shinmushin zuzō no juyō to 'Genpei tōsōroku' no Myōken setsuwa" 寺社縁起と美術—中世千葉氏による道教の真武神図像の受容と「源平闘争録」の妙見説話. *Kokubungaku kaishaku to kanshō* 国文学　解釈と鑑賞 12: 33–42.

———. 1998c. "Rokuji Myōō no shutsugen" 六字明王の出現. *Museum* 553: 1–34.

———. 2006. "Images of Stars and Their Significance in Japanese Esoteric Art of the Heian Period." In Dolce 2006b: 145–193.

———, ed. 2012. *Zuzōgaku I: imēji no seiritsu to denshō (mikkyō, suijaku)* 図像学 I ーイメージの成立と伝承 (密教、垂迹). Bukkyō bijutsu ronshū 1. Tokyo: Chikurinsha.

Tsuji Hidenori 逵日出典. 1970. *Murōji oyobi Hasedera no kenkyū* 室生寺及び長谷寺の研究. Kyoto: Seika gakuen.

———. 1979. *Murōji shi no kenkyū* 室生寺史の研究. Kyoto: Seika gakuen.

———. 2007. *Hachiman-shin to shinbutsu shūgō* 八幡神と神仏習合. Kōdansha gendai shinsho 1904. Tokyo: Kōdansha.

Tyler, Royall. 1990. *The Miracles of the Kasuga Deity.* New York: Columbia University Press.

———. 2007. "The True History of Shido Temple." *Asian Folklore Studies* 66, 1–2: 55–82.

Tyler, Susan. 1989. "Honji Suijaku Faith." *JJRS* 16, 2–3: 227–250.

Tylor, E. B. 1877: "Remarks on Japanese Mythology." *Journal of the Anthropological Institute of Great Britain and Ireland* 6: 55–60.

Uchida Keiichi 内田啓一. 2000. "Shoson zuzō, darani-tō (kokonoe no mamori) ni tsuite: Saidaiji-bon o chūshin to shite" 諸尊図像・陀羅尼等（九重守）について一西大寺本を中心として. *Kanazawa bunko* 305: 1–19.

———. 2006. *Monkan-bō Kōshin to bijutsu* 文観房弘真と美術. Kyoto: Hōzōkan.

———. 2010. *Go-Daigo tennō to mikkyō* 後醍醐天皇と密教. Shirīzu Kenryokusha to bukkyō 2. Kyoto: Hōzōkan.

———. 2012a. "Nezu bijutsukan-zō Dainichi Kinrin, Nyoirin Kannon zushi ni tsuite: Monkan-bō Kōshin to seisaku haikei" 根津美術館蔵大日金輪、如意輪観音厨子について―文観房弘真と制作背景. *Bukkyō geijutsu* 仏教藝術 324: 98–123.

———. 2012b. "Ryōzu Aizen-ō no zuzō to hensen: Aizen Myōō to Fudō Myōō" 両頭愛染王の図像と変遷―愛染明王と不動明王. In Tsuda 2012: 237–251.

Ueda Reijō 上田霊城. 1986. *Shingon mikkyō jisō gaisetsu: Shin'anryū o chūshin to shite* 真言密教事相概説―新安流を中心として. Kyōto: Dōhōsha.

Uemura Toshikuni 上村俊邦, ed. 2000. *Hakusan shinkō shiryōshū* 白山信仰史料集. Tokyo: Iwata shoin.

Ueno Kayoko 植野加代子. 2010. *Hata-shi to Myōken shinkō* 秦氏と妙見信仰. Minzokugaku sōsho 19. Tokyo: Iwata shoin.

Uesugi Bunshū 上杉文秀. 1973 (1935). *Nihon Tendai shi* 日本天台史. 2 vols. Tokyo: Kokusho kankōkai.

Uezumi Setsuko 上住節子. 1990. *Mikkyō senseijutsu* 密教占星術. Tokyo: Daizō shuppan.

Vanden Broucke, Pol, trans. 1992. *Hōkyōshō: "The Compendium of the Precious Mirror" of the Monk Yūkai*. Gent: Rijksuniversiteit.

———. 1994. "On the Title and the Translator of the *Yugikyō* (T. XVIII no. 867)." *Kōyasan daigaku mikkyō bunka kenkyūjo kiyō* 7: 184–212.

———. 1999. "The Twelve-Armed Deity Daishō Kongō and His Scriptural Sources." *Romanian Journal of Japanese Studies* 1: 57–78.

———. 2000. "The Yugitō." *Oriens Extremus* 42: 105–167.

van der Veere, Henny (Hendrik). 2000. *A Study into the Thought of Kōgyō Daishi Kakuban: With a Translation of His* Gorin kuji myō himitsushaku. Leiden: Hotei Publishing.

van Gulik, Robert H. 2006 (1935). *Hayagrīva: Horse Cult in Asia*. Orchid Press.

Varley, Paul H., trans. 1980. *A Chronicle of Gods and Sovereigns:* Jinnō Shōtōki *of Kitabatake Chikafusa*. New York: Columbia University Press.

Vernant, Jean-Pierre. 1982 (1962). *Les origines de la pensée grecque*. Paris: Presses Universitaires de France.

———. 1985 (1965). *Mythe et pensée chez les Grecs: Études de psychologie historique*. Paris: La Découverte.

———. 2006. *Myth and Thought among the Greeks*. Trans. Janet Lloyd and Jeff Fort. New York: Zone Books.

Viveiros de Castro, Eduardo. 2004. "Exchanging Perspectives: The Transformation of Objects into Subjects in Amerindian Cosmologies." *Common Knowledge* 10, 3: 463–484.

———. 2009. *Métaphysiques cannibales: Lignes d'anthropologie structurale*. Trans. Oiara Bonilla. Paris: Presses Universitaires de France.

Wada Tetsujō 和田徹城. 1918. *Inshi to jashin* 淫祠と邪神. Tokyo: Hakubunkan.

Wakabayashi Haruko 若林晴子. 1999. "From Conqueror of Evil to Devil King: Ryōgen and Notions of *Ma* in Medieval Japanese Buddhism." *Monumenta Nipponica* 54, 4: 481–507.

Wakayama kenritsu hakubutsukan 和歌山県立博物館, ed. 2012. *Kōyasan-roku inori no katachi* 高野山麓祈りのかたち. Wakayama: Wakayama kenritsu hakubutsukan.

Wakita Haruko. 2005. "Du mythe à la fiction et retour—La formation d'une 'mythologie médiévale': Le *Shintō-shū*; les récits de fondation des sanctuaires shintō et monastères bouddhiques; les pièces de nō." In Anne Bouchy, François Carré and François Lachaud, eds., *Légitimités, légitimations*, 45–65. Paris: École Française d'Extrême-Orient.

Waley, Arthur. 1932. "An Eleventh Century Correspondence." In *Études d'Orientalisme publiées par le Musée Guimet à la mémoire de Raymonde Linossier,* 531–562. Paris: Librairie Ernest Leroux.

Washio Junkyō 鷲尾順敬. 1930. *Nihon shisō tōsō shiryō* 日本思想闘諍資料. Vol. 5. Tokyo: Tōhō shoen.

Watanabe Kyōichi 渡辺匡一. 1999. "Zentsūji-zō 'Himitsu gentei kuketsu' honkoku, shōkai" 善通寺藏「秘密源底口決」翻刻、紹介. *Zentsūji kyōgaku shinkōkai kiyō* 善通寺教学振興会紀要 6: 118–130.

Wayman, Alex. 1965. "The Fivefold Ritual Symbolism of Passion." In Kōyasan daigaku 高野山大学, ed., *Mikkyōgaku mikkyōshi ronbunshū* 密教学密教史論文集, 117–144. Kyoto: Naigai Press.

Wayman, Alex, and R. Tajima. 1992. *The Enlightenment of Vairocana.* Delhi: Motilal Banarsidass.

Weinstein, Stanley. 1964. "The Concept of the *Ālaya-vijñāna* in Pre-T'ang Chinese Buddhism." In *Yūki kyōju shoju kinen bukkyō shisōshi ronshū* 結城教授頌壽記念佛教思想史論集, 33–50. Tokyo: Daizō shuppan.

———. 1974. "The Beginnings of Esoteric Buddhism in Japan: The Neglected Tendai Tradition." *Journal of Asian Studies* 34, 1: 177–191.

Werblowsky, R. J. Zwi. 2001–2002. "Catalogue of the Pantheon of Fujian Popular Religion." *Studies in Central and East Asian Religions* 12–13: 95–191.

Wessels-Mevissen, Corinna. 2001. *The Gods of the Directions in Ancient India: Origins and Early Development in Art and Literature.* Monographien zur indischen Archäologie, Kunst und Philologie 14. Berlin: Dietrich Reimer Verlag.

Wilson, William R. 2001. *Hōgen Monogatari: Tale of the Disorder in Hōgen.* Ithaca, NY: Cornell University East Asia Program.

Wittgenstein, Ludwig. 1960. *The Blue and Brown Books.* New York: Harper Torchbooks.

———. 1987. *Remarks on Frazer's Golden Bough.* Ed. Rush Rhees. London: Brynmill Press.

———. 1997. *Tractatus Logico-philosophicus.* New York: McGraw-Hill.

Wu Limin 呉立民 and Han Jinke 韓金科, eds. 1998. *Famensi digong Tang mi mantuoluo zhi yanjiu* 法門寺地宮唐密曼荼羅之研究. Hong Kong: Zhongguo fojiao wenhua chuban youxian gongsi.

Xiao Dengfu 蕭登福. 1982. *Daojiao xingdou fuyin yu fojiao mizong* 道教星斗符印與佛教密宗. Beijing: Xinwenfeng chuban gongsi.

Yamagishi Kenjun 山岸乾順. 1929. *Chintaku reifujin* 鎮宅霊符神. Kyoto: Daigakudō shoten.

Yamagiwa Teppei 山極哲平. "Chintaku Reifujin shinkō kenkyūshi no seiri" 鎮宅霊符神信仰研究史の整理. *Kokubungaku* 国文学 91: 143–153.

Yamamoto Hiroko 山本ひろこ. 1990. "Irui to sōshin: Chūsei ōken o meguru sei no metafā" 異類と双身ー中世王権をめぐる性のメタファー. In Ichikawa Hiroshi 市川浩 et al., *Erosu: gendai tetsugaku no bōken* エロスー現代哲学の冒険 4, 115–195. Tokyo: Iwanami shoten.

———. 1993a. *Henjō fu: Chūsei shinbutsu shūgo no sekai* 変成譜ー中世神仏習合の世界. Tokyo: Shunjūsha.

———. 1993b. *Daikōjin ju* 大荒神頌. Tokyo: Iwanami shoten.

———. 1997. "Chūsei ni okeru Aizen Myōō-hō: sono poritikusu to erosu" 中世における愛染明王法ーそのポリティクスとエロス. *Nihon no bijutsu* 日本の美術 376: 86–98.

———. 1998a. *Ijin: Chūsei Nihon no hikyō-teki sekai* 異神ー中世日本の秘教的世界 Tokyo: Heibonsha.

———. 1998b. *Chūsei shinwa* 中世神話. Iwanami shinsho 593. Tokyo: Iwanami shoten.

Yamaori Tetsuo 山折哲雄, ed. 1999. *Inari shinkō jiten* 稲荷信仰辞典. Shinbutsu shinkō jiten shirīzu. Tokyo: Ebisu kōshō shuppansha.

Yamashita Tatsuru 山下立. 1999. "Reiganji-kei Myōken bosatsu zō to sono yuirei" 霊巌寺型妙見菩薩像とその遺例. *Nihon shūkyō bunkashi kenkyū* 日本宗教文化史研究 3, 2: 64–77.

Yanagita Kunio 柳田國男. 1990a. *Yanagita Kunio zenshū* 柳田國男全集. Ed. Yanagita Tamemasa 柳田為正 et al. 32 vols. Tokyo: Chikuma shobō.

———. 1990b. *Santō mindan shū* 山島民譚集. In *Yanagita Kunio zenshū*, 5: 55–484.

———. 1990c. *Ishigami (Shakujin) mondō* 石神問答. In *Yanagita Kunio zenshū*, 15: 7–200.

Yano Michio 矢野道雄. 1986. *Mikkyō senseijutsu: Sukuyōdō to Indo senseijutsu* 密教占星術—宿曜道とインド占星術. Tokyo: Tōkyō bijutsu.

Yiengpruksawan, Mimi Hall. 1991. "In My Image: The Ichiji Kinrin Statue at Chūsonji." *Monumenta Nipponica* 46, 3: 329–347.

Yoshida Atsuhiko 吉田敦彦. 1961–1962. "La mythologie japonaise: Essai d'interprétation structurale." *Revue d'Histoire des Religions* 160: 47–66; 161: 25–44; 163: 225–245.

———. 1974. *Nihon shinwa to in-ō shinwa: kōzōronteki bunseki no kokoromi* 日本神話と印欧神話: 構造論的分析の試み. Tokyo: Kōbundō.

———. 1977. "Japanese Mythology and the Indo-European Trifunctional System." *Diogène* 98: 93–116.

Yoshida Mitsukuni 吉田光邦. 1970. *Hoshi no shūkyō* 星の宗教. Kyoto: Tankōsha.

Yoshida Takahide 吉田隆英. 1998. "Hikosan no engi" 彦山の縁起. *Kokubungaku: Kaishaku to kanshō* 国文学　解釈と鑑賞 12: 139–166.

Yoshida Yui 吉田唯. 2008. "*Aizen-ō jōryūki* ni okeru Aizen shinkō: Hosshōji kanren setsuwa o chūshin ni" 『愛染王紹隆記』における愛染信仰—法勝寺関連説話を中心に. In Ōtori Kazuma 大取一馬, ed. *Chūsei no bungaku to shisō* 中世の文学と思想, 381–400. Tokyo: Shintensha.

Yoshihara Hiroto 吉原浩人 and Wang Yong 王勇, eds. 2008. *Umi o wataru Tendai bunka* 海を渡る天台文化. Tokyo: Bensei shuppan.

Yoshino Hiroko 吉野裕子. 1975. *Kakusareta kamigami: Kodai shinkō to on'yō gogyō* 隠された神々—古代信仰と陰陽五行. Kyoto: Jinbun shoin.

———. 2000. *Tennō no matsuri: Daijōsai, tennō sokuishiki no kōzō* 天皇の祭り: 大嘗祭, 天皇即位式の構造. Kōdansha gakujutsu bunko 1455. Tokyo: Kōdansha.

Yoshioka Yoshitoyo 吉岡義豊. 1966–1967. "Myōken shinkō to dōkyō no Shinbushin" 妙見信仰と道教の真武神. *Chisan gakuhō* 14–15. Reprinted in *Yoshioka Yoshitoyo chosakushū* 吉岡義豊著作集, vol. 2. Tokyo: Gogatsu shobō, 1989.

Yü Chün-fang. 2000. *Kuan-yin: The Chinese Transformation of Avalokiteśvara*. New York: Columbia University Press.

Žižek, Slavoj. 2003. *The Puppet and the Dwarf: The Perverse Core of Christianity*. Cambridge, MA: MIT Press.

INDEX

ABOUT THE AUTHOR

Bernard Faure, who received his Ph.D. (Doctorat d'Etat) from Paris University, is interested in various aspects of East Asian Buddhism, with an emphasis on Chan/Zen and Tantric or esoteric Buddhism. His work, influenced by anthropological history and cultural theory, has focused on topics such as the construction of orthodoxy and heterodoxy, the Buddhist cult of relics, iconography, sexuality, and gender. He has published a number of books in French and English. His English-language publications include *The Rhetoric of Immediacy: A Cultural Critique of Chan/Zen Buddhism* (1991), *Chan Insights and Oversights: An Epistemological Critique of the Chan Tradition* (1993), *Visions of Power: Imagining Medieval Japanese Buddhism* (1996), *The Red Thread: Buddhist Approaches to Sexuality* (1998), *The Power of Denial: Buddhism, Purity, and Gender* (2003), and *Double Exposure* (2004). *The Fluid Pantheon* is the first in a planned four-volume work that explores the mythico-ritual system of esoteric Buddhism and its relationships with medieval Japanese religion. Faure has taught at Cornell University and Stanford University and is presently Kao Professor in Japanese Religion at Columbia University.